Victorian Fiction

Victorian Fiction

Edited and with an introduction
by *HAROLD BLOOM*
Sterling Professor of the Humanities
Yale University

CHELSEA HOUSE PUBLISHERS
New York ◇ *Philadelphia*

Printed and bound in the United States of America

10 9 8 7 6 5 4 3 2 1

∞The paper used in this publication meets the minimum
requirements of the American National Standard for
Permanence of Paper for Printed Library Materials,
Z39.48-1984.

Library of Congress Cataloging-in-Publication Data
Victorian fiction / edited and with an introduction by Harold
Bloom.
        p.   cm. — (The Critical cosmos series)
    Bibliography: p.
    Includes index.
    Summary: A collection of twenty-three critical essays on
English fiction from 1830 to 1880.
    ISBN 0-87754-980-X
    1. English fiction—19th century—History and criticism.
[1. English fiction — 19th century — History and criticism.]
I. Bloom, Harold.   II. Series: Critical cosmos.
PR783.V53   1988
823'.8'09—dc19   87-15529
                                                       CIP
                                                        AC

Contents

Editor's Note

This book aims to present a comprehensive collection of the best criticism available upon Victorian prose fiction, conceived here as covering the half century from 1830 to 1880, ending with the late Victorian novelist Thomas Hardy. A companion Critical Cosmos volume on *Edwardian and Georgian Fiction 1880–1914* can be said to form a natural unit with this volume.

The critical essays are arranged here, as far as is possible, in the order of the dates of the novelists' births. I am grateful to Marena Fisher and Susan Laity for their erudite assistance in editing this volume.

My introduction begins with a discussion of the relationship between Thackeray the narrator and Becky Sharp in *Vanity Fair,* and then passes to what Ruskin called "stage fire" in Dickens, particularly manifested in two of his masterpieces, *David Copperfield* and *Bleak House.* Following is an analysis of Emily Brontë's *Wuthering Heights* and Charlotte Brontë's *Jane Eyre* as Byronic "Northern romances." George Eliot's *Middlemarch,* perhaps *Bleak House*'s true rival as the great novel of the age, is read here as a romance of the Protestant will. My introduction then concludes with exegeses of two of Thomas Hardy's strongest novels, *The Return of the Native* and *The Mayor of Casterbridge.*

Studies of the individual novelists begin with an overview of the earlier political novels of Edward Bulwer-Lytton, seen by Elliot Engel and Margaret F. King as belated instances of High Romanticism, which enters again in Donald D. Stone's essay on Disraeli's Byronism.

Catherine Gallagher closely reads Mrs. Gaskell's *Mary Barton,* finding in it the need for a new form to embody the dialectic of free will and determinism. Thackeray receives two considerations, with Jack P. Rawlins emphasizing authorial self-awareness of the narrative voice and George Levine expounding Thackeray's realistic polemic against the fancifulness of Sir Walter Scott.

The great central voice of Victorian fiction, that of Charles Dickens, is studied in Garrett Stewart's analysis of irony in the first chapter of *Pickwick Papers*—Dickens's first major fiction. John Carey considers how Dickens energetically represents violence while John Kucich defends the novelist's much-maligned happy endings by assigning them to the realm of fairy tales.

Michael Riffaterre, studying Trollope's rhetoric, gives us a good sense of the vast scope of this novelist's writing, a sense confirmed by George Levine's account of Trollope's insights into love and marriage in *Can You Forgive Her?*

Wuthering Heights and *Jane Eyre* are coupled in Tony Tanner's essay on modes of narrative identity in the Brontë sisters, while Jan B. Gordon first reads Anne Brontë's *Tenant of Wildfell Hall* and then compares it to *Wuthering Heights,* in order to show how Anne attempted to individuate herself against her sister's fiercer vision.

George Eliot, Dickens's closest rival in aesthetic eminence, is shown by Barry V. Qualls to have been questing for a narrative strategy that might combine John Bunyan and William Wordsworth. In parallel ways, Daniel Cottom compares romance and realist elements in Eliot, and T. B. Tomlinson shows differences and similarities in the representation of "spiritual dread" between Eliot and some later novelists: Hardy (in *Jude*), Conrad (in *Victory*), and James (in *The Awkward Age*).

Charles Kingsley's *The Water-Babies* is rather surprisingly shown by Valentine Cunningham to have been an industrial reform novel in the context of its own time. In D. A. Miller's lively reading of Wilkie Collins's *The Woman in White*, we receive another surprise with the critic's revelation of the sexual strategies that pervade this novel.

George MacDonald, fantasist and Christian moralist, is surveyed by Humphrey Carpenter, who emphasizes both the violence and the religiosity of the fairy tales. A wonderfully different moralist, comic and secular, George Meredith is shown by Rachel M. Brownstein to have inverted the tradition of Samuel Richardson by concentrating upon the curious hero rather than the heroine of *The Egoist* and to have recreated the real-life model for *Diana of the Crossways*.

Lewis Carroll's Alice is uncovered by Nina Auerbach as an unusual representation of a Victorian female child, since she is so markedly and delightfully aggressive. Thomas L. Jeffers studies Samuel Butler's polemical reactions to the crucial and controversial evolutionary ideas of his age in the brilliant *Way of All Flesh*.

This book concludes with J. Hillis Miller's now classic account of Thomas Hardy's rhetorical and psychological detachment in his fiction and with Jean R. Brooks's reading of *Tess of the D'Urbervilles* as a dramatic conflict between personal and impersonal elements in Tess's distraught being.

Introduction

G. K. Chesterton, saluting Thackeray as the master of "allusive irrelevancy," charmingly admitted that "Thackeray worked entirely by diffuseness." No celebrator of form in the novel has ever cared for Thackeray, who, like his precursor Fielding, always took his own time in his writing. Thackeray particularly follows Fielding, who was the sanest of novelists, in judging his own characters as a magistrate might judge them, a magistrate who was also a parodist and a vigilant exposer of social pretensions. Charlotte Brontë, Thackeray's fierce admirer, in her preface to the second edition of *Jane Eyre* said that he "resembles Fielding as an eagle does a vulture." This unfortunate remark sounds odd now, when no critic would place Thackeray anywhere near Fielding in aesthetic eminence. Nor would any critic wish to regard Thackeray as Dickens's nearest contemporary rival, a once fashionable comparison. Thackeray, we all agree, is genial but flawed, and until recently he did not have much following among either novelists or critics. Trollope and Ruskin sometimes seem, respectively, the last vital novelist and great critic to regard Thackeray with the utmost seriousness. Splendid as he is, Thackeray is now much dimmed.

Though *Henry Esmond* is a rhetorical triumph in the genre of the historical novel, *Vanity Fair*, itself partly historical, is clearly Thackeray's most memorable achievement. Rereading it, one encounters again two superb characters, Becky Sharp and William Makepeace Thackeray. One regrets that Becky, because of the confusion of realms that would be involved, could not exercise her charms upon the complaisant Thackeray, who amiably described his heroine's later career as resembling the slitherings of a mermaid. Anyway, Thackeray probably shared the regret, and what I like best in *Vanity Fair* is how much Thackeray likes Becky. Any reader who does not like Becky is almost certainly not very likeable herself or himself. Such an observation may not seem like literary criticism to a formalist or some other kind of plumber, but I would insist that Becky's vitalism is the critical center in any strong reading of *Vanity Fair*.

Becky, of course, is famously a bad woman, selfish and endlessly designing, rarely bothered by a concern for truth, morals, or the good of the community. But Thackeray, without extenuating his principal personage, situates her in a fictive cosmos where nearly all the significant characters are egomaniacs, and none of them is as interesting and attractive as the energetic Becky. Her will to live has a desperate gusto, which is answered by the gusto of the doubtlessly fictive Thackeray who is the narrator, and who shares many of the weaknesses that he zestfully portrays in his women and men. Perhaps we do not so much like Becky because Thackeray likes her, as we like Becky because we like that supreme fiction, Thackeray the narrator. Sometimes I wish that he would stop teasing me, and always I wish that his moralizings were in a class with those of the sublime George Eliot (she would not have agreed, as she joined Trollope and Charlotte Brontë in admiring Thackeray exorbitantly). But never, in *Vanity Fair*, do I wish Thackeray the storyteller to clear out of the novel. If you are going to tour Vanity Fair, then your best guide is its showman, who parodies it yet always acknowledges that he himself is one of its prime representatives.

Does Thackeray overstate the conventional case against Becky in the knowing and deliberate way in which Fielding overstated the case against Tom Jones? This was the contention of A. E. Dyson in his study of irony, *The Crazy Fabric* (1965). Dyson followed the late Gordon Ray, most genial and Thackerayan of Thackerayans, in emphasizing how devious a work *Vanity Fair* is, as befits a narrator who chose to go on living in Vanity Fair, however uneasily. Unlike Fielding, Thackeray sometimes yields to mere bitterness, but he knew, as Fielding did, that the bitter are never great, and Becky refuses to become bitter. An excessively moral reader might observe that Becky's obsessive lying is the cost of her transcending of bitterness, but the cost will not seem too high to the imaginative reader, who deserves Becky and who is not as happy with her foil, the good but drab Amelia. Becky is hardly as witty as Sir John Falstaff, but then whatever other fictive personage is? As Falstaff seems, in one aspect, to be the child of the Wife of Bath, so Becky comes closer to being Falstaff's daughter than any other female character in British fiction. Aside from lacking all of the Seven Deadly Virtues, Becky evidently carries living on her wits to extremes in whoredom and murder, but without losing our sympathy and our continued pleasure in her company.

I part from Dyson when he suggests that Becky is Vanity Fair's Volpone, fit scourge for its pretensions and its heartlessness, of which she shares only the latter. Becky, like her not-so-secret sharer, Thackeray the narrator, I judge to be too good for Vanity Fair, though neither of them has the undivided inclination to escape so vile a scene, as we might wish them to do. Becky's most famous reflection is "I think I could be a good woman if I had five thousand a year." This would go admirably as the refrain of one of those ballads that Brecht kept lifting from Kipling, and helps us to see that Becky Sharp fits better into Brecht's world than into Ben Jonson's. What is most winning about her is that she is never morose. Her high-spirited courage does us good, and calls into question the aesthetics of our morality. Thackeray never allows us to believe that we live anywhere except in Vanity Fair, and we can begin to see that the disreputable Brecht and the reputable Thackeray die one another's lives, live one another's deaths, to borrow a formulation that W. B. Yeats was too fond of repeating.

Thackeray, a genial humorist, persuades the reader that *Vanity Fair* is a comic novel, when truly it is as dark as Brecht's *Threepenny Opera*, or his *Rise and Fall of the City of Mahagonny*. The abyss beckons in nearly every chapter of *Vanity Fair*, and a fair number of the characters vanish into it before the book is completed. Becky survives, being indomitable, but both she and Thackeray the narrator seem rather battered as the novel wanes into its eloquent and terribly sad farewell:

> Ah! *Vanitas Vanitatum!* Which of us is happy in this world? Which of us has his desire? or, having it, is satisfied?—Come children, let us shut up the box and the puppets, for our play is played out.

II

Courage would be the critical virtue most required if anyone were to attempt an essay that might be called "The Limitations of Shakespeare." Tolstoy, in his most outrageous critical performance, more or less tried just that, with dismal results, and even Ben Jonson might not have done much better, had he sought to extend his ambivalent obiter dicta on his great friend and rival. Nearly as much courage, or foolhardiness, is involved in discoursing on the limitations of Dickens, but the young Henry James had a critical gusto that could carry him through every literary challenge. Reviewing *Our Mutual Friend* in 1865, James exuberantly proclaimed that "*Bleak House* was forced; *Little Dorrit* was labored; the present work is dug out as with a spade and pickaxe." At about this time, reviewing *Drum-Taps*, James memorably dismissed Whitman as an essentially prosaic mind seeking to lift itself, by muscular exertion, into poetry. To reject some of the major works of the strongest English novelist and the greatest American poet, at about the same moment, is to set standards for critical audacity that no one since has been able to match, even as no novelist since has equalled Dickens, nor any poet, Walt Whitman.

James was at his rare worst in summing up Dickens's supposedly principal inadequacy:

> Such scenes as this are useful in fixing the limits of Mr. Dickens's insight. Insight is, perhaps, too strong a word; for we are con-

vinced that it is one of the chief conditions of his genius not to see beneath the surface of things. If we might hazard a definition of his literary character, we should, accordingly, call him the greatest of superficial novelists. We are aware that this definition confines him to an inferior rank in the department of letters which he adorns; but we accept this consequence of our proposition. It were, in our opinion, an offence against humanity to place Mr. Dickens among the greatest novelists. For, to repeat what we have already intimated, he has created nothing but figure. He has added nothing to our understanding of human character. He is a master of but two alternatives: he reconciles us to what is commonplace, and he reconciles us to what is odd. The value of the former service is questionable; and the manner in which Mr. Dickens performs it sometimes conveys a certain impression of charlatanism. The value of the latter service is incontestable, and here Mr. Dickens is an honest, an admirable artist.

This can be taken literally, and then transvalued: to see truly the surface of things, to reconcile us at once to the commonplace and the odd—these are not minor gifts. In 1860, John Ruskin, the great seer of the surface of things, the charismatic illuminator of the commonplace and the odd together, had reached a rather different conclusion from that of the young Henry James, five years before James's brash rejection:

The essential value and truth of Dickens's writings have been unwisely lost sight of by many thoughtful persons merely because he presents his truth with some colour of caricature. Unwisely, because Dickens's caricature, though often gross, is never mistaken. Allowing for his manner of telling them, the things he tells us are always true. I wish that he could think it right to limit his brilliant exaggeration to works written only for public amusement; and when he takes up a subject of high national importance, such as that which he handled in *Hard Times*, that he would use severer and more accurate analysis. The usefulness of that work (to my mind, in several respects, the greatest he has written) is with many persons seriously diminished because Mr. Bounderby is a dramatic monster, instead of a characteristic example of a worldly master; and Stephen Blackpool a dramatic perfection, instead of a characteristic example of an honest workman. But let us not lose the use of Dickens's wit and insight, because he chooses to speak in a circle of stage fire. He is entirely right in his main drift and purpose in every book he has written; and all of them, but especially *Hard Times*, should be studied with close and earnest care by persons interested in social questions. They will find much that is partial, and, because partial, apparently unjust; but if they examine all the evidence on the other side, which Dickens seems to overlook, it will appear, after all their trouble, that his view was the finally right one, grossly and sharply told.

To say of Dickens that he chose "to speak in a circle of stage fire" is exactly right, since Dickens is the greatest actor among novelists, the finest master of dramatic projection. A superb stage performer, he never stops performing in his novels, which is not the least of his many Shakespearean characteristics. Martin Price usefully defines some of these as "his effortless invention, his brilliant play of language, the scope and density of his imagined world." I like also Price's general comparison of Dickens to the strongest satirist in the language, Swift, a comparison that Price shrewdly turns into a confrontation:

> But the confrontation helps us to define differences as well: Dickens is more explicit, more overtly compassionate, insisting always upon the perversions of feeling as well as of thought. His outrage is of the same consistency as his generous celebration, the satirical wit of the same copious extravagance as the comic elaborations. Dickens's world is alive with things that snatch, lurch, teeter, thrust, leer; it is the animate world of Netherlandish genre painting or of Hogarth's prints, where all space is a field of force, where objects vie or intrigue with each other, where every human event spills over into the things that surround it. This may become the typically crowded scene of satire, where persons are reduced to things and things to matter in motion; or it may pulsate with fierce energy and noisy feeling. It is different from Swift; it is the distinctive Dickensian plenitude, which we find again in his verbal play, in his great array of vivid characters, in his massed scenes of feasts or public declamations. It creates rituals as compelling as the resuscitation of Rogue Riderhood, where strangers participate solemnly in the recovery of a spark of life, oblivious for the moment of the unlovely human form it will soon inhabit.

That animate, Horgarthian world, "where all space is a field of force," indeed is a plenitude and it strikes me that Price's vivid description suggests Rabelais rather than Swift as a true analogue. Dickens, like Shakespeare in one of many aspects and like Rabelais, is as much carnival as stage fire, a kind of endless festival. The reader of Dickens stands in the midst of a festival, which is too varied, too multiform, to be taken in even by innumerable readings. Something always escapes our ken; Ben Jonson's sense of being "rammed with life" is exemplified more even by Dickens than by Rabelais, in that near-Shakespearean plenitude that is Dickens's peculiar glory.

Is it possible to define that plenitude narrowly enough so as to conceptualize it for critical use, though by "conceptualize" one meant only a critical metaphor? Shakespearean representation is no touchstone for Dickens or for anyone else, since above all modes of representation it turns upon an inward changing brought about by characters listening to themselves speak. Dickens cannot do that. His villains are gorgeous, but there are no Iagos or Edmunds among them. The severer, more relevant test, which Dickens must fail, though hardly to his detriment, is Falstaff, who generates not only his own meaning, but meaning in so many others besides, both on and off the page. Probably the severest test is Shylock, most Dickensian of Shakespeare's characters, since we cannot say of Dickens's Shylock, Fagin, that there is much Shakespearean about him at all. Fagin is a wonderful grotesque, but the winds of will are not stirred in him, while they burn on hellishly forever in Shylock.

Carlyle's injunction, to work in the will, seems to have little enough place in the cosmos of the Dickens characters. I do not say this to indicate a limitation, or even a limit, nor do I believe that the will to live or the will to power is ever relaxed in or by Dickens. But nothing is got for nothing, except perhaps in or by Shakespeare, and Dickens purchases his kind of plenitude at the expense of one aspect of the will. T. S. Eliot remarked that "Dickens's characters are real because there is no one like them." I would modify that to "They are real because they are not like one another, though sometimes they are a touch more like some of us than like each other." Perhaps the will, in whatever aspect, can differ only in degree rather than in kind among us. The aesthetic secret of Dickens appears to be that his villains, heroes, heroines, victims, eccentrics, ornamental beings, do differ from one another *in the kinds of will that they possess*. Since that is hardly possible for us, as humans, it does bring about an absence in reality in and for Dickens. That is a high price to pay, but it is a good deal less than everything and Dickens got more than he paid for. We also receive a great deal more than we ever are asked to surrender when we read Dickens. That may indeed be his most Shakespearean quality, and may provide the critical trope I quest for in him. James and Proust hurt you more than Dickens does, and the hurt is the meaning, or much of it. What hurts in Dickens never has much to do with meaning, because there cannot be a poetics of pain where the will has ceased to be common or sadly uniform. Dickens really does offer a poetics of pleasure, which is surely worth our secondary uneasiness at his refusal to offer us any accurately mimetic representations of the human will. He writes always the book of the drives, which is why supposedly Freudian readings of him always fail so tediously. The conceptual metaphor he suggests in his representations of character and personality is neither Shakespearean mirror nor Romantic lamp, neither Rabelaisian carnival nor Fieldingesque open country. "Stage fire" seems to me perfect, for "stage" removes something of the reality of the will, yet only as modifier. The substantive remains "fire." Dickens is the poet of the fire of the drives, the true celebrant of Freud's myth of frontier concepts, of that domain lying on the border between psyche and body, falling into matter, yet partaking of the reality of both.

III

If the strong writer be defined as one who confronts his own contingency, his own dependent relation on a precursor, then we can discover only a few writers after Homer and the Yahwist who are strong without that sense of contingency. These are the Great Originals, and they are not many; Shakespeare and Freud are among them and so is Dickens. Dickens, like Shakespeare and Freud, had no true precursors, or perhaps it might be more accurate to say he swallowed up Tobias Smollett rather as Shakespeare devoured Christopher Marlowe. Originality, or an authentic freedom from contingency, is Dickens's salient characteristic as an author. Since Dickens's influence has been so immense, even upon writers so unlikely as Dostoevsky and Kafka, we find it a little difficult now to see at first how overwhelmingly original he is.

Dickens now constitutes a facticity or contingency that no subsequent novelist can transcend or evade without the risk of self-maiming. Consider the difference between two masters of modern fiction, Henry James and James Joyce. Is not Dickens the difference? *Ulysses* comes to terms with Dickens, and earns the exuberance it manifests. Poldy is larger, I think, than any single figure in Dickens, but he has recognizably Dickensian qualities. Lambert Strether in *The Ambassadors* has none, and is the poorer for it. Part of the excitement of *The Princess Casamassima* for us must be that, for once, James achieves a Dickensian sense of the outward life, a sense that is lacking even in *The Portrait of a Lady*, and that we miss acutely (at least I do) amidst even the most inward splendors of *The Wings of the Dove* and *The Golden Bowl*.

The Personal History of David Copperfield, indeed the most personal and autobiographical of all Dickens's novels, has been so influential upon all subsequent portraits of the artist as a young man that we have to make a conscious effort to recover our appreciation of the book's fierce originality. It is the first therapeutic novel, in part written to heal the author's self, or at least to solace permanent anxieties incurred in childhood and youth. Freud's esteem for *David Copperfield* seems inevitable, even if it has led to a number of unfortunate readings within that unlikely compound oddly called "Freudian literary criticism."

Dickens's biographer Edgar Johnson has traced the evolution of *David Copperfield* from an abandoned fragment of autobiography, with its powerful but perhaps self-deceived declaration: "I do not write resentfully or angrily: for I know how all these things have worked together to make me what I am." Instead of representing his own parents as being David Copperfield's, Dickens displaced them into the Micawbers, a change that purchased astonishing pathos and charm at the expense of avoiding a personal pain that might have produced greater meaningfulness. But *David Copper-field* was, as Dickens said, his "favourite child," fulfilling his deep need to become his own father. Of no other book would he have said: "I seem to be sending some part of myself into the Shadowy World."

Kierkegaard advised us that "he who is willing to do the work gives birth to his own father," while Nietzsche even more ironically observed that "if one hasn't had a good father, then it is necessary to invent one." *David Copperfield* is more in the spirit of Kierkegaard's adage, as Dickens more or less makes himself David's father. David, an illustrious novelist, allows himself to narrate his story in the first person. A juxtaposition of the start and conclusion of the narrative may be instructive:

> Whether I shall turn out to be the hero of my own life, or whether that station will be held by anybody else, these pages must show. To begin my life with the beginning of my life, I record that I was born (as I have been informed and believe) on a Friday, at twelve o'clock at night. It was remarked that the clock began to strike, and I began to cry, simultaneously.
>
> In consideration of the day and hour of my birth, it was declared by the nurse, and by some sage women in the neighbourhood who had taken a lively interest in me several months before there was any possibility of our becoming personally acquainted, first, that I was destined to be unlucky in life; and secondly, that I was privileged to see ghosts and spirits; both these gifts inevitably attaching, as they believed, to all unlucky infants of either gender, born towards the small hours on a Friday night.
>
> I need say nothing here, on the first head, because nothing can show better than my history whether that prediction was verified or falsified by the result. On the second branch of the question, I will only remark, that unless I ran through that part of my inheritance while I was still a baby, I have not come into it yet. But I do not at all complain of having been kept out of this property; and if anybody else should be in the present enjoyment of it, he is heartily welcome to keep it.
>
> And now, as I close my task, subduing my desire to linger yet, these faces fade away. But one face, shining on me like a Heavenly light by which I see all other objects, is above them and beyond them all. And that remains.
>
> I turn my head, and see it, in its beautiful serenity, beside me.
>
> My lamp burns low, and I have written far into the night; but the dear presence, without which I were nothing, bears me company.
>
> O Agnes, O my soul, so may thy face be by me when I close my life indeed; so may I, when realities are melting from me, like

the shadows which I now dismiss, still find thee near me, pointing upward!

No adroit reader could prefer the last four paragraphs of *David Copperfield* to the first three. The high humor of the beginning is fortunately more typical of the book than the sugary conclusion. Yet the juxtaposition does convey the single rhetorical flaw in Dickens that matters, by which I do not mean the wild pathos that marks the death of Steerforth, or the even more celebrated career of the endlessly unfortunate Little Em'ly. If Dickens's image of voice or mode of representation is "stage fire," then his metaphors always will demand the possibility of being staged. Micawber, Uriah Heep, Steerforth in his life (not at the end) are all of them triumphs of stage fire, as are Peggotty, Murdstone, Betsey Trotwood, and even Dora Spenlow. But Agnes is a disaster, and that dreadful "pointing upward!" is not to be borne. You cannot stage Agnes, which would not matter except that she does represent the idealizing and self-mystifying side of David and so she raises the question, Can you, as a reader, stage David? How much stage fire got into him? Or, to be hopelessly reductive, has he a will, as Uriah Heep and Steerforth in their very different ways are wills incarnate?

If there is an aesthetic puzzle in the novel, it is why David has and conveys so overwhelming a sense of disordered suffering and early sorrow in his Murdstone phase, as it were, and before. Certainly the intensity of the pathos involved is out of all proportion to the fictive experience that comes through to the reader. Dickens both invested himself in and withdrew from David, so that something is always missing in the self-representation. Yet the will—to live, to interpret, to repeat, to write—survives and burgeons perpetually. Dickens's preternatural energy gets into David, and is at some considerable variance with the diffidence of David's apparent refusal to explore his own inwardness. What does mark Dickens's representation of David with stage fire is neither the excess of the early sufferings nor the tiresome idealization of the love for Agnes. It is rather the vocation of novelist, the drive to tell a story, particularly one's own story, that apparels David with the fire of what Freud called the drives.

Dickens's greatness in *David Copperfield* has little to do with the much more extraordinary strength that was to manifest itself in *Bleak House*, which can compete with *Clarissa, Emma, Middlemarch, The Portrait of a Lady, Women in Love*, and *Ulysses* for the eminence of being the inescapable novel in the language. *David Copperfield* is of another order, but it is the origin of that order, the novelist's account of how she or he burned through experience in order to achieve the Second Birth, into the will to narrate, the storyteller's destiny.

IV

Bleak House may not be "the finest literary work the nineteenth century produced in England," as Geoffrey Tillotson called it in 1946. A century that gave us *The Prelude* and Wordsworth's major crisis lyrics, Blake's *Milton* and *Jerusalem*, Byron's *Don Juan*, the principal poems of Shelley, Keats, Tennyson, and Browning, and novels such as *Pride and Prejudice, Emma, Middlemarch*, and Dickens's own *Hard Times* and *Our Mutual Friend*, is an era of such literary plenitude that a single choice is necessarily highly problematic. Yet there is now something close to critical agreement that *Bleak House* is Dickens's most complex and memorable single achievement. W. J. Harvey usefully sketches just how formidably the novel is patterned:

> *Bleak House* is for Dickens a unique and elaborate experiment in narration and plot composition. It is divided into two intermingled and roughly concurrent stories; Esther Summerson's first-person narrative and an omniscient narrative told consistently in the historic present. The latter takes up thirty-four chapters; Esther has one less. Her story, however, occupies a good deal more than half the novel. The reader who checks the distribution of these two narratives against the original part issues will hardly discern any significant pattern or correlation. Most parts contain a mixture of the two stories; one part is narrated entirely by Esther and five parts entirely by the omniscient author. Such a check does, however, support the view that Dickens did not, as is sometimes supposed, use serial publication in the interest of crude suspense. A sensational novelist, for example, might well have ended a part issue with chapter 31; Dickens subdues the drama by adding another chapter to the number. The obvious exception to this only proves the rule; in the final double number the suspense of Bucket's search for Lady Dedlock is heightened by cutting back to the omniscient narrative and the stricken Sir Leicester. In general, however, Dickens's control of the double narrative is far richer and subtler than this.

I would add to Harvey the critical observation that Dickens's own narrative will in "his" thirty-four chapters is a will again different in kind than the will to tell her story of the admirable Esther Summerson. Dickens's (or the omniscient, historical present narrator's) metaphor of representation is one of stage fire: wild, free, unconditioned, incessant with the force of Freud's domain of those grandly indefinite frontier concepts, the drives. Esther's mode of representation is certainly not flat or insipid; for all of her monumental repressions, Esther finally seems to me the most mysteriously complex and profound personage in *Bleak House*. Her narrative is not so much plain style as it is indeed repressed in the precise Freudian sense of "repression," whose governing metaphor, in Esther's prose as in Freud's, is flight from, rather than a pushing down or pushing under. Esther frequently forgets, purposefully though "unconsciously," what she cannot bear to remember, and much of her narrative is her strong defense against the force of the past. Esther may not *appear* to change as she goes from little girl to adult, but that is because the rhythm of her psyche, unlike

Dickens's own, is one of unfolding rather than development. She is Dickens's Muse, what Whitman would have called his "Fancy," as in the great death-lyric "Goodbye, My Fancy!" or what Stevens would have called Dickens's "Interior Paramour."

Contrast a passage of Esther's story with one of Dickens's own narrative, from the end of chapter 56, "Pursuit," and towards the close of the next chapter, "Esther's Narrative":

Mr. Jarndyce, the only person up in the house, is just going to bed; rises from his book, on hearing the rapid ringing at the bell; and comes down to the door in his dressing-gown.

"Don't be alarmed sir." In a moment his visitor is confidential with him in the hall, has shut the door, and stands with his hand upon the lock. "I've had the pleasure of seeing you before. Inspector Bucket. Look at that handkerchief, sir, Miss Esther Summerson's. Found it myself put away in a drawer of Lady Dedlock's, quarter of an hour ago. Not a moment to lose. Matter of life or death. You know Lady Dedlock?"

"Yes."

"There has been a discovery there, to-day. Family affairs have come out. Sir Leicester Dedlock, Baronet, has had a fit—apoplexy or paralysis—and couldn't be brought to, and precious time has been lost. Lady Dedlock disappeared this afternoon, and left a letter for him that looks bad. Run your eye over it. Here it is!"

Mr. Jarndyce having read it, asks him what he thinks?

"I don't know. It looks like suicide. Anyways, there's more and more danger, every minute, of its drawing to that. I'd give a hundred pound an hour to have got the start of the present time. Now, Mr. Jarndyce, I am employed by Sir Leicester Dedlock, Baronet, to follow her and find her—to save her, and take her his forgiveness. I have money and full power, but I want something else. I want Miss Summerson."

Mr. Jarndyce, in a troubled voice, repeats "Miss Summerson?"

"Now, Mr. Jarndyce"; Mr. Bucket has read his face with the greatest attention all along: "I speak to you as a gentleman of a humane heart, and under such pressing circumstances as don't often happen. If ever delay was dangerous, it's dangerous now; and if ever you couldn't afterwards forgive yourself for causing it, this is the time. Eight or ten hours, worth, as I tell you, a hundred pound a-piece at least, have been lost since Lady Dedlock disappeared. I am charged to find her. I am Inspector Bucket. Besides all the rest that's heavy on her, she has upon her, as she believes, suspicion of murder. If I follow her alone, she, being in ignorance of what Sir Leicester Dedlock, Baronet, has communicated to me, may be driven to desperation. But if I follow her in company with a young lady, answering to the description of a young lady that she has a tenderness for—I ask no question, and I say no more than that—she will give me credit for being friendly. Let me come up with her, and be able to have the hold upon her of putting that young lady for'ard, and I'll save her and prevail with her if she is alive. Let me come up with her alone—a harder matter—and I'll do my best; but I don't answer for what the best may be. Time flies; it's getting on for one o'clock. When one strikes, there's another hour gone; and it's worth a thousand pound now, instead of a hundred.''

This is all true, and the pressing nature of the case cannot be questioned. Mr. Jarndyce begs him to remain there, while he speaks to Miss Summerson. Mr. Bucket says he will; but acting on his usual principle, does no such thing—following up-stairs instead, and keeping his man in sight. So he remains, dodging and lurking about in the gloom of the staircase while they confer. In a very little time, Mr. Jarndyce comes down, and tells him that Miss Summerson will join him directly, and place herself under his protection, to accompany him where he pleases. Mr. Bucket, satisfied, expresses high approval; and awaits her coming, at the door.

There, he mounts a high tower in his mind, and looks out far and wide. Many solitary figures he perceives, creeping through the streets; many solitary figures out on heaths, and roads, and lying under haystacks. But the figure that he seeks is not among them. Other solitaries he perceives, in nooks of bridges, looking over; and in shadowed places down by the river's level; and a dark, dark, shapeless object drifting with the tide, more solitary than all, clings with a drowning hold on his attention.

Where is she? Living or dead, where is she? If, as he folds the handkerchief and carefully puts it up, it were able, with an enchanted power, to bring before him the place where she found it, and the night landscape near the cottage where it covered the little child, would he descry her there? On the waste, where the brick-kilns are burning with a pale blue flare; where the straw-roofs of the wretched huts in which the bricks are made, are being scattered by the wind; where the clay and water are hard frozen, and the mill in which the gaunt blind horse goes round all day, looks like an instrument of human torture;—traversing this deserted blighted spot, there is a lonely figure with the sad world to itself, pelted by the snow and driven by the wind, and cast out, it would seem, from all companionship. It is the figure of a woman, too; but it is miserably dressed, and no such clothes ever came through the hall, and out at the great door, of the Dedlock mansion.

The transparent windows with the fire and light, looking so bright and warm from the cold darkness out of doors, were soon gone, and again we were crushing and churning the loose snow. We went on with toil enough; but the dismal roads were not much worse than they had been, and the stage was only nine miles. My companion smoking on the box—I had thought at the last inn of begging him to do so, when I saw him standing at a great fire in a comfortable cloud of tobacco—was as vigilant as ever; and as quickly down and up again, when we came to any human abode or any human creature. He had lighted his little dark lantern, which seemed to be a favourite with him, for we had lamps to the carriage; and every now and then he turned it upon me, to see that I was doing well. There was a folding-window to the carriage-head, but I never closed it, for it seemed like shutting out hope.

We came to the end of the stage, and still the lost trace was not recovered. I looked at him anxiously when we stopped to change; but I knew by his yet graver face, as he stood watching the ostlers, that he had heard nothing. Almost in an instant afterwards, as I leaned back in my seat, he looked in, with his lighted lantern in his hand, an excited and quite different man.

"What is it?" said I, starting. "Is she here?"

"No, no. Don't deceive yourself, my dear. Nobody's here. But I've got it!"

The crystallised snow was in his eyelashes, in his hair, lying in ridges on his dress. He had to shake it from his face, and get his breath before he spoke to me.

"Now, Miss Summerson," said he, beating his finger on the apron, "don't you be disappointed at what I'm a going to do. You know me. I'm Inspector Bucket, and you can trust me. We've come a long way; never mind. Four horses out there for the next stage up! Quick!"

There was a commotion in the yard, and a man came running out of the stables to know "if he meant up or down?"

"Up, I tell you! Up! Ain't it English? Up!"

"Up?" said I, astonished. "To London! Are we going back?"

"Miss Summerson," he answered, "back. Straight back as a die. You know me. Don't be afraid. I'll follow the other, by G—."

"The other?" I repeated. "Who?"

"You called her Jenny, didn't you? I'll follow her. Bring those two pair out here, for a crown a man. Wake up, some of you!"

"You will not desert this lady we are in search of; you will not abandon her on such a night, and in such a state of mind as I know her to be in!" said I, in an agony, and grasping his hand.

"You are right, my dear, I won't. But I'll follow the other. Look alive here with them horses. Send a man for'ard in the saddle to the next stage, and let him send another for'ard again, and order four on, up, right through. My darling, don't you be afraid!"

These orders, and the way in which he ran about the yard,

urging them, caused a general excitement that was scarcely less bewildering to me than the sudden change. But in the height of the confusion, a mounted man galloped away to order the relays, and our horses were put to with great speed.

"My dear," said Mr. Bucket, jumping up to his seat, and looking in again—"you'll excuse me if I'm too familiar—don't you fret and worry yourself no more than you can help. I say nothing else at present; but you know me, my dear; now, don't you?"

I endeavoured to say that I knew he was far more capable than I of deciding what we ought to do; but was he sure that this was right? Could I not go forward by myself in search of—I grasped his hand again in my distress, and whispered it to him—of my own mother.

"My dear," he answered, "I know, I know, and would I put you wrong, do you think? Inspector Bucket. Now you know me, don't you?"

What could I say but yes!

"Then you keep up as good a heart as you can, and you rely upon me for standing by you, no less than by Sir Leicester Dedlock, Baronet. Now, are you right there?"

"All right, sir!"

"Off she goes, then. And get on, my lads!"

We were again upon the melancholy road by which we had come; tearing up the miry sleet and thawing snow, as if they were torn up by a waterwheel.

Both passages are extraordinary, by any standards, and certainly "Pursuit" has far more stage fire than "Esther's Narrative," but this time her repressive shield, in part, is broken through, and a fire leaps forth out of her. If we start with "Pursuit" however, we are likelier to see what it is that returns from the repressed in Esther, returns under the sign of negation (as Freud prophesied), so that what comes back is primarily cognitive, while the affective aspect of the repression persists. We can remember the opening of *David Copperfield*, where Dickens, in his persona as David, disavows the gift of second sight attributed to him by the wise women and gossips. Inspector Bucket, at the conclusion of the "Pursuit" chapter, is granted a great vision, a preternatural second sight of Esther's lost mother, Lady Dedlock. What Bucket *sees* is stage fire at its most intense, the novelist's will to tell become an absolute vision of the will. Mounting a high tower in his mind, Bucket (who thus becomes Dickens's authorial will) looks out, far and wide, and sees the truth: "a dark, dark, shapeless object drifting with the tide, more solitary than all," which "clings with a drowning hold on his attention." That "drowning hold" leads to the further vision: "where the clay and water are hard frozen, and the mill in which the gaunt blind horse goes round all day." I suspect that Dickens here has a debt to Browning's great romance "Childe Roland to the Dark Tower Came," where another apparent instrument of human torture in a deserted, blighted spot is seen by a companionless figure as being in association with a starving blind horse, cast out from the Devil's stud, who provokes in Browning's narrator the terrible outcry that he never saw a beast he hated so, because: "He must be wicked to deserve such pain."

The ensuing chapter of "Esther's Narrative" brilliantly evokes the cognitive return of Esther's acknowledgment of her mother, under the sign of a negation of past affect. Here the narrative vision proceeds, not in the Sublime mode of Bucket's extraordinary second sight, but in the grave, meditative lyricism that takes us first to a tentative return from unconscious flight through an image of pursuit of the fleeing, doomed mother: "The transparent windows with the fire and light, looking so bright and warm from the cold darkness out of doors, were soon gone, and again we were crushing and churning the loose snow." That "crushing and churning" images the breaking of the repressive shield, and Dickens shrewdly ends the chapter with Esther's counterpart to Bucket's concluding vision of a Browningesque demonic water mill, torturing consciousness into a return from flight. Esther whispers to Bucket that she desires to go forward by herself in search of her own mother, and the dark pursuit goes on in the sinister metaphor of the sleet and thawing snow, shield of repression, being torn up by a waterwheel that recirculates the meaning of memory's return, even as it buries part of the pains of abandonment by the mother once more: "We were again upon the melancholy road by which we had come; tearing up the miry sleet and thawing snow, as if they were torn up by a waterwheel."

It is a terrifying triumph of Dickens's art that, when "Esther's Narrative" resumes, in chapter 59, we know inevitably that we are headed straight for an apocalyptic image of what Shakespeare, in *Lear*, calls "the promised end" or "image of that horror," here not the corpse of the daughter, but of the mother. Esther goes, as she must, to be the first to touch and to see, and with no affect whatsoever unveils the truth:

> I passed on to the gate, and stooped down. I lifted the heavy head, put the long dank hair aside, and turned the face. And it was my mother, cold and dead.

V

The three Brontë sisters—Charlotte, Emily Jane, and Anne—are unique literary artists whose works resemble one another's far more than they do the works of writers before or since. Charlotte's compelling novel *Jane Eyre* and her three lesser yet strong narratives—*The Professor, Shirley, Villette*—form the most extensive achievement of the sisters, but critics and common readers alike set even higher the one novel of Emily Jane's, *Wuthering*

Heights, and a handful of her lyrical poems. Anne's two novels—*Agnes Grey* and *The Tenant of Wildfell Hall*—remain highly readable, although dwarfed by *Jane Eyre* and the authentically sublime *Wuthering Heights.*

Between them, the Brontës can be said to have invented a relatively new genre, a kind of Northern romance, deeply influenced both by Byron's poetry and by his myth and personality, but going back also, more remotely yet as definitely, to the Gothic novel and to the Elizabethan drama. In a definite, if difficult to establish, sense, the heirs of the Brontës include Thomas Hardy and D. H. Lawrence. There is a harsh vitalism in the Brontës that finds its match in the Lawrence of *The Rainbow* and *Women in Love,* though the comparison is rendered problematic by Lawrence's moral zeal, enchantingly absent from the Brontës' literary cosmos.

The aesthetic puzzle of the Brontës has less to do with the mature transformations of their vision of Byron into Rochester and Heathcliff, than with their earlier fantasy-life and its literature, and the relation of that life and literature to its hero and precursor, George Gordon, Lord Byron. At his rare worst and silliest, Byron has nothing like this scene from Charlotte Brontë's "Caroline Vernon," where Caroline confronts the Byronic Duke of Zamorna:

> The Duke spoke again in a single blunt and almost coarse sentence, compressing what remained to be said, "If I were a bearded Turk, Caroline, I would take you to my harem." His deep voice as he uttered this, his high featured face, and dark, large eye burning bright with a spark from the depths of Gehenna, struck Caroline Vernon with a thrill of nameless dread. Here he was, the man Montmorency had described to her. All at once she knew him. Her guardian was gone, something terrible sat in his place.

Byron died his more-or-less heroic death at Missolonghi in Greece on April 19, 1824, aged thirty-six years and three months, after having set an impossible paradigm for authors that has become what the late Nelson Algren called "Hemingway all the way," in a mode still being exploited by Norman Mailer, Gore Vidal, and some of their younger peers. Charlotte was eight, Emily Jane six, and Anne four when the Noble Lord died and when his cult gorgeously flowered, dominating their girlhood and their young womanhood. Byron's passive-aggressive sexuality—at once sado-masochistic, homoerotic, incestuous, and ambivalently narcissistic—clearly sets the pattern for the ambiguously erotic universes of *Jane Eyre* and *Wuthering Heights.* What Schopenhauer named (and deplored) as the Will to Live, and Freud subsequently posited as the domain of the drives, is the cosmos of the Brontës, as it would come to be of Hardy and Lawrence. Byron rather than Schopenhauer is the source of the Brontës' vision of the Will to Live, but the Brontës add to Byron what his inverted Calvinism only partly accepted, the Protestant will proper, a heroic zest to assert one's own election, one's place in the hierarchy of souls.

Jane Eyre and Catherine Earnshaw do not fit into the grand array of heroines of the Protestant will that commences with Richardson's Clarissa Harlowe and goes through Austen's Emma Woodhouse and Fanny Price to triumph in George Eliot's Dorothea Brooke and Henry James's Isabel Archer. They are simply too wild and Byronic, too High Romantic, to keep such company. But we can see them with Hardy's Tess, and even more, his Eustacia Vye, and with Lawrence's Gudrun and Ursula. Their version of the Protestant will stems from the Romantic reading of Milton, but largely in its Byronic dramatization, rather than its more dialectical and subtle analyses in Blake and Shelley, and its more normative condemnation in Coleridge and in the Wordsworth of *The Borderers.*

VI

The Byronism of Rochester in *Jane Eyre* is enhanced because the narrative is related in the first person by Jane Eyre herself, who is very much an overt surrogate for Charlotte Brontë. As Rochester remarks, Jane is indomitable; as Jane says, she is altogether "a free human being with an independent will." That will is fiercest in its passion for Rochester, undoubtedly because the passion for her crucial precursor is doubly ambivalent; Byron is both the literary father to a strong daughter, and the idealized object of her erotic drive. To Jane, Rochester's first appearance is associated not only with the animal intensities of his horse and dog, but with the first of his maimings. When Jane reclaims him at the novel's conclusion, he is left partly blinded and partly crippled. I do not think that we are to apply the Freudian reduction that Rochester has been somehow castrated, even symbolically, nor need we think of him as a sacrificed Samson figure, despite the author's allusions to Milton's *Samson Agonistes.* But certainly he has been rendered dependent upon Jane, and he has been tamed into domestic virtue and pious sentiment, in what I am afraid must be regarded as Charlotte Brontë's vengeance upon Byron. Even as Jane Eyre cannot countenance a sense of being in any way inferior to anyone whatsoever, Charlotte Brontë could not allow Byron to be forever beyond her. She could acknowledge, with fine generosity, that "I regard Mr. Thackeray as the first of modern masters, and as the legitimate high priest of Truth; I study him accordingly with reverence." But *Vanity Fair* is hardly the seedbed of *Jane Eyre,* and the amiable and urbane Thackeray was not exactly a prototype for Rochester.

Charlotte Brontë, having properly disciplined Rochester, forgave him his Byronic past, as in some comments upon him in one of her letters (to W. S. Williams, August 14, 1848):

Mr. Rochester has a thoughtful nature and a very feeling heart; he is neither selfish nor self-indulgent; he is ill-educated, misguided; errs, when he does err, through rashness and inexperience: he lives for a time as too many other men live, but being radically better than most men, he does not like that degraded life, and is never happy in it. He is taught the severe lessons of experience and has sense to learn wisdom from them. Years improve him; the effervescence of youth foamed away, what is really good in him still remains. His nature is like wine of a good vintage, time cannot sour, but only mellows him. Such at least was the character I meant to portray.

Poor Rochester! If that constituted an accurate critical summary, then who would want to read the novel? It will hardly endear me to feminist critics if I observe that much of the literary power of *Jane Eyre* results from its authentic sadism in representing the very masculine Rochester as a victim of Charlotte Brontë's will-to-power over the beautiful Lord Byron. I partly dissent, with respect, from the judgment in this regard of our best feminist critics, Sandra M. Gilbert and Susan Gubar:

> It seems not to have been primarily the coarseness and sexuality of *Jane Eyre* which shocked Victorian reviewers . . . but . . . its "anti-Christian" refusal to accept the forms, customs, and standards of society—in short, its rebellious feminism. They were disturbed not so much by the proud Byronic sexual energy of Rochester as by the Byronic pride and passion of Jane herself.

Byronic passion, being an ambiguous entity, is legitimately present in Jane herself as a psychosexual aggressivity turned both against the self and against others. Charlotte Brontë, in a mode between those of Schopenhauer and Freud, knows implicitly that Jane Eyre's drive to acknowledge no superior to herself is precisely on the frontier between the psychical and the physical. Rochester is the outward realm that must be internalized, and Jane's introjection of him does not leave him wholly intact. Gilbert and Gubar shrewdly observe that Rochester's extensive sexual experience is almost the final respect in which Jane is not his equal, but they doubtless would agree that Jane's sexual imagination overmatches his, at least implicitly. After all, she has every advantage, because she tells the story, and very aggressively indeed. Few novels match this one in the author's will-to-power over her reader. "Reader!" Jane keeps crying out, and then she exuberantly cudgels that reader into the way things are, as far as she is concerned. Is that battered reader a man or a woman?

I tend to agree with Sylvère Monod's judgment that "Charlotte Brontë is thus led to bully her reader because she distrusts him . . . he is a vapid, conventional creature, clearly deserving no more than he is given." Certainly he is less deserving than the charmingly wicked and Byronic Rochester, who is given a lot more punishment than he deserves. I verge upon saying that Charlotte Brontë exploits the masochism of her male readers, and I may as well say it, because much of *Jane Eyre*'s rather nasty power as a novel depends upon its author's attitude towards men, which is nobly sadistic as befits a disciple of Byron.

"But what about female readers?" someone might object, and they might add: "What about Rochester's own rather nasty power? Surely he could not have gotten away with his behavior had he not been a man and well-financed to boot?" But is Rochester a man? Does he not share in the full ambiguity of Byron's multivalent sexual identities? And is Jane Eyre a woman? Is Byron's Don Juan a man? The nuances of gender, *within literary representation,* are more bewildering even than they are in the bedroom. If Freud was right when he reminded us that there are never two in a bed, but a motley crowd of forebears as well, how much truer this becomes in literary romance than in family romance.

Jane Eyre, like *Wuthering Heights,* is after all a romance, however Northern, and not a novel, properly speaking. Its standards of representation have more to do with Jacobean melodrama and Gothic fiction than with George Eliot and Thackeray, and more even with Byron's *Lara* and *Manfred* than with any other works. Rochester is no Heathcliff; he lives in a social reality in which Heathcliff would be an intruder even if Heathcliff cared for social realities except as fields in which to take revenge. Yet there is a daemon in Rochester. Heathcliff is almost nothing but daemonic, and Rochester has enough of the daemonic to call into question any current feminist reading of *Jane Eyre.* Consider the pragmatic close of the book, which is Jane's extraordinary account of her wedded bliss:

> I have now been married ten years. I know what it is to live entirely for and with what I love best on earth. I hold myself supremely blest—blest beyond what language can express; because I am my husband's life as fully as he is mine. No woman was ever nearer to her mate than I am; ever more absolutely bone of his bone and flesh of his flesh.
>
> I know no weariness of my Edward's society: he knows none of mine, any more than we each do of the pulsation of the heart that beats in our separate bosoms; consequently, we are ever together. To be together is for us to be at once as free as in solitude, as gay as in company. We talk, I believe, all day long: to talk to each other is but a more animated and an audible thinking. All my confidence is bestowed on him, all his confidence is devoted to me; we are precisely suited in character—perfect concord is the result.
>
> Mr. Rochester continued blind the first two years of our union: perhaps it was that circumstance that drew us so very near—that knit us so very close! for I was then his vision, as I am still his right hand. Literally, I was (what he often called me) the apple of

his eye. He saw nature—he saw books through me; and never did I weary of gazing for his behalf, and of putting into words the effect of field, tree, town, river, cloud, sunbeam—of the landscape before us; of the weather round us—and impressing by sound on his ear what light could no longer stamp on his eye. Never did I weary of reading to him: never did I weary of conducting him where he wished to go: of doing for him what he wished to be done. And there was a pleasure in my services, most full, most exquisite, even though sad—because he claimed these services without painful shame or damping humiliation. He loved me so truly that he knew no reluctance in profiting by my attendance: he felt I loved him so fondly that to yield that attendance was to indulge my sweetest wishes.

What are we to make of Charlotte Brontë's strenuous literalization of Genesis 2:23, her astonishing "ever more absolutely bone of his bone and flesh of his flesh"? Is *that* feminism? And what precisely is that "pleasure in my services, most full, most exquisite, even though sad"? In her "Farewell to Angria" (the world of her early fantasies), Charlotte Brontë asserted that "the mind would cease from excitement and turn now to a cooler region." Perhaps that cooler region was found in *Shirley* or in *Villette*, but fortunately it was not discovered in *Jane Eyre*. In the romance of Jane and Rochester, or of Charlotte Brontë and George Gordon, Lord Byron, we are still in Angria, "that burning clime where we have sojourned too long—its skies flame—the glow of sunset is always upon it—."

VII

Wuthering Heights is as unique and idiosyncratic a narrative as *Moby-Dick*, and like Melville's masterwork breaks all the confines of genre. Its sources, like the writings of the other Brontës, are in the fantasy literature of a very young woman, in the poems that made up Emily Brontë's Gondal saga or cycle. Many of those poems, while deeply felt, simply string together Byronic commonplaces. A few of them are extraordinarily strong and match *Wuthering Heights* in sublimity, as in the famous lyric dated January 2, 1846:

> No coward soul is mine
> No trembler in the world's storm-troubled sphere
> I see Heaven's glories shine
> And Faith shines equal arming me from Fear
>
> O God within my breast
> Almighty ever-present Deity
> Life, that in me hast rest
> As I Undying Life, have power in Thee

Vain are the thousand creeds
That move men's hearts, unutterably vain,
Worthless as withered weeds
Or idlest froth amid the boundless main

To waken doubt in one
Holding so fast by thy infinity
So surely anchored on
The steadfast rock of Immortality

With wide-embracing love
Thy spirit animates eternal years
Pervades and broods above,
Changes, sustains, dissolves, creates and rears

Though Earth and moon were gone
And suns and universes ceased to be
And thou wert left alone
Every Existence would exist in thee

There is not room for Death
Nor atom that his might could render void
Since thou art Being and Breath
And what thou art may never be destroyed.

We could hardly envision Catherine Earnshaw, let alone Heathcliff, chanting these stanzas. The voice is that of Emily Jane Brontë addressing the God within her own breast, a God who certainly has nothing in common with the one worshipped by the Reverend Patrick Brontë. I do not hear in this poem, despite all its Protestant resonances, any nuance of Byron's inverted Miltonisms. *Wuthering Heights* seems to me a triumphant revision of Byron's *Manfred,* with the revisionary swerve taking Emily Brontë into what I would call an original gnosis, a kind of poetic faith, like Blake's or Emerson's, that resembles some aspects (but not others) of ancient Gnosticism without in any way actually deriving from Gnostic texts. "No coward soul is mine" also emerges from an original gnosis, from the poet's knowing that her *pneuma* or breath-soul, as compared to her less ontological psyche, is no part of the created world, since that world fell even as it was created. Indeed the creation, whether heights or valley, appears in *Wuthering Heights* as what the ancient Gnostics called the *kenoma,* a cosmological emptiness into which *we have been thrown,* a trope that Catherine Earnshaw originates for herself. A more overt Victorian Gnostic, Dante Gabriel Rossetti, made the best (if anti-feminist) observation on the setting of *Wuthering Heights,* a book whose "power and sound style" he greatly admired:

It is a fiend of a book, an incredible monster, combining all the stronger female tendencies from Mrs. Browning to Mrs. Brownrigg. The action is laid in Hell,—only it seems places and people have English names there.

Mrs. Brownrigg was a notorious eighteenth-century sadistic and murderous midwife, and Rossetti rather nastily imputed to *Wuthering Heights* a considerable female sadism. The book's violence is astonishing but appropriate, and appealed darkly both to Rossetti and to his close friend, the even more sadomasochistic Swinburne. Certainly the psychodynamics of the relationship between Heathcliff and Catherine go well beyond the domain of the pleasure principle. Gilbert and Gubar may stress too much that Heathcliff is Catherine's whip, the answer to her most profound fantasies, but the suggestion was Emily Brontë's before it became so fully developed by her best feminist critics.

Walter Pater remarked that the precise use of the term *romantic* did not apply to Sir Walter Scott, but rather:

> Much later, in a Yorkshire village, the spirit of romanticism bore a more really characteristic fruit in the work of a young girl, Emily Brontë, the romance of *Wuthering Heights;* the figures of Hareton Earnshaw, of Catherine Linton, and of Heathcliff—tearing open Catherine's grave, removing one side of her coffin, that he may really lie beside her in death—figures so passionate, yet woven on a background of delicately beautiful, moorland scenery, being typical examples of that spirit.

I have always wondered why Pater found the Romantic spirit more in Hareton and the younger Catherine than in Catherine Earnshaw, but I think now that Pater's implicit judgment was characteristically shrewd. The elder Catherine is the problematical figure in the book; she alone belongs to both orders of representation, that of social reality and that of otherness, of the Romantic Sublime. After she and the Lintons, Edgar and Isabella, are dead, then we are wholly in Heathcliff's world for the last half-year of his life, and it is in that world that Hareton and the younger Catherine are portrayed for us. They are—as Heathcliff obscurely senses—the true heirs to whatever societally possible relationship Heathcliff and the first Catherine could have had.

Emily Brontë died less than half a year after her thirtieth birthday, having finished *Wuthering Heights* when she was twenty-eight. Even Charlotte, the family survivor, died before she turned thirty-nine, and the world of *Wuthering Heights* reflects the Brontë reality: the first Catherine dies at eighteen, Hindley at twenty-seven, Heathcliff's son Linton at seventeen, Isabella at thirty-one, Edgar at thirty-nine, and Heathcliff at thirty-seven or thirty-eight. It is a world where you marry early, because you will not live long. Hindley is twenty when he marries Frances, while Catherine Earnshaw is seventeen when she marries the twenty-one-year-old Edgar Linton. Heathcliff is nineteen when he makes his hellish marriage to poor

Isabella, who is eighteen at the time. The only happy lovers, Hareton and the second Catherine, are twenty-four and eighteen, respectively, when they marry. Both patterns—early marriage and early death—are thoroughly High Romantic, and emerge from the legacy of Shelley, dead at twenty-nine, and of Byron, martyred to the cause of Greek independence at thirty-six.

The passions of Gondal are scarcely moderated in *Wuthering Heights,* nor could they be; Emily Brontë's religion is essentially erotic, and her vision of triumphant sexuality is so mingled with death that we can imagine no consummation for the love of Heathcliff and Catherine Earnshaw except death. I find it difficult therefore to accept Gilbert and Gubar's reading in which *Wuthering Heights* becomes a Romantic feminist critique of *Paradise Lost,* akin to Mary Shelley's *Frankenstein.* Emily Brontë is no more interested in refuting Milton than in sustaining him. What Gilbert and Gubar uncover in *Wuthering Heights* that is antithetical to *Paradise Lost* comes directly from Bryon's *Manfred,* which certainly *is* a Romantic critique of *Paradise Lost. Wuthering Heights* is *Manfred* converted to prose romance, and Heathcliff is more like Manfred, Lara, and Byron himself than is Charlotte Brontë's Rochester.

Byronic incest—the crime of Manfred and Astarte—is no crime for Emily Brontë, since Heathcliff and Catherine Earnshaw are more truly brother and sister than are Hindley and Catherine. Whatever inverted morality—a curious blend of Catholicism and Calvinism—Byron enjoyed, Emily Brontë herself repudiates, so that *Wuthering Heights* becomes a critique of *Manfred,* though hardly from a conventional feminist perspective. The furious energy that is loosed in *Wuthering Heights* is precisely Gnostic; its aim is to get back to the original Abyss, before the creation-fall. Like Blake, Emily Brontë identifies her imagination with the Abyss, and her *pneuma* or breath-soul with the Alien God, who is antithetical to the God of the creeds. The heroic rhetoric of Catherine Earnshaw is beyond every ideology, every merely social formulation, beyond even the dream of justice or of a better life, because it is beyond this cosmos, "this shattered prison":

> "Oh, you see, Nelly! he would not relent a moment, to keep me out of the grave! *That* is how I'm loved! Well, never mind! That is not *my* Heathcliff. I shall love mine yet; and take him with me— he's in my soul. And," added she, musingly, "the thing that irks me most is this shattered prison, after all. I'm tired, tired of being enclosed here. I'm wearying to escape into that glorious world, and to be always there; not seeing it dimly through tears, and yearning for it through the walls of an aching heart; but really with it, and in it. Nelly, you think you are better and more fortunate than I; in full health and strength. You are sorry for me— very soon that will be altered. I shall be sorry for *you.* I shall be incomparably beyond and above you all. I *wonder* he won't be near

me!" She went on to herself. "I thought he wished it. Heathcliff,
dear! you should not be sullen now. Do come to me, Heathcliff."

Whatever we are to call the mutual passion of Catherine and Heathcliff,
it has no societal aspect and neither seeks nor needs societal sanction.
Romantic love has no fiercer representation in all of literature. But "love"
seems an inadequate term for the connection between Catherine and Heathcliff. There are no elements of transference in that relation, nor can we call
the attachment involved either narcissistic or anaclitic. If Freud is not applicable, then neither is Plato. These extraordinary vitalists, Catherine and
Heathcliff, do not desire in one another that which each does not possess,
do not lean themselves against one another, and do not even find and thus
augment their own selves. They *are* one another, which is neither sane nor
possible, and which does not support any doctrine of liberation whatsoever.
Only that most extreme of visions, Gnosticism, could accommodate them,
for, like the Gnostic adepts, Catherine and Heathcliff can only enter the
pleroma or fullness together, as presumably they have done after Heathcliff's
self-induced death by starvation.

Blake may have promised us the Bible of Hell; Emily Brontë seems to
have disdained Heaven and Hell alike. Her finest poem (for which we have
no manuscript, but it is inconceivable that it could have been written by
Charlotte) rejects every feeling save her own inborn "first feelings" and
every world except a vision of earth consonant with those inaugural
emotions:

> Often rebuked, yet always back returning
>   To those first feelings that were born with me,
> And leaving busy chase of wealth and learning
>   For idle dreams of things which cannot be:
>
> To-day, I will seek not the shadowy region;
>   Its unsustaining vastness waxes drear;
> And visions rising, legion after legion,
>   Bring the unreal world too strangely near.
>
> I'll walk, but not in old heroic traces,
>   And not in paths of high morality,
> And not among the half-distinguished faces,
>   The clouded forms of long-past history.
>
> I'll walk where my own nature would be leading:
>   It vexes me to choose another guide:
> Where the gray flocks in ferny glens are feeding;
>   Where the wild wind blows on the mountain side.
>
> What have those lonely mountains worth revealing?
>   More glory and more grief than I can tell:
> The earth that wakes *one* human heart to feeling
>   Can centre both the worlds of Heaven and Hell.

Whatever that centering is, it is purely individual, and as beyond gender as it is beyond creed or "high morality." It is the voice of Catherine Earnshaw, celebrating her awakening from the dream of heaven:

> "I was only going to say that heaven did not seem to be my home; and I broke my heart with weeping to come back to earth; and the angels were so angry that they flung me out, into the middle of the heath on the top of Wuthering Heights; where I woke sobbing for joy."

VIII

> *Even taken in its derivative meaning of outline, what is form but the limit of that difference by which we discriminate one object from another?—a limit determined partly by the intrinsic relations or composition of the object, & partly by the extrinsic action of other bodies upon it. This is true whether the object is a rock or a man.*
> —GEORGE ELIOT, "Notes on Forms in Art"

It was Freud, in our time, who taught us again what the pre-Socratics taught: *ethos* is the *daimon*, character is fate. A generation before Freud, George Eliot taught the same unhappy truth to her contemporaries. If character is fate, then in a harsh sense there can be no accidents. Character presumably is less volatile than personality, and we tend to disdain anyone who would say personality is fate. Personalities suffer accidents; characters endure fate. If we seek major personalities among the great novelists, we find many competitors: Balzac, Tolstoy, Dickens, Henry James, even the enigmatic Conrad. By general agreement, the grand instance of a moral character would be George Eliot. She has a nearly unique spiritual authority, best characterized by the English critic Walter Allen about twenty years ago:

> George Eliot is the first novelist in the world in some things, and they are the things that come within the scope of her moral interpretation of life. Circumscribed though it was, it was certainly not narrow; nor did she ever forget the difficulty attendant upon the moral life and the complexity that goes to its making.

Her peculiar gift, almost unique despite her place in a tradition of displaced Protestantism that includes Samuel Richardson's *Clarissa* and Wordsworth's poetry, is to dramatize her interpretations in such a way as to abolish the demarcations between aesthetic pleasure and moral renunciation. Richardson's heroine Clarissa Harlowe and Wordsworth in his best poems share in a compensatory formula: experiential loss can be transformed into imaginative gain. Eliot's imagination, despite its Wordsworthian antecedents and despite the ways in which Clarissa Harlowe is the authentic precursor of Dorothea Brooke in *Middlemarch,* is too severe to accept the formula of compensation. The beauty of renunciation in Eliot's fiction does not result from a transformation of loss, but rather from a strength that is in no way dependent upon exchange or gain. Eliot presents us with the puzzle of what might be called the Moral Sublime. To her contemporaries, this was no puzzle. F. W. H. Myers, remembered now as a "psychic researcher" (a marvelous metaphor that we oddly use as a title for those who quest after spooks) and as the father of L. H. Myers, author of the novel *The Near and the Far,* wrote a famous description of Eliot's 1873 visit to Cambridge:

> I remember how at Cambridge I walked with her once in the Fellows' Garden of Trinity, on an evening of rainy May; and she, stirred somewhat beyond her wont, and taking as her text the three words which had been used so often as the inspiring trumpet-call of men—the words God, Immortality, Duty—pronounced with terrible earnestness how inconceivable was the first, how unbelievable was the second, and yet how peremptory and absolute the third. Never, perhaps, have sterner accents confirmed the sovereignty of impersonal and unrecompensing Law. I listened, and night fell; her grave, majestic countenance turned towards me like a sybil's in the gloom; it was as though she withdrew from my grasp, one by one, the two scrolls of promise and left me the third scroll only, awful with inevitable fates. And when we stood at length and parted, amid that columnar circuit of forest trees, beneath the last twilight of starless skies, I seemed to be gazing, like Titus at Jerusalem, on vacant seats and empty halls—on a sanctuary with no Presence to hallow it, and heaven left empty of God.

However this may sound now, Myers intended no ironies. As the sybil of "unrecompensing Law," Eliot joined the austere company of nineteenth-century prose prophets: Carlyle, Ruskin, Newman, and Arnold in England; Emerson in America; Schopenhauer, Nietzsche, Kierkegaard, and finally Freud on the Continent. But this ninefold, though storytellers of a sort, wrote no novels. Eliot's deepest affinities were scarcely with Dickens, Thackeray, and Trollope, and yet her formal achievement requires us to read her as we read them. This causes difficulties, since Eliot was not a great stylist, and was far more immersed in philosophical than in narrative tradition. Yet her frequent clumsiness in authorial asides and her hesitations in storytelling matter not at all. We do not even regret her absolute lack of any sense of the comic, which never dares take revenge upon her anyway. Wordsworth at his strongest, as in "Resolution and Independence," still can be unintentionally funny (which inspired the splendid parodies of the poem's leech-gatherer and its solipsistic bard in Lewis Carroll's "White Knight's Ballad" and Edward Lear's "Incidents in the Life of My Uncle

Arly"). But I have seen no effective parodies of George Eliot, and doubt their possibility. It is usually unwise to be witty concerning our desperate need, not only to decide upon right action, but also to will such action, against pleasure and against what we take to be self-interest. Like Freud, Eliot ultimately is an inescapable moralist, precisely delineating our discomfort with culture, and remorselessly weighing the economics of the psyche's civil wars.

IX

George Eliot is not one of the great letter writers. Her letters matter because they are hers, and in some sense do tell part of her own story, but they do not yield to a continuous reading. On a scale of nineteenth-century letter-writing by important literary figures, in which Keats would rank first, and Walter Pater last (the Paterian prose style is never present in his letters), Eliot would find a place about dead center. She is always herself in her letters, too much herself perhaps, but that self is rugged, honest, and formidably inspiring. Our contemporary feminist critics seem to me a touch uncomfortable with Eliot. Here she is on extending the franchise to women, in a letter to John Morley (May 14, 1867):

> Thanks for your kind practical remembrance. Your attitude in relation to Female Enfranchisement seems to be very nearly mine. If I were called on to act in the matter, I would certainly not oppose any plan which held out a reasonable promise of tending to establish as far as possible an equivalence of advantages for the two sexes, as to education and the possibilities of free development. I fear you may have misunderstood something I said the other evening about nature. I never meant to urge the "intention of Nature" argument, which is to me a pitiable fallacy. I mean that as a fact of mere zoological evolution, woman seems to me to have the worst share in existence. But for that very reason I would the more contend that in the moral evolution we have "an art which does mend nature"—an art which "itself is nature." It is the function of love in the largest sense, to mitigate the harshness of all fatalities. And in the thorough recognition of that worse share, I think there is a basis for a sublimer resignation in woman and a more regenerating tenderness in man.
>
> However, I repeat that I do not trust very confidently to my own impressions on this subject. The peculiarities of my own lot may have caused me to have idiosyncrasies rather than an average judgment. The one conviction on the matter which I hold with some tenacity is, that through all transitions the goal towards which we are proceeding is a more clearly discerned distinctness of function (allowing always for exceptional cases of individual

organization) with as near an approach to equivalence of good for woman and for man as can be secured by the effort of growing moral force to lighten the pressure of hard non-moral outward conditions. It is rather superfluous, perhaps injudicious, to plunge into such deeps as these in a hasty note, but it is difficult to resist the desire to botch imperfect talk with a little imperfect writing.

This is a strong insistence upon form in life as in art, upon the limit of that difference by which we discriminate one object from another. I have heard feminist critics decry it as defeatism, though Eliot speaks of "mere zoological evolution" as bringing about every woman's "worse share in existence." "A sublimer resignation in woman" is not exactly a popular goal these days, but Eliot never speaks of the Sublime without profundity and an awareness of human loss. When she praises Ruskin as a teacher "with the inspiration of a Hebrew prophet," she also judges him to be "strongly akin to the sublimest part of Wordsworth," a judgment clearly based upon the Wordsworthian source of Ruskin's tropes for the sense of loss that dominates the Sublime experience. The harshness of being a woman, however mitigated by societal reform, will remain, Eliot tells us, since we cannot mend nature and its unfairness. Her allusion to the Shakespearean "art which does mend nature," and which "itself is nature" (*Winter's Tale*, 4.4.88–96) subtly emends Shakespeare in the deliberately wistful hope for a moral evolution of love between the sexes. What dominates this letter to Morley is a harsh plangency, yet it is anything but defeatism. Perhaps Eliot should have spoken of a "resigned sublimity" rather than a "sublime resignation," but her art, and life, give the lie to any contemporary feminist demeaning of the author of *Middlemarch*, who shares with Jane Austen and Emily Dickinson the eminence of being the strongest woman writer in the English language.

X

Henry James asserted that "*Middlemarch* is at once one of the strongest and one of the weakest of English novels." The second half of that judgment was evidently defensive. By common consent, *Middlemarch* is equal, at least, to any other novel in the language. Dorothea Brooke is a crucial figure in that great sequence of the fictive heroines of the Protestant Will that includes Clarissa Harlowe, Elizabeth Bennet, Emma Woodhouse, Esther Summerson, Hester Prynne, Isabel Archer, Ursula Brangwen, and Clarissa Dalloway, among others. James complained that "Dorothea was altogether too superb a heroine to be wasted; yet she plays a narrower part than the imagination of the reader demands." Yet this is surely true of Isabel Archer also, since, like Dorothea Brooke, "she is of more consequence than the action of which she is the nominal centre." It could be argued that only Hester Prynne is provided with an action worthy of her, but then the superb

Hester is called upon mostly to suffer. Dimmesdale, under any circumstances, seems as inadequate for Hester as Will Ladislaw seems too inconsequential for Dorothea, or as even Ralph Touchett seems weak in relation to Isabel. Except for Clarissa Harlowe confronting her equally strong agonist in Lovelace, the heroines of the Protestant Will are always involved with men less memorable than themselves. Lawrence attempted to defy this tradition, but failed, as we must acknowledge when we set the tendentious Birkin beside the vital Ursula.

"Of course she gets up spurious miracles," the young Yeats remarked in defense of Madame Blavatsky, "but what *is* a woman of genius to do in the Nineteenth Century?" What is Saint Theresa to do in the nineteenth century, and in England, of all countries? What is Isabel Archer, heiress of all the ages, to do in the nineteenth century? In America, is she to marry Caspar Goodwood, a prospect that neither she nor James can endure? In Europe, she marries the subtly dreadful Osmond, mock-Emersonian and pseudo-Paterian. Even Casaubon might have been better, George Eliot could have been sly enough to tell Henry James. The heroes of the Protestant Will may have existed in mere fact—witness Oliver Cromwell and John Milton—but they have not been persuasively represented in prose fiction.

Rereading *Middlemarch* makes me unhappy only when I have to contemplate Will Ladislaw, an idealized portrait of George Henry Lewes, George Eliot's not unworthy lover. Otherwise, the novel compels aesthetic awe in me, if only because it alone, among novels, raises moral reflection to the level of high art. There is Nietzsche of course, but then *Zarathustra* is not a novel, and *Zarathustra* is an aesthetic disaster anyway. The great moralists, from Montaigne through Emerson to Freud, do not write prose fiction, and yet George Eliot is of their company. If we can speak aesthetically of the Moral Sublime, then she must help inform our speaking. All versions of the Sublime seem to involve a surrender of easier pleasures in favor of more difficult pleasures, but the Moral Sublime, in Freud or George Eliot, necessarily centers upon a coming to terms with the reality principle.

How is it that Eliot can imbue her moralizings with an aesthetic authority, when such contemporary practitioners as Doris Lessing, Walker Percy, and even Iris Murdoch cannot? I think that there are two answers here, and they may be quite unrelated to one another. One is that Eliot is unmatched among all other novelists in cognitive strength; she has the same eminence in prose fiction as Emily Dickinson has in lyric poetry or Shakespeare in the drama. We ordinarily do not estimate imaginative writers in terms of intellect, but that may be one of the eternal weaknesses of Western literary criticism. And yet the puzzle is great. Walt Whitman, in my judgment, surpasses even Dickinson among American poets, yet compared to her he cannot think at all. Dickinson and George Eliot, like Blake, rethink everything in earth and in heaven for themselves, as Shakespeare, above all writers, would appear to have done for himself. Such cognitive originality clearly does become an aesthetic value, in combination with other modes of mastery, yet it scarcely exists in poets as superb as Whitman and Tennyson.

Unallied to her cognitive strength (so far as I can tell) is Eliot's other massive aesthetic advantage as a moralist: a lack of any of the crippling intensities of the wrong kind of self-consciousness concerning morals and moralization. We do not encounter hesitation or affectation in Eliot's broodings upon moral dilemmas. She contrives to be at once intricate and direct in such matters, as in the famous conclusion to *Middlemarch:*

> Certainly those determining acts of her life were not ideally beautiful. They were the mixed result of young and noble impulse struggling amidst the conditions of an imperfect social state, in which great feelings will often take the aspect of error, and great faith the aspect of illusion. For there is no creature whose inward being is so strong that it is not greatly determined by what lies outside it. A new Theresa will hardly have the opportunity of reforming a conventual life, any more than a new Antigone will spend her heroic piety in daring all for the sake of a brother's burial: the medium in which their ardent deeds took shape is for ever gone. But we insignificant people with our daily words and acts are preparing the lives of many Dorotheas, some of which may present a far sadder sacrifice than that of the Dorothea whose story we know.
>
> Her finely-touched spirit had still its fine issues, though they were not widely visible. Her full nature, like that river of which Cyrus broke the strength, spent itself in channels which had no great name on the earth. But the effect of her being on those around her was incalculably diffusive: for the growing good of the world is partly dependent on unhistoric acts; and that things are not so ill with you and me as they might have been, is half owing to the number who lived faithfully a hidden life, and rest in unvisited tombs.

Eliot is defending both of Dorothea's marriages, but I rapidly forget Dorothea, at least for a while, when I read and ponder that massive third sentence, at once a truism and a profound moment of wisdom writing: "For there is no creature whose inward being is so strong that it is not greatly determined by what lies outside it." Our overdetermination—by society, by generational position, by the familial past—could not be better expressed, nor could we be better reminded that we ourselves will overdetermine those who come after us, even heroines as intense as Saint Theresa, Antigone, and Dorothea Brooke.

Eliot's proleptic answer to Henry James's protest at the waste of the superb Dorothea is centered in one apothegm: "the growing good of the world is partly dependent on unhistoric acts." James might have agreed, but then would have murmured that the growing good of the world and of the art of fiction are somewhat different matters. It is George Eliot's peculiar strength that she comes closer than any other novelist to persuading us that the good of the world and of the novel are ultimately reconcilable.

XI

For Arthur Schopenhauer, the Will to Live was the true thing-in-itself, not an interpretation but a rapacious, active, universal, and ultimately indifferent drive or desire. Schopenhauer's great work *The World as Will and Representation* had the same relation to and influence upon many of the principal nineteenth- and early twentieth-century novelists that Freud's writings have in regard to many of this century's later, crucial masters of prose fiction. Zola, Maupassant, Turgenev, and Tolstoy join Thomas Hardy as Schopenhauer's nineteenth-century heirs, in a tradition that goes on through Proust, Conrad, and Thomas Mann to culminate in aspects of Borges and of Beckett, the most eminent living writer of narrative. Since Schopenhauer (despite Freud's denials) was one of Freud's prime precursors, one could argue that aspects of Freud's influence upon writers simply carry on from Schopenhauer's previous effect. Manifestly, the relation of Schopenhauer to Hardy is different in both kind and degree from the larger sense in which Schopenhauer was Freud's forerunner or Wittgenstein's. A poet-novelist like Hardy turns to a rhetorical speculator like Schopenhauer only because he finds something in his own temperament and sensibility confirmed and strengthened, and not at all as Lucretius turned to Epicurus, or as Whitman was inspired by Emerson.

The true precursor for Hardy was Shelley, whose visionary skepticism permeates the novels as well as the poems and *The Dynasts*. There is some technical debt to George Eliot in the early novels, but Hardy in his depths was little more moved by her than by Wilkie Collins, from whom he also learned elements of craft. Shelley's tragic sense of eros is pervasive throughout Hardy, and ultimately determines Hardy's understanding of his strongest heroines: Bathsheba Everdene, Eustacia Vye, Marty South, Tess Durbeyfield, Sue Bridehead. Between desire and fulfillment in Shelley falls the shadow of the selfhood, a shadow that makes love and what might be called the means of love quite irreconcilable. What M. D. Zabel named as "the aesthetic of incongruity" in Hardy and ascribed to temperamental causes is in a profound way the result of attempting to transmute the procedures of *The Revolt of Islam* and *Epipsychidion* into the supposedly naturalistic novel.

J. Hillis Miller, when he worked more in the mode of a critic of consciousness like Georges Poulet than in the deconstruction of Paul de Man and Jacques Derrida, saw the fate of love in Hardy as being darkened always by a shadow cast by the lover's consciousness itself. Hugh Kenner, with a distaste for Hardy akin to (and perhaps derived from) T. S. Eliot's in *After Strange Gods*, suggested that Miller had created a kind of Proustian Hardy, who turns out to be a case rather than an artist. Hardy was certainly not an artist comparable to Henry James (who dismissed him as a mere imitator of George Eliot) or James Joyce, but the High Modernist shibboleths for testing the novel have now waned considerably, except for a few surviving high priests of Modernism like Kenner. A better guide to Hardy's permanent strength as a novelist was his heir D. H. Lawrence, whose *The Rainbow* and *Women in Love* marvelously brought Hardy's legacy to an apotheosis. Lawrence, praising Hardy with a rebel son's ambivalence, associated him with Tolstoy as a tragic writer:

> And this is the quality Hardy shares with the great writers, Shakespeare or Sophocles or Tolstoi, this setting behind the small action of his protagonists the terrific action of unfathomed nature; setting a smaller system of morality, the one grasped and formulated by the human consciousness within the vast, uncomprehended and incomprehensible morality of nature or of life itself, surpassing human consciousness. The difference is, that whereas in Shakespeare or Sophocles the greater, uncomprehended morality, or fate, is actively transgressed and gives active punishment, in Hardy and Tolstoi the lesser, human morality, the mechanical system is actively transgressed, and holds, and punishes the protagonist, whilst the greater morality is only passively, negatively transgressed, it is represented merely as being present in background, in scenery, not taking any active part, having no direct connexion with the protagonist. Œdipus, Hamlet, Macbeth set themselves up against, or find themselves set up against, the unfathomed moral forces of nature, and out of this unfathomed force comes their death. Whereas Anna Karenina, Eustacia, Tess, Sue, and Jude find themselves up against the established system of human government and morality, they cannot detach themselves, and are brought down. Their real tragedy is that they are unfaithful to the greater unwritten morality, which would have bidden Anna Karenina be patient and wait until she, by virtue of greater right, could take what she needed from society; would have bidden Vronsky detach himself from the system, become an individual, creating a new colony of morality with Anna; would have bidden Eustacia fight Clym for his own soul, and Tess take and claim her Angel, since she had the greater light; would have bidden Jude and Sue endure for very honour's sake, since one must bide by the best that one has known, and not succumb to the lesser good.
>
> (*Study of Thomas Hardy*)

This seems to me powerful and just, because it catches what is most surprising and enduring in Hardy's novels—the sublime stature and aesthetic dignity of his crucial protagonists—while exposing also his great limitation, his denial of freedom to his best personages. Lawrence's prescription for what would have saved Eustacia and Clym, Tess and Angel, Sue and Jude, is perhaps not as persuasive. He speaks of them as though they were Gudrun and Gerald, and thus have failed to be Ursula and Birkin. It is Hardy's genius that they are what they had to be: as imperfect as their creator and his vision, as impure as his language and his plotting, and finally painful and memorable to us:

> Note that, in this bitterness, delight,
> Since the imperfect is so hot in us,
> Lies in flawed words and stubborn sounds.

XII

I first read *The Return of the Native* when I was about fifteen, forty years ago, and had reread it in whole or in part several times through the years before rereading it now. What I had remembered most vividly then I am likely to remember again: Eustacia, Venn the red man, the Heath. I had almost forgotten Clym, and his mother, and Thomasin, and Wildeve, and probably will forget them again. Clym, in particular, is a weak failure in characterization, and nearly sinks the novel; indeed ought to capsize any novel whatsoever. Yet *The Return of the Native* survives him, even though its chief glory, the sexually enchanting Eustacia Vye, does not. Her suicide is so much the waste of a marvelous woman (or representation of a woman, if you insist upon being a formalist) that the reader finds Clym even more intolerable than he is, and is likely not to forgive Hardy, except that Hardy clearly suffers the loss quite as much as any reader does.

Eustacia underwent a singular transformation during the novel's composition, from a daemonic sort of female Byron, or Byronic witch-like creature, to the grandly beautiful, discontented, and human—all too human but hardly blameworthy—heroine, who may be the most desirable woman in all of nineteenth-century British fiction. "A powerful personality uncurbed by any institutional attachment or by submission to any objective beliefs; unhampered by any ideas"—it would be a good description of Eustacia, but is actually Hardy himself through the eyes of T. S. Eliot in *After Strange Gods*, where Hardy is chastised for not believing in Original Sin and deplored also because "at times his style touches sublimity without ever having passed through the stage of being good."

Here is Eustacia in the early "Queen of Night" chapter:

> She was in person full-limbed and somewhat heavy; without ruddiness, as without pallor; and soft to the touch as a cloud. To see her hair was to fancy that a whole winter did not contain darkness enough to form its shadow: it closed over her forehead like nightfall extinguishing the western glow.

Her nerves extended into those tresses, and her temper could always be softened by stroking them down. When her hair was brushed she would instantly sink into stillness and look like the Sphinx. If, in passing under one of the Egdon banks, any of its thick skeins were caught, as they sometimes were, by a prickly tuft of the large *Ulex Europaeus*—which will act as a sort of hair-brush—she would go back a few steps, and pass against it a second time.

She had Pagan eyes, full of nocturnal mysteries, and their light, as it came and went, and came again, was partially hampered by their oppressive lids and lashes; and of these the under lid was much fuller than it usually is with English women. This enabled her to indulge in reverie without seeming to do so: she might have been believed capable of sleeping without closing them up. Assuming that the souls of men and women were visible essences, you could fancy the colour of Eustacia's soul to be flame-like. The sparks from it that rose into her dark pupils gave the same impression.

Hardy's Eustacia may owe something to Walter Pater's *The Renaissance*, published five years before *The Return of the Native*, since in some ways she makes a third with Pater's evocations of the Botticelli Venus and Leonardo's Mona Lisa, visions of antithetical female sexuality. Eustacia's flame-like quality precisely recalls Pater's ecstacy of passion in the "Conclusion" to *The Renaissance*, and the epigraph to *The Return of the Native* could well have been:

> This at least of flame-like our life has, that it is but the concurrence, renewed from moment to moment, of forces parting sooner or later on their ways.

This at least of flame-like Eustacia's life has, that the concurrence of forces parts sooner rather than later. But then this most beautiful of Hardy's women is also the most doom-eager, the color of her soul being flame-like. The Heath brings her only Wildeve and Clym, but Paris doubtless would have brought her scarce better, since as Queen of Night she attracts the constancy and the kindness of sorrow.

If Clym and Wildeve are bad actors, and they are, what about Egdon Heath? On this, critics are perpetually divided, some finding the landscape sublime, while others protest that its representation is bathetic. I myself am divided, since clearly it is both, and sometimes simultaneously so! Though Eustacia hates it fiercely, it is nearly as Shelleyan as she is, and rather less natural than presumably it ought to be. That it is more over-written than overgrown is palpable:

> To recline on a stump of thorn in the central valley of Egdon, between afternoon and night, as now, where the eye could reach

nothing of the world outside the summits and shoulders of heath-
land which filled the whole circumference of its glance, and to
know that everything around and underneath had been from pre-
historic times as unaltered as the stars overhead, gave ballast to
the mind adrift on change, and harassed by the irrepressible New.
The great inviolate place had an ancient permanence which the
sea cannot claim. Who can say of a particular sea that it is old?
Distilled by the sun, kneaded by the moon, it is renewed in a year,
in a day, or in an hour. The sea changed, the fields changed, the
rivers, the villages, and the people changed, yet Egdon remained.
Those surfaces were neither so steep as to be destructible by
weather, nor so flat as to be the victims of floods and deposits.
With the exception of an aged highway, and a still more aged
barrow presently to be referred to—themselves almost crystallized
to natural products by long continuance—even the trifling irreg-
ularities were not caused by pickaxe, plough, or spade, but remained as long as the very finger-touches of the last geological
change.

Even Melville cannot always handle this heightened mode; Hardy
rarely can, although he attempts it often. And yet we do remember Egdon
Heath, years after reading the novel, possibly because something about it
wounds us even as it wounds Eustacia. We remember also Diggory Venn,
not as the prosperous burgher he becomes, but as we first encounter him,
permeated by the red ochre of his picturesque trade:

> The decayed officer, by degrees, came up alongside his fellow-
> wayfarer, and wished him good evening. The reddleman turned
> his head and replied in sad and occupied tones. He was young,
> and his face, if not exactly handsome, approached so near to hand-
> some that nobody would have contradicted an assertion that it
> really was so in its natural colour. His eye, which glared so
> strangely through his stain, was in itself attractive—keen as that
> of a bird of prey, and blue as autumn mist. He had neither whisker
> nor moustache, which allowed the soft curves of the lower part
> of his face to be apparent. His lips were thin, and though, as it
> seemed, compressed by thought, there was a pleasant twitch at
> their corners now and then. He was clothed throughout in a tight-
> fitting suit of corduroy, excellent in quality, not much worn, and
> well-chosen for its purpose; but deprived of its original colour by
> his trade. It showed to advantage the good shape of his figure. A
> certain well-to-do air about the man suggested that he was not
> poor for his degree. The natural query of an observer would have
> been, Why should such a promising being as this have hidden his
> prepossessing exterior by adopting that singular occupation?

Hardy had intended Venn to disappear mysteriously forever from Eg-don Heath, instead of marrying Thomasin, but yielded to the anxiety of giving the contemporary reader something cheerful and normative at the end of his austere and dark novel. He ought to have kept to his intent, but perhaps it does not matter. The Heath endures, the red man either vanishes or is transmogrified into a husband and a burgher. Though we see Clym rather uselessly preaching to all comers as the book closes, our spirits are elsewhere, with the wild image of longing that no longer haunts the Heath, Hardy's lost Queen of Night.

XIII

Of Hardy's major novels, *The Mayor of Casterbridge* is the least flawed and clearly the closest to tragic convention in Western literary tradition. If one hesitates to prefer it to *The Return of the Native, Tess,* or *Jude,* that may be because it is the least original and eccentric work of the four. Henchard is certainly the best articulated and most consistent of Hardy's male person-ages, but Lucetta is no Eustacia, and the amiable Elizabeth-Jane does not compel much of the reader's interest. The book's glory, Henchard, is so massive a self-punisher that he can be said to leap over the psychic cosmos of Schopenhauer directly into that of Freud's great essay on the economics of masochism, with its grim new category of "moral masochism." In a surprising way, Hardy reverses, through Henchard, one of the principal *topoi* of Western tragedy, as set forth acutely by Northrop Frye:

> A strong element of demonic ritual in public punishments and similar mob amusements is exploited by tragic and ironic myth. Breaking on the wheel becomes Lear's wheel of fire; bear-baiting is an image for Gloucester and Macbeth, and for the crucified Prometheus the humiliation of exposure, the horror of being watched, is a greater misery than the pain. *Derkou theama* (behold the spectacle; get your staring over with) is his bitterest cry. The inability of Milton's blind Samson to stare back is his greatest torment, and one which forces him to scream at Delilah, in one of the most terrible passages of all tragic drama, that he will tear her to pieces if she touches him.

For Henchard "the humiliation of exposure" becomes a terrible pas-sion, until at last he makes an exhibition of himself during a royal visit. Perhaps he can revert to what Frye calls "the horror of being watched" only when he knows that the gesture involved will be his last. Hence his Will, which may be the most powerful prose passage that Hardy ever wrote:

> They stood in silence while he ran into the cottage; returning in a moment with a crumpled scrap of paper. On it there was pen-cilled as follows:—

"MICHAEL HENCHARD'S WILL

"That Elizabeth-Jane Farfrae be not told of my death, or made to grieve on account of me.

"& that I be not bury'd in consecrated ground.

"& that no sexton be asked to toll the bell.

"& that nobody is wished to see my dead body.

"& that no murners walk behind me at my funeral.

"& that no flours be planted on my grave.

"& that no man remember me.

"To this I put my name.

"MICHAEL HENCHARD."

That dark testament is the essence of Henchard. It is notorious that "tragedy" becomes a very problematical form in the European Enlightenment and afterwards. Romanticism, which has been our continuous Modernism from the mid-1740s to the present moment, did not return the tragic hero to us, though from Richardson's Clarissa Harlowe until now we have received many resurgences of the tragic heroine. Hardy and Ibsen can be judged to have come closest to reviving the tragic hero, in contradistinction to the hero-villain who, throughout Romantic tradition, limns his nightpiece and judges it to have been his best. Henchard, despite his blind strength and his terrible errors, is no villain, and as readers we suffer with him, unrelievedly, because our sympathy for him is unimpeded.

Unfortunately, the suffering becomes altogether *too* unrelieved, as it does again with Jude Fawley. Rereading *The Mayor of Casterbridge* is less painful than rereading *Jude the Obscure*, since at least we do not have to contemplate little Father Time hanging the other urchins and himself, but it is still very painful indeed. Whether or not tragedy should possess some catharsis, we resent the imposition of too much pathos upon us, and we need some gesture of purification if only to keep us away from our own defensive ironies. Henchard, alas, *accomplishes nothing*, for himself or for others. Ahab, a great hero-villain, goes down fighting his implacable fate, the whiteness of the whale, but Henchard is a self-destroyer to no purpose. And yet we are vastly moved by him and know that we should be. Why?

The novel's full title is *The Life and Death of the Mayor of Casterbridge: A Story of a Man of Character*. As Robert Louis Stevenson said in a note to Hardy, "Henchard is a great fellow," which implies that he is a great personality rather than a man of character. This is, in fact, how Hardy represents Henchard, and the critic R. H. Hutton was right to be puzzled by Hardy's title, in a review published in *The Spectator* on June 5, 1886:

Mr. Hardy has not given us any more powerful study than that of Michael Henchard. Why he should especially term his hero in his title-page a "man of character," we do not clearly understand. Properly speaking, character is the stamp graven on a man, and character therefore, like anything which can be graven, and which, when graven, remains, is a word much more applicable to that which has fixity and permanence, than to that which is fitful and changeful, and which impresses a totally different image of itself on the wax of plastic circumstance at one time, from that which it impresses on a similarly plastic surface at another time. To keep strictly to the associations from which the word "character" is derived, a man of character ought to suggest a man of steady and unvarying character, a man who conveys very much the same conception of his own qualities under one set of circumstances, which he conveys under another. This is true of many men, and they might be called men of character *par excellence*. But the essence of Michael Henchard is that he is a man of large nature and depth of passion, who is yet subject to the most fitful influences, who can do in one mood acts of which he will never cease to repent in almost all his other moods, whose temper of heart changes many times even during the execution of the same purpose, though the same ardour, the same pride, the same wrathful magnanimity, the same inability to carry out in cool blood the angry resolve of the mood of revenge or scorn, the same hasty unreasonableness, and the same disposition to swing back to an equally hasty reasonableness, distinguish him throughout. In one very good sense, the great deficiency of Michael Henchard might be said to be in "character." It might well be said that with a little *more* character, with a little more fixity of mind, with a little more power of recovering *himself* when he was losing his balance, his would have been a nature of gigantic mould; whereas, as Mr. Hardy's novel is meant to show, it was a nature which ran mostly to waste. But, of course, in the larger and wider sense of the word "character," that sense which has less reference to the permanent definition of the stamp, and more reference to the confidence with which the varying moods may be anticipated, it is not inadmissible to call Michael Henchard a "man of character." Still, the words on the title-page rather mislead. One looks for the picture of a man of much more constancy of purpose, and much less tragic mobility of mood, than Michael Henchard. None the less, the picture is a very vivid one, and almost magnificent in its fullness of expression. The largeness of his nature, the unreasonable generosity and suddenness of his friendships, the depth of his self-humiliation for what was evil in him, the eagerness of his craving for sympathy, the vehemence of his impulses both for good and evil, the curious dash of stoicism in a nature so eager for sympathy, and of fortitude in one so moody and restless, — all these are lineaments which, mingled together as Mr. Hardy has mingled them, produce a curiously strong impression of reality, as well as of homely grandeur.

One can summarize Hutton's point by saying that Henchard is stronger in pathos than in ethos, and yet ethos is the daimon, character is fate, and Hardy specifically sets out to show that Henchard's character is his fate. The strength of Hardy's irony is that it is also life's irony, and will become Sigmund Freud's irony: Henchard's destiny demonstrates that there are no accidents, meaning that nothing happens to one that is not already oneself. Henchard stares out at the night as though he were staring at an adversary, but there is nothing out there. There is only the self turned against the self, only the drive, beyond the pleasure principle, to death.

The pre-Socratic aphorism that character is fate seems to have been picked up by Hardy from George Eliot's *The Mill on the Floss*, where it is attributed to Novalis. But Hardy need not have gleaned it from anywhere in particular. Everyone in Hardy's novels is over-determined by his or her past, because for Hardy, as for Freud, everything that is dreadful has already happened and there never can be anything absolutely new. Such a speculation belies the very word "novel," and certainly was no aid to Hardy's inventiveness. Nothing that happens to Henchard surprises us. His fate is redeemed from dreariness only by its aesthetic dignity, which returns us to the problematical question of Hardy's relation to tragedy as a literary form.

Henchard is burdened neither with wisdom nor with knowledge; he is a man of will and of action, with little capacity for reflection, but with a spirit perpetually open and generous towards others. J. Hillis Miller sees him as being governed erotically by mediated desire, but since Miller sees this as the iron law in Hardy's erotic universe, it loses any particular force as an observation upon Henchard. I would prefer to say that Henchard, more even than most men and like all women in Hardy, is hungry for love, desperate for some company in the void of existence. D. H. Lawrence read the tragedy of Hardy's figures not as the consequence of mediated desire, but as the fate of any desire that will not be bounded by convention and community.

> This is the tragedy of Hardy, always the same: the tragedy of those who, more or less pioneers, have died in the wilderness, whither they had escaped for free action, after having left the walled security, and the comparative imprisonment, of the established convention. This is the theme of novel after novel: remain quite within the convention, and you are good, safe, and happy in the long run, though you never have the vivid pang of sympathy on your side: or, on the other hand, be passionate, individual, wilful, you will find the security of the convention a walled prison, you will escape, and you will die, either of your own lack of strength to bear the isolation and the exposure, or by direct revenge from the community, or from both. This is the tragedy, and only this: it is

nothing more metaphysical than the division of a man against himself in such a way: first, that he is a member of the community, and must, upon his honour, in no way move to disintegrate the community, either in its moral or its practical form; second, that the convention of the community is a prison to his natural, individual desire, a desire that compels him, whether he feel justified or not, to break the bounds of the community, lands him outside the pale, there to stand alone, and say: "I was right, my desire was real and inevitable; if I was to be myself I must fulfil it, convention or no convention," or else, there to stand alone, doubting, and saying: "Was I right, was I wrong? If I was wrong, oh, let me die!"—in which case he courts death.

The growth and the development of this tragedy, the deeper and deeper realisation of this division and this problem, the coming towards some conclusion, is the one theme of the Wessex novels.

(Study of Thomas Hardy)

This is general enough to be just, but not quite specific enough for the self-destructive Henchard. Also not sufficiently specific is the sympathetic judgment of Irving Howe, who speaks of "Henchard's personal struggle—the struggle of a splendid animal trying to escape a trap and thereby entangling itself all the more." I find more precise the dark musings of Sigmund Freud, Hardy's contemporary, who might be thinking of Michael Henchard when he meditates upon "The Economic Problem in Masochism":

> The third form of masochism, the moral type, is chiefly remarkable for having loosened its connection with what we recognize to be sexuality. To all other masochistic sufferings there still clings the condition that it should be administered by the loved person; it is endured at his command; in the moral type of masochism this limitation has been dropped. It is the suffering itself that matters; whether the sentence is cast by a loved or by an indifferent person is of no importance; it may even be caused by impersonal forces or circumstances, but the true masochist always holds out his cheek wherever he sees a chance of receiving a blow.

The origins of "moral masochism" are in an unconscious sense of guilt, a need for punishment that transcends actual culpability. Even Henchard's original and grotesque "crime," his drunken exploit in wife-selling, does not so much engender in him remorse at the consciousness of wrongdoing, but rather helps engulf him in the "guilt" of the moral masochist. That means Henchard knows his guilt not as affect or emotion but as a negation, as the nullification of his desires and his ambitions. In a more than Freudian sense, Henchard's primal ambivalence is directed against himself, against the authority principle in his own self.

If *The Mayor of Casterbridge* is a less original book than *Tess* or *Jude*, it is also a more persuasive and universal vision than Hardy achieved elsewhere. Miguel de Unamuno, defining the tragic sense of life, remarked that "the chiefest sanctity of a temple is that it is a place to which men go to weep in common. A *miserere* sung in common by a multitude tormented by destiny has as much value as a philosophy." That is not tragedy as Aristotle defined it, but it is tragedy as Thomas Hardy wrote it.

The Victorian Novel before Victoria: Edward Bulwer-Lytton

Elliot Engel and Margaret F. King

More than any other British novelist, Edward Bulwer-Lytton has been regarded as a mere literary weathercock, twirled first one way and then the other by the surface winds of popular taste. According to Edward Wagenknecht: "Bulwer was the most remarkable virtuoso in the history of English fiction. He could take up a line of fiction, exploit it for all it was worth, and then, just when he seemed to have written himself out, he could turn to an entirely different kind of fiction and repeat the performance. Bulwer was very shrewd in guessing which way the cat would jump." The fact that Bulwer's life followed the same frenzied veerings as his fiction—he was a poet, novelist, playwright, translator, editor, baronet and Member of Parliament all within a single decade—increased his vulnerability to the charge of dilletantism. The image of him as a vapid dabbler was unwittingly reinforced even by his own grandson, who once remarked: "The range of his writing was extremely wide, and one might say that he emptied his mind into his books as fast as he filled it." Coupled with Thackeray's brutal parodies of his fiction in *Fraser's* and Carlyle's castigations of it in *Sartor Resartus*, Bulwer's diversity has indeed diverted most modern readers and critics from his novels. (His very name offers diversity, with critics calling him "Bulwer," "Lytton" or "Bulwer-Lytton" [looking him up in an index requires patience]. We have chosen to call him "Bulwer" since he was known by that name for over half of his life.)

There is, of course, some justice in the fact that Bulwer has been largely ridiculed or ignored in the twentieth century. He is hardly a genius of the first order, and his humourless pretensions to such status, as reflected in his turgid, pompous prose, add a certain piquancy to the pleasures of

From *The Victorian Novel before Victoria: British Fiction during the Reign of William IV, 1830–37*. © 1984 by Elliot Engel and Margaret F. King. Macmillan, 1984.

denigrating him. On the other hand, Bulwer should not be dismissed as a mere charlatan, concocting cheap literary potions to fuel every fictional craze. Allan Christensen, in *Edward Bulwer-Lytton: The Fiction of New Regions,* has been the strongest and most recent voice in negating the image of Bulwer as a facile opportunist. Arguing that Bulwer was a dedicated artist, Christensen points to the underlying mythic or metaphysical conceptions in the novels which make their variety more apparent than real. Christensen is surely right that there is more unity than diversity among the novels, and we would argue, further, that there is an especially significant unity among those novels which he wrote from 1830 to 1837. All seven novels of this period, from *Paul Clifford* to *Ernest Maltravers* and its sequel *Alice,* try to answer the same question, perhaps the most fundamental question that early Victorian artists faced: how is the Romantic alien to function within a culture in transition, when many of the justifications for his rebellion against society are being eradicated by reform? Bulwer's fiction during the reign of William IV provides his broadest platform for addressing this issue, since in his earlier novels of the 1820s his heroes could still enjoy flaunting their disregard for society, and after 1837 he turned his enormous energies to drama and then took up a very different kind of fiction.

The Romantic protagonist, whose genius and aspirations set him at odds with a repressive society, preoccupied Bulwer from the outset of his career. His first four novels, written during the late 1820s, introduce all the Romantic prototypes which would be transmuted into his fictional heroes of the next decade: the Byronic hero, the dandy, the hero of the *Bildungsroman* and the hero of the historical romance. The morbidly brooding protagonist of *Falkland,* Bulwer's first novel, has been described by Park Honan as a "Bulwer Byronized." Never again would Bulwer create a hero who would reject all reality beyond the terrors and the grandeur of his own ego. Indeed, Bulwer would later refer to *Falkland* as a vehicle of personal catharsis through which he purged the "perilous stuff" of his youthful imagination. And he would point to *Pelham,* his second book, as a novel which "put an end to Byron's Satanic mania and turned the thoughts and ambitions of young gentlemen without neckcloths, and young clerks who were sallow, from playing the Corsair, and boasting that they were villains." In actuality, even though as a dandy Pelham out-Brummels Brummel, he is not as far removed from the Byronic rebel as Bulwer imagined him to be. As Ellen Moers notes in her study of this character type, the dandy is "an archetype of the human being in revolt against society," standing somewhat like the Byronic hero "on an isolated pedestal of self" and refusing to acknowledge any standards of dress and behaviour other than those imposed by his own will. Although Pelham was intended as an ironic undercutting of the dandiacal pose as well as a rejection of the Byronic, the satire is so ambiguous that Pelham appeared to many readers, among them Thackeray and Carlyle, not as the deviant from a more earnest norm but rather as the norm itself.

After these two contemporary and somewhat complementary portraits of Romantic aliens, Bulwer shifted to the recent past with *The Disowned*, set in the late eighteenth century. This novel has two heroes whose characteristics reflect in part the romantic traditions which Bulwer had exploited in the novels preceding them. Clarence Linden, the young hero, is something of a dandy, and his mentor Algernon Mordaunt is, for all his philanthropic idealism, rather Byronic. But Bulwer's allegorical treatment of such characters reveals his debt to a third type of Romantic alien—the hero of the *Bildungsroman* such as Goethe created in *Wilhelm Meister*. Unlike their Goethean predecessors, however, Bulwer's protagonists in *The Disowned* never move convincingly from alienation to assimilation. In *Devereux*, Bulwer's last novel of the 1820s and first historical romance, the author merges Scott's and Goethe's romantic heroes, but, once again, he departs from his models by creating a protagonist who never is absorbed into the social mainstream. By the time Devereux returns to and restores the family estate from which he was exiled, he lives almost wholly in his memories.

Bulwer's prefatory remark that Devereux is really "a child of the nineteenth century" suggests that Bulwer's last novel of the 1820s, like the three that preceded it, is concerned with the Romantic alien's inability to merge with his society in order to find a creative but practical outlet for his genius and his energies. The largely unresolvable conflict between the Romantic alien and his culture in Bulwer's novels of the 1820s reflects in part the nature of the decade. Although weakening, the Tory obstructionism against which Byron and Shelley had raged died slowly; and the mechanistic deism of the religious establishment offered little resistance to the mechanistic materialism of an industrial economy. Added to the alienating cultural forces was Bulwer's very personal sense of alienation during this decade. In 1825 the seat in Parliament which he had hoped to gain from Hertford went instead to a friend who had intrigued for it while Bulwer was in Paris. His mother's disapproval of his marriage to Rosina Wheeler, and his subsequent refusal to accept an allowance from his mother after he married against her wishes, forced Bulwer to retire to near seclusion at Woodcot, where he had to pour all his energies into writing to support himself and his new wife. And because Bulwer's success came first in the literary sphere rather than the political, or perhaps only because of his temperament, the influence of Byronic and German Romanticism remained strong upon him. The blatant autobiographical strains discerned by most critics in Bulwer's first four novels indicate that personal and cultural forces combined in the 1820s to keep both Bulwer's protagonists and their creator from moving effectively from Romantic self-consciousness to the earnest social consciousness of the Victorianism that began to emerge in the novels of the next decade.

As the 1830s began, Bulwer retailored his heroes to fit the changing patterns of his personal life and the cultural milieu. Many of the personal justifications for Bulwer's romantic alienation were vanishing: he had been reconciled with his mother, his allowance had been reinstated, he had settled into one niche in society as a successful novelist, and, most importantly, in 1831 he began carving out a second one as a Liberal Member of ·Parliament. Moreover, Regency and Tory indifference to the problems of the disadvantaged was being replaced by the social consciousness and reforming spirit of a Whig-dominated Parliament; changes could now be made by working within the system rather than attacking it from without. Therefore, the central issue which confronted Bulwer in the 1830s was whether the Romantic hero, without many of his traditional causes, was doomed to become an anachronism, or if he, like his culture, could be capable of fruitful transformation. By the end of William's reign, Bulwer had transformed his earlier prototypes of the romantic alien into the Carlylean romantic hero, who while maintaining his transcendent, anti-materialist vision is able to translate that vision into effective social action.

The transformation came gradually. Indeed, Bulwer's first two novels of this period (*Paul Clifford* and *Eugene Aram*) narrate stories of the quintessential rebel—the criminal—and in neither book can such a protagonist be effectively assimilated into his society. Nevertheless, *Paul Clifford* is considered the first *roman à thèse*, the first social problem novel, of the Victorian era. In it Bulwer merges two of his previous romantic prototypes, the dandy and the *Bildungsroman* hero, and tries to invest the resultant hybrid with a strong social conscience. According to his preface, Bulwer sees *Paul Clifford* as a novel about society's warping of a young man with great potential, who turns to crime because of the brutality and bad associates he encounters when he is unjustly incarcerated. At the very end of the novel, Paul makes a stirring four-page speech in which he blames the evils of the legal and penal systems for the unsavoury directions in which his "apprenticeship" has led him. However, little which occurs between the preface and those final pages in any way justifies classifying the novel as a *roman à thèse,* a Newgate novel or a *Bildungsroman.* Bulwer does not, for example, portray Paul as brutalized or corrupted by his prison experience; instead, he warns that "We do not intend, reader, to indicate, by broad colors and in long detail, the moral deterioration of our hero; because we have found, by experience, that such pains on our part do little more than make thee blame our stupidity instead of lauding our intention." In actuality, more than half of the few pages devoted to Paul's imprisonment allow Paul's mentor, the roguish highwayman Augustus Tomlinson, to narrate his autobiography. Tomlinson's manners, dress and even his ennui are so reminiscent of the Regency upper class that his prison conversations with Paul could as well have been set in a drawing room. Paul is not, therefore, corrupted by a Fagin-like criminal; rather, he is dazzled by a Pelham-like dandy. And after he escapes from prison with Tomlinson, he merely exchanges his earlier associations with rakish men about town for new relationships with dandified highwaymen who have similar elegant language, dress and upper-class pretensions. After adopting the alias of "Lovett," Paul rises to be the leader of the highwaymen because he *is* the dandy *par excellence:* handsome, well-tailored, clever and possessing impeccable manners.

Finding a life of crime delightful, Paul and his gang steal only from the cruel or the rich and share such an inspired devotion to their chivalric trade that any reader must find the lifestyle appealing. Viewed in the context of the entire novel, Paul's final stirring speech on social injustice seems very artificial and is clearly more fluff than substance, more nougat than Newgate. On the whole, the thrust and tone of the novel are much closer to eighteenth-century moral satire than to the earnest Victorian social-problem novels that followed. The rather frivolous social commentary implicit in Bulwer's parallels between highwaymen and Members of Parliament is much truer to the overall tenor of the novel than is Paul's reforming speech. And the society to which Paul speaks does not reform. Unable to be assimilated into an unreformed society, Paul must leave England for America where "men who prefer labor to dependence cannot easily starve" and where "his labors and his abilities obtained gradual but sure success; and he now enjoyed the blessings of a competence earned with the most scrupulous integrity, and spent with the most kindly benevolence."

Despite the fact that Clifford's dandyism is far more convincing than his social activism and that the society he attempts to reform remains utterly undisturbed in its corrupt leadership and agencies, the novel still represents Bulwer's first stage in the transformation of the Romantic alien. The title character is Bulwer's first hero to engage with intensity (though without adequate motivation) in an attempt to eradicate injustice. And for the first time Bulwer creates a romantic protagonist who, by giving passionate voice to the *Zeitgeist* of the era of reform, demonstrates his potential for becoming a responsible citizen. Bulwer's analysis of Clifford's character points towards a more Victorian figure than any he had created before: "The same temper and abilities which had in a very few years raised him in influence and popularity far above all the chivalric band with whom he was connected, when once inflamed and elevated by a higher passion, were likely to arouse his ambition from the level of his present pursuits, and reform him, ere too late, into a useful, nay, even an honorable member of society."

Eugene Aram, Bulwer's next novel, at first appears as a false step in the progression from his Romantic aliens to Victorian activists, a reversion to his earlier title characters with their paralyzing yet strongly appealing self-consciousness. Although Aram is a criminal like Paul Clifford, he is guilty of murder, a much more serious crime than Clifford's, but a crime that Bulwer portrays as a momentary aberration in an otherwise blameless life. Because of his guilty secret, Aram's alienation from society far surpasses Clifford's, from the beginning of the novel when he is virtually a hermit until the end when he is executed. Whereas Clifford's Romantic prototype is primarily the dandy, Aram is modelled on the Byronic solitary. And because his crime is not revealed to the reader until the third volume, his Byronism seems not only to explain his withdrawal from the world but also to justify that withdrawal on the basis of high-souled Romantic principles. Dubious of any one man's ability to alleviate the misery of the masses and fearing that the "world of men" would destroy the "wild liberty" he finds when alone in nature, Aram resists all pleas to devote his genius to public service: "he appeared to consider the pomps of the world as shadows, and the life of his own spirit the only substance. He had built a city and a tower within the Shinar of his own heart, whence he might look forth, unscathed and unmoved, upon the deluge that broke over the rest of the earth." Even the cabinet minister who urges Aram to enter the public sphere as his secretary praises him for the nobility of his refusal. Thus, the first two volumes of *Aram* seem not only to portray but also to applaud the Romantic hero's rejection of an active role in society in favour of cultivating the intellect and imagination through lonely communion with nature.

But the revelation of Aram's crime, while not invalidating the nobility of his character, most certainly undermines the nobility of his eschewing public service and embracing romantic retreat. Bulwer reveals in volume 3 that guilt and fear of public scrutiny, rather than Romantic idealism, have destroyed Aram's former ambition and his early desire to help mankind. And the burden of the crime is laid not on society but on Aram and his corrupter, Houseman. As Bulwer says in his preface: "Here, unlike the milder guilt of Paul Clifford, the author was not to imply reform to society, nor open in this world atonement and pardon to the criminal. . . . But I have invariably taken care that the crime should stand stripped of every sophistry, and hideous to the perpetrator as well as to the world" (Preface). Rather than applauding Aram's Byronism, therefore, Bulwer portrays the harm that results (both personal and social) when a Byronic hero decides to disregard the moral laws by which ordinary men are ruled.

Eugene Aram is Bulwer's first novel in which it is not the times which are out of joint but the man. As represented by the responsible cabinet member who tries to enlist Aram's talents in the service of the government, society is ripe for the intellect and "sun-eyed vision" of a romantic like Aram. The sympathy with which Bulwer portrays his protagonist is not primarily designed, as Thackeray sarcastically charged, "to show how Eugene Aram, though a thief, a liar, and a murderer, yet being intellectual was among the noblest of mankind"; rather, it underscores the tragic waste which occurs when an otherwise worthy man is ruined by his Byronic defiance of moral law and thereby rendered useless to a society eager for his contributions. The characters who can be assimilated effectively into this society are not the Byronic protagonist and his brilliant, otherworldly fiancée Madeline Lester but the less intense, less brilliant secondary characters, Walter and Ellinor Lester, who make a modest contribution to their age through public service and charitable works. Bulwer is not yet able to deflate sufficiently the wilful egotism nor the Promethean aspirations of his romantic protagonist to allow such a character to be assimilated, but in

Eugene Aram he does acknowledge the dangers of unconstrained Byronism and creates a society in which assimilation of an equally romantic but less towering hero would be possible.

In *Godolphin*, Bulwer again portrays his protagonist as outside the sociopolitical mainstream, and, far more explicitly than in his previous novels, his central concern is to demonstrate that the fault lies with the hero instead of the times. Rather than a criminal or Byronic protagonist like Paul Clifford or Eugene Aram, Percy Godolphin is a *Bildungsroman* hero whose alienation results from the influence of his early environment. Prefiguring the children of Arnold's famous simile in "Stanzas from the Grande Chartreuse," Bulwer's hero was raised in the shadow of Godolphin Priory, a Gothic ruin that epitomizes romantic withdrawal from the world. The magnetism of the priory is evident when even the practical and politically ambitious Constance Erpingham falls temporarily under its spell, remarking, "Methinks . . . while I look around, I feel as if I could give up my objects of life; renounce my hopes; forget to be artificial and ambitious; live in these ruins forever." Godolphin Priory nurtures the hero's obsession with pursuing "the Ideal, the Beautiful, and the Perfect," to the neglect of the pragmatic and the imperfect with which men committed to social and political action must grapple.

Despite the shaping influence of the priory on Godolphin, Constance Erpingham, the woman he loves, has the potential to direct his aspirations towards more practical, fruitful goals; however, her own alienation from society prevents her from exerting such a beneficial influence. In contrast to Godolphin, who recoils altogether from political action, Constance passionately pursues such action but for destructive ends. Warped like Godolphin by the experiences of her youth, she covets political power in order to keep a deathbed promise of revenge made to her father, who was ruined by political machinations earlier in the century. If Godolphin's idealism could merge with her political activism, he would be the perfect Carlylean hero, able to translate his idealism into action. But because marriage to a lord is essential to Constance's plans for vengeance, she refuses to marry Godolphin, and the embryonic influence of her practical activism upon him is aborted.

Thus, instead of having his romanticism retailored, Godolphin now has it gilded upon his soul as he withdraws from English society altogether and retreats into Italy, whose evocation of a romantic past is as narcotic in effect as Godolphin Priory. Here the sway of the "ideal" on Godolphin is enhanced by his encounter with Volktman, an astrologer who gives quavering voice to more abstract conceptions of Imagination and Truth than even the Bulwer of the 1820s could stomach. But more damaging is his liaison with Lucilla, the astrologer's daughter, a child of nature who will ultimately doom Godolphin when her Wordsworthian innocence curdles into a foreboding otherworldliness. The Italian countryside into which he escapes with Lucilla should be the romantic paradise he has longed for, but ironically it is a paradise without pleasure, because for all his romanticism and for all Lucilla's attractions, Godolphin still loves Constance. His relationship with Lucilla leaves him dissatisfied; his final lesson from his Italian experience seems to be the inadequacy of his romantic idealism, and he returns to Constance.

Just as Godolphin's break with Lucilla appears to represent his leaving behind an incapacitating romanticism, so his union with Constance (after the death of her first husband) would seem to herald his assimilation into English culture at a time when England could most use his talents—for the year is 1832. But Godolphin's union with Constance comes too late and is not strong enough to break the stronger union with his fatal romanticism. Constance herself finds that when the Reform Bill eliminates most of the abuses of power that ruined her father, she can finally work constructively rather than destructively within society; Godolphin, however, turns not to politics but to collecting *objets d'art*, again pursuing the Ideal, the Beautiful and the Perfect but under the most compromising circumstances since he must be subsidized by a begrudging Constance. Despite his love for her, Godolphin, unlike Carlyle's Teufelsdrockh, does not find, nor apparently desires to find, something he can work at. When at the end of the novel he finally decides to enter Parliament, it is not as a Liberal or Radical on the side of Reform, but as a Conservative, and even this gesture towards political activism is doomed. The reappearance of Lucilla, now mad, and her prediction of Godolphin's death, represent the stranglehold which Godolphin's romantic past has over him. His subsequent drowning, immediately after he has witnessed Lucilla's death, releases him from the new age which could not accommodate his lack of earnest purpose.

Although Godolphin is not assimilated into his society, his story represents a real advance in Bulwer's portrayal of the Romantic alien because Bulwer here recognizes more clearly than in any of his earlier novels the inadequacy of the purely romantic response to an age like his own. He is highly critical of Godolphin—and deliberately so, as reflected by his bizarre device of having the novel end with Constance writing Bulwer himself a letter in which she criticizes the injustice of his portrayal of Godolphin's character. In a footnote Bulwer responds to the letter by saying, "[The character of Godolphin] conveys exactly the impression that my delineation, faithful to truth, is intended to convey—the influences of our actual world on the ideal and imaginative order of mind, when that mind is without the stimulus of pursuits at once practical and ennobling." And, as in *Eugene Aram,* Bulwer can create a Victorian activist only within the more modest dimensions of a minor character, in this case Stanforth Radclyffe, who argues the merits of public service with Godolphin, denying that men enter politics for mere vanity yet emphasizing that the huge ego of a Romantic need not be swallowed up by the philanthropy of public duty:

> I see great changes are necessary: I desire, I work for these great
> changes. I am not blind, in the mean while, to glory. I desire, on

the contrary, to obtain it; but it would only please me if it came from certain sources. I want to feel that I may realize what I attempt; and wish for that glory that comes from the permanent gratitude of my species, not that which springs from their momentary applause. Now, I am vain, very vain: vanity was, some years ago, the strongest characteristic of my nature. I do not pretend to conquer the weakness, but to turn it toward my purposes. I am vain enough to wish to shine, but the light must come from deeds I think really worthy.

Godolphin's pathetic destiny prevents him from heeding Radclyffe's advice, but the lesson will not be lost upon Bulwer's future title characters such as Rienzi and Ernest Maltravers.

By 1833, Bulwer reached an impasse in his efforts to transform the romantic idealists of his early novels into the romantic pragmatists who could guide a society open to reforming leadership. *Paul Clifford, Eugene Aram* and *Godolphin* mark an advance over Bulwer's earliest novels in that they reflect the growth of Bulwer's interest in public service; here the romantic types presented so uncritically in his novels of the 1820s undergo limited transformations which allow Bulwer to accentuate the flaws in the alienated Romantic. The dandy, for example, is metamorphosed into a highwayman with a late-blooming social conscience, the Byronic hero into a Faustian overreacher whose guilty secret is a crime of intellect rather than of passion, and the *Bildungsroman* hero into a dreamy Platonist "wandering between two worlds"—the dead world of the romantic past and the world of social activism still powerless to be born, at least in Bulwer's fiction. But in none of these transformations are the heroes' Promethean egos and aspirations sufficiently diminished for credible fusion with a Victorian milieu based on compromise between an idealized vision of one's culture as it should be and a realistic appraisal of one's culture as it is. Bulwer was still unable to portray these protagonists as finding a place in the world outside themselves, where, as Carlyle says in "The Everlasting Yea" section of *Sartor*, "Conviction is worthless until it converts itself into conduct."

To advance his heroes beyond the confines of their own egos, Bulwer had to turn for his setting from contemporary England to ancient Rome. His trip to Italy in 1833 did not revive his moribund marriage, as he had hoped. But it did mark an important shift in his writing career by inspiring him to write two historical novels in which the remoteness of time and place finally gave him the perspective he needed to create a romantic hero capable of significant cultural assimilation—one whose colossal self-consciousness is no longer the sole motivating force of the narrative.

In *The Last Days of Pompeii*, Bulwer's first novel to feature a hero of modest proportions, the romantic prototype is the hero of historical romance, modelled on the protagonists of Walter Scott. In light of Bulwer's repeated attacks on Scott's "historical method" as well as on his brand of romanticism, such a choice seems ironic; and indeed in other aspects Bulwer is at pains in *Pompeii* to differentiate his historical romance as markedly as possible from Scott's. His elaborate footnotes, for example, are meant to underscore the painstakingly accurate nature of Bulwer's historical research, as opposed to what he regarded as Scott's cavalier manipulation of historical fact. But Glaucus, Bulwer's protagonist, is a bloodless brother to Scott's typical hero—bland, naively romantic in his view of the world, and thoroughly decent. This decency manifests itself in the stoicism with which Glaucus endures such miseries as being framed for murder, drinking a love potion which nearly drives him insane, and awaiting death in the lion's den.

Because of his decency (and his Greek heritage), Glaucus can never be absorbed into the decadent culture of Pompeii which Bulwer pointedly parallels to decadent Regency society. But the sense of honour that alienates him from such a culture, coupled with his stoic will to persevere, are precisely the qualities which would aid in the reception of such a hero into a reforming culture like Bulwer's own. And by escaping from the labyrinth of his hero's self-consciousness, Bulwer positions himself in this novel not in his hero's mind but rather in the forum; because of this shift in vantage-point, it is Vesuvius and not the volcanic ego of any hero which casts the largest shadow over the events of the narrative. Everything in the novel is subservient to the suspense that builds with the building pressure within the volcano. Bulwer's focus on external events is intensified by his determination to dissect with impressive accuracy the customs and structure of ancient Roman society. As external events loom larger, Bulwer's preoccupation with the inner world of his hero shrinks proportionately. As a result, the mind of the protagonist and the external events of his era impinge upon each other in a way that is more Victorian than Romantic, preparing the way for a protagonist who can acknowledge the claims of a world outside that of his own idealistic vision.

With *Rienzi*, the historical novel that followed *The Last Days of Pompeii*, Bulwer finally portrays a Romantic protagonist who can move beyond alienation to social activism. The novel is set in fourteenth-century Rome, an era at least as decadent as that of Pompeii, and even more desperate for a hero. Although Rome maintains an empty pageant of popular government, the plebeians are completely at the mercy of the patricians, who, as Bulwer says, are banditti in all but name. Their contempt for church as well as state had forced the pope to flee to Avignon, depriving Rome of religious as well as secular leadership. Stepping into this void is an historical figure whose prototype differs considerably from all Bulwer's previous romantic heroes. Rienzi's personality owes practically nothing to the influence of the dandy, Byronism, the *Bildungsroman* hero or the colourless young men of Scott. Rienzi is more nearly the Carlylean hero, a transcendental visionary who embodies his romantic ideals in social reform and social justice.

At the outset of the novel, Rienzi, reminiscent in some ways of Godolphin and Eugene Aram, is a dreamy scholar completely withdrawn from the world and obsessed with Rome's romantic past. But when his brother is murdered by the patricians, Rienzi is galvanized into a patriot and a revolutionary:

> From that bloody clay [his brother's corpse] and that inward prayer, Cola di Rienzi rose a new being. But for that event, the future liberator of Rome might have been but a dreamer, a scholar, a poet; the peaceful rival of Petrarch, a man of thoughts, not deeds. But from that time, all his faculties, energies, fancies, genius, became concentrated into a single point; and patriotism, before a vision, leapt into the life and vigor of a passion, lastingly kindled, stubbornly hardened, and awfully consecrated—by revenge!

Despite the fact that revenge helps mould his desire to re-establish Rome as a true republic, Rienzi sees himself as "the Instrument of Heaven." As he describes in retrospect his achievement to the Holy Roman Emperor, "I am that Rienzi to whom God gave to govern Rome, in peace, with justice, and to freedom. I curbed the nobles, I purged corruption, I amended law." His vocation is that of Carlyle's heroes—to wrest order from chaos as he incarnates through his leadership God's will for his society.

As Rienzi's efforts towards reform progress, romantic idealism obliterates his motive of revenge. His ennobling leadership is underscored by the contrasts between him and Walter de Montreal, the bandit leader of the Grand Company who aspires to conquer Rome. Although clever, courageous and resourceful—even chivalrous in his private life—Montreal is motivated purely by the desire for power. In politics, his guiding principles spring from Machiavellian cynicism; he will turn on his allies as easily as he supports his former enemies if either shift in allegiance will advance his own ambitions. His role as Rienzi's foil culminates when Rienzi comes to arrest him:

> And there, as these two men, each so celebrated, so proud, so able, and ambitious, stood, front to front—it was literally as if the rival spirits of force and intellect, order and strife, of the falchion and the fasces—the antagonist principles by which empires are ruled and empires overthrown, had met together, incarnate and opposed.

This contrast emphasizes that romantic idealism fosters not only efficient leadership but also an altruism that safeguards the welfare of the state. As a result, while Rienzi governs Rome, the power of the patricians is checked, and the arts flourish as luxuriantly as do justice and peace.

Despite his achievements, however, Rienzi is not Bulwer's ideal romantic protagonist. His first fall from power is as precipitous as his rise, and the fall which follows his brief second ascent is fatal. None of the reforms Rienzi instituted are preserved, and Rome lapses back into the chaos generated by the struggles among banditti, patricians, mercenaries

to it and is not so caught up in the events of the day that he loses his perspective or his attachment to values more timeless than topical:

> But while he withdrew himself from the insipid and the idle, he took care not to become separated from the world. He formed his own society according to his tastes: took pleasure in the manly and exciting topics of the day; and sharpened his observation and widened his sphere as an author, by mixing freely and boldly with all classes as a citizen. But literature became to him as art to the artist—as his mistress to the lover—an engrossing and passionate delight. . . . From LITERATURE he imagined had come all that makes nations enlightened and men humane. And he loved Literature the more, because her distinctions were not those of the world—because she had neither ribbons, nor stars, nor high places at her command.

Ernest is able to minister and prophesy to his culture out of his romantic idealism without being sacrificed to it, as Rienzi was.

In becoming an effective prophet, rather than a martyr or an ascetic recluse, Ernest masters a skill which eludes all his predecessors—the ability to compromise without being compromised. Paul Clifford, Eugene Aram, Percy Godolphin and Glaucus withdrew from their cultures because they refused to temper their romantic vision of what should be with at least a partial acceptance of what is; on the other hand, Rienzi was destroyed by his own people because his romantic vision of what should be blinded him to what was. By contrast, at the completion of his apprenticeship, Ernest is able to temper his Romantic vision with Victorian realism and to modify his Romantic idealism with Victorian pragmatism. In learning to compromise, a skill so central to the Victorian era that W. L. Burn has called its middle years "the age of equipoise," Ernest must steer a course between the Scylla and Charybdis of his "alter-egos," as Christensen calls them—Castruccio Cesarini and Lumley Ferrers. Castruccio represents the Romantic vision so turned inward upon itself that his rejection of reality leads ultimately to madness. Although a mediocre Italian poet who describes passions he has never felt, Castruccio strikes Byronic poses and exhibits an ego worthy of the most alienated of Bulwer's romantics, and in his outlandish dress he rivals Bulwer's early dandies. His romantic desire for revenge against Ernest and his egoistic naivety make Castruccio an easy dupe for Lumley Ferrers, who uses the poet as his accomplice in a scheme which, in deceiving Florence Lascelles about Ernest's true feelings for her, hastens her early death. From Castruccio's Byronic guilt, madness follows, and his withdrawal from reality is complete.

The alternative offered by Lumley Ferrers—pure pragmatic materialism—is portrayed as equally unpalatable. Where Castruccio is pathetic, Ferrers is despicable. Like Walter de Montreal in *Rienzi*, Ferrers is a man of great practical gifts but no scruples. Although just as self-centred as Castruccio, he is a thoroughgoing pragmatist, manipulating and often destroying any character who can be of use to him. And he represents the threat to the public weal of a leader in whom romantic idealism and altruism are totally lacking. Like Castruccio's unadulterated romanticism, Lumley's unadulterated materialism proves fatal; ultimately he is strangled in his bed by his dupe and accomplice in Florence Lascelles's death. Just as Ernest must cultivate romanticism undistorted by Castruccio's retreat from reality, he must also seek a pragmatism unalloyed by Lumley's cynicism—and he must develop a concern for the public good untainted by the self-seeking nature of both his antagonists.

As early as halfway through *Ernest Maltravers,* the hero seems well on his way to achieving a desirable compromise between Romantic idealism and Victorian earnestness. Unlike Bulwer's earlier heroes who resist too long the admonitions of socially responsible mentors, Ernest responds readily to those who urge him to discover his true vocation and to devote his genius to the good of his country: Monsieur de Montaigne, Lady Florence Lascelles and his guardian Frederick Cleveland. By the age of thirty Ernest has established himself both as a successful novelist and as a conscientious Member of Parliament. Yet he is miserable in both of his vocations. The sources of his misery are the flaws in his Romantic idealism, which has not yet been properly tempered to sustain the vocations he has chosen. The stress of trying to embody his Romantic vision in his writing is so great that it threatens his very life, his physician finally warning him to put his writing aside, at least temporarily. But the political career he turns to as an antidote disillusions him. His ideals of conduct are so lofty that the behaviour of his colleagues and other public figures inevitably disappoints him. Thus, unlike Bulwer's earlier Romantics, Maltravers's problem is not with entering the mainstream of society but rather with staying there. At the end of the first novel, the death of his fiancée makes him withdraw from the public sphere and remain withdrawn, first as a wanderer abroad and then as a recluse on his country estate, until the end of the second novel. During that time, he seems to regress towards the Byronic hauteur and misanthropy of many of Bulwer's earlier Romantics.

What Maltravers's romanticism lacks—the tempering element it requires if he is to resume his vocations and find them fruitful—is embodied in his first and last mentor, Alice Darvil Templeton. In an ironic reversal of *Godolphin,* Maltravers's proper soul-mate is not the politically ambitious Florence Lascelles (the counterpart of Godolphin's Constance Erpingham) but a personification of Wordsworthian Nature, like the earlier Lucilla. Unlike Lucilla, however, Alice does not tempt Ernest to withdraw still further from society. Rather, she infuses his soul with a Wordsworthian benevolence, becoming, like nature in "Tintern Abbey," the "anchor of [his] purest thoughts, the nurse, / The Guide, the guardian of [his] heart, and soul / Of all . . . moral being." Ernest's discovery of Alice's constancy to him during their eighteen years apart triggers an epiphany which humanizes his romantic idealism:

> Here have I found that which shames and bankrupts the Ideal! Here have I found a virtue that, coming at once from God and Nature, has been wiser than all my false philosophy, and firmer than all my pride! . . . you, alike through the equal trials of poverty and wealth, have been destined to rise above all triumphant,— the example of the sublime moral that teaches us with what mysterious beauty and immortal holiness the Creator has endowed our human nature when hallowed by our human affections! . . . And your fidelity to my erring self has taught me ever to love, to serve, to compassionate, to respect, the community of God's creatures to which—noble and elevated though you are—you yet belong!

Alice represents not only Nature in the Wordsworthian sense but also, as Allan Christensen points out, "Bulwer's version of Carlyle's natural supernaturalism. Beneath the apparently arid surfaces of the external and artificial world lies a beneficent, powerfully dynamic, and fertile principle, which . . . has been subtly guiding the artist back to herself even during the years of his seeming estrangement from her." And it is this principle which finally also equips Bulwer's Romantic alien to become a Carlylean hero:

> Maltravers once more entered upon the career so long suspended. He entered with an energy more practical and steadfast than the fitful enthusiasm of former years. And it was noticeable among those who knew him well, that, while the firmness of his mind was not impaired, the haughtiness of his temper was subdued. No longer despising Man as he is, and no longer exacting from all things the ideal of a visionary standard, he was more fitted to mix in the living World, and to minister usefully to the great objects that refine and elevate our race. His sentiments were, perhaps, less lofty, but his actions were infinitely more excellent, and his theories infinitely more wise.

If summarized and abstracted from his novels of the 1830s, Bulwer's concern with reconciling Romantic idealism with Victorian pragmatism should make him the third member of a triumvirate including Carlyle and Tennyson, who in respected works of the same decade (*Sartor Resartus* and "Palace of Art") were preoccupied with resolving this same conflict. Yet Bulwer's fiction is never mentioned as a complement to their prose and poetry. Indeed, when Bulwer is linked with Romanticism at all, it is most often in terms similar to those of Donald Stone who labelled him the "Dunciad-laureate" of "second-hand Romanticism." The cause for such denigration is, of course, his style—inflated by his sense of self-importance, turgid with circumlocutions and epic similes, and risible in its bathos and bombast. Bulwer's message is so deeply buried beneath his manner (or, actually, his mannerism) that few readers wish to unearth his timely themes by separating them from the rhetorical debris. How can we take seriously an author who is capable of creating in *Paul Clifford* the following simile when he simply wishes to relate that a character desired to leave a boarding house: "This idea, though conquered and reconquered, gradually swelled and increased at his heart, even as swelleth that hairy ball found in the stomach of some suffering heifer after its decease." Such writing leaves the reader's stomach in much the same condition as the heifer's.

Although Bulwer's style is certainly tainted by pretentiousness and poor taste, the most noxious contaminant is his overblown Romanticism. Bulwer writes novels with the sensibility and the style of a Romantic poet, very unlike the three major novelists of the Romantic period itself, who all eschewed the impassioned style of Shelley and Byron. Peacock's style is remembered for its biting satire; Austen's, for brilliant realism; Scott's, for beguiling congeniality. Only Bulwer is remembered for bloated grandiloquence, making him a sad contrast both to his predecessors and to the two greatest Romantic novelists of the Victorian period, Charlotte and Emily Brontë. Both writers carefully moored to reality the colossal aspects of Romanticism in their fiction. For example, although Charlotte's narrator in *Jane Eyre* has an ego as titanic as any of Bulwer's heroes, it is tethered to the everyday world by a harness of deadly earnest Victorian morality. Similarly, Emily filters the Romantic passions and aspirations of Heathcliff and Cathy in *Wuthering Heights* through the mundane lens of Nelly Dean's and Lockwood's perceptions. Many of Bulwer's novels, by contrast, sound as if they were written by a Heathcliff made articulate by university education, as in the following ejaculation from *Godolphin:*

> O much-abused and highly-slandered passion!—Passion rather of the soul than of the heart: hateful to the pseudo-moralist, but viewed with favoring, though not undiscriminating eyes by the true philosopher: bright-winged and august AMBITION! It is well for fools to revile thee, because thou art liable, like other utilities, to abuse! The wind uproots, it scatters a thousand acorns. Ixion embraced the cloud, but from the embrace sprang a hero. Thou, too, hast thy fits of violence and storm; but without thee, life would stagnate:—thou, too embracest thy clouds; but even thy clouds have the demi-gods for their offspring!

Unfortunately, the "passions" which prompt Bulwer's language to soar to such grandiose heights are not embodied convincingly in either Bulwer's characters or narrative personae; they have neither subjective nor objective correlatives. Because he has the grand manner without the grand matter, the image projected by Bulwer's style led to his being ridiculed [by G. K.

Chesterton] as a "lion in curl papers." The roar of such a lion is not likely to be heeded, respected, nor even remembered.

Despite his bombastic style, Bulwer still deserves study. Even G. K. Chesterton, after characterizing Bulwer's fiction as "mere polished melodrama," admitted that "there was an element indefinable about Lytton, which often is in adventures; which amounts to a suspicion that there was something in him after all." And according to Lionel Stevenson, it is only those novels written before 1838 which give Bulwer his chief significance. His merit lies partly in the fact that he was, like his heroes, a Romantic rebel, struggling against the tide of "materialistic" realism which he saw flowing from the novels of Sir Walter Scott. In place of the pleasant, tepid romantic values which Scott transposed to the sphere of the everyday, Bulwer insisted on searing his Romanticism with highest passion. By doing so, although Bulwer could hardly stem the tide of realism, he did create in it new currents of idealized, internalized meaning which would mark a crucial divergence between the realism of Victorian fiction and that of Scott. Moreover, by his insistence on anti-realistic digressions, authorial intrusions and dramatically gratuitous subplots and characters, Bulwer may have helped delay the imposition of much more restrictive standards until nearly the twentieth century, a delay for which the Victorian novel is no doubt the richer. Finally, as this chapter has shown, Bulwer mirrored the concerns of his contemporaries and anticipated a major theme in later Victorian fiction by portraying the difficulties faced by alienated Romantics in establishing fruitful, purposive roles for themselves in a culture that both welcomed and threatened them. By successfully directing his last fictional hero of the 1830s away from solely egotistical concerns, by tempering Ernest Maltravers's idealism with an other-centred and humane regard for social issues, Bulwer prefigured similar transformations in the novels of his more gifted successors, most notably Trollope and Eliot. Thus, it seems rather unfair that Edward Bulwer-Lytton should now be viewed as merely the weathervane of Victorian fiction since he usually stirred rather than reflected the necessary winds of change by his determined, though often wrongheaded, opposition to both realism and diluted romanticism. For better or, more typically, for worse, Bulwer was always his own man.

Benjamin Disraeli and the Romance of the Will

Donald D. Stone

The power of the passions, the force of the will, the creative energy of the imagination, these make life, and reveal to us a world of which the million are entirely ignorant.

—LOTHAIR

Historians have long recognized the Romantic element in Disraeli's political beliefs, and their view of his place in history has been considerably influenced by their attitudes toward those Romantic traits. Disraeli viewed a political career as a Romantic mission, as a vehicle for his Romantic artistry: in public service a Shelleyan devotion to the welfare of others could be united to a Byronic display of will and a Keatsian display of imagination. As one of the earliest English statesmen to capitalize on what Walter Bagehot called the public readiness to be governed by appeals to their imagination, Disraeli had many detractors who were disturbed by the ways in which he, in creating a myth of his own role and person for public consumption, occasionally disregarded humble matters of truth. The hero of Trollope's series of political novels, Plantagenet Palliser, was conceived, in large part, in protest against the manner in which Disraeli had risen to eminence. Everything about Palliser's political ideals and performance is at variance with Disraeli's:

> He was not a brilliant man, and understood well that such was the case. He was now listened to in the House, as the phrase goes; but he was listened to as a laborious man, who was in earnest in what he did, who got up his facts with accuracy, and who, dull though he be, was worthy of confidence. And he was very dull. He rather prided himself on being dull, and on conquering in spite of his dulness. He never allowed himself a joke in his speeches, nor attempted even the smallest flourish of rhetoric. He was very careful in his language, labouring night and day to learn to express

himself with accuracy, with no needless repetition of words, per-
spicuously with regard to the special object he might have in view.
He had taught himself to believe that oratory, as oratory, was a
sin against that honesty in politics by which he strove to guide
himself.

(*Can You Forgive Her?*)

Palliser's dullness and honesty lead him to only a limited success, as head
of the sort of coalition government that, Disraeli noted, England did not
love. Disraeli, by contrast, took advantage of his resources of imagination
and language to become one of the most popular, if also one of the most
mistrusted, of Victorian British leaders. The Romantic state of mind that
he brought to politics is candidly and often engagingly revealed in his
novels, and the connection between Disraeli's Romantic politics and his
literary endeavors provides an intriguing perspective on the allure and
dangers of the Romantic impulse.

Where Trollope sought to conceal or discipline his Romantic sensibility,
Disraeli delighted in exposing and making use of his. Although he was,
like his friend Edward Bulwer-Lytton, a second-generation Romantic, Disraeli gave his assent to many of the cardinal Romantic tenets, such as faith
in the supremacy of the will as controller of one's destiny and in the primacy
of the imagination as arbiter of reality and redeemer of mankind. However,
he also gave the impression, on occasion, that he was taking advantage of
these beliefs and of the credulity of his audience in order to create an effect.
In this respect, his championing of the rights of the imagination, for example, might be compared with the claims of his predecessors. The Romantic poets' refusal "to submit the poetic spirit" to what Wordsworth
called "the chains of fact and real circumstance" is well known: in Blake's
case, for example, "the things imagination saw were as much realities as
were gross and tangible facts." One of the most extreme instances involving
a Romantic poet's disregard for historical accuracy occurs in Keats's "On
First Looking into Chapman's Homer," where Cortez is substituted for
Balboa as the discoverer of the Pacific Ocean. However accidental the original slip may have been, once Keats's imagination had conjured up Cortez
he was obliged to leave the line as it stood: "Or like stout Cortez when
with eagle eyes / He star'd at the Pacific." Keats's claim for the "truth of
the imagination" is well known. "What the imagination seizes as Beauty
must be truth—whether it existed before or not," he says in a famous letter.
The imagination, as far as a Romantic poet is concerned, *creates* truth, rather
than reflects something that for a scientist or explorer is merely real. "The
Imagination may be compared to Adam's dream—he awoke and found it
truth."

Keats's words help to clarify a major theme in Disraeli's political life
and in his fiction: the supreme importance of the imagination as an instrument of redemptive power and the consequent irrelevance of facts. It is

this faith in the imagination (and in what Keats calls "the holiness of the Heart's affections") that prompts the words of Sidonia in Disraeli's best-known novel, *Coningsby*: "Man is only truly great when he acts from the passions; never irresistible but when he appeals to the imagination. Even Mormon counts more votaries than Bentham." The heroes of Disraeli's novels aspire to be leaders in a thoroughly Romantic fashion: by influencing their constituents through the magnetic force of their brilliantly endowed imaginations. Disraeli's popularity as a statesman was based on this real-ization; he claimed that his motive in writing the trilogy of *Coningsby*, *Sybil*, and *Tancred* was to recognize "imagination in the government of nations as a quality not less important than reason." But it was his resultant lack of interest in the factual details so dear to Utilitarian philosophers and realistic novelists that won him so many enemies as a statesman and a writer. "The intellectuals detested him almost to a man," as Robert Blake notes. Trollope's denunciation of the novels as having only the "flavour of paint and unreality" is the classic statement showing why the then Prime Minister and his novels should both be consigned to the dust bin:

> In whatever he has written he has affected something which has been intended to strike his readers as uncommon and therefore grand. Because he has been bright and a man of genius, he has carried his object as regards the young. He has struck them with astonishment and aroused in their imagination ideas of a world more glorious, more rich, more witty, more enterprising than their own. But the glory has ever been the glory of pasteboard, and the wealth has been a wealth of tinsel. The wit has been the wit of hairdressers and the enterprise has been the enterprise of mountebanks.
>
> *(An Autobiography)*

An answer to this line of attack (though not made in response to Disraeli) is to be found in Oscar Wilde's "The Decay of Lying," a defense of the creative power of the imagination and the need to divert from reality in the name of something better—which brings us back to Keats's premise quoted earlier. What to a Romantic-minded author is poetic license, to a realist is lying. When a Tory member of Parliament chooses to embellish the truth or discard it altogether, as Disraeli did on a number of occasions, he faces the resistance of opponents who are uninterested in whether he is speaking on behalf of what to him appears a larger and grander objective. "I like a lie sometimes," one of his fictional characters admits, "but then it must be a good one."

The second major component of Disraeli's Romanticism was his faith in the transforming power of the human will. If his associates in the Young England group "sought to revive a Toryism not the less potent for having never existed outside their imagination," Disraeli, with a mixture of ide-alism, ambition, and pragmatism, was uniquely able to transform some of their political fancies into concrete policy and action. The key Romantic personality for Disraeli (as for George Smythe, the leading figure in Young England and the model for Coningsby) was Byron, whose assertion of will in his life and whose celebration of will in much of his work were seen by repentant first-generation Romantics like Coleridge and Southey as a Satanic predilection: the liberated imagination and will finding expression in egoistic fantasies and questionable behavior. The Romantics were willing to admire heroes, as Carl Woodring notes, because "they lived in an atmosphere where will was ascendant. . . . In the actuality around them, reason subsided under the growing supremacy of will. The old Renaissance belief in man's freedom, immortality, and reason became less prudently belief in man's freedom, creative imagination, and illimitable power of will" (*Politics in English Romantic Poetry*). In Disraeli's case, however, the dangerous potential of the will was neutralized by his boyish faith in romance. No setback encountered by the future Prime Minister and his literary protagonists could make them abandon their sense of being ordained to occupy a dominating position. Thackeray spoke with admiration and mockery of Disraeli's "strong faith" in his heroes' ambitious fantasies: the reader "can't help fancying (we speak for ourselves), after perusing the volumes, that he too is a regenerator of the world, and that he has we don't know how many thousands a year." But if an individual has sufficient faith in his willpower, Disraeli repeatedly proclaimed, he will not go unrewarded: the prerogative of the romance hero—to come into good fortune "without any effort or exertion of your own"—accompanies the ambition of the Byronic hero.

Disraeli's huge political success—achieved in spite of the handicaps of his non-Christian birth and his nonaristocratic background—is a tribute to the possibilities of romance as well as to the hold that romance and Romantic values had on the Victorians. A reaction against the excesses of Romanticism is characteristic of what we think of as Victorianism: Victorian writers replaced the Romantic glorification of the individual will with an emphasis on communal and domestic values. "Close thy Byron, open thy Goethe" was Carlyle's shorthand way of arguing that English society would collapse if men and women saw themselves as superior to the world they lived in. The call for self-renunciation and a redirection of one's individual energies into social causes is the theme of that great work to which all Victorian fiction aspires, *Middlemarch*. But while Disraeli did open his Carlyle he never closed his Byron, and it was with reference to George Eliot that he tartly observed that when he wanted to read a novel, he wrote one. Unlike many of his contemporaries who worshipped Byron in the early nineteenth century but regarded him as one of the sins of their youth when they and the century reached middle age, Disraeli never lost his enthusiasm for the figure whom he once claimed to be "greater even as a man than a writer." There is a suggestion in Disraeli's first novel, *Vivian Grey* (1827), that if Byron had only lived longer and returned to England he might have become a political force to reckon with. (Byron himself had toyed with the idea of achieving fame in a political and military, as well as literary, capacity. After his eloquent speech in the House of Lords defending the rights of the people during the Frame-Work Bill debate, Byron noted that "Ld. H[olland] tells me I shall beat them all if I persevere." In later years, however, he denied being "made for what you call a politician, and should never have adhered to any party." The "intrigues" and "contests for power" that Disraeli delighted in Byron professed disgust for.) The hero of Disraeli's second novel, *The Young Duke* (1831), distinguishes himself politically by speaking in the House of Lords in favor of Catholic Emancipation, the subject of Byron's own speech in the same House in 1812. Disraeli's efforts on behalf of Jewish rights were an extension of Byron's pro-Catholic efforts, just as Disraeli's continuing and deliberately provoking references to "the sacred and romantic people from whom I derive my blood and name" were in line with Byron's great pride in his own ancestry.

Byron's hold on the public resembled Napoleon's: theirs seemed the triumph of men of destiny whose egotism was bold and splendid enough to speak for and direct the hidden wishes of the multitude. Disraeli associated himself with the assertive Byron, although in times of dejection he also identified with the thwarted Byron, the melancholy figure bumping his head against social convention and cosmic fate. Unlike Bulwer-Lytton, however, and greatly to his own advantage as novelist and statesman, Disraeli was able to adopt the role of the self-mocking Byron as well. Disraeli was later to identify himself with another Romantic statesman, Napoleon III, and just as Byron's rise to literary power provides the plot for his early novel *Venetia* (1837), Louis Napoleon's rise to political eminence is celebrated in his last novel, *Endymion* (1880). In both cases, Disraeli was fascinated by the spectacle of a man of strong will attaining influence over others. Louis Napoleon's determination to link "the rights of the people and the principles of authority" is similar to Disraeli's romantic Tory conviction that the aristocracy is the natural ally of the people; and where Louis Napoleon confidently invoked his uncle's name and his own "Star" as proof that he was "fated" to lead France, Disraeli interpreted his ambitions in a similarly romantic manner. Both leaders were hugely popular with multitudes hungry for a grand myth, and both were assailed as charlatans.

Disraeli gained greater prominence as a statesman than as a writer, but as a young man he hoped to win for himself the literary power that Byron had wielded and also to wield political power over others as a result of following the Byronic formula. To know oneself thoroughly, as Byron had known himself, meant to be aware of the passions that animate mankind. "Self-knowledge," as he notes of successful orators in *The Young Duke*, "is the property of that man whose passions have their play, but who ponders over their results. Such a man sympathises by inspiration with his kind. He has a key to every heart. He can divine, in the flash of a single thought, all that they require, all that they wish." "It is the personal that interests mankind," he writes in *Coningsby*, "that fires their imagination, and wins their hearts. A cause is a great abstraction, and fit only for students; embodied in a party, it stirs men to action; but place at the head of that party a leader who can inspire enthusiasm, he commands the world." It was Disraeli's fantasy to become the acknowledged and the unacknowledged legislator of the world: Shelley's famous line from "A Defence of Poetry" is quoted in the novel *Venetia*, which appeared just as Disraeli was finally preparing to enter Parliament. The Shelleyan echo should remind us that Disraeli's Romanticism was ultimately directed toward a goal of public service, not selfish gratification. In recent years the Byronic clinging to a position of "self-assertion in an alien universe" has been interpreted as an existential triumph, a heroic model of "humanistic self-reliance" (Peter Thorslev, *The Byronic Hero*); but the Byronic conquest of self-will, as displayed in his campaign for Greek independence, was hailed by many Victorians as an example of humanistic self-denial. By linking the Byronic will with the Shelleyan sympathetic imagination, Disraeli attempted to show that Romantic convictions could be made to serve the public interest. In his political speeches and his novels alike, Disraeli increasingly held up Romantic values as bulwarks against the anti-Romantic, socially corrosive forces of materialism, Utilitarianism, and nihilism.

In a diary entry for 1833, Disraeli, who had recently been twice defeated in bids for a Parliamentary seat, noted how difficult it would be to overcome the obstacles and prejudices lying in the way of the political success he craved. For the moment, he acknowledged, writing was "the safety-valve of [his] passions," but he panted "to act what" he wrote about. He then described three of his novels as "the secret history of [his] feelings." "In *Vivian Grey* I have portrayed my active and real ambition. In *Alroy* my ideal ambition. *The Psychological Romance* [*Contarini Fleming*] is a development of my poetic character." Despite differences in the books' backgrounds and subject matter, the theme in the trilogy is the same: the determination to achieve power in one form or another. There is a passage or two in each book in which the hero thinks of exerting power for humanitarian or libertarian ends, but this is only incidental to the grand ambition itself.

"Superior power, exercised by a superior mind," is the professed goal of Vivian Grey while yet a schoolboy; but this Byronic audacity gives way to Byronic melancholy when Vivian's schemes for political power are thwarted. In the second part of the novel, Vivian switches from an active to a passive role: he looks on while, in a memorable episode, a German minister, Beckendorff, achieves the very sort of power he has desired. Beckendorff himself sounds for the first time in Disraeli's writings the belief in the power of the will to achieve what it wishes. "If, in fact, you wish to succeed," he tells Vivian, "success . . . is at your command." In *The Wondrous Tale of Alroy* (1833), which was inspired partly by Disraeli's trip to the Middle East in 1831, partly by his fascination with a minor Jewish prince of the twelfth century who had declared himself the Messiah and achieved a brief success, Disraeli advanced the claim that his Jewish ancestry entitled him to be considered as worthy a claimant for English office as any nobleman. His hero, Alroy, describes himself as "the descendant of sacred kings, and with a soul that pants for empire"; and the escapades of the original princeling are blown up into the heroics of one who is a cross between Napoleon and Moses. Although the heroism comes to nothing, Disraeli protests that "a great career, although baulked of its end, is still a landmark of human energy."

Whether fantasying himself as a Metternichian minister of state in *Vivian Grey,* a Jewish Napoleon in *Alroy,* or a great writer in *Contarini Fleming* (1832), Disraeli's obsession in the trilogy is with power. Like Vivian Grey, Contarini Fleming spends his childhood dreaming that "life must be intolerable unless I were the greatest of men. It seemed that I felt within me the power that could influence my kind." In the course of the novel, Contarini indulges in a number of power games: in his schoolmates he sees "only beings whom I was determined to control" through the force of his eloquence; the creatures his youthful poetic imagination invents he sees as an army which will "go forth to the world to delight and to conquer"; even his beloved he regards with a possessive eye, and despite an operatic flourish of grief after her death, he consoles himself with the thought "that at the moment of departure her last thought was for me." By his father, who has achieved a political prominence not unlike that of Beckendorff in Disraeli's first novel, Contarini is advised to model himself upon "really great men; that is to say, men of great energies and violent volition, who look upon their fellow-creatures as mere tools, with which they can build up a pedestal for their solitary statue." An admirer of Napoleon, the elder Fleming represents the cynical extreme to which Disraeli's Byronic fancies might have led him. Looking upon people as brutes who can easily be manipulated, Fleming believes "all to depend upon the influence of individual character." The son rejects the political career his father has directed him toward, but he uses the same methods when he becomes a Shelleyan poet, determined to "exercise an illimitable power over the passions of his kind."

In no other Disraeli novel are the author's ambitions and self-conceit so profusely illustrated as in *Contarini Fleming.* It might be said that if Narcissus had been a novelist, this is the book he would have written. Everyone Contarini meets he longs to dominate, and everything he sees becomes a subjective correlative of his own feelings. Having crossed the Swiss Alps and visually absorbed the geographical and meteorological props so dear to a Romantic poet, he exults in the new images he can use to overwhelm his readers. Creativity is reduced to the status of a martial art. Contarini's exploits form a pattern-book of romantic behavior—a boyish version of Bulwer-Lytton's Maltravers novels. At one point, for example, he persuades his schoolmates to follow in the footsteps of Schiller's robbers. (They balk, however, at his proposal that they become Byronic pirates.)

Contarini defends his egotistical adventures as sentimental heroics in an "age of reality." The fictionalized Byron in Disraeli's novel *Venetia* similarly sees himself as having a "chivalric genius" in a "mechanical age." But while Contarini lusts after power, Disraeli has neglected to grant him conspicuous talents other than the audacity that demands to have whatever it wishes. When the young hero confesses his desire to be a poet to a successful artist whom he has just met, he is told, "when a mind like yours thinks often of a thing, it will happen." This artist figure, Peter Winter, is presented as a foil to Contarini's father; but while Contarini chooses the poet's career over the politician's, he still honors the advice his father has given him: "with words we govern men."

Disraeli's own dazzling career was established at the fortuitous moment when the protectionist wing of the Tory party lacked an articulate spokesman to argue its cause. Disraeli's desire to achieve success as a poet is evidenced in the poem he began about this time, *The Revolutionary Epick* (1834), which aimed at presenting Shelleyan principles in Miltonic form, and in the verse play *The Tragedy of Count Alarcos* (1839), which he undertook, as he claimed, in competition with Shakespeare. (The subject of both works is the attainment of power. In the poem the spirits of Burkean "Feudalism" and Shelleyan "Federalism" contend, but the narrative breaks off just as "that predestined Man [Napoleon],/Upon whose crest the fortunes of the world/Shall hover," arises—with perhaps the aim, like Disraeli's, of reconciling the claims of tradition and liberty. The protagonist of *Alarcos*, on the other hand, discovers that the price of political power is murder.) No reader of these turgid outpourings would wish that Disraeli had pursued a poetical career at the expense of his political goals; but perhaps the fairest way to interpret *Contarini Fleming* is in light of the political and personal frustrations its author was experiencing at the time. The colossal egotism of Contarini is a mask for Disraeli's insecurity. At one point dejectedly believing himself "the object of an omnipotent Destiny, over which I had no control," Contarini later consoles himself with the thought that "Destiny is our will, and our will is our nature." The boyish romance of an outsider who triumphs over everyone and everything was indeed a "safety-valve" for the energies of one who saw himself as an innately gifted individual in an age that lacked heroic grandeur. "I am only truly great in action," he confided to his diary in an effort at self-hypnotism. "If ever I am placed in a truly eminent position I shall prove this," he added prophetically; "I could rule the House of Commons, although there would be a great prejudice against me at first."

During the same decade in which Disraeli composed his autobiographical trilogy, he wrote three other novels with no higher aim in mind than making money to pay off his debts. But although *The Young Duke, Henrietta Temple,* and *Venetia* were initiated as hack works, they are a good deal more fun to read than Disraeli's serious novels of the period. They also express aspects of his active, ideal, and poetic ambition, but without the egotistical bombast and with a certain amount of mockery directed at his own high pretensions. The willingness to satirize his ambitions and posings is one of the most endearing of Disraeli's Byronic traits. In each of the books a young woman is the moral agent who converts a selfish young man to a sense of domestic or social responsibility. One might almost say that under the romantic trappings of these books a Victorian conscience is struggling to be heard. (*Henrietta Temple* and *Venetia* were published in 1837, the year Victoria ascended the throne.)

The hero of *The Young Duke* is an immensely wealthy young lord who spends his money lavishly and then converts to a serious sense of his duties as an aristocrat. The novel contains marvelous and witty set pieces of fashionable life—no less effective for being almost entirely the concoctions of Disraeli's imagination—and a description of a gambling den in which all the aristocratic forms are thrown off to reveal "hideous demons" lurking underneath. In the Romantic tradition, Disraeli saw Utilitarians rather than aristocrats as major threats to the moral and social well-being of the age. His animus against Utilitarian philosophers is humorously expressed in the description of the Benthamite writer whose hatred of aristocrats extends to a hatred of mountains: "Rivers he rather patronised; but flowers he quite pulled to pieces, and proved them to be the most useless of existences. Duncan Macmorrogh informed us that we were quite wrong in supposing ourselves to be the miracle of Creation. On the contrary, he avowed that already there were various pieces of machinery of far more importance than man; and he had no doubt, in time, that a superior race would arise, got by a steam-engine on a spinning-jenny." Disraeli's answer to the Utilitarian theories is the figure of the young duke at the end of the novel, whose feudal determination to take care of a people imaginatively enthralled by him is seen to be more effective in the long run than any Benthamite legislation.

Whether Disraeli himself could achieve political prominence is a matter for doubt in these books. Despite the will to be great, the heroes of Disraeli's early novels do not always achieve their objective or enjoy it for long. Those who do succeed, moreover, do so with the help, or at the will, of others. Disraeli interrupts the narrative of *The Young Duke* at one point to express his anguish that the most "supernatural" of energies—such as those of Byron or Napoleon—have been known to "die away without creating their miracles." A sense of personal insecurity is especially evident in *Henrietta Temple*. His hero, Ferdinand Armine, possesses "the power and the will" of his chivalric ancestors: as the "near descendant of that bold man who passed his whole life in the voluptuous indulgence of his unrestrained volition," Armine decides that he need only be willful himself for all to yield "to determination." Moreover, Armine possesses the requisite Romantic imagination: "His imagination created fantasies and his impetuous passions struggled to realise them." In the end, however, he attains his desires in large part because of Disraeli's own strong need for a fantasy of "acceptance" at this stage in his career. Armine achieves his goal because others are eager and determined to thrust greatness on him: "The most gifted individuals in the land emulated each other in proving which entertained for him the most sincere affection." The Romantic faith in will is overshadowed by the romancer's reliance on wish-fulfillment.

The twin heroes of *Venetia* are no less than Byron and Shelley, whom Disraeli renames Plantagenet Cadurcis and Marmion Herbert. Disraeli's defense of his Romantic idols is tempered, however, by his recognition that the same imaginative energies that produce great poetry can also find expression in questionable conduct. As a young radical poet and philosopher, Herbert has "celebrated that fond world of his imagination, which he wished to teach men to love." But despite intense idealism, Herbert's disbelief in conventional morality, his atheism, and his revolutionary politics wreck his marriage and exile him from England. It is intriguing to contemplate Matthew Arnold's "beautiful and ineffectual angel" becoming a general and fighting in the American Revolution against his native land; Disraeli sets his novel far enough in the past that his Shelley-figure can achieve that fate. However, the sight of his daughter Venetia and his wife Lady Annabel, from whom he has separated under conditions that echo Byron's separation from Lady Byron (Herbert's defense of American freedom is similarly reminiscent of Byron's crusade for Greek independence), is enough to make him cast off his past beliefs and sigh instead for "domestic repose" and "domestic bliss." "The age of his illusions had long passed"; in middle age Herbert cautions his poetic and political disciple Cadurcis that it is more important for a poet to "sympathise" with his fellowmen than to express his scorn for or exert his will upon them: "It is sympathy that makes you a poet. It is your desire that the airy children of your brain should be born anew within another's, that makes you create; therefore, a misanthropical poet is a contradiction in terms." Disraeli illustrates in Herbert's career the waste of an idealistic imagination and in Cadurcis's case the misuse of imaginative energies.

Despite his Romantic sympathies, Disraeli by 1837 had come to see, as Coleridge had earlier, that imagination and will have negative possibilities: by stressing Ferdinand Armine's passivity in *Henrietta Temple*, Disraeli disengaged his hero from any misexpenditure of will. (Scott had employed a similar strategy in the Waverley novels.) In Cadurcis, Disraeli embodies what to young Victorians appeared to be the quintessentially Byronic man of imagination and will. "If ever there existed a being who was his own master, who might mould his destiny at his will, it seemed to be Cadurcis." Yet Venetia's mother, quite rightly from a Victorian point of view, rejects Cadurcis's appeal for her daughter's hand on the basis of his "genius." "Spirits like him," Lady Annabel says, are swayed by a dangerous impulse: "It is imagination; it is vanity; it is self, disguised with glittering qualities that dazzle our weak senses, but selfishness, the most entire, the most concentrated." When Cadurcis insists to his friend Masham (modeled after

Bishop Wilberforce) that he must have Venetia, the Bishop replies that Cadurcis only really wants what his imagination has seized upon for momentary gratification. Once he had married Venetia, he "would probably part from her in a year, as her father parted from Lady Annabel." "Impossible!" replies Cadurcis, "for my imagination could not conceive of anything more exquisite than she is." "Then it would conceive something less exquisite," says the Bishop. "It is a restless quality, and is ever creative, either of good or of evil." The portrait of Cadurcis is the culmination of Disraeli's lifelong Byron-mania: we see Cadurcis evolve from a moody and willful child, whose mother is every bit as eccentric as Lady Gordon, to a young man of strange habits (including the famous diet of biscuits and soda water), misanthropic moods, and extraordinary literary success.

Disraeli collected information about Byron and Shelley from a variety of published and unpublished sources: among others, Thomas Moore's *Life of Byron*, Thomas Medwin's remembrances of Byron and Shelley, and anecdotes related by Edward Trelawny, Lady Blessington, and Byron's former manservant, Tita, whom Disraeli had acquired as a human souvenir during his trip to the East in 1831. But a recognition of Byron's genius did not prevent Disraeli from seeing an incompatibility between imaginative ambition and domestic virtues: if Medwin, Trelawny, and Moore were not sufficient witnesses to the improprieties of genius, his father Isaac D'Israeli's *The Literary Character, or The History of Men of Genius* was a treasure-trove of biographical episodes proving that men like Byron could not be "tamed" to fit the hopes of a character like Venetia. In the end, Disraeli was obliged to drown both his Byron and Shelley figures, despite their abrupt conversion away from their willful early lives, their Shelleyan unorthodoxy and Byronic "selfism." Although Disraeli himself was now in the process of toning down his Romantic rhetoric and posture in the hope of attaining recognition in the House of Commons, he was not about to show his poetic idols selling out. *Venetia* seems intended, as Disraeli's biographer [Robert Blake] observes, as a "last tribute to the Byronic myth . . . a final protest against the respectable world with which he now had to come to terms." But if Romantic flamboyance was no longer serviceable to Disraeli, the Romantic tradition of humanitarianism could now be turned to account.

The great trilogy of the 1830s represent Disraeli's major claim to be taken seriously as a novelist. In these works, for the first time, his heroes have a mission; they want not only power, like the early heroes, but something to direct that power toward. They want to see England governed by a real aristocracy, composed of talented and earnest young men who inspire others by their creative abilities. Noting a debt to Carlyle's idea of "Hero Worship" in *Coningsby*, Thackeray smiled at the "pining" of "Young England . . . for the restoration of the heroic sentiment, and the appearance of the heroic man." Indeed, the spirit of Carlyle and Scott had been joined to the spirit of Byron and Shelley, and the result—in *Coningsby* and *Sybil* at least—is the sort of work to please novel-readers who would perhaps rather be reading political tracts. Yet a Romantic quality permeates even these books. The appeal is to the imagination, but the imagination speaks not only the "language of power" (in Hazlitt's phrase) but the language of sympathy. A Byronic magnetic figure is still required to fire the passions of the public, but this figure also needs Shelley's humanitarian imagination. In defending the moral force of poetry, Shelley maintains, "A man, to be greatly good, must imagine intensely and comprehensively; he must put himself in the place of another and of many others; the pains and pleasures of his species must become his own. The great instrument of moral good is the imagination; and poetry administers to the effect by acting upon the cause." In *Coningsby, or The New Generation* (1844), Disraeli treats the political hero as Shelley regarded the poet: a great man, like a great book, produces "a magnetic influence blending with our sympathising intelligence, that directs and inspires it."

Coningsby himself exerts over his schoolmates "the ascendant power, which is the destiny of genius"; and he is granted a heroic will so that he and his friends can satisfy the English people's craving for great leaders to lead them in a time of crisis. "Surely of all 'rights of man,' " as Carlyle declares, somewhat less attractively, in *Chartism*, "this right of the ignorant man to be guided by the wiser, to be, gently or forcibly, held in the true course by him, is the indisputablest." For leadership, according to Carlyle and Disraeli, not only satisfies an instinctive need of the multitude—it also keeps the multitude from satisfying their passions in socially destructive ways. When Coningsby asks Sidonia, Disraeli's portrait of a wealthy Jewish Tiresias-figure who knows everything and everyone, whether "Imagination," which "once subdued the state . . . may not save it," Sidonia replies, "Man is made to adore and to obey: but if you will not command him, if you give him nothing to worship, he will fashion his own divinities and find a chieftain in his own passions."

In *Sybil, or The Two Nations* (1845), Disraeli shows to what a state the abdication of leadership by the aristocracy and the church has brought modern England. In that novel "a spirit of rapacious covetousness, desecrating all the humanities of life," has been spread by the newly powerful middle class. Their goal, as Disraeli sees it, is "to acquire, to accumulate, to plunder each other by virtue of philosophic [that is, Utilitarian, laissez-faire] phrases, to propose a Utopia to consist only of WEALTH and TOIL." Deserted by their natural allies, the upper classes, and exploited by the middle classes, the workers have been left totally degraded and at the mercy of Chartist slogans, which promise relief but lead only to destructive acts. It is precisely at such a time, as Sidonia urges, that great men are called for—not to follow the spirit of the age but to change it, to advocate reverence for heroic values in place of materialism, and to protect the poor who cannot defend themselves. Ten years earlier Disraeli had contended that "The Monarchy of the Tories is more democratic than the Republic of the Whigs. It appeals with a keener sympathy to the passions of the millions; it studies their interests with a more comprehensive solicitude." A political career for Harry Coningsby or Charles Egrement (the hero of *Sybil*) is seen as a romantic crusade, a chivalric adventure in which the successful hero slays Whig (or factitious Tory) dragons and ends up in Parliament making speeches in favor of the "rights of labour." The creator of these heroes draws at least as much from *Arabian Nights* fantasies of wish-fulfillment as from his observations of the actual political process. "Life was a pantomime," as Coningsby discovers; "the wand was waved, and it seemed that the schoolfellows had of a sudden become elements of power, springs of the great machine."

Tancred, or The New Crusade (1847) brings Disraeli's political trilogy to a brilliant, if also perplexing, climax. It is much less earnest in tone, though no less serious in purpose, than *Coningsby* and *Sybil*, and the seriousness is not deflected by Disraeli's many witty, and sometimes perverse, digressions. Tancred himself is an extremely earnest young nobleman, the descendant of crusaders, who wants "to see an angel at Manchester" and who does in fact see an angel on Mount Sinai. For Tancred, another Disraeli hero possessed of "indomitable will and an iron resolution," the achievement of political power is meaningless without a secure national religious faith to prop it up. "It is time to restore and renovate our communications with the Most High," he tells his astonished father. "What ought I to DO, and what ought I to BELIEVE?" To Coningsby and his friends, Tancred complains that without a magnetic religious influence directing human behavior "individuality is dead; there is a want of inward and personal energy in man; and that is what people feel and mean when they go about complaining there is no faith." Luckily for Tancred, Sidonia appears in time to encourage him to find the answer to his dilemma by penetrating "the great Asian mystery"—that is, by traveling to Palestine to discover why God chose to speak to mankind from there and not from Manchester.

Tancred's adventures in the Middle East are an odd sort of reverie to be coming from a member of Parliament who was about to assume the mantle of Tory leader Robert Peel. Yet the brilliant political invective Disraeli was using in his campaign against Peel and against the repeal of the Corn Laws at about this time was a product of the same imagination that created Tancred's "new crusade" to bring back religious principles to England and, at the same time, created the intrigues of the Arab prince Fakredeen to attain power for himself by any means possible. (Fakredeen's alliance of Arab princes, for example, may be a parody of Disraeli's own Young England Party.) Disraeli's gift for romantic image-making was matched by his brilliant ability to expose the sham underneath. If principle and opportunism appear almost inextricably connected in Disraeli's personality—as do the polar Romantic attitudes of reverential obeisance and heroic self-assertion—the novelist personifies and travesties this dualism in the contrasting characters of Tancred and Fakredeen.

Tancred's pilgrimage seems serious enough until he meets Fakredeen—

this "Syrian Vivian Grey," as Leslie Stephen calls him—who parodies Tancred's earnestness and utters many of Disraeli's sentiments. Fakredeen is ambitious, vain, and unscrupulous; but he is given many of the author's favorite ideas, including the maxim "everything comes if a man will only wait." While Tancred seeks to convert the world—as soon as he can find a principle of religious certainty for himself—Fakredeen wants only to conquer it. The two men join forces for a time in a preposterous plan to "conquer the world, with angels at our head," as Tancred explains, "in order that we may establish the happiness of man by a divine dominion." He settles in the end for domestic bliss, an angel in the house taking the place of the Angel of Arabia. (There is possibly an allusion to Keats's *Endymion* here: Tancred's beloved supplants the angel he has sought, while Endymion's Indian maid is the physical incarnation of Cynthia, goddess of the Moon.) Eva, his Jewish bride-to-be, comforts Tancred for the loss of some of his illusions. "Perhaps," she suggests, "all this time we have been dreaming over an unattainable end, and the only source of deception is our own imagination." The novel ends in confusion with Tancred still wanting to believe—and Disraeli wanting Tancred to want to believe—but with what to believe in still a matter for doubt.

What ultimately redeems the book is not its message (although Disraeli considered this his most important book) but its wit, seen in the political intrigues of Fakredeen, which mock the pretensions of many a Disraeli hero and the young Disraeli himself; in the epigrams, such as "Christianity is Judaism for the multitude"; and above all in the mockery directed against an English society that has lost all reverence for spiritual values. The parody of Robert Chambers's *Vestiges of the Natural History of Creation*, which had recently appeared and which offered in popular form an evolutionist's theory of history, is one of the great set pieces of Disraeli's comic spirit. Lady Constance hands Tancred a copy of " 'The Revelations of Chaos,' a startling book just published, and of which a rumour had reached him." "It is one of those books one must read," Lady Constance blithely declares. "It explains everything, and is written in a very agreeable style."

> "It explains everything!" said Tancred; "it must, indeed, be a very remarkable book!"
> "I think it will just suit you," said Lady Constance. "Do you know, I thought so several times while I was reading it."
> "To judge from the title, the subject is rather obscure," said Tancred.
> "No longer so," said Lady Constance. "It is treated scientifically; everything is explained by geology and astronomy, and in that way. It shows you exactly how a star is formed; nothing can be so pretty! A cluster of vapour, the cream of the milky way, a sort of celestial cheese, churned into light, you must read it, 'tis charming."
> "Nobody ever saw a star formed," said Tancred.

"Perhaps not. You must read the 'Revelations;' it is all explained. But what is most interesting, is the way in which man has been developed. You know, all is development. The principle is perpetually going on. First, there was nothing, then there was something; then, I forget the next, I think there were shells, then fishes; then we came, let me see, did we come next? Never mind that; we came at last. And the next change there will be something very superior to us, something with wings. Ah! that's it: we were fishes, and I believe we shall be crows. But you must read it."

"I do not believe I ever was a fish," said Tancred.

This famous passage should remind us that Disraeli was perfectly serious when, speaking at Oxford in 1864, he declared himself on the side of the angels, protesting that "instead of believing that the age of faith has passed, I hold that the characteristic of the present age is a craving credulity." Evolution, like Utilitarianism, deprived man of his power of volition; yet for Disraeli, as for Newman and Tennyson, the will to believe was a proof that there was something to believe in, something that affirmed the power of the will after all.

Like Keats in his substitution of Cortez for Balboa, Disraeli knew that the scientists' discoveries could not be discounted; in terms of the requirements of the imagination and the will to believe, however, such facts were irrelevant. "Craving credulity" is both the theme of and the danger in two of Disraeli's last three fictional works: *Lothair* (1870) and the unfinished "Falconet." The doubts and fears of the 1870s and 1880s find vivid expression in these books. Lothair, a young nobleman who like Tancred is searching for religious certitude, is characterized in terms of passivity rather than willfulness. "I often think . . . that I have neither powers nor talents," he laments at one point, "but am drifting without an orbit." He finds himself at the mercy of several opposing religious and political doctrines, all of which Disraeli treats with a certain amount of sympathy. The most troublesome temptation comes from Cardinal Grandison, whose endorsement of Roman Catholicism is an invitation for Lothair to resign his will altogether. The cardinal expresses Disraeli's fear that the rise of science has aided materialism and atheism. "The world is devoted to physical science," he charges, "because it believes these discoveries will increase its capacity of luxury and self-indulgence. But the pursuit of science leads only to the insoluble." For the cardinal, as for Sidonia, "all the poetry and passion and sentiment of human nature are taking refuge in religion." "Religion is civilisation," he argues later in the novel; "the highest: it is the reclamation of man from savageness by the Almighty. What the world calls civilisation, as distinguished from religion, is a retrograde movement, and will ultimately lead us back to the barbarism from which we have escaped." Like Dostoevsky, at about the same time, Disraeli is warning that when God is not believed to exist all things become permissible.

Lothair's susceptibility to Roman Catholicism does not lead to conversion only because he is even more susceptible to a strong-minded woman, Theodora, who wins him over to the cause of Italian freedom, and because Disraeli sees Jerusalem, not Rome, as the real fountainhead of religious truth. Action becomes the antidote for Lothair's morbid introspection; his romantic activity as a soldier in the cause of Italian unification is described as an "easy distraction from self-criticism." He is not the first troubled Romantic to come to that conclusion. "A region of Doubt . . . hovers forever in the background," Carlyle declared in 1831; "in Action alone can we have certainty." "The only tolerable thing in life is action," especially youthful action, as Theodora's friend the Princess of Tivoli says to Lothair. "You have many, many scrapes awaiting you. . . . You may look forward to at least ten years of blunders: that is, illusions; that is, happiness. Fortunate young man!" It is the princess who later sounds the theme of the romance of the will in opposition to the cardinal's doctrine of renunciation. "The power of the passions, the force of the will, the creative energy of the imagination," she proclaims, "these make life, and reveal to us a world of which the million are entirely ignorant." In the opposition between the romance of the will and the need for obedience and reverence, Lothair takes one side and then another, settling finally, like Tancred, for domestic bliss in a world of unresolved and unresolvable questionings.

There is no way of knowing what the outcome of "Falconet" would have been: before his death Disraeli had completed fewer than ten chapters of this novel, in which all values seem to be dissolving and only self-righteous hypocrites like Falconet (modeled after the Liberal leader Gladstone, whom Disraeli regarded as the "Arch Villain") or nihilistic philosophies seem to be thriving. England seems exhausted of her energies, and no youthful heroes have yet appeared when the manuscript breaks off to indicate how the visitors from the East and Germany, who turn up in the novel to preach a doctrine of "Destruction in every form," are to be thwarted—if they are to be thwarted. In one of the last scenes we are shown one of the invaders recommending a book by "a friend of Schopenhauer," a book that presumably offers Schopenhauer's message of the sublimation of the will.

Yet despite the sense that his was "an age of dissolving creeds" ("Falconet") and threats to civil order—or perhaps because of the realization that he himself had risen to power by seizing the initiative in a time of social instability—Disraeli's last completed novel, *Endymion* (1880), is the most romantic and optimistic of all his works. "It is a privilege to live in this age of rapid and brilliant events," he had exulted in 1864. "What an error to consider it an utilitarian age! It is one of infinite romance. Thrones tumble down and are offered, like a fairy tale, and the most powerful people in the world, male and female, a few years back were adventurers, exiles and demireps." Disraeli may have been describing the rise to power of men like Louis Napoleon, but he was also contemplating his own success, the fulfillment of the unrealistic ambition stated in the 1833 diary. By 1875 he was not only prime minister but Lord Beaconsfield. There is no mention of dissolving creeds in *Endymion*: indeed, Nigel Penruddock's rise to the position of Roman Catholic cardinal is celebrated here—though it would have been deplored in *Lothair*—because it is an assumption of power. All ways to eminence are to be admired, whether in the figure of Endymion, who becomes prime minister of the Whig, not the Tory, party; Vigo, who as a railway magnate is linked with what to the Victorians was the most visible symbol of material progress; or Prince Florestan, who is Disraeli's version of Napoleon III with touches added from the wondrous career of Alroy. "All you have got to do is to make up your mind that you will be in the next parliament, and you will succeed," Lady Montfort tells Endymion; "for everything in this world depends upon will." "I think everything in this world depends upon women," replies Endymion; to which Lady Montfort retorts, "It is the same thing."

Endymion expresses Disraeli's Romantic view of history, in which heroes triumph by the force of their will, buttressed by the spirit of romance, in which wishing for something to happen is enough to make it happen. Endymion rises from poverty to political power without having to engage in any of the intrigues and subterfuges necessary for climbing the "greasy pole." His only conspicuous qualities are youth, tact, and "the power and melody of his voice." Yet he is awarded the highest honors partly because of his intense desire for them and largely through the agency of a set of fairy godsisters. "If we cannot shape your destiny," his sister Myra contends of the power of women, "there is no such thing as witchcraft." Myra devotes her will, which Endymion recognizes to be "more powerful than his," to the great aim of making her brother prime minister. "I have brought myself, by long meditation, to the conviction that a human being with a settled purpose must accomplish it," she claims, "and that nothing can resist a will that will stake even existence for its fulfillment." In the end, all men and women of indomitable will have assumed power: Myra herself becomes the Queen of France, the bride of King Florestan. How little Disraeli decided to rely on reality in concocting *Endymion*—how much he chose to present a Keatsian set of imaginative values instead—can be seen in the way he used as prototype for Florestan's hugely successful career an emperor who in historical fact had been driven from power a decade earlier.

One might be tempted to dismiss *Endymion* as an exuberant piece of wish-fulfillment if not for the disconcerting links between the improbabilities of its plot and the historical improbabilities that saw the rise of so many self-proclaimed men of destiny in the nineteenth century. Despite the revulsion of Victorian intellectuals—many of them searching for an authentic principle of authority to replace the fallen gods of their ancestors, and in no mood to hail the exploits of a survivor from the Romantic period— Disraeli had discovered that his Romantic views were shared by many of his countrymen. By no means an original thinker, as Bagehot recognized, he was able to rise to power by demonstrating a force of personality and by *"applying* a literary genius, in itself limited, to the practical purpose of public life." His success indicates that in an age of disbelief people will follow a leader who believes in his own star and who is able to exert power over others with the right image and rhetoric. The power of words and images was a central Disraelian concern, as both a fictional and a national theme: "He thought in symbols," as Louis Cazamian noted, "and was acutely alive to the power of images over human thought and conduct, for he recognized it in himself." When Gladstone defeated Disraeli in 1880, he exulted that "the downfall of Beaconsfieldism is like the vanishing of some vast magnificent castle of Italian romance"; yet there occurred in the 1880s a revival of the romantic spirit, whether in the form of the fiction of Robert Louis Stevenson and H. Rider Haggard or in the form of imperial adventurism, which the Victorians had never really exorcised.

The adventurist and merely rhetorical aspects of Disraeli's Romanticism—the qualities that Trollope, for example, found so offensive—cannot be defended; but a more positive strain of Romanticism dominates his mature views. The negative aspect of his Romantic impulse is readily seen in the early novels, where his youthful narcissism and Byronic egoism are ingenuously revealed. In subsequent novels, however, he exhibited the humanitarian and reverential side of Romanticism; and in this respect, his development from self-preoccupation to concern for society may be said to parallel the development within Romanticism itself. The Romantic celebration of the powers of heroic will and sovereign imagination was transformed into a recognition of the need for responsible leadership and a sympathetic, morally attuned imagination. In the end, the country's political, economic, and spiritual interests and the imaginative desires of Coningsby, Egrement, and Tancred—and Disraeli himself—are seen to be synonymous. To Disraeli's credit, while he translated into political and fictional terms the romance of the will, his Byronic sense of self-mockery forbade his ever taking himself and the idea of leadership unduly seriously, and thereby insulated him from Carlylean delusions of grandeur.

A perennially boyish element in Disraeli accounted for his persistence in regarding life as a romance in which, like Aladdin, he had only to will things for them to happen. But this sense of wonder was related for Disraeli, as it was for Coleridge and Newman, to a belief in spiritual forces in the universe with which modern man seemed increasingly to be losing touch. Coleridge's Biblical reminder that "WHERE NO VISION IS, THE PEOPLE PERISHETH" is close to Disraeli's insistence on the role of imagination in the nation's life. Against the Utilitarian appeal to a self-interested populace in a materialistic universe, he offered a Romantic dream of human potentiality in a world of mutual respect. In the unfinished "Falconet," moreover, he seemed to be warning of a triumph of nihilism in a world that has lost faith in the Romantic values that sustain spiritual belief and that produce altruistic heroes. Uncharacteristic though it appears in theme and tone when compared with his other novels, "Falconet" betrays the sense of anxiety that underlies the euphoric fantasy of *Endymion*. Far more fearsome, as Disraeli realized, than the famous "leap in the dark" by which he had acted in 1867 to enfranchise members of the English working class, was the leap into darkness that might result from modern man's disenfranchisement from the visionary imagination.

Causality versus Conscience:
The Problem of Form in *Mary Barton*

Catherine Gallagher

As in the Religion of Causation, *Man seemed to be crushed into a mere creature, so was it on his behalf that remonstrance broke forth, and, at the bidding of Channing, the* Religion of Conscience *sprang to its feet. However fascinating the precision and simplicity of the Necessarian theory in its advance through the fields of physical and biological law, it meets with vehement resistence in its attempt to annex human nature, and put it under the same code with the tides and trees and reptiles. Our personality . . . is sure to recover from the most ingenious philosophy, and to reassert its power over the alternatives before it . . . ; and the second period of our theology is marked by this recovered sense of Moral Freedom.*
     —JAMES MARTINEAU, "Three Stages of Unitarian Theology"

No one seems to see my idea of a tragic poem; so I, in reality, mourn over my failure.
     —ELIZABETH GASKELL, Letter to Edward Chapman

When Elizabeth Gaskell wrote *Mary Barton* (1845–47), many Unitarians were revising their theories about free will. In those years James Martineau was trying to start what he later called the "second period of Unitarian theology," the period in which "moral freedom" was emphasized. James Martineau, Harriet's younger brother, was the most influential English Unitarian theologian of the nineteenth century. In their early childhood he and his sister Harriet established a profound emotional and intellectual bond that remained unbroken throughout their youth.

It was James who suggested she read Priestley, but once Harriet had arrived at her "grand conviction" of Necessarianism, she took every possible opportunity to impress the doctrine on her brother. According to James, Harriet dominated him intellectually throughout their adolescence and early adulthood. Describing their conversation while on a walking tour of Scotland in 1824, he reminisced:

> My sister's acute, rapid, and incisive advance to a conclusion upon every point pleasantly relieved my slower judgement and gave me courage to dismiss suspense. I was at that time, and for several years after, an enthusiastic disciple of the determinist philosophy . . . yet not without such inward reserves and misgivings as to render welcome my sister's more firm and ready verdict.

From *The Industrial Reformation of English Fiction: Social Discourse and Narrative Form 1832–1867.* © 1985 by the University of Chicago. University of Chicago Press, 1985.

Harriet managed to suppress James's "inward reservations and misgivings" until after she had become a well-known writer. R. K. Webb reports that in 1832 James still shared her views, and Harriet expressed the hope that James might also share her work of improving mankind: he by "lofty appeals to the guides of [Society], I by being the annalist of the poor."

As this proposed division of labor indicates, Harriet was conscious of certain intellectual and temperamental differences between herself and her brother, even while they espoused the same philosophy. She thought her own talent lay in logical cause-and-effect analysis, while his consisted of eloquence and intuition. In time the differences Harriet perceived in their modes of thinking developed into a philosophical disagreement that separated the intellectually intense siblings for life. As James recalled:

> While she remained faithful through life to that early mode of thought, with me those "reserves and misgivings," suppressed for a while, recovered from the shock and gained the ascendancy. The divergence led to this result,—that while my sister changed her conclusions, and I my basis, we both cleared ourselves from incompatible admixtures, and paid the deference due to logical consistency and completeness.

Harriet's Necessarianism finally led her to accept "free thought"; all organized religious practice came to seem incompatible with the logic of her determinism. James, on the other hand, rejected Harriet's basis, her "Religion of Causality," and reached down to "the springs of a sleeping enthusiasm" for a religion that could carry him "from the outer temple of devout science" to an inner conviction of the "greatness of human capacity, not so much for intellectual training, as for voluntary righteousness, for victory over temptation."

The change in James both symbolized and helped to bring about a vast transformation in the Unitarian Church. William Ellery Channing, the American Transcendentalist, converted James to the doctrine of a "free ideal life . . . which we know is in subjection to nothing inflexible." Channing's idea of the human will had been inspired by the writings of Coleridge, and James, in his turn, set about transforming English Unitarianism from a "Religion of Causality" to a "Religion of Conscience," emphasizing voluntary righteousness. He was not the first English Unitarian to believe in free will; Priestley's determinism had been modified and even opposed by many Unitarian theologians of the early nineteenth century. Indeed, Harriet Martineau's extreme Necessarianism was somewhat anachronistic in the 1830s, for by that decade most Unitarians either ignored the issue or settled for a moderate determinism. James Martineau's version of Transcendentalism, however, strongly insisted on the idea of free will, giving it a new emphasis within Unitarianism. Although James was not the acknowledged leader of English Unitarians until later in the century, during the 1840s and 1850s his thought was a powerful intellectual stimulus that led to the de-emphasis of "scientific" explanations of behavior and a new stress on the other side of Unitarianism—its exhortations to moral exertion.

Although Elizabeth Gaskell and her husband, William, stayed within the old school of Unitarianism on most issues and made no decided moves toward Transcendentalism, they were well acquainted with James Martineau. William Gaskell was a Unitarian minister and a colleague of Martineau's at Manchester New College in the 1840s, and their exposure to Martineau's brand of Unitarianism might easily have served to strengthen Elizabeth Gaskell's interest in the issue of moral responsibility. Moreover, in 1845, at the very time when she first began writing *Mary Barton*, she was deeply influenced by a close friend of Martineau's. Although not himself a Unitarian, Francis Newman, brother of John Henry Newman, associated almost exclusively with Unitarians in the 1840s, and on many issues his thinking closely resembled James Martineau's. Like James Martineau, Newman made much of man's "higher nature," his free moral life. Rejecting the psychological materialism of Priestley and Harriet Martineau, he argued that "human intelligence is a result of other intelligence higher than itself—is not a source, or a result, of what is unintelligent."

To Elizabeth Gaskell in the mid-1840s, Francis Newman seemed a living saint. She claimed to have hung on his every word, and it is quite probable that an 1844 booklet of his, *Catholic Union*, was an important source of inspiration for *Mary Barton*. This booklet, together with a series of lectures given in 1846, clearly reveals Newman's belief in a transcendent "moral energy." These works also, however, contain reminders of Unitarianism's earlier determinism, for in them Newman paradoxically insisted that morality does not exist in a realm apart from social and economic necessity. Thus he believed economic and spiritual issues interpenetrated one another, and like Gaskell in *Mary Barton*, he treated radical working-class movements sympathetically: Communism is called "one mode in which human nature is crying out for a new and better union than has yet been achieved." Although he strove to affirm the independence of the human spirit, he continually reversed himself and implied that spirit is chained to matter, that it does not exist in a separate realm of freedom: "to the support of moral energies," he wrote, "certain material conditions are required."

Elizabeth Gaskell absorbed this ambivalence about moral freedom not only from the works and conversation of Francis Newman, but also from the whole context of Unitarian intellectualism that surrounded her. The Unitarianism that shaped her perceptions was thus a different religion in several important respects from that which nurtured Harriet Martineau. Of course, because Gaskell's social experience also differed markedly from Martineau's, the dissimilarities in the two women's outlooks cannot be attributed solely to their religious beliefs. Nevertheless, important differences in their fiction can be traced to their disparate attitudes toward causality and free will. Martineau believed that Providence worked through natural laws that precluded human free will, whereas Gaskell, without abandoning the idea of Providence, tried to make room in her fiction for moral freedom. Gaskell's use of causality, like that of many other thoughtful Unitarians of the 1840s, was less consistent than Martineau's. It was, however, her very inconsistency, her refusal to be tied down to a single explanatory mode, that marked Elizabeth Gaskell's advance over Harriet Martineau in the craft of novel writing.

To move from [Martineau's] *Illustrations* to *Mary Barton* is to leave behind the narrowness of a unicausal interpretive scheme. The wider range of explanations available to Gaskell partly accounts for our sense that she is a more realistic novelist than Harriet Martineau. As James Martineau wrote, breaking away from the Necessarian doctrine constituted "an escape from a logical cage into the open air." And as he further pointed out, the escape entailed perceptual and stylistic changes: "I could mingle with the world and believe in what I saw and felt, without refracting it through a glass, which construed it into something else. I could use the language of men— of their love and hate, of remorse and resolve, of repentance and prayer— in its simplicity." The firm reliance on what is vividly seen and felt and an expanded use of the simple "language of men" are the hallmarks of Gaskell's realism. The "real" reality for her does not lie behind human behavior in a set of scientific laws; it is on the very surface of life, and although it is often obscured by conventional modes of perception, it can be adequately represented in common language. Indeed, Gaskell specifically objected to the kind of abstract language used by Harriet Martineau: she believed that presenting people as embodiments of labor and capital could only hide their true natures and the underlying motives of their actions.

In one important respect, however, Elizabeth Gaskell must be considered Harriet Martineau's heir: she intended John Barton's story, the story of a working man, to be a tragedy. "I had so long felt," she wrote in a letter, "that the bewildered life of an ignorant thoughtful man of strong power of sympathy, dwelling in a town so full of striking contrasts as this is, was a tragic poem, that in writing he was my 'hero.' " In several ways John Barton is a more successful working-class character than Martineau's William Allen, for many of Allen's characteristics seem inappropriate to a worker. His heroism relies, for example, on an elevated style of speaking, while Barton's tragic heroism gains poignancy from his working-class dialect. Adhering closely to classical models, Martineau presents Allen as far superior to other members of his class: she stresses how unusual his forbearance and intelligence are, and even makes him the victim of the striking workers. Barton, on the other hand, is presented as a typical worker. Indeed, his typicality is precisely what makes his story an important one to tell: "There are many such whose lives are tragic poems," Gaskell wrote, "which cannot take formal language." Moreover, Gaskell did not adopt the reversed chronology of Martineau's fiction, her tendency to reveal the ending at the beginning of the story, destroying suspense and precluding catharsis. In fact, Gaskell believed that the ordering of events was a major flaw in Martineau's work; she complained about one of Martineau's books that "The *story* is too like a history—one knows all along how it must end." Gaskell's own story, although it makes John Barton's decline seem inevitable, is not "like a history": she maintains suspense and seeks an intense emotional reaction from the reader. Barton has neither of Allen's defenses against suffering; he lacks both foreknowledge and stoicism. Barton thus seems more unequivocally victimized than did Allen.

Yet when the book came out, Gaskell complained that no one seemed to see her idea of a tragedy. She concluded that she had failed but could not identify the source of her failure. Her confusion is not surprising, for there are many ways in which Gaskell undercut her own intended tragic effects. One of these, a relatively minor one, reminds us again of the religious kinship between Gaskell and Harriet Martineau: the providential resolution of John Barton's story partly mitigates his tragedy. Although moral freedom was an increasingly important idea in Unitarian theology in the 1840s, Gaskell was still writing within a teleological tradition. John Barton feels responsible for his crime, but in the end the very intensity of his remorse leads to both his own and his enemy's spiritual regeneration. There is not even a hint of possible damnation in the novel; evil is eventually self-effacing and productive of good, although sin is not explicitly ordained by God. The close of Barton's life, therefore, hardly appears to be tragic; his life veers from its tragic course in the final episode, and readers are apt to agree with an early reviewer who complained that the ending was a religious homily, "twisted out of shape, to serve the didactic purpose of the author."

Long before the story's close, however, Gaskell's ambivalence about the tragedy she was writing manifests itself in the book's formal eclecticism, an eclecticism that cannot be traced simply to the contradiction between tragic and providential perspectives. For tragedy and theodicy both contain explanatory systems; both trace cause and effect. A dominant impulse in *Mary Barton*, however, is to escape altogether from causality, to transcend explanation. *Mary Barton* expresses both stages of the Unitarianism of the 1840s; it was inspired by both the "Religion of Causality" that Harriet Martineau advocated and the "Religion of Conscience" that her brother eloquently preached. It contains, therefore, an ambivalence about causality that finds its way into Gaskell's tragedy and creates an irresolvable paradox there: Barton's political radicalism is presented both as proof that he is incapable of making moral choices and as an emblem of his moral responsibility. The author consequently seeks refuge from the contradictions of her tragedy in other narrative forms, primarily melodrama and domestic fiction. The resulting formal multiplicity is most apparent in the first half of the book. Only in the second half, after the tragic action is complete, does she temporarily achieve a kind of generic consistency by retreating into the domestic mentality of her heroine. However, because the major action of these chapters is the suppression of the tragic narrative, the book seems to divide into not merely separate but mutually exclusive stories. In the conclusion, when the narrator must return to the subject of John Barton, she seems to have abandoned any attempt to give a consistent explanation of his development. Instead, we are given several stories that mix social criticism with religious homily, and we are then assured that, after all, causal interpretations are irrelevant to the story's meaning.

Gaskell's inability to commit herself to a causal scheme leads, therefore, to formal inconsistencies, but it also leads to a high degree of formal self-consciousness. Although she does not find a narrative form that satisfactorily reveals the reality of working-class life, she does identify several conventional genres that hide the reality. Her attempt to render the truth is beset by irresolvable difficulties, but some relief, some certainty, is secured in attacking what is obviously false. Thus *Mary Barton* is partly about the ways in which narrative conventions mask and distort reality; form becomes content by this process. But the criticism of false conventions does not succeed in deflecting attention from the absence of a stable, self-assured narrative posture. Rather, it makes us more acutely aware of that absence simply by emphasizing the issue of genre. Thus, in the very act of trying to evade certain narrative responsibilities, the book becomes peculiarly self-regarding.

Gaskell's use of contrasting narrative forms is one of the most interesting and overlooked features of *Mary Barton*. In a sense, the first half of the novel is about the dangers inherent in various conventional ways of organizing reality. The two most obviously false and destructive conventional perspectives on the novel's action are the sentimentally romantic and the farcical. The narrator herself never adopts these modes; rather, they enter the narrative as the distorted literary viewpoints of a few characters. Esther and young Mary hold the sentimental perspective; Sally Leadbitter and Harry Carson hold the complementary view of farce. Gaskell is careful to point out that the sentimental perspective originates in literature; Mary's "foolish, unworldly ideas" come not only from her Aunt Esther's talk about "making a lady" of her, but also from "the romances which Miss Simmonds's young ladies were in the habit of recommending to each other." And although the narrator excuses both Esther and Mary on the grounds of their youth, she indicates that their conventional literary delusions are truly pernicious. Esther's elopement ruins her and apparently also contributes to the death of Mary's mother, and Mary's desire to marry a gentleman brings her and almost all of the other characters in the book "bitter woe."

The complement to these sentimental notions, the convention that they play into and that makes them dangerous, is farce. Both Sally Leadbitter and Harry Carson see their lives and the lives of others as farce. Sally becomes a *farceuse* because she cannot be a sentimental heroine. Being "but a plain, red-haired, freckled, girl," she tries to make up for her lack of beauty "by a kind of witty boldness, which gave her, what her betters would have called piquancy." Sally is a working-class version of the witty female rogue: "Considerations of modesty or propriety never checked her utterance of a good thing." Her vision is entirely comic; it excludes any serious thought about the consequences of Mary's flirtation with young Carson at the same time that it denies the very possibility that Mary's romantic fantasies might be sincerely held: "Sally Leadbitter laughed in her sleeve at them both, and wondered how it would end,—whether Mary would gain her point of marriage, with her sly affectation of believing such to be Mr. Carson's intention in courting her." Harry Carson, of course, shares this farcical perspective on Mary's actions. Both he and Sally imagine her to be a character in their own farcical world—a "sweet little coquette," "a darling little rascal" with an "ambitious heart." For Sally and Harry Carson, this characterization gives a conventional authorization, indeed a conventional imperative, to Mary's seduction.

Moreover, Mary's is not the only reality that the farcical perspective distorts: everything that enters Sally's or young Carson's purview becomes comic material. Sally is always "ready to recount the events of the day, to turn them into ridicule, and to mimic, with admirable fidelity, any person gifted with an absurdity who had fallen under her keen eye." The ability to mimic "with admirable fidelity" is also a talent, indeed a fatal talent, of Harry Carson. Young Carson's farcical vision leads him to caricature not only Mary, but the whole of the working class as well, and as Gaskell points out, these comic caricatures both mask and perpetuate working-class suffering. In her exposition of the dangers inherent in farcical distortions, the author brings together the sexual and social themes of the novel: both Mary and the delegation of striking workers are victimized by Harry Carson's conventional blindness.

If working-class women are seducible "little rascals" for Harry Carson, working-class men are clowns. Young Carson exhibits his blindness to the human reality of working-class men on several occasions (for instance, in his treatment of Mr. Wilson, in his interview with Jem, and in his obstinate behavior at the negotiating table), but the conventional attitude that motivates his behavior is most clearly expressed in the action that precipitates his murder. He is killed for making a joke, for attempting to transform a workers' delegation into a troop of Shakespearean clowns:

> Mr. Harry Carson had taken out his silver pencil, and had drawn an admirable caricature of them—lank, ragged, dispirited, and famine-stricken. Underneath he wrote a hasty quotation from the fat knight's well-known speech in Henry IV. He passed it to one of his neighbours, who acknowledged the likeness instantly, and by him it was set round to others, who all smiled and nodded their heads.

The caricature, tossed away by Carson but retrieved by a curious member of the workers' delegation, so enrages John Barton that he conspires with the ridiculed workers to kill the caricaturist. It is significant that the fatal joke is as much Shakespeare's as it is Carson's: that fact emphasizes the unreal, literary nature of Carson's perception. It also stresses how deeply entrenched the farcical distortion of working-class life is in English culture. Carson's destructive use of Shakespeare reminds Gaskell's readers that although they have the best precedents for laughing at rags and tatters, they must now free themselves from the conventional association between "low" characters and comedy.

But the whole incident raises another question: what new associations should replace the old? It is quite clear that Gaskell intends to expose the dangerous falseness of both sentimental romance and farce; but the ground of her exposition, the narrative mode that she adopted because she believed that it did reflect working-class reality, is difficult to identify. Most literary practices calling themselves realistic rely on contrasts with other, presumably false and outdated narrative perspectives. In *Mary Barton* Gaskell purposely sets up false conventions for contrast, thereby calling attention to her own narrative method as the "true" perspective. The problem is that she then has trouble fixing on any one narrative mode; the ground of the contrast continually shifts in the first half of the book while the author searches for a mode of realism adequate to her subject matter. Thus, in her attempt to juxtapose reality and these false conventions, Gaskell employs several alternative narrative modes: tragedy, melodrama, domestic fiction, and finally religious homily.

The most obvious realistic contrast to both the sentimentality of Esther and Mary and the farce of Sally Leadbitter and Harry Carson is the tragedy of John Barton. Barton is the most active and outspoken adversary of both of these false conventions. It is from his perspective that we first see Esther's romantic folly; the story of the girl's elopement is completely contained within John Barton's gloomy interpretation of it: "bad's come over her, one way or another," he tells his friend Wilson. And his interpretation, of course, immediately undercuts all the story's romance. Moreover, his version of Esther's story makes it merely a part of a larger social tragedy. It includes the girl's social determinism: factory work, he is convinced, led to Esther's downfall by making her recklessly independent and giving her the means to buy finery. As Barton tells Esther's story, he reveals his perspective on the relationship between the classes, a perspective that is itself tragic and productive of tragedy. He opposes Esther's romantic dreams not only because they are dangerous, but also because he hates the class she wishes to join. Barton's is a completely polarized view of social reality: only rich and poor seem to exist, and the rich are the constant oppressors of the poor. The ubiquitous slavery metaphor makes its appearance here, attesting to Barton's radicalism, his polarized social vision, and the determinism that informs his thinking.

"We are their slaves as long as we can work; we pile up their fortunes with the sweat of our brows; and yet we are able to live as separate as if we were in two worlds; ay, as separate as Dives and Lazarus, with a great gulf betwixt us: but I know who was best off then," and he wound up his speech with a low chuckle that had no mirth in it.

Even this closing reference to heavenly justice is a gloomy prophecy of revenge, not a joyful anticipation of saintly rewards.

Barton's tragic perspective, therefore, contrasts sharply with Esther's and, later, with Mary's romantic fantasies. Moreover, his interpretation is corroborated by the plot itself; he is correct to note that Esther's romantic dreamworld is really a disguised stage for tragedy. Barton's relationship to the farcical viewpoint is similar: again he opposes it energetically, and again in his opposition he speaks the truth. In fact, in the most decisive moment of his own tragedy, Barton contrasts Harry Carson's caricature, his fixed, farcical representation, with the tragic reality that lies behind the conventionally ludicrous appearance:

"it makes my heart burn within me, to see that folk can make a jest of earnest men; of chaps, who comed to ask for a bit o' fire for th' old granny, as shivers in the cold; for a bit o' bedding, and some warm clothing to the poor wife as lies in labour on th' damp flags; and for victuals for the childer, whose little voices are getting too faint and weak to cry aloud wi' hunger."

Through Barton's eyes we see behind the cartoon images of the ragged men to the suffering of thousands of helpless people. The delegates caricatured by Harry Carson are tragic; they are compelled to strike by their noblest characteristics: their sympathy with and sense of responsibility to their hungry dependents. But Carson's Shakespearean joke attempts to freeze the imagination at the level of appearances, where the workmen become a troop of clowns. In Falstaff's speech, alluded to but not quoted, they are "good enough to toss; food for powder, food for powder; they'll fill a pit as well as better. Tush, man, mortal men, mortal men." Such dehumanization obscures the tragedy, making it perfectly appropriate that the story's central tragic action should be the destruction of this *farceur*, the murder of Harry Carson. Thus farce, the mask of tragedy, becomes its stuff, just as Falstaff's callous speech trails off into a sad and even leveling refrain: "Tush, man, mortal men, mortal men."

Tragedy, then, is the immediate realistic ground against which both romance and farce are contrasted. But the narrative method of this novel cannot be called tragic. As we will see, tragedy is forced to compete with other realistic forms in the book's first half, and in the last half it is present only as a suppressed reality. By examining the part of the story that Gaskell specifically intended as tragic—John Barton's own story—we can see why the author continually shifted to other modes of narration. For John Barton's tragedy is self-contradictory. Because she draws both on traditional ideas of heroic character and on determinist, Owenite ideas of character formation, the author encounters a paradox as she attempts to trace a continuous line of tragic development.

The causality Gaskell attempts to trace follows a traditional tragic pattern; it is the result of the interaction between the character's heroic qualities and external circumstances. As Gaskell told a correspondent after the book's publication, her original intention was to show the operations of inner and outer causes in the destiny of a Manchester weaver:

> I can remember now that the prevailing thought in my mind at the time . . . was the seeming injustice of the inequalities of fortune. Now, if they occasionally appeared unjust to the more fortunate, they must bewilder an ignorant man full of rude, illogical thought, and full also of sympathy for suffering which appealed to him through his senses. I fancied I saw how all this might lead to a course of action which might appear right for a time to the bewildered mind of such a one.

This was, she said, her original "design": the very qualities that made Barton a hero, his thoughtfulness and sympathy, were to combine with external circumstances to produce a tragic action.

The tragic design is certainly apparent in John Barton's story. We are often reminded by both Barton's speeches and the narrator's characterizations of him that his love for his family and his sympathy for the suffering poor cause his hatred of the rich. His unselfishness is emphasized repeatedly; he feels angry not on his own behalf, but on behalf of those who are weaker and poorer. The need to stress Barton's heroic unselfishness determines many of the plot's details; it is significant, for example, that he is not one of the workers caricatured by Harry Carson. His rude thoughtfulness, his desire to understand the suffering he sees, is a second admirable trait contributing to his downfall. Barton is the only character who consistently seeks causes for the world's phenomena, but his analyses are marred by his ignorance, by the fact that his understanding is circumscribed by his limited experience.

Gaskell carefully shows how these qualities of mind are impressed with a tragic stamp by external circumstances, by what comes to Barton "through [his] senses." The links in the tragic chain are clearly identified and labeled: his parents' poverty, his son's death, his wife's death, the trade depression and the consequent suffering of neighbors, his trip to London, his hunger, his opium addiction. Each of these incidents or circumstances is noted by the narrator as yet another cause of Barton's bitterness. The account of his wife's death, for example, concludes with the gloss: "One of the good influences over John Barton's life had departed that night. One of the ties which bound him down to the gentle humanities of earth was loosened, and henceforward the neighbors all remarked he was a changed man." The story of his son's illness and death also ends with emphasis on its consequences: "You can fancy, now, the hoards of vengeance in his heart against the employers."

Even the narrator's disavowals of Barton's ideas and feelings are intended to contribute to his story's tragedy. Remarks such as "I know that this is not really the case [that the workers alone suffer from trade depressions]; and I know what is the truth in such matters: but what I wish to impress is what the workman feels and thinks" may seem annoying intrusions to twentieth-century readers, but they were designed to keep the nineteenth-century readers' own opinions from interfering with their ability to follow Barton's tragedy. The disavowals are there to prevent the reader from becoming distracted by the issue of whether or not Barton's ideas are objectively true; Barton, we are told in these asides, reached the wrong conclusions, but the circumstances of his life did not allow him to reach any other.

Their very inevitability, however, creates a problem for the author. Unlike Harriet Martineau, Gaskell is not able to rest comfortably with the determinism she traces. Two obstacles present themselves: first, her idea of heroism entails moral freedom; and second, Gaskell's and Martineau's determinisms are of very different kinds. Martineau's does not explain the development of the protagonist's character. William Allen is a fully formed hero at the story's outset; the development of his character is unexplored and irrelevant to the story. He is a heroic, working-class *homo economicus* whose actions may be explained by his character, but whose character is not itself tragically determined. Gaskell's tragic vision, on the other hand, encompasses the formation and deformation of John Barton's character. Her social determinism is, in this sense, closer to Charlotte Elizabeth Tonna's than to Harriet Martineau's. Both use Robert Owen's brand of social theory, showing how the worker's environment and experiences shape his moral being. But unlike Tonna, Gaskell wishes to show us a worker who is a hero, not a monster; she wishes to give us a tragedy, not a freak show. As she traces Barton's inescapable decline, a decline that entails moral degeneration, she risks reducing him to a character without a will. In the words James Martineau used to describe the effects of Necessarianism, she almost "crushes" him "into a mere creature" with her causation.

Gaskell, then, was writing partly in the determinist tradition as it had been adapted by critics of industrialism, but her writing was also infused with the new Unitarian emphasis on free will. Consequently, a tension developed in her portrayal of John Barton, a tension between his social determinism and his tragic heroism. This tension increases as his crisis approaches until it finally emerges as an observable contradiction when the narrator directly confronts the political model of freedom Barton has come to advocate. His radical ambition to become a shaper of society, to cast off the role of a passive creature, acts as a magnet that draws both poles of the author's ambivalence about freedom toward one paradoxical center. The paradox is most clearly visible in the narrator's very last expository attempt to explain the causality of John Barton's story:

> No education had given him wisdom; and without wisdom, even love, with all its effects, too often works but harm. He acted to the best of his judgment but it was a widely-erring judgement.
>
> The actions of the uneducated seem to me typified in those of Frankenstein, that monster of many human qualities, ungifted with a soul, a knowledge of the difference between good and evil.
>
> The people rise up to life; they irritate us, they terrify us, and we become their enemies. Then, in the sorrowful moment of our triumphant power, their eyes gaze on us with a mute reproach. Why have we made them what they are; a powerful monster, yet without the inner means for peace and happiness?
>
> John Barton became a Chartist, a Communist, all that is commonly called wild and visionary. Ay! but being visionary is something. It shows a soul, a being not altogether sensual; a creature who looks forward for others, if not for himself.

All the elements of the tragedy are present in these metaphoric exchanges. Barton represents the uneducated, who are collected into the image of Frankenstein's tragically determined, larger-than-life monster. Then the monster, defeated and gazing at us, shrinks back to the dimensions of John Barton, the unselfish visionary. But these smooth metaphoric transitions do not quite cover the passage's central paradox: the "actions of the uneducated" grow out of their soullessness, their incapacity to make moral choices. Barton became a "Chartist, a Communist," a visionary in consequence of this soullessness. But the metaphor is too harsh, too denigrating to the hero, and the narrator pulls back and reverses herself: "But being visionary is something. It shows a soul." Suddenly John Barton's rebellious actions, instead of showing him to be a creature "ungifted with a soul," become the proof that he has a soul, the emblem of his humanity and this moral freedom. His heroism is saved, but only at the expense of the causality implied by the Frankenstein metaphor, a causality that traces Barton's crime to "us."

We can argue, therefore, that the paradoxical nature of Gaskell's tragic vision forces her to abandon it in the novel's second half. Even in the first half of the book, though, the narrator never confines her own view to this tragic dynamic, dangerous as it was to the very idea of moral freedom. Instead, she juxtaposes three "realistic" narrative modes in the book's early chapters: tragedy, melodrama, and a working-class domestic tale. The presence, indeed the competition, of the melodrama and the domestic tale allows two things. First, the author is able to avoid her tragic responsibilities, which are too contradictory to fulfill successfully; these other modes distract attention from and obscure the problematic causality of John Barton's story. Second, the presence of the melodrama, in particular, allows

Gaskell to extend her critical exploration of conventional ways of interpreting reality.

Gaskell's use of melodrama is skillful: she first invites us into a melodramatic narrative, sets up melodramatic expectations, and then reveals
that melodrama is a mere conventional distortion, a genre inappropriate
to modern reality. Critics have claimed that *Mary Barton* becomes melodramatic with the murder of Harry Carson, but this formulation is back-
wards. The first half of the book is much more seriously melodramatic than
the second because in the first half there is a melodrama just offstage, in
the wings, as it were, which threatens to take over the drama entirely.
Indeed, the reader cannot initially tell whether the early chapters are part
of a melodrama or of some other kind of narrative. They contain many
melodramatic characteristics. We view Esther's elopement not only from
Barton's tragic perspective, but also through the unarticulated, excessive
grief of her sister Mary, young Mary's mother. Her grief is so excessive
that it kills her, suddenly and surprisingly. It is the kind of parabolical
death that abounded in nineteenth-century melodramas, and it leads into
young Mary's potential melodrama—the threat of her seduction by the
rakish Harry Carson. The narrator, in true melodramatic manner, continually suspends any resolution of Mary's fate and makes dark prognosti-
cations about it: "Mary hoped to meet him every day in her walks, blushed
when she heard his name, and tried to think of him as her future husband,
and above all, tried to think of herself as his future wife. Alas! poor Mary!
Bitter woe did thy weakness work thee." The wholly conventional language
here ("Alas! poor Mary!") leads us to expect, mistakenly, that Mary's "bitter
woe" will also be of the conventional melodramatic kind.

Although romance and farce finally do turn into tragedy in *Mary Barton*,
they threaten repeatedly in the first half to turn into melodrama. Mary's
renunciation of Harry Carson, her abandonment of romance, brings the
melodrama even closer; for it is after his rejection that Harry Carson becomes truly villainous, indeed a potential rapist: "From blandishments he
had even gone to threats—threats that whether she would or not she should
be his." It is only after she has awakened from her romantic dream that
Mary is in danger of becoming a true melodramatic heroine: an innocent
girl sexually persecuted by a villain. Indeed, Mary registers the change
linguistically. As soon as she understands her true position she declares:
"If I had loved you before, I don't think I should have loved you now you
have told me you meant to ruin me; for that's the plain English of not
meaning to marry me till just this minute. . . . Now I scorn you, sir, for
plotting to ruin a poor girl." This is not "plain English," the language Mary
usually speaks. It is a popular stage English, and it temporarily throws a
melodramatic light across Mary's features. Harry Carson's murder, instead
of beginning the novel's melodrama, effectively terminates it. In fact, as
we will see, in the second half of the book melodrama joins romance and
farce as an overtly discredited convention.

In the first half, however, Mary's potential melodrama competes for our attention with her father's tragedy. Through the melodramatic mode of presentation, our concern is solicited for Mary in a way that it never is for John. Indeed, Gaskell so arranges her narrative that we end up looking for the catastrophic event in the wrong plot. The melodrama of Mary's story, therefore, makes us inattentive to the threatening nature of John's career. The careful tracing of his decline does not have the interest of Mary's melodrama because we are not expecting John's story to culminate in some disastrous event. Our sense of impending catastrophe, which is essential to a tragic narrative, is misplaced in *Mary Barton.* It is attached not only to the wrong plot but also to the wrong set of narrative conventions. We mistakenly expect a melodramatic catastrophe, one arising from a simple confrontation between good and evil, but we are given a tragic catastrophe, a complexly and carefully motivated revenge murder, the outcome of an inner as well as an outer struggle. The presence of the melodrama in the book's first half, therefore, prevents us from clearly seeing John Barton's decline as the successive complications of a tragedy, and his story, with its unresolved contradictions, tends to fade into the background.

In the book's second half, most of the characters repeat our mistake. They continue to interpret the plot according to a preconceived melodramatic pattern, assuming that Jem killed Harry Carson. It then becomes Mary's job to discredit their conventional assumptions. To save Jem is to disprove the melodramatic interpretation of the murder. Melodrama is, therefore, explicitly consigned to the category of false conventions. It is associated with other kinds of sensation-seeking, and Sally Leadbitter is its most determined spokeswoman. Because her cliché-ridden mind is only able to perceive situations in terms of popular stage conventions, after Carson's murder she moves with ease from a farcical to a melodramatic interpretation of the plot. She holds to her melodramatic version of the story even after Jem's acquittal. In explaining why Jem was dismissed from his job, she reveals the source of her opinions: "Decent men were not going to work with a—no! I suppose I musn't say it, seeing you went to such trouble to get up an *alibi;* not that I should think much the worse of a spirited young fellow for falling foul of a rival,—they always do *at the theatre"* (latter emphasis added). Mary, who is concerned for Jem, gasps, "Tell me all about it," and Sally continues, "Why, you see, they've always swords quite handy at them plays."

At this point in the story, Sally's melodramatic viewpoint is relatively harmless—the basis of a joke. But the same viewpoint predominates among the spectators at Jem's trial, almost costing him his life. It is Mary's hard task to disabuse the court of the notion that Jem was a "young fellow" who had "fallen foul of a rival." However, the courtroom, like Sally Leadbitter, seems receptive only to melodrama; even Mary's struggle to save Jem must be rendered melodramatically before it can be admitted: "The barrister, who defended Jem, took new heart when he was put in possession of these striking points to be adduced . . . because he saw the opportunities for a display of forensic eloquence which were presented by the facts; 'a gallant tar brought back from the pathless ocean by a girl's noble daring.' " This bit of parody points up the difference between the narrative we have just read and the same facts couched in melodramatic language.

Far from being melodramatic, therefore, the last half of the book takes melodrama as its specific point of contrast. The fact that we ourselves formerly shared the melodramatic assumption, however, allows us to understand what a natural reading of the events it is and how difficult it will be to overcome. Because Mary must overthrow the assumptions not only of the other characters, but also of one of the major narrative conventions of the book's first half, we feel that her task is almost overwhelming. The drama of Mary's plight, therefore, is heightened by the narrative reversal, and the reader's interest in Mary's story intensifies.

By discrediting melodrama, however, the later chapters raise the question of realistic narrative form even more insistently than do the earlier chapters. For the narrator's reversed attitude toward melodrama broadens her criticism of the conventional, a criticism that depends on a contrastingly realistic narrative ground. Again, the obvious candidate for such a ground is tragedy; the tragic interpretation of the murder is, after all, the truth that the melodramatic interpretation hides. But the tragic reality is precisely what all the actions of the book's second half are designed to conceal. The very causality that the narrator meticulously traced through the first half is hidden in the second. The events of the second half are more than an escape, an avoidance, of the tragic problem; they represent the problem's deliberate suppression.

In the second half of the book, Mary knows the truth, but she refuses to probe it, to ascertain its meaning. Instead, all her energies go into suppressing both public knowledge of her father's crime and her own consciousness of it. The "why" of the crime, the very substance of the tragedy is not even a subject for speculation in the later chapters: "[Mary] felt it was of no use to conjecture his motives. His actions had become so wild and irregular of late, that she could not reason upon them." In the chapters that are largely confined to Mary's consciousness, therefore, those that take place between the murder and Mary's return to Manchester after the trial, the narrator imposes a moratorium on reasoning about John Barton's life, on thinking about tragic causation. Mary's truth-concealing action takes the place of reason; finding an alibi substitutes for seeking the truth. Tragedy is still present as a narrative ground, but is increasingly shadowy; like melodrama, it is a genre Mary struggles against inhabiting. Thus, at precisely the moment when a stable, realistic narrative form is most needed, tragedy becomes unavailable and another genre emerges into prominence as Mary's special domain. Restricted almost entirely to Mary's viewpoint, the narrative becomes a working-class domestic tale that formally authorizes the suppression of tragic causality.

Elizabeth Gaskell was a pioneer of the working-class domestic tale. In 1837 she and her husband published a sketch of working-class life, *"rather in the manner of Crabbe,"* which tried to illustrate that the "poetry of humble life" exists "even in a town." Three short stories she published in *Howitt's Journal* share the intention of the sketch and are characterized by a wealth of domestic detail, illustrations of the charitable affection that the poor have for one another, and an emphasis on the trials and learning experiences of young women. All the women learn one thing: to do their duty, the duty obviously and immediately before them. These stories are also marked by some conspicuous absences: factories and other workplaces are alluded to but never shown, and people from other classes are almost entirely missing. The working-class domestic tales written by Gaskell combined the genres of homily and urban idyll; they were both exclusively domestic and exclusively working-class.

Much of *Mary Barton* is written in this same genre. The documentary realism for which Gaskell is often praised grows out of the impulse to compile domestic details. Thus she gives us elaborate and affectionate descriptions of working-class homes, clothes, and traditions, as well as careful transcriptions of working-class Lancashire dialect. Domesticity dominates the narratives told by old Alice and Job Leigh, narratives that are moving in the matter-of-fact spareness of their language and in the unobtrusiveness of their message: friends and family are all; duty is clear. Even Sally Leadbitter's farcical outlook is inspired by filial affection. Most of the working-class characters in the book share this domestic mentality: they think very little about the masters, they endure bad times, and they seek their satisfaction in the love of family and close friends. Margaret, Job Leigh, the Wilsons, and old Alice all belong to the domestic mode. This is the circle of duty and affection that Mary struggles to maintain.

But Mary is firmly established as a domestic heroine only after her interview with Esther, which reveals the truth about Harry Carson's murder, disabusing Mary of her melodramatic ideas. While the heroine glimpses the tragic abyss (a glimpse that speeds her on to the mental reality of a thoroughly domestic character), the narrator contrasts Mary's lot with Esther's. The contrast is explicitly between the domestic nature of Mary's working-class world and the territories of melodrama and tragedy that Esther inhabits. Just moments before, Mary believed she had driven Jem to murder; she is turned out of the Wilsons' home into the "busy, desolate, crowded street," and her own home seems to her "only the hiding place of four walls . . . where no welcome, no love, no sympathising tears awaited her." She thinks of herself melodramatically as an abandoned waif and longs for her mother, the absent center of a lost domestic idyll. She remembers "long-past times . . . when her father was a cheery-hearted man, rich in the love of his wife, and the companionship of his friend;— when (for it still worked round to that), when mother was alive." And while Mary longs, her mother actually seems to appear in the form of

Esther, who had hidden her own melodrama *cum* tragedy behind the costume of a working-class wife. From Esther we get an entirely different perspective on Mary's reality: Mary, who a minute before fancied herself a pathetic creature in a comfortless room, is seen by Esther as the lucky inhabitant of "that home of her early innocence." The house is Esther's "old dwelling-place, whose very walls, and flags, dingy and sordid as they were, had a charm for her," and Mary now seems to be a potential mother, the woman with power to heal: "For [Esther] longed to open her wretched, wretched heart, so hopeless, so abandoned by all living things, to one who had loved her once; and yet she refrained, from dread of the averted eye, the altered voice, the internal loathing, which she feared such disclosure might create." The poignant and ironic contrast firmly situates Mary in the narrative space between the distortions of melodrama and the abyss of tragedy. It identifies her as a domestic heroine, one still capable of becoming "the wife of a working-man" and thereby joining "that happy class to which [Esther] could never, never more belong."

The interview makes Mary a domestic heroine at the same time that it reveals the extent to which both her future and her present domestic worlds are threatened by the novel's other forms: the melodramatic lie that might condemn Jem and the tragic truth that might condemn her father. She emerges as a domestic heroine just in time to lock up her little house and embark on her mission to save these two men and rescue her personal life. For this reason, the events and settings of the book's second half are neither particularly domestic nor particularly working-class. We should not, however, let the public and adventurous events obscure the narrative mentality that pervades this part of the novel. As Kathleen Tillotson has pointed out, the thickness of domestic detail in *Mary Barton* makes its " 'big scenes'—the chase down the Mersey, the murder trial . . . seem simply emergencies that must occasionally arise in ordinary life."

Mary's existence is "ordinary," but it is also seriously threatened by the emergency she faces. A flawed social order has allowed melodrama and tragedy to break into Mary's world, and she must reestablish its domestic boundaries. Her task involves travel, public notoriety, and extraordinary events of all kinds, but these are necessary to combat melodrama, suppress tragedy, and save what little remains of her family. Mary's homelessness in the later chapters is symptomatic of the social evils the author is trying to illustrate. Mary's struggle to remain a domestic heroine is itself a social criticism with an ideal image of family life at its center. The domestic keynote of these later chapters sounds again and again: in Mary's relationship to Mrs. Wilson; in the minute but emotionally constrained accounts of Mary's tentative and fearful actions and reactions; in the descriptions of the lives and homes she encounters in Liverpool; and in the idyllic, domestic dreamworld that old Alice inhabits throughout the book's second half. Alice's reverie is both a vision of her own past and of Mary's future; Alice imagines the domestic world Mary's actions are retrieving.

For most of the book's second half, then, the domestic tale predominates and suppresses the tragedy, although the two genres are complexly
interrelated throughout the novel. Barton's tragedy is itself fundamentally
domestic. The loss of his son is the most decisive blow against him. Domestic also is the tragic reality behind the clownish appearance of the
workers' delegation, the barren rooms and the sickly wives and children
that *Mary Barton* tries to expose. The book was inspired by scenes of blighted
domestic life in the working class, and John Barton's narrative sketches the
disastrous course that such suffering might initiate.

Although reality is always domestic in *Mary Barton*, it is by no means
always tragic. Tragedy may grow out of working-class domestic life, but it
ultimately excludes that life. For the most part, *Mary Barton* is a domestic
tale, not a domestic tragedy, and the two genres present mutually exclusive
kinds of reality in this novel. Barton's tragic career, we are repeatedly told,
increasingly takes him away from home; furthermore, most of the working-
class characters, drawn in the domestic mode, are uninterested in Barton's
talk about social injustice. In fact, the book's first dialogue, between Barton
and Wilson, typifies the interaction between the hero and most of the
working-class characters. Barton rails on for half a page against the "gen-
tlefolk," but Wilson cuts him short: "Well neighbour, . . . all that may be
very true, but what I want to know now is about Esther." This kind of
exchange is repeated on other occasions with Jem Wilson and with Job
Leigh; the other men all express the assumptions that are built into Gaskell's
domestic convention: being too aware of social injustice only distracts one
from the principal realities of family and home; conversely, home and family
can protect one from the tragedy that attends class conflict.

His respondents never try to refute Barton's social analyses in these
exchanges. Rather, the other men quietly recur to their private preoccupations. Thus, after John Barton tells the sad story of his London journey
and concludes that "as long as I live I shall curse them as so cruelly refused
to hear us," Job Leigh tells his own London story, which includes his
daughter's death and his retrieval of his granddaughter Margaret. The
narrator confides that Job chose the domestic subject matter because it was
"neither sufficiently dissonant from the last to jar on the full heart, nor too
much the same to cherish the continuance of the gloomy train of thought."
The domestic tale suppresses the tragedy not by explicitly denying it, but
rather by eluding its causality. John Barton's tragedy, as we have seen, is
primarily concerned with cause and effect, with showing how and why
the hero became "a Chartist, a Communist, all that is commonly called
wild and visionary." Gaskell's domestic tales, on the other hand, aim at
showing how to circumvent tragic cause-and-effect logic by simply acting,
doing one's immediate duty, without stopping to ponder all of the
consequences.

Inevitability, the solemn basis of tragedy, is thus obscured by a flurry
of activity. On learning of her father's guilt, Mary first determines not to

speculate about his motives and then wades into the myriad activities of the book's second half. The causal logic of this part of the book is explicitly and enthusiastically stated by the narrator in the first person:

> Oh! I do think that the necessity for exertion, for some kind of action . . . in time of distress, is a most infinite blessing. . . . Something to be done implies that there is yet hope of some good thing to be accomplished, or some additional evil that may be avoided; and by degrees the hope absorbs much of the sorrow.

Thus action itself disproves inevitability: it gradually absorbs the tragic causality at the same time that it keeps that causality from emerging into conscious, public view. John Barton dies, but he dies, as Mary wished, at home.

The domestic tale, therefore, is to tragedy in *Mary Barton* as the "Religion of Moral Freedom" was to the "Religion of Causality" in Unitarian theology in the 1840s. Gaskell could not sustain Barton's tragedy, because in doing so she risked denying his freedom, his heroism, even his humanity. But, as the narrator points out, action implies freedom without overtly denying the tragic causality, without providing an alternate interpretation. The action in the book's second half is specifically anti-interpretative; it is designed to establish an alibi for Jem, not to set up a competing version of the truth. Similarly, the transcendental element in Unitarianism was not so much a competing causality as it was a suspension of the older deterministic causality.

Throughout the Liverpool chapters, however, the narrator reminds us that the suspension is merely temporary, that John Barton's terrible guilt is in no way affected by Mary's adventures. We know that once the alibi is established, there will be nothing left to do but confront the awful truth. Thus Will Wilson's arrival in the courtroom produces Mary's collapse. She breaks under the pressure of the suppressed truth, the truth to which the novel must recur once the melodramatic lie is overthrown. Mary's illness gives some reprieve from the inevitable confrontation with John Barton, as do old Alice's death and the settlements of numerous domestic details between Mary and the Wilsons. Each of these in its own way, however, conjures up the "phantom likeness of John Barton" and the problematic causality that attends his story.

Causation once again becomes an explicit theme in the book, one that haunts and perplexes the narrator. Indeed, at one point she attacks the reader for demanding causal explanations. After giving a somewhat unconvincing account of Jem's reasons for prolonging Mary's (and by extension, the novel's) separation from John Barton, she impatiently asserts that reality is not always amenable to clear cause-and-effect analysis: "If you think this account of mine confused, of the half-feelings, half-reasons, which passed through Jem's mind, . . . if you are perplexed to disentangle the real motives, I do assure you it was from such an involved set of thoughts that Jem drew the resolution to act." It is not, however, the reader, the threatening, skeptical, and ultimately guilty "you" of the novel, who demands cause-and-effect logic; it is the narrative itself. In the sentence quoted above, the narrator turns the novel inward by addressing the expectations that the book itself created and declaring both her inability and her unwillingness to meet them. It is a prominently placed sentence, standing at the end of the chapter between the courtroom scene and Mary's return to Manchester; it is an expression of failure, of liberation, and of formal self-consciousness that might well be taken as a motto for the chapters that follow.

The concluding chapters of *Mary Barton* return us to the story of John; Mary continues in the domestic mode, specifically refusing to think about causes. Indeed, where her father's story should be, there is nothing but a blank in Mary's mind: "He was her father! her own dear father! and in his sufferings, whatever their cause, more dearly loved than ever before. His crime was a thing apart, never more to be considered by her." The narrator, however, cannot so easily refuse to consider the causes of John Barton's suffering. Having returned to the subject, she must try to conclude it, but she faces the same bind she encountered earlier: she must indict society as the source of Barton's crime and still grant Barton his free will. Whereas her strategy in the Liverpool chapters was to suppress John Barton's story, her strategy in the concluding chapters is to tell different versions of the story. Since she has declared herself free from the necessity to "disentangle the real motives," she allows herself the luxury of presenting an "involved set" of interpretations without really striving after consistency. Thus the recapitulations contain elements of both social determinism and voluntarism. Finally, however, salvation comes in this novel not through retelling John Barton's story, but through making it irrelevant. All John Barton's and the narrator's explanations are for naught; his story is redeemed through the intervention of another story that makes all talk of causality superfluous.

In the terms of James Martineau's dichotomy, "conscience" is the key word in John Barton's development after the murder, just as "causality" had been before. The issue of John Barton's moral responsibility is partly settled by the mere description of the state in which Mary finds him on her return home: "He had taken the accustomed seat from mere force of habit, which ruled his automaton-body. For all energy, both physical and mental, seemed to have retreated inwards to some of the great citadels of life, there to do battle against the Destroyer, Conscience." John Barton now has no will; he acts from "mere force of habit." But the intensity of his remorse implies that in the past he was free. He takes full responsibility for his crime during his interview with Henry Carson, and his remorse intensifies in the course of conversation. So that remorse might appear a completely appropriate emotion, the narrator gives an account of the murder that makes it seem almost a voluntary political act rather than a desperate crime forced by the convergence of uncontrollable indignation and intolerable suffering. The version of Barton's crime given during his interview with Carson contains a causality compatible with freedom. It contains nothing of the intense suffering of the strikers or of Harry Carson's maddening arrogance: "To intimidate a class of men, known only to those below them as desirous to obtain the greatest quantity of work for the lowest wages,—at most to remove an overbearing partner from an obnoxious firm . . . this was the light in which John Barton had viewed his deed." The very word "cause" takes on a new meaning in this account of Barton's story: instead of implying a set of circumstances that led up to the fatal action, it comes to denote the partisan purpose of the trade unionists, the "cause he had so blindly espoused."

This description of the murder as a wholly political, indeed almost unemotional, act contains a social criticism, but one that increases our sense of Barton's guilty freedom. The account allows the narrator once again to argue that domesticity is the ultimate ground of reality. John Barton's reasoning had produced the distortion of human reality that always occurs when men are severed from their domestic contexts: "he had no more imagined to himself the blighted home, and the miserable parents, than does the soldier, who discharges his musket, picture to himself the desolation of the wife, and the pitiful cries of the helpless little ones, who are in an instant to be made widowed, and fatherless." The analogy links Barton's failing to Harry Carson's insensitivity: each in his own way was deaf to "the pitiful cries" of helpless relations. This plea for a more highly developed domestic consciousness is itself a species of social criticism, albeit a vague one. Barton's sin of abstracting Harry Carson from his domestic context is presented as the characteristic error of industrial society. By substituting this kind of broad criticism of an abstract and abstracting mentality for the careful descriptions of social relationships and experiences contained in earlier chapters, the author unites the classes on the basis of a shared human reality, the universal reality of family life. The account of Barton's story that emerges from the interview with Mr. Carson, therefore, makes a critical point, but the point does not relieve the hero of any guilt. Indeed, it increases Barton's crimes by adding to his faults of resentment and murder the crime of insensitivity to human suffering, which was previously attributed to the masters. In this account, the murder is no longer the result but the cause of suffering:

> The sympathy for suffering, formerly so prevalent a feeling with him, again filled John Barton's heart, and almost impelled him to speak . . . some earnest, tender words to the stern man, shaking in his agony.
> But who was he, that he should utter sympathy, or consolation? The cause of all this woe.

This version of Barton's story is concerned with causation, but not the kind of causation that the earlier chapters traced. In this retelling, "cause" comes to mean political purpose, and Barton himself becomes the cause of another's suffering. Causation in this version, therefore, is compatible with conscience and its corollary, free will.

Those circumstances formerly presented as the sources of Barton's action, however, are not completely ignored in the resolution of his story. After the unforgiving Mr. Carson leaves him, Barton gives an account of his own tragedy, an account which contains a heavy dose of the social determinism of earlier chapters. From him we hear once more about the moral effects of poverty and ignorance: "You see I've so often been hankering after the right way; and it's a hard one for a poor man to find. . . . No one learned me, and no one told me." Ignorance and poverty are two determining circumstances, and the hypocrisy of the upper classes is a third: "I would fain have gone after the Bible rules if I'd seen folk credit it; they all spoke up for it, and went and did clean contrary." And we hear again about the hatred inspired by his son's death from want of medicine and proper food: "wife, and children never spoke, but their helplessness cried aloud, and I was driven to do as others did,—and then Tom died."

The image of Barton as a driven man, however, competes in this deathbed account with yet another characterization, one quite new to the novel. Barton acknowledges that he is creating a new self in his story-telling; he describes the act of narration as "wrestling with my soul for a character to take into the other world." Although Barton's characterization of himself has elements of social determinism, it is not completely dominated by that model of causation. Even as he recapitulates the familiar circumstances, he subtly undermines their explanatory power by prefacing them: "It's not much I can say for myself in t'other world. God forgive me: but I can say this . . . ." This preface reminds us that John Barton's acknowledged guilt, his full moral responsibility, is the given context of his narrative; he is not rehearsing his story as a defense, as a proof of innocence. Instead, he is describing, somewhat inconsistently, the extenuating circumstances of a crime to which he has already pleaded guilty.

Accordingly, the focus of his narrative is not on the familiar circumstances of his decline, but on a new set of facts about his life, facts implying that he could have avoided his tragic course. We learn for the first time that the hero was once very devout, that he studied the Bible and tried to follow its precepts, that he even had a special comradeship with old Alice, who had tried to "strengthen" him. His faith, however, was not strong enough to survive the corrosive bitterness of his experience; the loss of faith, we are told, was the turning point of his career: "At last I gave it up in despair, trying to make folks' actions square wi' th' Bible; and I thought I'd no longer labour at following th' Bible myself. I've said all this afore; may be. But from that time I've dropped down, down,—down." Despair, itself a sin, becomes the decisive factor in this religious account of Barton's life. The character that Barton creates "to take into the other world" is thus a cross between the tragically determined John Barton we know and a John Barton we have never seen before, the free but erring subject of a religious homily.

The writer seems to have felt some uneasiness about introducing a completely new version of the story at such a late hour, especially one that fits imperfectly with the older deterministic version, for she has Barton suggest that "I've said all this afore; may be." If the sentence is meant to make the new facts seem less strange, it defeats its own purpose, for it conveys the self-conscious uneasiness of the writer by reminding us that in fact *no one* has "said all this afore," that we are being given a new story, one that is not easy to reconcile with the old. The sentence therefore increases our awareness of the discontinuities of these last chapters.

The issues tangled in the summaries of Barton's life and crime (whether he is fully responsible or not, free or determined) are never finally sorted out. We must accept this "involved set" of accounts, but we are also reassured that ultimately it does not matter how we interpret Barton's story. For the novel we have been reading is finally resolved by the introduction of a different book, the Bible. The narrator finds relief from the multiple reinterpretations of John Barton's story by superimposing the ending as well as the meaning of the Gospel onto her novel, and the meaning of the Gospel is that we need not choose among the several versions of John Barton's story.

While John Barton is recounting his failure to live "Gospel-wise," Henry J. Carson recreates himself (in both senses of the phrase) through the other story: "He fell to the narrative now, afresh, with all the interest of a little child. He began at the beginning, and read on almost greedily, understanding for the first time the full meaning of the story." The "full meaning" of the story turns out to be that John Barton should be forgiven, no matter what the sources or consequences of his crime. Henry Carson comes to forgive John Barton not because he has been told the hero's own story, but because Barton's words "I did not know what I was doing" referred him to the Gospel story. Forgiveness is mandated by the other narrative, and all versions of John Barton's life thus become irrelevant to the novel's concluding and redeeming action: Carson's forgiveness, which is a foretaste of the Christian spirit that the narrator assures us will allow Carson to effect industrial social change.

Thus the conclusion of John Barton's story points to narrative as an instrument of God's Providence without having to sort out the tangle of its own narrative threads. In the few episodes that remain, the characters settle in Canada, and the domestic tale is finally protected by distance from the tragedy caused by industrial vicissitudes. But the final episodes fail to settle the question that the novel repeatedly raises: the question of an appropriate narrative form. It is not surprising that, in Gaskell's words, no one "saw" her "idea of a tragic poem," for the tragedy is even more obscured by antagonistic interpretations at the end of the novel than in the early chapters. We must therefore agree with the author's judgment that she failed to express perfectly her tragic intentions. But we must also remember that her tragic purpose contained its own contradiction, which had definite historical roots in the Unitarianism of the 1840s and in certain features of the tradition of industrial social criticism that Gaskell inherited. We should also remember that her failure is the foundation of the book's formal significance, for its very generic eclecticism points toward the formal self-consciousness of later British realism.

The Narrative Voice
in Thackeray's Novels

Jack P. Rawlins

It is often felt that Thackeray's obtrusive narrator is an obstacle to the enjoyment of his novels; however, [elsewhere] we have seen that the conventional orientation toward narrator and narrative, which considers the teller something to be looked past, and the tale the thing to be looked at, does not work here. Thackeray's commentary on his fiction is so large a part of his work that to attempt to look past it as some sort of vehicle for telling a story is to ignore what to him is often primary. And even more— if we do succeed in looking past that voice to the novel it is telling, we will find the unsatisfying, confused congeries the previous chapter [of *Thackeray's Novels*] has examined. The narrator's novels are not very good; his commentary on them can be excellent. This chapter will examine the properties of that voice, eventually defining the use of the novel that the narrator by example is suggesting we make.

THE DISSERTATION ON THE NOVEL

We have seen that Thackeray's novels often refuse to obey the implicit commands of their own conventional form. An alternative to that outright rebellion from convention is for Pen to give us what convention demands, but to preface it with a discussion of novel writing, the demands of convention and a conventional public, and similar subjects. The method is basic to *Catherine*, where Thackeray prefaces his bloody consummation with a long denunciation of anyone who might like it and the literary customs that require it. In *The Virginians*, when Pen must write a love scene, we get pages, not of the scene itself, but of Pen's desire not to write it.

From *Thackeray's Novels: A Fiction That Is True.* © 1974 by the Regents of the University of California. University of California Press, 1974.

> Any man or woman with a pennyworth of brains, or the like
> precious amount of personal experience, or who has read a novel
> before, must, when Harry pulled out those faded vegetables just
> now, have gone off into a digression of his own, as the writer
> confesses for himself he was diverging whilst he has been writing
> the last brace of paragraphs. . . . When, I say, a lad pulls a bunch
> of amputated and now decomposing greens from his breast and
> falls to kissing it, what is the use of saying much more? . . .
>   And how came Maria to give it to Harry? And how did he come
> to want it and to prize it so passionately when he got the bit of
> rubbish? Is not one story as stale as the other? Are not they all
> alike? What is the use, I say, of telling them over and over?
> The incidents of life, and love-making especially, I believe to re-
> semble each other so much, that I am surprised, gentlemen and
> ladies, you read novels any more. Psha! Of course that rose in
> young Harry's pocket-book had grown, and had budded, and had
> bloomed, and was now rotting, like other roses. I suppose you
> will want me to say that the young fool kissed it next? Of course
> he kissed it,

and so on. This writing about writing, this eye upon himself as author,
becomes more pronounced in Thackeray's writings until it reaches the following apotheosis in *Philip:* Philip has lost his job at the Pall Mall Gazette,
and Pen's thoughts turn to the economics of journalism:

> Ah how wonderful ways and means are! When I think how this
> very line, this very word, which I am writing represents money,
> I am lost in a respectful astonishment. . . . I am paid, we will say,
> for the sake of illustration, at the rate of sixpence per line. With
> the words, "Ah, how wonderful," to the words, "per line," I can
> buy a loaf, a piece of butter, a jug of milk, a modicum of tea. . . .
> Wife, children, guests, servants, charwoman, we are all making a
> meal off Philip Firmin's bones as it were.

It is this apparent willingness to destroy the novel to make a point about
the business of reading and writing that makes us realize that we cannot
look past that voice as we look past the frame of a picture to the imagined
reality beyond. Thackeray's last group of essays, *The Roundabout Papers*,
makes this clear. Written when Thackeray was editor of the *Cornhill Magazine* in the years immediately before his death, they are largely about the
writing of essays, these essays particularly. "On Two Roundabout Papers
Which I Intended to Write" is paradoxically the treatment of two subjects
to show how completely unsuitable they are as essay topics; "On a Joke I
Once Heard from the Late Thomas Hood" is about Thackeray's refusal to
tell us the joke. "On Two Children in Black" is not so much about the
children themselves as about Thackeray's right to write about them, even

though there is no story to be told. It is an essay on the nature of the essay, using itself as an object for discussion—just as we have been maintaining that his novels use the conventional novel within themselves to make a point about novels and the assumptions about life that go into and come out of them. In these last essays, Thackeray begins with a defense of his right to be unorganized, egocentric, and trivial, and goes on to discuss the nature and responsibilities of the writer and reader. Here is a sample:

> *Linea recta brevissima.* That right line "I" is the very shortest, simplest, straightforwardest means of communication between us, and stands for what it is worth and no more. . . . When this bundle of egotisms is bound up together, as they may be one day, if no accident prevents this tongue from wagging, or this ink from running, they will bore you very likely; so it would to . . . eat up the whole of a ham: but a slice on occasion, may have a relish: a dip into the volume at random and so on for a page or two: and now and then a smile; and presently a gape: and the book drops out of your hand: and so, *bon soir,* and pleasant dreams to you.

The authorial self-awareness which these examples represent in its most overt form trains a similar objective critical scrutiny in the reader. Thackeray teaches us to attend to the rhetorical and dramatic processes of the novel as we experience them. The reader must share Thackeray's awareness of the artistic process; ultimately the degree of insight into the inner workings of fiction granted to the reader by Thackeray, and expected from him, is a very high one.

> Who knows any one save himself alone? Who, in showing his house to the closest and dearest, doesn't keep back the key of a closet or two? I think of a lovely reader laying down the page and looking over at her unconscious husband, asleep, perhaps, after dinner. Yes, madam, a closet he hath: and you, who pry into everything, shall never have the key of it. I think of some honest Othello pausing over this very sentence in a railroad carriage, and stealthily gazing at Desdemona opposite to him, innocently administering sandwiches to their little boy—I am trying to turn the sentence off with a joke, you see—I feel it is growing too dreadful, too serious.

> *(The Newcomes)*

Thackeray's intrusions are either infuriating or delightful, depending on whether we want to experience the fictive illusion or study it. Thackeray wants us to recognize, first, that Othello in a railroad carriage is rather absurd, and second, that the narrator is using that absurdity to avoid a darkness of moral vision that would violate the spirit of a light comedy of manners. He teaches us to attend to the distance between the verbal surface and the real meaning, the rhetorical effect and the means of achieving it, and it is this that makes Thackeray's novels demonstrably greater than Pen's evaluation of them. Thackeray gives us the tools by which we can come to a truer evaluation of the novel than Pen does.

THE UNDERCUTTING OF CONVENTIONAL RHETORIC

Thackeray began his career as a parodist of style [cf. the *Novels by Eminent Hands*], and he remains always supremely conscious of the distortive effect of style on subject matter; he habitually makes his meaning felt by the exaggeration of conventional rhetoric until its failure to describe accurately becomes unmistakable. When Barnes and his father discuss restraining the editorial hostility of the *Newcome Independent*, the liberal paper, Pen comments, "during the above conspiracy for bribing or crushing the independence of a great organ of British opinion, Miss Ethel Newcome held her tongue." "Great organ of British opinion" rings false enough to cause us to pause and consider the facts, which suggest that the paper is as unprincipled and selfish as the Newcomes. When Clive and Rosie are making their ill-conceived marriage, the source of the allusion directs our attention below the surface: "So, as a good thing when it is done had best be done quickly, these worthy folks went off almost straightway to a clergyman, and were married out of hand" [cf. *Macbeth* 1.7.1]. Frequently the language represents the spirit of the actors—"great organ of British opinion" is the newspaper's own conception of itself—and it reflects the actor's distorted self-image. Clive, for instance, when he is struggling to understand his love for Ethel, describes it entirely in a language taken from romantic art—ballad, novel, classical epic, and so on—and that use of an artificial language is definitely an attempt to take refuge in convention. Clive claims for his love a conventional heroic status it does not deserve. When J. J. tries to make him face the practical problems of courting above one's station with no money, Clive sings, "Her heart it is another's, she never-can-be-mine"; but Ethel is struggling with real-life problems she knows the romances cannot help her solve. Her heart is not another's; rather the barriers are the less romantic ones of birth, wealth, and profession.

And as the rhetoric of the romance is undercut, so the rhetoric of the pulpit is questioned by using it to deliver the narrator's best cynicism. Here is the conclusion of his description of the miseries of the Steyne household in *Vanity Fair*: "So . . . it is very likely that this lady [i.e. Steyne's wife], in her high station, had to . . . hide many secret griefs under a calm face. And let us, my brethren who have not our names in the Red Book, console ourselves by thinking comfortably how miserable our betters may be." The religion of righteous self-congratulation is uncovered. As with Clive's use of the rhetoric of romance, the presence of rhetoric represents an attempt to hide an unpleasant truth under an attractive surface, and Thackeray makes sure that it fails. An interesting nonverbal manifestation of this use of convention is in the illustrated majuscules which begin the chapters.

They often illustrate, not the story, but the conventional images, drawn from myth and romance, in which the actors see the story. Chapter 69, in which the Colonel gains his revenge against Barnes by defeating him in the parliamentary election, by the wholly unethical means of Fred Bayham and company, is headed with the Colonel's image of the affair, which the chapter belies—two knights jousting.

However, Thackeray's use of rhetoric is not as completely under control as we have so far suggested. That he uses rhetoric and undercuts it, everyone knows who reads his novels; but that he does so to any determinable purpose, one is not so sure. This problem has probably resulted in more critical dissatisfaction with Thackeray than any other, a dissatisfaction that is usually inadequately expressed by saying that Thackeray seems to be laughing at everything. John Forster says, in a review of *Vanity Fair*, "we are seldom permitted to enjoy the appreciation of all gentle and kind things which we continually meet with in the book, without some neighboring quip or sneer that would seem to show the author ashamed of what he yet cannot help giving way to" (*Examiner*, 22 July 1848). Robert Bell also suggests some inner conflict: "He cannot call up a tear without dashing it off with a sarcasm. Yet his power of creating emotion is equal to his wit, although he seems to have less confidence in it, or to have an inferior relish for the use of it" (*Fraser's*, September 1848). This is the role of sentimental cynic, in which Thackeray has so long been cast. We now have the insight necessary to put to sleep some of the myth. Thackeray's lack of conviction about the value of extreme sensibility is rather a lack of conviction about such feelings fictively aroused. No one who knew Thackeray personally suggests that he had any doubts about the value of tears, but he tells us in his fiction openly that he has severe doubts about the value of tears shed for heroines in books. He does like to dash away our tears, but usually with a reminder that our uncomplicated sympathy is a luxury provided by the pleasing distortions of romance.

But the critics are in spirit right; Thackeray undercuts his own rhetoric as well as the rhetoric of his characters, and in ways for which we cannot offer explanation or defense except in the general terms of an habitual ironic perspective. We know that he is being "ironic," without any sure knowledge of what the irony is meant to point to. We do not know what Thackeray means; we only know for sure that he does not mean what he says. In fact, we do not even know that for sure, as we shall see. Consider this description of the Brighton beach:

> Along the rippled sands (stay, are they rippled sands or shingly beach?) the prawn-boy seeks the delicious material of your breakfast. Breakfast—meal in London almost unknown, greedily devoured in Brighton! In yon vessels now nearing the shore the sleepless mariner has ventured forth to seize the delicate whiting, the greedy and foolish mackerel, and the homely sole.
>
> (*The Newcomes*)

Once we recognize the artificiality of the rhetoric, what explanation for it can we offer? When Thackeray slips into blank verse, can we say why? This is foolery only, but our very point is that no dramatic moment is free from the potential for such. We can make matters worse: If we explain the allusion to *Macbeth* quoted above as a directive to a moral interpretation of the marriage, how do we explain it when we discover it used repeatedly by Thackeray in the most innocent situations? Pen's use of allusion, then, is often morally equivalent to Clive's—as a "pre-fab" response to a situation, one that allows the user to avoid a personal moral involvement with the particulars. As the next paragraphs will show, convention is a mask, and, while both Clive and Pen are quick to acknowledge the existence and artificial nature of the mask, it still successfully allows them to avoid having to confront the face in the mirror.

Thackeray's enjoyment of artificial styles for their own sake, and without specific ironic intent, causes the critic serious problems. Here is the best of Thackeray's critics looking for a sure reading of perhaps the central passage in Thackeray's best book; failure here would have most serious implications indeed. The scene is Rawdon's confrontation with Becky and Lord Steyne; the critic is John Loofbourow.

> In the discredited context of criminal romance, a farcical Satan and a melodramatic Eve have played a primordial scene for laughs. The fallen Becky—"wretched woman" . . . "brilliants on her breast which Steyne had given her." . . . "I am innocent." . . . "All covered with serpents, and rings, and baubles." Steyne, the Tempter—"hanging over the sofa" . . . "grinding his teeth" . . . "fury in his looks." The "bald forehead" of the second-rate serpent is bruised by the clumsy Adam, Rawdon—"Steyne wore the scar to his dying day." In the parodic context, this biblical sequence is a moral nightmare.

Loofbourow is saying that Thackeray, by the use of a discredited rhetoric, alerts us to the distance between the verbal surface and the true moral nature of the scene. The rhetoric of criminal romance and the biblical machinery is a purposely noisy attempt to simplify the moral ambiguities of this moment, when all the challenges *Vanity Fair* makes to our complacency are becoming explicit. The rhetoric attempts to cast the characters as heroes and villains, and the artificiality of tone alerts us to that distortion as it is done. Becky's serpentine jewelry is an example of Thackeray's sense of a deluding style, of the lying power of the symbol—because Becky is not simply evil, though the scene is more comfortable to read if she is so cast.

Though this interpretation of Loofbourow's is fundamentally correct, it ignores a problem it raises. The rhetoric of this scene is certainly "discredited," or at least questioned, by Thackeray, but we have argued that Thackeray discredits all languages; thus the reader's task is not to determine whether or not the language at hand has been discredited—at which point he may conclude the passage to be "parodic"—but rather to determine how to establish criteria for evaluation of texts that are inevitably in one or another discredited rhetoric. Loofbourow implies that we reject the superficial reading of this scene because we recognize the presence of a discredited rhetoric; but the rhetoric only directs us to evaluate its assertions in the context of the novel; the novel proves the scene simplistic—the false rhetoric only asks us to find criteria for judgment other than itself. The distinction may seem small when dealing with a scene that in either system is a fraud, but when the scene is apparently legitimate the distinction becomes critical. Consider these passages, both in a "discredited" rhetoric, but neither revealing a "moral nightmare" behind the words.

> And this, at the end of threescore and seven or eight years, was to be the close of a life which had been spent in freedom and splendour, and kindness and honor; this the reward of a noble heart—the tomb and prison of a gallant warrior who had ridden in twenty battles—whose course through life had been followed by blessing, and whose career was to end here—here—a low furious woman standing over him and stabbing the kind defenseless breast with killing insult and daily outrage!
>
> (*The Newcomes*)

> The painter turned as he spoke; and the bright northern light which fell upon the sitter's head was intercepted, and lighted up his own as he addressed us. . . . The palette on his arm was a great shield painted of many colors: he carried his maul-stick and a sheaf of brushes along with it, the weapons of his glorious but harmless war. With these he achieves conquests, wherein none are wounded save the envious: with that he shelters him against how much idleness, ambition, temptation! Occupied over that consoling work, idle thoughts cannot gain the mastery over him; selfish wishes or desires are kept at bay. Art is truth: and truth is religion; and its study and practice a daily work of pious duty.
>
> (*The Newcomes*)

Clearly we need a more flexible way to deal with rhetoric than simply to divide it into two categories, discredited and still-undiscredited. Because it is a prominent feature of Thackeray's fiction that languages that have been "discredited" are somehow still available for use, and to great effect, as in the passage about Colonel Newcome quoted above. It is more helpful to say that Thackeray teaches us to scrutinize all styles, to look behind them and test them against a larger moral context; what is finally being discredited is not so much a language or languages, but the authorial process as an evaluative instrument. Rhetoric, in the most general sense, is being questioned: the use of persuasive language by an enthusiastic and short-sighted author to enforce his interpretation of fictive events upon the reader surreptitiously. Thackeray indicates surely that sometimes what his narrator says, or how his narrator interprets, is not the truth; it would seem that there is no logical end to that, and that once the question of authorial insincerity has been raised, all rhetoric must be tested with some correlative. Thackeray, by admitting that the rhetoric of his narrator is of dubious value, implies that there is some basic substratum of truth that rhetoric obscures, and that we have some means to determine that truth. This, however, is not obviously so. Wayne Booth, in *The Rhetoric of Fiction*, argues persuasively against the basic realist myth that fictive experience is somehow self-evaluative and that therefore the author should strive to remove himself as much as possible from the work and let it make its own meaning. As Booth observes, the ideal dichotomy between matter and manner is based on the fallacy that one is truer than the other. Both are equally fictional, and thus indistinguishable. Booth gives evidence for the confusion that arises when authors deny the reader sure rhetorical directives. Thackeray is between two stools—he neither gives us sure rhetorical directives, nor denies us rhetorical directives at all; rather he gives us the rhetoric and questions it. This makes him rather unique in Booth's scheme, because if an absence of rhetoric leads to confusion and unreadability, then Thackeray is made somewhat readable by his rhetoric, even if it is a specious sense of order that it brings.

One must learn to read back and forth between Thackeray's "realist" moral vision and his authorial commentary. Simply to discard the latter is to distort his work completely; to contain the two in one reading is difficult indeed. Becky's serpentine jewelry is a good instance of the difficulties involved. If we assume, as we did previously, that the serpentine symbolism is a fraud, designed to awaken us, by its convenient artificiality, to the moral ambiguities of her situation the symbol fails to represent, we are forced to "throw out" of *Vanity Fair* the large amount of text in which Thackeray describes Becky as simply evil. The famous mermaid metaphor at the beginning of Becky's dark history, for instance:

> In describing this syren, singing and smiling, . . . the author, with modest pride, asks his readers all round, has he once forgotten the laws of politeness, and showed the monster's hideous tail above water? No! Those who like may peep down under waves that are pretty transparent, and see it writhing and twirling, diabolically hideous and slimy, flapping amongst bones, or curling round corpses.

The question is, do we take the opportunity Thackeray gives us to say that this is a joke ("we had best not examine the fiendish marine cannibals, revelling and feasting on their wretched *pickled* victims," my emphasis), and thus forget it? Thackeray will always give us that opportunity, but there is no end to that, and if we laugh at this we will laugh always and never know when to stop laughing. It is this lack of confidence with which we take in his fiction that disturbed his contemporary critics and made them suspect they were being laughed at. This is perhaps the most fundamental way in which his fiction is confused and thus forgettable—because we never have complete confidence in the manner of our involvement with the text. Because, just as we have seen that the central moment of high drama in *Vanity Fair* is meant to discredit itself through the very height of the drama, similarly the presence of a joke does not mean the passage is meant to be funny—as we saw in the passage about Othello in the railroad carriage, where Thackeray tells us he is trying to be funny and achieves a moment of high seriousness by doing so.

Let us take George Osborne's death scene and seek an absolute authority among the various languages used to describe it. We begin with Jos showing the white feather. In two paragraphs George is dead. Jos's farcical cowardice is followed by a paragraph on the atrocity of war: "There is no end to the so-called glory and shame, and to the alternations of successful and unsuccessful murder, in which two high-spirited nations might engage." Then one paragraph in a magnificent heroic style: "unscared by the thunder of the artillery, which hurled death from the English line—the dark rolling column pressed on and up the hill. . . . Then it stopped, still facing the shot. Then at last the English troops rushed from the post from which no enemy had been able to dislodge them." Then the neutral announcement that "Amelia was praying for George, who was lying on his face, dead, with a bullet through his heart." The next chapter begins with the worldly Miss Crawley reading the promotions resulting from the battle in the Gazette, and speculating on Rawdon's chances, and missed chances, for advancement. We go from comedy to bitter philosophy to heroism to social pragmatism in five paragraphs, with George's death in the middle, surrounded by these alternative evaluations of the military drama in which he has been acting that fatal role. Is Jos right to run, if the battle was only "so-called glory and shame" and "successful and unsuccessful murder"? "So-called" implies that the battle is called glory and shame falsely—what is it truly called? Can a soldier be heroic in the doing of wicked deeds? Is Miss Crawley right to see the army as only an instrument of social advancement? The status of George's death in such a context becomes more interesting when we remember from Thackeray's letters that he had strong feelings about the death. He writes, "when [Amelia's] scoundrel of a husband is well dead with a ball in his odious bowels," Amelia will find true humility, as we noted [elsewhere]. So this is a moment in the drama with a clear dramatic function for Thackeray—retribution for a villain, almost—and he chooses to present it in a multiply ambiguous context, one that ignores George's function as Amelia's hateful husband and concentrates on his role as morally ambiguous soldier. And we should note that these issues are raised only here in the novel, as if to cloud our responses with a fresh subject. To approach these multiple languages of evaluation with an attitude toward choosing the correct one is to destroy a complexity that Thackeray is working to create.

By undercutting dramatic unity and authorial rhetoric, Thackeray denies the reader the two fundamental tools for the comprehension of fiction. What we witness may be only accident; what we are told may be insincere, ironic, mistaken, the product of a narrow mind or a perverse wit. Thackeray asks for a maximal amount of scrutiny from his reader; perhaps he asks for more than his fiction can bear. Do these novels have meaning above the level of personal friendships, accidental history, and Pen's need to earn a living? We can spontaneously answer yes, but locating the source of that meaning is proving difficult.

NOVELIST AS PREACHER

Thackeray likes to preface his sermons with the observation that sermons are out of place in novels, and that therefore he will not sermonize. "Sick-bed homilies and pious reflections are, to be sure, out of place in mere story-books, and we are not going . . . to cajole the public into a sermon, when it is only a comedy that the reader pays his money to witness. But, without preaching, the truth may surely be borne in mind, that . . ." [*Vanity Fair*]. The sermon follows. By doing what the "novelist" should not do, he implies that he is doing something else. Why is a sermon out of place in the archetypal "novel," and how accurately can we describe Thackeray's methods as those of the pulpit?

Thackeray, like the sermonizer, is a fundamentally rhetorical writer, in that he writes not in terms of any abstract truth, but in terms of the reader and his response, and particularly in terms of the moral effect of his writing. To consider a Thackeray pronouncement out of rhetorical context is often to misunderstand, and to take it as absolute truth is to convince oneself that Thackeray is merely foolish. One such misunderstanding is a matter of public record. In *Vanity Fair*, Thackeray says, "An alderman coming from a turtle feast will not step out of his carriage to steal a leg of mutton; but put him to starve, and see if he will not purloin a loaf." George Henry Lewes, in an article in the *Morning Chronicle*, took violent objection to this passage (March 6, 1848). Calling it "a detestable passage," he says,

> Was it carelessness, or deep misanthropy, distorting that other-
> wise clear judgment, which allowed such a remark to fall? What,
> in the face of starving thousands, men who literally die for want
> of bread, yet who prefer death to stealing, shall it be said that
> honesty is only the virtue of abundance! . . . Of all false-hoods,
> that about honesty being a question of money is the most glaring
> and the most insidious. Blot it out, Thackeray; let it no longer
> deface your delightful pages!

But Lewes has made the error of taking the remark as pertaining to human nature *in abstracto*. As such, it would be morally hideous, since it would be amorality, simple pragmatism—one steals as much as one must. But this is to ignore the message Thackeray finds in it: "If you take temptations

into account, who is to say that he is better than his neighbor?" The lesson
is not that all aldermen are potential thieves, but rather that we should
take no credit for our respectable virtue, which has never been tried by
adversity. Thackeray repeats the moral elsewhere: "Oh, be humble, my
brother, in your prosperity! . . . Think, what right have you to be scornful,
whose virtue is a deficiency of temptation . . . whose prosperity is very
likely a satire." And, in a letter to Lewes, he makes the difference in orientation clear:

> That passage which you quote bears very hardly upon the poor
> alderman certainly: but I don't mean that the man deprived of
> turtle would as a consequence steal bread: only that he in the
> possession of luxuries and riding through life in a gig, should be
> very chary of despizing poor Lazarus on foot, and look very hum-
> bly and leniently upon the faults of his less fortunate brethren.

In this sense, Lewes is like the little girl in Sunday School who, when asked
to explain the moral of the tale of the Good Samaritan, said that it was
"when I am in trouble someone should stop and help me." He has ignored
the thrust of the rhetoric and interpreted the statement about the alderman
as pure truth.

Thackeray's sense of the artist as preacher is not a superficial one.

> . . . this book is all about the world, and a respectable family
> dwelling in it. It is not a sermon, except where it cannot help itself,
> and the speaker pursuing the destiny of his narrative finds such
> a homily before him. O friend, in your life and mine, don't we
> light upon such sermons daily—don't we see at home as well as
> amongst our neighbors that battle between Evil and Good? . . .
> Which shall we let triumph for ourselves—which for our children?
>
> (*The Newcomes*)

His urge to sermonize is actually stronger than he admits here. Often his
sermons are not the natural consequences of the narrative at all; rather, he
uses the text as an excuse to sermonize to heights the text itself cannot
support. Here are Thackeray's reflections on Clive's preferring the company
of his friends to the company of his father:

> The young fellow, I dare say, gave his parent no more credit for
> his long self-denial than many other children award to theirs. We
> take such life-offerings as our due commonly. . . . It is only in
> later days, perhaps, when the treasures of love are spent, and the
> kind hand cold which ministered them, that we remember how
> tender it was. . . . Let us hope those fruits of love, though tardy,
> are yet not all too late. . . . I am thinking of the love of Clive
> Newcome's father for him; (and, perhaps, young reader, that of
> yours and mine for ourselves;) . . . Did we not say, at our story's

commencement, that all stories were old? Careless prodigals and
anxious elders have been from the beginning:—so may love, and
repentance, and forgiveness endure ever till the end.

The reflections are of a size and intensity the particulars of the drama do
not justify; Clive is not a careless prodigal, and, though Thackeray frequently invokes that myth as the pattern for his story, it does not fit. Clive
is a loving and thoughtful son, and, when Thackeray is less moved by his
own swelling language, much of the blame for the Colonel's suffering is
correctly fixed on the Colonel himself, who selfishly expects Clive to live
for him. The moral is so attractive to the preacher that he will state it in
defiance of the particular text. In other ways Thackeray's description of the
cause and effect of his sermonizing tendency seems inaccurate. If Thackeray
sees his sermon as a defense of Good in its battle with Evil, to insure its
victory, we must complain that his commentary often obscures the clear
division between those two elemental forces—in fact, we sometimes feel
that the narrator feels called upon to speak out when the reader is getting
too clear a sense of where Good and Evil are aligned on the issue at hand.
Here is Thackeray's analysis of Ethel's treatment of Clive. Ethel likes Clive,
but she is obviously destined by her family for a "great match"; she treats
Clive with a provoking mixture of honest affection and cynical
discouragement.

> I allow, with Mrs. Grundy and most moralists, that Miss New-
> come's conduct in this matter was highly reprehensible: that if she
> did not intend to marry Clive she should have broken with him
> altogether; that a virtuous woman of high principle, etc., etc.,
> having once determined to reject a suitor, should separate from
> him utterly then and there. . . .
>
> But coquetry, but kindness, but family affection, and a strong,
> very strong partiality for the rejected lover—are these not to be
> taken into account? . . . The least unworthy part of her conduct,
> some critics will say, was that desire to see Clive and be well with
> him . . . , and every flutter which she made to escape out of the
> meshes which the world had cast about her, was but the natural
> effort at liberty. It was her prudence which was wrong; and her
> submission, wherein she was most culpable: . . . do we not read
> how young martyrs constantly had to disobey worldly papas and
> mamas . . . ? Does not the world worship them, and persecute
> those who refuse to kneel? Do not many timid souls sacrifice to
> them; and other bolder spirits . . . bend down their stubborn knees
> at their altars? See! I begin by siding with Mrs. Grundy and the
> world, and at the next turn on the seesaw have lighted down on
> Ethel's side, and am disposed to think that the very best part of
> her conduct has been those escapades which—which right-minded
> persons most justly condemn.

Thackeray discredits the language of both arguments. In the first, the "etc., etc." is his indication that gammon is being spoken, and the invocation of Grundy is a sure telltale. The second argument is compromised in subtler ways. This is a fine example of Thackeray's habit of irrelevant dissonance. "Worldly papas and mamas" is flippant, and "persecute those who refuse to kneel" is offensive, but neither accomplishes anything more specific in the argument than to put us off our ease with it. Thus we may call such a method "ironic" only in a very vague sense, since the dissonance directs our attention to nothing particular beneath the textual surface. There is conflict within the argument, but no indication of how to resolve it. That conflict seems forced upon the argument by an irrelevant intrusion. To this point we probably feel we can choose between the two views of Ethel's behavior offered, but Thackeray continues with a final reversal.

> At least that a young beauty should torture a man with alternate liking and indifference; allure, dismiss, and call him back out of banishment; practice arts-to-please upon him, and ignore them when rebuked for her coquetry—these are surely occurrences so common in young women's history as to call for no special censure: and, if on these charges Miss Newcome is guilty, is she, of all her sex, alone in her criminality?

Here the lecture ends, in irresolution. This is the basic pattern of Thackeray's lectures—an argument, a change of mind, and a final turn of the screw that reduces everything to uncertainty.

This process of the self-destructive sermon works on a larger scale, between separate arguments to opposite conclusions. When Sir Pitt has a stroke and is confined to a wheelchair, Thackeray is moved to meditation: "As for Sir Pitt he retired into those very apartments where Lady Crawley had been previously extinguished, and there was tended by Miss Hester, the girl upon her promotion, with constant care and assiduity. What love, what fidelity, what constancy is there equal to that of a nurse with good wages?" And so on through a long paragraph, ending, "Ladies, what man's love is there that would stand a year's nursing of the object of his affection? Whereas a nurse will stand by you for ten pounds a quarter, and we think her too highly paid." Again, the argument is a central one in the scheme of *Vanity Fair*. But on the next page Thackeray tells us that all the above is a fraud; Hester waits until everyone else leaves the room and then torments the helpless old man as a cruel child teases a kitten. Thackeray, never lacking "face," now discourses on Hester's *dis*loyalty in the great scheme of Vanity. Thus he sermonizes on a text that he immediately identifies as spurious—and proceeds to sermonize on the opposite data with equal felicity. We can easily imagine him sermonizing on the implications of his having thus deceived us.

If Thackeray's preaching does not lead to moral clarification for the reader, why does he offer his text as a sermon? How do the preacher and Thackeray share a common approach to their material?

MYTHIC ARCHETYPES: "AN OLD STORY"

Ian Watt, in *The Rise of the Novel*, distinguishes between the novel's illusion of unique reality and the power of earlier fiction:

> Defoe and Richardson are the first great writers in our literature who did not take their plots from mythology, history, legend, or previous literature. In this they differ from Chaucer, Spenser, Shakespeare, and Milton, for instance, who, like the writers of Greece and Rome, habitually used traditional plots: and who did so, in the last analysis, because they accepted the general premise of their times that, since Nature is essentially complete and unchanging, its records, whether scriptural or historical, constitute a definitive repertoire of human experience.

In this context, we may note that Thackeray constantly relates his action to the archetypal pattern, in legend or literature, that is its source and authority. Superficially, his language, the language of the classically educated English gentleman, has a habit of classical and literary allusion which reminds us that the events we are witnessing are basically old stories. On marrying first loves: "Ask Mr. Pendennis, who sulked in his tents when his Costigan, his Briseis, was ravished from him" (*The Newcomes*). On the disreputable company at Baden's gaming tables: "There was not one woman there who was not the heroine of some discreditable story. It was the Comtesse Calypso who had been jilted by the Duc Ulysse. . . . It was Madame Medee, who had absolutely killed her old father by her conduct regarding Jason." The immediate drama is authenticated by appeals to the mythic sources, and Watt rightly notes that this is in violation of the spirit of novelistic realism. This habit of literary allusion is little more than the standard equipment of Thackeray's class. Yet Thackeray makes the technique a matter of thematic significance by interrupting his drama frequently to discuss it, and its implications about the usefulness of writing what ultimately are only retellings. He begins *The Newcomes* with a "farrago of old fables," and his hypothetical critic takes exception to such tired material. Thackeray replies:

> What stories are new? All types of characters march through all fables. . . . With the very first page of the human story do not all love, and lies too, begin? So the tales were told ages before Aesop; and asses under lions' manes roared in Hebrew; and sly foxes flattered in Etruscan; and wolves in sheep's clothing gnashed their teeth in Sanscrit, no doubt. The sun shines today as he did when he first began shining; and the birds in the tree overhead, while

I am writing, sing very much the same note they have sung ever since there were finches. . . . There may be nothing new under and including the sun; but it looks fresh every morning, and we rise with it to toil, hope, scheme, laugh, struggle, love, suffer, until the night comes and quiet. And then will wake Morrow and the eyes look on it; and so *da capo*.

And Thackeray keeps this fact before us by means disruptive to the dramatic illusion. A seduction scene is interrupted with a brief parenthesis: "(Surely the fable is renewed for ever and ever?)" (*The Virginians*). And sometimes he breaks off in disgust and refuses to tell the old story over again:

Is not one story as stale as the other? Are not they all alike? What is the use, I say, of telling them over and over? Harry values that rose because Maria has ogled him in the old way; because she has happened to meet him in the garden in the old way; because they have whispered to one another behind the old curtain (the gaping old rag, as if everybody could not peep through it!). . . . Whole chapters might have been written to chronicle all these circumstances, but *a quoi bon*? . . . What is the good of telling the story? My gentle reader, take your story: take mine. To-morrow it shall be Miss Fanny's, who is just walking away with her doll to the school-room and the governess (poor victim! She has a version of it in her desk): and next day it shall be Baby's, who is bawling out on the stairs for his bottle.

(The Virginians)

The tale has become rotten, like the curtain, with old age and over-use. And this reminds us of the techniques we observed in *Catherine* and *Vanity Fair* whereby the events of the text are validated by an appeal to the readers' common experience. "What is the good of telling the story? My gentle reader, take your story: take mine." There is a verbal formula which Thackeray uses to introduce this perspective: "Who does not know . . . ?" or "Have we not all . . . ?" What did Clive do when he met Ethel on the train to Brighton? Exactly what anyone would have done—what has been done by countless young men before—what you did when you met Mrs. Jones in your youth. The actions and events of the novel are explained by Thackeray in terms of general human nature; thus Clive is angry at Ethel for knowing Lord Farintosh because "nothing is more offensive to us of the middle class than to hear the names of great folks constantly introduced into conversation." Thackeray's characters, like Thackeray, respond to events with generalizing moral conclusions; Laura responds to the news of Ethel's rejection of Farintosh's suit in terms of the Condition of England: "It seems to me that young women in our world are bred up in a way not very different [from that of Indian dancing girls.] . . . They are educated for the world, and taught to display" and so forth. Thackeray seems to have created a context for his fiction that allows the universal moral relevance that Richardson erroneously claims.

This is the main feature in which Thackeray's fiction resembles a sermon: its attempt to achieve universal moral relevance at the expense of dramatic intensity. The concept of a finite repertoire of human experience is, after all, an idea as much about art's proper purposes as about life's experiences themselves. The assumption that art should be morally didactic limits its subjects to the fourteen Deadly Sins and Heavenly Virtues; idiosyncratic behavior always exists—it is simply not worth art's efforts to record. The modern sense of art's infinitely diverse canvas is a change, not only in our sense of the diversity of experience, but in our sense of art's uses as well. Thackeray, like the preacher, gets his sense of art's limited repertoire from his assumption about art's moral didactic purpose. In these terms, Ethel's story has value insofar as it represents the marriage situation in England. For the preacher, the sin of prodigality is more important than the Prodigal Son; the lesson is truer than the vehicle by which it is taught. As we have seen, Thackeray's commentary is so important that, far from arising from the drama, it can force the drama to accommodate it, however much the drama must be distended. And, as we have noted, the dramatic action is of such little importance that when the Condition of Marriage in England is discussed as fully as Ethel's experiences allow, the novel ends without her marriage to Clive, the completion of the drama.

DE TE FABULA

Thackeray's sense that the novel's truest object of attention is ourselves has more important consequences than his frequent whimsical instructions to the reader, that he take the book's lesson to heart—"Remember how happy such benefactions made you . . . , and go off on the very first fine day and tip your nephew at school!"; it also means that the responses by the reader to the text—his criteria for judgment—are always topics for discussion. For instance, in *Vanity Fair*, in the midst of Lord Steyne's characterization as a monster, when we have been taught to hate him most and take pleasure in the misery of his family, Thackeray interrupts to observe that our hatred is un-Christian.

> And let us, my brethren who have not our names in the Red Book, console ourselves by thinking comfortably how miserable our betters may be and that Damocles, who sits on satin cushions, and is served on gold plate, has an awful sword hanging over his head in the shape of a bailiff, or an hereditary disease, or a family secret, which peeps out every now and then from the embroidered arras in a ghastly manner, and will be sure to drop one day or the other in the right place.

Thackeray turns our attention to our own dramatic response, and its moral character—gratification at our betters' misery. But it is not truly that which we feel; rather, it is gratification at the serving out of poetic justice to a villain of a novel. The distinction seems a crucial one. Thackeray is using his own drama to "catch" us when we cooperate with its demands. The device is common in pulpit rhetoric, one that utilizes the difference between the easy, absolute judgments we make in experiencing fiction and the more pragmatic morality of living. The preacher will tell a tale of a deserter and then ask, are we not all deserters from God's army? The tale of the deserter, when offered as a drama, wins an easy condemnation from us, at which point we discover that the tale is not a drama, but an exemplum, and that we have condemned ourselves. But the preacher and Thackeray are playing a trick here, since the relationship between the sympathetic commitments we make in a drama and the moral judgments we make in life is not a simple one. Our judgments in the novel are controlled largely by our desire to share the dramatic experience, for one thing, and for another, fiction often serves as an opportunity to exercise an absolutism of judgment life never allows us. Thus we damn utterly characters for doing things we would excuse or do ourselves with little difficulty in life, and we take pleasure in being so uncompromising. Thackeray is playing on a fundamental confusion about the relationship between literature and life—that fiction serves as a training ground for the moral judgment. This error is furthered by our having only one word for the very different criteria by which we judge in fiction and in life—"moral."

An example from a simpler genre will make this clear. The conventions by which we read detective fiction are entirely artificial; we try to outguess the author by reading those signs—for instance, that the most suspicious suspect is almost surely not the killer—and a good author writes using those conventions knowledgeably, and perhaps surprising us by having the overtly sinister figure be guilty of the crime. But the drama and resolution are in terms of conventions that obviously have nothing to do with real life, and thus reading mystery stories does not at all prepare one for real-life detective work. And vice versa—no reader of mystery stories would suggest that in life the most likely suspect should be considered almost surely innocent. And if reading mysteries does not at all prepare us for finding the culprit in real life, that unsurprising fact questions one of fiction's basic grounds for self-justification—its use as exercise for judgment and sensibility. Thackeray makes the same point when he turns from the drama to our judgment of it and asks us to notice the ease with which we condemn others in novels and excuse ourselves in real life, and to account for the discrepancy. There is, of course, an easy answer: we must only reply that the moral system of a novel is something quite separate from life's morality, and therefore there is no reason why the two should be comparable. But to say so much is to grant Thackeray his contention, that conventional romantic drama is little more than a toy and an indulgence of fancy, which becomes a lie when it claims more for itself.

We have been talking, in the last pages, about the uses Thackeray directs us to make of his fiction, and the assumptions about the status of didactic fiction implicit in those directives. We have seen that he validates his art by an appeal to universals of character and experience, that he will interrupt or destroy the dramatic illusion to make a point about the reader, that he leads us to see Ethel's courtships, for instance, as a vehicle to a discussion about generalities more important than the vehicle itself. But a qualification is necessary: this is the status Thackeray asserts for his fiction; it is not necessarily the status on which it really exists. As we noted at the beginning of this discussion, Thackeray claims his characters are vehicles to facilitate general discussion, but they refuse to submit. Ethel will win a dramatic commitment from us, however much Thackeray may suggest that we put her to other uses; and Thackeray indicates in his conclusion to the novel that he knows quite well the dramatic power he has created; there he tells us he refuses to marry Clive and Ethel, yet hints unmistakably that they do marry. That conclusion which refuses to conclude, which we have used repeatedly as the apotheosis of his rejection of the demands of dramatic form, is a sham, since he declares his independence and then quietly gives us the dramatic resolution he knows we need. We have been talking, then, in these last pages, not about the power of Thackeray's material, but about the author's assertions about its power, and the two seem somewhat at odds. It is, in fact, a sign of Thackeray's ambivalence that, when he says we all know X, therefore he need not describe it, or, this is not a novel, so you have no interest in knowing X—a description of X immediately follows. "How they were married is not of the slightest consequence to anybody": a description of how they were married follows (*Vanity Fair*). These things are of interest to us, as Thackeray implicitly recognizes again and again. *Philip,* for instance, is an eight-hundred-page love story interrupted at intervals by Thackeray's assurance that no one wants to read a love story and therefore he will not give us one.

Most of the conflicts we have been looking at in these last two chapters can be contained, though not defended, in a theoretic opposition between the structural principles and artistic aims of the dramatic novel and the moral essay. Many of the difficulties we have encountered in Thackeray's style disappear if we absolve him of the responsibility of being consistent from page to page. For instance, in the matter of Sir Pitt's nurse: Both arguments are of unimpeachable moral value; that money buys a loyalty in this world that virtue or affection cannot win, and that bought loyalty is insincere and based on quicksand, we would not deny—we would only wish that the two arguments not be juxtaposed so dissonantly. Put each argument in its own essay and publish them a week apart, and our objections disappear.

Thackeray's interest in universal didactic relevance; his emphasis on the reader at the expense of the reading experience; his lack of a convincing or even specified location in time and space; his use of characters representative of a class; his appeal to universal patterns of experience and the finite repertoire of morally pertinent stories; his stance as preacher, and his offering his story as a fable or sermon; his freedom from the dramatic present, and his destruction of dramatic suspense by the glance at the future; his obedience to a willful pen, and his stubborn defense of his right to be irrelevant—all these, and many more, are only disturbing in the context of a thousand-page work which is supposed to justify our reading it as a coherent unit and a progressively developing narrative. If Ethel is a vehicle for a discussion about marriage, she is probably not worth a thousand pages of dramatic presentation. And conversely, if she does justify those pages, it must be on terms that Thackeray's authorial habits obstruct. Thackeray's theory of how literature has true meaning leads to the moral essay, while his experience of what literature is shaped like (and perhaps his knowledge of what literature would be bought and read) leads to the romantic novel. His lack of conviction about the value of that form leads him to hide from his novel behind an impenetrable irony, and his desire to make a work doctrinal to a nation leads him to obstruct the dramatic forces that assert the value of the story as a unique experience.

A sense of Thackeray's commitment to the methods and rhetorical aims of the occasional essay helps us understand his hostility to the conventional tools for the unification of the novel. Consider the famous bowl of rack punch at Vauxhall, and Thackeray's claims for it: "That bowl of rack punch was the cause of all this history." That is another of Thackeray's jokes, claiming for his fiction precisely the features it lacks. There is a force of formal determinism working in the novel, but it is not one of act and consequence; it is rather a determinism of character or fate, which will out, in spite of the rack punch and all other instruments of plot mechanics, instead of by means of them. The rack punch upsets Jos's and Becky's plans to marry—but to no avail; the monstrous union is achieved anyway, though it takes years and a trip to Pumpernickel. There is an inevitability operating in Becky's history, which the events of the plot seem to postpone instead of hasten. In this sense, the plot of the novel is something to be sloughed off—in Gombrich's terms, it is the distracting flux of expression and posture that hides the eternal truth of the subject. The plot is rack punch—a trick of coincidence that obstructs momentarily the characters in their pursuit of their inevitable ends.

We will pursue this idea of eternal truths beneath the vagaries of plot events [elsewhere]. But first let us determine where we have "located" Thackeray among his contemporaries. Beginning with a desire to explain the paradox of a thousand brilliant passages making up a whole of dubious quality, we located the force for disharmony in an extreme consciousness of the novelistic process at work and an extreme distrust of the moral value of conventional romance. His view of literature's moral value, which is basically an eighteenth-century one, is fundamentally antagonistic to his realist aesthetic, as we saw as early as *Catherine*. His lack of faith in his art leads him habitually to expose the artifice of his fiction, an action that is made more discomforting by the power of the realist illusion he creates and attempts to destroy. His insight into the processes of writing and reading would be entirely praiseworthy if it were not destroying a very compelling drama by its presence. An understanding of Thackeray does not lead to an understanding of his works, but rather to a full perception of the impossibility of locating sure meaning in the diffracted light of his self-consciousness.

In these terms we can treat a false sense of paradox that may result from a reading of these last two chapters [of *Thackeray's Novels*]: [an earlier chapter] seems to suggest that Thackeray is an innovator; [this chapter] seems to suggest that he is a reactionary. Is he looking forward or back? Is he writing a new kind of novel, or simply not writing a novel? Our discussion suggests that to describe Thackeray as defending an aesthetic, either old or new, is misleading; rather he brings the criteria of realism and didacticism to the contemporary novel as he characterizes it, in the furtherance of a disquisition on the novel as an instrument of social and moral education. Thus he is more concerned with the implications of conventional romance's absurdity in the perspective of realistic assumptions than he is in defending a realistic aesthetic as an artistic Truth. Thackeray is, after all, confused; in the case of this author at least, that assertion must surely be something more than an abdication of the critic's responsibility. His approach is therefore a pragmatic one—he can expose the absurdity of what his contemporaries ask the novel to be, without offering an example of what it should be. His narrative techniques, which perhaps have here been unavoidably given the character of innovations, are in fact the techniques of his fellow novelists, turned self-conscious and with their implications about writing and reading made explicit. We noted in the case of the preacher pose that Thackeray does not invent it; rather, he uses the convention to spark a discussion about the novel, by noting the novel's inability to support the rhetoric of that image. So we would wish to argue in the largest terms: Thackeray is not best described as a realist; the illusion of realism we have observed him creating is a rhetorical device, by which he may give the lie to his own narrator's claims for an apologic orientation, and to which he can give the lie via his narrator's self-conscious responsibility of authorship. The conflict between realism and didacticism within his novels is a parodic examination of the same conflict that rages unobserved in his contemporaries' novels, and thus he is neither ahead of nor behind his time, but precisely at the center of his own age. His novels do not point to new horizons; rather they lead us to the very heart of the novel in the middle of the nineteenth century.

Thackeray: "The Legitimate High Priest of Truth" and the Problematics of the Real

George Levine

> *How do you like your novels? I like mine "hot with," and no mistake: no love-making: no observations about society: little dialogue, except where characters are bullying each other: plenty of fighting: and a villain in the cupboard, who is to suffer tortures just before Finis. I don't like your melancholy Finis.*
>
> —W. M. THACKERAY, *Roundabout Papers*

I

Thackery loved Scott, but he disliked Ravenswood. I have never, he wrote "fetched [Ravenswood's] hat out of the water since he dropped it there when I last met him." The sentence is characteristic of the parodic Thackeray. Every word deflates Scott's conclusion to *The Bride of Lammermoor*. "Fetched" and "dropped" seem to have little to do with Caleb Balderstone's melancholy retrieval of Ravenswood's "large sable feather" (rather than quotidian "hat"), which he "took . . . up, dried . . ., and placed . . . in his bosom" (chap. 35). But the diminishment is part of Thackeray's self-mockery. For what he dislikes about *The Bride of Lammermoor* is certainly not its rhetorical inflations but its "melancholy Finis." Ravenswood's death in Kelpie's flow (not "water") is the death of romance. The childish pleasures of Scott, as Thackeray nostalgically talks of them, cannot be qualified by details, except of the pleasurable violences of romantic triumph and revenge. Ravenswood's death may have been too directly evocative of the sort of tragedy its abruptness averts, as George Eliot was to avert it in Maggie Tulliver's death by drowning—the realist's tragedy.

"I protest," says the narrator of *The Newcomes*—the compromised Arthur Pendennis himself—, "the great ills of life are nothing—the loss of your fortune is a mere flea-bite; the loss of your wife—how many men have supported it, and married comfortably afterwards? It is not what you lose, but what you have daily to bear, that is hard" (bk. 2, chap. 2). What you have daily to bear comes, rhetorically, not in the grandiloquent language of Scott's large romantic moments, but in the modern banalities of

From *The Realistic Imagination: English Fiction from* Frankenstein *to* Lady Chatterley. © 1981 by the University of Chicago. University of Chicago Press, 1981.

"fetched," "dropped," "last met him." And Thackeray's career begins in deflating every kind of social pretension, every sort of rhetorical falsification. He becomes a stylist of the ironic mode, comically asserting the pervasiveness of the ordinary, the vanity of self and society, writing fictions that wryly refuse to be "hot with." But he loved fictions and fantasies that relieved him of the burden of what we have daily to bear, and he loved Scott for the largeness of his scope, the distance of his action, the strength of his dark heroes.

Ironically, however, Scott's heritage for Thackeray was more in the novels he implied than in those he wrote. The popular Scott becomes an inevitable object of Thackeray's parody, as in *Rebecca and Rowena* he tries to imagine a yet more satisfying ending, in which Ivanhoe gets the vital, risk-taking, foreign-seeming, and dark-haired Rebecca, rather than the prim and prudish Rowena. But it is the skeptical Scott that informs Thackeray's fully developed fictional styles. This was the Scott Thackeray would not have liked very much: the self-deprecating Scott who deflated his own rhetoric, who substituted the pedestrian hero for the chivalric one, who disbelieved in the seriousness of fiction and unabashedly wrote for money: the Scott, in other words, who was too much like Thackeray.

Thackeray turned Scott's doubts into a pervasive self-consciousness that floods over from the framing devices of his fiction into the style and substance. Although one may find near the center of any Thackeray novel a Scott-like nostalgia for a lost and exciting past, Thackeray builds his career from a comic perception of that very past as it is embodied in the conventions of narrative. Like Austen, almost like Scott himself, he begins with parody, but his art is always importantly parodic, seeking to displace the delightful absurdities of literary conventions with the truths that lay beyond literature. The complications and emotional losses of such displacement make his fictions diffusively unstable and self-conscious.

The most obvious examples of this manner occur when Thackeray steps back from his own effective satire, and from the "truth" implicit in his satirical dismissals. If Miss Buskbody can enter Scott's *Old Mortality* to impose upon it the most conventional possible conclusion. Thackeray can move, at the end of *The Newcomes,* from behind Pen's voice to remind us that his antiheroic, antiromantic fiction is, after all, only a fiction and hence subject to the controls of desire: "But for you, dear friend, it is as you like. You may settle your Fable-land in your own fashion. Anything you like happens in Fable-land" (bk. 2, chap. 42).

Unlike Scott's casual dismissal of his own more romantic fiction, this sudden reversal, emerging from a context of plausible and recognizable details, is seriously discomfiting. Scott pokes fun at a certain kind of busybody novel reader but reflects no unease about giving the public what it wants. In Thackeray, it is not a joke, but a melancholy deprecation of the whole enterprise of fiction making and of novel reading. The apparently genial concession implies contemptuous rejection of the reader's unreflecting assumptions about narrative, and of the writer's attempt to take writing more seriously than Scott did. The distance between the dreams so simply fulfilled in Fable-land, and the possibilities of experience outside the fictions—in the silences of the "real"—becomes unbridgeable. The easy freedom of doing as we like is perhaps the most powerful reminder that we have no such freedom beyond literature. The marriage becomes our responsibility, not Thackeray's, and we are consequently forced to reflect that our desires have been composing the fiction all along; its reality is only a "sentiment." After nine hundred pages, Thackeray reminds us that he has told us so from the start, and that as *The Newcomes* began with a peculiar melange of animal fables, so it must end: "The frog bursts with wicked rage, the fox is caught in his trap, the lamb is rescued from the wolf" (bk. 2, chap. 42).

The last pages of *The Newcomes* constitute a disruptive gesture at some truth beyond fictions. The slow evolution of what felt like a realistic novel is suddenly denied. Thackeray casually confesses that he has made mistakes, as in his resurrection of Lord Farintosh's dead mother. We achieve the fullest realism in Thackeray when we see how it entails precisely the violation of illusion for which James criticized Trollope. If Thackeray's novels are in any way serious about the need for their protagonists to see beyond the fictions created by their own desires, they must be serious about their own fictionality as well. Thackeray's peculiar and unstabilizing self-consciousness leads to confusions in his art that cannot be explained away; but it is also intrinsic to what is most interesting in it.

Alexander Welsh calls the ending of *The Newcomes* a "failure" that is "something of an event in literary history." It is a moment when, says Welsh, Thackeray finds himself struggling with "the conventions of the novel." Here, the latent split between the conventions of narrative and the impulse of realism, delayed by Austen's sense of a meaningful world, by Scott's uses of history, becomes manifest. Thackeray uneasily recognized realism as no more real than the romances he so gleefully parodied. To have struggled with the limits of the novel form as Thackeray did—however awkward and inconsistent the results—was to write with special intelligence and to belie Henry James, Sr.'s, delightfully malicious remark that Thackeray's mind was "merely a sounding board against which his experiences thump and resound." In the course of the struggle, Thackeray helped not only to shape the conventions of the realistic novel, but to subvert them radically.

There is some irony in the reputation Thackeray developed. With the most complex sense of any of his generation of the untruth of fiction, he found his struggle to speak truth rewarded in relatively simple ways. His own formulations are less decisive than his critics': "The Art of Novels is to represent Nature: to convey as strongly as possible the sentiment of reality." Yet Charlotte Brontë spoke of him as "the legitimate high priest of Truth." Elizabeth Rigby saw *Vanity Fair* as "a literal photograph of the manners and habits of the nineteenth century." David Masson, in his obituary tribute to Thackeray, called him a writer "sternly, ruthlessly real." "If the power of producing the impression of reality were the test of the highest creative power," said W. C. Roscoe, "Thackeray would perhaps rank higher than anyone who ever lived."

This is the same Thackeray who, along with his very Victorian passion for truth and sincerity, felt the insincerity of the most sincere fictions and the attraction of fictions "hot with," which bend reality to the shape of desire. Reality, he believed, was no simple matter, and the price of pursuing it was likely to be great. He pursued it, like Jane Austen, from parody to novel, in the pattern described by Harry Levin: "from the imitation of art through parody to the imitation of nature" (*Gates of Horn*). And he pursued it further into self-parody and that striking consciousness of self and audience that seems invariably to accompany developments in realistic technique.

Unlike Austen, Thackeray could never get comfortable about incorporating the old conventions, which he admired as long as he did not have to believe in them. His novels become nostalgic commentaries on forms no longer possible. His comfort with serialization, and with the rambling, bathetic style it encouraged accorded with his realist's resistance to Scott's kind of crystallization of form required by action, resolution, narrative convention, and a Whig reading of history. Every movement of plot is a violence done to the multiplicity and variousness of experience, to the elusiveness of reality. In the interests of truth, Thackeray felt impelled to mute the violence and to imply its incompatibility with the diffuseness and aimlessness of the ordinary. Yet Thackeray was not only attracted to the passionate excesses of traditional romance forms; he saw how what we had daily to bear concealed another, perhaps a more horrible violence. There was a Bertha Mason in his attic, a mad wife who filled him with guilt and sorrow. The strategy of the ordinary, of satire, and of the diffuseness of time, was both an ironic dismissal of the imposed happy endings of traditional comic forms, and a protected diversion from the quite monstrous irrational energies that lay beneath the surface of the ordinary. By averting the one, he averts the other. Yet the result, in his strangely compromised narratives, is often the quotidian tragedy, the melancholy survival of what we have daily to bear. The characteristic resolution of Thackeray's novels is the muted and not quite satisfactory happiness of, say, Dobbin and Amelia. In his work the strange conjunction of realism with comic form is threatened. Even where the comic form emerges, it is half-mocked as a manifestation of Fable-land.

II

In what follows, I do not want to minimize his culture's common sense that Thackeray was talking to them about reality. To read his novels as "representations" is inevitable and important. Certainly, he was concerned to imagine ways to navigate the perplexities of personal life in Victorian

society, and his satire is pointed as directly at the insanities of social behavior as at the madness of art. But my concern here is to examine the
enormous difficulties that underlay the Victorian ideal of representation
and to emphasize the perplexities that manifested themselves not only in
the period's self-tormented poetry and intricate nonfiction, but in the apparently stable forms of realistic fiction, where "massive confidence" is
most striking only in its absence. The greatness of Scott's art lay primarily
in its capacity to extend experience, to find foci not only in the great historical moments, but in the minutiae of domesticity and personal conflict.
If anything, Thackeray's art, focus though it does on a relatively small range
of Victorian society (and some Scott-ish eighteenth-century society as well),
is more democratic than Scott's, more alert to an unmanageable multiplicity.
Scott can frame that variousness only with history; Thackeray tries it
through memory. But in the process, he reaches beyond the limits of the
literature he knew to take the risks of a reality he could not finally know
or frame. It is worth speculating on the implications for realistic fiction of
his peculiarly embracing and exclusive method.

In a recent discussion of the way narrative dominates our imagination
of the world, not only in fictions, but in all our modes of discourse, Leo
Bersani talks of Flaubert's critique of narrative, and the terms he uses seem
remarkably applicable to Thackeray. Flaubert's critique, says Bersani, was
not merely of the "expectations imposed on life by literary romantics," but
of "the expectations which those same romances raise concerning literature
itself" ("The Other Freud," *Humanities in Society* 1 [1978]). Narrative, he
says, encourages us into an "orgasmic" mode of reading, in which "the
mind would excite itself out of consciousness." Since the explanations of
experience and sensation that narrative offers imply a time-connected,
causal set of relationships, they are, in effect, secondary elaborations of a
primary experience that comes to us—and to the writer—with inexplicable
immediacy. Narrative organizes those experiences and, in Bersani's account, can become a satisfyingly climactic substitute—masturbatory and
orgasmic—for a dangerously unnameable experience.

There is no character in Thackeray quite as intent on such experience
as Emma Bovary, who succeeds, as Bersani says, in "producing ecstasy
from literary narration." But Fanny Bolton, particularly in her excitement
over Pen's novel, *Walter Lorraine*, produces at least a faint echo of Emma.
And Thackeray's fiction, like Flaubert's, is preoccupied with the mindless
triviality of narrative, and in particular with anticipating and thwarting
"orgasmic" readings. His novels, says Jack Rawlins, in what I read as a
very useful exaggeration, "are dissertations on the novel, with a novel
provided for discussion."

The parallels between the two novelists extend interestingly beyond
concern with characters who misapprehend both life and literature. As
Bersani's discussion suggests them, they help illuminate Thackeray's position in the tradition of realism I have been tracing. In particular, Bersani

can help us see that realism has strong connections to the modern tradition normally connected with an almost contemptuous rejection of realism. Realism, as we see it working in Thackeray's novels, is an impulse to get beyond the very conventions of literature modernists object to when they find them in nineteenth-century novels. Moreover, the distrust of narrativity that Bersani takes as a clear sign of Flaubert's modernity is evident in Thackeray's self-conscious manipulations of his narratives and his narrative voice. Realists themselves, in the very struggle to find a way to "represent," were intensely aware of the limitations placed upon them by the singleness of their vision, and the disparity between the verbal medium and the world they were struggling to name.

Bouvard and Pécuchet provides an excellent controlled analogue to the slovenliness of Thackeray's similarly pointless and meandering last books. Bersani calls *Bouvard and Pécuchet* "an unqualified mockery of any climactic significance at all." One might say of a novel like *Philip* that it is, at least, a qualified mockery of any climactic significance. Rawlins, for example, notes "a horrible tautological propriety" to its "badness." He suggests that Thackeray's distrust of plots and climactic scenes issued inevitably in fictions that could no longer create such scenes (even in parody) to give narrative shape and meaning. It is as though he had learned fully the lesson of the nonscene among the rebels at the end of *Redgauntlet,* taking it a step further by refusing the power even of anticlimax. Thackeray seems to have been engaged in a criticism of "orgasmic" fiction by means of the "gradual and finally radical denarrativizing of his own writing," of the sort Bersani attributes to Flaubert. It is precisely the enterprise implicit in Thackeray's earlier parodies, such as *Rebecca and Rowena*, where he builds to a union between Ivanhoe and Rebecca, only to settle it all in a paragraph. They were married, "of course," and the narrator does not think that they were "subsequently very boisterously happy."

The refusal of climax is accompanied by promiscuity of attention to the multiplicity of experience. Both Flaubert's narrators and his characters, says Bersani, are ready to "swerve" their attention "to the sides of its objects and linger over insignificant, irrelevant, and yet sensually appealing digressive activities." What is most striking is his characterization of Flaubert's tone; it is close to how one would be tempted to characterize the tone of some of Thackeray's most interesting narratives—*Pendennis, The Newcomes,* and (alas) *Philip.* The digressive enterprise, says Bersani,

> in Flaubert generally takes the form of a desultory discouragement, of a low-keyed but persistent and crippling bitterness about, precisely, the factitious nature of both the so-called big subjects of history and the essential feelings of individuals. Flaubert's famous sympathy for Emma Bovary can thus be re-defined as a longing for her longing for exciting stories, or as an envy of that naiveté which allows her to believe not only that life is novelis-

tically serious but also that literature consists of serious and meaningful fictions.

Thackeray's relation to his audience and to himself is rather more senti-mental than such a description will allow. But there is a developing air of fatigue about his novels that suggests a comparable attitude. *Philip*, for instance, seems a novel that does not want to get written. Turning through it randomly one finds everywhere evidences of distractions, discontinuities and, more important, disbelief in its own seriousness. Describing Philip's love of Agnes, for instance, Pen, the narrator, does all he can to avert both the passion and the language required for it, and to cut short any narrative investment the reader might make in it:

> And yet, if a novelist may chronicle any passion, its flames, its raptures, its whispers, its assignations, its sonnets, its quarrels, sulks, reconciliations, and so on, the history of such a love as this first of Phil's may be excusable in print, because I don't believe it was a real love at all, only a little brief delusion of the senses, from which I give you warning that our hero will recover before many chapters are over.
>
> (bk. 1, chap. 9)

But Philip's true love receives similar treatments: "Do gentle readers begin to tire of this spectacle of billing and cooing? I have tried to describe Mr. Philip's love-affairs with a few words and in as modest phrases as may be—omitting the raptures, the passionate vows, the reams of correspon-dence, and the usual commonplaces of his situation" (bk. 2, chap. 8). Thackeray proceeds with his usual invocation of our memory of such pas-sions and a kind of indulgence that seems inconsistent and ironic itself. Desire, in Thackeray, is distanced and diminished, trivialized by general-izing. Is it the passion or the writing which provides "the usual common-places"? Either way, the tone is more than disenchanted; it is so deflating that it implies a "desultory discouragement" about the possibilities of life and of literature. He cannot, at any rate, keep his eye on the object, but moves to speculating on his own feelings, on his readers' feelings, on what other people have done in similar situations. This paragraph ends, for example, with other imagined young people whose hearts are bent on marriage:

> There is the doctor's brougham driving away, and Imogene says to Alonzo, "What anguish I shall have if you are ill!" Then there is the carpenter putting up the hatchment. "Ah, my love, if you were to die, I think they might put up a hatchment for both of us," says Alonzo, with a killing sigh. Both sympathize with Mary and the baker's boy whispering over the railings. Go to, gentle baker's boy, we also know what it is to love!

This is funny, but self-indulgent, a cross between cynical parody and sentimentalism, but hardly a way to impel a narrative. It is Thackeray trapped in a narrative medium in which he no longer believes.

By this time, Pen, having been long married to Laura—providing Thackeray with occasions for long discussions which further forestall the narrative—has distanced passion so that at its most intense it will emerge as mere sentimental nostalgia. But Pen is himself a device by which Thackeray further distances passion and can refuse the strategies of narrative by which passion is reasserted. Pen, once a disenchanted protagonist, is a disenchanted narrator. Through him, Thackeray, unlike Flaubert, found strategies by which to sustain nostalgia (not merely bitterness) for the childish dreams he could no longer allow himself. The deflated Pen deflates experience, and protects Thackeray from the pain of his frustrated desires, from the risk of indulging them or believing them. Thackeray's realism becomes, in part, a way to protect dreams, as was Scott's antiquarianism; the way to sustain desire is *not* to satisfy it—"forever wilt thou love, and she be fair"—and in place of satisfaction we find ironic memories of desire. The deflating and retarding narrative forms are a way to postpone the confrontation with narrative climax, the recognition of "the factitious nature of both the so-called big subjects of history and the essential feelings of individuals."

The exuberance of youth, in Thackeray, is reported in the language of memory—memory of the innocence that allowed a character, or the narrator, to desire the consummation intensely enough to stake his life on it. The intensity of Emma Bovary's passionate dreaming gives her a dignity that belies the sordidness of her life and the absurdity of her dream. Less powerfully, Arthur Pendennis's adolescent love of the Fotheringay is the primary evidence that he is worth his novel's nine hundred pages. Arthur's rescue from marrying her is a turn of plot that spares him the consummation required by plotting, and the banalities required by realism. Here already, but increasingly down through *Philip*, Thackeray's novels are the enactments of desires or dreams that can be articulated only by being thwarted. Formally, this entails the attenuation of plot in the frustration of the characters' desires—totally unlike the sharpness of plot necessary to satisfy Catherine Morland.

In Austen, as I have argued, a romance form is required to resolve the realistic materials. Romance is the form in which plotting projects upon the narrative screen the lineaments of desire. But in Thackeray, the imagined satisfactions constructed from the manipulations of narrative are normally so blatantly artificial and so laden with ironies that they are unequal to the intensities of desire that precede. Consider the absurd resolution of *Philip*, or the killing off of Rosie at the end of *The Newcomes*, so that Clive will be free to marry Ethel, or Blanche Amory's attempt to marry Foker in *Pendennis*, which frees Pen to marry Laura.

In another context, Bersani has defined desire as "a hallucinated satisfaction in the absence of the source of satisfaction" (*A Future for Astyanax*). Plot is, as it were, the hallucination. The refusal of satisfaction to the audience is a refusal of plot, a refusal to impose the conventions of romance on the developing conventions of realism. Ironically, however, the refusal of satisfaction is a way of sustaining both desire and narrative because it keeps the quest alive and denies any ending. In a sense desire unsatisfied is the driving force of realistic fictions as of the protagonists within them.

Thackeray's characters, who attempt to live romances, are frustrated by plots that do not develop, events that do not take place (except when it is too late for passion). The narratives carefully enfold passion in layers of irony and of time that diminish passion and transform it into self-consciousness. The obligatory nineteenth-century plot in which Thackeray was trapped normally ends by providing surrogates for the protagonists' first desires. In his four best novels, Dobbin gets Amelia only when he has discovered the vanity of her selfishness; Esmond gets not the beautiful and sexually vital Beatrix, but her mature mother; Pen gets neither Fotheringay, nor Blanche, but a saccharine Laura who looks suspiciously like Rowena; and we bestow Ethel on Clive only after she has outgrown her youthful energy, and he has gone through the embittering experience of a loveless marriage.

But however elaborately Thackeray's novels resist the entrapment of romance, they cannot entirely avoid it. At the points of crisis, he can withdraw from the "literary form" by blaming it on his narrator, or, as at the end of *The Newcomes*, by stepping out of narration completely and reminding us that he has made up both the story and the narrator. Such moments may even contribute to the effectiveness of his realistic technique, as Rawlins argues. Thus realism, the modernist's scapegoat, the apparent superstition that literature can represent life, is in Thackeray a means beyond the limiting conventions required of any narrative form (and for which— especially in discussion of closure—realism is unjustly blamed), a stretching beyond literature, an elaborate and saving articulation of a modern consciousness of the fictionality of fiction.

Thackeray's realism thus provides us with strong evidence that the realism in mid-Victorian fiction bore within it elements of a fragmenting, unstable, and self-conscious art that radically challenged the terms of our common sense apprehension of reality and of the relation of language to that reality. Looking back on Victorian novelists, early modern writers detected a complacency, a moralism, an insistence on explaining everything and tying it neatly, a sentimental and self-indulgent impulse from which they had to free themselves. But fresh readings of Victorian fiction constantly turn up subversions of these qualities, and the discoveries are often not merely modish applications of current critical methods but readings of what the texts explicitly offer. The inconsistencies in realist art are part of the realist's exploratory enterprise; and the effort to find a containable, a nameable, order in reality was invariably compromised by the integrity that

led writers like Thackeray and George Eliot to confront the disruptive energies and elusively nonverbal texture of the "real."

It is possible to reverse the Jamesian judgment of the Victorian "large
loose baggy monster," and to find in the Victorian realist's mode—and, in
particular, in Thackeray's—a viable alternative to the more rigorously formal Jamesian aesthetic by which much Victorian fiction has been condemned. Here, for example, is the passage from the Preface to *The Tragic
Muse* in which the famous phrase occurs:

> A picture without composition slights its most precious chance for
> beauty, and is moreover not composed at all unless the painter
> knows *how* that principle of health and safety, working as an ab-
> solutely premeditated art, has prevailed. There may in its absence
> be life, incontestably, as "The Newcomes" has life, as "Les Trois
> Mousquetaires," as Tolstoi's "Peace and War," have it; but what
> do such large loose baggy monsters, with their queer elements of
> the accidental and the arbitrary, artistically *mean*? We have heard
> it maintained, we will remember, that such things are "superior
> to art"; but we understand least of all what *that* may mean, and
> we look in vain for the artist, the divine explanatory genius, who
> will come to our aid and tell us. There is life and life, and as waste
> is only life sacrificed and thereby prevented from "counting," I
> delight in a deep-breathing economy and an organic form.

Until recently, the assumptions about art implicit here have not required
articulation because we have all, with modifications, tended to be Jamesians
in our criticism of narrative. "Organicism" now is a bit suspect, too easily
identifiable as another kind of fiction. And there are other problems.

The leading assumption here is that satisfactory "composition" entails
artistic premeditation, and that it requires not only "selection" but a hierarchical arrangement of materials, all ultimately "counting," to be sure,
but nothing counting in its own right. Making things "count" and "mean"
is what distinguishes art from life, as James sees it, and he has no tolerance
for that more "democratic" energy of Victorian realism that aspires to make
all reality count. The unaccountable, the "accidental," the "arbitrary" are
in James's argument, waste, or life sacrificed. In Victorian realism, and
particularly in Thackeray's uneven art, all meaning that will not allow for
varieties of experience uncontainable within "premeditated art" must be
recognized as itself merely arbitrary and far too selective.

For James, the inevitability of form in language is not a concern, nor
is he interested in what Nietzsche has taught us to recognize as the Dionysian sources of art, the large, irrational energies that will not be teased
into form and are, indeed, falsified by language. Composition in this Jamesian sense (and I am not, of course, attempting to deal with the shifts and
complexities of James's entire theory or practice) can be seen not as an
aesthetic virtue but as a fundamental distortion of the multifarious inten-

sities of feeling and the resistant "wastes" of experience. Thackeray's art, like most Victorian fiction, was unquestionably anticlassical. While Arnold was seeking architectonics, novelists were finding the need to sacrifice architecture for particularities and to make their compromises with the "accidental and the arbitrary," compromises that for them reflected both the disruptive irrationality of experience and the convenience of prerealistic forms and conventions. Thackeray's usual refusal to premeditate, though it can be seen as a concession to his laziness, was a reasonable concomitant of his distrust of narrative and his uneasiness about making things "count."

James is insisting on the familiar distinction between art and life, and implying that recognition of it should lead to "art." We probably still find it easy to approve his rejection of the notion that the "life" in the large novels is somehow "superior to art." Yet James's terms imply his own acquiescence in the notion that there is, in novels, life without art, and one might well ask what *he* could mean by that. All "life" in art is artful, not merely selected, but created and shaped through the medium. Thackeray knew this well, and it filled him with misgivings about fiction writing. The Jamesian attempt to create illusion sufficiently powerful to make us forget we are reading a novel would have seemed to Thackeray misguided. His novels willfully remind us of the difference between art and life, and "the sentiment of reality" is not after all, "reality," but more like James's "verisimilitude," or Conrad's appeal to the "temperament." Trollope, describing Thackeray's art, calls it "realistic . . . by which we mean that which shall seem to be real." Such an awareness requires sophistication about the nature of the medium.

James talks as though the large loose monsters reflect no such awareness. He seems to be assuming that the art that places a Clive Newcome in a large and diverse context of other Newcomes, and that refuses to stay focused on a single Newcome and a single strand of relationships—that takes all Newcomes for its province—is somehow less an art than that whch does a single thing fully. We will put aside here the question of the means by which a novelist, who is preoccupied with the pressures of community and society on individuals (in the tradition established by Scott) and aware of how diverse, arbitrary, and elusive such pressures may be, can manage an art with so intense a focus as that which James requires. Thackeray cannot and does not want to place all the action inside, and thus his composition is looser, but composition it is. In tightness of composition there is implicit a commitment to "literary form" that Frye's analysis places with plot. Even in James, that is, one can detect the violence of narrativity that Thackeray was so self-consciously avoiding.

James cannot cope with the "queer elements of the accidental and the arbitrary." He asks, what can they artistically mean? Precisely. Thackeray's art, though it will retreat from its full implications, risks the not-meaning, and the denigration of literature itself. From the start, realism, in its antiliterary preoccupation with the real as opposed to the art that has always deformed it, found itself threatened by nonmeaning. Thackeray's strategy in *The Newcomes* is to imagine a world that resists the falsely explanatory and clarifying controls of art. The distinction between what counts and what is waste becomes increasingly artificial and arbitrary. If the deluge of details represses the monster latent for Thackeray and other Victorians in undisciplined desire, it also reveals the monstrously shapeless and unattainable nature of ordinary reality. Arbitrary and disruptive material keeps emerging.

In James, the artist becomes "the divine explanatory genius," and it is precisely such heroic claims for the artist that the realist attempts to exclude from his art. Thackeray, simply, does not take his art as seriously as James takes his, although he takes his responsibility to the truth with perhaps greater seriousness. The democracy of truth outranks the elitism of art, and Thackeray is thus less able to distinguish between what "counts" and what is "waste." Any narrative, he understands, "wastes" a background that might as well have been a foreground. By invariably asking the readers to remember whether they have not had experiences similar to those of his novels, Thackeray, in effect, transforms all into "waste." The ideal of his realism is to find its subject anywhere, amid the waste; and even when confined to a single narrative line, he swerves his attention to the infinite other novels that might be going on out there at the moment.

Obviously, Thackeray is no modernist, however susceptible his novels become to modernist readings. Yet it is important to complicate our ways of thinking about his work so that we can see in the midst of what has too often been taken as a Victorian "massive confidence" in the real, or a Victorian facility for boxing up experience into cubes of meaning, or a Victorian slovenliness about form, a viable, sophisticated realist art. His is a realist art that implies an aesthetic pluralism, a profound uncertainty about the nature of reality, a fine alertness to the complications of his medium and of his audience's expectations of the medium, and a persistent self-consciousness about the strategies by which desire imposes itself on narrative. In the midst of a genuinely experimental art form, Thackeray, like the other Victorians, normally exploited certain narrative conventions whose very conventionality is at odds with the realism. Moreover, in their explorations of "reality," beyond the literary conventions and against literature, Victorians were eager to disrupt complacencies of conventional order, to resist the irresistible conventionality of language, and to speak the truth. Thackeray belongs in the midst of this difficult aesthetic tangle. But if we step back from his work to locate the specific elements of the realist impulse evident there, we can identify an art that took large risks, anticipated modernism in many ways, and reflects what is, for me at least, a deeply moving effort to surprise the elusive fair maiden, even though, were she to turn around, she might show the face of the monster.

The Pickwick Case: Diagnosis

Garrett Stewart

"Eruct, Sancho," said Don Quixote, "means belch, and that is one of the coarsest words in the Castilian language, though it is very expressive; and so refined people have resorted to Latin, and instead of belch say eruct and for belches eructations . . . for that is the way to enrich the language."

—CERVANTES, *Don Quixote*, part 2

Dickens's precocious masterpiece, *The Posthumous Papers of the Pickwick Club*, is like no other novel. Its vision of innocence aside, it is in another way one of the purest books in our literature, pure because nothing has been refined or filtered off, pure precisely because nothing has been purified away. It is the essential, the instinctive Dickens, unhindered, eager, yet somehow miraculously mastered. By being in a sense all rough edges, it appears to have none. It is, at its finest times, full of those things Dickens does best and is to do better and better with the increase of his genius, but which he will never again do so freely. And the freedom of *Pickwick Papers* is not abandon, but discovery. It seems a freedom that has no second thoughts, that trumpets its own unimportance, yet, when they come, its significances can leave us gasping.

Pickwick is a book with secrets; like the best moments in Dickens after it, this entire first novel seems to take itself by surprise. Then, too, there is nothing like *Pickwick Papers* because while we are in it there seems to be nothing else. Its wholeness is not only complete but exclusive. The novel has a life of its own, a personality, the way only characters in most other books have such lives. In fact *Pickwick Papers* has a split personality, a divided nature that invites a kind of stylistic psychoanalysis. It has a nature that *speaks to us* in a rather literal sense, announcing mood and temper through its various voices. In no other Dickens novel is there quite so much dialogue, and in none is the surrounding prose so much like the talk it frames. To all this we must pay close attention, trying to catch the tone. Defined roughly for our purposes here, tone is the way style has us listen to narrative voice, and what we hear in *Pickwick Papers* we will hear over

From *Dickens and the Trials of Imagination*. © 1974 by the President and Fellows of Harvard College. Harvard University Press, 1974.

and over again in Dickens. From the intersecting and colliding styles of his first novel there results, among other things, a pervasive ironic tone discernible everywhere in that comic prose which will be his mainstay from *Pickwick* on out. There is another reason, too, for beginning at such length with *Pickwick Papers*. The primacy of tone in this first novel, with its implications about Mr. Pickwick's serene but guarded temperament, the limits imposed on his imagination, brings style and the themes of imagination into a revealing alliance.

[This essay] will explore Dickens's diagnosis, primarily in *Pickwick*, of the stylistic ills which plagued literature and public rhetoric in his day. Parody is most often his mode of analysis, and when he turns it against the Pickwickians, we begin to understand what ails the novel's opening not only in style but in implied mentality. Dickens's ironic diagnosis continues to probe the emotional make-up of Mr. Pickwick himself, discovering the symptoms of a temperamental strength that is also a peculiar kind of constitutional weakness—requiring what my [discussion elsewhere] will study as the quarantine of imagination. Style performs as the very means of isolation, setting the prevailing Pickwickian tone while alternately, in the interpolated tales, offering the means of experimentation for divergent forms of imaginative experience. The resolution of style and tone in the closing pages of the novel will be [discussed elsewhere], a release from quarantine which will then need comparison with the imaginations of Sam and Tony Weller—characters who have been exempt from the start of the book, and whose styles tell their stories.

There being no better place to start, let us attend (it is quite a syntactical performance!) the very first sentence, all by itself the first paragraph, of *Pickwick Papers*:

> The first ray of light which illumines the gloom, and converts into a dazzling brilliancy that obscurity in which the earlier history of the public career of the immortal Pickwick would appear to be involved, is derived from the perusal of the following entry in the Transactions of the Pickwick Club, which the editor of these papers feels the highest pleasure in laying before his readers, as a proof of the careful attention, indefatigable assiduity, and nice discrimination, with which his search among the multifarious documents confided to him has been conducted.

Whatever else this is, it is preposterous, a sodden prose in which gravity is overheard digging its own grave. Diction and syntax have together taken leave of at least one of their senses, and the result is tone-deaf eloquence. Clotted by the multiple passive forms and the five mechanical relative clauses, this is a lifeless, colorless rhetoric which it is never dreamed any of us will spot as verbosity. Except of course by Dickens, for it is all a joke, a parody. I have said it is this, "whatever else" it may be, in deference to Steven Marcus, who has deepened his own pioneering study of *Pickwick* in an important revisitation of Dickens's first novel. His interest at this homecoming is more than ever linguistic, his attention naturally drawn to that first replete sentence. "It is a parody, which later on and at length we learn is in part not a parody," but rather an embodiment of pure creative impulse. The novel's opening sentence "begins at the beginning, with 'creation' itself, with the Logos appearing out of 'obscurity'—that is, the 'earlier history . . . of the immortal Pickwick'—and into the light of creation. But it also dramatizes the fundamental activity of the Logos; it dramatizes the notion of cosmic creation as a word—which is how God, as the Logos, created the world: *fiat lux*, said God, when he was speaking Latin, and so it was ("Language into Structure"). Marcus is paying tribute here to the generative powers of Dickens's language, a just and subtle tribute which I would want to qualify only by insisting in more detail on the *quality* of the language in *Pickwick*, on the parody itself which we may later manage to see beyond.

The first words of *Pickwick Papers* are poor words. If the Logos is revealed, it is the Logos gone wrong. Dickens may well be orienting his first sentence entirely in verbal terms. He even appears to suggest that the antecedent chaos, the "gloom" upon which the initial words so blindingly dawn, was itself, somehow, a verbal disarray. There are two timid puns in the phrase "that obscurity in which the earlier history of the immortal Pickwick would appear to be involved," for "history," like its synonym "life," can refer either to experience itself or to biography, to events written down, and "involved" is a possible adjectival form not only for "involvement" but for grammatical "involution," of which this supposedly corrective sentence is a nasty sample. There seem to be more hints here than Marcus has picked up; from one angle, writing may indeed be the *only* subject of the novel's opening statement. Later in his essay, Marcus cleverly points out that with the chiseled motto "BILL STUMPS, HIS MARK," we may actually have inscribed for us a hidden truth about the novel: that it, too, like the carving on the stone, is "writing about writing." There is a duplicate clue in the chapter just before the stone is found, another hint Marcus himself does not mention. Enraged at Alfred Jingle, Mr. Pickwick throws an inkstand against the wall, leaving *his* mark, and Sam Weller is on hand to interpret: "Self-acting ink, that 'ere; it's wrote your mark upon the wall, old gen'lm'n"(chap. 10). In a novel where Dickens is "undertaking to let the writing write the book," the image of "self-acting ink" may indeed be a node of unexpected meaning. Faced with all this "writing about writing," I simply wish to place my emphasis on the kind of writing it is. The topic of *Pickwick Papers* is not writing per se, not language in general. What the novel seizes as its subject by (and in) its very first words is the kind of language that is self-aware in the worst sense, words not only self-generated but self-serving. The style of *Pickwick* is a monumental satire, conceived and executed with some specific targets in mind. For Marcus's case there may be more evidence than he needed; for mine much more is now in order.

One of Gissing's few negative comments about Dickens's style—that "facetiousness is now and then to blame for an affected sentence"—is a decidedly unhelpful remark, both in its understatement and in its own unfollowed lead. That more recent novelist-critic, Angus Wilson, is more specific in his distaste for what he thinks the disastrous opening of *Pickwick*, "one of the worst, most facetious chapters he [Dickens] ever wrote." We may well decide that Dickens overdid his opening, but we should first decide what it was he set out to do. The trouble with Gissing's criticism, or so it appears, is his failure to recognize "affectation" as the key to what becomes an elaborate stylistic parody, perhaps overly concentrated in this first chapter but meted out in smaller doses to almost every other chapter in Dickens. Of all the moral and personal failings the novelist attacks, affectation is the best suited for immediate translation into style, and Dickens detests affectation with a vigor that communicates itself undiminished to his parodic comedy, becoming one of the hallmarks of prose. Here is a debt in theory to one of Dickens's favorite authors; at one point in *Pickwick* there is an aphoristic comment on human passion which opens with the words "Fielding tells us" (chap. 8), but any reader familiar with English fiction will have long since recognized a more widespread influence. This is Fielding from his "Preface" to *Joseph Andrews:* "I might observe that Ben Jonson, who of all men understood the Ridiculous the best, hath chiefly used the hypocritical affectation." The subject of verbal hypocrisy in Dickens, of deceptive rhetoric after *Pickwick*, will get full-scale treatment [elsewhere], where the Jonsonian tradition will also come in for discussion. In *Pickwick Papers*, meanwhile, it is the other phase of Fielding's "ridiculous," the affectation of "vanity," which is most often in question and which prompts the linguistic "burlesque" in Dickens's own first and purest example of the "comic epic-poem in prose." In addition to Jonson, *Joseph Andrews* acknowledges a major debt to *Don Quixote* on its title page. What we are about to discover concerning Dickens's verbal satire will help place him in a tradition of linguistic comedy that dates back, as my epigraph testifies, to Cervantes, and that moves through Fielding, Smollett, and Sterne to Dickens himself, and from Dickens through Meredith to Joyce and Nabokov.

Circumlocution, the affected herding of as many words as possible into a given meaning, is one of the ways linguistic "vanity" often finds expression. Things do not amuse in *Pickwick*, they afford amusement; people do not agree, they express their concurrence. Instead of being shown a double chin, we are conducted more delicately to this observation: "his chin . . . had acquired the grave and imposing form which is generally described by prefixing the word 'double' to that expressive feature" (chap. 23). Elegant variation—in Dickens just a special case of eloquent elongation—makes a frequent appearance, with most errors into the ordinary soon valiantly set right. Jesperson cites several non-comic examples from Dickens where words of Latin or Greek derivation follow those of native origin as approximate synonyms, avoiding repetition. What Jesperson notices helps us to see something characteristic about Dickens's style. While capitalizing on the wealth of synonyms at his command, Dickens never loses sight of the possible excess, the ready comedy of circumlocution and variation. As with so many of his linguistic methods, he recognizes the laughable just around the corner from the habitual. And he takes this turn into comedy as often as possible. When one moment a character cannot "believe his eyes," the next moment we can hardly believe our ears as he is forced into "the painful necessity of admitting the veracity of his optics" (chap. 2). When Dickens writes of "the red-headed man with a grin which agitated his countenance from one auricular organ to the other" (chap. 5), he is of course inviting this very response from us by another mock-scientific periphrasis, one almost as ludicrous as Sterne's having Uncle Toby whistle by "directing the buccinatory muscles along his cheeks, and the orbicular muscles around his lips to do their duty." The satire is of course every bit as deliberate in Sterne, where the narrator Tristram at one point objects to the habit of placing "tall, opake words, one before another, in a right line, betwixt you and your reader's conception," and where Parson Yorick, arch-enemy of "gravity" and "affectation" and one of the book's true heroes, emerges as a standard-bearer for "plain *English* without any periphrasis."

Taking example from Sterne among other of his important masters, Dickens finds that epithets and honorific titles serve as an especially good proving-ground for his verbal satire. "The fat boy," on one of his appearances, has his title elegantly varied a paragraph later to "the bloated lad" (chap. 8), a typical bloating of phrase which will later be used to identify the book's main characters, Mr. Pickwick and Sam Weller respectively, as "the illustrious man, whose name forms the leading feature of the title of this work" and "that eccentric functionary" (chap. 10). The difference— we sense it at once—is that Sam, unlike his master, would get the joke, and might well have made it. Tony Weller is at one point called Sam's "progenitor," and on the same page Sam mocks the whole periphrastic habit by referring to his father, in direct address, as "corpilence" (chap. 33). Mr. Pickwick, however, has no ear for language, no playful spirit; and he is quite unable to savor with the proper grain of salt those colloquial idioms that come his way. As a complete literalist, the licensed metaphors of slang have no jurisdiction in his vocabulary, and when Bob Sawyer asks, "I say, old boy, where do you hang out?", this is what we hear: "Mr. Pickwick replied that he was at present suspended at the George and Vulture" (chap. 30). Dickens answers for him, but presumably by repeating his own words. In any case the point is made, for by now we realize that Mr. Pickwick's serious pronouncements sound alarmingly like Dickens's parodic prose.

In *Pickwick Papers* Dickens is especially wordy and roundabout when it comes to that communal act of ritualized significance, the meal. At one place we find Mr. Pickwick "deeply investigating the interior of the pigeon-pie" (chap. 4), and twice in one prandial paragraph the idea of eating is deftly circumnavigated with "yield full justice to the meal" and "do good execution upon a decent proportion of the viands" (chap. 19). On the same page where eating is termed "the work of destruction," we hear about the fat boy "abstracting a veal patty" (chap. 4), and with this locution we have moved, according to the *OED*, from circumlocution to euphemism—indirection for propriety as well as elegance, but mocking all the while the Victorian syndrome of delicate and evasive diction. "Excisable articles were remarkably cheap at all the public houses" (chap. 14), we are told, facetiously asked to swallow this substitute for "alcoholic beverages." Euphemism and periphrasis, of course, continually overlap in Dickens's prose, becoming a source of laughter previously sanctioned by Fielding in his program for the "comic epic-poem in prose." Though insisting on the differences between "the comic and the burlesque," Fielding did make this concession for the higher form of comedy: "In the diction, I think, burlesque itself may be sometimes admitted." Certainly both he and Dickens avail themselves of the leeway this offers, with comic euphemism as one of the chief forms of such "burlesque." It is interesting to speculate about an actual debt to Fielding's description of the sleeping Parson Adams, who "snored louder than the usual braying of the animal with long ears," when Dickens writes in the *Sketches by Boz* about one Mr. Alexander, who "was deservedly celebrated for possessing all the pertinacity of a bankruptcy-court attorney, combined with the obstinacy of that useful animal which browses on the thistle" ("Tales," chap. 7).

Throughout the *Sketches*, the concept of pants is taken on with great scrupulosity, and we hear trousers rechristened repeatedly as "inexplicables" or "unmentionables." Before the Victorian advent, Sterne could say "breeches" but makes fun of his inability to itemize their features, when that scabrous chestnut "fell perpendicularly into that particular aperture of *Phutatorius's* breeches, for which, to the shame and indelicacy of our language be it spoke, there is no chaste word throughout all *Johnson's* dictionary." The last euphemism for pants in *Pickwick Papers* is "symmetrical inexpressibles" (chap. 55), and it reminds us of the transparent farce in all such phrases. To write about "unmentionables," for instance, to mention them even in this way, or to express the symmetry of "inexpressibles," is to skirt paradox rather narrowly. The logical fallacy of such a linguistic trick is used earlier and even more pointedly in *Pickwick*, deliberately, in fact, to point up the hypocrisy of such euphemistic sleight of hand. "Mr. Trotter smiled, and holding his glass in his left hand, gave four distinct slaps on the pocket of his mulberry indescribables with his right" (chap. 16). It need hardly be said that "mulberry" is itself a descriptive adjective. Self-perjured, such a phrase is its own worst indictment. We also see that it evolves from mixed rhetorical motives; Dickens is poking fun not only at false modesty but at that periphrastic high style which so often goes hand in hand with euphemism. To George Orwell, who, like Dickens, views language morally, circumlocution and euphemism are partners in essentially the same crime:

"The inflated style is itself a kind of euphemism. A mass of Latin words falls upon the facts like soft snow, blurring the outlines and covering up all the details. The great enemy of clear language is insincerity. When there is a gap between one's real and one's declared aims, one turns as it were instinctively to long words and exhausted idioms, like a cuttlefish squirting out ink."

That self-accusatory item, "mulberry indescribables," is a tiny instance of Dickens at his most compressed and intuitive. I would like to introduce two other related examples that bear on the verbal satire of his first novel, two sentences that put the problem of language's "insincerity" very clearly before us and that, in the process, become unexpected paradigms, reflecting from their confined surfaces an entire linguistic issue. The first of these strangely reflexive sentences, seeded with its own satiric dissent, follows a speech by Alfred Jingle, as yet unnamed:

> "Come," replied the stranger, "stopping at Crown—Crown at Muggleton—met a party—flannel jackets—white trousers—anchovy sandwiches—devilled kidneys—splendid fellows—glorious."
>
> Mr. Pickwick was sufficiently versed in the stranger's system of stenography to infer from this rapid and disjointed communication that he had, somehow or other, contracted an acquaintance with the All-Muggletons, which he had converted, by a process peculiar to himself, into that extent of good fellowship on which a general invitation may be easily founded.
>
> (chap. 7)

Here the breathless and the long-winded face each other across a padded phrase, "system of stenography," which is meant to describe the telegraphic "shorthand" of the former but which in fact illustrates the circumlocution of the latter. With this minor self-critical phrase, Dickens scores against inflated prose in the very act of designating its opposite. In the chapter just before, we have already been teased into extrapolation from another loaded sentence, nominally describing a quiet evening at cards: "The rubber was conducted with all that gravity of deportment and sedateness of demeanour which befit the pursuit entitled 'whist'—a solemn observance, to which, as it appears to us, the title of 'game' has been very irreverently and ignominiously applied" (chap. 6). That first tumescent phrase, "gravity of deportment and sedateness of demeanour," borders on redundancy and then gives way to the elegant variation by which "pursuit," itself an ennobling synonym for game, is puffed up to "solemn observance." Could prose or point anywhere—either deportment of style or demeanor of meaning—possibly be rendered more grave, sedate, or solemn? Circumlocution has again located its own satire, and the sentence almost seems to take as its subject that excessive language itself by which it is drawn out. To talk in this stuffy way and be serious is to live in a closed "game" world, airless and immature, and when the satirist notices this he is of course acting "irreverently." It is his own corresponding "game," with few rules and no real restraints, in which the score is tallied against a satiric opponent embodied in the parodied style itself.

It is an irony Dickens must have enjoyed that there were critics in his day who made no objection to his satiric "game" until it was played with a mixed deck, until native diction began to spoil words "in themselves good and classical." This last is from a review in which are cited among Dickens's "various impurities of expression" and "gross offenses of the English language" such typically Dickensian transgressions, often contributing to the famous animism of his description, as *"impracticable* nightcaps . . . *inscrutable* harpsichords, *undeniable* chins, *highly geological* home-made cakes . . . and the *recesses and vacations* of a toothpick."* These offenders were arraigned from *Martin Chuzzlewit,* but Dickens's interest in such collocations, the nearest possible contact he can force between the high and the low styles, to the discomfiture of the former, was with him from the beginning. In the *Sketches by Boz* we hear of a gentleman with an "interrogative nose" ("Our Parish," chap. 4), and at our first meeting with Mr. Perker in *Pickwick Papers* we find that he too has an "inquisitive nose," with which he indulges in an "argumentative pinch of snuff" (chap. 10). Later in the book, an anonymous waiter provides the occasion for such irreverent verbal coupling by having over his arm a napkin that was a fortnight old, "and coeval stockings on his legs" (chap. 22). This sort of phrasing is so inveterate with Dickens that it turns up in his last completed novel, over thirty years later, when Silas Wegg leaves *Our Mutual Friend* by being thrown into a scavenger's cart with a "prodigious splash" (vol. 4, chap. 14). Dickens never ceased to enjoy making incompatible partners within a single phrase of the two sorts of diction, invariably at the expense of the "good and classical" words. Their nearness to the native consort becomes a slight ironical jab at their own staid usage, as they somehow shed importance on the domestic or commonplace Anglo-Saxon word while continuing to look a little awkward and silly for the company they are keeping.

This is part of what happens when Nabokov takes to this sort of phrasing for *Lolita.* Charlotte Haze incarnates an earthy bourgeois grossness which she tries ceaselessly to deodorize with her "polished words." It never works, and this nervous discord in her personality is captured perfectly by the narrator's Dickensian linkage of a Latinized status word and a subversive bit of homely onomatopoeia, in that "deprecatory grunt" with which Charlotte stoops to pick up a sock. A sentence later, however, the narrator himself has "surreptitiously fished" a train time-table from his pocket, and the linguistic satire (as it does constantly in Dickens) has widened free of its immediate personal object. In *Lolita,* the marriage of high and low is more than phrasal; it becomes in part the theme of Humbert's union with both Haze women. More centrally yet, it is of course the theme of *Pickwick Papers* and, before it, of *Don Quixote,* where "eruct" and "belch" are abutted in the same way that Quixote and his squire, that Pickwick and his man-servant later, must confront each other's opposite "styles," their divergent experience of the world. In the comic authors before Nabokov, and most strikingly in Dickens, it is both the down-to-earth vernacular and the worldly assurance it bespeaks which carry the day. The higher the style, the harder it falls.

It must not be thought that Dickens stood alone in his day as a champion of native English in all of its resource and vernacular energy. He was part of a strong nineteenth-century movement away from unquestioned deference to the classical standards of language, and he wrote a piece called "Saxon-English" for his periodical *Household Words* on the history of English, with an expressed bias toward native rather than imported diction, a preference for what we might in fact call "household words." Dickens shows his contempt for the author who makes "cavalry regiments of his sentences" and seeks abroad "for sesquipedalian words." He reminds us that we "can all read with comfort the works of Thomas Fuller, Swift, Bunyan, Defoe, Franklin, and Cobbett; there, sense is clear, feeling is homely, and the writers take care that there shall be no misunderstanding. But in Robertson, Johnson, and Gibbon, one word in every three is an alien; and so an Englishman who happens to have, like Shakespeare, 'small Latin and less Greek,' is by no means quite at home in their society." The reference to Johnson and his "alien" words is especially revealing in the light of the most important modern study of Johnson's diction. William K. Wimsatt discusses Johnson's use of difficult and many-syllabled "philosophic words," words originally "scientific," as part of a long tradition of "big words in English" which "has exhibited in its successive phases a generally constant stylistic value, of pomposity, grandiloquence, or impressiveness." Such lexical choices "were stylistically the same words that became 'Johnsonese' and were given various epithets of disparagement by Macaulay and other Saxonists of the nineteenth century" (*Philosophic Words: A Study of Style and Meaning in the* Rambler *and the* Dictionary *of Samuel Johnson*).

Dickens, as we have seen, is of this company, and more often than not his disparagement takes the form of parody. Wimsatt observes that even for Johnson, at times, there was "a smile behind the ponderosity, a ripple beneath the grave style." But when Dickens gets hold of Johnsonian words, the smile breaks into laughter, the ripple becomes a complete ironic upheaval. Wimsatt's closing section on "Philosophic Humor" is full of indirect application to Dickens's style. There is to be found in the *Rambler* a brand of humor toned down from Sterne and Smollett (authors we know to be among Dickens's favorites) but still retaining "a certain mild contrast, and at the same time a metaphorical juncture, between gravity of diction and homeliness of content, a shade of grimace at some meanness or pretense. It is humor that often involves the bigness of legal, political, or social vocabulary." Change "mild contrast" to an almost grotesque disproportion and you have a fair appraisal of Dickens's prevailing ironic style. It was a comic program to which Meredith, later in the century, could not subscribe, and which he attacked along with punning in his "Essay on Comedy" (1877), though without mentioning Dickens in either regard: "The sense of the comic is much blunted by habits of punning and of using humoristic phrase, the trick of employing Johnsonian polysyllables to treat of the infinitely little."

But Dickens was a Saxonist not just in his satire of Latinity. A man of words delighted by the authentic words of others, he had a deep curiosity about the intuitive metaphors of London vernacular, and he often interrupts his own narrative in the *Sketches* to offer a more colorful or engaging alternative expression, with such little varied explanations as "to use his own appropriate and expressive description" or "to use Mr. Gattleton's expressive description" or "to use his own emphatic language" or "to adopt his own figurative expression in all its native beauty." In this way Dickens's own characters become stylists with him, and a passion for expression is diffused through every level of his writing. The same mannerisms are carried only somewhat abated into *Pickwick*, where we pause over such semantic glosses and afterthoughts as "if we may use the expression," "in the strict acceptation of the term," and "in his own expressive language." This announced preoccupation with phrase can of course accompany stale satirized language as well as vital idiom, and was perhaps cultivated in part by Dickens from his reading of Fielding, where a similar formula is used to spotlight the Latinism of the bookish Parson Adams as he "(to use his own words) replenished his pipe." An even more elaborate glossing of linguistic sources occurs earlier in *Joseph Andrews*, a perfect example of "burlesque" admitted in "diction" but not in character, a mock-heroic episode in which Adams is beaten by an assailant until "he concluded (to use the language of fighting) 'that he had done his business'; or, in the language of poetry, 'that he had sent him to the shades below'; in plain English, 'that he was dead.' " This is exactly the sort of thing Dickens would have picked up.

Beyond the featured "expressiveness" of borrowed figures and idioms, however, and the preening "impressiveness" of mock eloquence, there is a third kind of specialized language in *Pickwick* and in all the novels after it: the sheer verbal gymnastics of words on vacation from the chore of meaning, the stylistic fun of language at play. The enjoyment is often written right into the prose, by way of charming over-analysis. A pun, for instance, is seldom given the chance to slip by unapplauded. When in *Pickwick* we come upon Mr. Pott described as "pot-valiant," we also get a gentle hint to accept this in "a double sense" (chap. 51). In the *Sketches* we have already encountered another variety of the pun, not two senses compressed into one occurrence of the word, but two meanings adjacent in separate occurrences. Thus "we do not hear that he was advanced to any other public post on his return, than the post at the corner of the Haymarket" ("Scenes," chap. 17). If there is any suspicion that Dickens loses interest in such word play as his artistry matures, we need only cite the description of Silas Wegg at his dusty corner years later in *Our Mutual Friend*, as it combines that "double sense" formula with the same pun on "post": "All weathers saw the man at the post. This is to be accepted in a double sense, for he contrived a back to his wooden stool by placing it against the lamp post" (vol. 1, chap. 5). Another doubling of language's expected sense takes place in those figures of speech which Dickens probably uses more often than any other English prose writer, syllepsis and zeugma. *Pickwick* offers examples in which the governing verb appears only once for both objects, as when Mr. Pickwick "fell into the barrow and fast asleep, simultaneously" (chap. 19), and also a variant form given here to Dickens's stand-in, Sam Weller, a form in which the verb appears once for each different sense: " 'This is a wery impartial country for justice,' said Sam. 'There ain't a magistrate goin' as don't commit himself; twice as often as he commits other people' " (chap. 25). Nabokov is again a disciple of Dickens in such verbal calisthenics and tells us near the end of *Lolita*, for instance, that Quilty "had half opened his mouth and the front door." As already suggested, I think it is a mistake to believe with G. L. Brook that Dickens's whole fondness for puns, turns, and other playful dexterities of style is the infatuation of a distinctly young writer. As in the case of Nabokov, the fondness abides from novel to novel, becoming a real insight into the surfaces and hidden recesses of language, of style itself, as it can be made to yield up parables of the ethical and imaginative life.

In his survey of "Surface Wit and Structural Rhetoric" in Dickens, H. P. Sucksmith pursues distinctions between incidental linguistic antics and verbal devices employed "structurally," by which he means put to some thematic use. But inutility itself is often the point of Dickens's word play. No one can deny the importance of seeing how Dickens's language *works*, but it is also important to notice in his prose a kind of verbal "fun" that is there largely to remind us that something exists which is the exact opposite of work, an impulse utterly non-utilitarian, a spirit of truancy and trifling. No one knew better than Dickens that the devices of style and rhetoric, in proper hands, become invaluable instruments for the probing of character and psychology. The countless appearances of "surface wit" as treated by Sucksmith—such as malapropism, cliché, hyperbole, syllepsis, pun, polysyllabic humor, personification, mock heroics, bathos, anticlimax—are not, however, thematically negligible when they are not directly analytic. For style itself has its own independent character, its own implicit psychology. This, too, no one knew better than Dickens, and this we must also watch for as we go.

But fun with words is a rarity, and except for such very rare creatures as Sam Weller, it is almost entirely in the charge of the narrative voice, just as it usually was in the earlier comic writers to whose linguistic satire I have been alluding. Too many characters in Dickens speak a language that is stiff, spent, joyless, a language anesthetizing rather than enlivening—and, what is worse, deliberately so. A travesty on this calculated inhibiting of the word, this deliberate abdication of the power of language, is of course the reason for those thick forests of woodenness with which, at intervals, Dickens landscapes his comic narrative. And when all traces of verbal restraint and integrity have been uprooted, Dickens's prose settles down into direct, unequivocal satire, with the abuse of language its acknowledged and only subject. It is my argument that this is essentially what happens in the opening chapter of Dickens's first novel, and there are other moments in *Pickwick,* as in the *Sketches* earlier, that take focus in this way. To some of these clearly marked satires I will now turn with a closer focus of my own, to see the ways in which Dickens puts under more direct fire the spoiled language of rhetoric and public address, whether its corrupt accents are heard in pulpit oratory, in Parliamentary declamation, in the written periods of the newspapers, or in the official "legalese" of the courts.

Our recent acquaintance from the *Sketches* with the "interrogative nose" happens to be a pulpit speaker of no small self-esteem who, as Dickens facetiously puts it, "prides himself, not a little, on his style of addressing the parishioners in vestry assembled" ("Our Parish," chap. 4). In his next sentence, Dickens shows that he himself is hardly seduced by such worn, snobbish inversion as "in vestry assembled" when he destroys the orator with a crisp, tightly balanced Johnsonian announcement: "His views are more confined than extensive; his principles more narrow than liberal." The orator stands accused in a clear-cut case of rhetoric as hypocrisy. In "A Parliamentary Sketch" ("Scenes," chap. 18) we meet a Member "deluding himself into the belief that he is thinking about something" and—here the mock grandiloquence is triggered off—providing a "splendid sample of a Member of the House of Commons concentrating in his own person the wisdom of a constituency." As usual, Dickens gets the Parliamentarian with his own style. Later still, there is a piece on "The Parlour Orator" ("Characters," chap. 5) which lambastes oratorical flourishes at their most absurd, deprived even of the public occasion of their sins. We hear the blowhard "gradually bursting into a radiating sentence, in which such adjectives as 'dastardly,' 'oppressive,' 'violent,' and 'sanguinary,' formed the most conspicuous words." Dickens, the master of exaggeration and hyperbole, an expert in some of these same high-pitched adjectives, still manages to expose their artifice in an empty and blustering rhetoric. Once again, the habitual is re-evaluated for satire.

But something else happens here with peculiar consequence for Dickens's own style. The "parlour orator" has received high praise from the gathered listeners as a "Wonderful man!" and a "Splendid speaker!" with "Great power!" The company soon disbands, and Dickens is alone with his mind. What takes place is an unusual revelation: "If we had followed the established precedent in all such instances, we should have fallen into a fit of musing, without delay . . . and we should have gone dreaming on, until the pewter pot on the table, or the little beer-chiller on the fire, had started into life, and addressed to us a long story of days gone by. But, by some means or other, we were not in a romantic humour; and although we tried very hard to invest the furniture with vitality, it remained perfectly unmoved, obstinate, and sullen." His characteristic imaginative power, his artist's ability to animate the inanimate, is strangely incapacitated, and strains without effect. That "romantic humour" so essential to Dickens's art is now beyond his grasp. And the fatuous style of the orator appears somehow to be at fault: "Being thus reduced to the unpleasant necessity of musing about ordinary matters, our thoughts reverted to the red-faced man, and his oratorical display." Dickens's own style is unavailable, it seems, because he continues to dwell on the charlatan's. False style has not only insulted an authentic imagination, but somehow poisoned it. Portrayed in a very personal way for Dickens, this is the real threat of rhetoric as an enemy of romantic fancy.

Following the *Sketches* there is certainly no sign of a cease-fire in the parodic bombardment of oratory, Dickens's war against the mongers of false eloquence. In the chapter on the Eatanswill election in *Pickwick Papers*, we are informed that "everybody and everything then and there assembled was for the special use, behoof, honour, and renown" (chap. 13) of a candidate for the House of Commons, and these two redundant noun pairs merely typify the verbal snowballing that goes on in campaign rhetoric. When, three pages later, a man tries publicly to "nominate a fit and proper person to represent them in Parliament," this prepackaged adjectival redundancy is another such ceremonial gesture of oratory, one hardly appreciated by the rowdy assembly, however, for the speaker was "repeatedly desired by the crowd to 'send a boy home, to ask whether he hadn't left his woice under the pillow.' " Dickens has here cleverly delegated his satire to this anonymous audience, and though they are not expected to heed the resonance of what they say, the idea of disembodied speech, the dichotomy of "woice" and person, suggests the specious, self-sufficient life that oratory seems to take on. Every irony is therefore intended when Sam Weller, that artist of talk whose style and personality do beautifully coincide, is accused by Mr. Smauker of being "unparliamentary" in his use of the plural "missises" (chap. 37). What else would we expect from Sam, whose sense of English is the exact opposite of official? His response to this accusation is, fittingly, a parody of "parliamentary" expression, as he promises to "amend the obserwation and call 'em the dear creeturs."

The orotund banalities of journalistic style also come in for Boz's early parody, and even that "Parliamentary Sketch" has subsidiary fun at the expense of the press when it records that "the mover of the address will be 'on his legs,' as the newspapers announce sometimes by way of novelty, as if the speakers were occasionally in the habit of standing on their heads" ("Scenes," chap. 18). In the lampoon of "Public Dinners" ("Scenes," chap. 19), Boz slips into his newspaper voice for some well-signaled parodies of the Victorian press. When "God Save the Queen" is rendered by the guests at a public banquet, we are told that they impart to the national anthem "an effect which the newspapers, with great justice, describe as 'perfectly electrical.' " And on the same page Dickens is also "compelled to adopt newspaper phraseology, and to express our regret at being 'precluded from giving even the substance of the noble Lord's observations.' " It is an invigorating historical fact that the same hack journalistic formula turns up in a newspaper review of the *Sketches* themselves: "We regret that our limits will not allow us to extract an inimitable specimen of the intense feeling he has displayed in the tale of the broker's man."

Stephen C. Gill has recently made an interesting suggestion about the style of *Pickwick,* tracing it back to the "penny-a-liners," those free-lance journalists who handled everyday reporting other than Parliamentary debates and who, since they were paid by the line, had a vested interest in expansive phrasing of all kinds. Gill mentions in passing the parody of these "chroniclers by the line" in the thirty-third chapter of *Bleak House,* and it is worth looking at this episode more closely here. Two of these reporters are preparing their copy on Krook's bizarre death, and they "note down . . . how the neighbourhood of Chancery Lane was yesterday, at about mid-night, thrown into a state of the most intense agitation and excitement by the following alarming and horrible discovery." In their characteristic use of "as many words as possible," their synonymous doublings of both nouns and adjectives, we have an example of those "syntactic doublets" Wimsatt mentions in his first study of Johnson's style as a special form of parallelism in the master's prose, a strategy for increasing the emphasis of certain weighty words by multiplication so promiscuously borrowed by the journalists of Dickens's time. When these same reporters in *Bleak House* proudly display their Latinized alliteration, "foetid effluvia," to describe the atmosphere after Krook's spontaneous combustion, they are also exposing another Johnson-derived bad habit which shows up, along with the doublets, in *Pickwick*'s own newspaper parodies.

Most frequent of such parodies are the quotations from the *Eatanswill Gazette,* and perhaps most outrageous of these is the prognostication for Mrs. Leo Hunter's party, the ornate promise that it "would present a scene of varied and delicious enchantment—a bewildering coruscation of beauty and talent—a lavish and prodigal display of hospitality—above all, a degree of splendour softened by the most exquisite taste; and adornment refined with perfect harmony and the chastest good keeping" (chap. 15). And so on, and on. . . . This is worse than just newspaper padding. With its deluxe syntax and showcase diction, this is in fact self-promotional prose; the very reflection of its author Mr. Pott, it is a culture-climbing style that strives after the same splendor and adornment it describes, but has forgotten all sense of "chastest good keeping" in the process. Two chapters before, Mr. Pott reads several of his "leaders" to Mr. Pickwick, and we are sarcastically assured that our hero "was perfectly enraptured with the vigour and freshness of the style," a confidence derived from "the fact that his eyes were closed, as if with excess of pleasure, during the whole time of their perusal" (chap. 13). There is, it seems, a style too overblown even for Mr. Pickwick. When the style of this same *Gazette* is again read to us near the end of the novel, a most interesting commentary is implicit. Again we are pelted with those "syntactic doublets," used to heighten both the calumny and the praise: "A reptile contemporary has recently sweltered forth his black venom in the vain and hopeless attempt of sullying the fair name of our distinguished and excellent representative" (chap. 51). This runs on for most of a page, and we learn that, like Mr. Pickwick before them, "Messrs. Bob Sawyer and Benjamin Allen . . . had irreverently fallen asleep during the reading," only to be "roused" at last "by the mere whispering of the talismanic word 'Dinner' in their ears." The language at once perks up, as "to dinner they went with good digestion waiting on appetite, and health on both, and a waiter on all three." It seems that a typical Dickensian play on words has been inspired by the belated arrival, after all the ready-made palaver of newspaper rhetoric, of a word that really does have meaning. When words tend to come cheaply packaged in redundant multiples, it *is* almost a miracle, something magic or "talismanic," when a word like "Dinner" can become an act of real communication.

To be of worth, Dickens is reminding us, the word must have a final cause beyond its own marketability; it must point elsewhere, at some meaning, rather than being itself the point. Too often, and nowhere more than in the press, language degenerates into a kind of wholesale commodity. A parody of the poet's autonomous handling of verbal entities, the word falls victim to the merchandizing spirit and becomes a thing. The debased "poet"—the journalist or the orator—trades on language, bartering it, hoarding it, making of his verbal stockpiles a second-rate inventory of words, to be sold off cheaply when occasion demands. In the same year that Dickens, in *Pickwick Papers,* was mounting this attack on the squandered economies of language, Emerson, waging the same war in the American theater, found a tempting fiscal metaphor for the decline of the word: "The corruption of man is followed by the corruption of language. When simplicity of character and the sovereignty of ideas is broken up by the prevalence of secondary desires, the desire of riches, of pleasure, of power, of praise . . . new imagery ceases to be created, and old words are perverted to stand for things which are not; a paper currency is employed, when there is no bullion in the vaults." Both Emerson and Dickens detested the spurious coinages and indiscriminate expenditures of language which were everywhere in the public writing of their day. To prolong Emerson's analogy, the "paper currency" of expression had become so inflated and devalued that it was already a kind of counterfeit. Yet such easy metaphors, as Emerson would have admitted, are themselves accessories to the crime. They are meant only to signal their own danger, to warn of the initial mistake one makes by thinking of language in this way at all, as if the exchange of words and ideas were a commerce, not a communication.

Journalism in Dickens's day is not only a good place to look for the styles he apes and parodies, but also for commentary on his style that is more likely than twentieth-century criticism to report the topical, contemporary nature of the satire. *The Saturday Review of Politics, Literature, Science, and Art*, for instance, not only offers samples of Victorian journalese in its own pages, but also tells us, in a review of Dickens, that his writing is "the apotheosis of what has been called newspaper English." Historical distance has, in this respect, done some disservice to modern commentary on Dickens's style. We are only now coming to realize the true scope of Dickens's symbolic and psychological explorations, but as verbal adventure his style has left its context behind. All too often we take it merely, gratefully, as "Dickensian." We are not well-equipped to judge its satire. For us, meretriciousness in style is a new and different thing. The chic flair of Madison Avenue copy, the pallid and platitudinous expanses of television dialogue, eighth-rate imitators of Hemingway, the ghost-written bluster of our own hustings, the stuffiness of literary scholarship itself, scientific jargon, and today's most influential brand of journalese, the contagious *Time*-style, are some of our favorite targets. Dickensian stylistic satire is another matter. Its force as parody of degenerate and popularized Johnsonian style, newspaper Gibbonese, Parliamentary rhetoric, political and domestic euphemism, and the whole cloying atmosphere of the High Style, the prose of false show and evasion, is considerably blunted for readers a century later. Here the critics of Dickens's own time provide a welcome adjustment for our updated approaches.

We have already discussed the importance as a negative standard for Dickens the Saxonist of the Johnsonian hard word. In matters of style apart from diction—in syntax, rhythm, tone—Johnson was also, even as late as the mid-nineteenth century, the acknowledged model for fine writing. Stripped of talent and sincerity, the same sort of self-assured style became Dickens's satiric model for pomp and hypocrisy. It is an interesting biographical coincidence that both Dickens and Johnson spent part of their apprenticeship in letters as notably fluent and successful Parliamentary reporters. The aura of confident eloquence aspired to in political oratory, and captured by Johnson when manufacturing whole debates out of his imagination on the basis of the scantest details, was further refined and sharpened over the course of his career to become one of the outstanding formal styles in English. Dickens's career, from similar beginnings, took quite a different turn. The parliamentary style's same rhetorical aspirations, when bereft both of intelligence and of integrity, become, in Dickens's hands, the parodic basis for the most versatile, the most successful comic writing in the language. It is a style lavished disproportionately on little things and little people. The result is indirect but unmistakable: affectation stands accused.

In his article on "Saxon-English," Dickens included Gibbon with Johnson among the brandishers of "sesquipedalian" words. In a notebook entry from 1875 quoted by Miriam Allott, Thomas Hardy also seems to link Gibbon, among others, with "*Times* leaders" as promulgators of "too much style." And Alice Meynell, too, stresses the influence of Gibbon on the style of the Victorian press that Dickens was forever satirizing. "The burlesque so gayly undertaken by Dickens rallies a lofty and distant Gibbon," the "wreck" of whose style "strewed the press" in Dickens's day. "It was everywhere. Dickens not only was clear of the wreckage—he saw it to be the refuse it was; he laughed at it, and even as he laughed he formed a style" (essay reprinted in Ford and Lane, eds., *The Dickens Critics*). Once again, the press itself was not wholly unable to see what was going on, and the article already mentioned from *The Saturday Review* came very near to a full appreciation; in spite of his "intentional fallacies," the reviewer did see that Dickens was attacking the moribund standards of English which followed in the wake of Johnson and Gibbon:

> *Pickwick* is throughout a sort of half-conscious parody of that style of writing which demanded balanced sentences, double-barrelled epithets, and a proper conception of the office and authority of semi-colons. . . . Whenever he can get an opportunity, Mr. Dickens rakes up the old-fashioned finery, twists it into every sort of grotesque shape, introduces it to all kinds of strange bedfellows, and contrives, with an art which is all the more ingenious because it was probably quite undesigned, to convey the impression that every one who tries to think, or to act by rule, is little more than a pompous jackass.

A just conclusion, except in its withholding of credit for conscious parodic design. The style is hardly "all the more ingenious" for being "quite undesigned." It is art that tries to look artless; it is the satiric mask of naiveté, the ingenious passing itself off as the ingenuous. This is its charm, and a large part of its comedy.

Meynell tells us that Dickens laughed at journalistic style and that "even as he laughed he formed a style." His satiric prose was shaped, however, by a laughter not only at the press, but also at the pulpit, the podium, and the bench. And it is Dickens's parody of legal jargon, which I have not yet discussed, that is both most crucial for *Pickwick Papers* and most accessible for the modern reader. It is still very much with us today. Indeed, we even recognize the familiar jammed cadences of "legalese" as far back as Mrs. Shandy's marriage settlement, from which, since Sterne pretends it would be a "barbarity" to translate it into other words, we get reproduced for us such redundant barbarisms as "doth grant, covenant, condescend, consent, conclude, bargain, and fully agree to and with," or "fall out, chance, happen, or otherwise come to pass." One of Dickens's later comic tactics is to render such repetitive phrasing all the more ridiculous by divorcing it from its legal context altogether, and so we hear (with my italics) that when Sam Weller settles down before a tavern fire for a glass of brandy and water, the barmaid "carried away the poker to preclude the possibility of the fire being stirred without the *full probity and concurrence* of the Blue Boar being first *had and obtained*" (chap. 33). Dickens's satire can of course be more directly aimed, and we find what *The Saturday Review* termed "double-barrelled" locutions treated as if they were themselves (the word as weapon) among the "ingenious machines put in motion for the torture and torment of His Majesty's liege subjects, and the comfort and emolument of the practitioners of the law" (chap. 31). It is no surprise that Dickens names an "eminent counsel" in *Pickwick* "Mr. Prosee," or that the prosiest of all the lawyers, the eloquent Buzfuz, buzzes continually with the fuzzy pseudo-distinctions of the "doublet" style. Dickens's general parodic voice points out the "majesty and dignity" of Buzfuz, and then sneaks into the lawyer's own identical two-for-one diction for an indirect report of the responsibility Buzfuz feels so humbly burdened by: "—a responsibility, he would say, which he could never have supported were he not *buoyed up and sustained* by a conviction so strong that it amounted to positive certainty that the cause of *truth and justice,* or, in other words, the cause of his *much-injured* and *most oppressed* client, must prevail with the *high-minded and intelligent* dozen of men whom he now saw in that box before him" (chap. 34, my italics). It is such a rhetorical climate Pickwick will attempt, and fail, to weather in the famous trial of Bardell vs. Pickwick, where he will be, in a sense, punished by words themselves for his own misuse of language.

To show how this comes about, I must turn again to the novel's first chapter, from whose excesses there is still much to be learned. I have strayed so far in order to bring a more widely trained sense of just what style has at stake there, and of what precisely is called into question about the morality of style, the ethic of imagination. G. L. Brook, in his chapter on "Language to Suit the Occasion," does not seem to realize the implicit scope of this particular rhetorical occasion when he says merely: "The first chapter of *Pickwick Papers* contains a parody of the minutes, prolix and full of clichés, of a small debating society, and Mr. Pickwick's speech to the members of the Pickwick Club is a parody of the sort of speech that such societies encourage." In *Dickens as Satirist,* Sylvia Manning sees in this opening chapter only a "satire on scientific associations and on parliamentary procedures," a "failure" that "is actually as eccentric to the whole design of the novel as the satire in the story of Prince Bladud is shown to be by its undisguised interpolation into the narrative." By slighting the linguistic implications of the chapter, this critic of satire is in fact closing off one of its most interesting arenas in Dickens, interesting for *Pickwick,* for his style generally, and for the comic tradition he works within and perpetuates. When, in *The Egoist,* George Meredith distinguishes between the speech of a professed "artist in phrases" and the plainer clarities of his heroine, who at one point had "not uttered words, she had shed meanings," he is taking a leaf from Dickens's own Book of Linguistic Egoism, where false artists of phrase like the Pickwickians—as we are about to see—

see—"shed" meanings in an opposite sense, casting them off in favor of the mere sounds of their words, discarding the proper and effective function of language for mere effect.

The climax of *Pickwick*'s first chapter holds the key. The altercation between Pickwick and Blotton brings to a head tensions naturally aroused by prolonged contact with a padded prose that makes of style the mere upholstery of an overstuffed rhetoric. Chanting his own praises over his "Tittlebatian Theory," Mr. Pickwick manages twice to use the word "celebrated" about his own achievement, and then, in the same sentence with its second appearance, twice "pride" and once "proudest" about his state of mind. He is roundly cheered, and then adds, again in the report of the editor, that he "was a humble individual (No, no)." His auditors, responding in parenthesis and apparently unanimous, mean, we must assume, that he is no ordinary or unimportant man. Only Dickens, one step beyond the editor, intends this negative response to deny Pickwick's modesty. Yet just as the word "humble" divulges two contrasted meanings, so the twin negatives of "No, no" may be found to part company, for after two more preening sentences from Pickwick, the next parenthetical record of his listeners' response is indeed sharply divided: "(Cheers—a voice: 'No')." The anomalous voice turns out to be Blotton's, and unless this is merely the implicit charge of vanity repeated—the satiric half of "No, no"—we are left without a guess as to the immediate force of its negation, suspended as it is without a referent. Finally, it would seem, the deflation can only be intended to generalize. When Pickwick is heckled with that obstreperous and entirely unfocused "No," it is as if, by a single daring monosyllable, all the windy and lavishly syllabled rhetoric has been sweepingly negated— blotted out by the matter-of-fact Blotton, who is later to puncture Mr. Pickwick's archeological reputation.

"Let that honourable Pickwickian who cried 'No' so loudly come forward and deny it if he could." Deny what? Or how? Since his vociferous exception was taken to nothing in particular, "it" will be hard to retract. On the other hand, there would seem to be no way for anyone to step forward as the confessed dissenter and, in the very process of doing so, "deny" the admitted act of dissent. Yet this, as we will see, is exactly what comes to pass through a semantic evacuation of the charge itself. First Mr. Pickwick adopts the oratorical pose of *praeteritio*—a blatant form of hypocrisy under rhetorical sanction—and proceeds on that well-worn model, "I will hardly lower and demean myself by telling you the following." Dickens devoted most of a long paragraph in the *Sketches* to this same trick of "parliamentary style" ("Our Parish," chap. 4), and we are to laugh just as hard at Pickwick: "Who was it that cried 'No'? (Enthusiastic cheering.) Was it some vain and disappointed man—he would not say haberdasher (loud cheers)." And so we do indeed see Pickwick "come forward and deny" what, only by so doing, would he get said at all. Not only rhetoric, however, but definition itself will soon be at stake in this scene. Pickwick next fires against Blotton with the doubled barrels of his rhetoric, terming Blotton's "mode" of attack "vile and calumnious," to which Blotton retorts on the principle of an eye for an eye, adjective for adjective, that Pickwick's counterattack against his accusation is itself a "false and scurrilous accusation." The carefully paired epithets are balanced against each other in an overarmed rhetorical standoff, and the linguistic broil is further escalated when Blotton's combative language revealingly divides one of his own sentences against itself by saying of Pickwick that the "hon. gent. was a humbug. (Immense confusion and loud cries of 'Chair' and 'Order.')" This dis-"order" is a kind of verbal anarchy, an "immense confusion" in the very idea of meaning. With it we have one of the first and clearest examples in the novel of self-incriminating rhetoric, for to call a man first "honourable" and then a "humbug" is in its own to speak duplicitously, to utter humbug. Of course "hon." is a null adjective in this context, endorsed uncritically by the Pickwickians like the title "gentleman," voided of meaning, but then so, we find, are almost all their words. The "order" just cried for is restored only when the accusatory style is neutralized by a remarkable evasion. After the charge of "humbug," the chairman "felt it his imperative duty to demand of the honourable gentleman, whether he had used the expression which had just escaped him in a common sense." But there is no room for "common sense" in this rhetorical fray. Words seem to have a deceptive life of their own; they are not called forth, they "escape," and once out in the open they defy literal interpretation. Personally, he vows with yet another doublet, Mr. Blotton "held the highest regard and esteem" for Mr. Pickwick; he had only "used the word in its Pickwickian sense . . . he had merely considered him a humbug in a Pickwickian point of view. (Hear, hear.)" Hear that indeed. Mr. Pickwick fast avails himself of the same shelter, explaining, of course, that his own remarks "had been merely tended to bear a Pickwickian construction. (Cheers.)" So before we learn any other meaning for "Pickwickian," we understand it stylistically, so to speak, as a kind of verbal nullification, a retroactive euphemism under whose aegis words are able to retreat from their own consequences.

The chapter has drawn to its inevitable crisis. Here we have a vain and evasive use of language that is the final symptom of the word's degeneration, deepening the stylistic parody which began with the novel's first sentence. Characterized from the start by writing rather thoroughly inoculated against meaning, the injection of the magic word "Pickwickian" into the chapter at this point simply reduces to the absurd a style that has never steered very far clear of it. And it is a perfect stroke for Dickens to choose as the word highlighted by the debate the very word which best characterizes it. The style of the first chapter and its culmination, in its leaden elevation and the hypocritical dodges of its semantic double standard, is indeed *humbug prose*. It is a style in which there is always more saying going on than meaning and which, when cornered, admits to meaning not even the little it seems to mean. This is language on the edge of disintegration, and only the control of comedy can hold it together. Sarcasm salvages the hypocrisy of Pickwickian double talk and makes a comic virtue out of saying the reverse of what is meant. "Mr. Pickwick felt much gratified by the fair, candid, and full explanation of his honourable friend," and Dickens, in the naive guise of editor, mocks this ploy by himself facetiously treating the conclusion of the debate as the arrival "at such a highly satisfactory and intelligible point." Early in this chapter, taking the hint from Fielding, I made a distinction between the verbal affectations of "vanity" on the one hand and "hypocrisy" on the other, a distinction it is now time to retract. The point of *Pickwick*'s first chapter is that the two faults overlap. The Pickwickians' humbug prose is more than just bogus eloquence; they are looking for a sort of verbal impunity, the middle ground between saying and meaning which "Pickwickian" implies. They think that by loosening the bond between saying and meaning, for the purposes of lofty and libelous speech, they are taking a merely rhetorical liberty. But Dickens wants to show us that the bond between expression and intention is not simply stylistic, but ethical as well; and that by forgetting this, the Pickwickians become not just pompous rhetoricians but moral humbugs.

The large resonance I am suggesting for this debate in the first chapter is further argued, it seems to me, by the fact that Dickens has composed two later scenes that echo the two keynotes struck in the first chapter— first the specific use of the term "humbug" and then the general misuse of vocabulary in its Pickwickian "definition." During the ice-skating fiasco in chapter 30, we hear an indignant Mr. Pickwick himself use the term "humbug" against a fellow Pickwickian in a "common sense" this time, capable of restatement with an unequivocal synonym. When Mr. Winkle's pretense of knowing how to skate is exposed, Pickwick "uttered in a low but distinct and emphatic tone these remarkable words: 'Your're a humbug, sir' " (chap. 30)—words "remarkable" for nothing so much as the contrast with how we have heard them before. Now plain-speaking is the intention, and when Winkle asks "A what?" Pickwick offers clarification, as if remembering his own complicity in the initial meaningless use of the term: "A humbug, sir. I will speak plainer if you wish it. An impostor, sir."

This dominant chord of Pickwickian semantics then finds an absurd comic transposition two chapters later, reminding us that we are never far from the collapse of verbal communication admonished against by the book's chaotic opening. The episode, in which Mrs. Raddle confronts Bob Sawyer about his bill, is full of Dickensian word play and implied linguistic commentary of all sorts. When a question about how long the bill has "been running" is posed, the narrator stokes the hidden metaphor until the bill becomes "the most extraordinary locomotive engine that the genius of man ever produced. It would keep on running during the longest lifetime, without ever once stopping of its own accord" (chap. 32). Mrs. Raddle herself turns the language of definition and tautology to her own advantage, though with a facile reliance on mere "calling" to corroborate character that reminds us of the questionable title "gent." in the first chapter: "every gentleman as has ever lived here, has kept his word, sir, as of course anybody as calls himself a gentleman, does." But the keeping of words in any kind of order is about to meet an impossible challenge. Ben Allen interrupts to call Mrs. Raddle an "unreasonable woman" and then at once opts for that standard "Pickwickian" dodge: "I didn't make use of the word in any invidious sense, ma'am." The honorific "ma'am" and the accusation itself are of course at odds here the way "honourable gentleman" and "humbug" were in the first debate, but this scene has gone even farther into semantic mayhem than the opening chapter. We are meant to be just as confounded as Mr. Allen when we discover that Mrs. Raddle, who has in fact recently referred to herself as "a hard-working and industrious woman," takes her objection not to the adjective "unreasonable" but, with sublime unreasonableness, to the other "invidious" word: " 'I beg your parding, young man,' demanded Mrs. Raddle in a louder and more imperative tone. 'But who do you call a woman? Did you make that remark to me, sir?' "

Long before this ironic echo of the first chapter, this parody of a parody, there is another more important extension of those linguistic themes with which the novel began. This is the famous scene in which Pickwick asks Mrs. Bardell whether it is "a much greater expense to keep two people, than to keep one?" (chap. 12), and she misreads the plans to make Mr. Weller his manservant as a proposal of marriage to herself. Steven Marcus has written that "Mr. Pickwick's use of the language is literal, abstractly symbolic, and almost entirely denotative and normative," that Pickwick "does not yet understand language, and his innocence is primarily a linguistic innocence." This is what we might call his comic rather than his tragic flaw, and it drives the novel to its first major crisis. When Mr. Pickwick speaks, as he is unaccustomed to, in metaphor, fate seems to retaliate, and Mrs. Bardell, who knows his characteristic use of language, takes him literally. Envisioning Sam as his valet, he alludes to "the person I have in my eye," and catastrophe follows because of the attendant literal circumstance that he "looked very hard at Mrs. Bardell" at the time. Language itself is bested, and when Mrs. Bardell faints publicly into the hero's arms, he is "struck motionless and speechless." So Mr. Pickwick is tried and sentenced to prison for breach of promise, dramatizing in an oblique way the first revenge of imagination in Dickens outside of the interpolated tales. For this over-spoken gentleman, who from the first page of *Pickwick Papers* represented a use of language held culpable by Dickens for not meaning what it said, is here punished—in an ironic reversal of guilt and innocence— for accidentally not saying what he meant.

The adjective "Pickwickian," as brought forward by the debate, has found its way into modern usage in two senses, both the verbal and the personal. It can suggest some esoteric or eccentric sense of a word's meaning, occasionally associated with the rhetorical license of parliamentary or congressional oratory, a definition owed specifically to the first chapter of *Pickwick*, or it can refer to the qualities of simplicity and benevolence which Mr. Pickwick himself comes to embody as the novel unfolds. The two meanings are simultaneous in the opening chapter; or rather, "Pickwickian" only exists for us at this point as a stylistic label, for words understood in no "common sense." Indeed, throughout *Pickwick Papers* the Pickwickian style and the Pickwickian personality remain much more closely fused than either modern vocabulary or Dickens criticism seems to have recognized. Style is the man, and helps us to understand the man. The opening chapter may be primarily a stylistic experiment, a full-dress verbal *tour de force*, but so are many things in *Pickwick*, many things in Dickens generally. His characterization only benefits from such experiments, for they are the ways mentality and imagination find portrayal.

The Violent Effigy: A Study of Dickens's Imagination

John Carey

INTRODUCTION

Dickens is infinitely greater than his critics. The point needs stressing because critics can, with unusual ease, appear intelligent at his expense. Shortcomings, ultimately irrelevant, in his own intelligence account for this, plus the presence of worthless elements in even his best novels. What makes him unique is the power of his imagination and, in Kafka's phrase, its "great, careless prodigality"—careless, because extending itself typically into odd angles and side-alleys of his subject. To take a single example, when Mrs. Jarley's caravan rolls into town one sultry afternoon, Dickens's narration passes swiftly over houses, inns and bystanders and lights on some insects: "the flies, drunk with moist sugar in the grocer's shop, forgot their wings and briskness, and baked to death in dusty corners of the window." Festive and forlorn in rapid succession, they are very Dickensian flies, and it took Dickens to notice them at all.

The second fact to bear in mind is that Dickens is essentially a comic writer. The urge to conceal this, noticeable in some recent studies, can probably be traced to a suspicion that comedy, compared to tragedy, is light. Comedy is felt to be artificial and escapist; tragedy, toughly real. The opposite view seems more accurate. Tragedy is tender to man's dignity and self-importance, and preserves the illusion that he is a noble creature. Comedy uncovers the absurd truth, which is why people are so afraid of being laughed at in real life. As we shall see, once Dickens starts laughing nothing is safe, from Christianity to dead babies. His instinctive response to tragic pretensions may be gauged from an early letter, in which he announces that he has just moved into a hotel room previously occupied by the celebrated actor Charles Kean:

> I am sitting at this instant in his wery chair!!! I was bursting into the water-closet this morning, when a man's voice (of tragic quality) cried out—"There is somebody here." It was his. I shall reserve this for his Biographer.

Humankind's attempts to surround its puny concerns with gravity and decorum seemed to Dickens hilarious. Contemplating them he was overcome, he confessed, by that "perverse and unaccountable feeling which causes a heart-broken man at a dear friend's funeral to see something irresistibly comical in a red-nosed or one-eyed undertaker." Institutions and organizations and the structure of government upon which civilized society depends provoked him to scornful merriment. Yet the effect of his mirth is curiously not sardonic. His investigation of fools and hypocrites radiates enjoyment. His comic figures claim our affection. The laughter, though devastating, revels in what it exposes. It is this crucial aspect of his genius that is omitted by moralistic critics who see in Quilp only "a study in sadistic malice" (the phrase is from Dr. and Mrs. Leavis's *Dickens the Novelist*), or in the portrayal of Fagin only "horror at the corruption of innocence."

Dickens's inability to take institutions seriously is one reason for believing that we shall miss his real greatness if we persist in regarding him primarily as a critic of society. There are other reasons, too. As has often been remarked, he warmly favoured the hanging of disaffected natives in Jamaica and the blowing of mutinous sepoys from the mouths of cannon. In America he regretted the "melancholy absurdity" of giving blacks the vote, and objected besides that "exhalations not the most agreeable arise from a number of coloured people got together." These traces of prejudice, though venial when placed in their historical perspective, are not encouraging if one wishes to recommend Dickens for his enlightened social views. A more serious drawback, in this respect, is his inconsistency. He reflects the popular mind in that he is able to espouse diametrically opposed opinions with almost equal vehemence. He urges compassion for the occupants of prison cells, yet feels outraged when convicts are given better accommodation than impoverished working men. In the *History of England* he wrote for his children he includes a lecture on the wickedness of warfare which, he insists, can never be "otherwise than horrible." But when he recounts the havoc King Richard wrought among the Saracens "with twenty English pounds of English steel," or celebrates the exploits of "bold Admiral Blake" who "brought the King of Portugal to his senses," it appears that the horrible side of war has somehow slipped out of sight. "He was very much a man of one idea," affirmed his friend John Forster, "each having its turn of absolute predominance." Almost any aberration, indeed, from drunkenness to wife-beating can be found eliciting at various times both Dickens's mournfulness and his amused toleration. It is noticeable, too, that though he customarily laments the inadequacy of the successive systems of Poor Relief, he congratulates those who would never deign to accept it. In *Our Mutual Friend* persons seeking public charity are likened to "vermin," while old Betty Higden, fleeing it, remains a "decent person." By encouraging this distinction Dickens could hardly ease the lot of the destitute, yet consideration for the destitute was commonly his cry. It seems clear that in reality he believed in "independent self-reliance" just as firmly as Lord Decimus Tite Barnacle, yet Lord Decimus is ridiculed for adhering to that belief in *Little Dorrit*. It has caused some surprise, too, considering the picture of industrialism presented in *Hard Times*, that Dickens should have paid tribute at a public banquet the year before the novel appeared to

> the great compact phalanx of the people, by whose industry, perseverance, and intelligence, and their result in money-wealth such places as Birmingham, and many others like it, have arisen.

These inconsistencies, and they are widespread, would be damaging if Dickens were prized as a social theorist. But they are symptomatic of a flexibility which, if he is regarded as an imaginative writer, becomes vital. It is this that impels him to see his dominant objects and landscapes—his locks and cages and crumbling mansions, his effigies and corpses and amputated limbs—in sharply contrasting lights. Precisely relevant here is Keats's argument about the poetic character: that it is essentially amoral and unprincipled: "It has as much delight in conceiving an Iago as an Imogen." Dickens, though more apologetically, recognized in himself the same bond between imagination and inconsistency: "the wayward and unsettled feeling which is part (I suppose) of the tenure on which one holds an imaginative life."

Regarding Dickens as an imaginative writer does not entail marking down his work as a sort of fanciful vacation from "real" experience. That might, admittedly, be the case if we were to accept the pronouncements about literature and reality offered in Mr. Robert Garis's influential study *The Dickens Theatre*. Mr. Garis regrets, in the first place, Dickens's tendency to "show off his style." It strikes him as an offence against "*good taste* and *good manners*," and would not be acceptable, he intimates, in the pieces of prose composition submitted by his own students. But his more substantial reason for deciding that Dickens is not a "serious" writer like George Eliot is that we are not allowed to see the "inner life" of his characters. We are not invited to analyse their motives or attend upon their cogitations. This disqualifies Dickens as a serious writer, Mr. Garis explains, for "we expect serious drama and serious literature in general to enact an approach towards human beings which accords with the way we approach the people we know in real life, when we are taking them seriously."

That Mr. Garis has a very cramped idea of literature will be apparent, yet something like it hovers behind many of the complaints about Dickens's "unreality." The power of imaginative literature to refashion the seen world, to fracture and recast the reader's circumscribed notions about what constitutes the "real," seems to have no place in Mr. Garis's calculations. The reader, he supposes, will be secure in the conviction that he has exhausted the available ways of "taking people seriously" before he starts his book, and he will expect the author not to venture outside these. Literature, on this reckoning, will restrict itself to imitating those views of other people's affairs, satisfying both to our curiosity and to our self-esteem, which acquaintances occasionally favour us with in moments of confidence.

Yet Mr. Garis, in denying Dickens's novels the status of serious literature, probably does them less of a disservice than the critics who labour to unearth their "meanings," as if great works of art were to be cherished, in the last resort, for whatever moral droppings can be coaxed from them. The fruits of this approach often provide the strongest argument for its discontinuance. Mr. A. E. Dyson, for instance, proposes as the kernel of *David Copperfield* the information that "the best marriages are between two deep yet not passionately tormented friends of opposite sexes." The objection to this is not so much its banality as that it belongs to a species of discourse and a mode of thought quite distinct from that in which Dickens's powers operate upon us. In consequence it is ludicrously unlike the gains which are actually to be reaped from entering the imaginative world of *David Copperfield*.

The main subject of the following [section], then, will not be Dickens's morals, social criticism or alleged inferiority to George Eliot, but the workings of his imagination.

DICKENS AND VIOLENCE

In Dickens's travel book *Pictures from Italy* he describes how on February 21, 1845, he, thirty-one guides, six saddled ponies and a handful of tourists made an ascent of Mount Vesuvius. The local people warned him it was the wrong time of year, especially for a night ascent. Snow and ice lay thick on the summit. Characteristically he ignored the advice of these "croakers," as he called them. His wife and another lady and gentleman had to be carried in litters. Dickens went on foot. As the party approached the top, blundering in the darkness over the broken ground, half suffocated with sulphurous fumes, Dickens's description of the sheets of fire, and the red-hot stones and cinders flying into the air "like feathers," becomes more and more excited. "There is something," he relates, "in the fire and the roar, that generates an irresistible desire to get nearer to it." Not that this desire was felt by the others. While Dickens, a guide and one other crawled to the edge of the crater, the rest of the party cowered below in the hot ashes yelling to them of the danger. "What with their noise," writes Dickens, and what with the trembling of the thin crust of ground, that seems about to open underneath our feet and plunge us in the burning gulf below (which is the real danger, if there be any); and what with the flashing of the fire in our faces, and the shower of red hot ashes that is raining down, and the choking smoke and sulphur; we may well feel giddy and irrational, like drunken men. But we contrive to climb up to the brim, and look down, for a moment, into the Hell of boiling fire below. Then, we all three come rolling down; blackened and singed, and scorched, and hot, and giddy: and each with his dress alight in half-a-dozen places.

On the way down one of the tourists falls—"skimming over the white ice, like a cannon-ball"—and almost at the same moment two of the guides come rolling past. Dickens is offended, unreasonably enough, by the cries of dismay the other guides send up. Luckily all three casualties are eventually recovered, none of them badly injured.

The anecdote is typical of Dickens. Typical of his disregard for other people—his "hard and aggressive" nature, "impetuous" and "overbearing," in Forster's words; typical of his enormous and unquenchable desire for activity, for something which would use up his dynamic energies; and typical of his fascination with fire as a beautiful and terrible destroyer, a visible expression of pure violence. In Rome on Easter Sunday he watches St. Peter's stuck all over with fireworks, and records his sense of exultation at seeing great, red fires suddenly burst out from every part of the building, so that the black groundwork of the dome "seemed to grow transparent as an eggshell." Railway trains and steamboats excite him as moving fires. In his American travel book he describes the engine which takes them across the country as a thirsty monster, a dragon, yelling and panting along its rails, scattering a shower of sparks in all directions. Crossing the Atlantic on board the *Britannia* in 1840 he was impressed at night by the way the light gleamed out from every chink and aperture about the decks "as though the ship were filled with fire in hiding, ready to burst through any outlet, wild with its resistless power of death and ruin."

In *Dombey and Son* the railway train becomes a fiery animal with "red eyes, bleared and dim in the daylight," which smashes Carker when he unwisely steps on its track. It "struck him limb from limb, and licked his stream of life up with its fiery heat, and cast his mutilated fragments in the air." But fire had been used to express violence in the novels before this. In *Oliver Twist*, in the scene where Nancy suddenly braves Fagin and Sikes, the signs of human passion—Nancy stamping her foot and going white with rage—are reinforced when she seizes Fagin's club and flings it into the fire, "with a force," Dickens notes, "that brought some of the glowing coals whirling out into the room." It's as if the human actors are inadequate to embody the violence of Dickens's idea, and he has to bring in fire to express it. This scene is recalled when Sikes murders Nancy. Afterwards he lights a fire and thrusts his club into it. Dickens vivifies the moment with an incandescent detail: "There was hair upon the end, which blazed and shrunk into a light cinder, and, caught by the air, whirled up the chimney." Running away from his murder, Sikes suddenly comes upon a conflagration:

> The broad sky seemed on fire. Rising into the air with showers of sparks, and rolling one above the other, were sheets of flame, lighting the atmosphere for miles around, and driving clouds of smoke in the direction where he stood.

It is, in fact, a house on fire, and Dickens fills in the circumstances with his usual enthusiasm for such subjects—the "molten lead and iron" pouring white-hot onto the ground, and so on. The episode seems an arbitrary intrusion, quite redundant so far as the plot is concerned, unless one sees it as a projection of the violence and torment within Sikes. Similarly in Peggotty's abode, when David Copperfield comes upon the lustful Steerforth snarling about "this Devil's bark of a boat," the malcontent seizes a piece of wood from the fire and strikes out of it "a train of red-hot sparks that went careering up the little chimney, and roaring out into the air"— just to impress upon the reader the dangerous state he's in. Fire spells peril as well as passion. In *Bleak House,* Esther first comes upon Ada and Richard "standing near a great, loud-roaring fire" with a screen "interposed between them and it." Our sense of destruction reaching towards youth and beauty becomes definite when this fire is given "red eyes" like a "Chancery lion."

The violence of a mob, which always intensely excites Dickens, is repeatedly conveyed through its fiery antics. In *Barnaby Rudge* the molten lead on Bill Sikes's house recurs in the magnificent scene where the rioters burn down Mr. Haredale's mansion:

> There were men who cast their lighted torches in the air, and suffered them to fall upon their heads and faces, blistering their skin with deep unseemly burns. There were men who rushed up to the fire, and paddled in it with their hands as if in water; and others who were restrained by force from plunging in, to gratify their deadly longing. On the skull of one drunken lad—not twenty, by his looks—who lay upon the ground with a bottle to his mouth, the lead from the roof came streaming down in a shower of liquid fire, white-hot; melting his head like wax.

Later in the novel, when Newgate prison is stormed, the mob build a fire against the main gate, and men can be seen in the middle of the flames trying to prise down the red-hot metal with crowbars. The same mob howls and exults as Lord Mansfield's Law library, with its priceless collection of manuscripts, goes up in flames. Seeing the violence directed against a prison and the law should remind us how much Dickens, the Dickens who was to write *Little Dorrit* and *Bleak House,* is imaginatively on the side of the rioters and wreckers, despite the dutiful expressions of dismay with which he surrounds the scene. "I have let all the prisoners out of Newgate, burnt down Lord Mansfield's, and played the very devil," he wrote exultingly to Forster, "I feel quite smoky." Similarly in *A Tale of Two Cities* the chateau, symbol of aristocratic oppression, is fired in a scene reminiscent of the St. Peter's firework display. At first the chateau begins "to make itself strangely visible, by some light of its own, as though it were growing luminous." Soon flames burst out of the windows, rents and splits branch out in the solid walls "like crystallization," and lead and iron boil in the marble basin of the fountain. The "illuminated village" rings its bells for joy.

Even when a mob can't actually burn things, Dickens gives it bits of fire to signify its rage and frenzy. The mob which hunts down Sikes is "a struggling current of angry faces, with here and there a glaring torch to light them up." Similarly, if a character can't be supplied with a blazing house to symbolize his violence, the fire can be conveyed in the imagery. When, in *Little Dorrit,* Mrs. Clennam is eventually goaded beyond endurance by Rigaud, she defies him, Dickens says, "with the set expression of her face all torn away by the explosion of her passion, and with a bursting from every rent feature of the smouldering fire so long pent up." Mrs. Clennam, like the steamship *Britannia,* shows fire at every porthole. Introducing Krook, the villainous rag and bottle dealer in *Bleak House,* Dickens draws attention to "the breath issuing in visible smoke from his mouth, as if he were on fire within." Unlike Mrs. Clennam and the *Britannia,* Krook does, of course, literally explode later in the novel, leaving nothing but oily soot on the walls of his room. Dickens regularly spoke of his own industry and his need for strenuous exercise in the same fiery terms. "I blaze away, wrathful and red-hot," he reported, at work on *The Chimes.* "If I couldn't walk fast and far I should just explode."

Great Expectations is another novel which plays with fire. The blacksmith's furnace, with its red-hot sparks and murky shadows, and its two giants, Joe and Orlick, one good, one bad, is an imaginative touchstone in the book. Walking home at night Pip notices the furnace "flinging a path of fire across the road." Out on the marshes the torches of the search party are intensely seen. "The torches we carried, dropped great blotches of fire upon the track, and I could see those, too, lying smoking and flaring. . . . Our lights warmed the air about us with their pitchy blaze." Pip's sister is murderously struck down by a blow on the head at a moment when, Dickens notes, "her face was turned towards the fire." Pip sees the face of Estella's mother "as if it were all disturbed by fiery air," like a face passing behind "a bowl of flaming spirits in a darkened room." Dickens intends this as an index, of course, of the criminal passions that lurk within. Miss Havisham goes up in flames, "shrieking, with a whirl of fire blazing all about her, and soaring at least as many feet above her head as she was high." She had, of course, tempted providence by becoming so fond of Joe's blacksmith song about fire "soaring higher," which Pip taught her. The image of her rouged corpse with fire bursting from its head had so strong an appeal, it seems, that Dickens attached it, rather gratuitously, to Magwitch as well. The disguise Magwitch contrives for leaving London includes a "touch of powder," which suggests to Pip

> the probable effect of rouge upon the dead; so awful was the manner in which everything in him, that it was most desirable to repress, started through the thin layer of pretence, and seemed to come blazing out at the crown of his head.

Miss Havisham on fire, and the fire of Joe's smithy, fuse in Pip's mind. Delirious, after his own narrow escape from being burned in Orlick's lime-kiln, he dreams of an iron furnace in a corner of his room, and a voice calling that Miss Havisham is burning within. Pip's sick fancy recalls Esther Summerson's dream, striking in one so uninflammable, that she is a bead on a "flaming necklace" in "black space," praying to be released from "the dreadful thing."

Joe is a good character, of course: the repository of those natural, human affections that Dickens dwells upon with such patronizing approval. His association with fire warns us that in Dickens's imaginative landscape fire is not simply the sign of violence and destruction. It is a leading characteristic of Dickens's mind that he is able to see almost everything from two opposed points of view. In his thinking about society this often makes him look confused and hypocritical, as we have noted. Even a major Dickensian property like the prison is viewed at different times as a hideous deprivation of freedom and as a snug retreat from the world. Some of the prisoners released from Newgate by the mob, creep back and "lounge about the old place." For them it's home. So, too, with fire. A violent, though enthralling destroyer on the one hand, it also becomes, in the innumerable cosy Dickensian inn parlours with their blazing logs, a natural accompaniment to comfort and security. The fire of Joe Gargery's forge represents the safety of the childhood home. It flings a path of fire across Pip's road as a friendly, domestic warning to turn him aside from his ruinous ambitions. With something of the same purpose, no doubt, it tries to cremate Miss Havisham, who has done her best to make Pip rebel against the values of home and fireside.

The episode in *The Old Curiosity Shop* where Nell and her grandfather make a brief excursion into the industrial midlands neatly illustrates Dickens's two ways of looking at fire. A lurid glare in the sky hangs over the neighbourhood, and the wanderers meet a factory worker, imagined by Dickens as a sort of smoky goblin, who lets them spend a comfortable night in the ashes beside his furnace. This touching scene is strangely out of key with the way the factory is described. It is said to be full of the "deafening" noise of hammers. Men move "like demons" among the flame and smoke, "tormented by the burning fires," and drag from the white-hot furnace doors sheets of clashing steel, "emitting an insupportable heat, and a dull deep light like that which reddens in the eyes of savage beasts." The factory worker proves communicative about his own particular fire. It has been alive, he says, as long as he has. He crawled among its ashes as a baby. It's his "book" and his "memory": he sees faces and scenes among its red-hot coals. In Dickens's terms this marks him as a good character. Only virtuous people in the novels practise this species of fire watching. We recall Lizzie Hexam in *Our Mutual Friend* who develops her imagination by looking at red-hot embers, in strong contrast to her selfish brother Charlie who wants to better himself by reading books. The fire in this episode, then, is both nurse and destroyer; the fire of home and the fire of Hell.

Dickens, who saw himself as the great prophet of cosy, domestic virtue, purveyor of improving literature to the middle classes, never seems to have quite reconciled himself to the fact that violence and destruction were the most powerful stimulants to his imagination. To the end of his career he continues to insert the sickly scenes of family fun, and seriously asks us to accept them as the positives in his fiction. The savages and the cynics, the Quilps and the Scrooges, who have all the vitality, are, in the end, tritely punished or improbably converted. His public championship of domestic bliss became so natural to him that he persisted in it even when his own actions wildly belied it. Starting a new magazine in 1859, he seriously proposed to call it *Household Harmony*, despite the fact that he had recently separated from his wife, had personally announced in the newspapers that she was an unsatisfactory mother disliked by all her children, and was himself having an affair with the actress Ellen Ternan. When Forster pointed out that the proposed title would be met with derision, Dickens was surprised and irritated.

With so much of his imaginative self invested in his violent and vicious characters, and so much of the self he approved of vowed to the service of home and family life, Dickens has a particular weakness for villains whose express intention it is to smash up happy homes. Silas Wegg in *Our Mutual Friend* walks to the Boffin house each evening in order to gloat over it like an evil genius, exulting in his power "to strip the roof off the inhabiting family like the roof of a house of cards." It was, says Dickens, "a treat which had a charm for Silas Wegg." For Dickens too, to judge from the vigour of the image. Steerforth, in *David Copperfield*, smashes the pure Peggotty home by seducing Little Em'ly. The old converted boat in which the Peggottys pursue their blameless existence is blown down on the night of the storm which drowns Steerforth. David finds him next morning, lying appropriately "among the ruins of the home he had wronged." Even Gabriel Varden in *Barnaby Rudge* indulges in some miniature home-smashing. Mrs. Varden has been in the habit of putting her voluntary contributions to the Protestant cause in a collecting box shaped like a little red-brick dwelling house with a yellow roof. When the riots show how mistaken her allegiance has been, Gabriel throws the little house on the floor and crushes it with his heel. So much for little houses, militant Protestants and meddling females. Apart from the home, the main haunt of Dickensian snugness is the inn. Of the Maypole Inn in *Barnaby Rudge* he writes: "All bars are snug places, but the Maypole's was the very snuggest, cosiest and completest bar, that ever the wit of man devised." A rhapsodic description of its neat rows of bottles in oaken pigeonholes, and its snowy loaves of sugar follows. It's appropriate that this veritable temple of snugness and security should be selected by Dickens for one of his wildest home-wrecking scenes. When the mob arrive at the Maypole, equipped with their usual flaring torches, they smash the glass, turn all the liquor taps on, hack the cheeses to bits, break open the drawers, saw down the inn sign and are divided in opinion whether to hang the landlord or burn him alive. Dickens's tone is predominantly comic, and there is no mistaking the pleasure with which he elaborates the details of pillage and destruction.

Early in his career Dickens began to produce narratives in which the figures who are regarded with the most intense fellow feeling are the murderers. He habitually speaks about murderers' mental habits with extraordinary self-confidence, as if he were one himself. The consequences of murder, he asserts in *Bleak House,* are always hidden from the murderer behind a "gigantic dilation" of his victim, and rush upon him only when the blow is struck. This "always happens when a murder is done." Similarly he is adamant that murderers like Sikes, who do not give "the faintest indication of a better nature," really do exist. "That the fact is so, I am sure." From where, we wonder, could he get such certainty? The conformist part of him repudiated his murderers with horror. But the artist delved with fascination into their responses, and particularly into how they feel when hunted down or at bay. In *Master Humphrey's Clock,* for instance, we find a first-person narrative in which Dickens casts himself in the role of a child slayer, telling what it was like to murder his brother's son. He stabs him in a garden, and as he does so he is struck not only by the look in his victim's eyes, but also by the eyes which seem to watch him, even in the drops of water on the leaves. "There were eyes in everything." He buries the child in a piece of ground which is to be newly turfed, but when the lawn has been completed over the grave he is haunted by visions of the child's hand or his foot or his head sticking up through the grass. He sits and watches the secret grave all day. "When a servant walked across it, I felt as if he must sink in; when he had passed, I looked to see that his feet had not worn the edges." Eventually he has a table set out on the lawn, and puts his chair directly over the grave, so that no one can disturb it. When he is entertaining some friends at this table, though, two great bloodhounds come bounding into the garden and circle about it excitedly, ending up snuffing at the earth directly under his chair. As his friends dragged him away, he says, "I saw the angry dogs tearing at the earth and throwing it up into the air like water." Bill Sikes, like this murderer, is haunted by eyes after his slaying of Nancy, and it is his dog's eyes gleaming from behind the chimney pot that send him plunging to his death. " 'The eyes again!' he cried in an unearthly screech." Similarly the elder Mr. Rudge, who has little to occupy himself with in the novel besides galloping furiously through the night, is brought to life for a moment when Dickens shows him remembering the circumstances of the murder he committed. He recalls how his victim's face went stiff, "and so fell idly down with upturned eyes, like the dead stags' he had often peeped at when a little child: shrinking and shuddering . . . and clinging to an apron as he looked." The flash of childhood recollection at the moment of murder is instantly convincing: the one convincing sentence about Mr. Rudge in the entire book. Again, Jonas Chuzzlewit isn't generally a figure we feel Dickens has managed to get inside. He is viewed from above as a vile, cringing specimen with whom we can all feel virtuously disgusted. But in the few pages where he commits murder he suddenly becomes the recipient of Dickens's imaginative sympathy. The details of the blotched, stained, mouldering room with its gurgling water-pipes in which Jonas locks himself are intently conveyed. When he unlocks the long-unused door in order to slink off and murder Montague Tigg, Dickens makes the reader attend to his tiniest movements:

> He put the key into the lock, and turned it. The door resisted for a while, but soon came stiffly open; mingling with the sense of fever in his mouth, a taste of rust, and dust, and earth, and rotting wood.

We know even what the murderer's mouth tastes like. After the murder, Jonas keeps fancying himself creeping back through the undergrowth to peer at the corpse, "startling the very flies that were thickly sprinkled all over it, like heaps of dried currants." The simile—added in the manuscript—shows Dickens's imagination entrapped by the scene, like Jonas's. But Jonas has to commit murder to get promoted from the status of a routine Dickensian villain and earn himself a page or two of great literature. No other human experience—least of all the positive human experiences, like being in love—will arouse Dickens to such intense imaginative sympathy as the experience of being a murderer. One of his most vivid studies in this mode is Fagin on trial for his life—a very different matter from Fagin in the death cell a few pages later, where he is transformed into a gibbering wretch for the unctuous Oliver to pity. Fagin's sensations in the courtroom are recorded as scrupulously as Jonas Chuzzlewit's:

> He looked up into the gallery again. Some of the people were eating, and some fanning themselves with handkerchiefs; for the crowded place was very hot. There was one young man sketching his face in a little notebook. He wondered whether it was like, and looked on when the artist broke his pencil point, and made

> another with his knife, as any idle spectator might have done. . . .
> There was an old fat gentleman on the bench, too, who had gone
> out, some half an hour before, and now come back. He wondered
> within himself whether this man had been to get his dinner, what
> he had had, and where he had had it. . . . He fell to counting the
> iron spikes before him, and wondering how the head of one had
> been broken off, and whether they would mend it or leave it as
> it was.

Here the hypersensitivity, combined with a strange feeling of detachment, common to people who find themselves at the centre of an accident, are conveyed by Dickens with absolute seriousness of intent and perfect artistic honesty. The temptation to use Fagin as the occasion for lofty moralizing is withstood, though Dickens succumbs to it soon afterwards. Oliver's reactions after the trial are, by contrast, wholly preposterous: " 'Oh! God forgive this wretched man!' cried the boy with a burst of tears. . . . Oliver nearly swooned after this frightful scene, and was so weak that for an hour or more, he had not the strength to walk." Dickens could furnish this type of saintly confection in unlimited quantities, but the triumphs of his art stick out of it like islands, and there is no difficulty about distinguishing them.

Before Oliver's visit Fagin's mind is seized with the details of how murderers are disposed of: "With what a rattling noise the drop went down; and how suddenly they changed, from strong and vigorous men to dangling heaps of clothes." A keen interest in the different methods of executing men, and the precise manner of each, was another aspect of Dickens's preoccupation with violence. The guillotine stands in the foreground of *A Tale of Two Cities*. Charles Darnay, in the condemned cell, realizes he has never seen it, and questions about it keep thrusting themselves into his mind: "How high it was from the ground, how many steps it had, where he would be stood . . . which way his face would be turned." Dickens could have enlightened him. When in Rome he went to see a man guillotined, and has left a minute account of the whole affair, from the behaviour of the various members of the crowd to the appearance of the scaffold: "An untidy, unpainted, uncouth, crazy-looking thing . . . some seven feet high, perhaps: with a tall, gallows-shaped frame rising above it, in which was the knife, charged with a ponderous mass of iron." The prisoner appears on the platform, barefoot, hands bound, the collar and neck of his shirt cut away. A young, pale man, with a small dark moustache, and dark brown hair.

> He immediately kneeled down, below the knife. His neck fitting
> into a hole, made for the purpose, in a cross plank, was shut down,
> by another plank above; exactly like the pillory. Immediately below
> him was a leather bag. And into it his head rolled instantly.
> The executioner was holding it by the hair, and walking with it

round the scaffold, showing it to the people, before one quite knew that the knife had fallen heavily, and with a rattling sound.

The head is set up on a pole—"a little patch of black and white" for "the flies to settle on." The eyes, Dickens notices, are turned up, "as if he had avoided the sight of the leathern bag." He stays on to see the scaffold washed down, observing "There was a great deal of blood," and to get a closer look at the body.

> A strange appearance was the apparent annihilation of the neck. The head was taken off so close, that it seemed as if the knife had narrowly escaped crushing the jaw, or shaving off the ear; and the body looked as if there were nothing left above the shoulder.

The eager, graphic brilliance of the writing throughout hardly prepares one for the moral stance Dickens hastily adopts at the end, complaining that the crowd were callous, and that several attempts were made to pick his pocket during the spectacle.

In July 1840 Dickens was one of the 40,000 people who witnessed the hanging of the murderer Courvoisier. Writing of it later he is again hot against the pickpockets, and stigmatizes the disgraceful behaviour of the crowd, whose motives for being there, he leaves us in no doubt, are altogether more reprehensible than his own. Opposed in principle to capital punishment, he plainly cannot admit to himself that he watches it out of curiosity, like everyone else. When Mr. and Mrs. George Manning were hanged together in 1849 on top of the Horsemonger Lane Gaol, Dickens was in attendance again to see them "turned quivering into the air." He recalls the curious difference in appearance between the two dangling bodies: "the man's, a limp, loose suit of clothes as if the man had gone out of them; the woman's, a fine shape, so elaborately corseted and artfully dressed, that it was quite unchanged in its trim appearance as it slowly swung from side to side." In Switzerland he went to see a man beheaded, and writes an account later in *Household Words*. The victim sits tied to a chair on a scaffold, and the executioner uses a huge sword loaded with quicksilver in the thick part of the blade.

It's plain that Dickens derives a considerable thrill, too, from visiting localities where executions and murders have occurred. The only thing that redeemed the city of Norwich, in his eyes, was its place of execution, "fit for a gigantic scoundrel's exit." After a tour of the prison at Venice he writes, "I had my foot upon the spot, where . . . the shriven prisoner was strangled." In the Tombs Prison in New York he has himself conducted to the yard where prisoners are hanged: "The wretched creature stands beneath the gibbet on the ground; the rope about his neck; and when the sign is given, a weight at its other end comes running down, and swings him up into the air—a corpse." Dickens preferred this method to the English—"far less degrading and indecent." By the time he visited America again, a former acquaintance of his had been able to assess its advantages. This was Professor Webster of Harvard, hanged for murdering a colleague, portions of whose body he had concealed about his lecture room. Dickens eagerly inspected the scene of the crime, sniffed the unpleasant odours of the furnace—"some anatomical broth in it I suppose"—and peered at the "pieces of sour mortality" standing around in jars. In *Sketches by Boz* he relates how he often wanders into Newgate Prison "to catch a glimpse of the whipping place, and that dark building on one side of the yard, in which is kept the gibbet with all its dreadful apparatus." Dennis the hangman in *Barnaby Rudge* provides Dickens with ample opportunity for anecdotes about the dreadful apparatus and its operation. The first feature of Dennis to which Dickens draws attention is his neck, with its great veins "swollen and starting." A neck for stretching, as Dennis himself would say, and at the end of the novel it is stretched—unlike that of the real-life Dennis, who was reprieved. Several aspects of the execution scene show that Dickens's imaginative powers have been aroused: Dennis between two officers, unable to walk for terror, his legs trailing on the ground; the room into which the prisoners are taken to have their irons struck off, so close to the gallows that they can plainly hear people in the crowd outside complaining of the crush; and the gallows itself, its black paint blistering in the sun, and "its nooses dangling . . . like loathsome garlands."

A form of violence more exotic and, to Dickens's way of thinking, more amusing than capital punishment was cannibalism, and we can see his thoughts straying towards it on several occasions. He was introduced to the subject by his nurse, Mary Weller, who used to take a fiendish delight in terrifying him with the story of a certain Captain Murderer whose practice it was to get his tender young brides to make a piecrust into which he would then chop them up, adding pepper and salt. The resultant pie he would eat, with his teeth filed sharp by the blacksmith for the occasion. He was finally thwarted by a bride who took deadly poison just before he killed her, so that after his meal he began to swell and turn blue, and went on swelling until he blew up with a loud explosion—an early version of Krook in *Bleak House*. The Fat Boy in *Pickwick Papers* has similar tendencies. He is about to consume a meat pie when he notices Mary, the pretty housemaid, sitting opposite. He leans forward, knife and fork in hand, and slowly enunciates: "I say! How nice you look." "There was enough of the cannibal in the young gentleman's eyes," Dickens remarks, "to render the compliment a double one." When Hugh in *Barnaby Rudge* has the delicious Dolly Varden and haughty Emma Haredale at his mercy, imprisoned in a closed carriage, he insists on speaking of them as delicate, tender birds, and stares into the carriage, we are told, "like an ogre into his larder." Furthermore Dickens is just as excited as Hugh and his confederates at the sight of tempting, helpless femininity, and hardly conceals the fact. "Poor Dolly! Do what she would, she only looked the better for it, and tempted them the more. When her eyes flashed angrily, and her ripe lips slightly parted, to give her rapid breathing vent, who could resist it?" Not Dickens, we gather, who is evidently salivating freely. It is by far his sexiest scene, which makes the cannibalistic hint more worth noting. Even Pecksniff, in *Martin Chuzzlewit*, has a cannibalistic impulse when forcing his attentions on the maidenly Mary Grant, having first got her alone in a wood, as Hugh does with Dolly Varden. Mary struggles but, Dickens comments, "she might as well have tried to free herself from the embrace of an affectionate boa-constrictor." Pecksniff clutches one of her hands, despite her attempts to pull it free, and gazes at it speculatively, "tracing the course of one delicate blue vein with his fat thumb." Eventually he holds up her little finger and asks, "in playful accents," "Shall I bite it?" But the tearful, trembling Mary doesn't get nibbled after all: Pecksniff kisses the finger and lets her have it back. In both these scenes the flutterings of female distress and the humbling of female pride are evidently so appetizing to Dickens that it is really hypocritical of him to pretend that the two men concerned are thorough rogues with whom he has no sympathy. But as usual he can preserve his moral composure only by foisting his violent imaginings onto another character, whom he then condemns for imagining them. A further edible heroine is Estella—or so it seems to Miss Havisham, who eyes the girl "with a ravenous intensity," "as though she were devouring the beautiful creature." In *Bleak House* the cannibal is the dyspeptic Vholes. Given to regarding Richard "as if he were making a lingering meal of him," he finally quits the novel with a gasp, suggesting that he has "swallowed the last morsel of his client." Opponents of legal reform defend Vholes's livelihood as though he and his relations were "minor cannibal chiefs" threatened by the abolition of cannibalism. "Make man-eating unlawful, and you starve the Vholeses!" Pip in *Great Expectations* is likewise an edible hero. Magwitch, on the marsh, is immediately tempted by his plumpness: " 'You young dog,' said the man, licking his lips, 'what fat cheeks you ha' got. . . . Darn Me if I couldn't eat 'em.' " He refrains, however, and instead tells Pip about the young man whom he is with difficulty holding back from tearing out Pip's heart and liver and eating them, roasted. Uncle Pumblechook's mouth seems to water too, at the sight of the succulent boy, and he takes pleasure in informing Pip that if he had been born a pig Dunstable the butcher would have come along and seized him under his arm and taken out his penknife from his waistcoat pocket and killed him for pork. "He would have shed your blood and had your life." "I'm a going to have your life!" declares Orlick, later in the novel, when he has Pip all ready trussed up in the sluice-house on the marsh: "He leaned forward staring at me, slowly unclenched his hand and drew it across his mouth as if his mouth watered for me." It's unusual to find a hero who has such difficulty keeping himself out of the stomachs of the other characters.

Dickens's need to express his violent and murderous instincts through his fiction can be seen, of course, as early as *Pickwick Papers*. But there the tales of savagery and slaughter are kept apart from the main narrative and

are quite untouched by the humour which pervades it. In the tale called
A Madman's Manuscript, for example, Dickens tries to imagine himself into
a demented wife-slayer: "Oh! the pleasure of stropping the razor day after
day, feeling the sharp edge, and thinking of the gash one stroke of its thin
bright edge would make!" Another of the inset tales concerns a man who
murderously avenges himself for the imprisonment of himself and his family in the Marshalsea. This, it has been conjectured, may mean that Dickens's resentment against society over his father's imprisonment is one of
the roots of his violence. But the *Pickwick* tales, particularly *A Madman's
Manuscript*, are forced and melodramatic, because Dickens's sense of humour, his greatest gift as a novelist, simply switches off when he starts to
tell them. Not until the writing of *The Old Curiosity Shop* in 1840 did he
create an embodiment of his violence who could also express his black and
anarchic laughter. This embodiment was Daniel Quilp, a magnificent invention who is able to embrace all the variations of violence Dickens can
desire.

Quilp is both dwarf and giant—a dwarf in body, with a giant's head.
For teeth he has a few discoloured fangs, and he is so filthy that when he
rubs his hands together the dirt drops off in pellets. Much of his time is
spent in driving to ludicrous excess the components of Dickensian cheer-
iness. Conviviality trails a hair-raising image of itself around with it. Food
consumption, for instance, is an indispensable accompaniment of Dickensian bliss. Quilp approaches meals with horrible ferocity. He eats hard-
boiled eggs shell and all. He devours "gigantic prawns with the heads and
tails on." He chews tobacco and watercress at the same time, and bites his
fork and spoon until they bend. He smokes pipes of hideous strength, and
forces his guests to do the same, warning them that otherwise he will put
the sealing-waxed end in the fire and rub it red-hot on their tongues. He
drinks boiling spirit, bubbling and hissing fiercely, straight from the sauce-
pan. He pinches his wife black and blue, bites her, and keeps her in constant
terror of the ingenious punishments he devises. For all this she is utterly
infatuated, and tells her lady friends that they would all marry Quilp to-
morrow if they had a chance. What's more, Dickens implies that she is
right. His corrected proofs show that Quilp was originally meant to have
a child by Sally Brass—an earnest of his exceptional virility. When amused,
Quilp screams and rolls on the floor. He delights in tormenting animals as
well as people. Finding a dog chained up he taunts it with hideous faces,
and dances round it snapping his fingers, driving it wild with rage. He
keeps a huge wooden figurehead of an admiral, sawn off at the waist, in
his room, and diverts himself by driving red-hot pokers through it. He is,
in short, a masterpiece of creative energy in comparison with whom Little
Nell and her grandfather and all their part of the novel are so much waste
paper.

Dickens was never able to create a second Quilp, but bits of him turn
up in the other novels. His treatment of his wife is reflected in Flintwinch

in *Little Dorrit*, who shakes Mrs. Flintwinch by the throat till she's black in the face, and twists her nose between his thumb and finger with all the "screw-power of his person." Cruncher in *A Tale of Two Cities*, who flings boots at his wife because she insists on saying her prayers, has Quilpish quality too. Quilp's taste for boiling spirit is something he shares with the maddened rioters in *Barnaby Rudge*. When a vintner's house catches light they lap up the scorching liquor which flows along the gutters, dropping dead by the dozen, rolling and hissing in a lake of flame, and splashing up liquid fire. Already in *Pickwick Papers*, in the story of the goblins and the sexton, the goblin king had drunk blazing liquor, his cheeks and throat growing transparent as he swallowed it. And the thrill of blistering beverages survives in *Our Mutual Friend*. Jenny Wren, saddled with a sottish parent, invents a short way with drunkards:

> When he was asleep, I'd make a spoon red-hot, and I'd have some boiling liquor bubbling in a saucepan, and I'd take it out hissing, and I'd open his mouth with the other hand—or perhaps he'd sleep with his mouth ready open—and I'd pour it down his throat, and blister it and choke him.

Quilp piercing the admiral with a red-hot poker is recalled in David Copperfield's vindictive fantasies relative to Uriah Heep. When Heep is audacious enough to fall in love with Agnes, David is tempted to seize the red-hot poker from the fire and run him through the body with it. That night he dreams so vividly that he's actually done this that he has to creep into Heep's bedroom to make sure he's still alive. Pip in *Great Expectations* recalls how Orlick drew a red-hot bar from the furnace and "made at me with it as if he were going to run it through my body." According to Dickens, one of his nurse's ghoulish tales featured a lady who slew her husband with a heated poker, so his interest in this topic began early.

Quilp is Dickens's way of avenging himself upon the sentimental set-up of *The Old Curiosity Shop*, upon all that part of his nature that revelled in angelic, plaster heroines, the deaths of little children, and touching animals. To aid her in her assault on the readers' hearts, for example, Nell has a little bird in a cage. Quilp threatens to wring its neck. He is salaciously inclined towards Little Nell herself, gloats over her blue veins and transparent skin, and invites her to become the second Mrs. Quilp. Nell trembles violently, much to Quilp's amusement. When he takes over Nell's grandfather's house, he chooses her own little bed to sleep in. Dickens offers violence to his own sexless heroine in these passages, and with aggressive enjoyment. Quilp's reduction of his wife to a mass of bruises gives an outlet to Dickens's punitive feelings towards women, which he felt the need to repress when speaking about them in his own person. In *Martin Chuzzlewit*, reporting that Jonas actually struck his wife, Dickens soars into virtuous indignation and the second person singular—always a bad sign with him: "Oh woman, God beloved in old Jerusalem! The best among us need deal lightly with thy faults." After the strain of such noble attitudes Quilp would clearly be a relief.

Both before and after 1840 Dickens attempted to create violent villains, but none ever rivals Quilp, because their violence seems stuck on, not essential to their natures, as Quilp's is. Monks, for instance, in *Oliver Twist*, has fits, writhes on the ground, foams at the mouth, bites his hands and covers them with wounds, and entertains the Bumbles to the accompaniment of thunder and lightning. But he lacks Quilp's humour and energy. On the one occasion he tries to hit Oliver, he falls over. Uriah Heep has an isolated moment of violent power. This is in the scene with David where he tells him he has Agnes's father, Mr. Wickfield, under his thumb:

> "Un—der—his thumb," said Uriah, very slowly, as he stretched out his cruel-looking hand above my table, and pressed his own thumb down upon it, until it shook, and shook the room.

Heep is a boy of fifteen, and nothing in his cringing gait or starved appearance suggests a figure who could shake a whole room merely by pressing the table with his thumb. In this instant he is about to turn into an altogether different and more violent creation, but Dickens doesn't forget himself again.

Thomas Wright notes that Quilp's mother-in-law Mrs. Jiniwin was modelled on Dickens's mother-in-law Mrs. Hogarth. Quilp was, in a sense, Dickens himself, as seen through his mother-in-law's disapproving eyes. In his last completed novel Dickens drew another violent villain, also to some degree a self-portrait—Bradley Headstone. Headstone's jealous love for Lizzie Hexam is usually taken to reflect Dickens's feelings for his young mistress Ellen Ternan, and the location of Headstone's school, Edgar Johnson has noticed, parallels that of the house, Windsor Lodge, which Dickens had rented for Ellen. Comparing Headstone with Quilp's fine demonic rapture allows us to see how much has been lost over the years. Headstone is presented as a man of terrible passions which lurk beneath a respectable exterior. When moved, his lips quiver uncontrollably, blood gushes from his nose, his face turns "from burning red to white, and from white back to burning red," and he punches a stone wall until his knuckles are raw and bleeding. When he hears of Lizzie's marriage he throws a fit, and bites and lashes about. As he sleeps, red and blue lightning and palpitating white fire flicker about his bed. On one of his particularly bad nights Dickens shows him sitting in front of the fire, "the dark lines deepening in his face . . . and the very texture and colour of his hair degenerating." Despite all these alarming physical symptoms, though, Headstone is utterly helpless and ineffective. He has no weapons against Eugene Wrayburn's cool irony, which goads him almost to madness. There is no glimmer of humour about him or his presentation. Compared to Quilp, he is a lamb for the slaughter. He is sexually null too. His desire for Lizzie is a dry, theoretic passion. There is nothing to show he even notices her body, as Quilp does Nell's.

The trouble is that Headstone is only partly a vehicle for Dickens's love for Ellen. He also has to serve as a diagram for certain social developments that Dickens deplores. From humble origins he has raised himself by hard work and is now a schoolmaster. Dickens, formerly a hearty advocate of universal education, now sees it as the breeder of pedantry and social pretensions. Once educated, the lower classes get above themselves. In his decent black coat and waistcoat Headstone looks, Dickens says, like a workman in his holiday clothes. He might have made a good sailor if, when a pauper child, he had taken to the sea instead of to learning. As it is, his learning is merely mechanically acquired. Needless to say, Dickens doesn't explain what the alternative ways of acquiring learning might be. When Headstone has committed, or thinks he has committed, murder, he is made into a model to illustrate another of Dickens's pet social theories: that the murderer is never sorry for his crime. All Headstone can think about is how he might have got rid of Wrayburn more efficiently. Dickens is no longer an opponent of capital punishment. Headstone proves a failure because he is fabricated out of his author's social prejudices, instead of being impelled, as Quilp is, by his author's savage humour, self-criticism and emancipation from the cant and sentimentality that were always threatening to kill Dickens's art.

It would be wrong to conclude that because Headstone is a violent character, and is disapproved of by Dickens, Dickens has grown disillusioned with violence. On the contrary, he retains to the end his perfectly simple faith in a strong right arm. Nicholas Nickleby is the first of the heroes to exercise his virtuous muscles on evil-doers. Though slight in appearance—John Browdie refers to him as a whipper-snapper—he makes an impressive showing when struck across the face by Squeers: "Nicholas sprang upon him, wrested the weapon from his hand, and pinning him by the throat, beat the ruffian till he roared for mercy." Mr. Lenville is the next victim: "Nicholas . . . suffered him to approach to within the requisite distance, and then, without the smallest discomposure, knocked him down." To complete the act Nicholas picks up Mr. Lenville's ash stick, breaks it in half, tosses him the pieces, and makes his exit. There follows a fine dramatic encounter between Nicholas and the dastardly Sir Mulberry Hawk: "Stand out of the way, dog," blusters Sir Mulberry. Nicholas shouts that he is the son of a country gentleman, and lays Sir Mulberry's face open from eye to lip. Finally Nicholas confronts the arch villain, Uncle Ralph. " 'One word!' cried Ralph, foaming at the mouth." But Nicholas, distrustful of words, knocks down Ralph's elderly fellow-conspirator Arthur Gride instead, picks up Madeline Bray, and rushes out with, as Dickens puts it, "his beautiful burden in his arms." Granted this is a very early novel, but the victory of righteousness is no less physical, and no less theatrical, at the end of *Martin Chuzzlewit*. Old Martin rises against Pecksniff and strikes him to the ground, "with such a well-directed nervous blow, that down he went, as heavily and true as if the charge of a Life-Guardsman had tumbled him out of the saddle." The soldierly simile here is, of course, meant to give the violence an especially decent flavour. A similar motive prompts Dickens to remind us, at the end of *Our Mutual Friend*, that John Harmon's "seafaring hold was like that of a vice," and that he takes a "sailor-like turn" on Silas Wegg's cravat, preparatory to knocking Silas's head against the wall. There is something healthy and patriotic about a sailor, which makes it all right to assault a cripple. Eventually Wegg and his wooden leg are carried downstairs and thrown into a muck cart. By such summary means is evil expelled from a Dickens novel.

We notice, in these examples, how the writing deteriorates once the violence becomes virtuous. The military images are shoddy subterfuge. Hopelessly dignified, the good characters brandish their sticks or fists, and the villains tumble. Dickens beams complacently. It is a dutiful, perfunctory business. Riot, murder, savagery have to be there before Dickens's imagination is gripped.

ENDPIECE

. . . What saves Dickens from [a] rather shrill surrealism is his humour— a humour so interfused with his creative processes that when it fails his imagination seldom survives it for more than a few sentences. His humour serves as weapon and refuge. It allows him both to cut through the fake of the "real world," as we have seen, and to keep the terrors of his imagination at bay. Consequently there is a feeling of strain when one applies words like "appalling" or "horrifying" to his creations. The materials of horror may be there, but they are transmuted by humour into something more spirited and resilient. Laughter establishes Dickens's confidence, his superiority to menacing forces, and the confidence is deeply unmodern, connecting him not with Sartre or Kafka but with the eighteenth-century writers—Fielding, Swift—who influenced him as a boy. "If I went to a new colony," he once asserted, "I should force myself to the top of the social milk-pot, and live upon the cream." This toughness helped to ensure his commercial success, but it can be traced, too, in the way he manipulates his imagination. Behind his defenceless children—David or Pip—there stands, smiling, the secure adult writer; it is the same figure who authoritatively converts his insidious scissored women into frumps and termagants. Dickens's imagination transforms the world; his laughter controls it.

The Fairy-Tale Endings
of Dickens's Novels

John Kucich

Everything possible to be believed is an image of truth.
—WILLIAM BLAKE, *The Marriage of Heaven and Hell*

If they have not died, they are still alive.
—Traditional fairy-tale ending

Dickens's stylistic freedom through excess is always a negative one, in the sense that all excess is negative; it is founded upon a loss. The energy released through Dickens's writing is negative energy because it is exhausted without being able to recuperate, in some valuable way, the artistic play that it generates. What distinguishes Dickens's parodic voice from his satiric voice is precisely its uselessness, its tendency to escape rational purpose and values. At its purest moments, the energy of that voice is expended without leaving the positive trace of a meaning behind. But Dickens did want to present some kind of final, positive image of this experience, which is why his novels always move from parody to romance. Though Dickens's novels may begin in absolute skeptical negativity, they end in unqualified images of satisfaction. In the presentation of these positive images, of course, Dickens is faced with the problem that haunts most novelists: the problem of imaging infinite (or "negative") novelistic experience in a finite form.

Dickens is usually assumed to have resolved the dissonances of his world in an image of the bourgeois marriage that is too conventional to be taken seriously. He thus fails to address either metaphysical or pragmatic issues satisfactorily, and he certainly never brings them into agreement. But as long as the question of conclusiveness is posed in this traditional way—as the problem of a disjunction between transcendent experience and meaning recuperated as a limited form of experience in the world— the question is self-circumscribing. What is at stake in Dickens is not a prescription for a final, transcendental positivity; what is at stake is the affirmation of a purity of loss. Since by definition loss does not want to be

From *Excess and Restraint in the Novels of Charles Dickens.* © 1981 by the University of Georgia Press.

recuperated, the question for the ending of Dickens's novels becomes: how does the narrative affirm loss as a form of human action in a way that mitigates its terror? Dickens *did* want to end his novels with a positive image, but not necessarily with a positive image of recuperated meaning, or even of recuperated loss. Rather, as we saw [elsewhere], Dickens wanted to present a positive image of loss itself, drained of its violent and aggressive qualities. Instead of simply retreating from impulses toward ultimate excess, in his endings Dickens wanted to image the very goal of excess—that which is beyond the limits of human life, the impersonal flux of union and continuity—in a desirable way. In Dickens's novels, this project extends beyond the symbolic level discussed previously in regard to endings and becomes also a question of stylistic enthusiasm, of voice: first, through certain stressed qualities of the positive images in Dickens's "happy endings," and second—but more importantly—through appeals to a narrative genre that renders even these images obviously mechanical, thus freeing the energy that animates them.

In the first place, Dickens's eternally conclusive image of the bourgeois marriage certainly does not express the violence of excess, but it does express the wish underlying all expenditure, the wish that loss may produce "union." In Dickens's endings, as in those of all Victorian novels, we are presented with marriage as an act, not as a state. As indicated [elsewhere], we should be careful to observe a difference between the social or ideological meaning of the state of marriage and the experience of timelessness that marriage as an act can produce for characters. Esther Summerson repeatedly insists on this timeless quality in her marriage, and her version of timelessness exceeds even the vehicle of marriage that creates it, since timelessness extends to everyone associated with Esther in *Bleak House,* married or unmarried. Of Charley, Esther says, "I might suppose Time to have stood still for seven years"; of Jarndyce, "I have never known the wind to be in the East for a single moment, since the day when he took me to the porch to read the name" (chap. 67). And even a disillusioned Pip at the end of *Great Expectations* sees "no shadow of another parting" (chap. 59) from Estella. In one way or another, all of Dickens's novels feature an ending moment that dissolves both the flow of time—which engenders separations—and the estrangements between characters, resolving them all into an uninterrupted state of bliss that Bataille would call "continuity," the eroticized formlessness that is ontologically prior to the discontinuity of human life. In his endings, Dickens takes positive—in the sense of nonviolent—images of expenditure, images of rest rather than of energy, and he pushes these images to the point at which they become images of a purer loss, irreconcilable with the world. This is the reason why Dickens's happy endings have a nostalgic quality to them; the happy ending is an image of loss contained now within a soothing metaphorics of union. We saw [elsewhere] how Dickens's endings are based in hidden movements of excess, but it is also important to recognize that the ending represents marriage itself as an act that ends experience, rather than as a beginning or a continuation of experience. Dickens's typical sorrow at taking leave of his characters is partly sorrow over their being rarefied beyond the range of his pen—that is, beyond the possibility of meaningful, alterable existence in the world.

In the second place, these positive images, in which loss is embodied in a conservative form, are treated stylistically in vaguely parodic terms similar to those Dickens uses to free the energy of narrative parody from the rigid, mechanical stereotypes that it animates. So it is that we feel Dickens's tone to be slightly condescending at the end of his novels even toward his good characters. The more affirmative way to put this is that Dickens miniaturizes his good society in a way that seems to remove it from the realm of plausibility. But to raise the issue of style in this way is to raise the great question always asked of Dickens's work: did Dickens really believe in his domestic conclaves as plausible images of blissful life on earth? What exactly is the status of the good society in Dickens's novels as an image of human action?

Surely, Dickens did believe in the values represented by hearth and home, but it is possible to see in his attitude two different levels of belief. We know, for example, that for all his defense of the home, Dickens was a less-than-perfect husband himself. Johnson points out that he never regarded his wife as an equal, and it is difficult to understand why he tortured Kate with his love for Mary, or why he made her visit Ellen Ternan after declaring to Kate his love for the actress. In addition, Dickens often neglected his children. His daughter Katie said of Dickens during the time of his separation from his wife, "He did not give a damn about any of us. We were the most miserable and unhappy household imagineable." We also know that Dickens had nothing but contempt for the ordinary domestic novel. These inconsistencies do not necessarily make Dickens a hypocrite, or a bad husband—whatever we understand that to mean—but they do tend to imply that there was some kind of doubleness in Dickens's attitude toward conventional marriage. Significantly, Forster tells us that Dickens could be convinced only with considerable difficulty that *Household Harmony* might be a bad title for a magazine about to appear immediately after his separation from Kate. Strangely, too, Dickens's audience at the first readings supported him wholeheartedly throughout the separation, continuing to cherish his stories of connubial bliss despite what they knew of the author's blasted home life. On both sides, belief in marriage as a value seems willing to dispense with the reality, or at least to have slightly different expectations from life and from literature, and to take slightly different satisfactions from the two. Dickens himself casts this doubleness in harsh terms through the artistic doubleness of Jenny Wren; the doll's dressmaker takes great pains in the construction and care of her dolls, yet she hates real children. This kind of doubleness indicates that the question of Dickens's actual beliefs is irrelevant to the novels; the real question is, what did Dickens do with the convention of bourgeois marriage as a writer? And what happens to the convention when it is projected in his novels? Very simply, such conventions operate only as fairy-tale values.

Dickens's fairy-tale marriages emerge from the same source as many of his stylistic idiosyncracies—in a parodic movement that expends energy profitlessly and experiences a pleasure in loss. How the fairy tale parallels Dickens's parodic voice will become apparent if we consider for a moment what a fairy tale is. From a certain perspective, the fairy tale can be seen as a substitute for, rather than a reflection of, reality. According to Jean Starobinski, for example, the fairy tale expresses what is literary about literature—its desire to stage experience that is not possible in the limited state of nature, but which is possible as an act of free consciousness. The goal of the fairy tale, Starobinski says, is to make the literal meaning of a story insubstantial and to emphasize instead its figural meaning. In this view, the fairy tale does not represent a state of affairs in nature, since it is obviously not true, and it does not take our credence on a mimetic level; rather, the fairy tale is an image of the kind of felicity man can imagine but can project only in language. For this reason, the fairy tale calls attention to its artificiality, its unreality, its claim to a separate, purely linguistic status. That is, by emphasizing its formal unreality, the fairy tale seems to embody desires without tying them to real and, therefore, inevitably limited solutions. In other words, through the fairy-tale device Dickens's stories are deliberately presented as mechanical, as artificial, to elide the conservative ideological content of the conclusions without actually negating that ideology. Paradoxically, by stressing their conventionality, their mechanicalness, these endings aspire to the more organic world of pure story.

Though we tend to think of fairy tales as naive, self-consciousness is actually indispensible to the form. As Starobinski points out, many great fairy tales—the *1001 Nights*, for instance, or the fables of Gozzi and Hoffmann—are framed by explicit hopes that the world of story can cure the melancholy of characters within the fairy tale. The fairy-tale story itself is often presented as the magical cure for the particular melancholy at hand. Something of this belief in the magically primal power of stories lies behind Captain Cuttle's announcement to Florence—"I know a story, Heart's Delight" (chap. 49)—as an introduction to his producing Walter; Cuttle's fairy-tale story echoes Polly's fairy tale at the beginning of *Dombey and Son*, in which she tries to present Florence with an image of the restoration of her mother, but Cuttle—a better storyteller—actually makes his story work. Cuttle's self-conscious fabrication of an innocent but potent world of story at the critical juncture of the novel is telling: the very naiveté of fairy tales is often deliberate, as an expression of their claim to primal truth. No wonder that even the most serious analysts of narrative often tend to think of fairy tales as being closer to the organic well-springs of narrative than to the literature generated by mere individuals. What this deliberate fabrication of naiveté implies, ultimately, is that the pretended naturalness of the fairy tale conceals very real, socially determined values; the purity of the fairy tale is illusory. But the illusion is powerful, and, in Dickens's case, it is an indispensible element in the effect of his endings.

The most important feature of the fairy-tale voice, then, for our purposes, is that it always tries to circumvent any subjective assertion of temporal values by aspiring to the pure world of story. In the fairy tale, we are asked to believe in the absence of merely personal authorship and of any personal avowal of values. By being traditional, and even mechanically formulaic, the fairy tale aspires to an objective or impersonal status, denying its partiality. And through this deliberate gesture toward the world of story, the fairy tale tries to break itself free of determined meaning. The consequence of this aspiration toward narrative purity is that even the figural meaning of the fairy tale is not meant to be reduced to temporal terms. Starobinski claims that when fairy tales do provide morals, these morals are either obviously tacked on or they are enigmatic, belonging to a different order of knowledge; even a psychoanalyst like Bruno Bettelheim, who is interested in the use fairy tales are put to by children, insists that fairy tales are never meant to be explained. Dickens himself hated the reduction of fairy tales to moral lessons—he protested vehemently, for example, against Cruikshank's use of fairy tales as lessons in temperance.

As an intention, at least, the fairy-tale voice does not remain tied to the conventions it employs—for the very reason that those conventions are so obvious—any more than the parodic voice is tied to the objects of satire it uses as a springboard. Instead, the fairy tale is a kind of benign parody of the real, deliberately stressing itself as intention and not as prescription. Like the parodic voice, the fairy-tale voice is a narrative machine; it uses the conventions of the happy ending, along with its other obvious clichés and repeated motifs, in exactly the same way that Dickens's parodic voice uses the conventions of mechanical behavior—that is, to elide the mimetic substantiality of those conventions in favor of mimetically ungrounded and therefore free images of continuity. Thus, John Harmon and Bella Wilfer's home is frequently described as a doll's house to express an impossible kind of harmony, one that negates any conceivable conflicts they might have—specifically, one wants to say, over Harmon's deception. Similarly, Jarndyce's fairy-tale role as Esther's guardian helps to eliminate questions about the plausibility of his nonsexual interest in her. Character psychology is partially suspended here in favor of a larger, purely formal, narrative resolution. Aside from these specific images of marriage, Dickens's endings generally insist on their pure existence as stories by calling attention to their fictional status. When Mr. Dombey and his grandson disappear into the ending of *Dombey and Son*, we are told, "as they go about together, the story of the bond between them goes about, and follows them" (chap. 62); the ending in *A Tale of Two Cities* is projected as a story told by Darnay to his future grandson; and besides telling us that the story of Nell is repeated by Kit to his children, and by Master Humphrey to his circle of friends, *The Old Curiosity Shop* ends, "Such are the changes which a few years bring about, and so do things pass away, like a tale that is told" (chap. 72).

A closer look will reveal all of Dickens's concluding marriages to be presented as fairy-tale marriages, as resolutions which lack psychological or social content because they are dictated by the naive power of story. Of John Westlock and Ruth Pinch we are told, "They went away, but not through London's streets! Through some enchanted city, where the pavements were of air; where all the rough sounds of a stirring town were softened into gentle music; where everything was happy; where there was no distance, and no time" (chap. 53). This enchanted city is not merely an ornamental way of describing Ruth's bliss; it posits a state of being that exists only on the level of story, as the negation of worldly space and time. The more prosaic descriptions of Tom and Ruth Pinch's bourgeois domestic economy earlier stress the difference between the substantiality of that arrangement and the insubstantial, purely fictional quality of Ruth's marriage. So, too, David Copperfield loves Agnes "with a love unknown on earth" (chap. 60). Even *Little Dorrit*, which ends more grimly, perhaps, than any other Dickens novel, concludes with a modest appeal to the fixed destiny of the fairy-tale world; before they leave the Marshalsea to be married, Arthur and Little Dorrit ritually burn his mother's letter, while Arthur asks, "Does the charm want any words to be said?" (vol. 2, chap. 34). And at the church, Little Dorrit's "old friend" holds open the worn marriage register for her to sign and comments, "This young lady is one of our curiosities, and has come now to the third volume of our Registers. Her birth is in what I call the first volume; she lay, asleep on this very floor, with her pretty head on what I call the second volume; and she's now a-writing her little name as a bride, in what I call the third volume." Earlier, the volumes of the registry had been called a "sealed book of Fate" (vol. 1, chap. 14). Then, too, Little Dorrit's marriage cannot but remind us of the fairy tale she had earlier told Maggy, about a "tiny woman" who possesses a "shadow of Some one," which she will take to her grave with her (vol. 1, chap. 24). Little Dorrit's fairy tale comes true in a way that even she had not foreseen; this fairy tale posits a union of the "tiny woman" and the "Some one" only in death. And, as we saw [elsewhere], Little Dorrit and Arthur must go through a kind of deathlike loss—the separation from the world both experience through the loss of their fortunes—before they can be united.

The marriage of John Harmon and Bella Wilfer is the union most explicitly merged with the conventions of the fairy tale. We are told that "the two walked away together with an ethereal air of happiness, which, as it were, wafted up from the earth and drew after them a gruff and glum old pensioner to see it out" (vol. 4, chap. 4). This character is then given a fairy-tale sobriquet, "Gruff and Glum"; Mr. Wilfer is so frightened by this apparition that "his conscience might have introduced, in the person of that pensioner, his own stately lady disguised, arrived at Greenwich in a car and griffins, like the spiteful Fairy at the christenings of the Princesses, to do something dreadful to the marriage service." Bella's movements are described as a fairylike gliding; "the church-porch having swallowed up Bella Wilfer for ever and ever, had it not in its power to relinquish that young woman, but slid into the happy sunlight, Mrs. John Rokesmith instead." And at the marriage dinner we are told that there are even "samples of the fishes of divers color that made a speech in the Arabian Nights"; that the dishes are "seasoned with Bliss"; and that "the golden drink had been bottled in the golden age." The fairy-tale references suffusing the wedding—barely glanced at here—are inexhaustible, making this marriage seem the focal point for all the fairy-tale motifs scattered throughout *Our Mutual Friend*; together they make this marriage, the last to be described in Dickens's novels, seem to address itself to the primitive world of story and to dissolve any reality in the love of John and Bella into a fairy-tale connection that exceeds the world.

In this way, Dickens uses the fairy-tale voice to move beyond the conventions of his happy endings—specifically, the resolution of marriage—into the world they intend, a world of rest that is on the other side of loss, a world which, as our study of expenditure makes clear, is something that consciousness can imagine, can even intend as the goal of action, but cannot fully realize in the world. The reader of Dickens's novels is not left with marriage as a meaning, a prescription for happiness—if he were, the bachelorhood of characters like Tom Pinch, Jarndyce, or Mortimer Lightwood would be disturbing. Instead, conservative, fairy-tale marriages become metaphors for an affirmed experience of timelessness and of satisfied, excessive desire; the fairy-tale marriage presents a positive image of that which surpasses or destroys meaning, exceeding significance by dissolving itself into the pure mechanism of narrative convention. Thus, for Dickens, the fairy tale is a terrorless image of loss itself, and fairy-tale marriages aspire to an absence of ideological or social content—they constitute a kind of infinite loss—by merging with traditional narrative structures. In other words, positive expressions of loss or rest in Dickens depend paradoxically on the operation of a linguistic and narrative machine that never ceases its operation.

Through the fairy-tale voice in Dickens, the happy ending is lifted above the status of a worldly economy, an image only of what can be retained. As if to insure this excess, there is no observable progress developed to produce the happy ending; it is not earned by any of the characters and therefore does not form a strategy of exchange or reward—it cannot realistically be reimplemented; it is "useless." In sum, Dickens employs an image of what recuperated loss might be like—marriage—only in a kind of recognition that thought cannot escape the necessity of temporal form, what Bataille calls "the self-evidence of meaning." That is, the restoration of a significance to loss is inevitable in thought and in language—

even in terms of this study of Dickens, which tries (despite an understanding of the paradoxical quality of the labor) to affirm a temporal, useful meaning in expenditure. But through the very predictability of fairy-tale marriage Dickens can use his conventional image in such a way as to push it, too, toward a euphoria of absence, toward a recognized fairy-tale impossibility that is the very condition of its value for Dickens and for his reader.

Trollope's Metonymies

Michael Riffaterre

After a century of criticism, much remains to be said about Trollope's technique. His approach to traditional or perhaps obsolescent concepts of the novel and his morality have been much studied. But relatively little is known of his writing practice other than what he himself revealed in his *Autobiography*. Indeed there exists no thorough, detailed analysis of the formal and semantic structures of his narrative and descriptive style. As a step in that direction I propose to examine Trollope's use of the descriptive detail in sketching his characters. The function of the detail is complex. It is not merely to add precision or color to the description. It is not merely to help the reader visualize the object depicted. Nor is it solely to make us marvel at some clever observation and at the author's keen way of noticing something that would have eluded most of us. Granted, the detail does all this. But its true function is to induce a semantic displacement. It refers to and ultimately symbolizes something other than its "natural" referent. I shall focus on those details that are used to represent a whole of which they are only a part—in other words on metonymies.

I shall not try to distinguish between metonymy and those figures that rhetorical tradition considers to be related to it, such as synecdoche, antonomasia and metalepsis. Traditional definitions in fact do little more than list different possibilities (*pars pro toto*, or the reverse; the cause for the effect, or the effect for the cause; the use of a proper name, which would designate a specific member of a class, to refer to any member of that class; etc.) and give them various labels. But in order to explain the phenomenon, a unifying principle is needed: one word is used for another with which, in usage, it already has a relation of contiguity. Metonymies are used dif-

From *Nineteenth-Century Fiction* 37, no. 3 (December 1982). © 1982 by the Regents of the University of California.

ferently according to genres. In the novel the trend has been to dissolve or disperse the image of a character into surrounding objects or to suggest a state of mind or the significance of a dramatic situation through physical details that invite certain deductions or inferences on the part of the reader.

In the specific case of portraits, the metonymic detail does not summarize the whole person so much as it does an ensemble of psychological or behavioral traits about which society and therefore the reader, more often than not, hold definite opinions. The reader will therefore react to those traits in accordance with social custom or his individual wont, and, as a consequence, empathize with the character who now embodies these traits. I shall concern myself with only one class of metonymies—those which cause the reader to infer all sorts of moral judgments about a character from his behavior or some minor feature of physical or sartorial appearance.

My field of inquiry may seem narrow, but Trollope so clearly favors this type of metonymy that its study is likely to identify factors truly typical of his style as a whole. To be sure, such devices are commonplace in Victorian novels. Yet further examination discloses traits that are uniquely Trollopian.

First, his metonymies are essentially comic devices. The apparently disproportionate attention Trollope lavishes on Mr. Rubb's gloves (*Miss Mackenzie*), or on Tom Tringle's "ornamental gilding" (*Ayala's Angel*), or on a hairdo never fails to produce a humorous effect. These comic devices, however, do not necessarily cease to be components of realism. Second, Trollope's metonymies generate textual amplifications turning sly humor into broad comedy. Third, this dual function, comic and descriptive, is the nub of a contradiction that is one of the earmarks of Trollope's manner. The descriptive function creates verisimilitude. The comic function tends to cancel it, for it literally points to the author's intrusion, suggesting that the novel does not so much represent reality as make use of it to a specific end. We can hardly avoid seeing the comic as a manipulation. In metonymy, therefore, the mimesis of reality coexists with a display of artifice. I hope to show that although artifice would seem to pose a threat to verisimilitude, the two nevertheless coexist comfortably. Indeed, the comic distortion or reduction remains harmless; it does not detract from the truth of a portrayal, for we come to recognize and accept it for what it is: a game, but not a gratuitous one, in other words, a factor of literariness. (As opposed to literature. Literature is a canon and a corpus. Literariness, of course, refers to the universals that must be found represented in any canonical rule of literature.)

The humorous or comical effect of metonymy is entirely caused by the trope's ability to lower its object by several degrees on the scale of values assigned that object in its normal, usage-regulated representation. If the portrait of a human being, for instance, substitutes a thing or a physical detail for a moral quality or psychological trait, this displacement is unfailingly perceived as reductionist. This very thing or physical detail may very well function as a symbol of the moral or of the psychological without being reductive so long as the text makes the relationship explicit and places the moral content and its material sign side by side. Again, there will be no caricature if the relationship is customary and so established in usage that convention makes up for the implicitation of the moral content. Metonymy, on the other hand, need not be conventional. If it is not, content implicitation emphasizes the explicit physical detail—the way a throne loses its majesty if it is not named a throne but is described as a gilded chair. In *The Small House at Allington* Trollope portrays the vanity of a minor railroad functionary thus:

> A stern official who seemed to carry the weight of many engines on his brow; one at the very sight of whom smokers would drop their cigars, and porters close their fists against sixpences; a great man with an erect chin, a quick step, *and a well-brushed hat powerful with an elaborately upturned brim.* This was the platform-superintendent, dominant even over the policemen. (Emphasis added.)

Even though "powerful" applies literally to the headgear's bold design, we cannot help feeling that the adjective acquires its strength from the hat wearer himself, and that, as a consequence, the hat metonymically stands for the superintendent. He himself is seen a few lines further "keeping on his hat, for he was aware how much of the excellence of his personal dignity was owing to the arrangement of that article." But in this sentence, of course, since it is explanatory and makes explicit the rationale for wearing such a hat, "that article" has ceased to be a metonym and has become a symbol.

Metonymic reductionism need not apply directly to man. It works just as well when it affects the established values of any kind of symbol. So it is with the following sketch of a man about to jilt his fiancée and pledge his troth to a socially more prominent bride. The cad is lying in a canopied bed as he meditates his deed:

> He repented his engagement with Lilian Dale, but he still was resolved that he would fulfil it. He was bound in honour to marry "that little girl," and *he looked sternly up at the drapery over his head,* as he assured himself that he was a man of honour. Yes; he would sacrifice himself.
>
> (*The Small House at Allington,* chap. 18; emphasis added)

Supine as he is, he perhaps cannot help but gaze upwards. But this is not reality. The mimesis specifies "sternly," an adverb that activates the symbolism of his bold eyes: they bespeak unwavering steadfastness and firm purpose. "Upwards," however, or "uplifted" alone would do to describe a stern gaze. The metonymic substitution of the real and decidedly down-to-earth curtain ironically undercuts the connotations of firmness and announces vacillation and betrayal.

This *vis comica* of metonymy does not weaken when the metonym blossoms into a metaphor. Rather it increases. Witness the following passage in *Rachel Ray*, in which a nephew is described as the heir to a tradition begun by his uncle, on the model of a commonplace double metonymy—a chip off the old block. The commonplace is humorous as is; Trollope's rephrasing is even more so, since it substitutes for chip and block the names of wooden objects typical of the uncle's trade. He is a brewer.

> Who had taught him to brew beer—bad or good? Had it not been Bungall? And now, because in his old age he would not change these things, and ruin himself in a vain attempt to make some beverage that should look bright to the eye, he was to be turned out of his place by this chip from the Bungall block, this stave out of one of Bungall's vats! *"Ruat coelum, fiat justitia,"* he said, as he walked forth to his own breakfast. He spoke to himself in other language, indeed, though the Roman's sentiment was his own. "I'll stand on my rights, though I have to go into the poor-house."

Substitution particularizes and emphasizes the fact that there is no similarity in reality between a father or uncle and a block, and between a son or nephew and a chip. The whole trope rests on an abstract analogy; the commonplace image does no more than suggest a make-believe similarity; the nephew is to the uncle what the chip is to the block. Without the buffer of the commonplace, the same abstract relationship, now actualized with "stave" and "vat," will appear even more remote from the human, the reductionist strategy, more artificial, and its effect, decidedly funny. As if this were not enough, another make-believe textual strategy seems to attribute the learned quotation to a tradesman who presumably had little Latin. This new contrast sets "vat" and "stave" in relief, closing the frame, as it were, and emphasizing the playful artificiality.

The second characteristic of Trollope's metonymies is their ability to generate texts. The transformation of a word into a text (that is, a multi-sentence semiotic unit ending on closure) (a complete definition of the *text* should of course comprise the opposition *significance* vs. *meaning*, and the whole intertextuality network) can be described as a simultaneous process of conversion and expansion. Expansion consists in making explicit one or more semes, or semantic features, of the matrix word in the form of periphrastic sentences. Expansion does not in itself give formal unity to the text. It does no more than record a mental process, equating an undeveloped implicit signification (usually no more than a word) with its explicit development (always a set of sentences). The equivalency, however, would remain unperceived in most cases. It would be lost in the thicket of descriptive details, which might be mistaken for a description or a narrative in its own right. Its complex syntactic structure would not immediately be recognized as a mere variant of the matrix word. The equivalency becomes inescapable through conversion. Conversion creates the equivalency by modifying every constituent of the expansion-generated text with the same factor. The working of conversion is especially evident in the following passage in *Miss Mackenzie.* The whole paragraph is the complex syntactic equivalent of two family names. As patronyms, these names designate two attorneys, both fairly typical, familiar characters in the nineteenth-century novel. Both names also function as the first actualization of the text's matrix, for both are emblematic of the slow pace of justice—again a familiar theme, but one that lends itself to many representations:

> Mr. Slow was a grey-haired old man. . . . He was a stout, thickset man, very leisurely in all his motions, who walked slowly, talked slowly, read slowly, wrote slowly, and thought slowly; but who, nevertheless, had the reputation of doing a great deal of business, and doing it very well. He had a partner in the business, almost as old as himself, named Bideawhile; and they who knew them both used to speculate which of the two was the most leisurely. It was, however, generally felt, that, though Mr. Slow was the slowest in his speech, Mr. Bideawhile was the longest in getting anything said.

At first, one might think that a mere repetition of "slow" or its synonyms is comical and that this comical portrayal progresses, like all depictions, from detail to detail. In fact, there is no more real progression than there is any difference between the two partners. Their two portraits are but a variation on the first phrase, which develops the implications of Mr. Slow's name: "very leisurely in all his motions." The variation consists in repeating *procrastination,* an essential seme of the word "attorney." That there is no progression becomes evident when the first attorney, the only one who actually plays a part in the novel, is suddenly divided into two. Aside from the fact that law partners come in pairs (at least), there is not a shadow of a narrative motivation for Mr. Bideawhile's presence, unless one recognizes in this scissiparity a "legal" variant of the stereotype "six of one and half a dozen of the other." Had Trollope chosen the oxymoron rather than the tautology as his motivating trope, we would have had an attorney Swift and his partner Quick. Be that as it may, both synonymous names and the description of their bearers make the characters metonyms of human justice, or rather of its literary representation that progresses *pede claudo.* The significance of this double portrait—the irony of Themis's "deliberate speed"—could make a whole novel the equivalent of this vignette: from a transformational viewpoint there is no difference between an expansion from "Slow" into two patronyms and an expansion from the pithy Trollope portrayal into a protracted narrative like *Bleak House.*

Derivations similar to the one I have just discussed are the factors that guide the reader's interpretation of a novel. They are longer and more complex but are always generated by metonymies. Because they reflect the long fictional narrative in miniaturized form, as it were, they make it easier for the reader to identify the significance and perceive the unity of the novel. They are fragments of the larger text, immersed in it and mirroring the whole. I shall therefore call them subtexts.

A subtext must actualize the same matrix as the whole narrative, or a matrix structurally connected with that of the encircling text. These subtexts operate as units of reading, so to speak, not unlike themes or motifs, except that a theme or motif has a matrix of its own, born elsewhere and existing before that of the larger text, so that theme or motif functions like a quotation, or borrowing, or, rather, like an embedding in the syntax of the narrative. The subtext obtrudes on the reader as a segment that could stand alone and be remembered as a passage representing the whole and representing the author, as an episode may be remembered; only an episode is a link in a chain of events, while a subtext is no such thing, since it can be omitted without unraveling the fabric or obscuring the logic of the narrative. The subtext works like those units of reading or fragments or vectors in a reading sequence that Roland Barthes called *lexies*, except that Barthes's lexies depend upon the individual's choice, upon his ideological grids. The subtext, by contrast, is objectively defined and resists subjective, reader-initiated segmentation. The subtext itself, and its limits—in particular the connection between closure and incipit—are identified when the reader becomes retroactively aware that one textual component is echoing another component, formerly read and now remembered. The component from out of the past, thus recollected or reread with the eye of memory, takes on features not noticed during the first or primary reading, for they are noteworthy only because they are the first step or rung in a repetitive series. For the same logical reason that a rhyme is perceived only when the eye or ear has reached the second rhyming word, a narrative prolepsis is perceivable only after the fact. It carries nothing in itself pointing to its proleptic function until the narrative sequence arrives at the consequences of the premises posited in the prolepsis. For the subtext to be noticed, then, there must be homologues within the narrative from which flow recognizable, well-marked derivations constituting the formal and semantic constants any literary text must be able to show. When the reader does finally stumble upon one or more of such homologues, but a homologue whose shape and meaning indicate that the series is coming to an end—for instance, when this latest homologue reverses the order of components in the initial one— then the subtext closes.

Subtexts, however well defined by closure, are hardly ever solid, uninterrupted verbal sequences. They usually overlap other subtexts, or are simply disseminated throughout the novel.

Subtexts derived from metonymies are thus not foreign bodies inserted into the fictional text but playful variants of that text, concentrating the realistic features dispersed throughout the narrative continuity. These features form a network of signs on which the mimesis of a way of life is built. Whenever Mr. Neefit, the breeches-maker, appears in *Ralph the Heir,* allusions are made to his trade and words quoted from the language of that trade. Soon, entire chapters become saturated by these references to the tailor's art. Nothing could be easier, since the tradesman intends to make a lady of his daughter by forcing the aristocratic protagonist to marry her: Ralph's inordinate fondness for riding habits has made him Mr. Neefit's debtor. Not only the characters' language but their whole life becomes inseparable from breeches-making. This specialized language is no longer limited to the depiction of a milieu; it becomes a code for any representation. Similarly, everything and everybody coming in contact with Sir Thomas, the former Solicitor-General, becomes tinged with his dryness. Like old Casaubon in *Middlemarch,* he pursues an impossible dream of scholarship in his chambers. A *dust* code seems to permeate the contexts in which he figures.

We may say that linguistic forms, especially lexical ones, are used as a code when they do not designate their habitual object, the referent they seem to have in common usage, or when their normal reference now plays only a secondary role: this is the case when words suggest an atmosphere rather than represent a specific scene or setting. (Trollope's metalanguage occasionally underscores the displacement from denotation to connotation, e.g.: "she had no regret, no uneasiness, no conception that any state of life could be better for her than that state in which an *emblematic beefsteak* was of vital importance" [*He Knew He Was Right,* chap. 96; emphasis added].) More specifically, a fragment of discourse, or a lexical set, becomes a code when its connotations displace its denotation. When this occurs, the descriptive or narrative discourse appears less motivated in context, more loosely connected with the sequence of events, and less justified by the exigencies of the mimesis. The most obvious instance of such a displacement of meaning is the symbolic or metaphorical use of discourse. But the displacement is just as real when there is a shift from the denotative to the connotative rather than from the literal to the figurative. An apparently descriptive sentence may thus be no more than a grammatical frame, the sole purpose of which is to provide space for a sequence of connotation-laden words. For instance:

> They all walked home gloomily to their dinner, and ate their cold mutton and potatoes in sorrow and sadness.
>
> (*Rachel Ray,* chap. 4)

It is clear that the epithet in "cold mutton" is culinary at the level of denotation, but pathetic at the level of connotation. Similarly, "mutton" and "potatoes" denote a menu and connote inglorious mediocrity. Thus, the seemingly descriptive sentence merely prolongs the pejorative paradigm of "gloomily," "sorrow," and "sadness."

Rachel Ray is a novel characterized by a *food* code. The central conflict between a brewer and his young business partner is naturally enough linked to a controversy over the quality of beer and the respective merits of cider and beer. Before long, the whole novel turns into a mock epic of beer. The election subplot is also couched in a *food* code, since no election-eering can take place without many banquets and much potation. Likewise, family life revolves around menus, party preparations, and the taming of husbands with clotted cream (chap. 14)—clearly a reduction this, since literary strategies of seduction are usually sexual. Everything, including spiritual matters or less worldly concerns, is translated into terms of eating and drinking. Witness this stab at a minister's hypocrisy:

> [Mr. Prong's] teapot was still upon the table, together with the debris of a large dish of shrimps, the eating of small shell-fish being an innocent enjoyment to which he was much addicted.
>
> (chap. 9)

While the *food* code gives the whole novel the atmosphere of the earthly living and of robust healthy appetites that one associates with English country life and the denizens of rural counties, the subtexts color the whole tableau with its humorous tinge, and at times, its ironic overtones. One such subtext is a series of "tea" episodes—tea both in the British sense of an afternoon meal with tea, and tea as the accompaniment to a social call. We cannot suppose that the series merely reflects the routine of Devonshire afternoons. While the routine in the reality of everyday existence may remain as inconspicuous a regulator of life as a clock's chime, its literary depiction must be visibly symbolic and connotative. For repetitiveness in a text cannot remain inconspicuous and must represent, as a sign in its own right: as "tea" represents food and custom, its recurrence represents comforting continuity or the rut of boredom. In *Rachel Ray* it links together the main plot, with its central drama and love interests, and the consequent tribulations of Mrs. Ray, the heroine's mother. It does so in a mildly comical way, for tea taking and tea pouring come to stand for Mrs. Ray herself and her moral outlook. Tea as a pleasurable occasion in her uneventful life metonymically becomes equivalent to her very relative moral weakness (she is sweet-tempered, good-humored, and enjoys life) and to her dilemmas as a devout and timid Christian ("she would have taught herself to believe this world to be a pleasant place, were it not so often preached into her ears that it is a vale of tribulation"; chap. 1). Because this equation of a moral outlook and tea cannot fail to amuse, the subtext provides an ironical commentary, a tale bordering on tragedy and a comic counterpoint to the sorrows of the protagonist.

The subtext unfolds at regular intervals from the very beginning of the novel to its last pages. It appears when we are introduced to the small pleasures of Mrs. Ray, a lady in reduced circumstances:

> She could gossip over a cup of tea, and enjoy buttered toast and hot cake very thoroughly, if only there was no one near her to

whisper into her ear that any such enjoyment was wicked. . . .
When the clergyman in his sermon told her that she should live
simply and altogether for heaven . . . and that nothing belonging
to this world could be other than painful . . . she . . . would be-
think herself how utterly she was a castaway, because of that tea,
and cake, and innocent tittle tattle with which the hours of her
Saturday evening had been beguiled.

(chap. 1)

Her enjoying tea may still appear to be only an example of sin, but the
very next page completes the metonymic substitution, by the same stroke
of pen that shows a discrepancy between the parson's own conduct and
his doctrine:

Twice or thrice a year Mrs. Ray would go to the parsonage, and
such evenings would be by no means hours of wailing. Tea and
buttered toast on such occasions would be very manifestly in the
ascendant.

(chap. 1)

Grammar gives "tea" the initiative, as it were, or an independence that
makes it a synecdoche of *creature comforts* and therefore a metonym of
worldly pleasures—the token for the class. In later passages, tea will therefore
symbolize Mrs. Ray's weakness as she vacillates between encouraging her
daughter's love for a worthy young man and yielding to her minister's
strictures. Conversely, tea will represent puritanical contrariness:

There was no hot toast, and no clotted cream. . . . In truth, such
delicacies did not suit Mrs. Prime. . . . She liked the tea to be
stringy and bitter, and she liked the bread to be stale. . . . She
was approaching that stage of discipline at which ashes become
pleasant eating, and sackcloth is grateful to the skin.

(chap. 5)

As metonymy begets more details, the descriptive grammar allows for
reversals of the symbolism: all that is needed is for the verbs to be modified
with negations and for the adjectives to turn pejorative. The very continuity
of this practice emphasizes its artifice and therefore its comical nature.
Hence the development of a discreetly farcical sequence, in which Rachel
Ray's growing unhappiness at being kept apart from her beloved is ex-
presssed through her preparing increasingly austere and spare teas for her
mother.

The metonymic subtext is now so well established as a grammatical
frame representing Mrs. Ray's mental constitution that the scene in which
she learns to appreciate her daughter's worthy suitor appears in a chapter
titled "Luke Rowan Takes His Tea Quite Like a Steady Young Man." Significantly, as metonymy evolves towards symbolism and may lose its re-

ductionist tendencies, subsidiary metonyms spring up, maintaining the comic discrepancy between man and thing: the wearing away of Mrs. Ray's reservations about the young man and his progress in her esteem are marked by the jerky motions of the "tea-caddy" in her hands (chap. 11).

As the novel comes to a close, so does the subtext. When her daughter goes away to her husband, Mrs. Ray experiences the sadness of a parent left behind, but not directly in terms of loneliness: "those little evening festivities of buttered toast and thick cream were over for her now" (chap. 29).

The subtext's recurrence acts as a catalyzer of the metonymy's comic potential. A mere hint of whimsy at the beginning becomes outrageously funny by dint of repetition. Outrageously so since the realistic facet of metonymy tends to become less convincing as reduction becomes more ludicrous. Verisimilitude and farce are hardly compatible. Trollope nonetheless is easily carried away, perhaps less by the lure of comedy (although what we know of him suggests that the man's sense of humor, if not the author's, tended to uproarious slapstick) than by the accelerating momentum of phrases building into periphrases, and of these into hilarious playlets. This accelerating tempo is almost a verbal automatism, deeply ingrained in techniques of composition, namely rhetorical *amplificatio*, that have been basic school training ever since antiquity and part of our Latin heritage in the humanities. To be sure, at any point Trollope could have checked this momentum, but the fact is that he did not. Far from it, subtexts increase in scope from the rapid notation of a potentially funny detail to comedy to elaborate mock epic. As subtext grows larger and more complex, the reader is less able to hold back. Even if he were to resist the comedy (but he does not), the subtext would still orient his interpretation and its irony would continue to serve as a hermeneutic guideline.

Such a development can be seen in *Miss Mackenzie* with the "squint" subtext. The most obsessive and most mercenary of the heroine's suitors is a Reverend Maguire, a preacher whose physical charms and spellbinding eloquence she would be unable to resist were it not for his eye:

> Mr. Maguire she did notice, and found him to be the possessor of a good figure, of a fine head of jet black hair, of a perfect set of white teeth, of whiskers which were also black and very fine, but streaked here and there with a grey hair,—and of the most terrible squint in his right eye which ever disfigured a face that in all other respects was fitted for an Apollo.
>
> (chap. 4)

He is by no means the only fictional character whose inner flaws are comically externalized by an inability to look you in the eye. A certain Miss Pucker's pharisaic mentality, in *Rachel Ray*, is suggested by a squint to which the novel briefly alludes. In *Harry Heathcote of Gangoil* suspicions are aroused against a foreman turned arsonist by this concession to the emblematic obviousness of moralistic literature. The motif does little for the narrative—the detail generating no more than reactions of watchfulness and hostility among the other characters. The cross-eyed arsonist is simply a sign of evil, like the one-eyed Squeers in *Nicholas Nickleby*. In *Miss Mackenzie*, however, the subtext is fully integrated in the sequence of events and functions as a figurative gloss on the narrative. The eclipses and reappearances of that fearful strabismus add suspense to the seduction scenes. The reader alternately trembles for the heroine and hopes for her salvation depending on whether the Reverend is able to enthrall her when she can see only his good profile or whether she is trapped in a position where she finds it "impossible to avert her eyes from his eye" (chap. 4).

It is significant that when Trollope is at his artistic best we should find him working with metonymy. I am well aware of my perils here and how facile this subjective impressionism must seem. I can at least shore up my value judgments by invoking a consensus. Most critics, for instance, would agree that unity in a work of art, manifesting itself both in form and content, is a criterion of esthetic excellence. Such, at any rate, is the view shared by the interpretive community in Trollope's time, and it still is a perception of a majority of academic Trollopians. How significant then to find this unity most successfully achieved in those metonymic subtexts that mesh the descriptive and the diegetic portrayal and narration. And to find unity again in the way metonymy turns into symbol, smoothly combining a light, incidental satire of mores and penetrating psychological analysis, for the metonymic derision has become the viewpoint of the characters themselves—it is the way they see themselves and others. Such is the case in the "chignon" subtext, one of the principal props of the narrative in *He Knew He Was Right*, and a hermeneutic model that dictates the reader's interpretation of the novel's main subplot.

The central plot spins out the tragic tale of a marriage destroyed by a sincere, honest, but prideful wife whose unbending spirit drives her husband literally to madness. The subplot contrasts this with the happily ending story of a wedding won by sincere, honest, but meek Dorothy whose modesty conquers the hearts of both her lover and her wealthy and cantankerous spinster aunt, old Miss Stanbury. The subplot also brings comic relief to the high drama of the plot. Comedy stems from a subplot within the subplot: Dorothy's modesty, freshness, and guileless good nature are contrasted to the cunning affectations of two sisters past their prime, who have learned the hard way "that of all worldly goods a husband is the best" (chap. 50), "the two Miss Frenches from Heavitree, who had the reputation of hunting unmarried clergymen in couples" (chap. 15). They vie with each other in trying to catch Mr. Gibson, a minor canon of the cathedral, who in turn is trying to catch Dorothy's dowry. When Dorothy turns him down, Camilla French manages to net him. This is where the derivation from a metonymy transforms the stagy farce—the clergyman's shuttlecock to the Miss Frenches' battledores— into high comedy with psychological truth. The purely mechanical accidents of a circular chase give way to the language of symbolism and emotions.

Dorothy's natural freshness and artlessness are symbolized by her "soft hair which [her aunt] loved so well,—because it was a grace given by God and not bought out of a shop" (chap. 73). Her opposite's crafty snares have a chignon for their emblem, a postiche purchased by Arabella French in an attempt to repair the injuries of Time and to remain fashionable. Note that the thing is more than just a grotesque detail: it does give its bearer some claim to the reader's sympathy. The anxieties and yearnings it betrays in her are actually moving:

> It was natural enough that he shouldn't want her. She knew herself to be a poor, thin, vapid, tawdry creature, with nothing to recommend her to any man except a sort of second-rate, provincial-town fashion which,—infatuated as she was,—she attributed in a great degree to the thing she carried on her head. She knew nothing. She could do nothing. She possessed nothing. She was not angry with him because he so evidently wished to avoid her. But she thought that if she could only be successful she would be good and loving and obedient,—and that it was fair for her at any rate to try.
>
> (chap. 47)

The subtext opens with Miss Stanbury bitterly railing at this headdress, for her religion finds such secular adornments iniquitous. Comedy shifts into high gear when Mr. Gibson in his anxiety to escape Arabella focuses on the ghastly thing that was meant to be his bait. As the threat of matrimony comes closer, the chignon takes on epic proportions. As the victim has to face the thought of connubial intimacies, the chignon nightmarishly replaces and embodies the bride. We come as close to lifting the veil on nuptial mysteries as Victorian prudishness would allow:

> And as he regarded it in a *nearer and dearer light,*—as a chignon that might possibly *become his own,* as a burden which in one sense he might himself be called upon to bear, as a domestic utensil of which he himself might be called upon to inspect, and, perhaps, to aid the shifting on and the shifting off, he did begin to think that that side of the Scylla gulf ought to be avoided if possible. (Emphasis added.)
>
> (chap. 47)

(The Miss Stanbury satire has been mentioned before [chap. 22]. The reader will recognize phrases where "she" is the normal pronoun. As one indication of the perfect symmetry of the novel and of Trollope's memory and planning, this revelatory glimpse of what a bridegroom never says aloud echoes phrase for phrase what had come to Dorothy's mind when Mr. Gibson proposed to her and the "feeling of the closeness of a wife to her husband" had occurred to her and conjured up unbearable images [chap. 42].)

Verbal fireworks now signal the rise of paranoia in the poor clergyman as he feels the trap shutting on him. Significantly, Trollope had just abandoned all stylistic restraints and used the fish and bait metaphor literally, daring to say things such as "landing the scaly darling" caught in the "bucket of matrimony" "out of the fresh and free waters of his bachelor stream" (the "bucket of matrimony" appears in chap. 13. Another sign of the cumulative power of the subtext derivation is that metaphors are now mixed together). Poor Gibson hallucinates seeing the chignon as a "shapeless excrescence," as "that distorted monster," growing "bigger and bigger, more shapeless, monstrous, absurd, and abominable, as he looked at it" (chap. 47). Such are the dynamics of this accelerating verbal derivation that the writer's taste and sense of balance seem to desert him, and that the text explodes into fantastic literary allusions: English no longer suffices, Vergil is called into play, and the chignon looms above Gibson as Polyphemus over Ulysses:

> He thought that he never in his life had seen anything so unshapely as that huge wen at the back of her head. "Monstrum horrendum, informe, ingens!" He could not help quoting the words to himself.
> (chap. 47)

By now the reader is carried along irresistibly and finds it natural for the metonymy to have become the hallucination of an evil presence: "Poor young woman,—perishing beneath an incubus which a false idea of fashion had imposed on her!" (chap. 47). (When Arabella sacrifices her chignon [in vain], she is compared to a ship lowering her flag in sign of surrender [chap. 48].) That we accept this can be explained by the sheer rhetorical impact of accumulation, but also by our sense that Trollope, in pulling out all the stops, is indulging simultaneously in verbal giddiness and in a very conscious parody of it. Above all, our acceptance is guaranteed by truth in portrayal: the exaggerated style escapes being ridiculous since it no longer seems the writer's sin but rather a reflection of the character's attitudes. Trollope simply records Mr. Gibson's *idée fixe*. Better still, his panic, the obsessiveness of the metaphors, and their very hysteria are the ultimate but thoroughly logical and justified consequence of verisimilitude much earlier in the novel. These derivations, which have by now invaded the narrative and contaminated all the involved characters, and the very metonymy that triggers them are motivated almost four hundred pages earlier by old Miss Stanbury's principles of Christian living. As she prepares to do her duty by a poor relative and take her under her roof as her adopted daughter, she is afraid Dorothy may have been spoiled by worldly fashions:

> [She] was intensely anxious as to the first appearance of her niece. Of course there would be a little morsel of a bonnet. She hated

those vile patches,—dirty flat daubs of millinery as she called them; but they had become too general for her to refuse admittance for such a thing within her doors. But a chignon,—a bandbox behind the noddle,—she would not endure.

(chap. 8)

Dorothy *is* unspoiled, but a rule of derivative grammar has been formulated that will also apply to any description of the people Miss Stanbury encounters later on. In this way a subtext shapes up, one that will help to overdetermine the unfolding of the novel.

The esthetic and mimetic anomalies of the metonymic derivation tend to increase geometrically as the derivation extends from phrase to sentence to text. But even so, its efficacy and its acceptability to the reader are insured, guaranteed, so to speak, by the constant presence of a compensatory factor. In the case of the chignon, this factor is a convincing representation of the characters' mental quirks or prejudices. There is, however, a more permanent and more generally applicable guarantee for the derivation's stylistic vagaries, for its ungrammaticality (in the sense that it comes to flout the rules of verisimilitude, of prevailing taste, and occasionally of common sense). This guarantee is the authority of language and of the mythology of commonplaces it embodies, in short, the authority of the sociolect.

The subtext's lexicon is generated by a metonymy, but its syntax is modeled on a stereotype, cliché, or proverb already established in usage— the linguistic equivalent of a symbol of truth. My example is from *The Warden*. A campaign is being waged by radical newspapers against what they regard as the excessive material wealth of the Church of England. A zealous reformer discovers that the salary paid to the warden of an institution for old pensioners is absorbing altogether too much of the endowment by the founder. These disclosures arouse in the thickheaded old beadsmen a not unnatural desire for a larger share for themselves. Archdeacon Grantly, the warden's son-in-law, will not hear of it: the archetypal worldly cleric, a rich man, son of a bishop, he sees nothing wrong with a Church whose cup runneth over. He comes to the almshouse to address the disgruntled pensioners:

As the archdeacon stood up to make his speech, erect in the middle of that little square, he looked like an ecclesiastical statue placed there as a fitting impersonation of the church militant here on earth; his shovel hat, large, new, and well-pronounced, a churchman's hat in every inch, declared the profession as plainly as does the Quaker's broad brim; his heavy eyebrow, large open eyes, and full mouth and chin expressed the solidity of his order; the broad chest, amply covered with fine cloth, told how well to do was its estate; one hand ensconced within his pocket, evinced the practical hold which our mother church keeps on her temporal possessions;

and the other, loose for action, was ready to fight if need be in her defence; and below these the decorous breeches, and neat black gaiters showing so admirably that well-turned leg, betokened the decency, the outward beauty and grace of our church establishment.

(chap. 5)

The reader's interpretation is strictly controlled by the incompatibility between the genre that the subtext actualizes and the manner of its actualization. This piece fits into the moral allegory in its narrow sense as personification: a character represents an abstract idea, and the reader knows how to identify the idea from this character's symbolic attributes. If a woman in long skirts holds a sword and a pair of scales, she must be Justice; if she holds a sword and shield, she must be War, and so forth. A written rather than visual allegory is free to extend the range of significant attributes: a representational verb may posit an equation between details describing the character and aspects of the ethical reality it represents, even though there may be no natural analogy to justify the symbolism. Such metalinguistic statements, of course, lead to parody and lend themselves to comic interpretation. On the one hand is a statue allegorizing the Church Militant; on the other, we are told its attributes correspond to the virtues of the Church—but the reader finds the correspondences by and large unacceptable: equating the beauty of breeches and gaiters with the moral beauty of the Church, for instance. A polarization pulling further apart the tenor and the vehicle of comparison makes the satire more pungent. For the vehicle—breeches and gaiters—is emphatically unspiritual; these garments lack the acceptability of a standard clerical metonym like *cloth*, used earlier in the passage. Whereas the tenor—*grace*—is more spiritual than mere *outward beauty*. Thus tension exists between two codes, the allegorical, the *statue* discourse, and the literal, the *clothing* discourse, the clergyman depicted metonymically through his professional accoutrements. This forced equivalency, however, does not seem gratuitous, because it is predicated on a verbal double authority: the authority of a cliché or quotation, and the authority of the text from which it is culled—*The Book of Common Prayer*: "Let us pray for the whole state of Christ's Church militant here on earth." What is kept of the prayer's phraseology generates the whole parody. The allegorical code, the statue's belligerent stance, is derived from the words "Church militant." The clothing code derives from a sly misprision of the words "here on earth" to mean "all-too-earthly." Again *The Book of Common Prayer* generates the subtext's closure: the metonymies substituting the outward symbols of self-interest for the signs of spiritual militancy form a sequence concluded by the words "archdeacon militant"(intertextual overdetermination is reinforced here by the latent presence of yet another model—the cliché "from head to toes," translated into ecclesiastical code [from "shovel hat" to "gaiters"]). No reader can help noticing it as a well-marked clausula, a violent substitute for "church militant." First, because of the unusual word order. Second, because of a sociolect tradition that views the image somewhat ironically. Third, because replacing "church," open to spiritual interpretation, with "archdeacon," associated only with hierarchy and temporal matters, is the same as replacing the spirit that quickens by the letter that deadens.

Nor is this all: yet another commonplace overdetermines the derivation and gives the initial metonymy the weight necessary to authorize the subtext's fanciful imagery. Indeed the entire allegorical sequence is but the expansion of the proverbial phrase "clothes make the man." The incipit of the subtext is found long before its allegorical climax: the initial metonymy is a vernacular reduction of the archdeacon to his calling, of the calling to the cloth that symbolizes it, and of the cloth to a satirical synecdoche of it—equating the divine with his gaiters: as Cavaliers used to reduce Puritans to Roundheads, so an insurgent beadsman calls him "Calves." Adds Trollope: "I am sorry to say the archdeacon himself was designated by this scurrilous allusion to his nether person." Another rebel upbraids his timid confederates: "some men is cowed at the very first sight of a gen'leman's coat and waistcoat" (chap. 4), only to doff his own hat to the "black coat and waistcoat of which he had spoken so irreverently" (chap. 5) when actually face to face with the archdeacon. Within such a context the whole allegory has to be interpreted the way it is because it functions as if clothes really and literally did make the man, as if the relationship between spirituality and gaiters were indeed akin to that uniting soul and body. That such is the mechanism of satire is proven by the transformation of a sentence about the archdeacon, "he was every inch a churchman," forty pages earlier, into "a churchman's hat in every inch" (chap. 3, chap. 5).

Without giving too much weight to one aspect of Trollope's art, it seems to me that his choice of metonymy as a favorite tool explains neatly how he can be at one and the same time an objective observer, faithfully depicting reality, and a satirical one, artfully distorting it. This is made possible by the two-faceted nature of the trope. On the one hand, metonymy focuses precisely on suggestive details. On the other, its reductive function makes the selfsame details (seen as substitutes rather than taken in their own rights) the words of humorous discourse.

Finally, it appears that the generative power of metonymy is what makes this figure most fundamentally germane to the novel as a genre. Metonymies can be found in texts other than fictional ones. What seems peculiar to the novel is the combination of metonymy and the subtext periphrastically derived from it. The fact that the subtext derivation proceeds from word to word, rather than from word to nonverbal referent, as well as the fact that this derivation is facilitated by preexisting linguistic models, may explain how Trollope could write so fast and so unerringly.

Can You Forgive Him?: Trollope's *Can You Forgive Her?* and the Myth of Realism

George Levine

The vast and casual terrain of Anthony Trollope's fiction has persistently resisted easy classification of both its texture and quality. His *Autobiography,* which seems at times a calculated attempt to *épater les intellectuels*, is probably—both in its humility and its arrogance—a not unreasonable summation of his qualities. It is hard to imagine, even in spite of some recent very interesting and serious attempts at revaluation and reconstruction, that we can ever take Trollope as seriously as an artist as we take some of the other major Victorians. Technically, he accepted the terms of the realistic technique he adopted, and there is little sign in his fictions, early or late, that the demands of his subjects, or of his own considerations of his work, led him to test out the limits of that technique in any direction. He was, for better or worse, a conventional artist—that is, a writer who unquestioningly accepted the conventions he inherited. His emphasis was on character and story, more the former than the latter, on plain tales plainly told, a touch of melodrama permissible, only the most moderate sort of heroism, and a sense of character sharply defined by social context.

Yet he told so many stories in his lifetime that those who come to him expecting only a comfortably clumsy Victorian moderation in both style and subject tend to be in for surprises. One way to talk about such surprises, of course, is by returning to Trollope's realism, by taking seriously the notion that, as a realist, he was simply reflecting the society he had chosen to describe. And that society was full of submerged violence, potential madness, charlatans and hypocrites and not so virtuous young ladies. But Trollope is no more accurate a "reflector" of society than Dickens or George Eliot, and "realism" is as conventional, that is, as literary, a mode as any other. Its allegiance is, finally, not so much to the "outside world" as to

From *Victorian Studies* 18, no. 1 (September 1974). © 1974 by Indiana University.

credibility, and not so much to credibility as to certain conventions of the credible. The realist is as much bound to invent his world as the fantasist, and he depends in similar ways, on how earlier writers invented their worlds. My argument is, then, that to judge Trollope fairly one is obliged to consider the nature of his "invention," to begin, that is, not by testing his vision of society against what we can know of the realities of Victorian life, but by examining the rules of his game. To the historian Trollope may remain interesting as a writer who portrayed with remarkable accuracy the nuances of Victorian upper middle-class society. But he is interesting in another and more satisfying way. As one of the few writers of competence who wrote comfortably and almost exclusively within the range of the conventions of English realism, Trollope can illuminate for us many of the central problems of realism: the tension between credibility and form, the dependence of the realist on extra-realist conventions, the internal contradictions which arise when moral questions are at stake, or when credibility demands, in both subject and style, a movement beyond conceptions of "normality."

The techniques of realism in English fiction tend to release energies to which the techniques themselves are unequal. For Trollope, these techniques are expressions of that myth of the real which is more pervasive in his fiction than in the work of any other English realist. This is the myth that wisdom resides in learning the rules of society and acquiescing in them. Within the movement to wisdom there is, of course, a great deal of room for individual variation and for recognition of the inequity of society and the importance of individual needs which society seems unwilling to accommodate. Realistic techniques imply the value of surfaces, of social manners, of objects, of appearances; but they also tend to force careful notation of thought and feeling as surfaces and characters meet and conflict. Yet in its concentration on these things, realism tends to treat feelings and ideas which cannot accommodate themselves to "reality"—that is, to surfaces and social conventions—as aberrations. Thus, while inviting, almost requiring, critical perceptions of the irrationalities and cruelties of surfaces and societies, realism in English has almost always invited an anti-romantic, anti-ideal compromise, an ultimate rejection of ideals as "aberrations." Trollope, who invites us in *Can You Forgive Her?* to see well beyond the hypocrisies and irrationalities of social conventions, to understand the brutality of society's treatment of women, the hypocrisies of respectable society, the viciousness of the money game, the centrality of money to power, invites us as well to accept the necessity for accommodation. Strong enough to show us the incompleteness of the relation between his protagonists, he requires that we take as beautiful and satisfying the impossible accommodations they try to make to each other.

He will not, like George Eliot, or Dickens, or Hardy, reach beyond the techniques and the myth, and thus, though there are impressive elements of moral subversion in his art, his novels become comforting, conservative documents, easy in the ways of the middle class, admiring of the ways of the aristocracy, worldly wise in their acceptance of the inevitabilities of compromise. He gives us—as does George Eliot, Dickens, or Hardy—a vision of society organized according to incorrigible self-interest, sanctioning, in its business and its parties, greed and hypocrisy, engaged in violent if quietly respectable repression of women and of the poor. In this he is rather like the other and greater realists who were his contemporaries. Like them, too, he understood that society's rules could never deal adequately with the variety and complexity of human nature. In the quest for the possibility both of community and individual fulfillment all but Trollope were forced beyond the realistic mode where their greatest aesthetic lapses and their most intensely felt needs and aspirations sought a place. Trollope remained within the realistic mode, and his realism almost perfectly reflects not the "reality" of Victorian society, but the myth of pragmatic worldly wisdom which supported it. There are, in Trollope's world, certain ways to play the game, and though one is allowed a great deal both of sophistication and cynicism about the game itself, one is not allowed to violate the rules, either as a novelist writing, or as a character acting. Trollope's fiction is dominated by a social myth: even if one knows society's rules of decorum, gentlemanliness, and order to be wrong and repressive in any given situation, those rules are essential to society's survival. And that survival is the ultimate value because the well-being, even the identity, of all people is dependent upon it.

To choose any novel to represent the possibilities of Trollope's art and the nature of his realism is necessarily to be almost absurdly arbitrary. But *Can You Forgive Her?*, which contains much of the best of Trollope, can, without fully representing the variety of Trollope's worlds, tell us a good deal about the way his realism expresses a particular political and social mythology while it appears to be splendidly dispassionate. At the same time it seems to share and transcend many of the qualities of Trollope's narrative art. It has a loose structure, which I take to be generally characteristic, but it has a stronger than normal thematic coherence among the various plots. It has, moreover, one of those rare, essentially symbolic moments, the presence of which might help define its absence in other works, and its essential irrelevance to Trollope's mode. And finally, it deals as seriously as Trollope ever did with the tension between private feeling and social responsibility while revealing with almost uncanny sensitivity (up to a point) the plight of women and the submerged violence of the gentlemanly ideal. *Can You Forgive Her?* shows as clearly as any of Trollope's novels the special kind of achievement available to a writer for whom the stakes are not too high.

Partly because it strives so much for coherence, almost in spite of itself, *Can You Forgive Her?* is a perfect example of the way in which Trollope never, as Henry James would have put it, "does" a subject. The problems inherent in the relationship of Alice Vavasor and John Grey are, as it were, transferred and inverted in the relationship of the Pallisers. It is almost as though Trollope lost interest in the initiating plot (based on that of an early unperformed play he had written) and so shifted the focus. With the obvious transference of focus, Trollope seems to have felt obliged to do something about connecting the two plots, and so we have quite conscious and repeated parallels between the problems of the two women. The nature of the parallels is complicated and very rich—almost altogether unusual for a Trollope novel. Trollope's narrative mode does not usually entail that the relationships among subplots be tight. In his *Autobiography,* he says that "Every sentence, every word, through all those pages, should tend to the telling of the story," and that "subsidiary plots" should "all tend to the elucidation of the main story, and . . . take their places as part of one and the same work." Yet by his own quite convincing testimony, character is the primary interest of fiction, and once Trollope introduces an interesting character, the requirements of his own commitments lead to what looks like an altogether new story. In fact, it is frequently very hard to know what the "story" of some of the novels is supposed to be.

Can You Forgive Her? is an important example of the mode and the problem. Its three narratives focus on three women who must in different ways test their personal inclinations, their "wilful" desires for freedom, against social conventions and public morality. The title suggests, as it is picked up through the book, that the true subject is Alice Vavasor, who in the early stages of the plot jilts John Grey. But the question can be asked equally of Lady Glencora, who loves Burgo Fitzgerald while she is married to Plantagenet Palliser. Lady Glencora, who as he himself indicates is Trollope's favorite character in the book, does not appear in it until chapter 18, and does not reappear until chapter 22, but she is the center of focus in the book from that point on while Alice, whose problem began as a genuinely complicated one, becomes less and less attractive, less and less substantial. The tension soon goes out of her story, and its resolution in her marriage to Grey seems almost a formality. It is difficult to know how Trollope would have reconciled this structure to his own statement, "every word . . . should tend to the elucidation of the main story," because it is almost impossible to know what the main story is. On the whole, I would argue, unity is not a real problem for Trollope, because his real preoccupation is with following out in time the developments of the characters whom he regards as worthy of interest.

The juxtaposition of the two plots creates a striking potential thematic and dramatic coherence—and the theme has very little to do with the question the title asks. Nor is it merely (though it is partly) another Trollopean exploration of the meaning of marriage. Happily, the theme or themes cannot be stated in any simple formula. The novel begins, in the story of Alice Vavasor, to explore the possibilities of personal freedom—even at the expense of love—within a society which transforms love by marriage into a contract of submission for the wife. Equally, it questions both moral and gentlemanly perfection, and allows us to see these qualities in terms of power. Of course, at the center of all this is Trollope's complicated and sensitive but ultimately thoroughly masculine perception of the difficulties of being a woman in so arbitrarily constructed a society. In this novel, as in many others, Trollope allows a much greater sympathy with wilful women than almost any other male Victorian but Meredith and Hardy. Even Alice Vavasor, universally condemned by critics and by Trollope himself as unattractive, is a potentially fascinating figure until the entrance of Glencora, when her role in the exploration of these problems is largely taken away from her. Our interest in her is precisely in her resistance to the perfect marriage, and in her reasons for resistance. She self-consciously asserts her will in a vague and indecisive rejection of love. But her latent reasons are thoroughly comprehensible: a fear of and consequent resistance to power, even to the power of goodness. It is symptomatic that as Trollope shifts his own interest, he begins to be unclear himself about why Alice rejected John Grey and thus fudges all the issues he had delicately and insightfully raised.

But the two stories do have common preoccupations, held together not only thematically but by the interesting role of "duenna" which Alice unwittingly takes and by the curious inversion of the love relationships. Glencora, under pressure from Lady Midlothian and others, rejects the man she loves, who is wicked, for a man she does not love, who is almost perfect. Alice, under the pressure of Lady Midlothian and others, is being persuaded to marry the man she loves, but whom she has rejected almost because of his goodness; and she is turning to a man she doesn't love, who is wicked. Palliser has money, Burgo does not; John Grey has money, George Vavasor has not. Both women, for radically different reasons, are driving themselves towards the impractical and the dangerous and the violation of all the rules the society sanctions. Very rarely, in Victorian novels within the realistic tradition, are the problems of personal feeling, social restrictions, and resistance to power more extensively dealt with.

Even the third plot, more characteristically separate, has a role in this cluster of preoccupations, and it too has been rather hardly or inadequately treated because Lady Glencora so entirely steals the show. Mrs. Greenow is little better than she should be. Beginning life in society as an apparently dangerous flirt, she makes a prudential marriage with an old and wealthy man, and in the novel is an entirely free woman since her husband has died and left her rich. But she also has two choices in love—either a wealthy and pompous man who is hardly lovable but, because he is part of a comic subplot, is not altogether vicious, or a total scapegrace with charm and wit. In the long run, of course, Mrs. Greenow's presence is not at all important to the "story," whichever one decides *is* the story, and certainly, some of the attempts at amusement through description of picnics and buffoonery by Cheesacre, Bellfield, and Greenow are altogether digressions, and clumsily unfunny ones, at that. The novel strains, here, after diverting comedy that may be the mark of Trollope's formulaic sense of what should go into a novel.

Yet Mrs. Greenow, too, is a wilful woman, a woman who has the worldly wisdom essential to survival and success, and who cannot be moved by arguments as to decorum, by exposures of her own lies, or by anything but consideration of what would be best for her. She is nevertheless not a lost woman, merely a prudent one, who knows how to bend the rules or how to get away with pretending that she is observing them. She recommends flirtations for girls in their youth, but prudence in actual commitment. She has an un-Victorian frankness that is quite satisfying. "Some women," she says, "look as though matrimony itself were improper, and as if they believed the little babies were found about in the hedges and ditches. They talk of women being forward! There are some of them a deal too backward according to my way of thinking." She sees that power and comfort are available only with "means," and, as she says, "I want things to be comfortable." But Trollope makes Mrs. Greenow something more than a scheming prudential woman. Though she can bring tears to her eyes on any occasion, it seems clear that some of the tears for dear departed Mr. Greenow are authentic, if only because he was the means to her power. She feels free, now that she is wealthy, to find some of the romance she couldn't have with her first husband, and thus she surrenders the wealthy Mr. Cheesacre, who represents "bread and cheese," for the impecunious Bellfield, who represents "rocks and mountains." But only on the condition that she can keep Bellfield, about whom she is thoroughly knowledgable, from squandering her fortune and ruining her. In the forthcoming marriage, she will obviously be in control. "Of course," she says, "bread-and-cheese is the real thing. The rocks and valleys are no good at all, if you haven't got that. But enough is as good as a feast." And thus she decides to take Bellfield because she can afford to and because, as she honestly says, "I do think he's fond of me,—I do indeed."

In choosing Bellfield, Mrs. Greenow acts out, on a small and comic scale, the possibilities open to Alice and Glencora of taking George Vavasor and Burgo Fitzgerald. But unlike Alice, Mrs. Greenow does not offer her money to her lover unconditionally. She uses it to keep control. And unlike Glencora—were she to have run off with Burgo—she is willing to sacrifice nothing in the way of social acceptance or respectability. Romance becomes available to her because she is rich and because her husband is dead. Burgo would have ruined Glencora, just as Vavasor was on the verge of ruining Alice. With the confidence of worldly wisdom, and money, Mrs. Greenow makes her bargain with romance, achieves that kind of Trollopean compromise which is almost a model of the cynical warmth that characterizes so much of the Trollopean world. And although the Greenow story is rather clumsily interlarded among the two major plots, Mrs. Greenow achieves the kind of compromise between prudence and warmth which is echoed in more complicated ways in the relationship that develops between Palliser and his wife. They are compromises possible because of a recognition within the narrative of the arbitrariness of the rules of social life. Mrs. Greenow's special sort of pleasantly cynical frankness is only open to a realist like Trollope because he almost never concerns himself much about ideals.

In the story of Alice Vavasor, who does concern herself with ideals and who cannot endure her own falling short of them, there is not the slightest indication that either romance or comfort is very important. To Jeffrey Palliser she says, during her first visit to the Palliser's house at Matching, "Romance usually means nonsense, I believe." And although she is sensible enough to be unwilling to give all her private fortune to George Vavasor, she will insist on retaining only enough to keep her from starving. It is perhaps this resistance both to the calls of excessive personal feeling and of simple prudence that made Alice unattractive to Trollope. But the Alice we meet at the beginning of the story has an interest outside either prudence or romance. Her first act in the novel is a decision to take a trip to Switzerland with her former lover and her sister while she is engaged to Mr. Grey. If not exactly warm—there are very early signs of prudishness—she is strong and willing to take risks, to be regarded, as Lady Macleod says, as "wicked." As Trollope depicts her, of course, she is also to be seen as quite weak and badly educated in the ways of society although trained to obey them instinctively. Before the novel opens, we later learn, Alice refuses to allow Glencora and Burgo to meet in her house. This propriety is the aspect of Alice that dominates once Glencora enters the novel, but until that time, we can see in Alice a convincingly uncertain girl, attempting to respond to her own private needs though repressed by the very conventions which have almost become instinct and conscience to her. What she is really trying to do in going off to Switzerland, though she is not altogether aware of this herself, is to find a way to keep from having all her options closed, all her possibilities circumscribed by a marriage. One bit of clear evidence for this view is the discomfort she feels at John Grey's perfection. "Would that he had some faults! Would that he had!" she thinks desperately. (And this is a reflection that will be echoed in Glencora's feelings about *her* husband.) Alice tells herself that she could not—being herself full of faults—make so perfect a creature as Grey happy. With remarkable acuity, Trollope shows us Alice disappointed that her fiancé does not forbid her to take the trip, because by forbidding her, he would open a way to her breaking the engagement. "If he does not trust me he is quite free to go," she had thought, perhaps hoped, as she anticipated Grey's refusal.

When talking to her Aunt MacLeod, Alice formulates that fear of final restraint. Refusing to be pushed into an early marriage, she tells her aunt: "People always do seem to think it so terrible that a girl should have her own way in anything. She mustn't like any one at first; and then, when she does like someone, she must marry him directly she's bidden. I haven't much of my own way at present. But you see, when I'm married I shan't have it at all." This may, in Trollope's view, be a simple rationalization for perversity, but her attitude is confirmed by almost every action in the book, and echoed by Mrs. Greenow's utter refusal to submit to such a state of things. Alice herself is ambitious, unwilling to accept a quiet, merely domestic life. And Grey demonstrates, in his interview with Alice before she leaves for Switzerland, that he has neither understanding of this difference, nor compassion for that spirit of action and freedom which gives Alice her essential character at the start. Grey's presence tends to overpower her arguments, both because she has genuine affection for him and because he is clearly behaving like a gentleman, according to the rules.

> Now that he was with her she could not say the things she had told herself that she would utter to him. She could not bring herself to hint to him that his views of life were so unlike her own, that there could be no chance of happiness between them, unless each could strive to lean somewhat towards the other. No man could be more gracious in word and manner than John Grey; no man more chivalrous in his carriage towards a woman; but he always spoke and acted as though there could be no question that his manner of life was to be adopted, without a word or thought of doubting, by his wife.

This is far more convincing than the earlier argument that she could not marry him because she was flawed and he perfect. Grey plays according to the rules of society, he is a perfect gentleman. But in this relationship we see that from the woman's point of view, to be a gentleman is to be at best a benevolent tyrant, and Alice is too strong to bear even that kind of tyranny.

All of this is handled delicately, and Alice's refusal to submit not only does not provoke the question Trollope seems to think it provokes—*Can You Forgive Her?*—but positively justifies her, except according to those arbitrary rules of society, which ultimately control the shape of all Trollope's novels. Being free to see the arbitrariness of the rules and to understand how they pull against individual needs, he can allow us to understand the plight of women within these rules without allowing himself to reject them. Far from being the weakest parts of the book, the opening chapters are highly promising, suggesting that Trollope, in working out Alice's fate, will be forced to put to the test those qualities of compromise, that almost cynically quiet acceptance of society's rules, which regularly mark his work.

The pressure of the Trollopean myth, however, gradually diminishes the intensity of Alice's story, and transforms her inarticulate aspiration for freedom and scope into something utterly impractical and imprecise. Thus, once Alice has chosen to reject Grey, the book takes sides and assumes both that Alice is wrong and that all sensible people will see this to be the case. Allowing himself the casual freedom as narrator to shift his narration among dramatic recordings of his characters' thoughts, an equal's perception of those thoughts, and an author's judgment of them, Trollope slips—in chapter 11—into a strong, implicitly condescending rejection of the position that Alice has taken up. Alice, he says,

> had by degrees filled herself with a vague idea that there was a something to be done; a something over and beyond, or perhaps altogether besides that marrying and having two children;—if she only knew what it was. She had filled herself, or had been filled by her cousins, with an undefined ambition that made her restless without giving her any real food for her mind. When she told herself that she would have no scope for action in that life in Cambridgeshire which Mr. Grey was preparing for her, she did not herself know what she meant by action. Had any one accused her of being afraid to separate herself from London society, she would have declared that she went very little into society and disliked that little. . . . When she did contrive to find any answer to that question as to what she should do with her life,—or rather what she would wish to do with it if she were a free agent, it was generally of a political nature. She was not so far advanced as to think that women should be lawyers and doctors, or to wish that she might have the privilege of the franchise for herself; but she had undoubtedly a hankering after some second-hand political maneuvering. She would have liked, I think, to have been the wife of the leader of a Radical opposition, in the time when such men were put into prison, and to have kept up for him his seditious correspondence while he lay in the Tower. . . . John Grey had no politics. . . . What political enthusiasm could she indulge with such a companion down in Cambridgeshire?
>
> She thought too much of all this,—and was, if I may say, overprudent in calculating the chances of her happiness and of his. For, to give her credit for what was her due, she was quite as anxious on the latter head as on the former. "I don't care for the Roman Senate," she would say to herself. "I don't care much for the Girondists. How am I to talk to him day after day, night after night, when we shall be alone together."

Even the condescension here cannot altogether mask the reality of the difficulty which Alice envisages and Trollope, with the stance of worldy wisdom, is in fact pooh-poohing. And it is part of Trollope's peculiar stature as a novelist that he is rarely so heavily judgemental that he keeps out of his books alternative possibilities. But that special angle from which Trollope sees with cynical warmth reduces reality for any woman to marrying and having two children and being honest with an honest husband. As we can see from the later political novels and from the others, and from the Mrs. Proudie sequences in the Barsetshire novels, Trollope is nevertheless fascinated by the way women enter politics through—occasionally over—their husbands. In any case, woman's political role has nothing to do with any genuine political understanding, but exclusively with what Trollope surely sees as quite special feminine qualities of concreteness, irrationality, romance, and affectionate loyalty. In his handling of Alice's aspirations, Trollope suggests, only to disallow, a quest which in the hands of less worldly-wise but more intelligent novelists became the central subjects of great novels. Dorothea Brooke and Isabel Archer both take romantic stances which disallow, disastrously, conventional marriages to good men. The pressure of this theme pushed James beyond the limits of the realistic conventions which he explicitly espoused and provided George Eliot with material verging on tragedy. But for Trollope, Alice's incompletely imagined desires are merely childish and, from his perspective, feminine. She is protected against her own worst self by John Grey, who surreptitiously provides George Vavasor with the money Alice has promised him. And since George himself turns out to be precisely the bounder and wild man Trollope warns us of at the start, no possibility for real usefulness remains open to Alice.

The conclusion of Alice's story is—for anyone who has allowed himself to take her aspirations seriously—a confirmation of the horror of her condition. Alice is one of those figures, like Jane Austen's Emma, George Eliot's Gwendolen Harleth, James's Isabel Archer, for whom genuine freedom seems to be available only—and powerfully—through frigidity, or at least through mistaken resistance to men who love them. The resistance to sexuality is a resistance to being mastered, penetrated, taken. But we are reminded that Alice is a sexual being. Her inability to force herself to marry George Vavasor is primarily sexual: "Was she to give herself bodily—body and soul, as she said aloud in her solitary agony,—to a man whom she did not love. Must she submit to his caresses,—lie on his bosom,—turn herself warmly to his kisses? 'No,' she said, 'no.' " On the other hand, John Grey is really dangerous to her because she feels his sexual attraction. When he "had come and had touched her hand, . . . the fibers of her body had seemed to melt within her at the touch so that she would have fallen at his feet." Grey means surrender of self in sexual surrender. And the surrender is made, in depressingly appropriate language, near the end of the book:

> of course she had no choice but to yield. He, possessed of power of force infinitely greater than hers, had left no alternative but to be happy. . . . And it may be that there was still left within her bosom some remnant of that feeling of rebellion which his masterful spirit had ever produced in her. He was so superior in his tranquillity, he argued his question of love with such a manifest preponderance of right on his side, that she had always felt that to yield to him would be to confess the omnipresence of his power.

Alice surrenders, though by this time in the book it is a little difficult to care or believe in the problem of power and submission so effectively raised at the start.

Of the three plots, then, only the story of Glencora is worked out fully and satisfactorily. This may be in part because Glencora is imagined as more thoroughly a child than Alice, whose romantic aspirations are always mixed with prudence and are always quite specially and threateningly serious. Glencora is a woman of far more vivacity than Alice, and of a mind much less theoretical and abstract. Because she is less prudent and less serious, she is also in greater danger of violating one of society's rules in a disgraceful and self-destructive way, but her qualities as character allow a far more satisfying, less condescending stance. Glencora, from the point of view of Trollope's world, is thoroughly a woman, and therefore Trollope, with his worldly wisdom, can allow that she is sexually attracted to a beautiful man (and one might point out as well that another virtue of Trollope's special worldly sympathy with basic human drives outside the rules is manifest in the fact that he is the only male nineteenth-century novelist I can remember who allows himself to use the word "beautiful" about a man). But though Glencora, too, is wilful, and though she too would like to reject authority, she is shown to have a becoming weakness— a capacity to be governed which we may see, if Trollope does not, as an aspect of the fragility of women within the arbitrarily ruled society Trollope imagines. Glencora, unlike Alice, has succumbed to the pressures of her relatives and has married a man she doesn't love, just as she later ends her defiance only short of running off with her lover.

Some critics have suggested that as Trollope imagined Glencora, she would have run off with Burgo Fitzgerald. But this is to ignore Trollope's quite remarkable insight into her powerlessness and weakness. Part of what is so attractive about Glencora is that her fits of independence and defiance—in relation at least to the man's world—are necessarily fruitless. In later novels she will learn something of how to wield power. But while she can annoy her husband, she cannot really win over him at any point where he is determined to take a stand. His chivalry allows few stands, but he remains unquestionably the master. There is, in Glencora's defiance, pathos as well as comedy. Even Glencora's romance is tempered in a way that makes it less threatening to society. Like Mrs. Greenow, she likes her "rocks and mountains." "Lady Glencora herself had a love for the mountains and lakes, but it was a love of that kind which requires to be stimulated by society, and which is keenest among cold chicken, picnic-pies, and the flying of champagne corks." Even the language here recalls Mrs. Greenow's plein-air picnics. She remains far less of a threat to Trollope's realistic mythology than Alice might have been, and when, in *Can You Forgive Her?*, she learns the art of compromise, it is a far more convincing and satisfying education than that which Trollope allows Alice.

This is not to suggest anything of the quality of the Palliser sections of the novel, but merely to indicate the kind of materials that Trollope's special vision and literary technique are most comfortable with. In fact, there is much in the Palliser section which is quite wonderful, not only because it deals, with an almost non-Victorian frankness, with sexual possibilities, but because it manages to create characters of great depth in the process of growth. Even that happy coincidence which gives Glencora the child she has wanted in time to save the marriage and get Palliser back to accept his position in the cabinet is not merely a trick of plotting to ring down the curtain happily. It is a perhaps unconscious recognition of the society's idea of women. Glencora and Mr. Palliser have, before this happy moment, learned to do what Alice Vavasor saw correctly as being essential to marriage. They learned "that there could be no chance of happiness between them, unless each could strive to lean towards the other." Plantagenet has striven, at great expense, even to the surrender of the political prize he had spent his life in earning, and Glencora has surrendered her lover. With nothing in common but the will to try to make it work, they learn something of each other. Palliser expresses his love and Glencora learns that the love is there, awkwardly but almost heroically present. Plantagenet learned to come to terms, almost to sympathize with Glencora's perversity, however painful. The act of travelling through Europe together, of forcing themselves to be in each other's company, is also the act of bringing the marriage to fruition through the conception of an heir.

In the relation between Glencora and Plantagenet, Trollope has invented a subject which needs almost no overt manipulation. Although through the coming birth of the child the conventional happy ending is achieved, Trollope creates an almost altogether unsentimental story which can have no genuine ending until the death of one of the partners—and in *The Duke's Children*, written sixteen years later, Glencora's presence is felt even in her absence. It is a story which does not end in marriage but begins in it, a quite natural development from the really incongruous comic ending in marriage of traditional realistic fiction. It is a development which one can see also in the works of George Eliot, and which was coming in Thackeray as well. For the natural direction of the realist vision is toward a sense that there are no endings, only constant shiftings and developments in time. The inadequacy of the comic ending in marriage in the Trollopean world is manifest in the thorough bathos of the culminating marriage of John Grey and Alice Vavasor. This culmination almost entirely ignores precisely those problems of incompatibility, of long silences on domestic evenings that are the test of marriage. Only the fortuitous conversion of Grey to a willingness to stand for Parliament at the instigation of Palliser does anything to deal with the problem. And by accepting the importance of this step for the success of Alice's marriage, Trollope implicitly concedes the validity of the romantic notions to which he condescended in the early passages of the novel. The resistance to finality is a natural consequence of the realistic myth, and it allows Trollope to open his stories again and again into new novels. In the realistic myth, death is the only possible ending, and prior to death all experience struggles through time toward formlessness. The novel of epic breadth, stretching across generations, is one of the ends towards which realism moves.

But it would be wrong to treat this novel simply as a part of the great Palliser saga. It contains within itself quite remarkable sequences chronicling the growth of Glencora and Palliser and of their relationship, but since by the very nature of this sort of subject, these sequences sprawl through time and the novel, it will be difficult to do more than hint at the nature of the technique, which is Trollope's most distinctive virtue as a writer, and his own natural development of the techniques of realism.

Glencora's wilfulness of spirit is manifested in the energy of her language, which contrasts very sharply, and immediately, with Alice's. Where Alice restrains and controls her feelings, and uses language sparingly and with apparent calculation and reserve, Glencora reveals almost everything about herself immediately, either by implication or direction. In Glencora's first scene, as she takes Alice to Matching with her, she confesses, after a long period of uninterrupted talk, that "I'm one of those who like talking, as you'll find out. I think it runs in families; and the Pallisers are non-talkers." Here, as almost everywhere, she suggests something of the incompatibility between her and her husband, and we become aware, in Alice's reserved silences, that Glencora's later only half-facetious comment to Alice is correct: after being read one of those lectures which begin to mark Alice as a prig, about the "reticence which all women should practice," Glencora responds by saying that "it was a pity she [Alice] had not married Mr. Palliser." But one of the marks of Glencora's desire for spontaneity, directness, and honesty of speech is that she is almost powerless to act out her independence any way but verbally.

The contrast between Alice and Glencora is extremely important for Glencora's story, though it comes, as I have suggested, at the expense of Alice's story. Alice understands that verbal control is essential to the rules of society, and she serves constantly to warn Glencora of the dangers of violating those rules through frankness. Alice is a supreme verbal compromiser, and a persistent interpreter of the rules. The irony of the relationship is that though Alice obeys the verbal rules, she has in fact violated a rule of behavior in breaking with John Grey. Glencora, though she persistently violates the verbal rules, has not quite broken the rules of behavior. And this contrast gives to Glencora's verbal energy an attractive touch of pathos—it is the fluttering of wings in a cage. "I hate all these rules. Don't you, Alice," she asks. But "Alice did not hate them, therefore she said nothing." In fact, with all her threats and imaginations of improper actions, through the whole book Glencora manages only three violations of the rules: she walks in the cold moonlight among the Priory ruins; she gambles in Baden; and she waltzes with Burgo. The futility of the first two of these is patent—they are the extent to which Glencora actually indulges her impulses to take chances. The dance with Burgo is, of course, genuinely dangerous, but the very openness of it reduces the possibility of the actual elopement, which is what Alice and society fear. Glencora, however much wing-fluttering she does, is entirely trapped by the rules.

In fact both girls—equally wilful in their own ways—are struggling against aspects of themselves which would allow them to fly free. Trollope repeats, with variations, a scene near the beginning and ending of the book which points up the contrast and the similarity. When Alice is in Basle, standing on a bridge over the Rhine, she turns to George Vavasor and says, "Wouldn't you like to be swimming down there as those boys were doing when we went out into the balcony. The water looks so enticing . . . I should so like to feel myself going with the stream, . . . particularly by this light. I can't fancy in the least that I should be drowned. . . . It would be so pleasant to feel the water gliding along one's limbs, and to be carried away headlong." But those swimmers, who had been "glorying in the swiftness of the current," are not particularly attractive to George Vavasor, her companion. "I can't say I should," he replies. Sitting on a balcony in Basle, overlooking the Rhine once more, Glencora sees the swimmers just as Alice had seen them earlier. "Oh how I wish I could do that," she exclaims. To which Mr. Palliser replies much as George had earlier, "It seems to be very dangerous . . . I don't know how they can stop themselves." "Why," says Glencora, "should they want to stop themselves? . . . Think how cool the water must be; and how beautiful to be carried along so quickly and to go on, and on, and on! I suppose we couldn't try it?" She receives no reply, and we have once again the pathos of her aspirations to break loose. It isn't even clear that, were anyone to have taken her up, she would have acted out her wishes.

The pathos of the desire is repeated for Glencora in the gambling hall, where the full extent of her rebellion comes in the betting of one piece of gold. "There are moments," Glencora had said, "when I almost make up my mind to go headlong to the devil,—when I think it is the best thing to be done. It is a hard thing for a woman to do, because she has to undergo so much obloquy before she gets used to it." At this point, the prudent Alice asserts all the priggishness with which Trollope endows her in the later sections of the novel, and threatens to leave if Glencora bets. She acts the role Palliser himself would have acted, a very different one from that suggested by her desire to swim in the Rhine. But neither girl, at any point, can do more than "almost" make up her mind to go to the devil, to surrender to the personal desires which society restrains.

This desire not to be restrained, the longing for some excitement, however minimal, distinguishes Glencora from her husband as much as does her talkativeness. Palliser wonders, in characteristic banal fashion, how the swimmers will stop themselves. And his whole career has been a quiet steady application to study and work and soporific six-hour speeches in Parliament which win him a reputation while nobody listens. Where Glencora is excitedly involved in particular people and particular moments, these things bore Palliser, who yawns unless he can apply himself to his blue books and documents. Where Glencora is demonstrative, he is reticent; where she is careless, he is prudent. We have almost a high society reflection of the relation of Sissy Jupe to Mr. Gradgrind in *Hard Times* but without the satirical judgment implied in the Dickensian portraits.

One can only suggest here how Trollope keeps from giving to the relation a forced, diagrammatic and obviously manipulated structure. But the following passage, describing part of the quietly funny psychological warfare Glencora wages during the European travels, manages to sustain the contrast without making it parody because the narrative compassion circumscribes both Glencora and her husband:

> They stayed in Paris for a week, and during that time Alice found that she became very intimate with Mr. Palliser. At Matching she had, in truth, seen but little of him, and had known nothing. Now she began to understand his character, and learned how to talk to him. She allowed him to tell her of things in which Lady Glencora resolutely persisted in taking no interest. She delighted him by writing down in a little pocketbook the number of eggs that were consumed in Paris every day, whereas Glencora protested that the information was worth nothing unless her husband could tell her how many of the eggs were good, and how many bad. And Alice was glad to find that a hundred and fifty thousand female operatives were employed in Paris, while Lady Glencora said it was a great shame, and that they ought all to have husbands. When Mr. Palliser explained that was impossible, because of the redundancy of the female population, she angered him very much by asserting that she saw a great many men walking about who, she was quite sure, had not wives of their own.
>
> "I do so wish you had married him!" Glencora said to Alice that evening. "You would always have had a pocket-book ready to write down the figures, and you would have pretended to care about the eggs, and the bottles of wine, and the rest of it. As for me, I can't do it. If I see an hungry woman, I can give her my money; or if she be a sick woman, I can nurse her; or if I hear of a very wicked man, I can hate him;—but I cannot take up poverty and crime in the lump. I never believe it all. My mind isn't big enough."

This sequence is immediately followed by an argument about whether they should all have a plan or travel spontaneously. And so it goes through Europe. Trollope's own untheoretical and non-logical mind obviously was greatly sympathetic to Glencora's. But he allows moments into the relationship between husband and wife which transform it from simple domestic comedy, and in which Palliser has it much his own way. The male, however awkward, shy, and inexpressive, cannot but win, in this world, over the feminine, whose imagined concreteness, emotionalism, and capriciousness can be attractive only when it is guided.

The crisis of the relationship between the two comes, of course, in the scenes following Glencora's dancing with Burgo Fitzgerald. Until that time, we are told much of Palliser's distinction, but he is presented dramatically as far worse a prig than Alice ever becomes and as a man cruel in his insensitivity to other people's emotional needs while he is utterly absorbed in self. But his calculated coldness is not worse humanly than his unwillingness or incapacity to think ill of his wife or worry about his marriage. There is some question whether his trust of Glencora is more noble than cruel. When Glencora, before the marriage, explained that she loved Burgo Fitzgerald, Palliser's total response was, "You must love me now." "And then, as regarded his mind, the thing was over." His preoccupation with work of government and developing "ascendancy over other men" is apparently total: "To lose his influence with his party would be worse to him than to lose his wife, and public disgrace would hit him harder than private dishonour." Because of his politics, we are reminded, "He could thus afford to put up with the small everyday calamity of having a wife who loved another man better than she loved him." Glencora thinks of the "deadness in life" which she endures with Palliser, and it is easy to share the feeling. The passages in which the deadness of the relationship is worked out are too diffuse to quote, but one moment will do for many here. At one point Glencora complains that Palliser shouldn't be angry with her. "I am not angry," he replies. "You speak like a child to say so."

Yet the fault is surely not all on one side, and the scope of Palliser's special strength comes convincingly, when it comes, during the interview between him and Glencora after the dance. When he re-enters the party to find Fitzgerald with Glencora, he responds to Glencora's first remark that she thought he had gone home, almost casually: "I did go home, . . . but I thought I might as well come back for you." And then he immediately decides to go off—leaving Fitzgerald and his wife together—to fetch Glencora's scarf. Glencora is touched by the "chivalry of his leaving them again together," and quietly returns home with him. Seven chapters awkwardly intrude between this scene and the interview between Glencora and Plantagenet on the following morning, as the two plots drift apart once again. But the chapter that describes the interview is worth waiting for, and we are made aware of a depth in Palliser's character which, we can assume, has always been there, but which as yet had found no occasion for expression.

Appropriately, it is not jealousy that provokes Palliser to talk to his wife about the events of the preceding evening—Trollope tells us that Palliser is incapable of jealousy—but the fact that Glencora had, on the ride home, "defied him by saying that she would see his friends no more."

These friends, Mr. Bott and Miss Marsham, she regards as spies—and quite correctly—but what matters to Palliser is the violation of husbandly authority, another aberration from the rules. The Palliser we already know, apparently incapable of deep personal feeling, is initially altogether in control: "He would rather have to address the House of Commons with ten columns of figures than utter a word of remonstrance to his wife." His sense of himself as a gentleman prohibits him from even admitting his own feelings, but he has moved, in dealing with the personal and concrete rather than the public and abstract, onto Glencora's ground, and to start with she has all the better of it.

> "If anybody is angry with me I'd much rather they should have it out with me while their anger is hot. I hate cold anger."
> "But I am not angry."
> "That's what husbands always say when they're going to scold."
> "But I am not going to scold. I am only going to advise you."
> "I'd sooner be scolded. Advice is to anger just what cold anger is to hot."
> "But my dear Glencora, surely if I find it necessary to speak—"
> "I don't want to stop you, Plantagenet. Pray, go on. Only it will be nice to have it over."

The interview proceeds in such a way as to prevent Palliser from giving the speech he wants, and Glencora breaks through the veneer of cold propriety. He arises "from his chair with a gesture of anger," and it is only then that Glencora apologizes. Only manifest feeling can touch her. But as he proceeds and she interrupts, the anger heightens and the nature of the discussion begins to change. "Glencora," he says, "you are determined to make me angry. I am angry now,—very angry." The pathos and the dignity of Palliser are precisely in the stiff and explicit language in which he is forced to announce his anger. Slowly he is drawn into the emotional center of the crisis. "If it were ever to come to that, that I thought spies necessary, it would be all over with me." At this point, the flippancy dies from Glencora's arguments. She is driven to confess that Burgo has asked her to run away with him.

> He was startled and stepped back a pace, but did not speak; and then stood looking at her as she went on.
> "What matter it whether I drown myself, or throw myself away by going with such a one as him, so that you might marry again, and have a child? I'd die;—I'd die willingly. How I wish I could die! Plantagenet, I would kill myself if I dared."
> He was a tall man and she was short of stature, so that he stood over her and looked upon her, and now she was looking up into his face with all her eyes. "I would—I would! What is there left for me that I should wish to live?"

> Softly, slowly, very gradually, as though he were afraid of what
> he was doing, he put his arm around her waist. "You are wrong
> in one thing," he said. "I do love you."
>
> She shook her head, touching his breast with her hair as she
> did so.
>
> "I do love you," he repeated. "If you mean that I am not apt
> to telling you so, it is true. My mind is running on other things."
>
> "Yes," she said, "your mind is running on other things."
>
> "But I do love you. If you cannot love me, it is a great misfortune
> for us both. But we need not therefore be disgraced. As for that
> other thing of which you spoke,—of our having, as yet, no
> child"—and in saying this he pressed her somewhat closer with
> his arm—"you allow yourself to think too much of it;—much more
> than I do. I have made no complaints on that head, even within
> my own breast."

The moment is carefully imagined both in dialogue and in physical context.
The minimal movements are all recorded, and the fact of the comparative
stature of the two is crucial to the effect. Palliser is here, surely, a man
capable of feeling, but he never becomes other than the man oriented to
his own public standing. He sustains aristocratic dignity, and the act of
putting the arm around Glencora's waist is, therefore, full of implications.
The scene is alive with physicality and an alertness to sexual reality which
makes us aware that both characters and Trollope himself know full well
that, as Mrs. Greenow puts it, babies are not found in a ditch. Yet the
coming together never minimizes the still almost hopeless distance between
the two. If this is, almost literally, the moment of conception, it is nevertheless, in keeping with the texture of the realistic myth, anything but final.

In the last three lines of the chapter, the old motif of the too-noble
man is reiterated, and we see precisely how a husband's generosity and
trust can become a special weapon for his victory. He proposes that they
take a European trip:

> "Perhaps your friend, Miss Vavasor, would go with us?"
>
> He was killing her by his goodness. She could not speak to him
> as yet; but now, as he mentioned Alice's name, she gently put up
> her hand and rested it on the back of his.
>
> At that moment there came a knock at the door,—a sharp knock,
> which was quickly repeated.
>
> "Come in," said Mr. Palliser, dropping his arm from his wife's
> waist, and standing away from her a few yards.

That touch is quintessential Trollope, and quite splendid. It is a moment
which draws brilliantly on the realistic technique which sees character in
terms of physical action and context, and it reminds us of the distance that
remains between him and Glencora, of the gentleman's decorous refusal

to allow private feelings to become visible, and of the fact that for Palliser, the publicly seen gesture can reveal nothing about his personal feelings except that they are not what is visible. It is a lesson Glencora begins, in this scene, to learn.

This is Trollope almost at his best, although no single passage can capture the quality of the long, extended time-bound growth and revelation of character. Throughout the tradition of realism, overt gesture, the surface of experience, is meaning; and, therefore, that surface provides the essential form of the realistic novel. The price paid in tedium, casualness, bagginess is, surely, high, but it makes possible such moments as these, of which there are many in *Can You Forgive Her?* It also allows Trollope, when he is faithful to the technique, to avoid those gross lapses into false or excessive feeling, and particularly into sentimentality, by which so much remarkable work in the tradition is marred. Trollope and Palliser and John Grey are content with compromise, and they teach the lesson of contentment even to such as Glencora and Alice. The slow, casual duplication and variation of plot suggest no intense, demonic romantic reality immanent in it, forcing its way over the obstacles of material detail and quotidian life. All intensity is precisely in those details, details which never rise to ritual or to symbolic concentration. One of the reasons the Palliser plot is more effective than the Alice Vavasor one is that the latter has a pretense to finality that nothing in the world of the novel can allow. The distance between Alice and John Grey can no more be obliterated than that between Glencora and Planta-genet; but the Alice plot is bound conventionally within the comic structure that implies the resolution of all in marriage, while the Palliser plot is released from that restraint, first, because it begins after marriage and, second, because it is comfortably encased within a narrative which provides just that satisfactory conclusion that Trollope imagined his audience re-quired. His special development of realistic technique and mythology is manifest in the Palliser sections of the story, sections which are capable of moving in and out of such moments as that which we have just looked at in detail. Even the wholly happy ending which provides an heir to the Pallisers is appropriately mixed with the tensions that come from Planta-genet's excessive protectiveness (amounting almost to imprisonment) dur-ing his wife's pregnancy.

Can You Forgive Her?, as it deals with the three separate stories on which it is built, comes close to being a novel of disenchantment. And it is toward a vision of unembittered disenchantment that most of Trollope's fiction tends to move. Its peculiar quality lies not so much in the special knowledge acquired by the particular characters: Mrs. Greenow's aware-ness of and willingness to accept a lover who is surely after her money and may, at the same time, have some feeling for her; Alice's acceptance of a love which surely means the end of the freedom she had wanted, though it also may mean happiness; Glencora's acceptance of a marriage in which she is still to try to learn to love her husband. Rather, it is in the surprise of discovery, when one steps back and looks at the world Trollope has created here, that there really isn't terribly much goodness, or love, or freedom in it. Trollope's delight in the details of such a world does not suggest depression. There is a pleasure in survival in such a world, a pleasure in its variety, a greater pleasure in success, even if it is a success rather different from what one might have hoped in one's brightest moments. The vision of worldly wisdom is precisely the vision of comfortable disenchantment.

And this is the reach of Trollopean aspiration, Trollopean need. The special desire that informs these books does not link Trollope with his heroes or heroines as George Eliot is surely linked to Dorothea, Hardy to Henchard, Lawrence to Ursula Brangwen in *The Rainbow*. Overt manipulation of plot is not critically necessary here for the working out of possibilities which society and the limits of each man's nature seem inevitably to block.

All Trollope need do is demonstrate convincingly the dangers of stepping beyond the pragmatic. One example of this, of necessity, uncharacteristic of Trollope, is the symbolic, almost fortuitous, hunting scene in which Burgo Fitzgerald participates. That it is symbolic is appropriate not only because Burgo represents some of the false energy of romance, but because Trollope must, without allowing Glencora to suffer the consequences, show where romance must lead. Trollope manages to get in his almost obligatory chapter on hunting and to achieve, quite surprisingly, symbolic concentration:

> Then came poor Burgo! Oh, Burgo, hadst thou not have been a very child, thou shouldst have known that now at this time of day,—after all that thy gallant horse had done for thee,—it was impossible to thee or him. But when did Burgo Fitzgerald know anything? He rode at the bank as though it had been the first fence of the day, striking his poor beast with his spurs, as though muscle, strength, and new power could be imparted by their rowels. The animal rose at the bank, and in some way got upon it scrambling as he struck it with his chest, and then fell headlong into the ditch at the other side, a confused mass of head, limbs, and body. His career was at an end, and he had broken his heart! Poor noble beast, noble in vain! To his very last gasp he had done his best and had deserved that he should have been in better hands. His master's ignorance had killed him. There are men who never know how little a horse can do,—or how much!

The application to Glencora is almost too obvious, but we are reminded of it, more delicately, when she dances with Burgo later. "Then she put up her nostrils,—as ladies do as well as horses when the running has been severe and they want air." The analogous demonstration for Alice occurs when George Vavasor breaks his sister's arm, a demonstration that he is, indeed, a wild man. But Alice is spared—as Glencora is spared the broken arm and back—and Kate Vavasor, who is partly responsible for bringing George and Alice together, must suffer the consequences of this false aspiration.

Passionate energy toward shape and meaning, toward freedom and the absolute, is simply not to be taken seriously. So Trollope sees both Alice's vague wish for freedom and Glencora's desire for a beautiful and physical love as altogether childish, though winning and understandable. Like John Grey with Alice and Palliser with Glencora, Trollope with his characters kills by goodness. He generously allows his favorites their childishness, their romance, because he knows that the depiction of the contingent, enmeshed world of social existence will deprive them soon enough of their childishness.

The morality of his novels, is, thus, far more interesting and complicated than anything he himself had to say about it in his nonfiction. He gives us the morality of tolerance. Thus the title, *Can You Forgive Her?*, though in some ways misleading, is actually fully appropriate. His two heroines have both violated the rules, as young girls are wont to do. But as the rules themselves are arbitrary and the girls' desires are entirely comprehensible and touching (if unacceptable and dangerous), his narrative forces his readers into sympathy with them. And as long as they don't remain outside the rules, they should be accepted, even loved. Even poor Burgo Fitzgerald is not utterly damned because he did not manage what he planned, and Palliser's generosity to him is the type of the book's morality, indeed, of the morality implicit in the myth of realism.

The Trollopean ideal, Plantagenet Palliser, is relatively comfortable in such a world, and Palliser, with all his nobility, is really—one should remember—something of a hypocrite and a cynic. While telling his wife what is proper, he omits to tell her of his bumbling attempt (recorded in *The Small House at Allington* but alluded to several times in *Can You Forgive Her?*) to run off with the wife of Lord Dumbello, the former Griselda Grantly. And his morality not only depends on sustaining an outward demeanor altogether remote from the reality of his personal feelings and commitments, but self-consciously antagonistic toward at least one Christian ideal. "A desire for wealth," he tells Jeffrey Palliser, "is the source of all progress. Civilization comes from what men call greed. Let your mercenary tendencies be combined with honesty and they cannot take you astray." If this sounds much like the Trollope of the *Autobiography*, it is surely no accident. Here, as elsewhere, Trollope knows and is capable of dramatizing that each man is essentially locked within himself, that society depends—as I have already suggested—on the personal ambition and greed of these isolated people.

He seems to believe not that society should be re-imagined, reconstructed, but that there must be rules. Only if people live according to the rules—whatever they may be—can society and its members survive. Thus

Palliser's supreme virtue is trust, and Trollope only becomes bitter in his novels and with his characters if they violate the rules of trust. This is a morality of surfaces, of behavior, not of ideals. And Trollope acts out that trust in his fictions by abjuring surprises and mysteries, and even in his prose style, which faithfully, clearly, ploddingly records objects and events, with no flourishes, no pretenses. He dislikes George Vavasor because Vavasor loves mysteries. He loves Glencora because her feelings are visible.

Trollope's is an act of acceptance, an act which will not struggle with its materials. *Can You Forgive Her?* takes in on the edges of its vision the possibility of other realities, but it circles three times around them and dismisses those possibilities with a pat on the head. And it achieves its special success by working out the fates of Glencora and Plantagenet Palliser, with utter consistency to the implications of the vision, while it fails most seriously at the point where it begins to challenge, in the story of Alice Vavasor, the compromised pragmatism of a contingent, greedy, and complacent world. Alice, unlike Isabel Archer or Dorothea Brooke, takes her comfortably wealthy and indulgent lover. Trollope, in the society he aspired successfully to join, takes his.

Passion, Narrative and Identity in *Wuthering Heights* and *Jane Eyre*

Tony Tanner

We learn from Elizabeth Gaskell's incomparable biography of Charlotte Brontë that one day the father of the Brontës wanted his children to reveal their true feelings to him. So he put masks on their faces and, thus concealed, invited them to give absolutely truthful answers to his questions. To be honest, his questions were not such as to bring out the secret inner life of his children, but we may take the occasion as in one way being a prophetic paradigm of what the children, and most importantly Emily and Charlotte, would subsequently do. They put on narrative masks and revealed feelings and problems and inner contestations which could never surface in Haworth Priory. We are exceedingly familiar with the idea of "masks" by now. But I want to start by suggesting that the different choices of narrative devices made by Emily and Charlotte are not only intimately related to what the books are about: these decisions, I think, already latently contain the ultimate meaning of the novels. In this sense the chosen form really is in large part the content. Let us consider the adopted narrative techniques in the two novels in question. Neither uses an omniscient third-person authorial voice. Emily chooses as a narrator a figure who is in all crucial respects her opposite—male, emotionally etiolated, and a product of the modern city. He in turn gets most of his evidence from Nelly Dean. That is to say that between us and the experience of Catherine and Heathcliff there is Lockwood's journal and Nelly Dean's voice—a text and a tongue, thus effecting a double translation, or refraction of the original story. Catherine and Heathcliff are as far as possible away from the narrative, and they recede into terminal dissolution when nothing can be narrated because nothing can be differentiated. They become rumour and

From *Teaching the Text*, edited by Susanne Kappeler and Norman Bryson. © 1983 by Tony Tanner. Routledge & Kegan Paul, 1983.

legend as they cease to be corporeal identities. Charlotte chose a precisely opposite technique. Jane Eyre—a potentially passionate woman with some experiences not unlike her creator's—tells her own story not only in but on her own terms. Her narrative act is not so much one of retrieval as of establishing and maintaining an identity. She survives. She is her book. Catherine and Heathcliff escape—from houses, from identity, from consciousness, and indeed from the book. This gives some indication of the different ways in which the two imaginations worked.

Wuthering Heights has often been regarded as pure romance, a timeless drama which has no particular reference to nineteenth-century England. Yet we notice that the book does not start "Once upon a time . . ." but with a date—1801. And, in addition, it is Lockwood we encounter first. Why? I think there are a number of reasons which make the book immeasurably richer than it would otherwise have been, but two comments by other authors might help us here. They are both addressing themselves to the problem of how to write about the supernatural or the demonic, the timeless, the utterly non-civilised. Thomas Mann (referring to his narrative method in *Dr Faustus*) succinctly says that for ironic purposes it was better "to make the demonic strain pass through an undemonic medium." Henry James, writing about ghost stories, asserts that "[supernatural] prodigies, when they come straight, come with an effect imperilled; they keep all their character, on the other hand, by looming through some other history." So the demonic intensity of Heathcliff is refracted through the very undemonic, emotionally timid, Lockwood. By showing us Lockwood and Heathcliff as inhabitants of the same universe, Emily Brontë, it seems to me, increases the impact of her story. Because part of the force of the book comes from the fact that a passionate yearning for timelessness and placelessness is forced to inhabit time and place, 1801. By making us see Lockwood and Heathcliff existing in the same space, Emily Brontë can show how space can become uneasy, problematical, holding incompatibles.

Let us look a little at the way the novel opens, for a good deal of the novel is contained, in embryo, in the first three chapters, in which Lockwood describes his first meeting with Heathcliff and his first entrance into Wuthering Heights. As Lockwood records his penetration into the house, considerable ironies are generated. For instance, he thinks of Heathcliff as a gentleman like himself, who prefers not to manifest his good feelings; or again, his domesticated eye can only see the wild dogs as tame pets (an error he will pay for when they set on him!). He even tells about a recent amorous incident in his own life which is comically the reverse of the story we are to hear. He reveals that he once found himself attracted to a girl, but when he managed to draw her glance, "I shrank icily into myself, like a snail." This is a good example of the attenuation and deadening of feeling which can be a result of "civilised" existence, where individuals live more and more separately and their passions diminish into egotistic self-withdrawal. On Lockwood's second visit to the house he sees Cathy (the daughter) and makes two embarrassingly wrong guesses as to her relationship with the other men. This only serves to show what an utterly alien world he has moved into: he can have no notion of what goes on in this house. He gets it all wrong. His urban/urbane discourse cannot comprehend the wild exiled depths he has stumbled into. He thinks in terms of a bland and tempered sociability, but in the house all is hatred, violence and anarchy. There is an additional point. He thinks in terms of conventional relationships. But Heathcliff is disruptive of genealogy and the whole web of familial relationships which make for social clarification and continuity.

Again Lockwood is set upon by the dogs and has to stay the night. This effectively takes him deeper into the secret of the house, for he is shown into a bedroom which, in turn, contains a small sort of closet (rooms within rooms) which makes a panelled bed. In this Lockwood seeks security. "I slid back the panelled sides, got in with my light, pulled them together again, and felt secure against the vigilance of Heathcliff, and every one else." It is a revealing gesture. Lockwood, as a civilised man, likes to secure himself, to shut out possibilities of darkness and violence. In every sense he locks the wood. However, inside his refuge he notes various things. Some writing for a start—"a name repeated in all kinds of characters, large and small," or rather three names, Catherine Earnshaw, Catherine Linton, Catherine Heathcliff. Here indeed is Catherine's problem—she cannot reconcile the three identities, and in which of them shall she find her self? The varying experimental inscriptions point to the insoluble dilemma of her life. Then Lockwood finds some diary entries by Catherine. They describe Catherine and Heathcliff's revolt against institutionalised religion and even civilisation itself. The fanatical Calvinist Joseph apparently forced two books on them—*The Helmet of Salvation* and *The Broad Way to Destruction*. In a gesture of revulsion they fling their books into the dog kennel. It is a crucial repudiation of the Word. And to fling the books into the dog kennel suggests an inversion with larger implications. If they put the books in the dog kennel, where would they put the dogs? From an early age it would seem that Heathcliff and Catherine were associated with an inclination to reject the controls of orthodoxy and to "unkennel" things more usually boxed up and confined.

Lockwood then goes to sleep and dreams and in his second dream he comes into contact with the drama of the book. Catherine, gripping his hand through a broken window, cries to be let into the house from the moors. Lockwood, in his dream, is hideously cruel: "I pulled its wrist on to the broken pane, and rubbed it to and fro till the blood ran down and soaked the bed-clothes." When he gets his hand free he tries to bar the window and cries out: "I'll never let you in, not if you beg for twenty years." It is notable that he tries to keep her out by piling up *books* to block up the gap in the window, trying to use print to stem the penetration of passion. He dreads any possibility of emotional leakage, any threat to his snail's shell. It is striking that Emily Brontë should use a dream to involve

Lockwood in the violence and cruelty of Wuthering Heights, and I don't think it is just a matter of his somehow tapping the atmosphere of the place while unconscious. It is surely significant that the apparently "civilised" Lockwood dreams of doing just about the cruellest and most sadistic act in a book full of cruelty. It suggests that Emily Brontë knew very well that in the most civilised effete mind there may well lurk a distorted and perverse proclivity to violence. The kind of extreme passional impulses embodied in Catherine are usually "kept out" by society, disavowed and repressed by the individual. But in dreams—"the return of the repressed" in a frighteningly grotesque form—Catherine represents a passion which society has excluded, cannot accommodate—just as Lockwood tries to keep her *out*. But in the world of this book the window which separates the house from the moor, the civilised from the uncivilised, consciousness from unconsciousness, ultimately life from death, this window has been broken. Much of the power of the book stems exactly from this "breaking of the window": things that are normally "kept out" clamour for admission or come flowing in.

Let me turn now to the end. Again, we have three chapters from Lockwood and another date, 1802. The book started in storms and mists and snow, the very dead of Winter. It ends in "sweet warm weather": wildness has given way to peace, storm to calm, and all kinds of savage disruptions and molestations to an image of a reconstituted society. To remind you of the picture Lockwood brings us, we have a new relationship between the young Cathy and Hareton, the legal inheritor whose *name* stands over the door of the house (remember Catherine's trouble with names). For a period Heathcliff has come between the house and the name, causing an antisocial rupture. This is now being healed. The new couple present a purely domestic scene of pleasant harmless peace. Hareton's "ignorance and degradation" have dropped away from him under the civilising care of Cathy. Significantly, they come together over books—"I perceived two such radiant countenances bent over the page of *the accepted book*, that I did not doubt the treaty had been ratified, on both sides, and the enemies were, thenceforth, sworn allies" (my italics). The "accepted" book is to be set against the *rejected* book—as in the gesture of Heathcliff and Catherine. Books, the written word, are the very essence of civilisation. To put it very simply, they accept human separation and recognise that we can communicate only indirectly—via sign systems. Accepting the book (in this novel) amounts to accepting the conditions of socialisation. Heathcliff and Catherine had no time for books—because they were not interested in any form of mediated communication. They desired actually to become one another—indeed, insisted on that identity. Such an impulse for total identification and assimilation is necessarily inimical to anything we can call society.

A word, now, about Heathcliff. He is a figure who in some way seems to transcend history—he is certainly not at home in it. He is the dark stranger from outside the home, the eternal alien of no known origin. He is found wandering in the streets of the great anonymous modern city (Liverpool), a gypsy child, an outlaw. Note that when Mr Earnshaw carries him home—i.e., to the *inside* of the domestic circle—he is utterly exhausted by the effort. More, in the process of carrying Heathcliff, Mr Earnshaw finds that all the toys he had bought for his own legitimate children have been broken. We may sense that, from the beginning, Heathcliff, if contained, is more prone to cause destruction than further creation. (It is, for instance, unthinkable that he should have Catherine's child; he has no connection with social and familial continuity. He is himself alone: no parents, no successors. The son he has inherits none of his power—he is really the negative of a child, and dies before coming to life.) While Heathcliff and Catherine are children they are utterly happy. They live as one person inside what Emerson called "the magic circle" of unselfconscious nature, sleeping together as they run together. But the essence of growing up is that individuals grow aware of their own separateness, their otherness and apartness from all other men and women. And it is exactly this severance— this emergence into separateness—which proves such a torment for Heathcliff and Catherine. Inevitably, one way or another, their energies will be devoted to breaking all the boundaries which make for this separation, to recapture some of that wild delight when, as one person, they ran over the moors all night.

Cathy is in some ways more complex than Heathcliff. She wants to be a "double character," and indeed she suffers from something like schizophrenia as she tries to reconcile marriage (Edgar) and passion (Heathcliff). The division of energies is fatal and she dies between them (with Edgar, significantly, at his books). In her famous speech to Nelly just before her marriage she asserts that she and Heathcliff are inseparable and concludes: "Nelly, I *am* Heathcliff!" For his part Heathcliff asserts that "I cannot live without my life! I *cannot* live without my soul!" In effect they are both saying, I exist only because the other exists. Catherine feels her real self to be Heathcliff: Heathcliff feels that his life and soul are Catherine. This is the extreme form of that romantic passion which attempts to merge completely with another person—to end the inevitable, intolerable separation between two people. To be deprived of this kind of union, in Emily Brontë's world, is to suffer an utter hell of isolation and destitution (her poems return constantly to this sort of suffering). Clearly, there is in this sort of passion a drive towards death. As Catherine says, if she cannot have Heathcliff she will choose to die. On the other hand, if she could merge totally with Heathcliff that too would mean death—the annihilation of the boundaries which contain and separate the living individual. This is hinted at in the one passionate embrace of Catherine and Heathcliff, which is at the same time an embrace of love and an embrace of death. Heathcliff seems to be crushing Catherine into himself, to be merging himself into her. After she dies his one real desire is to share her grave—an event he prepares for by having one side of her coffin removed. Death is the final release from separateness, the individual merging back into the endless continuum of sheer matter and Being. There Heathcliff and Catherine can merge into each other and become one, because there everything is merged with everything else. Unconscious nature is a pure unity and, even from the beginning of their lives, Heathcliff and Catherine are really seeking to rejoin it. Their energies are ultimately aimed at destroying the "shell" of the separate self.

At the end Heathcliff and Catherine are once more sleeping peacefully in the same bed, as they did as children; though now they have entered the second stage of unselfconsciousness: death. The second Cathy and Hareton "accept" separateness and survive as restorers of a calm society. They will find their identities in marriage: Heathcliff and Catherine lose their identities in an unsocialised and unsocialisable passion. In their way they finally elude Lockwood's narrative "framework"—he works with traces and indirect evidence for much of the time—just as, in a different way, Cathy and Hareton conclude it.

Matthew Arnold saw in *Jane Eyre* only "hunger, rebellion and rage," while a contemporary reviewer considered the book "preeminently an anti-Christian composition" and associated the novel with Chartism and the threat of social rebellion. Yet we can now see that the novel is most importantly about the creation of a self out of nothing except consciousness and sensation—and language. That is to say, Jane Eyre has none of the things that most people have to help them establish their first sense of reality—no family, no friends, no ties, no house (she is made to feel utterly unwanted and alien in the Reed household—aptly named Gateshead Hall, for they do indeed lock Jane up and try to imprison her mind). She has no connections, no context. She is alive but has no place in which to live. Let me remind you that the book starts in winter in extremes of cold, and this mood continues well into the book; while when Rochester "proposes" it is mid-summer. The important point about this is that all of Jane's early experiences are of cold, literal cold, shivering freezing fingers, no bodily comfort, but also icy looks, harsh hands, cold treatment, the chilling deprivation of warm contacts and real mutuality. I stress this because when she comes to write her life she in effect arranges her experience according to a range of metaphors drawn from these early physical and mental experiences. Experience is usually cold, too cold. This of course leads to a yearning for some kind of warmth, melting, and fire, and I shall say more about this later on. But in her experience she also notes that if things thaw too suddenly they overflow, and that if fire gets out of hand—literal fire but also mental and emotional fire—it consumes and destroys. Experience can be too cold, but it can also be too hot—the geographic realms of the West Indies and India are equivalents of emotional and psychic areas of excessive heat leading either to madness and derangement or a loss of self through scorching aridity.

Now let me bring in language and narrative. Jane Eyre has to write her life, literally create herself in writing: the narrative act is an act of self-definition. Given her social position, the only control she has over her life is narrative control. She is literally as in control of herself as she is of her narrative. Early in the book when she tells her life story to new friends—like Helen Burns—she is liable to lose control, become incoherent with resentment and rage and suppressed emotions—just as she is driven "out of herself" by being locked up in the red room. Helen tells her that she must learn to tell her story with more control, and this is a crucial lesson. For what Jane's narrative can contain, and order, and control, she herself can. A loss of narrative control is analogous to a loss of self-arrangement. From this point of view her identity is her text. This is particularly important in her dealings with the two key men in her life: they each in different ways try to take her to extremes, in effect to take her into non-lingual areas where the elemental annihilates the societal. Jane Eyre instinctively knows that if she allows herself to be taken into these extreme areas she will not be able to maintain her identity—though she has that in her which is drawn to such nonlingual extremes, to passional dissolutions of the self. What she has to do is to assimilate aspects of these extremes into her narrative. You can regard narrative—particularly "autobiographical" narrative—as an exercise in assimilation and exclusion. The narrator decides what enters his/her narrative world, and in what form it enters; hence Jane's metaphoric and symbolic treatment of her experience. In *Wuthering Heights* Heathcliff and Catherine try to get beyond language—they throw away their books—and by the same token try to get beyond identity—they finally throw away their social roles. And they die. But Jane, aware of what lies outside language and identity, struggles to assimilate and contain the nonlingual and translingual aspects of experience in her narrative—and she lives. Lives not as some false self or distorted role that other people try to impose on her, but lives with her own self-created, self-defined identity.

One other point here about Jane's narrative. Jane is nourished on nursery tales by Bessie (with the usual fantastic figures to be found in such stories): one of her favourite books is *Gulliver's Travels* which, let me just remind you, proposes the creation of extreme fictive realms in which people are impossibly small or impossibly large (or are animals—horses and apes). In addition, Jane Eyre admits that she needs a kind of compensatory fantasy world to make up for the boring routines of her actual one (as we know Charlotte Brontë needed, for a time, her "Angria" fantasies). Thus, when Jane hears something strange on the "third story" at Thornfield, she is drawn to it as a realm which nourishes her imagination, starved by the stagnation of the lower two storeys. "Then my sole relief was to walk along the corridor of the third story . . . and, best of all, to open my inward ear to a tale that was never ended—a tale my imagination created, and narrated continuously; quickened with all of incident, life, fire, feeling, that I desired and had not in my actual existence." The general point I am making is that Jane has a gift for narrative—imaginative, given to "enlargement" and symbolic extremes—which is larger than the very constricted compass of her actual social existence, or indeed almost non-existence (she is "nobody"). In her life she is subjected to pressure which would take her beyond the boundaries of her imaginary narrative altogether—into another kind of non-being, not inside society but outside it. What she needs is somehow to make her life both as ample and controlled as her narrative. The domestic must be intensified; at the same time, the elemental must be socialised. The medium for this is language and imagination—that "third story" which brings meaning and significance to the two below it. But there is also madness on the third storey (Mrs Rochester): this indispensable dimension of consciousness is necessarily ambiguous, and Jane has to tread—and fantasise   carefully.

So while there is much in the book that is drawn to wildness, abandon, the unhindered release of accumulating emotion, there is also much that contests the imperatives of passion and asserts the need for control and containment. Domestic and civilised realities are honoured and acknowledged at the same time as internal and external storms are raging. We often see Jane Eyre in different houses and rooms standing close to the window, more involved with the unstructured space and the climatic extremes outside the glass than with the often painful routines and orderings within the house. Yet the one time she leaves all houses and abandons herself to the elements—in her flight from Rochester—she is brought close to death, and at the nadir of her exhaustion she stands outside a house looking enviously *in* at the comfortable domestic routine. Jane Eyre has to learn how to control the dialectic of inside and outside, containment and release, structure and space, just as she has to establish for herself a sort of middle psychological geography, avoiding the extremes of the West Indies and India, and even the wicked south of France where Rochester would take her as a mistress but not as a wife. From one point of view her narrative is an act of psychological cartography. And at the end Jane is safe, inside a house having negotiated the outside; in England, a psychological England, not in the West Indies or France or India; and honoured by a legal marriage, not enslaved as a mistress or an object to be used.

When we first see Jane she is standing apart, prevented from "joining the group"; she retires into the window seat behind the red curtains and studies, first, the cold winter landscape outside and then Bewick's *History of British Birds*. Inevitably "birds" communicate a sense of liberty, a free circling in the immense spaces of the air. (And of course, Jane's surname contains a pun on that freest of elements—and more than once she is described as a bird—e.g., by Rochester: "I see at intervals the glance of a curious sort of bird through the close-set bars of a cage." But Bewick's book has another significance. Musing on the illustrations, Jane's imagination is drawn to the notions of the Terrible Arctic Zone—"those forlorn regions of dreary space": she thinks about "death-white realms"; she is drawn to the picture of "the rock standing up alone in a sea of billow and spray; to the broken boat stranded on a desolate coast; to the cold and ghastly moon glancing through bars of cloud at a wreck just sinking." The lonely rock, the broken boat, the sinking ship—these images of the threatened promontory and boat with no firm land at hand adumbrate various stages of her life and the continuous threat to Jane's precariously emerging sense of her own identity. If "air" is the element which attracts her, water is the one which warns of possible dissolution. On one occasion before Helen Burns dies, and just after a moment in the woods feeling how pleasant it is to be alive, she suddenly has a moment of what we may call metaphysical dread, or in Laing's term "ontological insecurity." Her mind tries to understand the idea of life after death—"and for the first time it recoiled baffled; and for the first time glancing behind, on each side, and before it, it saw all around an unfathomed gulf: it felt the one point where it stood— the present; all the rest was formless cloud and vacant depth; and it shuddered at the thought of tottering, and plunging amid that chaos." This feeling of being "at sea," of not having any certain ports behind or ahead in life (which equals a loss of a sense of origin and destination), of their being only the palpable "now" that one can be sure of—this is a basic and recurrent predicament for Jane. At another time she experiences temporal dislocation, a sort of existential amorphousness: "I hardly knew where I was; Gateshead and my past life seemed floated away to an immeasurable distance; the present was vague and strange, and of the future I could form no conjecture." That is, she cannot bring definition to the tenses of her life—was, is, will be. Awash in time, her life is in danger of losing all grammar and syntax. She also experiences a comparable spatial dislocation: "It is a very strange sensation to inexperienced youth to feel itself quite alone in the world, cut adrift from every connexion, uncertain whether the port to which it is bound can be reached, and prevented by many impediments from returning to that it has quited." At the end she is not only in possession of Rochester's house, Ferndean, she also has his watch in her keeping; i.e., she is finally in control of time and space. (Her own paintings reveal something of her fears: one "represented clouds low and vivid, rolling over a swollen sea: all the distance was in eclipse; so, too, was the foreground, or, rather, the nearest billows, for *there was no land*" [my italics]. There is only a wreck, a cormorant holding a bracelet, and a sinking corpse. This is the very image of that "formless cloud and vacant depth" into which she fears she might plunge. Other paintings, of a wild woman's face in the sky, of a face "blank of meaning but for the glassiness of despair" resting on an iceberg, likewise reveal her dreads and dreams. They portray wild or miserable lone human faces being reabsorbed into the elements—sinking into the sea, rising into cloud. They hinge on the notion of the evaporation or dilution and vanishing of the distinct human form.)

Given that she has no assured place, no fixed location, Jane Eyre's sense of identity is necessarily very vulnerable. When Rochester tries to deceive her into a false marriage he effectively tries to appropriate her by an illicit act of renomination, calling her "Jane Rochester." But it only makes her feel "strange"—as though she cannot find herself in the name. When the potentially bigamous marriage is revealed she is even more lost. "Where was the Jane Eyre of yesterday?—where was her life?—where were her prospects?" This loss of a sense of her own self goes even further when she is in flight from Rochester and wandering in the "outside" world of nature. The birds she sees are no longer an attractive image for her but a reproach: "birds were faithful to their mates; birds were emblems of love. What was I?" Not "who"—but "what"? Her sense of her own distinct being and human actuality is close to annihilation. The "outside," then, offers her no sphere for self-realisation. But when she is "inside" for the most part people try to "imprison" her in different ways. When she is locked up in the red room—a traumatic experience—it is felt to be a "jail." There are other dungeons in the book—Lowood School, Thornfield as described by Rochester, even her little school in Yorkshire, while St John Rivers turns her mind into a "rayless dungeon." In a crucial scene a game of charades is played at Thornfield, and the word chosen to be enacted is "Bridewell." Bridewell was in turn a royal palace, an hospital, and a house of correction or prison. The name focuses Jane's problem. She must "bride well" (i.e., make the right marriage), otherwise she will find herself in one kind of prison or another—her sense of self negated by the volition of a more powerful other. It is worth noting that only twice in the novel does she make the clear and confident assertion, "I am Jane Eyre," and these are both moments when a character who has at one time been a dominant and powerful menace to her unhelped independence appears before her weak, helpless, crippled or dying. I will return to these moments.

To summarise a little, the book is organised around five separate establishments, the names of which suggest a progression through a changing landscape—Gates(head),(Lo)wood, Thornfield, Moor(house) also known as Marsh(End); and Fern(dean Manor). In each of these establishments except the last, various pressures, influences and threats are brought to bear on her sense of her own identity. Initially she is regarded as—or "transformed" into—an "interloper and alien." But the main threats come from the two men who try to impose "bad" marriages on her. Rochester tries to impose a false identity and role upon her, turning her into a make-pretend wife whom he really wants for his mistress (his references to harems and "seraglio" indicate his "eastern" proclivities). That is the point of his efforts to heap all sorts of clothes and jewels on her before the "wedding": he is literally trying to deceive her by dressing her up as a "bride," i.e., to make her play a role in his fantasy. But she resists: "I can never bear being dressed like a doll." He calls her his "angel" but she refuses this: "I am not an angel . . . I will be myself"; and later: "I had rather be a *thing* than an angel," intimating she would prefer petrifaction to idolisation. Rochester thinks he has the "power" to change the rules of society—indeed, to change reality itself. Two of his comments are pertinent here: "unheard-of combinations of circumstances demand unheard-of rules." Jane resists this line of argument, sensing that "unheard-of rules" would be no rules at all. Concerning his mad wife, Rochester says: "Let her identity . . . be buried in oblivion." Jane recognises that if he thinks he can do this to one woman he can do it to any woman—hence her flight, a flight from identity-oblivion. Passionally, she is all but lost, but "mentally, I still possessed my soul, and with it the certainty of ultimate safety." In her flight she discovers that "I have no relation but the universal mother, Nature." It is not enough. We have come too far. We must find our identities in some kind of society, not simply in nature. Because of thought and reflection. We may decay with and in nature and mingle with its processes—but at the cost of a living identity. "Life, however, was yet in my possession; with all its requirements, and pains, and responsibilities. The burden must be carried; the want provided for; the suffering endured; the responsibility fulfilled. I set out." There it is. "I set out." The human obligation.

Refusing Rochester and the "stage-trappings" he tries to impose on her, Jane asserts: "I shall not be your Jane Eyre any longer, but an ape in a harlequin's jacket—a jay in borrowed plumes," and insists instead: "I will be myself." She would rather be a real Jane Eyre—no matter what the privations—than a false "Mrs. Rochester." With St John Rivers the problem and threat take another form. Whereas Rochester offered—or threatened—too much fire, St John Rivers is at various times likened to a glacier, marble, stone, glass. His eyes are like "instruments"; he speaks at key moments "like an automaton." He is a man of iron who forges his own chains: he locks too much up. His beauty is that of a dead classic statue; his religion is bitter and deathly. As he significantly says: "I am cold: no fervour infects me," while Jane replies "Whereas I am hot, and fire dissolves ice." Rivers gradually subdues her and she feels an "iron shroud" gather round her. His ice and iron seem to be winning over her innate fire. She gets to the point where she agrees to go with him to India—but not as his wife. "I abandon half myself," she meditates—but only half. She will not marry him, and in her answer to his pressing proposal she makes a distinction which is central to the issues I have been discussing. "And I will give the missionary my energies—it is all he wants—but not myself . . . my body would be under rather a stringent yoke, but my heart would be free. I should still have my unblighted self to turn to: my natural unenslaved feelings with which to communicate in moments of loneliness." This is the crucial act of resistance and assertion of her own identity. Her inner life is to be her own; whatever else she gives she will hold on to her "unblighted self." Her response to the telepathic call from Rochester indicates a sure intuition of where life lies for her. In leaving Rivers she is fleeing from ice, stone, iron, and an inflexible religious will which is corrupted by detectable sadomasochistic impulses: she is fleeing, that is, from everything that

threatens the death of her self and the cold, relentless extinction and obliteration of her inner life, her passional integrity.

Her journey to Rochester is marked by a symbolic suggestiveness. The
way gets darker and more constricted with trees until she feels she has lost
her way. There are no longer any roads—indeed, there is "no opening
anywhere." It is as though she is returning to some pre-social space where
all the conventional definitions are erased and where she can begin again.
In the "formlessness" of Ferndean she at last can re-form relationships and
roles on her own terms. When she finds Rochester he is of course the
helpless one now, in a semi-impotent state (blindness being a recognised
symbol for some degree of castration)—his imperious desire and antinom-
ian energies now tamed. And this is the second moment when Jane asserts
her full free-standing independent identity as she announces to him, "I am
Jane Eyre." Rochester has of course throughout been associated with fire
by Jane, where she sees Rivers in terms of ice. The latent fire—and need
for warmth—in Jane is roused by the perceptible flames in his own temperament. Her worry is that she must not be consumed and annihilated
in one sudden conflagration (such as partially blinded and crippled Rochester). Fire of course has always been the most ambiguous metaphor drawn
from the elements. It has meant so many contradictory things: it is the very
stuff of life and the most deadly agent of destruction; it is the gift of the
gods and the eternal punishment of hell; it is Promethean illumination and
the source of civilisation; and it is apocalypse, holocaust, judgment day.
This radical ambivalence is suggested by the large number of references to
fire in the book—indeed, David Lodge in an admirable essay has counted
them: eighty-five references to domestic fires, forty-three references to figurative fires, ten literal conflagrations, and four references to hell fire. I
simply want to refer to two key uses of fire. The "fire" of uncontrolled
passion (such as destroys Thornfield) is of course something which Jane
must avoid, but that does not mean that Jane is to be seen as opposing the
fire-element. Certainly she knows that she will die in extreme heat, or
utterly lose her identity; but that does not mean she would be more at
home in arctic wastes, geographically or psychologically. Indeed, we would
perhaps do best to see her as a spirit of *controlled* fire. Let me point to a
notable coincidence. I mentioned that it is when two of the once-dominant
opposing or coercive forces in her life appear before her humbled and
incapacitated that Jane asserts her full identity: "I am Jane Eyre." Well, it
is precisely at those two moments that we see her kindling a fading fire.
In Mrs. Reed's house the action seems merely an unconsidered reflex—
"the fire was dying in the grate. I renewed the fuel." But note that this is
exactly when she is thinking of Mrs. Reed dying upstairs. Jane is in charge
of the fire in the house which once imposed on her a cold and miserable
isolation. Again, when she returns to Rochester (who earlier had tried to
draw her too close to the fire until she complained that "the fire scorches
me"—see chapter 19), it is now her turn to be guardian of the fire while

he sits by, helpless and passively grateful. "Now let me leave you an instant, to make a better fire, and have the hearth swept up." And soon, through his dimmed eyes, he sees "a ruddy haze." It is in just such a nourishing but non-annihilating warm glow that Jane will now lead her life with Rochester. Not suffering extinction in either the extremes of cold (a dead marriage) or heat (an adulterous liaison), but completely and fully her own self, sustained by a controlled warmth of passion which is essential to the well-being of her inmost life. The excluded orphan has finally become that crucial domestic figure: the mistress of the hearth.

It is worth noting that one of the first lessons that Jane Eyre masters is "the first two tenses of the verb *être*"—I am, I will be, or I was. This is indeed exactly what she has to learn to say with full confidence and authority, to know what the self is in time, to stabilise the self in its relation to what is around it. If you can say "I am" then you can also say "You are"—self-apprehension leads to proper recognition of the other. Learning to articulate and define and hold on to her own identity, Jane Eyre is also able accurately to identify others. In this way she is able to resist being absorbed into, or transformed into, false selves which other people wish to make of her for their own selfish means. She can resist the kind of manipulation, reification, and falsification which threaten her at every key stage of her life (her narrative devices are an inscription of this resistance). Catherine and Heathcliff want to say "I am you," which may be good passion but is bad grammar: they want to destroy pronouns, tenses, genders, prepositional distances and differentiations—indeed, they want to get out of grammar altogether. On the other hand, Jane Eyre's achievement, and not only the subject of the book but the reason she wrote it, is the proper mastery of the verb *être*, or the attainment of the unchallenged ability to say "I am Jane Eyre."

Gossip, Diary, Letter, Text: Anne Brontë's Narrative *Tenant* and the Problematic of the Gothic Sequel

Jan B. Gordon

The frame, however, is handsome enough; it will serve for another painting. The picture itself I have not destroyed, as I had first intended; I have put it aside.
—*The Tenant of Wildfell Hall*

Anne Brontë's *The Tenant of Wildfell Hall* quickly calls attention to itself as the longest single-narrative, enclosing epistolary novel of the nineteenth century. Beginning "dear Halford," it concludes four hundred and fifty pages later with a "Till then, farewell, Gilbert Markham." It is not the characters of the individual subjects of the novel nor the contents of Markham's narrative that shape the meaning of *The Tenant of Wildfell Hall*, but rather the relative dispensation of alternative narratives competing for our attention and hence for a textual priority. Each mode of discourse must confront the recognition that in any scheme of recovery, "voice" is a privileged aspect of language, that the intrusion of the "otherness" of the listener is a necessary constitution of meaning. The engagement of a narratee is achieved by sublating a variety of second- or third-hand discourse: community gossip; the narrator's own source, a "faded old journal"; the incomplete manuscript of Helen Huntington's diary, given to the narrator because she cannot *speak* her story; a cluster of failed correspondence between Gilbert and Helen; and finally, a sort of running commentary on another and historically prior text, Helen's exegesis of the Bible, which serves to foreground all the other narratives. Each of the enclosed varieties of discourse appears as a supplement, an attempt to amend or correct either the inadequacy or the social threat posed by another "version" of the same

From *ELH* 51, no. 4 (Winter 1984). © 1984 by the Johns Hopkins University Press, Baltimore/London.

events. Rather than seeking to establish their primacy or priority by creating a discontinuity among narratives that would furnish a ground for deconstruction, however, Anne Brontë's narrator presents the reader with another situation: a world of proliferating "texts" which cannot be contained, except by a desperate and arbitrary act of enclosure. The formal rivalry between narratives has its genetic parallel in the way *The Tenant of Wildfell Hall* encloses its originary, *Wuthering Heights,* as it strives to supplant it. This structural belatedness is paralleled by a historical belatedness—a nineteenth-century epistolary novel.

The enclosing letter to Halford with which Gilbert Markham opens and closes his narrative occupies a curious structural position, partially inside and partially outside the body of *The Tenant of Wildfell Hall.* For the novel makes a clear distinction between its temporal, chronological "beginning" (chapter 1) and its narrative commencement in front of the first chapter. Formal priority is chronologically posterior, a relationship that holds throughout the novel, an inversion that points to the necessary belatedness of the novel as a form. It is always attempting to recover a prior text; hence it opens with six paragraphs, not part of any chapter, to Markham's friend, Halford, sandwiched between Anne Brontë's "Preface to the Second Edition" and the actual commencement in chapter 2 of the events that the novel purports to describe. This enclosed, "framed" nature of the narrative points to its provisionality, an arbitrariness that separates the beginning of the novel from the commencement of the act of writing:

> I have not my memory alone to depend upon; in order that your credulity may not be too severely taxed in following me through the minute details of my narrative.—To begin then, at once, with Chapter First, for its shall be a tale of many chapters.

And then begins the narrative *per se:* "You must go back with me to the autumn of 1827." Anne Brontë, by the framing device of the letter, suggests a feature of writing to which the characters of *The Tenant of Wildfell Hall* continually defer: that writing is always belated, always attempting to "recover" and bring into the present what remains forever lodged in the past. The vestige of this urge to recovery is a kind of narrative residue, a beginning before the beginning. It is a narrative device common to Gothic fiction with its plethora of found letters, scraps of documents in attics, texts as clues to a prior and whole truth which must somehow be pieced together. It is the formal corollary to the structures of the *ruin* and the *monstrous* which seem to belong to the beginning before the beginning. Stated in another way, the dialectic that Gilbert's letter enacts depends upon the way it flamboyantly plays on a temporal distance between the world it creates and the world in which the apparatus of invention is constructed.

Chapter 1 begins with a discussion of Gilbert's prospects. His father's deathbed wish is that the "paternal lands" be "transmit[ted]" to his own grandchildren, intact and unentailed, through the mediation of his son and our narrator, Gilbert Markham. The novel begins, then, with the death of paternity—a theme that continues throughout—and the gesture of transmission, that maintenance of property from one generation to the next that made the Victorian will such an instrument of social control and order. In fact, the setting of the first chapter is almost entirely devoted to ritual images of Victorian order: afternoon tea; visits by the curate, Millward; Guy Fawkes Day parties (which use a celebration to control the memory of subversion); knitting projects; and plans for a spring outing. Social order is a function of rituals whose meanings are communally shared and hence capable of being transmitted, more or less intact, to others. Stability is a function of the transactional nature of human discourse. But this seemingly endless round of trivial socialization is interrupted by the announcement that there is a new arrival in the neighborhood; like Heathcliff before her, she is dressed in black, and has recently moved into Wildfell Hall, now lapsing into the run-down condition of abandonment that characterizes the ruin:

> "Well," resumed Rose; "I was going to tell you an important Piece of news I heard there—I've been bursting with it ever since. You know it was reported a month ago, that somebody was going to take Wildfell Hall—and—what do you think? It has actually been inhabited above a week!—and we never knew!"
> "Impossible!" cried my mother.
> "Preposterous!!!" shrieked Fergus.
> "It has indeed!—and by a single lady!"
> "Good gracious, my dear! The place is in ruins!"

The woman is single with a child, did not attend Sunday church services, and is clearly a tenant rather than an owner of property, all of which serves to establish Mrs. Graham's subversiveness in Linden-Car.

But perhaps the most pointed signifier of her role as a potentially disruptive outsider in the community is the speech that relates her intrusion, for it is the first of many instances in which the force of gossip makes itself felt. In fact, the first ten chapters of the novel are really nothing more than the attempt of gossip to come to terms with meaning. Almost everyone in Linden-Car speculates about the past of the mysterious Mrs. Graham, and, although at the outset, only Mrs. Wilson is labelled "a tattling old gossip," eventually almost all of the characters come to participate at one time or another in that mode of discourse. There is the suspicion that Mrs. Graham is linked with some scandal, that she is poverty-stricken, that she is unsociable. All of these reports are incomplete and inadequate, not because of the inscrutability of their object, but because of the nature of the discourse.

As Heidegger understood, gossip, like the nineteenth-century novel itself, circulates, floating about the culture as *Geschwätz*, a kind of metalanguage. And, as a metalanguage, it has a number of features that particularly endear it to the residents of Linden-Car. In *The Tenant of Wildfell Hall,* as with the arena of most gossip, "overheard language" has no authorship that can be readily identified. It is a speculative language thrown out at that which is only incompletely understood, and its origins can never be traced or determined. Whenever anyone in the novel attempts to identify the source of a given rumor, it seems to recede into the folds of progressive narrative enclosure:

> "Well, tell me then," I answered, in a lower tone; "what is it you mean? I hate enigmas."
> "Well, you know, I don't vouch for the truth of it—indeed far from it—but haven't you heard—"
> "I've heard nothing, except from you."
> "You must be wilfully deaf then; for anyone will tell you that— but I shall only anger you by repeating it, I see; so I had better hold my tongue."
> She closed her lips and folded her hands before her with an air of injured weakness.
> "If you had wished not to anger me, you should have held your tongue from the beginning; or else spoken out plainly and honestly all you had to say."

The author of gossip tends to be an anonymously democratic "anyone" who cannot be identified as an origin and hence held responsible. All who participate in gossip are mediators, who invariably heard it from someone else. And it is potent in shaping reputations and responses to people or events in direct proportion to the dilution of its author(itative) base. Because it is essentially a speech-act, gossip can never be "recovered" in either sense in which we typically use that word—recaptured in its original form or covered over and stopped. As many Victorians must have understood, gossip is a deployment of discourse that is forever enlarging and expanding the field of its domain. As the volume of gossip in *The Tenant of Wildfell Hall* increases, it begins to affect almost everyone; people seem to live as if they were always being talked about. To fear gossip is to fear that one is becoming a character, an "other," in someone else's fiction:

> The pair had now approached within a few paces of us. Our arbour was set snugly back in a corner, before which the avenue, at its termination, turned off into the more airy walk along the bottom of the garden. As they approached this, I saw, by the aspect of Jane Wilson, that she was directing her companion's attention to us; and, as well, by her cold sarcastic smile, as by *the few isolated words of her discourse* that reached me, I knew full well that she was impressing him with the idea that we were strongly attached to each other. (My italics.)

Gossip, by its very nature, is isolated and unenclosed, which has the effect of tempting closure. "Anyone" can become a collective participant in a depersonalized speech-act, can in fact become an author, merely by supplementing a prior version. The widow Graham constantly seeks to remove herself from the range of what she calls "small talk"—the various "spicy piece[s] of scandal" that engage the narrative powers of the community. But the greater her distance, the more quickly the range of gossip is enlarged. It is as if language takes the place of the object of discourse and is itself "passed along." Gossip presents the illusion of transaction.

In one sense, gossip represents a kind of collective conspiracy to gain access to that which is spatially or socially hidden, and tends to be subversive precisely because it challenges our private spaces, because it treats history as a kind of property. The lower classes tend to gossip about the upper classes, but not vice versa, a feature of gossip which enabled Nelly Dean to be such a complex narrator in *Wuthering Heights,* gradually supplanting Lockwood. If the love of Heathcliff and Cathy represented unmediated desire, then Nelly Dean's narrative, tainted with the envy of a servant's gossip, represents mediation passing itself off as direct knowledge.

Forever seeking to establish its authenticity, gossip in *The Tenant of Wildfell Hall* threatens cultural values as it establishes its textuality. First of all, gossip can be directed. If the mere spatial contiguity of any two people of the opposite sex gives rise to the speculation that is gossip, then characters can effect, even initiate gossip by manipulating proxemics. Its apparently random circulation may not be so random after all. Late in the novel, Arthur Huntington refuses to accede to his wife's request for an end to their marriage on the grounds that such an estrangement would make him "the talk of the country"—a marvelous euphemism for gossip. Ralph Hargrave, who wishes to accompany Helen and her child as a guardian, attempts to convince her of his worth as protector and lover. In the process of kneeling before her, he notices that there is a witness:

> "That is Grimsby," said he, deliberately. "He will report what he has seen to Huntington and all the rest, with such embellishments as he thinks proper. He has no love for you, Mrs. Huntington—no reverence for your sex—no belief in virtue—no admiration for its image. He will give such a version of this story as will leave no doubt at all, about your character, in the minds of those who hear it."

Has her husband used a common friend to manipulate his wife into a compromising position in order to feed gossip? In that case gossip would have a beginning and an end, in the sense that it could be purposive, used for directed revenge.

Gossip always attempts to be what it is not by incorporating the patterns of relatedness appropriate to the novel; i.e., it creates plots where none exist. One of the most remarkable accomplishments of gossip in Anne Brontë's novel occurs when the community becomes aware of the frequent conversations between Frederick Lawrence, a familiar bachelor in the neighborhood, and the dark Helen Graham. Searching for clues to her past life, the Millward girls spread the story that Frederick Lawrence is her secret lover, a revelation that tempts Gilbert Markham into an assault. As it turns out, of course, Frederick and Helen are not lovers, but brother and sister. In generating lovers out of a relationship of consanguinity, gossip conspires to create the disappearance of difference that is incest. Hence it is not only that gossip obscures sources or "versions" of a story as well as the authors of a story, but also that it blurs the internal relationships of its objects. In a novel filled with references to the "value" and "investment" of a good marriage, to the transactional and contractual nature of the marriage "bond," gossip always appears as a threat to value: it either "speculates" or exaggerates by "inflating." In short, gossip devalues because it has nothing standing behind it. Lacking the authenticity of a definable source, it is simultaneously financially, theologically, and narratively unredeemable:

> "And who gave you this piece of intelligence, Miss Eliza?" said I, interrupting my sister's exclamations.
> "I had it from a very authentic source, sir."
> "From whom, may I ask?"
> "From one of the servants at Woodford."
> "Oh! I was not aware that you were on such intimate terms with Mr. Lawrence's household."
> "It was not from the man himself, that I heard it; but he told it in confidence to our maid Sarah, and Sarah told it to me."

Gilbert Markham's attempts to discover who Helen Graham is must initially discount the community's gossip. In order somehow to get behind the collective speech attempting to establish its dominance, Gilbert resorts to the expediency of using the text as a pre-text. In order to prevent other churchgoers from guessing at his admiration of Mrs. Graham's beauty, he somewhat sacrilegiously hides his own blushing face behind the prayer book at church, even as the Rev. Millward is conducting a commentary. Later, on an outing, he encounters the elusive widow, sketch-book in hand, "absorbed in the exercise of her favorite art," drawing copies from nature. Gilbert takes the opportunity to question her about life at the lonely and desolate habitation, and her response makes the role of the book as a potential instrument of repression obvious:

> "On winter evenings, when Arthur is in bed, and I am sitting there alone, hearing the bleak wind moaning round me and howling through the ruinous old chambers, no books or occupations can repress the dismal thoughts and apprehensions that come crowding in."

The course of their friendship is initially defined in terms of the exchange of books:

So we talked about painting, poetry, and music, theology, geology, and philosophy: once or twice I lent her a book, and once she lent me one in return: I met her in her walks as often as I could; I came to her house as often as I dared. My first pretext for invading the sanctum was to bring Arthur a little waddling puppy of which Sancho was the father, and which delighted the child beyond all expression. . . . My second was to bring him a book which, knowing his mother's particularity, I had carefully selected, and which I submitted for her approbation before presenting it to him.

Quite literally, Gilbert's knowledge of Helen, apart from that revealed by gossip, is derived entirely from their exchange of books: "She called me Gilbert, by my express desire, and I called her Helen, for I had seen that name written in her books." Any transgression of the highly limited nature of their friendship is measured in terms of a violation in the conditions of their book-loan agreement. Knowing that Helen Graham would like to be entertained by reading Scott's *Marmion*, Gilbert orders a copy from a London publisher, only to discover on presenting it to her that she demands to pay him for it:

"I'm sorry to offend you, Mr. Markham," said she, "but unless I pay for the book, I cannot take it." And she laid it on the table.
"Why cannot you?"
"Because—" She paused, and looked at the carpet.
"Why cannot you?" I repeated, with a degree of irascibility that roused her to lift her eyes, and look me steadily in the face.
"Because I don't like to put myself under obligations that I can never repay—I am obliged to you, already, for your kindness to my son; but his grateful affection, and your own good feeling must reward you for that."

The attempt to use books to get behind the community's gossip, as it turns out, has severe limitations. For instead of using the contents of the book to reveal more about herself, Helen Huntington deflects the status of the book from *clue* to *occasion* of exchange. Using the economic imagery of indebtedness and redemption in keeping with her religious convictions, Helen always demands the "exchange" of discourse: "I hate talking where there is no exchange of ideas or sentiment, and no good given or received." She wants a world where obligations and duties are faithfully recognized and discharged, as opposed to the world of "small talk" that achieves the opposite, inflationary effect.

Although Gilbert Markham is relatively immune from gossip, he does fall victim to the assumption that every text exchanged is a representation of love exchanged. One day, visiting Helen's parlor whose "limited but choice collection of books was almost as familiar to me as my own," he discovers an intruder among the volumes. There is an edition of Sir Humphrey Davy's *Last Days of a Philosopher* on whose fly leaf Frederick Lawrence's name appears. Although texts have a specificity that gossip does not have, Gilbert is plunged into the same speculation about their relationship as the rest of the community is. Demanding an explanation, he gets another text:

> She did not speak, but flew to her desk, snatching thence what seemed a thick album or manuscript volume, hastily tore away a few leaves from the end, and thrust the rest into my hand, saying, "You needn't read it all; but take it home with you."

Gilbert rushes home in accordance with her instructions, and discovers, in the process of reading it, the contraceptive to the community's gossip, except that its unfinished nature—unfinished at precisely the point of engaging his own "otherness"—tends to make him an object of gossip. He encloses it within his own narrative, repressing in the process the progressive failure of marriage and the subversion that it represents:

> I have it now before me; and though you could not, of course peruse it with half the interest that I did, I know you would not be satisfied with an abbreviation of its contents, and you shall have the whole, save, perhaps *a few passages here and there of merely temporal interest to the writer,* or such as would serve to encumber the story rather than elucidate it. It begins somewhat abruptly, thus—but we will reserve its commencement for another chapter, and call it,— (My italics.)

The process of enclosing one narrative within another serves to deflect the act of recovery, because the text now occupies a different disposition in the field of discourse. Helen retains a "few pages from the end" at her end of the narrative transaction and Gilbert selectively edits what remains. Hence her attempt to use the private confessional form to combat the metalanguage of the community is only partially successful, because the diary has some of the limitations of gossip: once exchanged, it tends to be replicated in successive versions; in the process of disclosure, the private world becomes public, making for more or less equal access; and finally, the diary, once having gone from her hands, cannot return to her in the same way. It suddenly has a "currency," an exchange value that is quite different from its value as self-reflection *for her*.

In a society where gossip seems to determine relationships, Helen Huntington's diary/ms. is an attempt to set the record straight, but it leaves gaps in testament and chronology that cry out for closure much as does gossip. Hers is a language that reveals its necessary incompleteness and hence its inadequacy at every turn. The dilemma of textuality, succinctly stated, is this: in their belatedness, texts are necessarily incomplete agents of recovery. Gossip has all the power of speaking as opposed to writing:

it is democratic, spontaneous, all-encompassing in the sense of participating in that which it purports to describe. But it has no author(ity) which might give it a basis in transaction. It cannot be bequeathed or inherited *as is*. Texts, on the other hand, can be "passed on," incorporated within other discourse which gives them form. Texts have a repository, either in other texts or in libraries, which means that they can be put aside in ways that gossip cannot. The community's gossip serves to give Helen Huntington a past which her diary/ms. attempts to counteract. When she gives her diary to Gilbert Markham and he "frames" it within his enclosing letter (novel) to Halford to create the layered narrative that is *The Tenant of Wildfell Hall*, his object, to borrow from the language of psychoanalysis, is to make her past definitively past, so that he might marry her. Her object had been to make present her past. Hence, his narrative can never enclose her intentionality.

But even were that problem solvable by accommodating intentionality in the doubtful way in which E. D. Hirsch recommends, there is something in the very composition of her diary/ms. that prevents it from ever severing itself from gossip. The burden of the scriptural passages she incessantly cites—and often misinterprets—is that life on earth is a kind of endless preparation for a glorious afterlife. Hence the suffering on earth that her diary details is necessary in order for the sequel to be enacted. Arthur Huntington's agony and the genuine physical horror of a life of *delirium tremens* is less threatening to Helen than is his refusal to live within the dialectic of constant preparation. When Huntington's guest, Hattersley, promises to make amends for a life of profligacy, Helen replies:

> you *cannot* make amends for the past by doing your duty for the future, in as much as your duty is only what you owe to your maker, and you cannot do *more* than fulfil it—another must make amends for your past delinquencies.

Her diary, by self-consciously omitting the final three pages, postpones the ending, becoming in the process an exercise synchronous with her theological condition: it is always in preparation, desperately seeking a narratee to complete the necessary fiction of a bond, a covenant between texts and their recipients.

In *The Tenant of Wildfell Hall*, the composition of Helen's diary/ms. takes up an enormous amount of space. As her marriage fails and Arthur's drunken bouts increase in frequency, she seeks recourse in writing. It would seem that private writing not only provides a refuge against that other public language, gossip, but becomes her only joy, as it must have indeed been for the Brontës:

> I have found relief in describing the very circumstances that have destroyed my peace, as well as the little trivial details attendant upon their discovery. No sleep I could have got this night would

have done so much towards composing my mind, and *preparing me* to meet the trials of the day—I fancy so, at least;—and yet when I cease writing, I find my head aches terribly. (My italics.)

Her own text becomes a structural and thematic companion to the other text, an indispensable aide in preparation. The progressive life of debauchery led by Arthur Huntington and his assorted household guests—Grimsby, the Hattersleys, Lord and Lady Lowborough—is always seen as a conspiracy against both texts: "none of our gentlemen had the smallest pretensions to a literary taste." Helen finds herself spending ever larger amounts of time in that repository of Victorian repression, the library. It is not only that her husband, Arthur, hurls books at the dog (in distinction to her future second husband, Gilbert Markham, who brought books and dogs), but that his role as the demon of the anti-text prompts him to invade the privacy of her diary:

> Jan. 10th, 1827. While writing the above, yesterday evening, I sat in the drawing-room. Mr. Huntington was present, but as I thought, asleep on the sofa behind me. He had risen, however, unknown to me, and, actuated by some base spirit of curiosity, been looking over my shoulder for I know not how long; for when I had laid aside my pen, and was about to close the book, he suddenly placed his hand upon it, and saying—"With your leave, my dear, I'll have a look at this," forcibly wrested it from me.

Given such a history of textual predation, her sudden offer of it to Gilbert Markham as an explanation of her past and an attempt to put an end to gossip represents an astonishing urge to go public. But, of course, she does not give him all of the diary. Her private manuscript from which she has torn away pages at the end, concludes thusly, as Gilbert relates in his enclosing epistle to Halford:

> November 3rd—I have made some further acquaintance with my neighbors. The fine gentleman and beau of the parish and its vicinity (in his own estimation, at least) is a young. . . .
>
> *   *   *   *
> *   *   *   *
>
> Here it ended. The rest was torn away. How cruel—just when she was going to mention me! for I could not doubt it *was* your humble servant she was about to mention, though not very favorably of course—I could tell that, as well by those few words as by the recollection of her whole aspect and demeanor towards me.

Helen's manuscript, because it is unfinished (and it is unfinished because it has been given to Gilbert) can never enact the otherness of its recipient. Instead, the gift of her private history to Gilbert displaces his role *in* the diary, and creates once again the idle speculation that is gossip. Was she about to talk about me, or someone else? Was she to mention me favorably or not? The very fact that he has the diary ironically prevents him from knowing the crucial detail of her history—his role in it: "I had no right to see it: all this was too sacred for any eyes but her own." Its failure to enact his otherness, ironically, becomes the ground for its sacredness.

What is really being engaged here is the potential paradox involved in the stance of a narrator who is suddenly an owner of someone else's private narration. The framing device must stabilize the incommensurable relation between an author conceived of as somehow outside his creation and a privileged but fictitious consciousness within that imagined world. Gilbert's role as an owner, in the bourgeois sense at least, succumbs to a logic of inertia and permanence, whereas his own narration to Halford is rooted in change. In *The Tenant of Wildfell Hall* Gilbert Markham's narrative letter to Halford, as a belated response to Halford's request for a renewal of correspondence, constitutes potential exchange as the basis for textuality. The novel itself, as we read, is the record of a private text entering the public, novelistic domain—which it can do only when it is resubmerged within Gilbert's enclosing narrative to his friend, Halford. Otherwise, Helen's diary/ms. in its drawer in the library remains a potential source of violence, either from her husband or the community.

The recovered text tends to transform reality itself into a kind of lost or fallen text, the ironic result of a reading which surrenders to the centripetal powers of an enclosing fiction. This transformation also effects a kind of currency or exchange value in Helen Huntington's diary. The fallen woman and the fallen world can be redeemed only by a narrative transaction, by creating a text that makes room for the intrusion of the other. Helen's creation, unlike that of the God she worships, can no longer be indifferent or neutral as soon as it is part of a narrative contract that includes Gilbert as a party. Her history must be made eligible for a narrative consumption, in order that the private history which had been such a threat to community stability might become part of the community's collective fiction. That is surely part of the socialization of Helen Huntington, part of her eventual acceptance within that other of society's exchange contracts—remarriage. The passing on of her diary to Gilbert, along with its subsequent resubmergence within his own epistolary novel, paves the way for discourse based on exchange because it recognizes the arbitrary nature of beginnings and endings. Gossip can never be so exchanged, because each speaker adds to the whole; it is discourse as perpetual supplement, in the same way that Helen's unenclosed diary could be said to be discourse in perpetual preparation.

And yet, neither Gilbert nor Helen immediately recognizes that the framed enclosure will ensure the contractual nature of both their lives and their discourse. Dispossessed of her private diary and still the object of speculation, Helen Huntington at last wishes to put an end to their relationship, by elevating it to the level of "a spiritual intercourse without hope or prospect of anything further." This radical act seeks to replace the world of perpetual beginnings and perpetual supplements with the heady realm of pure spirit. Such is a peculiar affection, somewhat like that of Cathy and Heathcliff, unmediated, but infinitely distant. Resigned to that end, Gilbert Markham proposes a discourse appropriate to such an agreement: " 'Is it a crime to exchange our thoughts by letter? May not kindred spirits meet and mingle in communion, whatever be the fate and circumstances of their earthly tenements?' " As community gossip had earlier transformed a brother and sister into lovers, so Helen Huntington consents to use the discourse of the letter in order that she might convert a relationship of lovers to one of brother and sister: *kin*-dred spirits. As if to make that change more obvious to poor Gilbert, she requests that they communicate to each other only through her brother, Frederick Lawrence, as she wishes that her "new abode should be unknown to you as to the rest of the world." The letters, like gossip, will have no point of origin, and in an attempt to avoid rumor, she embargoes all exchange of letters for six months, cautioning him to "maintain a correspondence all thought, all spirit, such as disembodied souls or unimpassioned friends might hold." Her wish for disembodied discourse is the antipode of enclosed discourse, and exchange is reduced to a mere vehicularity as letters float about the countryside— often delayed or undelivered. The lovers are asking the letter to be pure spirit, a task for which it is hopelessly inadequate.

The last quarter of the novel is filled with the intermittent and irregular news of Helen Huntington ministering to her husband in his terminal illness at Grassdale, repeated through the agency of Frederick Lawrence's selective narration of her letters. In one sense, the letters have no object; because she is writing to her brother, who agrees to relay any important news to Gilbert, Helen Huntington cannot use the mode of discourse appropriate to lovers. In an attempt to escape community conjecture about her whereabouts, she is forced to strip her language of its specificity. But the more she "purifies" her language through incompleteness, the more she erases any trace of a narratee, the more Gilbert Markham must treat her letters as fallen texts which he must somehow enclose, as he looks for clues of his own presence:

> "May I keep this letter, Lawrence?—you see she has never once mentioned me throughout—or made the most distant allusion to me; therefore, there can be no impropriety or harm in it."
> "And, therefore, why should you wish to keep it?"
> "Were not these characters written by her hand? And were not those words conceived in her mind, and many of them spoken by her lips?"
> "Well," said he. And so I kept it; otherwise, Halford, you could never have become so thoroughly acquainted with its contents.

Gilbert Markham is almost forced into a kind of nominalism—the word *is* Helen—in order to enclose discourse. His problem is that the letter participates in a modality of time, and hence meaning is partially a function of frequency. To create unexplained gaps in the frequency is to add to or subtract from meaning, and these gaps must occur because the agent of conveyance is not disinterested in the same way that she desires language to be. The exchange value of a letter is not what is said, but the occasion(s) of its delivery. Intentionality is a function neither of narrative subject nor narratee, nor its formal construction, nor its contents, but of something "outside" the letter. Helen's letters act as social signifiers not because their contents are lacking, but because their real function (as reminders of her presence) is less dependent on the knowledge or non-knowledge of their contents than Gilbert believes.

Gilbert Markham, like so many lovers, must resort to attempting to recover the *occasion* of the letter's composition, since he receives only mediated contents. And the result is collapse back into speculation and gossip. After Arthur Huntington's death, there is an interruption in the regular flow of letters, and Gilbert comes to blame his old adversary, Frederick Lawrence, for perhaps plotting to intercept his epistles to Helen: "I would wait, and see if she would notice me—which of course she would not, unless by some kind of message entrusted to her brother, that, in all probability he would not deliver." When the hiatus in the exchange of letters continues, he decides not to write, but to wait for news. And he discovers that Lawrence does not positively withhold communication, but confines himself to a literal interpretation of Markham's enquiries that again leaves no room for his own inclusion in her discourse:

> Ten weeks was long to wait in such a miserable state of uncertainty, but courage! it must be endured;—and meantime I would continue to see Lawrence now and then, though not so often as before, and I would still pursue my habitual enquiries after his sister—if he had lately heard from her, and how she was, but nothing more.
>
> I did so, and the answers I received were always provokingly limited to the letter of the enquiry: She was much as usual: She made no complaints, but the tone of her last letter evinced great depression of mind:—She said she was better:—and finally;—She said she was well.

The problem with the letter is always the same for Gilbert. Does she not mention me because she does not want her brother to know? Or, does the authority for my omission rest with him? The problematic of the letter is how to raise it from a residue of distant desire to a cipher of spiritual presence, given the conditions of its mediated vehicularity.

Throughout *The Tenant of Wildfell Hall* there is the recurrent suspicion that writing can be justified only if raised to some spiritual level. Otherwise it continues to exist as "re-crimination," the repetitive enlargement of plots and suspicion that moves discourse closer to gossip with all of its threat to human relationships. And the solution that the novel somewhat conservatively proposes is that of valorizing writing by exchange, which encloses and supplants other types of discourse, in the process making distinctions among them. Figuratively speaking, Gilbert Markham must get hold of all her writings—diary as well as letters—because only then can the unfinished, mediated status that always threatens to turn her life into gossip be put to an end. Gilbert must himself write the textual supplement to her life's diary—which cannot accommodate the otherness of the listener—and pass it on in order to prevent it from lapsing back into speech or gossip. Without that transactional frame, Anne Brontë's novel threatens to revert to the world of the narrative fragment, Gothic monsters, incestuous relationships, and, of course, whispered gossip—all of which call out for the completion of a closure that will restore differentiation. And in fact, as soon as Gilbert Markham's frame encloses all the other more subversive varieties of discourse, he marries Helen and the community's gossip vanishes. This takes place contemporaneously with the settlement of the dead father's farm upon Gilbert's brother Fergus, thus maintaining a legacy and keeping it from falling into other hands. The restoration of the narrative frame takes place at the same time as the investiture of the paternal lands, falling into disrepair during the plague of gossip. Just as the Victorian novel used a finalizing marriage, the fairy-tale ending, as an antidote to the threat of less socially acceptable forms of intercourse that threatened it, so *The Tenant of Wildfell Hall* equates a sort of narrative contract—the give-and-be-given of discourse—with the marital bond: both keep other monstrous plots at bay. The burden of my argument, in contradistinction to the thrust of much poststructuralist thought—is that the framed discourse that encloses more free-floating, incomplete, or discontinuous discourse in Gothic structures is not a formal component of the radical thematics of the mode, but rather serves to restrain and repress. The salvation of texts by arbitrary supplements, the recovery of subversive discourse, does for "fallen" writing what the Rev. Brontë's sermons did for the unregenerate soul: they define an ending that restores the fiction of a distinction between the elect and the babble of tongues. Closure restores metaphor—and hence likeness and difference—at the cost of containing a crisis in discourse.

Almost. There is a curious way in which Anne Brontë's novel by itself serving as a kind of supplement to *Wuthering Heights*, makes problematic the strategy of enclosure by belatedness. Not only does Anne Brontë's novel repeat its predecessor's initials and amplify its aspirant *h*'s of names and its climatic conditions, but there is something in the circumstances of its genesis that suggests more than the normal anxiety of sisterly influence. In her "Preface to the Second Edition," Anne Brontë betrays the fact that the struggle for primacy between gossip, letter, and textuality may well have been a feature of the novel's very composition. Largely because of the popular commercial success of *Jane Eyre*, Newby attempted to capitalize on the gossip among publishers and some readers that all three "Bells" were one and the same person. As if answering these charges, "The Preface" commences as a kind of letter to those who would discredit the novel's authenticity. But, like Helen Huntington's private letters to Gilbert Markham, it is a letter that must remain anonymous in two senses: it has a generalized rather than a specific object of address, and she must set herself apart from her sisters while simultaneously withholding revelation of her true identity:

> Respecting the author's identity, I would have it to be distinctly understood that Acton Bell is neither Currer nor Ellis Bell, and therefore let not his thoughts be attributed to them. As to whether the name be real or fictitious, it cannot greatly signify to those who know him only by his works.
>
> ("The Preface to the Second Edition")

In this remarkable paragraph, Anne Brontë says, in effect, "I am different from them, but you cannot know how because I am also different from my writing." In other words, the maintenance of her self as a narrative object is dependent upon the erasure of self as a narrative subject. Just as all the eponymous narratives within the novel threaten to collapse into one another, so Anne Brontë senses the pressure of publisher's gossip that threatens to create a univocity out of their separate and diverse achievements. Gossip threatens to turn a relationship of consanguinity into one of contractual identity (the three Brontë sisters are really one person) much as village gossip turns Lawrence and Helen (brother and sister) into one (lovers) or does the same thing later by erroneously replacing the news of Lawrence's upcoming betrothal by the false rumor of Helen's. The novel's genesis participates in the same crisis of discourse that it describes.

And in fact, *The Tenant of Wildfell Hall* is always on the verge of collapsing back into its originary, *Wuthering Heights*. Both novels make use of the crossed marital lines of two neighboring families: Helen's son, Arthur Huntington, marries her own namesake, Helen Hattersley, repeating in the second generation the names but not the facts of the first marriage— Arthur (Huntington) and Helen (Graham). Like the second Cathy and Hareton Earnshaw in *Wuthering Heights*, it is a repetition of the form of the earlier marriage, suggesting that a passing beyond the passionate hell of the first is necessary to a second generation's salvation. Both novels make abundant use of the servant figure, as Rachel and Nelly Dean echo one another in their manipulative faithfulness. In both *Wuthering Heights* and *The Tenant of Wildfell Hall* the puritanical hypocrisy of those who believe in the literal truth of the Text, transmittable of course only by memorization, Joseph and Rev. Millward, respectively, is posed against the possibility of other, more subversive texts. And both novels early on raise the possibility of incest as an explanation of obscured or absent origins: in *The Tenant of*

Wildfell Hall by the gossip-created union of Frederick and Helen; and in *Wuthering Heights* by Heathcliff's obscure origins when he is adopted by the elder Earnshaw, by the fact that he and Cathy wear each other's clothes as children, and that as adults they define their love in terms of identity as in Cathy's infamous "I *am* Heathcliff."

But surely the area where resemblance between *Wuthering Heights* and its supplement, *The Tenant of Wildfell Hall*, is most acute lies in their exploration of the problematic of textuality itself. That Anne Brontë, like Emily before her, used the framed narrative to raise a fallen metaphor is intriguing. Just as the urbane Lockwood, forced to seek refuge at *Wuthering Heights* during a storm, uses the first Cathy's diary as a source for his own biased narrative, so Gilbert Markham is handed Helen's diary as a refuge against the storm of community gossip, a clarification of a legend. The texts of both novels come to have the structural features of the Gothic house—that "penetralium" that J. Hillis Miller first noticed: one text lies enclosed by another, then another, as the boundaries between narratives are blurred. The whole question of belatedness and priority threatens to collapse all the narratives back into a single narrative in much the same way that genealogy threatens to collapse back into the disappearance of difference that produces the monstrous, the ruin, or the fragment—the ontic status of lacking paternity or succession.

One way of thinking about *Wuthering Heights* is to envision the novel as a struggle for supremacy between and among competing texts. There is of course Joseph's Text that on a fateful day he finds rejected by two children who, in refusing to memorize, flee to a different world, that of Thrushcross Grange. There, they are introduced to Edgar Linton whose virtual emblem is the library that provides him with an uninterrupted flow of textuality forever distancing his response to the passions. Nelly Dean's self-serving gossip is the mode of speech appropriate to outsiders, as is Lockwood's speculation; the former is an outsider by virtue of class, the latter, as a result of geography. There is Cathy's diary in its repository, the private closet, like Helen Huntington's in its drawer, increasingly vulnerable to being transformed into a "source" by Lockwood. And finally there is the culminating text on the novel's last page, the one read by the second Cathy to the illiterate Hareton Earnshaw: the emblem of writing—probably the novel we read, *Wuthering Heights*—itself being transformed into speech, a replication of the act that the novel phonetically attempts by its use of the Yorkshire dialect. In reading to her husband the second Cathy is doing what the first Cathy could never do for Heathcliff, committed as she was to the authorship of her private, closet diary: transforming private discourse into speech by a gesture of transaction, enacting the inheritance of literacy by those less fortunate. An added side benefit is the repression of all the earlier violence by this last, best text which combines the belatedness of textuality with the spontaneous presence of speech.

Similarly, the question posed by the narrative structure of *The Tenant of Wildfell Hall* is how a textuality inclusive of the varieties of discourse which comprise it is to be transmitted without a threat. What is the process by which the proliferation of discourse is prevented from being subversive to a culture? Gossip, Helen's increasingly vulnerable diary, and the curiously mediated letters whose contents Frederick Lawrence orally edits—all equate the *process* of literary production with the product itself. They make no distinction between production and consumption since they are all part of what might be called "folk discourse." As a result of that equation, none of the forms of latent communication that float about the novel can ever enter the domain of a possible consumption; they can never be appropriated by an "other" and used for the same purpose as that which initiated them. In much the same way that gossip can never be "used up," so it is with Helen's private, unfinished diary or the flow of the mediated, yet "pure speech" letters from Grassdale. The novel in one sense traces that gesture by which an audience is defined and a narratee is given a fixed address, thereby enabling threatening discourse to be co-opted. Gilbert Markham's extraordinarily long cover letter, however, does for *The Tenant of Wildfell Hall* what the second Cathy's reading does for Hareton Earnshaw in *Wuthering Heights:* it enables narrative once again to become an instructional device, to be legitimized within a corpus. This saving of the text (to borrow from Derrida through the mediation of Geoffrey Hartman) by an act of supplementary enclosure would hint at another problem for the student of Victorian discourse: what are the implications of this salvational gesture for the history of the novel? Formally, the process of "passing on"—the logical succession in textuality—is obviously related to the restoration and revaluation of writing-as-containment. It restores a lineage of sorts to forms of writing and speech which seemed increasingly discontinuous from an originating authority. In both Emily and Anne Brontë's novels the suggestion is always present that the gradual disappearance of religious orthodoxy, with its emphasis upon the primacy of a single, authoritative text, is responsible for the proliferation of texts and tongues. The church at Gimmerton Slough has fallen into disrepair at the conclusion of *Wuthering Heights,* and in *The Tenant of Wildfell Hall,* the hypocritical Rev. Millward has died, his living having passed into the hands of his milder scholarly successor, Richard Wilson, himself a devotee of classical texts.

The immense popularity of the Gothic mode in the late eighteenth and early nineteenth centuries in effect created a world of fragmentary texts, incomplete manuscripts, unfinished diaries—all traces of decentered writing. Its equivalent in the so-called mainstream Victorian novel would have been the proliferation of the orphan, who, having no genealogical lineage, was the perfect emblem of discontinuous discourse—the gossip, diaries, partial letters, and other fragments of floating writing or speech to which the frame restores historicity.

There is abundant evidence that for all the Brontës, writing itself was a kind of conspiracy against the dictates of another, prior text. Writing was simultaneously pleasurable and an activity to be kept secret, as the existence of the Angria legend and its later successor, the Gondal poems, attests. The publication of first *Wuthering Heights* and then, in July 1848, *The Tenant of Wildfell Hall*, with the advertisement implying that all the Bells were one and the same, prompted the notorious ride to London in the same month, and the disclosure of their true identities to the publisher. In that crucial period, sometime between 1846 and 1848 the close relationship between Anne and Emily Brontë which Ellen Nussey had termed "like twins" in 1833, clearly underwent a sea change. In June of 1845 Anne had given up her employment and returned to Haworth, resuming a life she had known six years earlier in the Brontë household. But something had clearly changed, and Anne Brontë's poem "Self-Communion" is almost certainly a partial record of the disappearance of the "genial bliss that could not cloy" (*Poems*, "Self-Communion," 1.179) but apparently did. In that lengthy poem, Anne catalogued the causes of the "jarring discords" that came between the sisters:

> But this was nothing to the woe
> With which another truth was learned:—
> That I must check, or nurse apart
> Full many an impulse of the heart
>   And many a darling thought:
> What my soul worshipped, sought, and prized,
> Were slighted, questioned, or despised;—
>   This pained me more than aught.
>   (*Poems*, "Self-Communion," ll. 188–95)

In imagery that seems partly derivative of one of the famous scenes in *Wuthering Heights*, the speaker describes a separation:

> I saw that they were sundered now
> The trees that at the root were one:
> They yet might mingle leaf and bough,
> But the stem must stand alone.
>   (ll. 204–7)

The destruction of the Gondal saga (December 1846?) and with it, the virtual cessation of communal projects between Emily and Anne, plus the gradual but discernible replacement of an editorial "our" in the pre-1846 poems with the emergence of first person singular possessive pronouns in the later poems by Anne—all would suggest that the public disclosure of separate identities by the Brontë sisters was but the making public of what had already happened in private: a rift. The publication of *Wuthering Heights* had been a betrayal of the private, albeit communally shared imaginative world of the Brontës. *The Tenant of Wildfell Hall* was a belated attempt to domesticate the damage. Like all enclosures, it has not been entirely successful because of a perceived distance between the supplement and its originary. Hence, the disparagement of even Charlotte Brontë, on grounds of its historical displacement, of Anne's quietness:

> Anne's character was milder and more subdued. . . . She wanted the power, the fire, the originality of her sister, but was well endowed with quiet virtues of her own.

The Tenant of Wildfell Hall supplements and encloses *Wuthering Heights* partially, of course, by parodying it. It does in one sense what sequels always do to the Gothic impulse, from Hogg's *The Confessions of a Justified Sinner,* which supplants and justifies the "found" manuscript which is its originary, "The Private Memories and Confessions of a Sinner," to the celluloid *Jaws II,* which supplants and justifies an early version by "passing it on." It contains potentially independent, straying texts by keeping them within the same generic family. The very book we read, Anne Brontë's *The Tenant of Wildfell Hall,* simultaneously enacts a transformation in the reader, in the narratee, Halford (who, as part of the "exchange," marries Markham's sister, Rose), and in the new Mrs. Markham all by calling attention to itself as a framed narrative. The belated, embodied nature of narrative has finally triumphed, enclosing those forms of speech and writing whose pretense to a counterfeit currency threatened the framing sequel. Enclosure does for Mrs. Huntington's past what *The Tenant of Wildfell Hall* does for *Wuthering Heights:* by giving it a new name, it reestablishes for it a rightful place within a family. Contrary to Benveniste's assertion that narrative erases or conceals signs of the narrator, Anne Brontë's use of Gilbert Markham's enclosing cover letter allows for the reintrusion of the narrator, whose role had been threatened by a range of anonymous, floating discourse. Narrative enclosure is part of a process of extension without subversion, a reminder of the importance of "our contract" in controlling the inflation of orality—gossip.

The impulse to "enclose" sweeps all before it, including the wind and the weather that swirl about Wildfell Hall and its environs. At the beginning of Anne Brontë's novel, nature itself is part of the imperfection of the fragmented, fallen world. Wildfell Hall is shielded from the war of wind and weather only by a group of scotch firs, "themselves half-blighted with storms." It is clearly an environment of incomplete closure where "the close green wall of privet, that had bordered the principal walk, were two-thirds withered away." By the time we reach the novel's end, however, a marvelous image of the conservative powers of enclosure appears. Helen Huntington wishes for her future husband, Gilbert, to be accepted by her aging aunt, now, like Helen, a widow. He must agree to the aunt's residence at the Staningley household, which has passed into Helen's inheritance. The aunt's avocation is the gentle nurturing of flowers out of season, a pastime made possible by the existence of an indoor *conservatory* to which Gilbert must pay homage. It is a fitting supplement to the bluebells in the gentle breeze which blows on the last page of *Wuthering Heights.* This arrangement enables three generations to live under one roof, much as Gilbert Markham's framing letter to Halford, a letter outside the novel's first chapter, enables discontinuous narrative to become suddenly continuous. The domestication of potentially anarchic nature, the nurture of roses in winter, is achieved by the same gesture that brings the civilizing influence of inheritance, marriage, the enclosure of unfinished texts, and the containment of the narrative rivalry that was part of the publication history of Anne Brontë's novel. Only then, safely passed on, is the fiction of the family and the family of fictions secure against those forces which would confuse narrative or generational lines.

Speaking through Parable:
George Eliot's Search
for a Narrative Medium

Barry V. Qualls

> *In the old days there were angels who came and took men by the hand and*
> *led them away from the city of destruction. We see no white-winged angels*
> *now. But yet men are led from threatening destruction: a hand is put into*
> *theirs, which leads them forth gently towards a calm and bright land, so*
> *that they look no more backward; and the hand may be a little child's.*
> —*Silas Marner*, chap. 14

No passage in Victorian fiction better illustrates the coming together of the biblical and Romantic traditions than this from *Silas Marner*. George Eliot's "sort of legendary tale" is a Wordsworthian *Pilgrim's Progress,* beginning with a lone individual carrying some "mysterious burden" on his back and closing with that burden gone and the man firmly rooted in a new community of fellow-feeling because of the coming of the golden-haired child. With its image of a journey towards some "bright land," this novel is characteristic of all of George Eliot's fiction. Whether her subjects be the Church people and Methodists of the century's beginning or the very modern men and women surveying a Gwendolen Harleth who has never registered "religious nomenclature" (*Daniel Deronda*, chap. 8 [all further references to this text will be abbreviated as *DD*]) as part of her inner life, George Eliot needs for adequately exploring her themes the structures that Bunyan and Wordsworth used.

Yet throughout her career George Eliot worries that she will be too schematic in her "teaching," too much a Bunyan. To Frederic Harrison she wrote in 1866 that as a "writer of novels"—"books which the dullest and silliest reader thinks himself competent to deliver an opinion on"—she had always to try to make her ideas "thoroughly incarnate, as if they had revealed themselves to me first in the flesh and not in the spirit."

> I think aesthetic teaching is the highest of all teaching because it
> deals with life in its highest complexity. But if it ceases to be purely
> aesthetic—if it lapses anywhere from the picture to the diagram—
> it becomes the most offensive of all teaching. Avowed Utopias are

From *The Secular Pilgrims of Victorian Fiction: The Novel as Book of Life.* © 1982 by Cambridge University Press.

not offensive, because they are understood to have a scientific and expository character: they do not pretend to work on the emotions, or couldn't do it if they did pretend . . . Well, then, consider the sort of agonizing labour to an English-fed imagination to make art a sufficiently real back-ground, for the desired picture, to get breathing, individual forms, and group them in the needful relations, so that the presentation will lay hold on the emotions as human experience.

Teaching is her emphasis, as it was for Bunyan and the later religious writers (whom she read during her intensely evangelical early years). And George Eliot constantly searches for the modes of using language which will allow her "to urge the human sanctities." She wants no diagrams, yet she insists that characters and incident be "typical" in order to "secure one's lasting sympathy"; and she grows more and more attracted to the opera—"a great, great product"—and its ways of rendering the emblematic (this interest we see fully used in *Daniel Deronda*).

Her fictions chart her continuing efforts to find a means of taking the novel beyond the level of mere entertainment. In *Adam Bede* and *The Mill on the Floss* she presents "George Eliot" as one who lives amongst the people he observes. Then she becomes in *Silas Marner* a storyteller and writes a romance which openly brings together the traditions of Wordsworth and Bunyan, in all their typicality. From this tale she moves into history, and into the role of historian and poet who, like Herodotus or Virgil, sees the relation of the fictive and the real. Finally, in *Daniel Deronda* she creates again the same "vision" she had offered in the overtly fabular *Silas Marner*. Far more sophisticated in its techniques and ideas, the deep structure of *Deronda* is nevertheless the same as that of the fable; George Eliot is a sacred romancer. Each of her novels, indeed, consolidates the ideas and methods used in the work which has preceded it. But in the consonance of vision which they all share, they underline George Eliot's determination to show her readers the "right road" towards natural supernaturalism.

Late in her career, shortly after *Daniel Deronda* had appeared, George Eliot insisted that "the principles" which went into creating Mordecai were the same as those governing Dinah Morris in *Adam Bede*. Yet her novels also belonged, as she said in 1861, to "successive mental phases" because they examined those same "principles" under different lights and from different angles. All were "experiments in life."

> But my writing is simply a set of experiments in life—an endeavour to see what our thought and emotion may be capable of—what stores of motive, actual or hinted as possible, give promise of a better after which we may strive—what gains from past revelations and discipline we must strive to keep hold of as something more sure than shifting theory. I become more and more timid—with less daring to adopt any formula which does not get itself clothed

for me in some human figure and individual experience, and perhaps that is a sign that if I help others to see at all it must be
through that medium of art.

"What gains from past revelations and discipline" we need, and the sense
of becoming "more and more timid"—the phrases offer a key to her evolving fictions and to her turn in the end towards the Jews with (as Mordecai
defines it) their "divine principle" of "action, choice, resolved memory"
(*DD*, chap. 42). Each of George Eliot's novels is a spiritual biography or
Bildungsroman focusing on Bunyan's question "What shall I do?" and charting the "civil war within the soul" (*Middlemarch*, chap. 67, epigraph [all
further references to this text will be abbreviated as *M*]) as answers are
sought. From George Eliot's narrative perspective each novel is also a new
station in her meditation on English life over a period of seventy years,
and thus on a world in such flux that anything "sure" is rarely discernible.
She wrote in 1862 that she required "freedom to write out one's own varying
unfolding self." Barbara Hardy has noted her "process of rewriting one
novel in the next." Each novel, as it focuses on the myths, fictions, histories—on the art—that human beings require to live, is a meditation intended to make its readers share the process of *seeing* that foundation in
memory of action and choice. This chapter is an examination of those
themes, situations, and narrative devices that constitute George Eliot's meditation on nineteenth-century English life.

I

"In the old days": the phrase from *Silas Marner* calls attention to the setting
of all of George Eliot's English novels except the last. Each looks back to a
time before any reader had been "to Exeter Hall, or heard a popular
preacher, or read *Tracts for the Times* or *Sartor Resartus*" (*Adam Bede*, chap.
52 [all further references to this text will be abbreviated as *AB*]); each recalls
a time of "history" set in "what we are pleased to call Merry England"
(*Silas Marner*, chap. 1 [all further references to this text will be abbreviated
as *SM*]). Yet the voice which places and focuses our attention always speaks
out of an intense awareness of *Sartor* and of Darwin, and with a sense that
"Merry England" is part of the religious *myth* that we—readers and author—need to confront the modern world. Like Carlyle's, the voice is constantly concerned to discover the filaments uniting past and present and
tying them together in a community's life and in an individual's. Five years
before *Silas Marner*, in her review of W. H. von Riehl's *Natural History of
German Life* (*Westminster*, July 1856), George Eliot had stated her sense of
developing English society. The ideas in this essay govern her representation of the cultural scene in all of her work:

> Language must be left to grow in precision, completeness, and
> unity, as minds grow in clearness, comprehensiveness, and sym-

pathy. And there is an analogous relation between the moral tendencies of men and the social conditions they have inherited. The nature of European men has its roots intertwined with the past, and can only be developed by allowing those roots to remain undisturbed while the process of development is going on, until that perfect ripeness of the seed which carries with it a life independent of the root. This vital connexion with the past is much more vividly felt on the Continent than in England, where we have to recall it by an effort of memory and reflection; for though our English life is in its core intensely traditional, Protestantism and commerce have modernized the face of the land and the aspects of society in a far greater degree than in any continental country.

George Eliot urges, as Carlyle had in *Heroes and Hero-Worship* and in *Past and Present*, that English society strive to be what von Riehl saw European society to be, *"incarnate history"*; "any attempt to disengage [society] from its historical elements," she warns, "must be simply destructive of social vitality."

George Eliot wants her fictions to incarnate history imaginatively and concretely, to show—as the phrase itself suggests—the transformation of the natural through the workings of the supernatural. Her novels present, in fact, the most incisive "natural history of English life" available. The metaphors of seeds and roots from this early essay resonate throughout her career (*Deronda*'s last book is called "Fruit and Seed"). Indeed, in her early novels she wellnigh insists that the way to the Celestial City is through the country (if not up the Delectable Mountains). But that "natural history" she writes is more a portrayal of dissociation and dislocation than any depiction of the "vital connexion" of past and present that she believes in. Her writing shows us the increasing severance of an individual from his heritage and of a community from its past. George Eliot cannot find, in a *real* English setting, a "Merry England" which will allow her questing protagonists to relate the community's evolving life to their spiritual needs, or to realize the place of the supernatural within the natural processes of their own lives or in the natural world itself. Dislocations, uprootings kill all possibility for incarnating history—except in a very individual and private sense. Only the fairy-tale structure of *Silas Marner* allows her to present a "history" where any "fruit," any resolution, occurs—and that tale begins with a slashing of past and present which is never reconciled.

George Eliot's first novel tries to deal with a community where dislocations look impossible. *Adam Bede* offers us in Hayslope a "Merry England" where there is "no rigid demarcation" (chap. 9) between classes or sects within the community. But central to this novel is the problem of discovering roots which while natural are not merely natural. The two women protagonists embody at once two sides of the dilemma and underline George Eliot's inability to resolve it within the world of the novel. Hetty Sorrel's frightening inability to conceptualize beyond the narrow range of her egoism suggests the terrible limits of a nature which is merely natural. "There are," George Eliot says of Hetty, "some plants that have hardly any roots" (chap. 15); and the sorrel plant is associated with bitterness and acidity. Hetty has utterly no sense of community, relationship, or God; she sees nothing beyond her image in a mirror.

But Hetty's opposite in this novel, Dinah Morris, is for George Eliot equally limited in her sense of having only heavenly roots rather than those firmly tied to the earth. Dinah's Methodism and her insistence on seeing a community as irrevocably divided between "the children of light" and "the children of this world" (chap. 10) clearly bind her to the Bunyan tradition (and *Pilgrim's Progress* begins with a denial of earthly spiritual community). She calls the Hayslope area the "land of Goshen" (chap. 3), comparing its life to Israel's contented home in Egypt before the Exodus became a necessity. And she renders a Bunyanesque judgment on the "comfortable" world Mrs Poyser happily attributes to communion in the Established Church: "I've noticed, that in these villages where the people lead a quiet life among the green pastures and still waters . . . there's a strange deadness to the Word," Dinah tells the Reverend Irwine (chap. 8). George Eliot does not endorse the judgment, finding instead that those "select natures who pant after the ideal . . . are curiously in unison with the narrowest and pettiest" (chap. 17).

She also develops a contrast between Dinah's Methodist ministry and that of the Established Church's Reverend Irwine to show the unnatural severing of past and present which sectarianism—and later commercialism—will inflict upon English life. Christopher Herbert, examining the "Schemes of Nature" in *Adam Bede,* has argued that Eliot in her two preachers is juxtaposing two "differing interpretations of the idea of Nature."

> Dinah's Methodism rests ultimately on the doctrine that Nature in all its aspects is corrupt, by virtue of Adam's sin; for her the goal of religious faith is to renounce and to overcome, therefore, whatever is natural (starting with all human instincts). . . . In contrast to this otherworldliness Mr. Irwine stands principally for a grateful acceptance of Nature, including human nature with all its imperfections.

The contrast is, essentially, between the Calvinistic and the Wordsworthian ideas about the natural world. And what we notice most strikingly in this novel is the destructive consequences for English society of the split between these two traditions; religion itself threatens to become a dividing force. The awful case of Hetty sufficiently refutes the Wordsworthian idea of the beneficence of nature without human connection and concern (and we might remember that Hetty's journey has striking affinities with Wordsworth's "The Thorn"); and the miserable death of her child undermines

Mrs Poyser's pious notion that "there's One above 'ull take care o' the innicent child, else it's but little truth they tell us at church" (chap. 40).

But while George Eliot can, in *Adam Bede*, adequately diagram the problem, she cannot convincingly project an image of its solution. She tries with Dinah and Adam, who ostensibly provide the book's central focus. In presenting them she is very concerned to shape their histories on models that her readers will recognize. We do not need to know of her wish to give Carlyle pleasure with her novel to see the Carlylean emphasis in the portrait of Adam himself: this "Saxon" (chap. 1; he also appears as a Celt) is a spiritual son of Abbot Samson. He has no patience with Methodist self-scrutiny ("But t' hear some o' them preachers, you'd think as a man must be doing nothing all's life but shutting's eyes and looking what's a-going on inside him"—chap. 1); his work has "always been part of his religion" (chap. 50); and when his own suffering comes, it brings a "baptism of fire" which yields "a soul full of new awe and new pity" (chap. 42).

If Adam's ideas and suffering suggest a Carlylean background, Dinah Morris's sermon and her account of her "Calling" to the Reverend Irwine (chap. 8) are straight out of Methodist memoirs and testimony (even to Dinah's being an orphan). And the entire prison experience of the novel, as Valentine Cunningham has shown, is a central image of Methodist confessional literature and hymns, which reflected the Methodists' "awareness that conversions effected in prison were an appropriate acting out of New Testament metaphor: salvation was a release from the bondage and captivity of sin." Hetty, of course, experiences no religious conversion; her sense of the godlike is nonexistent. But George Eliot appeals to the typical, and to the readers' recognition of it, even as she varies its resolution to make her *human* case.

Dinah and Adam provide two modes of existence in this world, modes which may be modified as the novel progresses but which are formed when we meet them. Dinah's work is to try like Bunyan to help others see the rewards of the next world; Adam is determined, like Teufelsdröckh, "to do my work well, and make the world a bit better place for them as can enjoy it" (chap. 48). Their union, in a fine pastoral scene, is meant to tell thematically. But it never makes the human case of the novel as do the stories of Arthur and Hetty.

In these two unformed "children" we have the true *Bildung* possibility, and its thwarting. Each begins life with little sense that the world is not an extension of his or her own personality. Arthur Donnithorne constantly announces his concern for others, but his alliance with Adam, in its superficiality, underlines the ease with which he utters his concern. His education will simply burn into his soul the meaning of those words he so glibly utters. But Hetty, as the famous mirror scene suggests (chap. 15), never sees anything beyond her own self, and never sees that very adequately. Her journey is so horrifying because it so darkly parodies Dinah's vision of her salvation and Calling. It is an egoist's journey into a self where there is only a vacuum (Christopher Herbert calls it "an allegorical journey to the core of human nature, stripped of all its lendings"), a "journey in despair" rather than hope, a cruel inversion of Israel's or Christian's march towards some promised land. She is without a sense of the past (the plant with no roots); she has never read a novel and cares not a whit for what the pictures in *Pilgrim's Progress* signify. Her lack of response to words is part and parcel of her lack of response to human beings: in George Eliot the two are inseparable (thus we know from Dinah's language what she reads, we see Adam reading Bunyan and Baxter, we hear Arthur on the "twaddling" *Lyrical Ballads*). Hetty's lack of education has left her no "shape for her expectations" (chap. 13). Her final journey is such an awful inversion of a pilgrim's progress because it is an "objectless wandering" (chap. 37). Hetty, like the malign Grandcourt later, terrifies because she is so utterly—and unknowingly—soulless: she has no models, no myths of *living* which pull her beyond her own vision in the mirror and force her to acknowledge her connection with her fellows. As the animal imagery associated with her suggests, she has only an empty human self.

Maggie Tulliver's journey is "objectless" too, but she has fictions, words, that animate her, that give some "vision" even if limited and finally without sustenance. Indeed, *The Mill on the Floss* reworks an emphasis begun in *Adam Bede*: a focus on the way the mind works with the myths—religious and Romantic—available to it, on the way it accepts or alters or rejects them as it tries to find a *ground* for belief in the modern world. A passage of commentary states this explicitly. George Eliot is discussing the needs of working men and women, of those who form "a wide and arduous national life" which supports a nation in its well-bred ease:

> This wide national life is based entirely on emphasis—the emphasis of want. . . . Under such circumstances, there are many among its myriads of souls who have absolutely needed an emphatic belief . . . , something that will present motives in an entire absence of high prizes, something that will give patience and feed human love when the limbs ache with weariness, and human looks are hard upon us—something, clearly, that lies outside personal desires, that includes resignation for ourselves and active love for what is not ourselves.
>
> (bk. 4, chap. 3)

The passage, with its Carlylean emphases, at once summarizes *Adam Bede*'s conclusion and urges us to see the new ways *The Mill* explores the same issues. In this second novel there is no golden pastoral Hayslope, nor any Reverend Irwine to make life whole and "comfortable." St Ogg's is a perfect town of Carnal Policy, and it illustrates the wedge between past and present and between classes which the combination of commerce and Protestantism has forced into community life. Its Protestantism is not evangelical, but the much more deadened and deadening religion of "respectability" (and George Eliot adds Carlyle's notation—"proud respectability in a gig of unfashionable build" (bk. 4, chap. 1)—to illuminate her point about the "pagan" nature of this "variation of Protestantism unknown to Boussuet"). The narrator warns the reader that in the Dodsons and their St Ogg's peers we find "a kind of population out of keeping with the earth on which they live" (bk. 4, chap. 1). There is an "oppressive narrowness" about the "religion" where no real harmony exists between man and nature. The ineffective Reverend Venn, with so little aid to offer Maggie, notes the dislocation: "At present everything seems tending towards the relaxation of ties—towards the substitution of wayward choice for the adherence to obligation, which has its roots in the past" (bk. 7, chap. 2). It is a truth which we have, under a different rubric, seen enacted in the lives of Hetty and Arthur Donnithorne, and which we see once again in Maggie's history. To Stephen Guest's assertion that "natural law surmounts every other," she replies: "If the past is not to bind us, where can duty lie? We should have no law but the inclination of the moment" (bk. 6, chap. 14). This statement suggests how much Maggie's history is a rewriting of Hetty and Arthur's story.

Maggie's quest is for some sense of what this *past* is, what its structures and foundations are. She wants an "emphatic belief." Her frustrated efforts to find some creed to live by, to make what Deronda will call "that hard unaccommodating Actual" (*DD*, chap. 33) sensible and bearable, provide the novel's focus. And the narrator dwells on Maggie's use of fictions to explain her world, or to provide grounds for hope: the eight-year-old girl amongst the gypsies wants her father to rescue her, but if not him then "Jack the Giant-killer, or Mr Greatheart, or St George" (bk. 1, chap. 11). The Maggie who at thirteen sees her father in despair finds that the "world outside the books was not a happy one" (bk. 3, chap. 5), and turns to Thomas à Kempis's words to make it bearable. Then, as a young lady in Lucy Deane's "fairy tale," Maggie finds herself "in her brighter aërial world again," in "a world of love and beauty and delight, made up of vague, mingled images from all the poetry and romance she had ever read" (bk. 6, chap. 3). Her internalizing of the images and languages of books is an expression of her "blind, unconscious yearning for something that would link together the wonderful impressions of this mysterious life, and give her soul a sense of home in it" (bk. 3, chap. 5). The Word gave Bunyan one home; words give Maggie many, but no permanent one.

The book titles within the novel call our attention to the sources of George Eliot's presentation of Maggie's progress. The first two—"Boy and Girl" and "School-Time"—suggest a Romantic childhood, with its *Bildungsroman* emphasis on education and its Wordsworthian glow around Maggie and her brother at that age when still "the outer world seemed only an extension of our personality" and they had not "known the labour of choice" (bk. 2, chap. 1). But then come titles—"The Downfall," "The Valley of Humiliation"—that invoke Bunyan and man's fall, and underline

Maggie's metaphysical homelessness. The naming of the novel's central book "The Valley of Humiliation" places Bunyan's pilgrimage firmly in the novel's texture—for counterpoint. Here we see the consolations available to Maggie as she seeks "some explanation of this hard, real life" (bk. 4, chap. 3). Significantly, the book opens with Dodson Protestantism, which Maggie's brother embraces without question, but it closes with Thomas à Kempis. Or rather, with Maggie's version, for George Eliot warns us (in Carlyle's language) that Maggie's celebration of "renunciation" as a key to "happiness" mistakes what renunciation centers on: "sorrow borne willingly" (bk. 4, chap. 3). For Maggie, Apollyon assumes no certain shape except that of the absence of "established authorities and appointed guides" (bk. 4, chap. 3). Bunyan's Christian survived the Valley of Humiliation only to face the Valley of the Shadow of Death, and then Vanity Fair. Maggie seems to escape the Humiliation (with Philip Wakem's aid), then survives her father's death, only to arrive in Vanity Fair ("Duet in Paradise")—and get very little beyond. Her final prayer, "O God, what is the way home?" is her hard and unflinching acknowledgment of her failure (even Philip's offer to be her Hopeful will not serve). There is, in the end, a Wordsworthian reunion with her brother and a pastoral frame supplied by George Eliot's commentary. But they do not efface the futility of Maggie's effort to break from her imprisonment, to fuse the world of words and the world of hard and harsh living.

George Eliot does not, however, intend us to see *The Mill* as only Maggie's biography. Two other figures share her pilgrimage, and make their own as well, and together their three *Bildungsromane* make the novel's emphasis. Tom Tulliver, in the "Valley of Humiliation," takes up Dodsonism and never looks back. He becomes a "character at unity with itself," one with "no visions beyond the distinctly possible" (bk. 5, chap. 2). His is the Utilitarian answer, a worldling's knowledge of "what is right and respectable"—and the answering "faith" in a world of change. "I don't find fault with change," says Mr Deane; "Trade, sir, opens a man's eyes" (bk. 6, chap. 5). It is the modern *vision*. And Tom Tulliver's.

It is Philip Wakem, Tom's schoolmate and Maggie's Greatheart (the "opening in the rocky wall which shut in the narrow valley of humiliation"—bk. 5, chap. 3), who gives us the novel's one real—because living and practicable—definition of vision. From his first appearance, this hunchback is seen as even more isolated than Maggie. Yet he breaks out of that isolation. His final letter to Maggie, though it cannot save her from being forever the "lonely wanderer" (bk. 7, chap. 5) she feels condemned to being, narrates his battle with his own Apollyon:

> In the midst of my egoism, I yet could not bear to come like a death-shadow across the feast of your joy. . . . The new life I have found in caring for your joy and sorrow more than for what is directly my own, has transformed the spirit of rebellious mur-

muring into that willing endurance which is the birth of strong sympathy. I think nothing but such complete and intense love could have initiated me into that enlarged life which grows and grows by appropriating the life of others; for before, I was always dragged back from it by ever-present self-consciousness. I even think sometimes that this gift of transferred life which has come to me in loving you, may be a new power to me.

(bk. 7, chap.3)

This "new life," "that enlarged life": it is Teufelsdröckh's language when he has broken into freedom. We do not read *The Mill* as George Eliot guides us to read it—with Philip's consciousness closing the novel at the point of *his* vision, his apocalypse—unless we see his education, his passage from the narrowness of egoism into "transferred life," as central to the meaning of the novel.

> His great companionship was among the trees of the Red Deeps, where the buried joy seemed still to hover—like a revisiting spirit.
>
> (bk. 7, Conclusion)

What George Eliot means by memory, by choice founded in "the deep immovable roots in memory," is in that phrase "buried joy." Certainly words have been part of its formation, but they have been animated—incarnated—by human relationship. The conjunction tells in the most liberating way.

But still the ending of *The Mill* does not resolve the issues of the strife of nature and God and man that Maggie's case raises any more than does the marriage which concludes *Adam Bede* (indeed, the cleansing flood touches the questions even less). The next year's *Silas Marner* does satisfactorily resolve them, and in precisely the way the case of Philip Wakem had pointed to. In this novel the words of supernatural creeds find illustration and confirmation not in religious worship but in the appearance of a child. The motto, from Wordsworth's "Michael," announces the theme:

> A child, more than all other gifts
> That earth can offer to declining man,
> Brings hope with it, and forward-looking thoughts.

Wordsworth and Bunyan are united in this "legendary tale." In the history of the weaver of Raveloe George Eliot juxtaposes—and reconciles—the Poysers' "comfortable" world and Mr Tulliver's "puzzlin' " one, Dinah's "prison" and the Dodsons' solid world.

The novel is something of a *jeu d'esprit* (it was done in a moment of inspiration while she labored on *Romola*), and it is a perfect construction. George Eliot's pilgrim is Israel outcast (men of his type "looked like the remnants of a disinherited race" we hear in the novel's first paragraph). The burden on the back of this poor nineteenth-century Christian is not, however, original sin; as Q. D. Leavis notes, it is the "loss of faith and of a community," a particularly Victorian dilemma. The pilgrim comes to his promised land from a place where "the currents of industrial energy and Puritan earnestness" (chap. 3) are strong indeed, even as they are quite foreign to a Raveloe that becomes "home" in a very Old Testament way; it becomes a "land of milk and honey" for Marner. (We note the characteristics of the novel's "Egypt"—its linking of Protestantism and commercialism—even to the factory standing where Lantern Yard's chapel once did.) In his new environment—"Merry England"—Marner is forced to see that the sources of "emphatic belief" are placed quite differently from what his early religious training had indicated. Starting out amidst the most emphatic of religious sects, he has his faith in God and his fellow-feeling shattered by a magical—and Bible ordained—drawing of lots; the Bible will never again be a source of literal truth for him. Going into exile, weaving for the gold which commands his only worship, Marner's life "narrow[s] and harden[s] itself more and more into a mere pulsation of desire and satisfaction that had no relation to any other being"; it reduces "itself to the functions of weaving and hoarding, without any contemplation of an end towards which the functions tended" (chap. 2). The mechanical and animal language describes his state: he seems another Hetty, on an "objectless" journey and reduced to satisfying only "natural" needs. But unlike her and like Maggie, he has known—felt—in that Lantern Yard sect the structures and the language and the situations that some "far-echoing voice" existing beyond the self can suggest. Thus, he never hesitates to think of the "golden" child who comes to him as Providentially sent; he has never been able to cut himself off from the biblical heritage and its supernatural agencies that are the foundation of his memories. And though he is "quite unable, by means of anything he heard or saw, to identify the Raveloe religion with his old faith" (chap. 14), "that new self" (chap. 16) to which Eppie's coming gives birth allows him an integration into Raveloe's "communion" (chap. 14).

The child's appearance reinstates even as it redefines Silas's supernatural understanding of his natural world—and both natural and supernatural worlds then lose their isolation and terror. His is a redemption underlining the source of Eppie's name, Isaiah 62:4: "Thou shalt no more be termed Forsaken; neither shall thy land any more be termed Desolate: but thou shalt be called Hephzibah, and thy land Beulah: for the Lord delighteth in thee." The supernatural and the natural join in the child Eppie—and "save" Marner, literally. He recovers "a consciousness of unity between his past and present" (chap. 16) and a "presentiment of some Power presiding over his life" (chap. 12). It is Carlyle's "new Mythus," and perfectly embodied.

But if Eppie gives palpable life to belief, she does not answer the questions that the severed past has raised. Silas constantly meditates on that past, and uses the Bible's language to frame his experience ("mine own famil'ar friend, in whom I trusted, had lifted up his heel again' me, and worked to ruin me"—from Psalm 41:9 [chap. 16]). This language is

Silas's means of bearing the burden of the past. But the very fact that the words can no longer promise an answer as they did for the Psalmist is telling. And we note that the "good" people of Raveloe are quite ignorant of the Bible's language; it is the church service and the songs they have heard there that they respond to (the same response is made by Adam Bede and the Poysers to the communal worship, and by Daniel Deronda in the synagogue). Dolly Winthrop has told Silas, after his gold had vanished, that a carol in church, amidst so many ills in the world, caused one to think "you've got to a better place a'ready" (chap. 10). Eppie's coming animates this idea for Silas, and integrates him into the established communion even as he uses "other" language to explain what is happening. The Bible serves him as a source for ordering his experiences, a means allowing him to transcend the natural world of chance and function and to find continuity between his past and present.

If Eppie's coming awakens in Silas "old impressions of awe at the presentiment of some Power presiding over his life," it also forces the same recognition on her father. Godfrey Cass and his wife form the "respectable" (chap. 19) part of *Marner*'s history, and their story points the full implications of Eppie's name. Isaiah, in calling the Hebrews Hephzibah, had prophesied: "And the Gentiles shall see thy righteousness, and all kings thy glory" (Isa. 62:2). Godfrey Cass is forced to see Marner's "righteousness." This man who had seen his brother's absence and his first wife's death as simply his own luck finds the child's presence with Silas a guarantee of his own future "as a promised land" (chap. 15). But that Beulah turns barren when he finds his home childless. He is forced, finally, to acknowledge himself "in no sense free" (Deronda's phrase), and to see in his childlessness a "retribution," an announcement that the past does tell in the present, that no law takes precedence over natural feeling.

> "What you say is natural, my dear child—it's natural you should cling to those who've brought you up," [Godfrey's wife] said mildly; "but there's a duty you owe to your lawful father."
>
> (chap. 19)

The Law—and in so allegorical a book that word carries Old Testament resonances—must give way to the relationships of feeling; Bunyan must give way before Wordsworth even as his idea of a jealous God is softened into a sense of some Power presiding over our lives (the New Testament substitute of Love for Law is part of the novel's "Morality Play"). Godfrey's recognition involves his own resignation to lifelong sorrow. The Gentiles *do* see Israel's righteousness, and Christ's love.

All ends then with "emphatic belief" defined as that "something, clearly, that lies outside personal desires, that includes resignation for ourselves and love for what is not ourselves." For Silas Marner and Godfrey Cass, as for Dolly Winthrop, this involves the Judeo-Christian promise of a "better place"; for George Eliot and her readers, this place seems quite established with Silas and Eppie in the Actual. But the point is that the human beings of this "legendary tale" need the words and structures of myths they know if they are to find meaning in their everyday experience (and to break out of personal selfishness and isolation). David Carroll has said that "the subject of the novel is the different ways in which we create myths, valid and invalid," to help us to understand "the mystery of the worlds in which we live." The two plots of *Silas Marner* allow George Eliot to explore two modes of living: one which sees nothing but what the eye focuses on; the other which acknowledges the power of the unseen, for good or ill. This "structural division" of the novel, Carroll notes, "creates an area of mystery which George Eliot says is an inescapable condition of human existence."

> This area is the testing-ground of the protagonists' myth-making faculties and within it George Eliot demonstrates that valid myths of order are a direct expression of love, while invalid myths of chance result from an absence of love. The former act as inter- mediaries between the individual and the realities of life, and the latter seek to deny these realities.

Importantly too, these plots together incorporate those worlds of "above and below" (chap. 16) which Silas had found so indifferent to him. They incorporate the worlds of romance and of history.

II

Without the fairy-tale wonders of *Silas Marner* or its Wordsworthian nature, George Eliot's next two English novels do precisely what that book did: though set during the period of the first Reform Bill, both *Felix Holt* and *Middlemarch* explore the myths, fictions, and lies that men and women create or expropriate in order to confront and survive change. Nothing in the early 1830s offers the soul's-aid that a tradition-centered community had in the earlier novels. Indeed, religion and its ministers have become one more of the controversies of the day, a very obvious source of division and contention ("But now, if you speak out of the Prayer-book itself, you are liable to be contradicted"—Mrs Farebrother [*M*, chap. 17]), or else a supporter of worldly comfort (a "way of conciliating piety and worldliness, the nothingness of this life and the desirability of cut glass, the conscious- ness at once of filthy rags and the best damask"—*Middlemarch*, with Bun- yan's language, chap. 27). By the time of *Deronda*, set in the readers' present, religion for the English ceases even to be controversial; "religious nomen- clature" becomes an unnoticed part of secular language. And because of this deforming of mythic language, George Eliot returns in this novel with- out hesitation to the overt "romance" structure of *Silas Marner*, with its basis in Israel's history. She has, indeed, "become more and more timid" in insisting that the myths which offer a basis for action and choice be anchored in the chief narrative of Western man's religious experience. But she is bolder than ever in garbing this traditional religious myth in the forms of romance.

To understand why *Daniel Deronda* had to be centered in Hebraism and the Zionist revival, we need to trace George Eliot's evolving narrative voice and to view that voice as the chief indicator of her "successive mental phases." As we have seen, she conceives of human life in the pattern of Carlyle's *Bildungsroman* with its emphasis on the possibility of visionary experience even when life seems trapped in an Everlasting No. Like *Sartor*'s Editor, she constantly guides the readers' interpretation of the words at hand even as she urges them to acknowledge how much a part of their own lives these fictions are. "Art is the nearest thing to life," she had written in the essay on von Riehl; "it is a mode of amplifying experience and extending our contact with our fellowmen beyond the bounds of our personal lot," of "surpris[ing] even the trivial and the selfish into that attention to what is apart from themselves, which may be called the raw material of moral sentiment." Through her changing narrative voice, George Eliot searches out ways to effect this self-extension in her readers. In effect asking herself again and again "What shall I do?" she grows into that final guiding voice which we think of as George Eliot's. From *Adam Bede*'s remembrancer, settled amongst the characters he is describing, George Eliot moves to the historian and then to the romancer. The "strong terrible vision" that forces attention to what is apart from ourselves is, finally, effected only by that guide who is also prophet or seer.

Silas Marner is her first experiment with sheer romance. The fairy tale that the characters themselves experience is the medium for rendering the "history" (chap. 2). Indeed, this story of "Merry England" is so wonderfully successful because it is so spare in its narrative techniques. Its narrator is George Eliot's most repressed—no fireside chats, no historical comparisons and speculations, few allusions beyond Bunyan, Wordsworth, and the Bible, beyond the common literary possession of readers. The mythic nature of the story relieves George Eliot completely from any need to insist on the reality of her common people, or from any need to supply titles and epigraphs to guide us. The belief of the "you" so often referred to is assumed—as in any Puritan allegory where the real and the symbolic are so inextricably connected by means of familiar biblical correspondences.

But what anchors this "Merry England" tale in the probable is its double plot, George Eliot's "device for telling the same story twice, with different endings" (Barbara Hardy, *The Novels of George Eliot*). It allows her the necessary freedom to use romance without apology, and to juxtapose it with the real in order to show their resemblance and the necessity of each for the "truth" of the other. The tale of Silas Marner and his golden child is romance; the history of Godfrey Cass is petty reality. Cass's life is inseparable from Marner's, the weaver's inseparable from Cass's. The landowner's story toughens Marner's and grounds it in the real; Marner's "history" forces Cass—and us—to acknowledge the place of visionary experience in man's life, whether he would see it or not. We see that [in Carlyle's words] "in these hard, unbelieving utilitarian days," the "Unseen but not unreal World" exists, that "the Actual and the Ideal," the real and the romantic, are not separable if we are to live wholly, adequately. Indeed, to sever them is to make life sterile and barren.

The novels before *Silas Marner,* told by solidly characterized narrators insisting on the "real" nature of their narratives, do not so easily or successfully render the path towards the visionary. Dinah Morris through her sermons and meditations gives this element to *Adam Bede.* Maggie and Philip in *The Mill* discuss the need to acknowledge "the divine voice within us" rather than "indulge ourselves in the present moment" (bk. 6, chap. 14). But next to these pleas for recognizing the need of vision in one's life stands George Eliot's voice—and it curiously qualifies the assertions of the novels' protagonists, even as it makes the same plea.

Because each "story is told as the thing remembered, not the thing invented" (Barbara Hardy), George Eliot talks directly to the reader, much as Bunyan or the overtly religious writers had done as they recounted their experiences and instructed their readers. Yet this explicitly didactic voice, which by its very nature implies that "art" is not its purpose, is forced again and again to discuss "art," to claim the "real" as its province and to defend fiction as its means of rendering truth. In *Adam Bede* George Eliot's belief that "Art is the nearest thing to life" is stated overtly in the invoking of Rembrandt, in the requests that we sympathize with plain Methodists and "old women scraping carrots" at least as readily as we would with "heroines in satin boots" and "heroes riding fiery horses" (chap. 3), and in the interview with the title protagonist (chap. 17). George Eliot is concerned that we know that she moves amongst—not above—her men and women. In *The Mill* she is again the remembrancer, but she also emphasizes that she is a dreamer (and her characters are oblivious to her). Art itself—literature, music—is not part of her commentary here, though it is part of the lives of her characters: George Eliot simply notes their (mis)interpretations.

Yet in working with her narrative voice in these first novels, George Eliot discovers how hard it is to extend sympathy to those whose aims and feelings are utterly opposed to her own. In her first novel she is imaginatively devoted to a "Merry England," a fiction that allows her to present a "comfortable" world where nature and man *seem* at strife neither with each other nor with God. In *Adam Bede* George Eliot so loves the community around the Reverend Irwine and Mrs Poyser that she tries to keep at bay all disturbing elements. She energetically defends them against her sense that modern (1859) readers will see them as "pagans." And she even more vigorously defends them against the onslaught of the self-centered Arthur and Hetty. Hetty receives almost no sympathy. We get harsh analogies ("One begins to suspect at length that there is no direct correlation between eyelashes and morals"—[chap. 13]) and little acknowledgment that Mrs Poyser's "comfortable" environment might have warped this woman's development. (There is surely some indictment in the question raised after Hetty's inability to read is mentioned: "How then could she find a shape for her expectations?"; the community has participated in her isolation.) George Eliot's voice is one quite at odds with Dinah's damnation of the natural self, yet her very harshness of tone when Hetty appears makes us doubt her judgment of Dinah (Dinah would make the same analysis of Hetty). Even the epigraph for *Adam Bede,* from Wordsworth's *The Excursion,* finally tells against her:

> And when
> I speak of such among the flock as swerved
> Or fell, those only shall be singled out
> Upon whose lapse, or error, something more
> Than brotherly forgiveness may attend.

Adam and Dinah do come together in extending this forgiveness to Hetty—and in their own resulting recognition and abandonment of pride in their ways. George Eliot tries to focus her emphasis on their conversion, on their education for daily living with awe and pity amongst their fellows. The closing marriage and the verbal Constable accompanying it are meant to underline this. But her interest in Arthur and Hetty, her often arch irony towards them, and her resort to melodramatic contrivances to get them off the stage undercut this focus—and show us the problems she has with "Merry England." That devotion to the memory of Mrs Poyser's England—to the country in all its Wordsworthian significance—sits uneasily beside the story of "natural" lives like Hetty's and Arthur's.

In *The Mill on the Floss* George Eliot faces the ways memory distorts, and the ways she has used it for comfort rather than truth or vision. Within the story itself Maggie insists on the sacredness of the past and of the community that has grown out of it, and she damns a life lived completely for itself: "If the past is not to bind us, where can duty lie? . . . but I can't believe in a good for you, that I feel—that we both feel is a wrong towards others" (bk. 6, chap. 14). But beside her voice emphasizing the "sanctity" of memory is George Eliot's, and there is a tension between its perceptions and Maggie's emphatic beliefs which emphasizes their transitoriness. George Eliot simply does not care about the St Ogg's community as she did about Mrs Poyser's world. As a result she is able to examine through Maggie that belief in memory which had been so signal a part of *Adam Bede.*

She constantly evokes memory, reminiscing again and again. In the opening pages she pronounces the river "a living companion," "the voice of one who is deaf and loving." But suddenly the reader finds this only a dream. Then he is launched *in medias res,* into Mr Tulliver's talk (a talk singularly devoid of any idea of harmony) and into Maggie's life. And in that life the river is anything but a companion; from her earliest days her mother predicts her end will come in those waters. (George Eliot throughout acknowledges nature's unreliability: she is "cunning," "not unveracious, but . . . ") Constantly, George Eliot's voice interrupts the action to place the events in some frame that will extend their meaning beyond the specific instance and make them a part of some larger order where suffering did have significant meaning (thus the references to Bunyan from the middle of the novel onward, even though George Eliot admits that Maggie's journey towards the "Promised Land" is "thirsty, trackless, uncertain"—(*The Mill on the Floss*, bk. 4, chap. 3).But these allusions only underline Maggie's needs—*and* George Eliot's. She needs Bunyan to make sense of—and even to elevate—Mr Tulliver's "puzzlin' world"; she requires Wordsworth to mark the end of childhood and preserve it as a resource of memory: "They had entered the thorny wilderness, and the golden gates of their childhood had for ever closed behind them" (bk. 2, chap. 7). It is a Romantic recollection of early childhood—except that this is not the way we have experienced what the novel tells us. Indeed, our experience is quite the reverse. From the time we meet Maggie she is different, and aware of her difference. Like Jane Eyre and Lucy Snowe, she never enjoys a state of innocence. Maggie is a "wild thing," her black hair and her reading do set her apart— really and imaginatively—from the Lucy Deanes of her world (and from their fictional counterparts; Maggie notices that black-haired heroines do not live happily ever after!—bk. 5, chap. 4). No hazes of memory nor natural imagery can obscure her isolation.

What happens to George Eliot's handling of her narrative voice in *The Mill* is that she herself is questioning the value of memory and the value of the memories. The concern about what memories afford us elicits those often shrill apologies for this "history of unfashionable families" and the efforts to share the readers' attitudes even as she seems uncertain what those attitudes are: "I share with you this sense of oppressive narrowness; but it is necessary that we should feel it, if we care to understand how it acted on the lives of Tom and Maggie—how it acted on young natures in many generations, that in the onward tendency of human things have risen above the mental level of the generation before them" (bk. 4, chap. 1). Surely no one thinks Tom Tulliver above the "mental level" of the previous generation, surely the only "onward tendency" we see in *The Mill* is the rush of business and of Maggie's hopes. There is confusion here, between George Eliot's beliefs and perceptions (as there is in Maggie's). This confusion is focused for us by George Eliot's surprise that readers found the Dodsons "mean and uninteresting." In their talk and action they certainly are not; indeed they are great fun even as they register quite thoroughly the indictment. It is George Eliot's apologetic labelling, her "unfashionable families" versus "good society," that blurs the emphasis and creates the negative impression. She is herself unsure about the Dodsons, and about the readers who will react to them. She is even more uncertain of what

Maggie's sense of the past is, for she finds it unattractive in all of its "respectability." The respectable people do not care a whit for this past, except as it supports their position. Maggie believes in it as she does in the God she calls on: it is sanctified by the fictions she knows if not by the chaotic experience she has suffered.

Although George Eliot acknowledges at the "Conclusion" that "To eyes that have dwelt on the past, [Nature makes] no thorough repair" (bk. 7), she avoids facing what the epigraph with which she begins and ends Maggie's story actually means. Surely, "In their death they were not divided" implies no victory over death for Maggie and Tom (even though the dwelling on Tom's "Magsie" and on the "new revelation to his spirit" urges us to accept their end as visionary apocalypse). The epigraph is from David's elegy on Saul and Jonathan, father and son divided in life by questions of familial loyalty; David speaks in sadness of the irony of death. Only Philip Wakem has gained this Davidic understanding by seeing the effect Maggie's life and its close have had on his vision. He sees that the unity of the end, in the mythic history or in the specific lives, is real only in that it gives the seer (and Philip is an artist) perception of "enlarged life." His story, completed, allows the reader to see. But Philip Wakem's victory is too private, too "inward" for George Eliot's purposes here. She is too devoted to an "enlarged life" that is community-centered. And not until *Felix Holt* and *Middlemarch* will she fully chart the separation of personal vision and communal life which Philip Wakem's case first illustrates.

In *The Mill on the Floss* George Eliot displaces the unpleasant past (which Philip accepts, with resignation) through memory; she renders "respectable" life bearable by fictionalizing it, by putting it in the shadow of larger myths that have told on experience. Maggie never comes to the vision she has sought, and which books have promised her is possible; she never sees how the past can "bind" one in a liberatingly human way. George Eliot, with hesitation and certainly with regret, of course sees this. But to her, memory is—in Carlyle's words—"beautiful, sad, almost Elysian-sacred"; there "the haggard element of Fear" vanishes. Memory fictionalizes the past for our comfort; it does not propel us towards strong vision. George Eliot, however, will not create a fiction urging this truth until she considers Daniel Deronda.

The English novels which follow *Silas Marner* (and George Eliot's work with history in *Romola*) underline the narrative discoveries that *Marner* showed. A remembrancer is not necessarily a guide; *vision* can indeed be hindered when devotion to "fictions"—of nature, of community—refracts truth. The question "What shall I do?" can be answered honestly—in life and in art—only by *forms* which acknowledge their fictiveness by telling the reader that the words before him do distort, but that they also show and share his experience—its unity with the past—as at once unique and common. "Wouldst read thy self . . . ?/ . . . Oh then come hither,/And lay my Book, thy Head and Heart together." Thus, George Eliot gives up the remembrancer figure and begins her search for a voice which is at once historian and seer, an investigator of our communities and of our inner lives—and always our guide.

Finding the appropriate figure for this task in Wordsworth's Wanderer and Dante's Virgil, she devotes the Introduction to *Felix Holt* to discussing their importance as narrators. Her story-teller in this Introduction is a coachman giving a tour of England over a thirty-year period. As we hear him, we know immediately that "Merry England" is not his binding fiction:

> The coachman was an excellent travelling companion and commentator on the landscape: he could tell the names of sites and persons, and explain the meaning of groups, as well as the shade of Virgil in a more memorable journey; he had as many stories about parishes, and the men and women in them, as the Wanderer in the "Excursion," only his style was different. His view of life had originally been genial, and such as became a man who was well warmed within and without, and held a position of easy, undisputed authority; but the recent initiation of Railways had embittered him: he now, as in a perpetual vision, saw the ruined country strewn with shattered limbs. . . . Still he would soon relapse from the high prophetic strain to the familiar one of narrative.
>
> (chap. 9)

Vision and prophecy versus narrative—we come here to what for George Eliot art in a shattered age must be if it is to deserve our attention. Not mere narrative, but language forcing us to open our eyes and selves to vision. It must make us see in new ways, expose us—in Klesmer's words— to a "breadth of horizon" beyond ourselves, force onto us, willing or not, a "sense of the universal." This is what the Wanderer does, and Virgil. They guide us beyond that indifference which is "self-satisfied folly"; they show us the "right road" (*DD*, chaps. 5, 23):

> Midway this way of life we're bound upon,
>   I woke to find myself in a dark wood,
>   Where the right road was wholly lost and gone.

It is the opening of the *Inferno*, but it could as easily translate the beginning of *Pilgrim's Progress*: "As I walk'd through the wilderness of this world, I lighted on a certain place, where was a Denn." There is one signal difference: Bunyan had the Word to show him the right road while Dante needed a Virgil who could show others a Promised Land he himself would never enter. And modern man, as Maggie's case had shown, needs human guides as well in an age when the Word and all words are so many "*mere words.*"

For George Eliot, such guides will not be remembrancers who glorify the past but voices which have, Carlyle-like, meditated on past and present unflinchingly, have seen that even in days without machines and rickburners there was a *"via media of indifference"* in those church-centered communities quite opposite to any sincere fellow-feeling (*Felix Holt*, chap. 6 [all further references to this text will be abbreviated as *FH*]). A narrator must show more than George Eliot's remembrancers have because he sees—he must see—more:

> The poets have told us of a dolorous enchanted forest in the under world. The thorn-bushes there, and the thick-barked stems, have human histories hidden in them; the power of unuttered cries dwells in the passionless-seeming branches, and the red warm blood is darkly feeding the quivering nerves of a sleepless memory that watches through all dreams. These things are a parable.
>
> (*FH*, chap. 11)

"These things are a parable"—George Eliot will repeat the line in *Middlemarch*, and she will write her own in *Daniel Deronda*. She will assert that "histories" are parables, not just compilations of "mere *words*" presenting facts. Prophecy springs from narrative at the moment when indifference is replaced by "the pity and terror of men," and by fellow-feeling. George Eliot notes that Sampson the coachman often gossiped of "fine stories," "stories not altogether creditable to the parties concerned."

> And such stories often come to be fine in a sense that is not ironical. For there is seldom any wrong-doing which does not carry along with it some downfall of blindly-climbing hopes, . . . some tragic mark of kinship in the one brief life to the far-stretching life that went before, and to the life that is to come after, such as has raised the pity and terror of men ever since they began to discern between will and destiny.
>
> (*FH*, chap. 11)

In a time when sectarian disputes and politics have divided communities, George Eliot's guide must be a Wanderer who sees and shows us the connections of past and present all around us, he must be a Virgil who will lead us into the demon-empires of ourselves and—perhaps—out of them towards health. Her narrator should be the historian of our consciousness and the seer of our unconsciousness, the Wanderer and the Virgil who will show us the way to vision.

And that way, as Dante shows us, very clearly involves the conjunction of the fictive and the real. The chapter epigraphs which George Eliot uses in each of her last three novels constantly and allusively place the "real" people before us in the context of Bunyan, Burton, Homer—in literary contexts which at once generalize experience and make us see connections that the men and women whose lives we are reading can at best only dream about. The *Purgatorio* epigraph to chapter 64 of *Deronda* connects Gwendolen's experience and her victory to Dante's journey. The Bunyan epigraph to chapter 85 of *Middlemarch*, with its picture of Vanity Fair's jury, places Mr Bulstrode's critics even as it offers an inverted parallel to his case. The constant references to Greek tragedy in the *Holt* epigraphs point out the "tragic mark of kinship" even as the characters seem incapable of (and too mean for) real tragic exaltation. The result: our pity and terror are required.

Furthermore, George Eliot asks us to acknowledge that even history and biography, the books Victorian readers accept as truth rather than artful lies, are not fundamentally different from poetry; there are no rigidly separated literary genres. Science and "[h]is less accurate grandmother Poetry" both have to choose a beginning point and then set "off *in medias res*": "Men can do nothing without the make-believe of a beginning" (*DD*, epigraph, chap. 1). In *Middlemarch*, where Lydgate makes so much of scientific discovery, George Eliot, as the historian-narrator also striving for accuracy, notes: "Even with a microscope . . . we find ourselves making interpretations which turn out to be rather coarse" (chap. 6). No wonder she links herself, without apology, to Fielding as well as to Herodotus:

> In fact, much the same sort of movement and mixture went on in old England as we find in older Herodotus, who also, in telling what had been, thought it well to take a woman's lot for his starting-point; though Io, as a maiden apparently beguiled by attractive merchandise, was the reverse of Miss Brooke, and in this respect perhaps bore more resemblance to Rosamond Vincy.
>
> (*M*, chap. 11)

The historian begins his history with myth; the novelist begins her tale with history. "Feigned truth and historical truth coalesce" here, as U. C. Knoepflmacher notes in discussing this passage.

George Eliot in *Middlemarch* constantly emphasizes how fact takes on quite another shape entirely once it gets itself lodged in our consciousness; to articulate is to interpret, and to distort:

> There is always a good number who once meant to shape their own deeds and alter the world a little. The story of their coming to be shapen after the average and fit to be packed by the gross, is hardly ever told even in their consciousness; for perhaps their ardour in generous unpaid toil cooled as imperceptibly as the ardour of other youthful loves, till one day their earlier self walked like a ghost in its old home and made the new furniture ghastly. Nothing in the world more subtle than the process of the gradual change! In the beginning they inhaled it unknowingly: you and I may have sent some of our breath towards infecting them, when we uttered our conforming falsities or drew our silly conclusions: or perhaps it came with the vibrations from a woman's glance.
>
> (chap. 15)

"What is truth?" as Jesting Pilate asked, with "Thick serene opacity" veiling his eyes (*Past and Present*). For George Eliot modern man has much less chance of discerning an answer. Memory itself, as she discovered in the early novels, is selective, and thus fiction-making. "There's no disappointment in memory," Daniel Deronda says, "and one's exaggerations are always on the good side" (*DD,* chap. 35). Interpretations too, because they are our means of ordering random experience, also help us relieve disappointment and comfort ourselves.

> We sit as in a boundless Phantasmagoria and Dream-grotto; boundless, for the faintest star, the remotest century, lies not even nearer the verge thereof: sounds and many-coloured visions flit round our sense. . . . Then, in that strange Dream, how we clutch at shadows as if they were substances; and sleep deepest whilst fancying ourselves most awake! . . . This Dreaming, this Somnambulism is what we on Earth call Life; wherein the most indeed undoubtedly wander, as if they knew right hand from left; yet they only are wise who know that they know nothing.
>
> (*Sartor Resartus*)

Like Teufelsdröckh, George Eliot in her later novels insists that we see what dream-worlds we require for living; in that consciousness there is vision.

So Virgil's shade takes Dante through his own Inferno, and Christian with the Word's direction encounters the *real* aspects of himself that would keep him off the "right road." But for modern man it requires "a good strong terrible vision" (*FH,* chap. 27) if he is to escape the "danger of absorption within the narrow bounds of self" and keep to his "best self" (*FH,* chap. 15). Only such a vision answers the cry of the lost, "What shall I do?" And for George Eliot no novelist can show this vision except by parable, by making "mere *words*" speak *sub specie aeternitatis.* Her multiple plots, as *Silas Marner* illustrates, allow the reality and the Romance to merge into this parable.

Lest we miss the "Morality Play" beneath her narratives (Barbara Hardy), George Eliot increases her use of the Pilgrim's first question, "What shall I do?" Certainly it is used for expediency, for protecting the self from its mistakes and petty failures. But it is also used for a scrutiny of the soul, for finding a path to take one beyond the trivial and the selfish into "enlarged life," into the typical life. The very commonness of this question—in literature and in our lives—forces us to share with the narrator's men and women, to see how they incorporate themselves into the fabric of our lives. In the novel's Morality Play, George Eliot provides us with the same frame of reference that she uses for valuation. Her epigraphs and allusions, her parallel structuring of the narratives, all take us beyond the surface differences until we see how we—readers, characters, author—participate in fictions for good or ill.

George Eliot knows, says David Carroll, "that the mind in its own defence must create a theory by which to mediate with the outer world."

But what she demands is that we become sensitive to the exact point where the mind meets the outer world, where the hypothesis comes into contact with the facts it is trying to explain, where the deduction begins to mould the evidence, where for example, Mrs Cadwallader's caustic tongue and sharp epigrams begin cutting reality into the shape she desires.

("Middlemarch and the Externality of Fact")

Silas Marner showed Godfrey Cass moulding the evidence to fit his own happily planned Promised Land. And it showed the vision of the real pushing its way into his self-enclosed consciousness. But for George Eliot this story was too "legendary." It did not correspond to the way we live now, amidst rick burnings, trains, reform bills, Catholic questions, *Sartor Resartus* and Strauss. In *Felix Holt* and *Middlemarch* she makes her narrative voice consciously that of an historian who will chart these signs of the times even as, like Dante's Virgil, he will gaze into those areas of the self where vision originates. These novels and *Deronda* explore that moment when vision comes and we see who we are and what we must do; and they explore the continuing moments when we deny that we "dream"—and thus imprison ourselves.

Felix Holt introduces this concentration on the way towards vision—the word is everywhere—and the self-created prisons which prevent it. Mrs Transome is in "bondage" (chap. 8) utterly and forlornly as anyone in Dante's infernal forest. The Reverend Rufus Lyon, minister of the Independent Chapel, sees in his own history an example of a wanderer who for a time left the "right road" for an earthly paradise. A later epigraph (chap. 45) summarizes his experience for us, and the experiences of Mrs Transome as well.

> We may not make this world a paradise
> By walking it together with clasped hands
> And eyes that meeting feed a double strength.
> We must be only joined by pains divine,
> Of spirits bent in mutual memories.

It is an epigraph that marks for us how much George Eliot has matured since the "paradise" she insisted on seeing in those early novels.

The Reverend Lyon's revelation to his daughter Esther that she is not in fact his child begins her progress towards understanding what Felix Holt means by "vision," and how much it is tied to our relation with our fellows ("Very slight words and deeds may have a sacramental efficacy, if we can cast our self-love behind us"—[chap. 13]). Like Jane Eyre's orphanage, that of Esther begins her journey into the self. In the process this young woman for whom Byron, to Holt's disgust, offered visions of the happy life gives up the poet with Carlylean fervor (chap. 22), and more and more finds it "impossible to read": "her life was a book which she seemed herself to be constructing—trying to make character clear before her, and looking into the ways of destiny" (chap. 40). In casting his life into the biblical paradigms, Bunyan would have said the same thing. But the guides Esther needs are human: Felix with his kind of vision, her father with his (again, the Carlyle and Bunyan contrast). She is not like Maggie, stymied by books which she cannot see round, but like Philip Wakem: there are human voices to awaken her and pull her forward. Esther has the Dantes to force her towards those "strong visions" which will not be found in the well-bred ease of her daydreams (chap. 49).

The importance of the human will be Dorothea Brooke's experience too. This woman whose central concern, "Tell me what I can do" (*M*, chap. 30), has a Bunyanesque resonance far beyond its immediate application, breaks out of her "theoretic" imprisonment, out of self-absorption: "I used to pray so much—now I hardly ever pray. I try not to have desires merely for myself, because they may not be good for others, and I have too much already" (chap. 39). And finally, in chapter 80, with its epigraph from "Ode to Duty," Wordsworth and Bunyan come together in her life:

> The objects of her rescue were not to be sought out by her fancy: they were chosen for her. She yearned towards the perfect Right, that it might make a throne within her, and rule her errant will. "What should I do—how should I act now, this very day, if I could clutch my own pain, and compel it to silence, and think of those three?"
>
> It had taken long for her to come to that question, and there was light piercing into the room. She opened her curtains, and looked out towards the bit of road that lay in view, with fields beyond, outside the entrance-gates. On the road there was a man with a bundle on his back and a woman carrying her baby. . . . Far off in the bending sky was the pearly light; and she felt the largeness of the world and the manifold wakings of men to labour and endurance. She was a part of that involuntary, palpitating life, and could neither look out on it from her luxurious shelter as a mere spectator, nor hide her eyes in selfish complaining.
>
> (*M*, chap. 80)

It is the process of the visionary moment for all who are saved in George Eliot's novels, this breaking out of self-fancy, this understanding of how we dream, and this insight about the burdens that we must all carry and share *here*. Lydgate too may see momentarily, but he is denied the healing vision. He will live and die in the Slough of Despond (epigraph to chapter 79), imprisoned by that early belief in the factual truth of his "scientific views" of tissues and of his romantic views of women. He has no eyes to see that "the vision is all within" (*FH*, chap. 45), and no guide, finally, to take him beyond the depths of his demon-empire into a higher world of freedom: "He must walk as he could, carrying that burthen painfully" (*M*, chap. 8). His burden is there forever. We note the emblem. He, Casaubon, and Bulstrode, like Mrs Transome, will feel "the fatal threads" about them (*FH,* chap. 8) and have no more chance of escape than the souls in Dante's trees. "These things are a parable" (*M,* chap. 27).

In directing our attention to the parabolic nature of these *Bildungsromane,* George Eliot ties them to plots that are as conventional as Marner's tale. Only the endings surprise. *Felix Holt's* plot is as clanking as that in any Victorian melodrama; George Eliot is not adept in using to her story's advantage the theatrical contrivances of the laws of inheritance and entail in the way Dickens often does. But the plot's very conventionality tricks the readers: the expected resolution does not follow the conventions. There is no certain pattern to trust, in 1832 or 1866. The Cinderella of the tale cares not a whit for the prince of *her* palace. Her happy-ever-after life is based on her rejecting that myth of self-fulfillment. Esther's "last vision" has directed her away from this grand material world of fairy-tale comfort towards "the life where the draughts of joy sprang from the unchanging fountains of reverence and devout love" (chap. 50).

The ending of *Felix Holt* is radical from George Eliot's narrative perspective as well (and has little in common with the conclusions of the earlier novels). There is irony about the prosperity of Treby Magna (accompanied "doubtless" with "more enlightenment") and about the "all-wise" newspapers setting standards, an irony which quite undercuts a Trebian's summation of the effect of Esther's marriage: "It's wonderful how things go through you—you don't know how. I feel somehow as if I believed more in everything that's good" ("Epilogue"). But the sources of vision—new and old, Felix and the Reverend Lyon—leave the community. As does George Eliot. She tells us that she can not say whether the people are better, or whether "the publicans [are] all fit, like Gaius, to be friends of an apostle—these things I have not heard, not having correspondence in those parts." Although the language is patterned after the Apostle Paul's (see Romans 15:23), there is the sense of having done no work "in those parts," and this sense is reinforced by the refusal to give Felix's exact residence. George Eliot here seems to hint little belief in the lasting efficacy of her *spiritual* letters or of Felix's work.

It is a profoundly disconcerting close. The plotting and allusions in *Felix Holt* promise that tendency towards apocalypse which George Eliot's previous work had shown, but its ending denies that promise. The great vision is allowed only in an inward and individual sense; there is no reintegration into the community, no (more than momentary) social healing effected at all by Holt's work and Esther's "vision." Reality as George Eliot perceives it does not allow the "reconciliation" between the individual and the world, and between man and the sacred. Like Bunyan, these characters must choose between communal life in all of its constricting narrowness, and spiritual wholeness. Only romance, as *Silas Marner* showed, allowed both together. Israel's exodus towards a Promised Land is not a national paradigm that operates in the real world of rickburners and Dissent. The paradigm applies only in individual cases. And George Eliot, with her Pauline revisions, refuses to gloss over that discovery with pastoral painting.

Middlemarch is George Eliot's great meditation on the resignation that the ending of *Felix Holt* required of her. In this novel the one conventional plot—Bulstrode's—counterpoints and reinforces two biographies which tell the same "history," a history of the necessity of resigning our fictions, our aerial dreams which agree with nothing outside our own fancies and which will paralyze every action in life unless recognized as fictions. Esther gave up her books, and so must Dorothea and Lydgate. They come to the insight of Mary Garth—whose story is the fourth plot and the constant in this "experiment in life"—that "things were not likely to be arranged for her peculiar satisfaction" (chap. 33). But they come to this "vision" too late to remain a part of the community. In the significant consonance of the novel, they end along with Bulstrode in exile, uprooted or rootless forever. The old plot exiled the bad; the new and less fixed ones force out the good as well.

And the narrative voice who has told us this "parable" (and that of the pier glass)? George Eliot's voice here is that of an historian resigned to the need to tell of "hidden" lives lived in a "medium" so deadening that the "ardent deeds" of a Theresa or Antigone will never be possible. It is a parable of a very limited "vision" that she has to tell; there is not even the promise of a heavenly community. Fellow-feeling, mutual memories: they are not enough for the "strong vision" that will result in something greater than the "incalculably diffusive." Dante's vision is not possible if his guide is bound to that reality which is always limiting. If a parable is to be effective, it should make its readers feel the world Tennyson "saw" and expressed in those lines which form the epigraph to chapter 43 of *Felix Holt,* and it should allow the men and women who illustrate its meaning the vision too:

> Dear friend, far off, my lost desire,
> So far, so near, in woe and weal;
> O, loved the most when most I feel
> There is a lower and a higher!
>
> (*FH,* chap. 43)

This world, where the "lower and higher" form a thread that pulls us out of ourselves and unites us with the "enlarged life," is the world of parable, for a parable allows us a vision of the "higher" operating in the simplest "medium." But *Middlemarch*'s historian, even as she notes the fictive nature of history, can find no medium to support such parabolic work. George Eliot turns in *Daniel Deronda* to confront head-on the subject of art and vision. And in sacred romance she finds a means of creating vision out of the meanest reality.

The Romance of George Eliot's Realism

Daniel Cottom

> *Man can do nothing without the make-believe of a beginning.*
> —*Daniel Deronda*, chap. 1

In all of its features Eliot's fiction consists of a commentary upon an art antithetical to her own. At times this art is evoked through literary allusions, at other times Eliot makes reference to it through her reflections upon the work she has in hand, while in still other cases the actions, attitudes, words, and thoughts of her characters suggest that they would be happier in the world of this antithetical art than they are in hers. This other art may be called Romance to distinguish it from Eliot's own Realism, but in thus distinguishing them one also must note that each seems necessary to the articulation of the other as the argument between them is played out in every aspect of her narratives. As the genre she pursues and that against which she reacts are made to appear stages of social development and levels of human consciousness as well as aesthetic modes more or less accurately representing reality, each is ironically implicated in the other, but also dependent upon the other for its own full expression.

In Eliot's conception, then, Realism transcends Romance, but not by a simple rejection of its values or reversal of its stylistic characteristics. It transcends Romance as liberal intellectuals such as Eliot transcend society in general: by interpreting it, understanding it, and so gaining the power to patronize it. Unlike an intellectual such as Burke, who could feel free dogmatically to condemn certain historical events, situations, or representations, a liberal intellectual like Eliot would insist that nothing be lost from history. Even if they appeared to her to be misguided, all historical conflicts and the arts associated with them had to be recuperated within the understanding of her art so as to maintain its claim to comprehensive sympathy and disciplined understanding. Such was the rhetorical logic that Eliot drew from her assumption of her position as a modern intellectual.

From *Genre* 15, no. 4 (Winter 1982). © 1982 by the University of Oklahoma.

Therefore, in order to understand the art that she was pursuing, one must understand this antithetical art against which she was reacting.

Of course, in its broader terms this situation is no news to students of the history of the novel. In fact, it is arguably contemporaneous with or even definitive of the beginning of the novel as a genre, whether one cares to locate this in the eighteenth century or as far back as the time of *Don Quixote*. However, for this very reason it is less important to ask about the history of this situation than it is to ask how Eliot in particular used an antithetical art to prop up the terms of her fiction and then further to consider why the way she manipulated these terms was so influential in her own time and continues to seem so vital to any understanding of the Victorian period. As the history of the Realism versus Romance distinction shows—with works shuffled back and forth between these two pigeonholes depending on what person in what historical situation is doing the sorting—it is a distinction useful to the production of literature but only nominally relevant to its understanding unless this is directed to specific cases under specific social conditions. Like all generic distinctions, it requires historical analysis because it repesents the procedures by which texts may be institutionalized as if these depended upon properties intrinsic to the texts and so encourages an idealist conception of things. Moreover, the articulation of Realism versus Romance seems especially problematic in this regard because it was so frequently taken to be more than a formal distinction. Whether one was Hawthorne saluting the claims of Romance or Eliot those of Realism, the allegiance was likely to be made one to morality and knowledge as well as to style. And, of course, Eliot's great admiration for Hawthorne and the fact that her own Realism has often been analyzed for its Romance elements may serve to indicate just what a slippery customer this truth that everyone was arguing over really was. Even apart from a historical understanding of genres, this difficulty which is always found in rigorously classifying the features of an author's work ought to call into question schemes of generic classification.

Furthermore, in Eliot's case the art against which she was reacting could be referred to without explicit mention of any titles at all, or with mention of only one or two, because she was writing against her own image of such an art more than she was against any material that might actually be said to belong to it. In other words, it is not the accuracy of her classification and interpretation of the genre of Romance that is at issue in understanding her writing (even assuming that the notion of accuracy could legitimately enter into this situation), but rather the role that her construction of this antithetical art plays within her writing. This is an image at least as much imagined as real, one called forth from the necessities of her own argument as much as it is the source of her argument. True, Felix Holt might refer specifically to Chateaubriand's *René* when he says, " 'Your dunce who can't do his sums always has a taste for the infinite,' " and he might excoriate Byron in similar terms. However, as the nature of Felix's comments indicates, much more is at stake in these aesthetic judgments than formal aesthetic distinctions, just as one would expect in the work of a writer who conceived true art to be "a real instrument of culture" and as such a social vocation facilitated by individual inspiration. For example, it is evident that one issue involved in Eliot's rejection of this antithetical art is the nature of her readership in an age when this was likely to appear much more mysterious to an author than it had previously been, and the anxiety on this score expressed through her running commentary upon the appeal of this art opposed to hers shows that the proper denomination of art within her writing raises issues involving the organization of all of society.

In effect, then, Romance is Eliot's "make-believe of a beginning." In her delineation of this art antithetical to her own, it is finally middle-class morality rather than literary or historical analysis that guides Eliot's pen, as is only to be expected, again, in a writer who took this morality to constitute the essence of literature and history. It is for all the foregoing reasons that the significance of Romance in Eliot's writing does not lie in the similar function that such an image plays in many other novels—not in literary history analyzed in formal terms indebted to the aesthetic tradition to which Eliot sought to contribute—but rather in the history of a time and place, nineteenth-century England, when the way that Eliot used this image could appear so important as to make her an exemplary novelist of the age. Therefore, one needs to conceive of this antithetical art of Romance as one needs to conceive of Realism itself. It is not a generic term that has a potential for being definitive and universal if only it can be clarified theoretically, but rather a term used historically within the configurations of a discourse without which it would be entirely empty. Rather than being trapped in a hermeneutic circle of texts and theory like some Casaubon put into the service of the Borgesian sublime, then, one needs to look to the discourse within which Eliot was institutionalized as an author in order to see the significance that such terms as Realism and Romance could have in her writing.

Of course, the problem in analyzing an antithetical art so thoroughly implicated in Eliot's own aesthetics as to be coextensive with her Realism is that its scope extends beyond any summary term. Probably the word Eliot most often associates with Romance is "egoism," while occasionally she does identify it as "romance" proper; but the nature of this antithetical art is variously indicated in her writing by references to trashy literature, superstition, magic, gambling, unenlightened religious enthusiasm, aristocratic mastery, infant narcissism, and sensual pleasure, to name just a few. Although her statement that all of us are "born in moral stupidity, taking the world as an udder to feed our supreme selves" (*Middlemarch*, chap. 1 [all further references to this text will be abbreviated as *M*]) might serve as a summary description of the attitude informing Romance, so might many others whose diction and imagery offer quite distinct cultural references. Thus, in *Adam Bede* she anticipates Felix Holt in a slightly different idiom by referring slightingly to "that order of minds who pant after the ideal" (*Adam Bede* [all further references to this text will be abbreviated as *AB*]). In an early story, she suggest that readers who find her works uninteresting may find others more to their tastes, since, as she writes, "I learn from the newspapers that many remarkable novels, full of striking situations, thrilling incidents, and eloquent writing, have appeared only within the last season" ("The Sad Fortunes of the Reverend Amos Barton"). Elsewhere, she speaks ironically of the hero "who believes nothing but what is true, feels nothing but what is exalted, and does nothing but what is graceful" ("Janet's Repentance" [all further references to this text will be abbreviated as "JR"]). Or, to give a last example, she criticizes Gwendolen Harleth for wanting to be "the heroine of an admired play without the pains of art" (*Daniel Deronda*, chap. 1 [all further references to this text will be abbreviated as *DD*]). While it is true that Felix Holt refers to this antithetical art under the summary name of "Byronism," even to Felix this poet's name is only a broadly generic label, since he thinks *René* the same claptrap as Byron's works. And the fact that it is not a particular author or even a specific tradition of writing that is at issue in Eliot's work but rather the make-believe image of an antithetical art becomes even more clear when the references in question do not bear upon art except in figurative terms. Otherwise disparate elements in Eliot's fiction such as superstition and magic become aesthetic references as they are made to suggest within their contexts an artistic practice, a style of representing the world, contrary to her own. Thus, even though Gwendolen's gambling may not in itself be a form of art, it is taken to represent one by this novel which opens with the image of her playing in a casino and asks the question, "Was she beautiful or not beautiful?" (*DD*, chap. 1).

The affiliation of such passages in Eliot's writing is formally marked by their common opposition to her "own" art, then, and thematically by their cumulative evocation of a world opposed to Eliot's. As the quotations cited above indicate, this world is characterized by the separation of the individual from society at large, the exaltation of the individual above others through this separation, and the growth of luxurious feelings within this exalted transcendence. The argument of Eliot's fiction is always antagonistic towards this world of Romance and yet vitally bound to it. In fact, the terms of Romance and Realism in Eliot's writing are so closely bound to each other that her critical position can only be embodied in her characters as a form of masochism. Not only must they take pains to improve themselves, as students must even in a conception of education like Rousseau's, but they must cure themselves through the experience of sickness and undergo extreme suffering in seeking to purge themselves of Romance. It is according to this reasoning that the decision is made that Gwendolen is not beautiful as she appears in the casino, as far as Deronda is concerned, while the marriage in which she is sickeningly brutalized will make her appear much more attractive.

From examples such as this one it is evident that Romance is not wrong, as far as Eliot was concerned, but rather is only too right. It represents as a desirable world one that everyone does indeed desire, and that is precisely the problem. Everyone is a figure of Romance—and so Romance is untenable. In other words, in her image of Romance Eliot displayed a paradox in the idea of the individual. In her telling, as desire makes Romantics of everyone, it also individuates everyone according to his egoistic desires. Such is the common ground that Romance gives to all of human existence. Everyone may make Romantic claims for himself on the Romantic assumption that he is a singular figure in relation to society even though every other individual also may make quite incompatible claims based on the same assumption. Thus, the paradox is that of a conviction of singularity that may be shared by all of humanity. As Eliot writes, "Will not a tiny speck very close to our vision blot out the glory of the world, and leave only a margin by which we see the blot? I know no speck so troublesome as self" (*M*, chap. 1).

According to Eliot, unless it is received into the culture that she represents such a paradox can only result in either of two basic plots. One possibility is that it will lead to a disabling self-consciousness as egos inevitably collide and so suffer the realization that their dreams are common and competitive, not unique and transcendental. The other is an end in isolation, a lonely entombment of the individual in a private world shared by no one else, and thus a tragic fate of the most common sort imaginable. The former result may be represented by the fate of Gwendolen before she is reclaimed by Deronda, while examples of the latter are Silas Marner in his period of misanthropy or the Reverend Casaubon burying himself in his dusty scholarship. In Eliot's presentation, then, the cultural solution can only be suffering, which appears within the design of her art as the thematic equivalent to that tragic formal difference between particular and universal, individual and society, text and genre, which resonates in her continually reiterated distinction between Realism and Romance. As she puts it, we are all "children of a large family, and must learn, as such children do, not to expect that our hurts will be made much of—to be content with little nurture and caressing, and help each other the more" (*AB*). We must not be led into "fancying our space wider than it is "(*AB*), but instead must surrender the gossamer dream of transcendence to the unpleasant labor of life—and thus rediscover it in a form calculated to make the original dream look like the shoddiest of goods, in accordance with Eliot's humanized *felix culpa*.

Such is the moral thematics that Eliot developed from the discourse in which she was implicated, which demanded that the term of the individual be basic to society and yet be subject, along with all the other terms of social life, to society as a whole as this was conceived of in accordance with middle-class notions of universal nature and reason. Thus it is that another possible end to this paradox of individual desire suggested by works that might seem to fit Eliot's image of Romance—that of demonic evil acted out towards others—is never canvassed by Eliot except as a figurative rather than a dramatic fate involving her characters. For to accept such a possibility would mean accepting the idea that society actually could be a margin to singularity rather than the source of an imperative normality. It would mean that one truly could become exceptional, in corruption if not in virtue, while the rejection of this idea is precisely what constitutes the argument to which Eliot is committed. So Eliot's villains are such as the weak but essentially good Arthur Donnithorne in *Adam Bede* or the merely craven Raffles and the pathetic Bulstrode of *Middlemarch*. Even the brutal, wife-beating Dempster in "Janet's Repentance" is allowed a full measure of humanity and is shown to be as much his own victim as is Mr. Featherstone in *Middlemarch*, Tito in *Romola*, and Grandcourt in *Daniel Deronda*—all of whom are made pitiable, if not positively sublime, through death. For one of Eliot's intellectual persuasion, the first assumption of all understanding had to be that the individual is always a social figure, however singular he may feel himself in spirit or make himself in body. It was on this assumption that any idea of what was human had to proceed because society within her conception had been given over to the middle classes, to which she owed the possibility of her social position as a novelist and intellectual and the universal reasoning which developed from and justified this position. To have argued otherwise would have been to argue as a figure of Romance, which, like egoism, serves within Eliot's reasoning to signify the persistence of the past in the present and thus the disturbance of the modern world by forces, such as the untutored lower classes, which may threaten the middle-class assumption of its power as much as the traditions of the past had.

It is in accordance with this scheme of representation that in its absence of demonic agency and of superlative heroism Eliot's fiction characteristically shows its comprehensiveness. Such elements as it may seem to reject from representation—the unrespectable lower classes and the immoralities that she thought ought not to be represented in art—are actually disqualified from meaning, as far as Eliot was concerned. They are systematically excluded from representation for the same reason as the more violent actions of characters such as Tito are disqualified from signifying anything except the loss of self. Violence or evil on the one hand and extraordinary heroism on the other are not allowed within her scheme of representation except in the absence of characters from the truth of their ordinary selves— that is, in the temporary appearance of Eliot's Realism and Romance— because such elements would imply that society might not be adequate to its own conception, might be blind to or mistaken in its elements, might not possess itself within a controlling comprehension, and so might show that alienation of Eliot's characters to be a transfiguration of her own intellectual condition.

Here, though, is where one should note the permanent complicity between the opposing arts that form the argument of Eliot's writing. They can form a coherent narrative despite their antithetical relation because both are based upon the question of the individual's relation to the whole of society. As Eliot writes of Maggie Tulliver's discovery, by way of Thomas à Kempis, that this relation is a central dilemma of her life,

> It flashed through her like the suddenly apprehended solution of a problem, that all the miseries of her young life had come from fixing her heart on her own pleasure, as if that were the central necessity of the universe; and for the first time she saw the possibility of shifting the position from which she looked at the gratification of her own desires—of taking her stand out of herself, and looking at her own life as an insignificant part of a divinely guided whole.
>
> (*The Mill on the Floss* [all further references to this text will be abbreviated as *MF*])

Or, as she describes the virtues of the concept that Evangelical teaching opposed to the concept of man as "a mere bundle of impressions, desires, and impulses,"

> Evangelicalism had brought into palpable existence and operation in Milby society that idea of duty, that recognition of something to be lived for beyond the mere satisfaction of self, which is to the moral life what the addition of a great central ganglion is to animal life.
>
> ("JR")

Synecdoche was the most problematic trope for Eliot, as for so many Victorians. What was the Relationship of the part to the whole? In what ways might the part be taken adequately to represent the whole, and in what ways might such a representation be misleading, "merely" a trope, and hence dangerous? Although Eliot explicitly addressed this problem in terms of the broader issue of metaphor—"for we all of us, grave or light, get our thoughts entangled in metaphors, and act fatally on the strength of them" (*M*, chap. 1)—the problem she identified in the omnipresence of metaphor is that problem of synechdoche. The problem is not metaphor as such, but that people have so many different metaphors which in their irreconcileable diversity are still taken as adequate approaches to the whole of life. Eliot argued that a way was needed to relate all the parts of society to the whole of society without leaving any remainder and yet without reducing the idea of society to the anarchy of the lowest common denominator of its constituent parts. So Raymond Williams has written in reference to Eliot that "part of a crucial history in the development of the novel" occurs when "the knowable community—the extended and emphatic world of an actual rural and then industrial England—comes to be known primarily as a problem of relationship: of how the separated individual, with a divided consciousness of belonging and not belonging, makes his own moral history."

That this was a problem characteristic of her age and not just of Eliot's work certainly can be seen by examining other literary works of the period and by considering the religious, political, and scientific arguments that wracked it, but also by noting the circumstances of the production and consumption of literature in the nineteenth century. As J. A. Banks has noted, by the middle of this century "the social circumstances of the literate had begun to present an appearance of considerable diversity; and it is possible that his own self-consciousness of being part of a massive society which was not at all easy to grasp had increased the writer's sensitivity to the similar plight of others." Moreover, this was a question especially impressed upon the consciousness of people like Eliot by the huge growth of urban populations in this period. As Asa Briggs writes,

> It was the question of the relation of the constituent parts of the whole which gave point to most of the other questions contemporaries were asking about London. What was the whole? Did its constituent parts have a real life of their own? Was there any real sense in which London was one? These were questions about society which were intimately bound up also with questions about government.

But the fact that the question of social life was commonly and understandably posed in this form does not mean that Eliot's attachment to this form was only natural. To accept her positing of the question in this way would also mean accepting her assumption that there is a natural discontinuity between the individual and society that justifies giving them supreme importance as conceptual categories. Furthermore, one would accept the obverse assumption to this. There would seem to be no other category of equal importance to that of the individual in analyzing the problems of social life. And, finally, one would accept the assumption that what the individual most dramatically experiences to be different from or in conflict with himself, at least until such time as he may experience the reconciling growth of the education Eliot would give to him, is a whole society. That is to say, one would assume that the idea of society as a whole constitutes a reality specific and coherent enough so that one can rely upon it for guidance and trust it to guarantee the stability of values. It is thus that society is supposed to constitute experience in a universal form, despite the fact that this experience shows itself in Eliot's writing as an allegory of middle-class will.

As they are shared equally by Eliot's image of Romance and by the Realism she develops against this, these assumptions can be seen to stake out fundamental limits to her imagination. Given this understanding, it is only by analyzing the formation of these limits as an effect of the discourse to which she belonged, not as the "themes" or "ideas" that she or her culture developed, that one can avoid being lured into the same trap that locks Eliot's writing into such complicity with the very art whose image she seems to oppose. For these assumptions are not simply some elements among the others involved in Eliot's writing. Rather, along with the other specifications of her discourse, such as the superiority of "feeling" to "science" or the division among "private" and "public" worlds in society, they mark the possibility of this writing in the form in which it comes to us. They are the frontiers of its intelligibility. To put it crudely, then, as Romance is the Maggie Tulliver to Realism's Tom, the argument between the two is as coherent as it is logically interminable because these two share the same imaginative grounds in discourse, despite all their differences. After all, it was not for nothing that Eliot insisted that she had just as much sympathy for Tom as for Maggie, as she indicated within the novel by drawing each of these figures closer to the other's grounds until they finally consummated their implicit identity in death.

The argument is coherent and interminable because at every point of its articulation, on the side of Romance as on that of Realism, it is drawn from a society encouraging the idea of itself as a whole in contrast to the individual as a consequence of its organization into an increasingly urbanized and competitive capitalist order. As the economic order of an industrial society grows rapidly in scale and concentration, the desire for self-gratification is likely to appear privatized, narcissistic, culpable, and even illusory because the grounds of social commitments swell with this economic change to a scale incommensurate with any pleasures with which the generality of individuals can identify in their daily lives. In Eliot's words, the "local system" of life is supplanted by "the great circulating system of the nation" (*Felix Holt* [all further references to this text will be abbreviated as *FH*]). One cannot say of the laborer in the modern world what Eliot says of the peasant in the past, that his "solar system was the parish" (*FH*). Although this division makes the historical changes that occurred in England over the eighteenth and nineteenth centuries appear as they were neatly rationalized after the fact, it remains true that these changes commonly had the effect of removing society from the horizon of the individual and that this removal had consequences both material and ideological.

Concretely, this increasing abstraction of society may be epitomized by the gradual fading of local traditions, festivals, and folk holidays throughout the nineteenth century and their supersession by a pattern of work and play keyed to changing commercial and industrial demands—the change that Thomas Hardy memorialized in the club-walking at the beginning of *Tess of the D'Urbervilles* as well as in many other novels. As Marx noted, "Even the ideas of day and night, of rustic simplicity in the old statutes, became so confused that an English judge, as late as 1860, needed a quite Talmudic sagacity to explain 'judicially' what was day and what was night." Or perhaps an even better example of this change may be taken from James Plumptre's popular revision of Shakespeare's songs, first published in 1805, in which he changed *As You Like It*'s "Under the greenwood tree / Who loves to lie with me" to "Under the greenwood tree / Who loves to work with me." Many historians have described the changing nature of time and life-rhythms in this period, and a major effect of such changes was to make the economic theory and practice of this time appear as the power of nature. Thus, as people were likely to be increasingly divorced from the face of society in this way, a need was created for a morality based upon the rationalized idea of society as a whole. As nature came to be promoted as economic law and abstract commercial and industrial demand rather than appearing in the local figures of the church, the squire, and so on, as it was pictured as appearing in that memorialized past when streets were laid out "before inches of land had value, and when one-handed clocks sufficiently subdivided the day" (Thomas Hardy, *Tess of the D'Urbervilles*), the middle classes "naturally" felt a need for new modes of figuration that would bring home this modern nature to the generality of the people in society. This need was broadly satisfied by the modern conception of education brought forth by the middle classes and by the moralized transfiguration of the traditional idea of gentility that accompanied this, and on a more detailed scale by the myriad ways that middle-class discourse would seem independently or "naturally" to appear in the social life of the time. In the suppression of traditional customs and in the invention of new ones as well as in the educational theory and practice of the time, society came to be promoted by the governing classes as a moral idea opposed in its abstract nature to the daily experience, desires, and needs of individuals. This ideological change was embodied especially in the attitude taken by the middle classes towards the working and lower classes (no longer "the poor" within the eighteenth-century conception), as in Andrew Ure's argument that every mill-owner should *"organize his moral machinery on equally sound principles with his mechanical"* so as to discipline laborers to see their work as " *'a pure act of virtue.'* " For good reason, this argument sounds very like the ethos of Adam Bede and of Mr. Garth in *Middlemarch*. Moreover, it is still more fully recapitulated in the address that Eliot had Felix Holt make to the workingmen of her own time, by way of the readers of *Blackwood's*, on the occasion of the 1867 Reform Bill. To put it simply, in this address the claims of these people for redress as a class are made to be subordinate to their moral development as individuals. As far as Eliot and her class were concerned, such people were not allowed to understand their situation in society except in terms of a conflict between their culpable self-indulgence, on the one hand, and the order of society as a whole, on the other.

Hence Eliot's comment upon Caleb Garth's attempt in *Middlemarch* to "reason with" a laborer who, along with several others, has interfered with the surveyors for the railroad coming through Middlemarch:

Timothy was a wiry old laborer, of a type lingering in those times—who had his savings in a stocking-foot, lived in a lone cottage, and was not to be wrought on by any oratory, having as little of the feudal spirit, and believing as little, as if he had not been totally unacquainted with the Age of Reason and the Rights of Man. Caleb was in a difficulty known to any person attempting in dark times, and unassisted by miracle, to reason with rustics who are in possession of an undeniable truth which they know through a hard process of feeling, and can let it fall like a giant's club on your neatly carved argument for a social benefit which they do *not* feel.

(*M*, chap. 2)

As a figure of the transition from past to present, Timothy is not devoted to the duties of either and so perfectly represents the individual at odds with society—albeit in a vulgar and so amusing form. His "hard process of feeling" is represented by his argument that the railroad and other such changes in his lifetime have done nothing to help him or others of his kind: such is the violent interference, the unmeaning irrationality, with which reason must contend. The references to Paine of course situate him on the far side of democracy against which the middle classes were consolidating their power in this age, but more significant in the present context is the sociological assurance with which Eliot can approach this situation as she generalizes from Caleb's position to that of "any person attempting in dark times, and unassisted by miracle, to reason with rustics." Otherwise so intent upon making the rhetoric of feeling transcend even reasoned opinion as it shows the utopian fulfillment of reason, in this situation Eliot can denature Timothy's feeling. She makes it "hard" and as destructive as "a giant's club" demolishing a fine piece of rhetorical art which is made to belong to her readers as well as to Caleb ("your neatly carved argument"), because this feeling represents the configuration of an individual opposed to society as a whole and ignorant of this whole to which he is opposed. Timothy's argument is granted no meaning whatsoever simply because it does not take form in relation to society as a whole but rather in relation to himself and to others of his kind. Timothy can see only what Hawthorne saw of the railway when he described the English countryside in 1857— that its line "is perfectly arbitrary, and puts all precedent things at sixes and sevens"—whereas Caleb, the author who comments sociologically upon his case, and the reader formally placed into agreement with her would have Timothy recognize that modern miracle of reason which can make the advantage of the middle classes appear as benefits paid to—and thus duties owed by—such a one as Timothy.

The point, then, is that the individual is not conceived in the grasping terms of Eliot's image of Romance until the power of society has been made to appear more abstract than it has been in the past and yet appears still in the process of being accommodated to the ideologies—scientific, sociological, technological, and so on—of modern rationality. The conception of Romance in this grasping form occurs when their perception of this transitional situation makes those who speak for society feel that they must solicit people to their various duties by promoting a common idea of duty identified with the interests and manners of society as a whole. Or, to look at it the other way, this solicitation to an abstract moral duty does not make sense except in opposition to a degraded sense of localized and spiritualized duties. Individuals do not appear as random atoms before society becomes an order removed from the horizon of their perceptions, materially and ideologically demanding its perception as an imperative ideal rationally opposed to the generality of the daily experiences, conditions, and relations of a people in a local environment. Hence the structure of duty as Eliot conceives it to be a "supremely hallowed motive"—one which transcends all of society—and yet a motive "which can have no inward constraining existence save through some form of believing love" (*Romola*, chap. 2)—that is, which cannot be effective unless its transcendence is also its immanence in feeling. Society is thus systematically made a whole while being systematically displaced beyond and within the surface of its appearance in social life. In short, it is made a cultural figure that may appear imperative in terms of the actions of individuals because it is made elusive in relation to the social satisfaction of individual desires. This structure explains the significance of Eliot's attack upon egoism, which serves to elevate rationalized procedures over the effects of personalities but also over local effects of social life of all sorts. This figure of egoism is not conceived in relation to society as a whole: it produced the imperative moral effect of society as a whole. It marks a boundary of discourse constitutive of that discourse. This egoism that Eliot describes as an unfortunate source of the deviation of truth into rhetorical figures is required to produce the appearance of truth within her art just as the unreality of Romance is required for the articulation of Realism within this art. Thus it is that the conception of error within Eliot's writing is inextricably implicated within its construction of truth and so may be seen to reveal the politics of that truth just as a historical analysis of generic distinctions may reveal the purposes applied to idealist schemes of reading.

So Realism and Romance are dependent upon each other because individuals cannot be comprehended as sharing the common ground of Romance, within Eliot's delineation of this world, until society demands a rational understanding of its laws of the sort that Eliot defines as the basis of her Realism. Romance is to Realism as past to present, but also as unconsciousness to enlightenment and as trope to rhetorical ground; and therefore it also represents the persistence of the retrograde past in the progressive modern world. Thus it is that desire does not appear categorically egocentric—even though it may be represented as having this quality all the while—until society, within the governing discourse of the time, insists on its own image as a whole that can only be grasped through the public mind. Understandably, then, the first technique of the middle-class moralist is to establish the grounds of every argument in the domain of common experience so that the figure of the individual is defined as that which tends to exceed or deviate from the common interest. Insofar as this technique prevails, society will not be judged through its actual state, organizations, institutions, and practices as these may be experienced by such figures as Timothy. Instead, it will be judged within the public mind, and the individual correspondingly judged according to the extent to which this mind dominates him and continuously translates his experience into cultural generalities. The individual must be read into society just as Eliot's readers, within the self-conscious elaborations of her art, are read into their proper places—are even forced to feel Timothy's hard feeling attacking their property. It is for this reason that parallel distinctions will be drawn between the educated and the general public, respectable and rough workers, and the deserving and undeserving poor as the individuals in question do or do not show adherence to the cultural ideal. One need not actually possess culture as long as one shows oneself submissive to its rule, which is made to cut across all classes as the reality of society. Just as Realism and Romance ultimately are not separate conceptions but rather the articulations of a single discourse, so are these divisions which culture observes in the various classes in society most significant for the identity they signify—the identity they demand—through their production of differences in society.

In the promotion of this cultural ideal, then, the surface of modern society must be turned to invisibility and inwardness. In effect, its disturbing railroads must be transfigured into preserving sentimental figures. This is the solution commonly offered to the problem of synechdoche in the governing discourse of Eliot's time, and this is the solution in her novels. As Eliot puts it in *Adam Bede*, commenting upon the relation of the individual part to the social whole,

> Desire is chastened into submission; and we are contented with our day when we have been able to bear our grief in silence, and act as if we were not suffering. For it is at such periods that the sense of our lives having visible and invisible relations beyond any of which either our present or prospective self is the centre, grows like a muscle that we are obliged to lean on and exert.

True, in contrast to her image of Romance, in which people typically are made to appear as extreme or ideal types, Eliot presents her work as a historical discovery of the individual in whatever state or condition he may be found. And yet, at the very moment in which art thus comes to understand the individual, or rather to create the individual in the modern sense of the term, it does so by placing him in relations beyond his grasp. It defines his concrete individuality in terms of a mysterious sociality and identifies his true interests with the generality of social interest, in accordance with Adam Smith's brilliant myth. The individual is discovered so that he may be disciplined in Eliot's fiction as in nineteenth-century English society, in which the individualistic doctrine of laissez-faire economics was used not only to deny workers recognition as a class and to resist class activity through unions and other working-class organizations, but generally to assert that such conflicts as may appear in a competitive society are in reality not conflicts at all. According to this reasoning, this fable of consensus, to take conflicts as such is to exalt one's self and one's local situation at the expense of society, whereas the proper course is to recognize that one's true interest lies in the ends of competition and thus is the future of society as a whole. In effect, the individual is created, and society created in a relation to him that is at once greatly distant and absolutely vital, so that all conflicts can be made individual and all truths social. Romance is the falsity of individual conflict that must be recognized so that Realism may be recognized as this social truth.

Given the assumptions of her discourse, Eliot could not accept any idea of the self that was not from the very beginning included within the category of society and, therefore, had to invent a mystery—this invisibility and inwardness of social truth—because she needed it as a sponge with which to soak up such conflicts and contradictions as were evident within society. It is thus that she probed the problematic boundaries of the discourse in which she was involved and turned them into representations of social history. In a time in which "balloon views" of cities were popular as a way of seeking "a new and more ordered vision" of them, the universal vision of the public mind was designed to control, even to efface, the more immediate panorama of society. Hence Felix Holt's trust in public opinion over political measures and Eliot's general antagonism to any rule except that of her own narrative supervision, which sees everyone in his circumstantial particularity and yet at the same time dissolves this particularity within the breadth of a mind beyond circumstantial constraints. That same supervision which identifies the individual as an utterly unique subject also pulverizes him into the most general of abstractions:

> The great problem of the shifting relation between passion and duty is clear to no man who is capable of apprehending it: the question whether the moment has come in which a man has fallen below the possibility of a renunciation that will carry an efficacy, and must accept the sway of a passion against which he had struggled as a trespass, is one for which we have no master-key that will fit all cases. The casuists have become a by-word of reproach; but their perverted spirit of minute discrimination was the shadow of a truth to which their eyes and hearts are too often fatally sealed—the truth that moral judgments must remain false and hollow, unless they are checked and enlightened by a perpetual reference to the special circumstances that mark the human lot.
>
> All people of broad, strong sense have an instinctive repugnance to the man of maxims; because such people early discern that the mysterious complexity of our life is not to be embraced by maxims,

and that to lace ourselves up in formulas of that sort is to repress all the divine promptings and inspirations that spring from growing insight and sympathy. And the man of maxims is the popular representative of the minds that are guided in their moral judgment by a ready-made patent method, without the trouble of exerting patience, discrimination, impartiality—without any care to assure themselves whether they have the insight that comes from a hardly earned estimate of temptation, or from a life vivid and intense enough to have created a wide fellow-feeling with all that is human.

(MF)

Supervision is opposed to patent methods as discovery to creation, passive understanding to active comprehension, inspired to imposed knowledge. Thus, while patent methods might be put to use as analytic tools by the individual, this supervision is to be accepted as a unbreachable limit. This is the limit that defines the particular individual within society and yet at the same time establishes society as that which will not tolerate differences, particularities, or partialities. It is in this contradiction that the vacancy of the individual appears like a glimmering form on the horizon of Eliot's fiction, waiting to "grow," to be filled with ideological substance, and thus to be materialized as the Realistic image of a living and breathing human being. As its denomination as an "instinctive" component of good sense indicates, this supervision of the individual represents nature. Indeed, in the drag it places upon all actions, it is, in effect, that tragic principle of nature which is nothing more nor less than the rhetorical design of all of Eliot's writing, the "logic" of its rationality, the "experience" of humanity. "Naturally" this same understanding which recognizes the individual also neutralizes him, just as the form of Eliot's argument in this passage illustrates the understanding it recommends as it opposes itself to casuistry and yet draws truth from the shadows of this opposing method. It is thus that Eliot's writing understands the individual only as long as he is not a creature of desire pursuing individual ends, which is to say, only as long as he is not a separate individual but rather a knot in the great social fabric, and having no significance apart from the culture that has gone into the weaving, design, and printing of this fabric.

In other words, according to this supervision which runs through all of Eliot's writing in the distinction between the art she is pursuing and that against which she is reacting as in all the other vital differences productive of its meaning, the individual is such only as long as this figure is a transfiguration of middle-class will. It is for this reason that perpetual reference to special circumstances may be demanded and yet may be contradicted by perpetual reference to the generality of "all that is human" which signifies that comprehensiveness that the liberal intellectual constructs upon the denial of class differences, the exclusion of violence, the protocols of taste, and so on. To put the matter crudely but not inaccurately, this contradiction is not represented as such within Eliot's fiction for the same reason that it was not felt to be a contradiction within her society to demand that workers offer themselves to employers as individuals and not as a class while supporting this demand with the argument that, as a class, workers were too unenlightened to know their own best interests. *Felix Holt* perfectly represents this reasoning.

Since Eliot demands the recognition of individuality but refuses to allow any space to this recognition, the individual is so constituted in her writing that he must appear in conflict with himself if he is in conflict with society. Regarding "self-satisfaction" as "an untaxed kind of property" (*M*, chap. 1), Eliot takes her mission to be that of socializing the self by taxing it with society. And thus, as Eliot's society is made to be seamless and all-encompassing, it seems only natural that her individuals can only find a private space for themselves in an image of Romance that is nothing but an empty reflection of themselves.

"Fits of Spiritual Dread":
George Eliot and Later Novelists

T. B. Tomlinson

Middlemarch concentrates the strengths and weaknesses of the English middle class more steadily than probably any other novel before or since. And it does this in a way that gathers together some of the stablest forces evident even in later, more "modern" and complex novels by people as different as Conrad, James, and Lawrence. But before discussing some of these later writers, it is important I think to look a bit more closely at some of the *unstable,* even threatening, components evident in George Eliot's own writing and in the life around her. By this, I don't mean so much the notorious sentimentalities that weaken parts both of *Middlemarch* and lesser George Eliot novels; but, rather, a sense in her work that both the mistakes she makes, and, more interestingly, some of her strongest writing, are of a kind that cannot be entirely comprehended or explained in terms of her more widely acknowledged virtues, such as her engagement with society and the challenge and choices it presents to the individual.

There is a passage early on in *Daniel Deronda* that lingers constantly in the mind in this connection: "What she [Gwendolen] unwillingly recognised, and would have been glad for others to be unaware of, was that liability of hers to fits of spiritual dread." This is from the scene in chapter 6 in which one of Klesmer's "thunderous chords" from the piano opens the movable panel to disclose—for the second time, but now very unexpectedly—the picture of "an upturned dead face, from which an obscure figure seemed to be fleeing with outstretched arms." If the phrasing here is a shade melodramatic, the effect of the scene as a whole is not. Everybody is surprised; but Gwendolen actually collapses, and this in a way that none of the offered explanations—even, perhaps, George Eliot's own at the end of the chapter—quite comprehends.

From *The English Middle-Class Novel.* © 1976 by T. B. Tomlinson. Macmillan, 1976.

Klesmer's comment ("A magnificent piece of plastik that!") comes first, and is obviously intended kindly, though not as offering any complete understanding of what has happened. Gwendolen's mother and friends conclude simply that these "fits of terror" to which Gwendolen is subject are the result of her sensitive and excitable nature. But this is close to tautology, and one is struck by the fact that Gwendolen's own private admissions, which she would do anything rather than make public, or confess even to her mother, cut closer to the bone. To herself, though only half consciously, Gwendolen admits a quite general "susceptibility to terror." She then immediately tries to bury this fact about herself in a piece of wishful thinking that lays the blame for her timidity on her circumstances and upbringing: "this shortcoming seemed to be due to the pettiness of circumstances, the narrow theatre which life offers to a girl of twenty, who cannot conceive herself as anything else than a lady, or as in any position which would lack the tribute of respect."

This brings into play, comically but very pertinently indeed, the difficulties, not just of provincial life in general, but of women in particular. However spirited and independent by nature the heroines of many nineteenth-century novels may be, their position in life forces them into a kind of idleness and subjection that even Lydgate, for instance, is not subjected to. Whatever its frustrations and restrictions, Lydgate's life has, as he himself acknowledges, wider boundaries than the house and home that Rosamond—or if it comes to that Dorothea herself—is bound to. However, what is interesting about Gwendolen's reflections here is that, though they bring considerations of this kind once again very sharply to mind, they also include an element that operates almost independently of any sociological considerations. Thus, the fact that Gwendolen's statements about the "pettiness of circumstances," and the "narrow theatre which life offers to a girl of twenty," are for all their truth essentially rationalisations, is underscored by her more private thoughts turning, at precisely *this* point, to the still more compelling reflections about "that liability of hers to fits of spiritual dread."

George Eliot's own explanation or comment follows immediately; and, though it reads perhaps a shade literal-mindedly, it clearly builds on—is in fact really part of—Gwendolen's own innermost, half-recognised admissions. It also offers these as of much more general significance than any that could be attributed simply to a girlish sensitivity constricted by the circumstances of county society. Clearly, this side of Gwendolen's character would have been much the same, no matter what class or circumstances she had been born into:

Solitude in any wide scene impressed her with an undefined feeling of immeasurable existence aloof from her, in the midst of which she was helplessly incapable of asserting herself. The little astronomy taught her at school used sometimes to set her imagination at work in a way that made her tremble: but always when some one joined her she recovered her indifference to the vastness in which she seemed an exile; she found again her usual world in which her will was of some avail, and the religious nomenclature belonging to this world was no more identified with those uneasy impressions of awe than her uncle's surplices seen out of use at the rectory. With human ears and eyes about her, she had always hitherto recovered her confidence, and felt the possibility of winning empire.

The mention here, and earlier in chapter 6, of the fact that religion has had no meaning at all for Gwendolen other than the externals of an Anglican service is an uneasy reminder of ways in which not merely Gwendolen, but unfortunately George Eliot herself later on, takes refuge in Daniel; or worse still, in George Eliot's own case, in Mordecai's empty phrase-making ("Seest thou, Mirah . . . "). By the time we get to Mordecai's interminable sermons, George Eliot's critical intelligence has weakened to fits of defensive irony only, coming the more faintly because channelled through the sentimentalised Mirah:

> "In this moment, my sister, I hold the joy of another's future within me. . . . I recognise it now, and love it so, that I can lay down this poor life upon its altar and say: 'Burn, burn indiscernibly into that which shall be, which is my love and not me.' Dost thou understand, Mirah?"
> "A little," said Mirah faintly.
>
> (chap. 61)

Yet the failure of virtually the whole of the Daniel/Mordecai/Mirah sections of the book has at least the negative interest of pointing exactly what it is that both Gwendolen and George Eliot are running away *from*. And that is best recollected in terms of the accuracy with which, in the more public scenes earlier on, Gwendolen's boredom at the prospect of domestic life meshes with her strongly physical repulsion to any form of love or tenderness—the scene giving us Rex's proposal is brilliantly done—and also with the "sick motivelessness" that attacks her from time to time, and that is so tellingly close to certain states of mind that Grandcourt, both before and after he marries Gwendolen, shows. Grandcourt and Gwendolen are the centre of this novel; and they are so in wholly positive ways that make a silly nonsense of both Mordecai's and Daniel's ostensibly more constructive behaviour and ideals. At first sight most of Gwendolen's behaviour, and Grandcourt's, looks passive, indeed "motiveless." It looks as if what George Eliot is saying is that these two people exemplify, in different ways, the boredom and pointlessness of contemporary life; a life, that is, in which even the riches of a yacht on a Mediterranean cruise can do nothing to alleviate, and may indeed exacerbate, the feeling of helplessness that can assail people who lack the positive assurances of a religious, or quasi-religious, belief of the kind that Mordecai, Daniel, Mirah differently ex-emplify. And so, indeed, part of her wants to say. But the fact is that the scenes in the novel that render Grandcourt's and Gwendolen's boredom are so telling, and so memorable, that any accurate and fair reading must surely remember these scenes as in some way positively charged. Gwen-dolen, for all her disadvantages, and quite certainly Grandcourt, are forces to be reckoned with. Both of them far exceed any merely diagnostic reading of what can happen to people who, given certain circumstances, have either too little money, and/or too little to do with the money they acquire or inherit.

In her early life, Gwendolen has of course always been in command of the small world around her. Indeed, her fits of loneliness apart, she cannot merely command other people—servants at a hotel, her mother's household, her own family—but, for all that her life lacks any sense of direction or purpose, she can effortlessly instil alacrity and life into others, whether family or servants or friends. It is simply part of her nature to feel herself perfectly confident, "well equipped for the mastery of life." And the fact that she fails, unequivocally, in the end does not, somehow, make her power over people and things illusory. Because almost all the way through the book, the very unusual thing one notices about Gwendolen is that her very weaknesses—as for instance the physical repulsion she feels to Lush, or to Rex's very different intimacy, or, finally, her utter failure to master Grandcourt—carry also a wholly positive charge. There is, for in-stance, the extraordinary scene in chapter 11 when the "physical antipathy" she feels to Lush's prominent eyes, fat person and grey-sprinkled, frizzy hair prompts her instantly effective repulsion when he offers the burnous she had asked for: "holding up the garment close to Gwendolen, he said, 'Pray, permit me?' But she, wheeling away from him as if he had been a muddy hound, glided on to the ottoman, saying, 'No, thank you.' "

It is much the same with the more serious scene, cutting still closer to the bone, of her reaction to Rex's proposal earlier. In both cases, Gwendolen is clearly in the grip of an irrational, physical repulsion that she cannot control, and that is I think strongly linked with her more general feelings of loneliness and dread. But one never feels that scenes of this kind, at least up to and including the yachting "accident," make her the slightly sad spectacle that Lydgate for instance is in some of his moments of defeat, or Bulstrode at the end of *Middlemarch*. The scene with Rex, and with her mother after Rex has left (chap. 7), is one of the most powerful in this connection, because here the physical antipathy is quite explicitly linked with those feelings of "spiritual dread"—of a contact, however devastating, with powerful, inimical forces in the very universe around her—that over-come Gwendolen occasionally. These are frightening moments, certainly, but Gwendolen's, and George Eliot's, response to a certain blankness in the universe has an electricity in it that makes their sensitivity quite different from that focused on Lydgate's failure of nerve and will:

> "Should you mind about my going away, Gwendolen?"
>
> "Of course. Everyone is of consequence in this dreary country," said Gwendolen, curtly. The perception that poor Rex wanted to be tender made her curl up and harden like a sea-anemone at the touch of a finger.

The "certain fierceness of maidenhood" in Gwendolen then makes her come out explicitly and more curtly still with her "Pray don't make love to me! I hate it"; and then finally, after Rex has left, there is the sudden and devastating collapse—quite out of proportion to her careless feeling for Rex himself—and the confession to her mother that she feels there is "nothing worth living for," and that "I shall never love anybody. I can't love people. I hate them."

The whole scene is psychologically very acute; but more important still than this, it has a probing, investigatory quality in it that is directly and positively in touch, through Gwendolen's sensitive but highly charged nature, with a certain threat that the universe (rather than *just* the intractable nature of middle-class county society) poses. And it is instinctive feelings and perceptions of this kind, rather than simply the need for money, security and power, that make Grandcourt first of all so attractive to Gwendolen, and then, when she has discovered that he is virtually a human embodiment of all that she has feared as powerfully alien in the world around her, make her hate him, and finally kill him, or at least let him drown without throwing the rope that might well have saved him.

Grandcourt is an extraordinarily powerful figure. At first sight, of course, he is simply the embodiment of a cultured, quite undemonstrative boredom that must appeal to Gwendolen after Rex's youthful eagerness and naivety. But we hardly need the very excellent scene at the beginning of chapter 12, where Grandcourt and Lush are at breakfast, to sense the threat and power in his quiet, effortlessly contemptuous mastery over men and animals alike. He is like Gwendolen in that he has both a sure and quick intelligence, and an instinctive response to the powerful and quite unmalleable forces that must, in the end, govern even his strong will. But he is much more advanced in his experience of these, and of course of the world in general, than she is, and he uses this experience to govern her almost as easily as he has used it earlier on with Lydia Glasher and Lush. What is remarkable about him—what makes him, for instance, both more menacing and more interesting than James's Gilbert Osmond in *The Portrait of a Lady*—is the quality at once of an extremity of boredom, and at the very same time of a latent quick activity, that invests all the images George Eliot uses to describe his states of mind and behaviour. His is a very powerful boredom, and the "lotus-eater's stupor" that invades him in chapter 13 during the ride at Diplow very quickly and actively invades ("benumbs") Gwendolen and others too. The same is true of his appearance—"as natural as an alligator"—after Gwendolen has been frightened away by Lydia; of his state of mind when lazily following her back to England, and when

Lush notices that the likelihood of poverty making Gwendolen accept him after all has induced a familiar state of mind where "the certainty of acceptance was just 'the sort of thing' to make him lapse hither and thither with no more apparent will than a moth"; and, finally, of his still more powerfully effective inactivity in the close confines of the yacht, when Gwendolen finds that quarrelling with Grandcourt is not merely ineffective, but actually impossible: "and even if she had not shrunk from quarrelling on other grounds, quarrelling with Grandcourt was impossible: she might as well have made angry remarks to a dangerous serpent ornamentally coiled in her cabin without invitation."

Even more positively than Gwendolen's states of "sick motiveless-ness," Grandcourt's behaviour —apparently negative, but actually strongly and powerfully active—testifies to impulses beyond the bounds of his own personality and situation. There are forces at work here that neither character can wholly control, but that demand, even in their most destructive vein, some kind of assent, both from the writer and I think from the reader:

> Gwendolen's will had seemed imperious in its small girlish sway; but it was the will of a creature with a large discourse of imaginative fears: a shadow would have been enough to relax its hold. And she had found a will like that of a crab or a boa-constrictor which goes on pinching or crushing without alarm at thunder.

Daniel Deronda was completed in 1876, and was of course the last of George Eliot's novels. Given the wisdom of hindsight, one can see why she was tempted, towards the end of her life, to try for the broadness and sublimity of vision that the Mordecai sections—as it turned out, most unfortunately—outline. In *Middlemarch*, a few years earlier, she had written a novel that is at once much livelier and more readable than popular estimate usually allows, and also a normative, *directing* experience as to both the difficulties, and the sheerly solid possibilities, in ordinary day-to-day living. But of course both *Middlemarch* and earlier novels had also contained, however imperfectly, sections that pointed to some quite different kind of awareness: a sense of "otherness" (the more modern word, "alienation," would be too definitive) that some of the characters experience. Mrs Transome's musings are a case in point, as also are some of the scenes concerning Casaubon, quite cut off from any of the life around him, or Bulstrode towards the end of the novel, or even Farebrother, man-of-the-world in some ways though he is. Presumably, the element of threat—again, it is quite independent of class circumstances or of social pressures—in each of these scenes pressed on George Eliot so much that she tried to conceive a life that would either transcend these threats, or offer some answer to them that might gather all "lesser" lives into an encompassing whole.

That the "Mordecai" sections (excepting some scenes where Daniel is talking, not to Mordecai or Mirah, but, interestingly enough, to the much more worldly Gwendolen)—that these scenes fail so badly is a tragedy for

George Eliot, but also, one cannot help feeling, for the nineteenth-century English novel as a whole. Or, since "tragedy" is far too melodramatic a word for what is happening to the English novel at this time (1876), it represents a severe limitation as to what the distinctively English novel can do. Neither Dostoevsky nor Tolstoy would have been troubled to write very interesting scenes that could arise from the worries that assail Daniel early on in his life, or the events that happen to Mirah and Mordecai early on in theirs. George Eliot fails abysmally.

What, then, might she have done? Short of suggesting that she attempt another novel, one cannot answer this question, since it encompasses far more than merely the metaphysical doubts and speculations that both Mordecai and Daniel indulge. What one can do is keep in mind what she has indeed done, and done well; and perhaps link this with some of the prevailing impulses in other quite distinctively English novelists—writers, that is, who are for the most part temperamentally sceptical of the worth of any abstract or conceptual thinking.

Of the writers before George Eliot, Jane Austen must clearly be the most interesting in this connection. With the possible exception of *Mansfield Park*, she does not attempt anything at all like the sort of "answer" to doubts and queries that George Eliot attempts in the Mordecai sections of *Daniel Deronda*. But throughout her career, as D. W. Harding has shown, she is most sharply aware of the possibilities in human nature for inconsistent, even vicious behaviour of a kind that is not unconnected with impulses that dominate some of the best of the Gwendolen/Grandcourt scenes. The two writers are separated by a very telling half-century that makes George Eliot closely and intimately aware of the impact on English culture of the German Idealist philosophers who, in Jane Austen's day, were unregarded by, and indeed probably quite unknown to, most important English writers except Coleridge. It is only later on that a John Stuart Mill can see and write about the significance that this un-English activity might have for everybody in England, including even the most unaware of natively Anglo-Saxon writers and readers of literature, politics, and philosophy. It is largely this difference—a difference of horizon, influence, awareness—that deepens the tone at least of the more "serious" passages in George Eliot's writing. And yet, though Jane Austen would never have been tempted to say of one of her own characters that "solitude in any wide scene impressed her with an undefined feeling of immeasurable existence aloof from her, in the midst of which she was helplessly incapable of asserting herself . . ."—though such a sentence would be inconceivable in a Jane Austen novel, the hard core of doubt, much more Anglo-Saxon in origin than it is Germanic-metaphysical, is common to both novelists, and furthermore inspires some of the very best writing of each.

Jane Austen's "hatred" for certain traits that she clearly regards as permanently embedded in human nature, and that tend therefore to isolate people even within the close communities she describes; and George Eliot's sense of a threatening loneliness that is equally engrained, though by this time it is seen to be so within the wider frame of the universe generally—at first glance these tendencies in both, and differently again in some later writers like Hardy, Conrad, James, could well represent some sort of Achilles' heel in the developing middle-class confidence and solidity on which, I have been claiming, the quality of all the great nineteenth-century novels largely rests.

What is remarkable about the novelists, however—and indeed about some other prose writers in English—is the way in which they can turn such threats, and the resulting doubts and fears, to wholly productive ends. When Dr Johnson kicked the stone and simply said, of Berkeley's theory of perception, "I refute it *thus*," he may have been wrong about Berkeley, or misinterpreting him, but he was surely very right—and characteristically English—in placing so much of his faith in the solid ordinariness of simple, obvious, everyday existence. The English middle-class novel is very like Johnson in this regard; and it is like him too in that its trust in simple fact and common sense is an active, enquiring—even, at points, aggressive—quality, not a passive or purely defensive one. What is interesting in the Johnsonian response as it lives on through the next century is not that it dispels all shades of doubt and speculation (it doesn't), but that it is prepared actively to participate in these. Thus even the middle-class (and in many respects rather un-Johnsonian) confidence so clearly there in the densely populated area of *Middlemarch* is rendered, not in terms of a bulwark of stoicism against an encroaching blankness and alienation, but as a way of life much more actively interested in the forces threatening it than any such metaphor would imply, and prepared in consequence to gain from these, rather than simply retreat, defensively, before them. And many later novels, even ones which, like *Daniel Deronda*, fail badly in segments, continue just such an active participation.

To test this claim and make it more specific, I want now to look briefly at three very different novels, none of which seems to me quite as good as the novels I will be discussing [elsewhere], but each of which is responding very clearly to specific forms of modern life—or better still, life itself—as, at least in part, a threat. In Hardy's *Jude the Obscure* (1895), James's *The Awkward Age* (1899) and Conrad's *Victory* (1915), we have middle-class figures (together with Jude, who is of course a working-class man trying to master middle-class attainments) all either killed or driven into some form of retreat in the face of problems of modern living and modern unbelief, doubt, alienation. Quite clearly the problems these people face are not new. The social inequalities and religious doubts that Jude faces, the brittle rootlessness of the small (and dwindling) group in *The Awkward Age*, and Heyst's inability finally to trust even Lena—all these have been either prefigured, or at least given some impetus, in both the breakdown of social conventions (of the kind Mr Longdon, for instance, had known) and the ramifications of a by now well-established mechanistic science and philosophy that, however genuinely impressive, has tended to emphasise man's relative helplessness—even unimportance—in the face of a universe seemingly dominated by principles enunciated by Lyell, Darwin, Huxley and others. On the other hand, each of these novels shows such a strong and continuing base in Victorian middle-class certainties that they can afford to be almost as exploratory in the realm of Victorian *un*certainties as later, more technically experimental, novels are in the problems they tackle.

What singles out Hardy, first of all, in such a context, is his naivety. What I mean here is the kind of "naivety" in *Jude* that results in some melodrama, certainly, and some over-specific writing that is close to mere propaganda against "the iron contract" of marriage, but that results also in a story and scenes with quite unusually strong lineaments. The best and the worst scenes, as in Hardy generally, are separated by a hair's breadth, and what they share is a strong simplicity that makes the melodrama of Father Time's hanging of himself and Sue's children ("Done because we are too menny") quite as memorable, and in its way as close to the heart of the novel, as the splendid scenes in which Sue is shown as driven to torment both Jude and Phillotson (and in these we remember also, of course, the story of the undergraduate earlier on in Sue's life). Admittedly, the details of Sue's relationships with her young (and not so young) men have a complexity about them that reminds one of later, rather than earlier, novels. Nevertheless, what lingers in the mind from Hardy's rendering of these scenes is just such a clarity of outline as characterises the presentation of Father Time in the train, his walk to Jude's house, and later on his suicide.

And this remains true, I think, even in those scenes in which Hardy himself is probably only partly conscious of what is going on. One of the most remarkable things that he renders about Sue (and I think this is indeed unconscious, rather than fully conscious, on his part) is her tendency to give one excuse after another, and each of them different, for not marrying Jude and for thinking marriage in general disastrous. These "excuses" include her claim that marriage is a "dreadful contract to feel in a particular way," enforced by an inflexible modern civilisation (the rather crude but telling analogy with the rabbit caught in a steel trap follows this outburst of Sue's in chapter 2 of part 4); that she and Jude are ahead of the times, and an "irrevocable path" is doubly risky for them (part 5, chap. 4); that a bride can be nothing but a heifer led to sacrifice, the flowers wilting in her hand (same chapter); that popular disapproval of her will ruin Jude's career (part 5, chap. 6); that in conscience she must return to Phillotson (part 6, chap. 3); and so on.

As Freud remarked some years later (and as his colleague Ernest Jones detailed in the case of Hamlet), when somebody gives a number of different excuses for not doing something, it is more than likely that they are hiding, even from themselves, whatever the real reason is. Sue does glance at the real reason (her tendency to destroy men by some kind of sado-masochistic "flirting"), but only to reject it immediately. Even Hardy himself, perhaps, is unwilling to keep this fact about Sue in the forefront of his *conscious* mind for long. But in his telling of her tale he does place it—whether consciously or not doesn't matter—at the centre. In fact, the best scenes between Jude and Sue are a very telling mixture on Hardy's part of certain quite real difficulties in the way of the marriage—most of them put to us by Sue, but real none the less—and Hardy's own recurrence, again and again, to the fact of Sue's fastidious, "Shelleyan" nature being at the same time rapacious, driven all the time, no matter what the social circumstances or obligations acting upon it, towards actions that turn her ethereal qualities into the pretty vicious cruelty of scenes like the mock-wedding she forces on Jude just before her actual marriage to Phillotson. What Hardy is doing in these scenes, then, is recognising the relevance, to people like Jude and Sue, of the social, conventional pressures symbolised in the marriage bond; and at the same time insisting on the primacy of certain instinctual forces of the kind here concentrated in Sue's very nature, "quite unfitted by temperament and instinct to fulfil the conditions of the matrimonial relation with Phillotson, possibly with any man" (part 4, chap. 3). The social bonds and pressures that Hardy renders are quite real (more so, I think, than Lawrence, in his "Study of Thomas Hardy," is prepared to admit); at the same time, it is clear that Sue herself would be much the same no matter what society she was born into, and the clear, single-minded (or single-spirited) strength with which Hardy renders this fact is the most telling thing about the book.

In all this, Hardy is indeed rather unusual in the nineteenth-century landscape, fictional or otherwise. And within Hardy's own works, *Jude* stands out—warts and all—as exceptional. Certainly no other nineteenth-century writer one can readily think of renders sex as a single, driving impulse in men and women as strongly or as openly as he does. Yet there are certain aspects of this quality in Hardy that do make one turn back and reflect, however tentatively, on the most un-Hardy-like nineteenth-century novels. Because in the first place, even Hardy's open and frank rendering of sexual drives and impulses is still done very much, and at its best, very impressively, in nineteenth-century terms. Even in *Jude*, his is a *pre*-Freudian, rather than a Freudian, analysis—much simpler and more telling, in fact, than that of many more complex novels since. And he is not merely perfectly happy with, but actually very good at, the "old stable *ego* of the character" that binds even the most exceptional people strongly to the society around them, dismayingly and massively immovable though this may be. In the second place, and given Hardy's quite distinctively nineteenth-century characteristics, one is bound I think to reflect that both the most apparently conformist of novels, like most of Jane Austen's some eighty years before *Jude*, and the most discreetly "un-Freudian," like those of Henry James's that were written about the same time as Hardy's, all render, and indeed depend in part upon, certain aspects of human behaviour that cannot be *entirely* explained by, or even referred to, the social circumstances that were nevertheless so clearly important to all these writers.

Henry James's *The Awkward Age* came out just after *Jude*; Conrad's *Victory* some sixteen years later still (1915). One thing I would like to stress about the James, because it is reflected also in the other two (clearly very different) novels, is that, whatever the importance to Nanda of local circumstances—and the vicious inbreeding of much of her mother's circle clearly is important, both to her and to James—it is not these that *cause* her self-condemnation to perpetual spinsterhood. It is all too easy to read this novel (as it is to read Conrad's *Victory* or Hardy's *Jude*) as if the author were saying, "Had circumstances been different. . . ." Yet in fact, like both the other novelists, James is saying, I think very clearly, that local circumstances, though they are indeed definitive in certain ways as far as his characters are concerned (Nanda, but also Mitchy, Mrs Brookenham, Van and the rest), are nevertheless not a first cause of the self-imposed isolation that most of these people—especially Nanda—in the end exemplify. The same is true of the Conrad: Heyst's father, and all that he exemplifies in the way of nineteenth-century rationalist/determinist thinking, moulds his son's character and beliefs into inescapable patterns; and though Conrad's recurring to the father is a trifle forced or even unnecessary, his presentation of the shaping element of rationalism in modern life is crucial to the novel's success. Even in this case, however, there is a residual, instinctual element that is finally self-sufficient as a cause of Heyst's inability to admit his love for Lena, or to make it real. Heyst might very well have agreed with Sue Bridehead's virtual confession that it is her very nature not to be able to love any of the men she tempts; just as he might also have agreed with Nanda's proclamation to Mr Longdon, "I shall be one of the people who don't" (that is, marry). And in each of these three cases, Gwendolen's sudden confession to her mother springs again to mind: "I can't love people, I hate them."

But *The Awkward Age* is in some ways *the* crucial example here, because it is one of the most closely involved of all English novels with the very texture and substance of the society into which the characters are born or (in Mitchy's case at least) precipitated. Even on first reading, and with a comparatively dim understanding therefore of exactly what is going on, one is aware from the start of the close-knit texture of the life these people are living. Mr Longdon's first late-evening talk to Van, bringing together as it does Mr Longdon's half-idealised memories of the past, and Van's oblique, crowded references to the Brookenhams' house in Buckingham Crescent, the mystery of what they live on, the four puzzling children, his own impulse (which he calls a necessary part of London "friendship") to betray Mrs Brookenham's real age as a bit older than what she has claimed— all this testifies to what we are to see, even in the larger gatherings later on, of the hot-house atmosphere which the group has fostered, and on which it depends for its continued, if rather precarious, existence. Actually, the whole thing is much better done by James than any phrase like "hot-house atmosphere," relevant though it is in a way, can possibly render; because all through the novel one is struck by the fact that what might so easily have turned into a bitter but rather facile denunciation of "modern" London life, yields instead the most striking combinations of, for instance, the sheer enmity between Mrs Brookenham and her son Harold, and a kind of honesty in both of them—like most of the rest of Mrs Brook's circle, they are devious but far too intelligent to be less than honest—that is too striking to be condemned as simply degenerate. If Harold's stealing of his mother's five pounds, and his open admission of having done so, are unpleasant, the resulting dialogue between the two, in the first chapter of book 2 ("Little Aggie"), so far from betraying any note of tired resignation or complaint on James's part, registers very clearly an open enquiry into just what will be revealed if, in a closed society, people's intelligence and intuition are such that literally nothing at all either can be, or need be, concealed. The deviousness of it all is an essential part of the game being played, but the intelligent people concerned—and they certainly include the apparently listless Mrs Brook—know all the moves, and all the intimate details of others' making the moves; and furthermore face, at least as far as they can, the consequences of such a "knowing."

This is a novel, then, in which the dense atmosphere of *Middlemarch* (particularly its second, more concentratedly urban, half) is narrowed to a fraction of the area George Eliot explores, but in which the resulting intensity of vision—bringing people as close together as they could possibly be brought without the social group simply exploding into fragments—is still essentially that of the social novel. *The Awkward Age* could not have been written if it had not been for James's close involvement with both the possibilities and the impossibilities of and in certain kinds of communal life.

Yet what is most interesting about this novel (and in a different way about *Victory* later on) is James's also bringing into play certain states of mind that *look* as if they are wholly the result of, say, the kind of upbringing that Nanda has had, and that the Duchess so much and so spitefully objects to, but that on inspection turn out to be also, and independently, the product of James's own feelings about certain indelible qualities in life itself. Like others of its kind, this "middle-class" novel clearly knows that human nature—or, in wider terms, nature itself—produces behaviour that can, in certain cases, run parallel to socially induced actions, motives, feelings, but that is in fact alarmingly autonomous. Some examples from *The Awkward Age* include, for instance, Mitchy's exchange with Mrs Brookenham about himself and Nanda:

"I like her as much as I dare to—as much as a man can like a girl when, from the very first of his seeing her and judging her, he has also seen, and seen with all the reasons, that there's no chance for him whatever. . . . "

"I think you exaggerate," his hostess replied, "the difficulties in your way. What do you mean by 'all the reasons'?"

"Why, one of them I've already mentioned. I make her flesh creep."

(chap. 3)

There could be an echo here of the comic phrase from Dickens's Fat Boy ("I wants to make your flesh creep"), but I doubt it. Mitchy's comic guise (mainly his clothes) cuts much closer to the bone than the horror-fun in *Pickwick*; and though part of the reason for it is indeed his origin as a wealthy shoe-maker's son who must feel something of a raw newcomer in the West End, both his very acute intelligence, and his honesty, reflect also the range of James's own intelligence: Nanda's antipathy to Mitchy is an antipathy that could perfectly easily be overcome if social origins were all that was in question—indeed, she likes Mitchy very much; what she can't overcome is firstly her own love for Vanderbank, and secondly a physical reaction that Mitchy's slightly comic but surely very acute phrase catches immediately: "I make her flesh creep."

This reaction of Nanda's is very close to Gwendolen's reaction (also quite removed from any social considerations) to Rex's too timid overtures. The parallel is not complete, because Gwendolen is never shown by George Eliot to be in love with anyone in the way Nanda clearly is with Van; and in addition, Nanda's very intelligent, but much quieter, personality means that her motives are not so much on public display as Gwendolen's, for all their tangled and partly hidden nature, sometimes are. Of the two however Nanda's motives are at least *as* telling as Gwendolen's (in the sense that they have a general, rather than just a local and psychological, interest); and in some ways the quieter presentation perhaps allows a slightly more flexible and suggestive exploration of the ways in which even the most closely knit social groups are subject to tensions, impulses, emotions that have a quite non-social origin, and so are finally beyond the control of the group itself or of anyone in it.

In this sense, perhaps the most commanding, and puzzling, fact about Nanda is her clear choice of spinsterhood, most obviously at the end of the novel, but also in fact much earlier ("I shall be one of the people who don't"). Certainly the brittleness of modern life that Mr Longdon detects and so distrusts, even as early as his first talk to Van ("You don't care, you don't care!" he says when Van airily dismisses "friendship" to Beccles and the countryside)—this, clearly, is a determining factor. Nanda's nature is too serious to fit at all into this world. But there are other worlds, and over the run of the story as a whole the clear impression is not that Nanda is being driven into exile by London life, but that it is her own *nature* driving her to it, and so to the very sad future at the end.

It is an impulse in Nanda very close to the self-destructive, and its significance is widened by the rest of the novel giving us different, but clearly related, impulses in others of the group. Most of these are people who fit much more easily and willingly into the London life James is giving us than Nanda ever could, and so they are the more fully moulded by it. But even so, there is often a marked suggestion that their actions are more precipitate, or more extreme, than the situation necessarily demands. Thus Harold's sheer delight in a career of sponging might have been changed a bit had his upbringing been healthier, but it surely would not have been wiped out of his nature; while his father's choice of a completely separate life, ironically distanced from all the goings-on around him, is indeed *his* choice, not merely something dictated by circumstances and Mrs Brook.

But at the end of the novel, and despite her apparent control of many of the events in it, it is Mrs Brook herself who is left as the book's most isolated figure. And, paradoxically, the reasons that have driven her to this isolation have an odd kinship with the impulses in Nanda that have left her (one takes it) a perpetual spinster. Paradoxically, because the moments when Mrs Brook's self-isolating impulses are most clearly apparent tend also to be those when she is most actively concerned to close off her daughter's future.

One of the most striking scenes in this regard—one where, quite suddenly and unexpectedly, Mrs Brook seems almost as intent on bringing the whole house of cards tumbling about her own head as on keeping it up, or drawing her friends more closely round her—is the one in book 2 ("Mrs Brook"), chapter 2, where she "blurts out" to Mitchy, in Van's presence, the fact that Mr Longdon has offered Van money if he will marry Nanda. Mr Longdon, of course, has been quite uncorrupt—idealistic, even—in making this offer, which is in any case one in which Mitchy not merely concurs, but wishes to share. They both wish to see any impediment there may be to Nanda's happiness removed.

Mrs Brook's interest in the matter is, however, very different from theirs. Clearly her main purpose, or one of her main purposes, is indeed to bind Van closer to her by "exposing" him publicly, or at least in Mitchy's presence, as a man who has been made an offer of money which he has then kept to himself. She wants Van to stay with her, the star in her *own* orbit, rather than marry her daughter. If therefore she brings out the fact of Mr Longdon's offer before Van himself has told Mitchy about it (supposing he ever would), it must make Van feel so exposed, so much like a man who has been bribed to marry Nanda, that he will never do so. And, in her boldly devious way, Mrs Brook capitalises further on this by stating aloud what must indeed be Van's own near certainty: "He thinks I want him myself." This forces the normally safely reticent Van into an impossible situation: he must now either deny the accusation (which he cannot, because everyone present knows it is true—he does think Mrs Brook wants him herself); or he can admit it, thus increasing even further the, for him, quite unusual state of embarrassment into which Mrs Brook has forced him. Either way the marriage, always unlikely, is now definitely off because, as Mrs Brook again explains (tightening the noose still further), Van's pride will make it impossible for him to propose under these circumstances. Her parting dig at Van (actually just after he has left) is almost contemptuous: in his presence, she and Mitchy have agreed that the likelihood is that Mr Longdon will leave even more to Nanda if Van does not propose; and Mrs Brook keeps Mitchy behind for a moment simply to add, "Now—by that suggestion [that is, that Nanda will benefit financially by Van's *not* proposing to her]—he has something to show. He won't go in."

So much would seem to leave Van virtually a prisoner in Mrs Brook's circle. But the oddest twist to the whole scene is that it is Mrs Brook herself who really knows, more clearly and certainly than any of them, that this badgering of Van is quite unnecessary. In the previous chapter she has told Van, quite directly, that she is scheming for Mitchy's help as well as Mr Longdon's for Nanda's "desolate old age"; and when he asks why, she comments:

> "What can relieve me of the primary duty of taking precautions . . . when I know as well as that I stand here and look at you—"
> "Yes, what?" he asked as she just paused.
> "Why that so far as they count on you they count, my dear Van, on a blank. . . . You won't do it."

Very true. But the more we see this, the more we must see Mrs Brook's tormenting of Van as something supererogatory. The only end it really achieves is that of making life in her drawing-room impossible for him, and so breaking up the small circle which has been her main—indeed, her only—interest in life outside the gossip provided by the carryings-on of Petherton, Mrs Donner, and others.

Nanda only cuts her*self* off from life—no doubt depriving Mitchy and others of her company, but not doing this perversely. In her mother, the same impulse is stronger still, and includes the uncontrollable and contradictory urge to twist all her moves to draw Van closer, into ones that will in fact drive him away. Mitchy's proffered explanation, that the modern girl (specifically, Aggie) "knows too much," is part of the truth, and it is clearly meant to touch all of them, not just the women and, as Mitchy comically admits, himself. The life these people lead is so intellectual, and so very much on the defensive about emotions like the "friendship" and love Mr Longdon wants for Nanda, that it must be unstable. But what even these facts cannot explain quite by themselves is the eagerness with which they all—particularly their leader, Mrs Brook—embrace the final isolation that comes to seem for all of them (to use that favourite, and telling, Jamesian phrase) "a doom."

The degree of sophistication and self-consciousness in all this—the characters' self-consciousness, but also James's own—is clearly a long way on from that given us in any of Jane Austen's novels, even the more persistently reflective ones like *Persuasion*. But this progression (in any case far from unambiguously in favour of the much more modern world rendered by James) should not be allowed to conceal the presence in the work of both writers of certain rather similar, because permanently *un*social, and unselfconscious, feelings. And I think the comparison is strengthened if we add to it some of those apparently wayward impulses in people and in nature itself that also command part of Conrad's *Victory*. Indeed reading a book like this, as also reading some of the Tales like "The End of the Tether" or "The Secret Sharer," brings out some key facts about Conrad rather more obviously than does a book like *Nostromo*, though this is certainly a more massive, and also I think far greater, work. Like the rest of Conrad, the *Tales* and *Victory* realise very strongly the stabilising force of a conventional, "middle-class" society and even economy; but they also put a bit more into prominence both the strains inherent in the very notion of such societies (Heyst's upbringing is a case in point), and the strongly *un*balancing but potentially productive forces of some impulses in human—and indeed non-human—nature itself. In terms of *Victory*, what I mean here is not so much the paragraphs of rather over-declamatory prose about every age being "fed on illusions, lest men should renounce life early and the human race come to an end," and "Man on this earth" being "an unforeseen accident which does not stand close investigation"—these, like roughly comparable passages in Hardy, spoil the author's best insights by turning them into stiffish, rather literal-minded pronouncements that are not nearly adaptable enough to fit the changing facts that the tale itself produces. What strikes one much more forcibly is Conrad's ability to call to mind certain totally ordinary, day-to-day things in such a way as to put the solid realities of life cheek-by-jowl with its totally unpredictable qualities. For instance, chapter 9 of part 4 gives us Heyst's rage at the absurdity of his having nothing better than blunt kitchen knives to defend Lena against the three bandits: "Absolute rubbish—neither edge, point, nor substance. I believe one of these forks would make a better weapon at a pinch. But can I go about with a fork in my pocket?"

This is the very best of Conradian comedy, and it is continued in Heyst's reflections that there might perhaps be a crowbar or so in one of the sheds, but he has given up the keys anyway. "And then, do you see me walking about with a crowbar in my hand? Ha, ha!" One might call it pre-absurdist comedy, and indeed it is a kind of comedy that has all the unstressed but perfectly real element of pain that Beckett, for instance, renders in his plays thirty or forty years later. But what differentiates Conrad from later writers in roughly the same vein is that, in *Victory*, the notion of the 'absurd' is only one element (though admittedly crucial) in an otherwise stable universe. To a Beckett, the spectacle of gentleman Jones in his dressing-gown "executing a dance of rage in the middle of the floor" would be the centre of the whole tale: "Heyst looked on, fascinated by this skeleton in a gay dressing-gown, jerkily agitated like a grotesque toy on the end of an invisible string. It became quiet suddenly" (part 4, chap. 11).

To Conrad—as the sanity of his prose, in particular, demonstrates— Jones is only one element in the story. He is crucial certainly, but crucial in the sense that he is, like Pedro, Ricardo, Schomberg, one of those things that just will not fit into what is nevertheless a solid, logically predictable world. Conrad sees the world (as Hardy, though in very different terms, also sees it) as a place where most things fit together and make sense, but where a few do not and never will. And it is not that we haven't yet learnt or seen why they do not. Neither of these writers is tempted to look to some "beyond" where, when all is known, all will be made clear. Indeed, very few English novelists are. To all these writers it is the collocation of the stability of things, and a certain oddness—even instability—in them, which is permanent, challenging and far beyond the reach either of any social change, or of any metaphysical or religious insight.

Soiled Fairy:
The Water-Babies in Its Time

Valentine Cunningham

"What is the story of the Water-Babies about?," an Admiral Sir George Back wrote to a friend. "This extraordinary book," he called it—and well he might. For *The Water-Babies: A Fairy-Tale for a Land-Baby* (1863) is an exceedingly curious, overdetermined, heavy-laden, oddly multivalent text. Its omnivorous crankiness, its weird omni-comprehensiveness reflected, well, of course, the impulsive, hot-headed, manic-depressive, often nearly hysterical charging about from cause to cause, issue to issue, of its author the Reverend Canon Charles Kingsley—all at once, or at one time or another, a sanitary reformer, Christian Socialist, poet, novelist, parish priest, Cambridge Professor, Cathedral Canon, heated Protestant, fervid Briton, befriender of the poor, tutor to the Prince of Wales, devoted re-reader of Rabelais and bondage fetishist. But the heatedness and hysterias are not just Kingsley's own. They coincide frequently with those of his age, and the results are, often, conceptually and textually messy. Kingsley's texts are generally ragged, baggy, tugging sharply against regularities of order and form, and *The Water-Babies* is even more chaotic than the usual run. No wonder the good Admiral was a bit taken aback when he actually got around to reading the book:

> I think I told you that no one, lady or gentleman, could give me anything like a satisfactory answer to the question of "What is the story of the *Water-Babies* about?" And now that I have read it, the reason is clear enough, for in the playfulness of a charming fairy-tale is included the most amusing allusions to different branches of science. Of plants, fresh-water and sea, of waterflies, dear to an old fisherman, and especially the gorgeous dragon-fly, of fish,

From *Essays in Criticism* 35, no. 2 (April 1985). © 1985 by Stephen Wall.

321

birds and shells . . . , of species, of gorillas, theories, specific grav-
ities, latitudes and longitudes, minute computations, philosophers, examiners, etc. etc., and some poetry that did one's heart
good to read.

I will honour the shadow of the shoe-tie of any Land-baby, age *à
discretion,* who will do full justice to the merits of this extraordinary
book.

Doing *full* justice to *The Water-Babies,* getting near to tying up all its shoe-
ties in a single essay is impossible. But there are some approaches to its
more important meanings—particularly its meanings in and for its own
age—that deserve immediate engagement.

The Water-Babies has been, and is still, much read. It has often been
reprinted—indeed, so far as one can tell, it's never been out of print. While
Kingsley was undoubtedly an irredeemably secondhand alarmist in the
matter of social problems, always coming belatedly to the scandals of the
tailoring trades, or to sewage provision and water supply, or the employment of children, well after a Mayhew or a Chadwick, or the Children's
Employment Commissioners and all the other compilers of the Blue Books,
had done their work, he nonetheless provided what none of his forerunners
managed to provide: a powerful, readable, mythic text read by, and to,
simply every bourgeois child. Powerful fictions have never had to depend
upon factual originality for their power. Nor have powerful children's books
had to rely for their impact on what their childish readers have been able
consciously to absorb. Like other texts that one first encounters in childhood
(*Robinson Crusoe* and *Gulliver's Travels,* for example) *The Water-Babies* turns
out when one looks at it again as an adult to be full of extremely weird
things that one never noticed as a child-reader, or skipped over (perhaps
even had skipped over for one by some adult reader, parent or teacher),
and that one certainly would have been in no position to weigh as a juvenile
reader. *The Water-Babies* has the capacity to yield further meanings, respond
to later interpretative squeezes; it is a great hermeneutical sponge, rather
like a dream, as strong mythical texts frequently are. It is in fact the dreamland that Kingsley sometimes sought consciously to enter in his fiction.
His *Alton Locke* (1850), for instance, has a dream experience of backward
evolution (chap. 36) that is a pre-run for much of what happens in *The
Water-Babies.* That chapter of *Alton Locke* is entitled "Dreamland." It is as
strange and mixed as *The Water-Babies.* (And, of course, consciously wishing
for the dream condition in a writing does not guarantee one conscious
control over the bizarre unconscious meanings prevailing there.)

Kingsley admired Fairy Stories. Children should be given "the old
fairy-tales and ballads," he thought, in preference to "French novels, and
that sugared slough of sentimental poetry": fairy stories were more "manful
and rational"; they were good stuff, in other words, for tiny muscular
Christians. And *The Water-Babies* wears its affinities to classic fairy-story

motifs quite openly. Tom the chimney-sweeping boy immediately took his place as one more among the scores of versions to be found the world over of what in Britain is known as the Cinderella story: tales of the neglected child who makes good after a period of difficulty and problem-solving, a testing time that involves consignment to the place of ashes, dirt or soot that the names of these heroes and heroines bear witness to—Cendrillon, Cenerentola, Aschenputtel, Pisk-i-aske, Askepott, Aschenbrödel, Ashpit, Ashiepattle, Pepeleshka, Chernushka, Zamaraschka, and so on.

In *The Water-Babies* Ashiepattle (as the Brothers Grimm call the heroine of this story) comes heavily Christianised. And, because Christianity is never an absolute, monodic affair, he comes Christianised according to the peculiar idioms and pattern of mid-Victorian protestant and Anglican Christianity, especially of Kingsley's own mid-Victorian Christianity—the ex-Christian Socialist's Christianity, the present Natural Historian's Christianity, the anti-papist, Muscular Chauvinist's hunting-shooting-fishing, pond-trawling, insect-watching Christianity. The peculiar slantings of Kingsley's religious postures add their peculiar markings to the usual slantedness of fiction.

There is no fiction that does not in some measure stand askew to the world. This is perhaps especially true of those powerful myths that have survived and thrive among us as the well-known fairy-tales. Peter Laslett is, of course, right to detect in the Cinderella story evident components of mere historical actuality: "stories like Cinderella are a sharp reminder of what life was once like for the apprentice, the journeyman, the master and all his family in the craftsman's household" (*The World We Have Lost*). But as we're now being forcefully persuaded, not only by literary critics but also by historians like Hayden White and Karel Williams, all texts, even so-called historical ones, are only readings and so are all problematically related to what we think of as the signified or even the given world. One wants fiercely to challange Karel Williams's denigration of the given world as it is written out in the nineteenth-century texts of social concern ("Engels's 'Manchester' is not a real city nor a representation of that city, but a discursive figure in a text" [*From Pauperism to Poverty*]: Hayden White never makes this extremist mistake). Engels's Manchester and Dickens's Preston or London are properly to be considered, and with more theoretical finesse, as both word *and* world, figures in a text but also figures from context. But Williams's point has some force. And it's a force that gets stronger when it shifts from Engels's *Condition of the Working Class in England in 1844* to a text like *The Water-Babies* which is all at once consciously myth-mongering—cannily endeavouring to draw on the forces of fairy and inevitably operating within the framework of Kingsley's Christian my-themes—and, also, more or less unconsiciously sunk into strong personal and collective neuroses about the condition of the Victorian Cinderella (Richard Schoenwald's reflections on the neurotic aspects of Victorian social reform offer possibly illuminating insights here) as well as tapping even wider human anxieties and prevailing ritualised assumptions about the orders and hierarchies of cleanliness and pollution such as Mary Douglas and Julia Kristeva have investigated.

The story of Ashiepattle had been theologised before Kingsley did *The Water-Babies* (I shelve, for the moment, the interesting question of how far Christian assumptions are built intrinsically into the Cinderella story) and by an even more eminent Protestant than Kingsley ever managed to be. Bruno Bettelheim has pointed out that Martin Luther himself had detected the Biblical analogues for this old story of sibling rivalry. In his *Table Talks* Luther talked of Abel as the little ash-brother (the *Aschebrüdel*) to the more powerful, aggressive, and in the end murderous older brother Cain. In a sermon Luther also called Esau the ash-brother of Jacob because he was cheated out of his rightful inheritance. I don't suppose that Kingsley knew this (though he greatly admired "that glorious Luther"), but his polemic on behalf of the ash-brother of Victorian England is backed continually by reference to Cain's question to God after he has killed off Abel, the question which Kingsley won't ever allow his fellow-bourgeois citizens, legislators and Christians to get away with: "Am I my brother's keeper?" They were their ash-brother's keeper, he kept arguing, because "It is not the will of your Father in Heaven that one of these little ones should perish." Three times in the extremely important sermon that Kingsley preached in June 1870 in Liverpool on behalf of the Kirkdale Ragged School (at least, three times in the bit of the sermon that Mrs Kingsley published in her *Letters and Memories of His Life*), Kingsley repeated that saying of Christ's. This Liverpool sermon is known as the sermon on "Human Soot." The Human Soot consisted of God's little ones: the ash-brothers, the multitude of which Tom the chimney-boy had, by the time Kingsley preached that sermon, become Victorian England's, and Victorian literature's, most famous type and exemplum.

The ash-brother—whether Abel, Esau, Aschenbrödel, or Cinderella— is that member of the family who is neglected, not-cherished, cast-out, defrauded of his/her birthright, and who is severely put-upon, exiled in various ways, even done to death, by some more prosperous, lucky, cunning, powerful, better-organised member or group of members of the family. As a model for the Victorian working-class, especially its children, in relation to the Victorian bourgeoisie, the figure of the ash-brother could not be more apt.

The essence of the ash-brother's plight is that he has been driven away to the margin, the border, the edge: that place (in Mary Douglas's and Julia Kristeva's analyses) for doubtful, feared people and substances, the place of the physical exuviae that are ejected and rejected at the margins of the human body, the skin (that edge), the exits at the borderline of the body, the place of human debris and castaways, people construed as discardable and inferior, the place where sanity is at hazard ("on the border"), and where the wholeness of societies, individuals, and writings is most in question. At the edge is where safety, security, happiness and prosperity for people, communities and even for language itself, are at risk, are minimalised, and threatened with total extinction.

The preoccupation with, and the rhetoric of this set of margins, this kind of marginalisation, recur obsessively in Victorian contemplations of poverty, class, industrialization, political economy. They make one of the commonest of analytical tropes. There is, for example, the awareness of the marginalisation of the northern and midlands industrial towns. There's the marginalisation of the slum district and the way the industrial proletariat is shown to have been driven to the edge of humanity, to the condition of beasts, the condition of that notorious old man observed by Engels in Salford subsisting in a cowshed, himself a piece of human refuse, scraping a living by "removing dung, etc. with his handcart"; and the way (in Marx's very moving analysis of The Working Day) that the worker's paid-for share of his day's labours is thinned progressively, driven down and down to the margins of non-existence—a process whose logical end is very few or no wages at all, an exile into the vast pool of casual or partial unemployment or no employment at all. There's even that drama of the margin noticed with horror by Dickens in his article "Ground in the Mill" in *Household Words* in 1854, in which the Victorian ash-brother has his fingers, arms, hands, his actual bodily peripheries, invaded, violated, torn off by his master's unfenced machinery: an incursion across the physical borders of the ash-brother that results in what Dickens can envisage as sacks of discarded human bits (one hundred and six lives have been lost, one hundred and forty-two arms and hands have been chopped off, one thousand three hundred and forty bones smashed up, and one thousand two hundred and eighty seven fingers severed: "in bulk, how many bushels" does that number of fingers come to? Dickens wants to know). And even the most common offer of salvation—the way out—that good hearted people like Mrs Gaskell or Kingsley or William Booth of the Salvation Army could imagine for these people of the margin, was yet further marginalisation: a new home on the margins, as it were, of Britian, in the colonies or the Americas.

So the marginal location of Kingsley's Tom the Sweep is just another—albeit an extremely memorable and potent—version of the ash-brother's edgy, edged-out existence. If, in a sense, as *The Water-Babies* asserts (chap. 2), we're all on edge ("the wisest man . . . is, as the great Sir Isaac Newton said, only a child picking up pebbles on the shore of a boundless ocean"), that member of the human family whom the rest of us have turned into the ash-brother is even more so. And thus is Tom presented. His working day is timed for the edge of the lives of "fine gentlemen and ladies." He gets up at 3 A.M., so that he's "just ready to get up when the fine gentlemen and ladies were just ready to go to bed" (chap. 1). In classic Cinderella fashion he's laughed at and rudely pointed at by the more fortunate boys at the little Dame's School on the river bank (chap. 2). The girl pupils at the School cry when he shows up. The Dame herself pities him alright. But she nevertheless puts him in "an outhouse" because he's too dirty for anything better. "If thou wert a bit cleaner I'd put thee in my own bed, for the Lord's sake. But come along here": even the Good Samaritan flinches from the ash-brother and seals him in the outcast position. The cause of Tom's flight was being chased away from the Great House for having got into Miss Ellie's all-white bedroom. Mistakenly he'd gone down the wrong chimney. But even in that bedroom—construed by the aroused household as a dangerous act of trespass, a fearful act of quitting the cindery margin to which he was usually consigned—he'd never actually left the physical and social edge which was deemed his proper place. "The boy had taken nothing in the room; by the mark of his little sooty feet, they could see that he had never been off the hearth-rug till the nurse caught hold of him." The hearth, the uncomfortable edge of the room in which other members of the family lodge in greater comfort, is Cinderella's traditional place. If the ash-brother ventures away from it, he's treated like a criminal. What happens to Tom shows that he's regarded as a criminal even if he never actually leaves the blackened hearths of the rich.

The edge, the margin is, of course, interpreted by the sympathetic observer as a place of sorrow. William Blake's pair of poems each entitled "The Chimney Sweeper"—the first of which has a little sweep actually called Tom who dreams of washing in a river and rising "naked and white" into the sky to converse with angels—no doubt provided a keynote for Charles Kingsley. They clearly also set the tone of sorrowfulness with their "little black thing[s]" crying "'weep! 'weep!'"—that is, an ironic variant of "sweep! sweep!" And the margin is read as sorrowful above all because it's perceived as a grim place of waste, of degraded, discarded people and stuff, the worrying abode of human waste matter. Characteristically, Preston becomes *Coke*town in Dickens's *Hard Times* (1854). Coke is filthy residue, a kind of waste. Coketown's red brick houses, again typically, are dismayingly blackened with soot, just as its canal and river are polluted with other sorts of filth. This pollutedness is "The Key-Note" of the northern industrial condition (chap. 5 of *Hard Times*). The key-note of the writings about Manchester in the 1840s was, Steven Marcus has pointed out, the chimney: the place where soot was emitted, an emblem of wealth, but also of that wealth's by-product, dirt, ash, cinder, soot, filth. Engels's Mancunians, human discards, chuck-outs of the bourgeois family, live in quagmires of discarded human waste: amidst excremental oozes and filths, malodorous smells and piles of ordure—waste matters that are mirrors of their condition. Southwood Smith, one of the keenest sanitary investigators and delvers into the courts and alleys of Britain's great cities, found the accumulations of waste stuff, human, animal and vegetable, hard to find words for. The open middens of Manchester were drowning in trash, skins, and discarded stuff of the edge: "besides the privy matter, the house slops, the more solid house refuse, potatoe parings, cabbage leaves, bones, and offal . . . a thick layer of mingled ashes and night-soil." This, Southwood Smith wound up his 1860 report, was "the condition of the creators" of the "enormous wealth" of the richer classes—wasting away amidst heaps of offal. Kingsley's Human Soot sermon—itself enjoying a curiously marginalised existence (never published in its entirety, even though numerous volumes of Kingsley's lectures and sermons did get published; only allowed a partial airing among the wider public in Mrs Kingsley's *Letters and Memories*; eventually dropped from the one volume edition of those Letters)—makes the same sort of point about waste, human and material, as the discarded product of the money-making industrial process. Kingsley's reflections are more radical, though, than Southwood Smith's. He suggests that the wasting is not accidental. The waste is hardly a *by*-production. It is a calculated part of industrial production, one of the factory society's main products:

> Our processes are hasty, imperfect, barbaric; and their result is vast and rapid production, but also waste, refuse, in the shape of a dangerous class. We know well how, in some manufactures, a certain amount of waste is profitable—that it pays better to let certain substances run to refuse, than to use every product of the manufacture—as in a steam-mill every atom of soot is so much wasted fuel; but it pays better not to consume the whole fuel and to let the soot escape. So it is in our present social system; it pays better. Capital is accumulated more rapidly by wasting a certain amount of human life, human health, human intellect, human morals, by producing and throwing away a regular percentage of human soot—of that thinking and acting dirt which lies about, and, alas! breeds and perpetuates itself in foul alleys and low public-houses, and all and any of the dark places of the earth.

"Human refuse," "human soot," "human poison gases," "brutal, ignorant, degraded, helpless people," living not "in the light of common day" but "sunk into the darkness of the common sewer": the humanly polluted and polluting are pushed into social apartness. And *The Water-Babies* offers a potent drama of the apartness of waste and the degradation of apartness and margins. Wasteful and dirty men will, the novel tells us, "let sewers run into the sea . . . or throw herrings' heads, and dead dog-fish, or any other refuse into the water; or . . . make a mess upon the clean shore" (chap. 5). And Tom's long experience of apartness involves him in the course of the novel in a whole sequence of waste-matter processes. He's taught by the Fairy about what happens to people who seek only pleasure for themselves. The Doasyoulikes, he learns (chap. 6), are consumed and covered in the "ashes, and slag, and cinders" from a dangerously smoking mountain (an analogue of Manchester's chimney-beset condition) whose existence they have ignored. The fate of the Doasyoulikes is a protracted parable of degradation. The Cinders consume them. Then those who remain turn into ape-like savages (like the Irish who compose such a great part of the population of Manchester and Liverpool: "poor Paddies" who have to live on potatoes). Then they get more animal-like still, swinging from trees with their toes (reminding Kingsley of "Hindoo tailors" who use their toes to thread their needles). Finally they go completely ape. "And that was the end of the great and jolly nation of Doasyoulikes." Tom is told: "You were very near being turned into a beast once or twice, little Tom." The dreamland vision of *Alton Locke*, which in general got transformed into Tom's whole devolutionary experience of being turned into a fish, is here transmogrified in particular into a nightmare of what "a great and jolly nation" may do to itself once it steps onto the cinder-path to the condition of the primitive human and the beast.

Tom, of course, was rescued before the cinder-path could take him that far. But he still has to go through other discomforting waste-matter experiences, intended to bring home to us the revoltingness of trash. He's made to travel through Waste-paper-land, for instance (chap. 8). There people dig and grub among heaps of "stupid books." And "he went by the sea of slops, to the mountain of messes, and the territory of tuck . . . full of deep cracks and holes choked with wind-fallen fruit . . . nasty things which little children will eat if they can get them . . . trash . . . poisons." Then there's Oldwivesfabledom, where children are frightened by the ghosts and bogies that pop out of the Powwow man's box. He is ugly and black; he speaks "fire and smoke"; his tears are "boiling pitch" (he's another variant on the Manchester chimney). And his box is (of course) called a "thunderbox"—a Victorian word for a portable lavatory. It's a repository of wastes.

Unsurprisingly, Tom has to go through a curious lot of what (at the instance of what Mary Douglas has called "the sad wit of pollution" [*Purity and Danger: An Analysis of the Concepts of Pollution and Taboo*]) one can only think of as back-passage experiences. Tom is blown up through the sea by forces coming from "a vast hole in the bottom of the sea." Later (in chap. 8) he wonders how he is "to get up that great hole again, now the steam has stopped blowing." And he's taken up the backstairs by Mrs Bedonebyasyoudid, after an oddly Rabelaisian passage about the universal desire to know the secret of the "great backstairs." He must go up blindfold and ignorant, else how should he resist the universal clamour to be told the secret; everyone "crying to you":

> "Only tell us the great backstairs secret, and we will be your slaves; we will make you lord, king, emperor, bishop, archbishop, pope, if you like—only tell us the secret of the backstairs. For thousands of years we have been paying, and petting, and obeying, and worshipping quacks who told us they had the key of the backstairs, and could smuggle us up them; and in spite of all our disappointments, we will honour, and glorify, and adore, and beatify, and translate, and apotheotize you likewise, on the chance

of your knowing something about the backstairs, that we may all go on pilgrimage to it; and, even if we cannot get up it, lie at the foot of it, and cry;

'' 'Oh backstairs,   aristocratic backstairs,
precious backstairs,   respectable backstairs,
invaluable backstairs,   gentlemanlike backstairs,
requisite backstairs,   ladylike backstairs,
necessary backstairs,   commercial backstairs,
good-natured backstairs,   economical backstairs,
cosmopolitan backstairs,   practical backstairs,
comprehensive backstairs,   logical backstairs,
accommodating backstairs,   deductive backstairs,
well-bred backstairs,   orthodox backstairs,
comfortable backstairs,   probable backstairs,
humane backstairs,   creditable backstairs,
reasonable backstairs,   demonstrable backstairs,
long-sought backstairs,   irrefragable backstairs,
coveted backstairs,   well-bred backstairs,

                potent backstairs,
                all-but-omnipotent backstairs,
                     etc.

Save us from the consequences of our own actions, and from the cruel fairy, Mrs Bedonebyasyoudid!' ''

The backstairs must not in truth be spoken about. They're strictly unspeakable, not least because Kingsley and the others like him are poking about in their own taboos. They're busy making public what part of them at least believes should remain privy matters. That these privinesses have become so awfully public in the ash-brother's world of the open sewer and midden and the unprivate privy is what is so offensive to the prudish bourgeois sense of the necessary connexion between individual wholeness and maintaining secrecy and seclusion during defecation. These privy matters are unspeakable too because they're construed as evil, a national evil (as the sanitary campaigners all kept on saying), the work of Satan, the Lord of the Flies of the dungheap. This evil makes the ash-brothers dangerous—the "dangerous classes" no less—and not just because they might in the end revolt, but because right now they are poisonous, that is revolting in the other sense, to sensitive bourgeois nostrils and susceptibilities. There is a Nemesis attendant upon neglecting the ash-brother's disgusting condition. Ignore him and the poisons of his margin may well come to affect the health of the whole body politic. Hence the Dame's fear of Tom and the chasing of Tom away from Ellie and her pure white bedroom. This message about Nemesis was Carlyle's and Dickens's. It is Kingsley's recurrent and obsessive worry that the poisons from the secluded margin, and back passages, the privies and the middens at the social rear, the backs of slummy houses where the wastes accumulate, will come out from the back, the hidden-away places, and affect everyone, but especially himself and his bourgeois readers. Kingsley's implied theories of how pestilences spread were a rich and contradictory mixture concocted out of the going contagionist and anticontagionist suggestions of his time, but their unifying thread was a fixated horror of the dangers of the dark margin at the back. *Alton Locke*'s account of the London slums of St Giles (one of English literature's most visited slums: its potent threats from the back of respectable society even survive into the "Whitechapel" chapter of Virginia Woolf's little ironic life of Elizabeth Barrett Browning's dog *Flush: A Biography*, 1933: "Behind Miss Barrett's bedroom . . . one of the worst slums in London"),— *Alton Locke*'s description of St Giles (chap. 8) envisions multiplex contagions from that rear:

> Blood and sewer-water crawled from under doors and out of spouts, and reeked down the gutters among offal, animal and vegetable, in every stage of putrefaction. Foul vapours rose from cowsheds and slaughter-houses, and the doorways of undrained alleys, where the inhabitants carried the filth out on their shoes from the back-yard, into the court, and from the court up into the main street.

Kingsley's pamphlet about tailoring, *Cheap Clothes and Nasty* (1850), is, like *Alton Locke*, obsessed too with diseases from another, but connected and equally frightening margin: the filthy skins of the sweated tailors. The very name "sweated tailor" indicated the source of the horror. That untouchable skin was in constant contact with the clothes of the rich customer. The sweaters covered their own otherwise unclothed, wasted, diseased skins with the garments they sewed, and these thus polluted garments transported the illness of the social and bodily margin to the bodies of the "main" social body. Kingsley opened *Cheap Clothes* in a passage of extreme horror and fascination over French Revolutionary "tanneries of human skins." Tanneries worry Kingsley and the other sanitation writers as peculiarly abhorrent polluters of the urban waterways. How much more distressing to them was a tannery of human skins. And the English Mammon in Kingsley's presentation is a human tanner. He may be a good Liberal who deplores the flogging of a soldier (that skin problem), but he still "adorns his legs with the flesh of men and the skins of women." He takes the tailors' lives, but also their illnesses and shame. "So Lord ————'s coat has been seen covering a group of children blotched with small-pox. The Rev D———— finds himself suddenly unpresentable from a cutaneous disease, which it is not polite to mention on the south of Tweed," because the "shivering dirty" tailor who made his coat wore its sleeves as he sewed it. Nemesis could not be more direct. As Kingsley put it in the Human Soot sermon:

The Nemesis comes swift and sure. As the foul vapours of the mine and manufactory destroy vegetation and injure health, so does the Nemesis fall on the world of man—so does that human soot, those human poison gases, infect the whole society which has allowed them to fester under its feet.

Importantly, though, *The Water-Babies* does not stop at this point. What it also represents is Kingsley's faith that the margin can be redeemed. The edge can be the place of cleanness as well as filth; the place where waste is turned into usefulness and profit. Tom passes through the waters of cleansing and testing. They are analogues of Christian baptism. Grimes, the Master Sweep, weeps tears of repentance—those traditionally good bodily exuviae—and his tears wash him clean, and free. There is seen to be cleansing for the filthy at the watery margin of the river and seashore, and upgrading there for the degraded. Just as, in the dramatic emblem of Christian Baptism (especially in adult Baptist Baptism) the Christian goes down, is immersed, "buried with Christ" in order to rise again to newness of life, so Kingsley's Tom "went downward into the water." And his enormous plunge downward towards and into the waters of purification—three hundred feet down a craggy descent, smudging and dirtying the rocks, but all the while getting cleaner through his sweat (sanctified and sanctifying sweat on this occasion)—is nicely echoed in the passage in the book by Kingsley's friend the naturalist and adult-Baptising Philip Henry Gosse called *Sacred Streams: The Ancient and Modern History of the Rivers of the Bible* (1850; revised 1878) in which Gosse meditates on the baptism of Christ in the River Jordan. Christ was, he says, "plunged out of sight beneath the mystic waters; but, lifted up out of them straightway, a figure of resurrection." The Jordan, Gosse reveals, is a very low river, "far below the sea-level" and "Throughout the Scripture this wonderous river stands as the type of *penal death*. . . . Its very name is significant, whether we accept the etymology which reads 'the descender,' the downward-plunger, or that, which seems the better one, of 'the River of Judgement' " (Gosse, 1878 edition). Kingsley, evidently, takes the river as the place of both downward plunging and judgement. Tom's river of baptism is also the place of justice and punishment, the zone where moral readjustments occur. In this watery realm presided over by Mrs Bedonebyasyoudid cruel doctors, mothers, nursemaids, and schoolmasters get punished (chap. 5)—through a curious combination of backpassage work ("she dosed them with calomel, and jalap, and salts, and senna, and brimstone and treacle; and horrible faces they made; and then she gave them a great emetic of mustard and water, and no basins; and began all over again"); and of skin torments (tight stays, tight boots; pins stuck in; beatings and birchings).

Fairy writing was cleansing writing, Kingsley thought. The Professor in his story who doesn't believe in water-babies has to write fairy nonsense, which then cures him of his skin affliction (Bumpsterhausen's blue follicles) and clears the "foul flood-water in his brains"—"till very fine clean fresh-run fish did begin to rise in his brains." Clean water, which the rivers and seas ought to consist of, is particularly healthful in Kingsley's obsessive view of such things. The combination of fairy with water in *The Water-Babies* signifies Kingsley's deep desire for the margin to be a good place and his sense of it as at least potentially good.

The human body, naked as Tom becomes, is also perceived as good in a great deal of Kingsley's theology. Kingsley was an overt enemy of Manichaeanism. The body was thought by him to be especially good at its touchable margins. He hated women to be bound in by corsets. In *The Water-Babies* tight stays are used to punish cruel women, as we've just noted. The children of the four great bogies (Self-Will, Ignorance, Fear and Dirt) in chapter 7 are said to include Tight Stays. Mrs Doasyouwouldbe-doneby certainly doesn't wear corsets. Nor is she one of Kingsley's sick seamstresses. She's the ultimate Kingsley fantasy of naked, blissful, mothering female flesh: "nice, soft, fat, smooth, pussy, cuddly, delicious" (chap. 5). And when Tom shall have learned not to torment sea-beasts he'll get cuddled once more by this "pussy mamma" and lie "in the softest place of all." Tom's story is, in fact, an illustration of the Biblical stress on the moral accountability of life in the body: upon judgement of "deeds done in the body," but also upon the redemption and resurrection "of the body." One's not surprised to find the novel contains advice against treating children only as mental creatures, the mistake made on "the Isle of Tomtoddies, all heads and no bodies" (chap. 8).

On this view the margin, the river bank and sea-shore, is a very good place. Tom is a kind of Glaucus—that mythic figure who sustains Kingsley's popular sea-shore book *Glaucus, or The Wonders of the Shore* (1855). Tom's immersion is a fulfilment of Kingsley's Glaucan yearnings:

> Often, standing on the shore at low tide, has one longed to walk on and in under the waves . . . and see it all but for a moment; and a solemn beauty and meaning has invested the old Greek fable of Glaucus the fisherman: how, eating of the herb which gave his fish strength to leap back into their native element, he was seized on the spot with a strange longing to follow them under the waves, and became for ever a companion of the fair semi-human forms with which the Hellenic poets peopled their sunny bays and firths.

Kingsley adapted Greek legend to the glory of his Christian God in *Glaucus*. The shore declared the glory and purposes of God. *Glaucus* is full of tributes to and quotations from the shore books of Philip Henry Gosse—*Tenby* and *A Naturalist's Rambles upon the Devon Coast*. Gosse rejoiced in his rugged marginality as a member of a small sect and a scientist who stood out against evolutionary doctrine. His writings continually dwell on the delights of river-banks and coastlines—watery margins where God especially reveals himself. Kingsley responded enthusiastically to this line of thought. "I like your Tenby more and more," he wrote to Gosse on May 13, 1856. "Your larvae of Echinoderms have thrown me into such a state of astonishment, that if I could make my people understand them, I would preach a sermon on them, and ask them . . . how men can doubt the mysteries of grace, coming from a God who has created such mysteries of nature?" And Kingsley's *Glaucus* became in its turn, as Mrs Kingsley put it, "a blessing and an inspiration to so many."

In the same way, geology, "the science which explains to us the rind of the earth," "the mere rind of this earth-fruit," also shows forth the majesty of God. God's rind was no mere offal or waste-matter, trash to be chucked away. America too, like the other distant margins in the colonies (such as the West Indies, which Philip Henry Gosse travelled in, as did Kingsley just before preaching his Human Soot sermon), was, in this vein, thought of as composing a set of good margins, sabbatical places offering sabbath rest to God's rescued ash-children, places of wealth currently going to waste for want of Britain's waste-people to go and reap their fruits:

> If you have courage and wisdom, emigrate you will, some of you, instead of stopping here to scramble over each other's backs for the scraps, like black-beetles in a kitchen. And if you emigrate, you will soon find out, if you have eyes and common sense, that the vegetable wealth of the world is no more exhausted than its mineral wealth . . . precious timbers, gums, fruits, what not, enough to give employment and wealth to thousands and tens of thousands, wasting for want of being known and worked.

The place of the scavenger could be thought of, in short, and on this set of views, as a place of great potential and honour. *Glaucus* has a long passage of tribute to the sea-shore's Maia Squinado that lives on nuisances, the perfect hoopsnake of the sanitary reformers' highest imaginings which feeds on trash ("so having neither cart nor barrow, he just began putting it into his stomach") and is a beautiful creature into the bargain. *The Water-Babies* repeats the tribute in very similar words (chap. 5). On both occasions the honoured, beautiful scavenger is presented as the enactment of Fourier's notion that "scavengers, chimney sweeps, and other workers in disgusting employments" should receive signal public tributes for their work. (Charles Fourier's utopian, cooperative socialism seems to lie strongly behind Kingsley's Christian Socialism, his efforts to encourage cooperation among working-class men, his interest in the Cooperative Movement, and so on.)

And if Victorian chimney sweeps are in fact black and filthy rather than ravishingly decorative like the Squinado they can be washed and upgraded and turned to profit. Kingsley the naturalist is at pains to inform the world that "Madame Nature" is always transforming such trash to profitable ends: this is her way of neutralising the "dangerous classes."

Kingsley's lectures on Town Geology are all about the transformation of waste stuff into precious and useful commodities: "bone earth" can be dug up and used as fertilizer ("not a gold-mine . . . but a food-mine": "The Stones in the Wall"); decayed leaves and trees have turned into coal, graphite and diamond ("The Coal in the Fire"); ugly lumps of "soft and shapeless ooze" are now unrecognisable as slate ("The Slates on the Roof"). What's more, it is Kingsley's constant contention, there is profit to be made out of sewage. The waste matter from the back alleys, privies and dark passages is good stuff, useful for agriculture, saleable for money. "Thifty" and "reasonable souls," *The Water-Babies* tells us, "put . . . the stuff" of sewers "upon the fields" (chap. 5).

In the Human Soot sermon, Kingsley looks forward to a time when the concept of waste will have withered entirely away, when no Chimney Sweep will be despised and discarded, when in fact the rehabilitation that he effected for Tom will have been generalised:

> I can yet conceive a time when, by improved chemical science, every foul vapour which now escapes from the chimney of a manufactory, polluting the air, destroying the vegetation, shall be seized, utilized, converted into some profitable substance, till the Black Country shall be black no longer, and the streams once more run crystal clear, the trees be once more luxuriant, and the desert which man has created in his haste and greed, shall, in literal fact, once more blossom as the rose. And just so can I conceive a time when, by a higher civilisation, founded on political economy, more truly scientific, because more truly according to the will of God, our human refuse shall be utilised like our material refuse, when man as man, even down to the weakest and most ignorant, shall be found to be (as he really is) so valuable that it will be worth while to preserve his health, to the level of his capabilities, to *save him alive,* body, intellect, and character, at any cost; because men will see that a man is, after all, the most precious and useful thing in the earth, and that no cost spent on the development of human beings can possibly be thrown away.

But, of course, and despite the brave assurances about what "really is," the ambivalences of Kingsley's position—and not least in that passage—are abundantly clear. They are never really concealed in any of his writings, and least of all in *The Water-Babies,* a novel whose would-be playful trade in reluctances and refusals to come clean never quite masks the genuine doubleness of mind they skirt (if Cousin Cramchild—one of the storey's bogeymen—"says things cannot degrade, that is, change downwards into lower forms, ask him, who told him that water-babies were lower than land-babies? But even if they were, does he know about . . . ? And . . . if he says . . . that. . . . And so forth, and so forth. . . . Am I in earnest? Oh dear no. Don't you know that this is a fairy-tale, and all fun and pretence;

and that you are not to believe one word of it, even if it is true?" [chap. 2]). And at their heart Kingsley's misgivings are not just bourgeois ones, but Christian-bourgeois ones.

To be sure, the non-Christians cannot avoid doubts about what Kristeva has called the "ambivalence of residues"—which are "pollution *and* potential for renewal," "remainder and fresh start" all at once (*Powers of Horror: An Essay on Abjection*, translated by Leon S. Roudiez). It would be odd anyway if Marx were able to shrug off these ambivalent feelings which his native Judaism inscribed in Christian belief and ritual. Not all the working-class is ready for the revolution. We find the *Lumpenproletariat* being invented: a concept and a social group that's very close to being history's unredeemable waste stuff. But for all this, there is no doubt that Marx and Engels were fairly decided about the value of "waste" people. *Mehrwert*, Surplus Value, is *real* value. The presently wasted worker is the basis for all Capitalism's profit. He and his labours *are* profit. So he doesn't need renewing; only his conditions and rewards need righting. In this regard it is perhaps important to compare Kingsley's Christian approach to valuable stuff dug out of the earth with Marx's. Kingsley concentrates on decay and ooze which only evolve slowly and under immensely tough physical conditions into diamond, coal and slate. Marx for his part saw the intrinsic value, the beauty of gold and silver as such, that was there more or less from the start. "They appear," he writes in *Towards a Critique of Political Economy* (1859), "in a way, as pure light brought up from the underworld, since silver reflects all rays of light in their original combination and gold reflects only the colour of highest intensity—red." It's a different fairy story, as it were. "Jacob Grimm," Marx goes on, "in his *History of the German Language*, has demonstrated the etymological connection between the names of the precious metals and colour-relationships in the different Indo-Germanic languages." The axiomatic worth of gold and silver is built into the Germanic languages themselves. This is not, *per contra*, what Kingsley went to the Brothers Grimm for. In any case, Christian theology brought other considerations to bear.

Religious doubts have traditionally flourished precisely at the watery margins both of Christian initiation and of Christian conclusion. Is one's salvation utterly secure? Will one eventually turn out to be, as St Paul feared he might, and as the Reverends Brocklehurst and St John Rivers threaten the young Jane Eyre with becoming, a "castaway" from grace? Will one get over the river of death safely—as Bunyan's pilgrims worried? And anyway was one's baptism authentic?—a concern that keeps animating *Father and Son* (1907) by Philip Henry Gosse's son Edmund, who was allowed to be baptised very young and probably without real faith, and who delights in the story of the girl who "fell" into the baptismal waters and so was "baptised" despite a parental ban. Also, the evil that is supposed to be ended at baptism always proves signally hard to erase: pollution is tenacious in its hold. Kingsley's scavengers have, of course, to keep busy even on the purified margin: they're locked into the Christian struggle with the old sinful nature (chap. 5). Kingsley's observation is like the reflections of the sanitary commissioners who note poignantly that the increase of water-closets and sewer facilities has actually increased the pollution of the rivers. Dirty salt-water will perhaps always await the modern Nausicaa who goes for a bathe at the seaside, Kingsley noted gloomily. And since this is the case the scavenger, however beautiful, begins to look distinctly shaky as a basis for rejoicing about the divine economy. Certainly, if Tom is as honourable a civic functionary as Kingsley's thoughts about scavenging sea-creatures suggest, one wonders why he has to undergo such a long and arduous purgation before he is thought fit to consort with bourgeois Ellie. And one is continually in doubt as to precisely where Tom is intended to be in his underwater progress. Is he in a Paradiso or a Purgatorio? Isn't some of his experience a little like parts of the Inferno? Why does he have in effect to die before he can be socially and spiritually upgraded? Why, for that matter, is Tom not allowed to marry Ellie ("Don't you know that no one ever marries in a fairy-tale, under the rank of a prince or princess?")? Visiting her on Sundays hardly seems the sort of reward his cleansing was set up to provide. Bourgeois reluctance to let the sweep have the princess overwhelms the story's ending. But the dilemma finds its excuse in, as it is a reflection of, traditional Christian problematic. Kingsley's story founders between its sense of the value of the wasted person, the waste matter (i.e., the sinner for whom Christ died) and its repugnance for the evil of that waste (the sin that besmirches the sinner). It's as though Kingsley's cheerful anti-Manichaeanism tells him that the world, the flesh, the ash-brother are good or at least redeemable, whilst the implicit Manichaean tendencies of Christian theology keep providing nagging reminders of their evil and the difficulty of redemption without long trial and harsh processes of purging. So they remain sources of guilt, confusion, a sense of sin. Looked at another way, it is as if Kingsley is hesitating between Old Testament pollution fears that believe excrement, waste, menstruating women, the dirty and sweating belong "outside the camp" of the righteous in obedience to laws "which the wild cat of the wood, burying its own excrement apart from its lair, has learnt by the light of nature," and New Testament insistences that nothing or nobody is to be rejected as polluting and unclean. Kingsley hesitates in other words just at Christianity's most taboo-challenging point, where Christ is presented as the symbolic revaluer of pollution: crucified, wasted, becoming waste on the margin where the wasted have traditionally been consigned, "outside the camp," in order to redeem and recuperate the rejected waste matter of the old ritual's order—lepers, Samaritans, women with "an issue of blood," Gentiles of all sorts, blackened chimney sweeps, Human Soot.

Kingsley wasn't alone. His hesitations are even built into the various versions of the Cinderella/Ash-brother stories—at least if one accepts Bruno Bettelheim's observation that in these tales ashes and cinders are ambivalently mixed (ashes he sees as "the very clean powdery substance which is the residue of complete combustion," whilst cinders are "the quite dirty remnants of an incomplete combustion"). Soot could be sold for fertilizer, but its blackness and filthiness made it hard for it ever to escape being an emblem of evil. This dubiety surrounds the fortune that Dickens's Golden Dustman has procured by his trade in night-soil in *Our Mutual Friend* (1864–65). In fact the literature concerned with the putting of sewage to profitable use is rifted by similar reluctances. Sewage can be sold as fertilizer. It can be recycled usefully. It has an undoubted money value, even if this cannot be calculated with any precision. But it is still evil, noxious stuff whose evils have to be combatted vigorously with expensive chemicals, machines, gadgetry and massive human ingenuity. And if the value of human refuse remained objectively in doubt (the old man Engels described didn't make much of a living by anybody's reckoning), subjectively the anxieties about pollution were even harder to cope with. In July 1859 Kingsley was complaining that the farmers wouldn't take the available human manure, and so his pet scheme to run pipes along the railway lines into "barren" Surrey and Berkshire looked too risky to tempt the railway companies into investing in it. As narrator of *The Water-Babies* Kingsley declares that he has never found any water-babies at "any watering-place which I have ever seen" because "wasteful and dirty" men "let the sewers run into the sea, instead of putting the stuff upon the fields" (chap. 5).

But if shuffling about "man's dirt" (as *The Water-Babies* has it) was common, with Kingsley the fudging reached spectacular levels. He simply will not, or cannot, make up his mind between the belief "that commerce is the will of God" and that Human Soot "is not the will of God"; between his inclination to blame those responsible ("Somebody must be whopped for this," he wrote, quoting Sam Weller, of London's insanitariness in November 1849) and his wish not to blame his bourgeois congregations ("I do not blame you, or the people of Liverpool" he said in his Human Soot discourse); between his deep involvement in his own class (the implied reader of *The Water-Babies* is a British boy who's expected to grow up into a hunting gent just like Sir John Harthover, that "fine old English gentleman, with a face as red as a rose, and a hand as hard as a table, and a back as broad as a bullock's"—[chap. 2]) and his contrary sympathy for the little ash-brother who sweeps the chimneys of that class and who was driven out over hill and dale, even to death, by Sir John Harthover and his servants and allies. It's noticeable that Mrs Bedonebyasyoudid herself punishes the bourgeois offenders against children, the teachers and doctors and such, because, she says, they know not what they do: "they were only stupid and impatient." The working-class persecutors, the butties and nailers and master-sweeps, villains Kingsley has read about in the Blue Books, are however punished far more severely elsewhere because they're thought of as much more evil: "they knew they were doing wrong" (chap. 5).

Kingsley's anti-Manichaean insistence that all that is given, all the real, is God's—including the whole British class system and the works of capitalist enterprise—conflicts sharply with his efforts to get things changed. Kingsley's Christian, Fourieresque radicalism goes soft—or worse—when it runs up against what Kingsley also believes to be God's will: class distinctions, profit-making, the importance of not striking, the debasement of Irish people and negroes, the wickedness of foreigners, the need for, and the glory of, war:

> Just read, read the last three chapters of the Revelations, and then say, whether these same organs of destructiveness and combativeness, which we nowadays, in our Manichaeism, consider as the devil's creation, may not be part of the image of God, and Christ the Son of God, to be used in His service and to His glory, just as much as our benevolence or our veneration.

Not the least sinister aspect of Kingsley's interest in granting health to the wasted population of ash-brothers is his desire to make soldiers, ready for more Crimeas.

> Verily, the days are coming (they have not been of late years) when, as the Prophet says, "a man shall be more precious than fine gold"; when the lives and manhood of the citizens will be found more valuable to a nation, after all, than the wealth of a few, or even than the mere brute physical employment of vast numbers. And if we are to furnish many more levies of men who will equal the heroes of Inkerman, we must open our eyes, and first keep them alive when they are infants, and next, give them such an atmosphere to grow up in, that they shall become men and not rickety monkeys. . . . It is a sad thing that "food for powder" requires to be of the best quality; but so it is.

The Human Soot can (perhaps) be turned into or revalued as a set of truly "profitable servants," like faeces recycled as fertilizer. But when wasted workers are fattened up as food for powder, who profits from that but the old profiteers and systems of profit that Kingsley professed to find so ungodly in the first place? Or, put another way, what price the revaluing of those polluted creatures "outside the camp" through a social ethic and a faith incited by the mercifulness of the scapegoat Christ, only so that those recuperated men can be dispatched to some military camp to fight putative enemies beyond England's margin?

The Cinderella stories are all riddling tales. Like the Oedipus story they impose the task of solving puzzles on their ash-brothers and sisters. In its form as the nineteenth century "Industrial Novel," the ash-brother/ash-sister story is about the widespread failure to solve the riddle of how reason and the will of God might prevail within a capitalist economy. Again and again Stephen Blackpool's response in *Hard Times* is the typical and baffled comment: it's "aw a muddle." So *The Water-Babies* is not alone in compounding rather than clarifying the riddles it begins with. Its increasing complications, fragmentation, Rabelaisian encyclopedism, signify a mounting rather than disappearing set of analytical (not to mention formal) difficulties. Tom's fictional trouble begins when he gets lost in a labyrinth of chimneys, a dark set of what Kingsley calls—in a manner very startling to readers more familiar with the word as it occurs in *Ulysses* as a signal of Joyce's modernist apprehension of difficulty—*anastomoses*. And Tom's story continues anastomotically, in a darkening series of anastomosing stories, informations, forms. "Come read me my riddle, each good little man," the novel's epigraph urges: "If you cannot read it, no grown up folk can." But the question arises: can Charles Kingsley read his own riddle? Fairy, we learn, is supposed to be the cure of the sceptical Professor's "subanhypaposupernal anastomoses of peritomic diacellurite in the encaphalo digital region." But, we wonder, are Tom's and his author's anastomotic conditions actually to be solved by resort to fairy conditions and plottings? Kingsley tried hard for firm conclusions. He even provided a final section entitled "Moral." But the finale's throwaway tone indicates that even Kingsley can't muster much confidence in his own resolutions. And one has, regretfully, to conclude that Kingsley's reflections about margins founder precisely at the social margins they scrutinise, just as the better novel *Alton Locke*—itself hesitant, blurry, rewritten, hedged about with apologies, changes of mind, failures of nerve—also foundered at the margin, with its hero never making it to the exotic, beautiful, natural, virgin lands of South America, dying on the sea voyage, to the sound of "the 'Good Time Coming,' " the narrative breaking up into fractured utopian visions, fragmentary jottings, incoherence, and final incompleteness of story and statement.

Cage aux Folles:
Sensation and Gender in Wilkie Collins's *The Woman in White*

D. A. Miller

There is nothing "boring" about the Victorian sensation novel: the excitement that seizes us here is as direct as the "fight-or-flight" physiology that renders our reading bodies, neither fighting nor fleeing, theatres of neurasthenia. The genre offers us one of the first instances of modern literature to address itself primarily to the sympathetic nervous system, where it grounds its characteristic adrenalin effects: accelerated heart-rate and respiration, increased blood pressure, the pallor resulting from vasoconstriction, etc. It is not, of course, the last such instance, and no less current than the phenomenon is the contradictory manner in which, following in the Victorians' footsteps, we continue to acknowledge it. On the one hand, a vulgar salesmanship unblinkingly identifies hyperventilation with aesthetic value, as though art now had no other aim or justification than its successful ability to rattle what the French would call, with anatomical precision, our *cage*. That the body is compelled to automatism, that the rhythm of reading is frankly addictive—such dreary evidence of involuntary servitude is routinely marshalled in ads and on backcovers to promote entertainments whose Pavlovian expertise has become more than sufficient recommendation. On the other hand, an over-nice literary criticism wishfully reassures us that these domineering texts, whose power is literally proved upon our pulses, are not worth a thought. By a kind of Cartesian censorship, in which pulp-as-flesh gets equated with pulp-as-trash, the emphatic physicality of thrills in such literature allows us to hold them cheap. Accordingly, the sensation novel is relegated to the margins of the canon of approved genres, and on the infrequent occasions when it is seriously discussed, "sensation"—the modern nervousness that is as fun-

From *The Nineteenth-Century British Novel* (Stratford upon Avon Studies), edited by Jeremy Hawthorn. © 1986 by Edward Arnold (Publishers) Ltd.

damental to this genre as its name—is the first thing to be dropped from the discussion. What neither view of sensation fiction questions—what both views, it might be argued, become strategies for not questioning—is the natural immediacy of sensation itself. The celebration of sensation (as a physical experience to be enjoyed for its own sake) merely *receives* it; the censure of sensation (granting it the obviousness of something about which there is nothing to say) refuses to *read* it. In either case, sensation is felt to occupy a natural site entirely outside of meaning, as though in the breathless body signification expired.

To be sure, the silence that falls over the question of sensation seems first enjoined by the sensation novel itself, which is obsessed with the project of finding meaning—of staging the suspense of its appearance—in everything except the sensations that the project excites in us. Yet in principle the sensation novel must always at least imply a reading of these sensations, for the simple reason that it can mobilize the sympathetic nervous system only by giving it something to sympathize with. In order to make us nervous, nervousness must first be represented: in situations of character and plot which, both in themselves and in the larger cultural allusions they carry, make the operation of our own nerves significant in particular ways. The fiction elaborates a fantasmatics of sensation in which our reading bodies take their place from the start, and of which our physiological responses thus become the hysterical acting out. To speak of hysteria here, of course, is also to recall the assumption that always camouflages it—that what the body suffers, the mind needn't think. "So far as my own sensations were concerned, I can hardly say that I thought at all" (*The Woman in White*). The efficacy of psychosomatisms as "defences" presupposes a rigorously enforced separation in the subject between *psyche* and *soma*, and hysteria successfully breaches the body's autonomy only on the condition that this autonomy will be felt to remain intact. Reading the sensation novel, our hystericized bodies "naturalize" the meanings in which the narrative implicates them, but in doing so, they also nullify these meanings as such. Incarnate in the body, the latter no longer seem part of a cultural, historical process of signification, but instead dissolve into an inarticulable, merely palpable self-evidence. Thus, if every sensation novel necessarily provides an interpretation of the sensations to which it gives rise in its readers, the immediacy of these sensations can always be counted on to *disown* such an interpretation. It may even be that the non-recognition that thus obtains between our sensations and their narrative thematization allows the sensation novel to "say" certain things for which our culture—at least at its popular levels—has yet to develop another language.

Wilkie Collins's *The Woman in White* (1860)—of all sensation novels the best-known and considered the best—seems at any rate an exemplary text for making this case. For what "happens" in this novel becomes fully clear and coherent only, I think, when one takes into account the novel's implicit reading of its own (still quite "effective") performative dimension and thus restores sensation to its textual and cultural mediations. For the reason given above, the attempt to do so must be prepared to seem rather "forced"—as unprovable as a connotation and as improbable as a latency—but it is worth undertaking for more than a better understanding of this particular text. The ideological valences with which sensation characteristically combines in the novel do not of course absolutely transcend the second half of the Victorian period in which they are elaborated—as though the social significance of nervousness (itself an historical construct) were fixed once and for all; but neither are they restricted to this period. Collins's novel continues to be not just thoroughly readable, but eminently "writable" as well. If it is still capable of moving readers to the edge of their seats (and how sharp a sense of this edge may be is suggested when one character starts from his own seat "as if a spike had grown up from the ground through the bottom of [his] chair"), this is because its particular staging of nervousness remains cognate with that of many of our own thrillers, printed or filmed. It thus offers a pertinent, if not exhaustive, demonstration of the value, meaning, and use that modern culture—which in this respect has by no means broken radically with Victorian culture—finds in the nervous state.

Without exception, such a state affects all the novel's principal characters, who are variously startled, affrighted, unsettled, chilled, agitated, flurried. All sooner or later inhabit the "sensationalized" body where the blood curdles, the heart beats violently, the breath comes short and thick, the flesh creeps, the cheeks lose their colour. No one knows what is the matter with Mr Fairlie, but "we all say it's on the nerves," and in widely different ways, his niece Laura is "rather nervous and sensitive." The "nervous sensitiveness" of her double and half-sister Anne Catherick, the "woman in white," issues in the aneurism that causes her death. Characters who are not constitutionally nervous become circumstantially so, in the unnerving course of events. Unsettled by the mystery surrounding Anne, fearful that Laura may be implicated in it, suspecting that he is himself being watched, Walter Hartright develops a "nervous contraction" about his lips and eyes, which he appears to have caught from Laura herself, whose "sweet, sensitive lips are subject to a slight nervous contraction." At first "perfect self-possession," Sir Percival Glyde degenerates after his marriage to Laura into "an unsettled, excitable manner . . . a kind of panic or frenzy of mind." And Marian Halcombe, Laura's other half-sister, has already lost the "easy inborn confidence in herself and her position," that initially characterized her by the time of the first anxious and "sadly distrustful" extract from her diary. In the course of keeping that diary, of gathering the increasingly less equivocal evidence of a "plot" against Laura, she literally writes herself into a fever. It is a measure of Count Fosco's control over these characters that he is said to be "born without nerves," though his "eternal cigarettes" attest that even here nervousness is not so much missing as mastered, and mastered only in so far as its symptoms are masked in the banal practices of civilized society.

Nervousness seems the necessary "condition" in the novel for perceiving its real plot and for participating in it as more than a pawn. The condition is not quite sufficient, as the case of the wilfully ignorant Mr Fairlie shows, but otherwise those without the capacity to become nervous also lack the capacity to interpret events, or even to see that events require interpreting. The servants, for instance, also called (more accurately) "persons born without nerves," are uniformly oblivious to what is or might be going on: the "unutterably tranquil" governess Mrs Vesey, the maid who "in a state of cheerful stupidity" grins at the sight of Mrs Catherick's wounded dog, the housekeeper Mrs Michelson, whose Christian piety prevents her from advancing "opinions." It is not exactly that the novel uses nervousness to mark middle-class status, since the trait fails to characterize the "sanguine constitution" of Mr Gilmore, the family lawyer, who "philosophically" walks off his "uneasiness" about Laura's marriage. Rather the novel makes nervousness a metonymy for reading, its cause or effect. No reader can identify with unruffled characters like Gilmore or Mrs Michelson, even when they narrate parts of the story, because every reader is by definition committed to a hermeneutic project that neither of these characters finds necessary or desirable. Instead we identify with nerve-racked figures like Walter and Marian who carry forward the activity of our own deciphering. We identify even with Anne Catherick in her "nervous dread," though she is never capable of articulating its object, because that dread holds at least the promise of the story we will read. Nervousness is our justification in the novel, as Mrs Michelson's faith is hers, in so far as it validates the attempt to read, to uncover the grounds for *being* nervous.

The association of nervousness with reading is complicated—not to say troubled—by its coincident, no less insistent or regular association with femininity. However general a phenomenon, nervousness is always gendered in the novel as, like Laura's headache symptom, an "essentially feminine malady." Of the novel's three characters who seem "born" nervous, two are women (Anne and Laura), and the third, Mr Fairlie, an effeminate. "I am nothing," the latter pronounces himself, "but a bundle of nerves dressed up to look like a man." No one, however, is much convinced by the drag, and Walter's first impression—"he had a frail, languid-fretful, over-refined look—something singularly and unpleasantly delicate in its association with a man"—never stands in need of correction. Even in the less fey male characters, nervousness remains a signifier of femininity. At best it declares Walter still "unformed," and Sir Percival's imposture—that he is not, so to speak, the man he is pretending to be—is already in a manner disclosed when Mrs Michelson observes that "he seemed to be almost as nervous and fluttered . . . as his lady herself." Fosco himself, Marian informs us, "is as nervously sensitive as the weakest of us [women]. He starts at chance noises as inveterately as Laura herself."

The novel's "primal scene," which it obsessively repeats and remembers ("Anne Catherick again!") as though this were the trauma it needed to work through, rehearses the "origins" of male nervousness in female contagion—strictly, in the woman's touch. When Anne Catherick, in flight from the asylum where she has been shut away, "lightly and suddenly" lays her hand on Walter Hartright's shoulder, it brings "every drop of blood in [his] body . . . to a stop." Released from—and with—the Woman, nervousness touches and enters the Man: Anne's nervous gesture is at once sympathetically "caught" in Walter's nervous response to it. Attempting to recover himself, Walter tightens his fingers round "the handle of [his] stick," as though the touch—"from behind [him]"—were a violation requiring violent counteraction, and what was violated were a gender-identification that needed to be reaffirmed. Yet Anne Catherick impinges on him again: "the loneliness and helplessness of the woman touched me." His formulation hopefully denies what is happening to him—Anne's weak femininity is supposed to evince *a contrario* his strong masculinity—but the denial seems only to produce further evidence of the gender slippage it means to arrest. Even in his classic gallantry, Walter somehow feels insufficiently manly, "immature": "The natural impulse to assist her and spare her got the better of the judgement, the caution, the worldly tact, which an older, wiser, and colder man might have summoned to help him in this strange emergency." He is even "distressed by an uneasy sense of having done wrong," of having betrayed his sex: "What had I done? Assisted the victim of the most horrible of all false imprisonments to escape; or cast loose on the wide world of London an unfortunate creature, whose actions it was my duty, and every man's duty, mercifully to control?" Walter's protection has in fact suspended the control that is "every man's duty" to exercise over the activity of the neuropathic woman. Thanks to his help, Anne eludes a manifold of male guardians: the turnpike man at the entry-gate of the city; the two men from the asylum including its director; the policeman who, significantly, is assumed to be at their disposal; and even Walter himself, who puts her into a cab, destination unknown. "A dangerous woman to be at large": the female trouble first transmitted to Walter will extend throughout the thick ramifications of plot to excite sympathetic vibrations in Laura and Marian, and in Sir Percival and even Fosco as well. And not just in them. "The reader's nerves are affected like the hero's," writes Mrs Oliphant in a contemporary review of the novel; in what I have called the novel's primal scene, this means that "the silent woman lays her hand upon our shoulder as well as upon that of Mr Walter Hartright." As the first of the novel's sensation effects *on us*, the scene thus fictionalizes the beginning of our physiological experience of the sensation novel as such. Our first sensation concides with—is positively triggered by—the novel's originary account of sensation. Fantasmatically, then, we "catch" sensation from the neuropathic body of the woman who, no longer confined or controlled in an asylum, is free to make our bodies resonate with—like—hers.

Every reader is consequently implied to be a version or extension of the woman in white, a fact which entails particularly interesting consequences when the reader is—as the text explicitly assumes he is—male. (For example, Walter, the master narrator who solicits the others' narratives and organizes them into a whole, speaks of Laura to the reader: "Think of her as you thought of the first woman who quickened the pulses within you." The same identification is also sustained implicitly, as in the equation between the reader and a judge.) This reader willy-nilly falls victim to an hysteria in which what is acted out (desired, repressed) is an essentially female "sensation." His excitements come from—become—her nervous excitability; his ribcage, arithmetically Adam's, houses a woman's quickened respiration and his heart beats to her skittish rhythm; even his pallor (which of course he cannot see) is mirrored back to him only as hers, the woman in white's. This reader thus lends himself to elaborating a fantasy of *anima muliebris in corpore virili inclusa*—or as we might appropriately translate here, "a woman's breath caught in a man's body." The usual translation, of course, is "a woman's soul trapped . . .," and it will be recognized as nineteenth-century sexology's classic formulation (coined by Karl Ulrichs in the 1860s) for male homosexuality. (It may also be pertinent here to note that turn-of-the-century sexology is almost universally agreed on "a marked tendency to nervous development in the [homosexual] subject, not infrequently associated with nervous maladies" [Edward Carpenter, *The Intermediate Sex,* 1908, in *Selected Writings,* vol. 1, London, Gay Men's Press, 1984]. Criticizing Krafft-Ebing for continuing to link homosexuality with " 'an hereditary neuropathic or psychopathic tendency"— *neuro[psycho]-pathische Belastung,"* Carpenter remarks that "there are few people in modern life, perhaps none, who could be pronounced absolutely free from such a *Belastung!"* His ostensible point—that nervous disorders are far too widespread in modern life to be the distinctive mark of homosexuals, whose "neuropathic tendency" would bespeak rather a social than a metaphysical fatality—is still [*mutatis mutandis*] worth making. Yet in a discursive formation that insistently yokes male homosexuality and neuropathology together [in the femininity common to both], his observation might also be taken to conclude that this homosexuality *too* [if principally in its reactive, homophobic form] is a general modern phenomenon.) I cite it, not just to anticipate the homosexual component given to readerly sensation by the novel, but also, letting the phrase resonate beyond Ulrichs's intentions, to situate this component among the others that determine its context. For if what essentially characterizes male homosexuality in this way of putting it is the woman-in-the-man, and if this "woman" is *inclusa,* incarcerated or shut up, her freedoms abridged accordingly, then homosexuality would be by its very nature homophobic: imprisoned in a carceral problematic that does little more than channel into the homosexual's "ontology" the social and legal sanctions that might otherwise be imposed on him. Meant to win a certain intermediate space for homosexuals, Ulrichs's formulation in fact ultimately colludes with the prison or closet drama—of keeping the "woman" well put away—that it would relegate to the unenlightened past. And homosexuals are not the only souls to be imprisoned in male bodies; Ulrichs's phrase does perhaps far better as a general description of the condition of nineteenth-century women, whose "spirit" (whether understood as intellect, integrity, or sexuality) is massively interned in male corporations, constitutions, contexts. His metaphor thus may be seen to link or condense together (1) a particular fantasy about male homosexuality; (2) a homophobic defence against that fantasy; and (3) the male oppression of women that, among other things, extends that defence. All three meanings bear pointedly on Collins's novel, which is profoundly about enclosing and secluding the woman in male "bodies," among them institutions like marriage and madhouses. And the sequestration of the woman takes for its object not just women, who need to be put away in safe places or asylums, but men as well, who must monitor and master what is fantasized as the "woman inside" them.

II

Like *The Moonstone*, *The Woman in White* accords itself the status of a quasi-legal document.

> If the machinery of the Law could be depended on to fathom every case of suspicion, and to conduct every process of inquiry, with moderate assistance only from the lubricating influences of oil of gold, the events which fill these pages might have claimed their share of the public attention in a Court of Justice. But the Law is still, in certain inevitable cases, the pre-engaged servant of the long purse; and the story is left to be told, for the first time, in this place. As the Judge might once have heard it, so the Reader shall hear it now. . . . Thus, the story here presented will be told by more than one pen, as the story of an offence against the laws is told in Court by more than one witness—with the same object, in both cases, to present the truth always in its most direct and most intelligible aspect.

The organizational device is a curious one, since nothing in the story ever appears to motivate it. Why and for whom does this story need to be thus told? At the end of the novel—after which Walter Hartright presumably gathers his narratives together—neither legal action nor even a para-legal hearing seems in the least required. And it is of course pure mystification to preface a mystery story with a claim to be presenting the truth "always in its most direct and most intelligible aspect." But the obvious gimmickiness of the device offers only the crudest evidence of the limited pertinence of the legal model that the text here invokes. On the face of it, despite its conventionally bitter references to oil of gold and the long purse, the text is eager to retain the law—the juridical model of an inquest—for its own narrative. It simply proposes to extend this model to a case that it wouldn't ordinarily cover. The explicit ideal thus served would be a law which fathomed every case of suspicion and conducted every process of inquiry. But what law has ever done this, or wanted to? Certainly not the English law, which like all non-totalitarian legal systems is on principle concerned to limit the matters that fall under its jurisdiction. The desire to extend the law as totally as the preamble utopically envisions—to *every* case of suspicion and *every* process of inquiry—would therefore supersede the legal model to which, the better not to alarm us, it nominally clings. For the project of such a desire makes sense only in a world where suspicion and inquiry have already become everyday practices, and whose affinities lie less with a given legal code or apparatus than with a vast multifaceted network of inquests-without-end. Under the guise of a pedantic, legalistic organization, the novel in fact aligns itself with extra-, infra- and supra-legal modern discipline.

Not, of course, that *The Woman in White* represents the world of discipline in the manner of either *Bleak House* or *Barchester Towers*. Its most important relationship to this world, at any rate, does not come at the level of an "objective" portrayal, either of institutions (like the Court of Chancery and the Detective Police in Dickens) or of less formal means of social control (like "moderate schism" and the norm in Trollope). It would be quite difficult to educe a sociological understanding of Victorian asylums from Collins's novel, which, voiding a lively contemporary concern with the private madhouse, describes neither its structure nor the (medicinal? physical? psychological?) therapies that may or may not be practised within it. Anne never says, and Laura finds it too painfully confusing to recall, what goes on there. The asylum remains a very black "black box," the melodramatic site of "the most horrible of false imprisonments," where the sane middle-class might mistakenly be sent. The asylum, in short, is available to representation mainly in so far as it has been *incorporated:* in Walter's "unsettled state" when he first learns that Anne is a fugitive from there, in Anne's nervous panic at the very word, in the difference between Laura's body before she enters the place and after she leaves, in the way we are invited to fill in the blank horror of what she cannot remember with the stuff of our own nightmares. What the example may be broadened to suggest is that the novel represents discipline mainly in terms of certain general isolated effects on the disciplinary *subject*, whose sensationalized body both dramatizes and facilitates his functioning as *the subject/object of continual supervision*.

These effects, together with the juridical metaphor under which they are first inscribed, are best pursued in the contradiction between the Judge and the Reader who is supposed to take his place. "As the Judge might once have heard [the story], so the Reader shall hear it now." The pronouncement, of course, confers on the latter role all the connotations of sobriety and even serenity attached to the former. That "wretches hang that jurymen may dine" will always give scandal to our Western mythology of justice, in which the judge—set above superstition, prejudice, "interest" of any kind—weighs the evidence with long and patient scruple before pronouncing sentence. Nothing, however, could be less judicial, or judicious, than the actual hermeneutic practice of the reader of this novel, whose technology of nervous stimulation—in many ways still the state of the art—has him repeatedly jumping to unproven conclusions, often literally jumping at them. Far from encouraging reflective calm, the novel aims to deliver "positive personal shocks of surprise and excitement" [as Mrs. Oliphant puts it] which so sensationalize the reader's body that he is scarcely able to reflect at all. The novel's only character with strictly judicial habits of mind is the lawyer Gilmore, who judges only to misjudge. Hearing Sir Percival's explanation of his dealings with Anne Catherick, he says: "my function was of the purely judicial kind. I was to weigh the explanation we had just heard . . . and to decide honestly whether the probabilities, on Sir Percival's own showing, were plainly with him, or plainly against him. My own conviction was that they were plainly with him." Characters who rely on utterly unlegal standards of evidence like intuition, coincidence, literary connotation, get closer to what will eventually be revealed as the truth. In her first conversation with Walter, Anne Catherick nervously inquires about an unnamed Baronet in Hampshire; Walter later learns that Laura is engaged to a Baronet in Hampshire named Sir Percival Glyde. "Judging by the ordinary rules of evidence, I had not the shadow of a reason thus far, for connecting Sir Percival Glyde with the suspicious words of inquiry that had been spoken to me by the woman in white. And yet, I did connect them." Similarly, when after Sir Percival's explanation, Gilmore wonders what excuse Laura can possibly have for changing her mind about him, Marian answers: "In the eyes of law and reason, Mr Gilmore, no excuse, I dare say. If she still hesitates, and if I still hesitate, you must attribute our strange conduct, if you like, to caprice in both cases." The competent reader, who does not weigh evidence so much as he simply assents to the ways in which it has been weighted, fully accepts the validity of such ungrounded connections and inexcusable hesitations: they validate, among other things, the sensations they make him feel. And this reader is capable of making what by the ordinary rules of evidence are comparably tenuous assumptions of his own. We can't know, just because Sir Percival's men are watching Somebody, and Walter may be being watched, that Walter is that Somebody; and yet, we are convinced that we do know this. Or again, the loose seal on the letter that Marian recovers from the postbag after she has seen Fosco hovering about it does not establish the fact that Fosco has opened and resealed her letter; but we take it firmly for granted nonetheless. Our judgements are often informed by no better than the silliest folk wisdom. Laura's pet greyhound shrinks from Sir Percival; "a trifle" Gilmore considers it even though Nina later jumps eagerly enough into his own lap. In the strange court of justice over which we preside, we consider her evidence unimpeachable. Yet neither adhering to ordinary rules of evidence nor inhering in a decisive institutional context (except of course that provided by the conventions of this kind of novel), such "acts of judgement" are in fact only entitled to the considerably less authoritative status of *suspicions,* whose "uncertainty" in both these senses makes it easy to discredit them. Walter is the first to refer his hypotheses to their possible source in "delusion" and "monomania." Like the characters who figure him, the reader becomes—what a judge is never supposed to be—paranoid. From trifles and common coincidences, he suspiciously infers a complicated structure of persecution, an elaborately totalizing "plot."

What a judge is never supposed to be? Yet the most famous paranoid of modern times *was* a judge, and his paranoia was triggered precisely when, at Dresden, he entered on his duties as Senatspräsident. Schreber's case suggests that paranoia is "born" at the moment when the judge, without ceasing to be judge, has also become the accused, when he is both one and the other. It was, of course, his homosexuality that put Schreber in this institutionally untenable position, since the law he was expected to administer would certainly include, as [Guy] Hocquengham has pointed out, interdictions against homosexuality itself. Schreber's delusion does nothing so much as elaborate the paradoxical aspect of his actual situation as a judge who might well have to judge (others like) himself. The Rays of God, having constituted his monstrosity (literally: by feminizing his constitution via the nerves), taunt him with it thus: "So *this* sets up to have been a Senatspräsident, this person who lets himself be f——d!" In *The Woman in White,* another case of feminization via the nerves, Mrs Michelson's article of unsuspecting faith—"Judge not that ye be not judged"—postulates an inevitable slippage between subject and object whenever judgement is attempted. The slippage is in fact far more likely to occur when judgement, no longer governed by an institutional practice with established roles and rules of evidence, has devolved into mere suspicion. Unlike legal judgement, suspicion presupposes the reversibility of the direction in which it passes. The novel abounds with suspicious characters, in the telling ambiguity of the phrase, for what Anne, Walter, and Marian all suspect is that *they are themselves suspected.* Why else would Anne be pursued, Walter watched, Marian's correspondence opened? They are suspected, moreover, precisely, *for being suspicious.* For Walter to notice that Anne's manner is "a little touched by suspicion" is already to suspect her, as she instantly recognizes ("Why do you suspect me?"). Hence the urgency, as well as the futility, of the suspicious character's obsessive desire *not to excite suspicion,* since the act of suspecting always already implies the state of being suspect. The whole vertiginous game (in which I suspect him of suspecting me of suspecting him) is meant to ward off—but only by passing along—the violation of privacy that it thus at once promotes and resists. In what Roland Barthes would call the novel's symbolic code, this violation connotes the sexual attack whose possibility "haunts" the novel no less thoroughly than the virginal presence—insistent like a dare—of the woman in white. What stands behind the vague fears of Anne and Walter during their first encounter; what subtends Mr Fairlie's malicious greeting of the latter ("So glad to possess you at Limmeridge, Mr Hartright"); what Sir Percival sadistically fantasizes when he invites his wife to imagine her lover "with the marks of my horsewhip on his shoulders"; and what Fosco finally accomplishes when he reads Marian's *journal intime*, is virtual rape. We might consider what is implied or at stake in the fact that the head-game of suspicion is always implicitly transcoded by the novel into the body-game of rape.

Perhaps the most fundamental value that the novel as a cultural institution may be said to uphold is privacy, the determination of an integral, autonomous "secret" self. Novel-reading takes for granted the existence of a space in which the reading subject remains safe from the surveillance, suspicion, reading, and rape of others. Yet this privacy is always specified as the freedom to read about characters who oversee, suspect, read, and rape one another. It is not just that, strictly private subjects, we read about violated, objectified subjects, but that, in the very act of reading about them, we contribute largely to constituting them as such. We enjoy our privacy in the act of watching privacy being violated, in the act of watching that is already itself a violation of privacy. Our most intense identification with characters never blinds us to our ontological privilege over them: they will never be reading about *us*. It is built into the structure of the novel that every reader must realize the definitive fantasy of the liberal subject, who imagines himself free from the surveillance that he nonetheless sees operating everywhere around him.

The sensation novel, however, submits this panoptic immunity to a crucial modification: it produces repeated and undeniable evidence—"on the nerves"—that we are perturbed by what we are watching. We remain of course unseen, but not untouched: our bodies are rocked by the same "positive personal shocks" as the characters are said to be. For us, these shocks have the ambivalent character of being both a kind of untroubled pleasure (with a certain "male" adventurism we read the sensation novel to *have* them) and a kind of less tame and more painful *jouissance* (with a certain "female" helplessness we often protest that we can't *bear* them, though they keep on coming). The specificity of the sensation novel in nineteenth-century fiction is that it renders the liberal subject the subject of a *body*, whose fear and desire of violation displaces, reworks, and exceeds his constitutive fantasy of intact privacy. The themes that the liberal subject ordinarily defines himself against—by reading *about* them—are here inscribed into his reading body. Moreover, in *The Woman in White* this body is gendered: not only has its gender been *decided*, but also its gender-identification is an active and determining *question*. The drama in which the novel writes its reader turns on the disjunction between his allegedly masculine gender and his effectively feminine gender-identification (as a creature of "nerves"): with the result that his experience of sensation must include his panic at having the experience at all, of being in the position to have it. In this sense, the novel's initial assumption that its reader is male is precisely what cannot be assumed (or better, what stands most in need of proof), since his formal title—say, "a man"—is not or not yet a substantial entity—say, "a real man."

By far the most shocking moment in the reader's drama comes almost in the exact middle of the novel, when the text of Marian's diary, lapsing into illegible fragments, abruptly yields to a postscript by the very character on whom its suspicions centre. Not only has Count Fosco read Marian's "secret pages," he lets her know it, and even returns them to her. In a fever which soon turns to typhus, Marian is in no condition even to take cognizance of this revelation, whose only immediate register is the reader's own body. Peter Brooks articulates our state of shock thus: "our readerly intimacy with Marian is violated, our act of reading adulterated by profane eyes, made secondary to the villain's reading and indeed dependent on his permission." It is not just, then, that Marian has been "raped," as both the Count's amorous flourish ("Admirable woman!") and her subsequent powerless rage against him are meant to suggest. We are "taken" too, taken by surprise, which is itself an overtaking. We are taken, moreover, from behind: from a place where, in the wings of the ostensible drama, the novelist disposes of a whole plot machinery whose existence—so long as it didn't oblige us by making creaking sounds (and here it is as "noiseless" as Fosco himself)—we never suspected. (We never suspected, though the novel has trained us to be nothing if not suspicious. Surprise—the recognition of what one "never suspected"—is precisely what the paranoid seeks to eliminate, but it is also what, in the event, he survives by reading as a frightening incentive: he can never be paranoid enough.) To being the object of violation here, however, there is an equally disturbing alternative: to identify with Fosco, with the novelistic agency of violation. For the Count's postscript only puts him in the position we already occupy. Having just finished reading Marian's diary ourselves we are thus implicated in the sadism of his act, which, even as it violates our readerly intimacy with Marian, reveals that "intimacy" to be itself a violation. The ambivalent structure of readerly identification here thus condenses together—as simultaneous, but opposite renderings of the same powerful shock—homosexual panic and heterosexual violence.

This is the shock, however, that, having administered, the novel (like any good administration) will work to absorb. The shock in fact proves the point of transition between what the narrative will soothingly render as a *succession:* on one side, a passive, paranoid, homosexual feminization; on the other, an active, corroborative, heterosexual masculine protest. Marian alerts us to this succession ("our endurance must end, and our resistance must begin"), but only towards the end of her narrative, since the moment of "resistance" will need to be effectively sponsored not just by a male agent, but by an indefectibly composed male discourse as well. The master narrator and actor in the second half of the novel is therefore Walter: no longer the immature Walter whose nerve-ridden opening narrative seemed—tonally at any rate—merely continued in Marian's diary, but the Walter who has returned from his trials in Central America a changed man: "In the stern school of extremity and danger my will had learnt to be strong, my heart to be resolute, my mind to rely on itself. I had gone out to fly from my own future. I came back to face it, as a man should." Concomitantly, the helpless paranoia of the first half of the novel now seeks *to prove itself*, as Walter aggressively attempts to "force a confession" from Sir Percival and Fosco "on [his] own terms." Shocks decline "dramatically" in both frequency and intensity (our last sensation: its absence) as characters and readers alike come to get answers to the question that sensation could never do more than merely pose of the event occasioning it—namely, "what did it mean?" Foremost on the novel's agenda in its second half is the dissolution of sensation in the achievement of decided meaning. What the narrative must most importantly get straight is, from this perspective, as much certain sexual and gender deviancies as the obscure tangles of plot in which they thrive. In short, the novel needs to realize the normative requirements of the heterosexual ménage whose happy picture concludes it.

This conclusion, of course, marks the most banal moment in the text, when the sensation novel becomes least distinguishable from any other kind of Victorian fiction. Herein, one might argue, lies the "morality" of sensation fiction, in its ultimately fulfilled wish to abolish itself: to abandon the grotesque aberrations of character and situation that have typified its representation, which now coincides with the norm of the Victorian household. But the project, however successful, is nothing here if not drastic. In *Barchester Towers*, by contrast, the normative elements of heterosexual coupling—the manly husband, the feminine wife—are ready-to-hand early on, and the plot is mainly a question of overcoming various inhibitions and misunderstandings that temporarily prevent them from acknowledging their appropriateness for one another. In *The Woman in White*, however, these elements have to be "engendered" in the course of the plot through the most extreme and violent expedients. The sufficiently manly husband needs to have survived plague, pygmy arrows, and shipwreck in Central America, and the suitably feminine wife must have been schooled in a lunatic asylum, where she is half-cretinized. Such desperate measures no doubt dramatize the supreme value of a norm for whose incarnation no price, including the most brutal aversion therapy, is considered too high to pay. But they do something else besides, something which Victorians, in thrall to this norm, suspected when they accused the sensation novel of immorality, and which we, more laxly oppressed than they, are perhaps in a better position to specify. This is simply that, recontextualized in a "sensational" account of its genesis, such a norm risks appearing *monstrous*: as aberrant as any of the abnormal conditions that determine its realization.

III

"It ended, as you probably guess by this time, in his insisting on securing his own safety by shutting her up." Male security in *The Woman in White* seems always to depend on female claustration. Sir Percival not only shuts up Anne in the asylum, but successfully conspires with Fosco to shut up Laura there as well. In a double sense, he also shuts up Anne's mother, whose silence he purchases with a "handsome" allowance and ensures by insisting she not leave the town where she has been shamed and therefore "no virtuous female friends would tempt [her] into dangerous gossiping at the tea-table." Thanks to "the iron rod" that Fosco keeps "private," Madame Fosco, who once "advocated the Rights of Women," now lives in a "state of suppression" that extends to "stiff little rows of very short curls" on either side of her face and "quiet black or grey gowns, made high round the throat." She walks in a favourite circle, "round and round the great fish pond"—the Blackwater estate is in any case already "shut in— almost suffocated . . . by trees"—as though she were taking yard-exercise. The novel does not of course approve of these restraining orders, which originate in unambiguously criminal depravity, but as we shall see, it is not above exploiting them as the stick with which to contrast and comple- ment the carrot of a far more ordinary and acceptable mode of sequestration.

Gilbert and Gubar have argued that "dramatizations of imprisonment and escape are so all-pervasive in nineteenth-century literature by women that . . . they represent a uniquely female tradition in this period." Male carceral representations, "more consciously and objectively" elaborated, tend to be "metaphysical and metaphorical," whereas female ones remain social and actual" (*The Madwoman in the Attic*). Yet at least in the nineteenth- century novel, the representation of imprisonment is too pervasive to be exclusively or even chiefly a female property, and too consistent overall to be divided between male and female authors on the basis of the distinctions proposed. On the one hand it is a commonplace that Dickens's carceral fictions are grounded in actual social institutions, and there is little that is metaphysical in Trollope's rendering of social control: what little there is, in the form of "religion" or "providence," merely sanctions the social mech- anisms concretely at work. On the other, Charlotte Brontë's "dramatiza- tions of imprisonment" do not deal with literal prisons at all, as Gilbert and Gubar themselves demonstrate. In so far as these critics endorse a familiar series of oppositions (masculine/feminine = abstract/concrete = conscious/unconscious = objective/subjective) that, even graphically, keeps women behind a lot of bars, their attempt to isolate the essential paradigm of female writing unwittingly risks recycling the feminine mystique. We are nonetheless indebted to them for posing the question of the specific historical configuration, in the nineteenth-century English novel, of what might be called the "feminine carceral." As they convincingly show, this configuration centres on the representation, in varying degrees of alienation, of the "madwoman," and if this representation is not a uniquely female tradition, one readily grants that it is dominantly so. *The Woman in White*, however, with impressive ease incorporating the story of female "imprisonment and escape" (again, *anima muliebris inclusa*), suggests that there is a radical ambiguity about the "madwoman" that allows the feminist concerns she often voices to have already been appropriated in anti-feminist ways. To the extent that novelists (or critics) underwrite the validity of female "madness," as virtually the only mode of its subject's authenticity, they inevitably slight the fact that it is also her socially given *role*, whose quasi-mandatory performance under certain conditions apotheosizes the familiar stereotypes of the woman as "unconscious" and "subjective" (read: irresponsible) that contribute largely to her oppression. The madwoman finds a considerable part of her truth—in the corpus of nineteenth-century fiction, at any rate—in being implicitly juxtaposed to the male *criminal* she is never allowed to be. If, typically, *he* ends up in the prison or its meta-phorical equivalents, *she* ends up in the asylum or *its* metaphorical equiv-alents. (As a child perusing the shelves of a public library, I thought *The Woman in White* must be the story of a nurse: it at least proves to be the story of various women's subservience to "the doctor," to medical domi-nation.) The distinction between criminal men (like Sir Percival and Fosco) and innocently sick women (like Anne and Laura) bespeaks a paternalism whose "chivalry" merely sublimates a system of constraints. In this light, the best way to read the madwoman would be not to derive the diagnosis from her social psychology ("who wouldn't go crazy under such condi-tions?"), but rather to derive her social psychology from the diagnosis: from the very category of madness that, like a fate, lies ever in wait to "cover"—account for and occlude—whatever behaviours, desires, or tendencies might be considered socially deviant, undesirable, or dangerous.

The achievement of blowing this cover belongs to *Lady Audley's Secret* (1862), the novel where, writing under the ambiguous stimulus of *The Woman in White*, Mary Elizabeth Braddon demonstrates that the madwom-an's primary "alienation" lies in the rubric under which she is put down. Not unlike Anne Catherick, "always weak in the head," Lady Audley appears to have been born with the "taint" of madness in her blood. She inherits the taint from her mother, whose own madness was in turn "an hereditary disease transmitted to her from her mother, who died mad." Passed on like a curse through—and as—the woman, madness virtually belongs to the condition of being female. But the novel is not so much concerned to conjoin madness and femininity, each the "truth" of the other, as to display how—under what assumptions and by what procedures—such a conjunction comes to be socially achieved. For in fact the text leaves ample room for doubt on the score of Lady Audley's "madness." Her acts, including bigamy, arson, and attempted murder, qualify as crimes in a strict legal sense; and they are motivated (like crime in English detective fiction generally) by impeccably rational considerations of self-interest.

When her nephew Robert Audley at last detects her, however, he simply arranges for her to be pronounced "mad" and imprisoned accordingly in a *maison de santé* abroad. The "secret" let out at the end of the novel is not, therefore, that Lady Audley is a madwoman, but rather that, *whether she is one or not*, she must be treated as such. Robert feels no embarrassment at the incommensurability thus betrayed between the diagnosis and the data that are supppposed to confirm it; if need be, these data can be dispensed with altogether, as in the findings of the doctor ("experienced in cases of mania") whom he calls in for an opinion:

> "I have talked to the lady," [the doctor] said quietly, "and we understand each other very well. There is latent insanity! Insanity which might never appear; or which might appear only once or twice in a lifetime. It would be a *dementia* in its worst phase, perhaps; acute mania; but its duration would be very brief, and it would only arise under extreme mental pressure. The lady is not mad; but she has the hereditary taint in her blood. She has the cunning of madness, with the prudence of intelligence. I will tell you what she is, Mr. Audley. She is dangerous!"

The doctor's double-talk ("the cunning of madness, with the prudence of intelligence") will be required to sanction two contradictory propositions: (1) Lady Audley is criminal—in the sense that her crimes must be punished; and (2) Lady Audley is not criminal—in the sense that neither her crimes nor her punishment must be made public in a male order of things. ("My greatest fear," Robert tells the doctor, "is the necessity of any exposure— and disgrace.") "Latent insanity, an insanity which might never appear" nicely meets the requirements of the case. At the same time that it removes the necessity for evidence (do Lady Audley's crimes manifest her latent insanity? or has the latter, quite independently of them, yet to make its appearance?), it adduces the grounds for confining her to a madhouse. Lady Audley is mad, then, only because she must not be criminal. She must not, in other words, be supposed capable of acting on her own diabolical responsibility and hence of publicly spoiling her assigned role as the conduit of power transactions between men. (A Victorian reviewer, W. Fraser Rae, criticizes the characterization of Lady Audley thus: "In drawing her, the authoress may have intended to portray a female Mephistopheles; but if so, she should have known that a woman cannot fill such a part" ["Sensation Novelists: Miss Braddon," *North British Review* 43 (1865) quoted in *The Woman Question*]. Ray might have spared himself the trouble [not to mention, in our hindsight, the embarrassment of failing to read the text that nonetheless proves quite capable of reading him], since his objection merely rehearses the same principle that, within the novel, Robert Audley victoriously carries in having Lady Audley confined.) Whatever doubts the doctor entertains in pronouncing her mad do not affect his certainty that she is, at all events, dangerous, and this social judgement entirely suffices to discount the ambiguities which the properly medical one need not bother to resolve.

Lady Audley's Secret thus portrays the woman's carceral condition as her fundamental and final truth. The novel's power as a revision of *The Woman in White* consists in its refusal of the liberal dialectic whereby the latter thinks to surpass this truth. Up to a certain point—say, up to the success of the conspiracy to confine Laura—Collins's novel is willing to tell the same story as Braddon's: of an incarceration whose patriarchal expediency takes priority over whatever humane considerations may or may not be invoked to rationalize it. (Anne's mental disorder, though real enough, is ony a plausible pretext for confining her on other grounds; and Laura's confinement has no medical justification whatsoever.) But unlike Lady Audley, Lady Glyde *escapes* from her asylum, and there fortunately proves somewhere else to go. The asylum has an "alibi" in Limmeridge House (twice called an "asylum" in the text), where in the end Laura settles happily down with Walter. Whereas in the first movement of the novel, the woman is shut up, in the second, she is liberated, and it is rather the "feminine carceral" that is put away instead. Laura thus follows a common itinerary of the liberal subject in nineteenth-century fiction: she takes a nightmarish detour through the carceral ghetto on her way *home*, to the domestic haven where she is always felt to belong. Yet while her history plainly dichotomizes carceral and liberal spaces, the asylum that keeps one inside and the "asylum" that keeps others out, it also gives evidence of continuities and overlappings between them. If her situation as Mrs Hartright throws domesticity into relief as relief indeed from the brutalities of the asylum, her state as Lady Glyde (at Sir Percival's "stifling" house) merely anticipates the asylum, which in turn only perfects Sir Percival's control over her. The difference between the asylum-as-confinement and the "asylum"-as-refuge is sufficiently dramatic to make a properly enclosed domestic circle the object of both desire and, later, gratitude; but evidently, it is also sufficiently precarious to warrant—as the means of maintaining it—a domestic self-discipline that must have internalized the institutional control it thereby forestalls. The same internment that renders Laura's body docile, and her mind imbecile, also fits her to incarnate the norm of the submissive Victorian wife. (Sir Percival might well turn in his grave to see his successor effortlessly reaping what, with nothing to show but acute frustration, *he* had sown.) Collins makes Laura's second marriage so different from her first that he has no reason to conceal the considerable evidence of its resemblance to what can be counted upon to remain its "opposite."

This evidence comes as early as when, virtually at first sight, Walter falls in love with Laura. "Think of her," he invites the reader who would understand his feelings, "as you thought of the first woman who quickened the pulses within you." As here, so everywhere else his passion declares itself in the language of sensation: of thrill and chill, of pang and pain, of "sympathies" that, lying "too deep for words, too deep almost for thoughts," have been "touched." Concomitantly, in the associative pattern we have already established, his sensationalized body puts him in an essentially feminine position. His "hardly-earned self-control" is as completely lost to him as if he had never possessed it, and "aggravated by the sense of [his] own miserable weakness," his situation becomes one of "helplessness and humiliation"—the same hendiadys that Marian will apply to herself and Laura at Blackwater Park. This is all to say that, notwithstanding Walter's implication, Laura Fairlie is *not* the first woman to quicken his pulses, but rather the object of a repetition compulsion whose origin lies in his (sensationalizing, feminizing) first encounter with the woman in white. Walter replays this primal trauma, however, with an important difference that in principle marks out the path to mastering it. He moves from an identification with the woman to a desire for her, heterosexual choice replacing homosexual surprise. The woman is once more (or for the first time) the other, and the man, who now at least "knows what he wants," has to that extent taken himself in charge.

Yet the sensational features of Walter's desire necessarily threaten to reabsorb it in the identification against which it erects itself as a first line of defence. Something more, therefore, is required to stabilize his male self-mastery, something that Walter does *not* know that he wants. "Crush it," Marian counsels him: "Don't shrink under it like a woman. Tear it out; trample it under foot like a man!" But the eventual recipient of this violence will be as much the object of Walter's passion as the passion itself. From the very beginning of his exposure to it, Laura's "charm" has suggested to him "the idea of something wanting":

> At one time it seemed like something wanting in *her*; at another, like something wanting in myself, which hindered me from understanding her as I ought. The impression was always strongest in the most contradictory manner, when she looked at me, or, in other words, when I was most conscious of the harmony and charm of her face, and yet, at the same time, most troubled by the sense of an incompleteness which it was impossible to discover. Something wanting, something wanting—and where it was, and what it was, I could not say.

This is not (or not just) a Freudian riddle (Q. What does a woman want? A. What she is wanting), though even as such it attests the particular anxiety of the man responsible for posing it: who desires Laura "because" (= so that) she, not he, is wanting. For shortly afterwards, with "a thrill of the same feeling which ran through [him] when the touch was laid upon [his] shoulder on the lonely high-road," Walter comes to see that the "something wanting" is "[his] own recognition of the ominous likeness between the fugitive from the asylum and [his] pupil at Limmeridge House." Laura's strange "incompleteness" would thus consist in what has made this likeness imperfect—namely, that absence of "profaning marks" of "sorrow and suffering" which alone is said to differentiate her from her double. Accordingly, the Laura Walter most deeply dreams of loving proves to be none other than the Anne who has been put away. It is as though, to be quite perfect, his pupil must be taught a lesson: what is wanting, what Laura obscurely lacks and Walter obscurely wishes for, is her sequestration in the asylum.

Courtesy of Sir Percival and Fosco, the want will of course be supplied, but long before her actual internment, Laura has been well prepared for it at Limmeridge House, where, on the grounds that her delicacy requires protection, men systematically keep their distance from her. Rather than deal with her directly, Sir Percival, Mr Gilmore, Mr Fairlie and Walter himself all prefer to have recourse to the mannish Marian who serves as their intermediary. "I shrank," says Walter at one point, "I shrink still—from invading the innermost sanctuary of her heart, and laying it open to others, as I have laid open my own." His many such gallant pronouncements entail an unwillingness to *know* Laura, the better to affirm without interference the difference between him and her, man and woman. ("Me Tarzan, you Jane": notice how male solipsism overbears the very opposition that guarantees male difference. Laura is a closed sanctuary/Walter is an open book, but it is Walter here who empowers himself to decide, by his shrinking reticence, what Laura shall be.) More than anything else, this "respect" is responsible in the text for rendering Laura—even in terms of a genre that does not specialize in complex character studies—a psychological cipher. (An English translation of the French translation of the novel might be entitled, precisely, *The Woman as Blank*). From turbid motives of her own, Marian is more than willing to do her part in drawing round Laura this *cordon sanitaire*. Like an efficient secretary in love with her boss, she spares Laura all troublesome importunities, and she is no less aggressive in forbidding an interview between Laura and Anne ("Not to be thought of for a moment") than in dispatching Walter from Limmeridge House, "before more harm is done." Laura's subsequent experience of the asylum only further justifies the imperative to isolate her. "The wrong that had been inflicted on her . . . must be redressed without her knowledge and without her help." And now a self-evident opposition between parent and child is available to overdetermine what had been the all-too-doubtful difference between man and woman. "Oh, don't, don't, don't treat me like a child!," Laura implores, but Walter immediately takes the plea for more evidence of her childishness and accordingly gives her some pretend-work to do. When she asks him "as a child might have" whether he is as fond of her as he used to be, he reassures her that she is dearer to him now than she had ever been in the past times. His profession carries conviction, and no wonder, since his passion for her, now become a part-parental, part-pedophilic condescension, no longer makes him feel like a woman. Though the text takes perfunctory notice of "the healing influences of her new life" with Walter, these have no power to produce a Laura who in any way exceeds men's (literal or "liberal") incarcerating fantasies about her. It is not just, as the text puts it, that the mark of the asylum is "too deep to be effaced," but that it has always already effaced everything else.

The same could not be said of Marian Halcombe, whose far more "interesting" character represents the only significant variation on business-as-usual in the novel's gynaeceum. As the conspicuously curious case of a woman's body that gives all the signs of containing a man's soul, Marian figures the exact inversion of what we have taken to be the novel's governing fantasy. Yet we must not conceive of this inversion standing in opposition to what it inverts, as though it implied not just the existence of a rival set of matching *female* fears and fantasies, but also the consequent assurance that, in the love and war between the sexes, all at least was fair: *così fan tutte*, too. No less than that of the woman-in-the-man, the motif of the man-in-the-woman is a function of the novel's anxious male imperatives ("*cherchez, cachez, couchez la femme*") that, even as a configuration of resistance, it rationalizes, flatters, and positively encourages. Thus, however "phallic," "lesbian," and "male-identified" Marian may be considered at the beginning of the novel, the implicit structuring of these attributes is precisely what is responsible for converting her— if with a certain violence, then also with a certain ease—into the castrated, heterosexualized "good angel" of the Victorian household at the end.

Our memorable first view of her comes in the disappointed appraisal of Walter's idly cruising eye:

> The instant my eyes rested on her, I was struck by the rare beauty of her form, and by the unaffected grace of her attitude. Her figure was tall, yet not too tall; comely and well-developed, yet not fat; her head set on her shoulders with an easy, pliant firmness; her waist, perfection in the eyes of a man, for it occupied its natural place, it filled out its natural circle, it was visibly and delightfully undeformed by stays. She had not heard my entrance into the room; and I allowed myself the luxury of admiring her for a moment, before I moved one of the chairs near me, as the least embarrassing means of attracting her attention. She turned towards me immediately. The easy elegance of every movement of her limbs and body as soon as she began to advance from the far end of the room, set me in a flutter of expectation to see her face clearly. She left the window—and I said to myself, The lady is dark. She moved forward a few steps—and I said to myself, The lady is young. She approached nearer—and I said to myself (with a sense of surprise which words fail me to express), The lady is ugly!
>
> Never was the old conventional maxim, that Nature cannot err, more flatly contradicted—never was the fair promise of a lovely figure more strangely and startlingly belied by the face and head

that crowned it. The lady's complexion was almost swarthy, and the dark down on her upper lip was almost a moustache. She had a large, firm, masculine mouth and jaw; prominent, piercing, resolute brown eyes; and thick, coal-black hair, growing unusually low down on her forehead. Her expression—bright, frank, and intelligent—appeared, while she was silent, to be altogether wanting in those feminine attractions of gentleness and pliability, without which the beauty of the handsomest woman alive is beauty incomplete. To see such a face as this set on shoulders that a sculptor would have longed to model—to be charmed by the modest graces of action through which the symmetrical limbs betrayed their beauty when they moved, and then to be almost repelled by the masculine form and masculine look of the features in which the perfectly shaped figure ended—was to feel a sensation oddly akin to the helpless discomfort familiar to us all in sleep, when we recognize yet cannot reconcile the anomalies and contradictions of a dream.

Though the passage develops all the rhetorical suspense of a strip-tease, in which, as Barthes has written, "the entire excitation takes refuge in the hope of seeing the sexual organ" (*The Pleasure of the Text*, trans. Richard Miller), the place of the latter seems strangely occupied here by Marian's "head and face." What Barthes calls the "schoolboy's dream" turns into a far less euphoric "sensation" of "helpless discomfort" when, at the climactic moment of unveiling, the woman's head virtually proves her a man in drag. Banal as this kind of revelation has become in our culture (where it is ritualized in a variety of spectacles, jokes, and folkloric anecdotes), it never ceases to be consumed, as here, "with a sense of surprise." The surprise would perhaps better be understood as a stubborn refusal to recognize how unsurprising it is that an obsessively phallocentric system of sexual difference, always and everywhere on the lookout for its founding attribute (if only in the case of women to make sure it isn't there) should sometimes, as though overcome by eyestrain, find this attribute even in its absence. Yet Walter's sense of surprise exceeds the more or less conscious ruse that serves to divorce his quasi-heterosexual identity from its quasi-homosexual genealogy. Surprise is also the text's figure for the violence of that double metamorphosis which overtakes this identity and thus calls for such a ruse. Marian's sudden transformation from the object that Walter looks at into the subject whose "piercing" eyes might look back at him—look at his back—simultaneously entails the reverse transformation in him. In a context, then, where the positions of subject and object are respectively gendered as male and female, and where the relation between them is eroticized accordingly, the nature of Walter's surprise, "which words fail [him] to express," may go without saying. Necessarily, his recovery has recourse to the affect of *repulsion*, which will reinstate the distance that surprise has momentarily abolished between him and the amphibolous figure of the "masculine woman." Walter's recoil carries the "instinctive" proof—more than welcome after his unnerving encounter with the woman in white—both of his competence in a male code of sexual signs (which Marian's monstrosity, far from compromising, offers the occasion for rehearsing and confirming) and of his own stable, unambiguous position in that code (as a man who judges with "the eyes of a man"). On such a basis, he succeeds in containing his potentially disturbing vision within the assured comic effects ("The lady was ugly!") of a worldly raconteur to whom Marian's sexual anomalousness presents no threat of contagion.

For Marian's "masculine look" may be seen in two ways, as not just what poses the problems she embodies, but also what resolves it. Precisely in her "masculinity," she incarnates that wit which men familiarly direct against women who are "altogether wanting in those feminine attractions of gentleness and pliability." We notice, for a characteristic example of such wit, that someone—an erring Nature, if not the anxious drawing-master who faithfully copies Nature's work—*has drawn a moustache on her*. However perturbed Walter may be that Marian lacks the lack, he is also plainly gratified to take inventory of the numerous phallic signs on her person, as though these could finally only mock the absence of the penile referent. The well-known anxiety attaching to male jokes about the "masculine woman" in no way extenuates the strategy that it energizes: which is to render the woman who is their target external to the system of sexual difference that gets along quite well without her. Unable to compete (when the chaps are down), she cannot be "male"; unable to attract (as though the derisive signs remained persuasive after all), neither can she be "female." What is thereby neutralized, in the root as well as derived senses of the word, is any sexuality—female and/or male—which cannot be reduced to either term of a phallic binarism.

Yet Walter's aggressive indifference to Marian as a relevant sexual counter is eventually belied when Count Fosco—who is as helpful in acting out the implications of Walter's fantasy here as he is in the case of Laura—takes a pronounced, even violent erotic interest in her. How does this ugly, neutered woman come to be targeted for what, as we have seen, the novel encodes as "rape"? We noticed that, though Walter's portrait of Marian abounds in phallic *signs*, it nowhere offers a phallic *symbol*: only later, too late, will the novelist hand her "the horrid heavy man's umbrella." Where, then, *is* the phallus so bountifully signified? If it isn't *on* Marian, whose unimpeachably curvilinear body (like the perfect waist that is its synecdoche) is "visibly and delightfully undeformed by stays," then it must be *in* her, the iron in the soul that manifests itself only through the soul's traditional windows: those "prominent, piercing, resolute brown eyes" with their "masculine look." (Even her moustache suggests that the masculine signs defacing her body have pushed through from within.) Psychoanalysis and the male adolescent alike are familiar with the castration fantasy in which—act one—the penis gets "locked" in the vagina during intercourse and—act two—having broken off, remains inside the female body. *Anima virilis in corpore muliebri inclusa:* Marian is not just the "dog" that no self-respecting male adolescent would be "caught with"; she is also—the "evidence" for act one of course being canine—the dog that he would not be caught *in*. (The novel's elaborate canine thematics more than justify this slang usage, which of course postdates it. Marian's first lesson at Blackwater Park, for instance, involves being instructed in the destiny of dogs there. A housemaid thus accounts to her for the wounded dog found in the boat-house: " 'Bless you, miss! Baxter's the keeper, and when he finds strange dogs hunting about, he takes and shoots 'em. It's keeper's dooty, miss. I think that dog will die. Here's where he's been shot, ain't it? That's Baxter's doings, that is. Baxter's doings, miss, and Baxter's dooty.' " "Baxter's" doings indeed: if the keeper is little more than a name in the novel, the name nonetheless contains almost all the elements in the novel's representation of female containment. For one thing, the suffix *-ster* originally designates a specifically feminine agency [in Old English, a "baxter" means a female baker]: whence perhaps Baxter's violence, as though he were protesting the femininity latently inscribed in his name. For another, in the context of the novel's insistence on "the touch from behind," the name would also signify the person who handles [its gender-inflection keeps us from quite saying "manhandles"] the hinder part of the body.) As the focus of fears of *male* incarceration, Marian's body becomes the operational theatre for the two tactics of "men's liberation" that usually respond to these fears. She is firmly abandoned by Walter's erotic interest and forcibly seduced by Fosco's. Both tactics cohere in a single strategy, since perhaps the most important fantasy feature of rape is the reaffirmation of the rapist's unimpaired capacity to withdraw, the integrity of his body (if not his victim's) recovered intact. (Fosco, we recall, returns to Marian the journal he has indelibly signed, and she, evidently, is stuck with it.) (In this context one must read Fosco's dandiacal lament after the episode where—"to the astonishment of all the men" who watch him—he successfully intimidates "a chained bloodhound—a beast so savage that the very groom who feeds him keeps out of his reach": " 'Ah! my nice waist-coat! . . . Some of that brute's slobber has got on my pretty clean waist-coat!' ") As its sexual variant, seduction-and-abandonment would thus in both senses of the word "betray" the constitutive myth of the liberal (male) subject, whose human rights must include the freedom, as he pleases, to come and go.

The meaning of Marian's "rape" is of course further determined by another, better known figure of the *anima virilis:* the lesbian. "She will be *his* Laura instead of mine!," writes Marian of the bride of Limmeridge—having taken the precaution, however, of promoting rather this faint-hearted marriage to Sir Percival than the obvious love-match with Walter, as if already anticipating the consolation that an unhappy Lady Glyde will not fail to bring to her closet: "Oh, Marian! . . . promise you will never marry, and leave me. It is selfish to say so, but you are so much better off as a single woman—unless—unless you are very fond of your husband—but you won't be very fond of anybody but me, will you?" Important as it is not to censor the existence of erotic feeling between women in the text (in any of the ways this can be done, including a certain way of acknowledging it), it is perhaps more important to recognize that what would also get absorbed here under the name of lesbianism is a woman's unwillingness to lend her full co-operation to male appropriations of her, as though Marian's "gayness" were the only conceivable key to passages like the following:

> "Men! They are the enemies of our innocence and our peace
> they drag us away from our parents' love and our sisters' friend-
> ship—they take us body and soul to themselves, and fasten our
> helpless lives to theirs as they chain up a dog to his kennel. And
> what does the best of them give us in return? Let me go, Laura—
> I'm mad when I think of it!"

In general, the "lesbianism" contextualized in *The Woman in White* amounts mainly to a male charge, in which the accusation is hard to dissociate from the excitation. In particular, the novel most effectively renders Marian "lesbian" in the sense that it makes her suffer the regular fate of the lesbian in male representations: who defiantly bides her time with women until the inevitable and irrevocable heterosexual initiation that she, if no one else, may not have known that she always wanted. One recalls this exchange from *Goldfinger*, after James Bond has seduced Pussy Galore: "He said, 'They told me you only liked women.' She said, 'I never met a man before.' " Not dissimilarly, Marian's "half-willing, half-unwilling liking for the Count"—what in a rape trial would be called her "complicity"—provides the novel's compelling, compulsive proof of the male erotic power that operates even and especially where it is denied. "I am almost afraid to confess it, even to these secret pages. The man has interested me, has attracted me, has forced me to like him." Fosco's eyes "have at times a clear, cold, beautiful, irresistible glitter in them which forces me to look at him, and yet causes me sensations, when I do look, which I would rather not feel." Like Pussy Bonded, Marian Foscoed (hearing the metathesis in the name of the "wily Italian," we need not even consider resorting to what Freud called Schreber's "shamefaced" elision) is a changed woman. If it is not her ultimate destiny to roll up the Count's endless cigarettes "with the look of mute submissive inquiry which we are all familiar with in the eyes of a faithful dog," as she abjectly fantasizes, he has nonetheless well trained her to be another man's best friend. "What a woman's hands *are* fit for," she tells Walter, whom she entrusts with her avengement, "early and late, these hands of mine shall do. . . . It's my weakness that cries, not me. The house-work shall conquer it, if *I* can't." The old signs of

Marian's "masculinity"—the hands that were "as awkward as a man's," the tears that came "almost like men's"—now realize what had always been their implied potential to attest a "weakness" that (like the housework she takes on "as her own right") refeminizes her. In the novel's last image, almost exactly according to the proper Freudian resolution of *Penisneid,* Marian is able to "rise" only on condition that she "hold up" Walter's son and heir "kicking and crowing in her arms." Almost exactly, but not quite, since the child is not of course her own. It is as though the woman whom Fosco "rapes" and the woman whom Walter "neuters" prove finally one and the same odd thing—as though, in other words, a woman's hetero-sexuality ("hetero-" indeed) were no sexuality of hers.

Even as the victim of terrific male aggression, however, Marian is simultaneously the beneficiary of considerable male admiration. Walter aptly imagines that she "would have secured the respect of the most au-dacious man breathing," and apart from Fosco, who eventually embodies that hypothetical man, apart even from Walter, who at once finds in the ugly lady an old friend, the novelist himself unexceptionally portrays Mar-ian as a "positive," immensely likable character. Demonstrably, then, *The Woman in White* accords a far warmer welcome to the fantasy of the man-in-the-woman (which, fully personified, the novel works through to a nar-rative resolution) than to the apparently complementary fantasy of the woman-in-the-man (which, as we have seen, the novel only broaches ob-scurely, in the blind spot of "non-recognition" between textual thematics and male reading bodies). This is doubtless because the *anima virilis* in-cludes, in addition to the aspects aforementioned, a male identification. "I don't think much of my own sex," Marian admits to Walter on their first meeting; "no woman does think much of her own sex, though few of them confess it as freely as I do." As though misogyny were primarily a female phenomenon and as such justified the male phenomenon that ventrilo-quially might go without saying, Marian's voice becomes the novel's prin-cipal articulation of that traditional code according to which women are quarrelsome, chattering, capricious, superstitious, inaccurate, unable to draw or play billiards. For all the pluck that it inspires, Marian's male identification consistently vouches for her female dependency. Thus, de-termined "on justifying the Count's opinion of [her] courage and sharp-ness," she bravely makes her night-crawl onto the eaves of the house at Blackwater to overhear Fosco's conversation with Sir Percival. But—per-haps because, as the male-identified woman necessarily comes to think, her "courage was only a woman's courage after all"—this determination obliges her to remove "the white and cumbersome parts of [her] under-clothing" and so to prepare herself for the violation that, on one way of looking at it, follows soon afterwards, but that, on another, has already succeeded. If the woman-in-the-man requires his *keeping her* inside him, the man-in-the-woman takes for granted her *letting him* inside her. The sexual difference that the former endangers, the latter reaffirms: by determining a single view of women—men's—to which women accede in the course of constructing a male-identified femininity. Fosco "flatters" Marian's vanity "by talking to [her] as seriously and sensibly as if [she were] a man," and she more than returns the favour by addressing Fosco, Walter, and the male reader on the same premise, reassuring all concerned that even the woman who speaks as "freely" as a man remains the prolocutor of a masculist discourse that keeps her in place. Finally, therefore, Marian may be taken to suggest how the novel envisions that *female* reader whom, though it nominally ignores, it has always taken into practical account. For the same sensation effects that "feminize" the male reading body also (the quotation marks are still indispensable) "feminize" the female: with the difference that this feminization is construed in the one case to threaten sexual identity and in the other to confirm it. Implicitly, that is, the text glosses the female reader's sensationalized body in exactly the terms of Marian's erotic responsiveness to Fosco: as the corporal confession of a "femininity" whose conception is all but exhausted in providing the unmarked term in opposition to a thus replenished "masculinity." If only on its own terms (though, when one is trembling, these terms may be hard to shake), the sensation novel constitutes proof of women's inability, as Marian puts it, to "resist a man's tongue when he knows how to speak to them" and especially, we might add with Marian emblematically in mind, when he knows how to speak through them.

IV

Precisely in so far as it does not fail, the project of confining or containing the woman cannot succeed in achieving narrative quiescence or closure. Safely shut up in the various ways we have considered, women cease being active participants in the drama that nonetheless remains to be played out (for over a hundred pages) "man to man." For when the text produces the configuration of incarcerated femininity, it simultaneously cathects the congruent configuration of phobic male homoeroticism: thus, for instance, its "paradoxical" rendering of Fosco, who is at once "a man who could tame anything" and "a fat St Cecilia masquerading in male attire." Accordingly, the novel needs to supplement its misogynistic plot with a misanthropic one, in which it will detail the frightening, even calamitous consequences of unmediated relations between men, thereby administering to its hero an aversion therapy calculated to issue in a renunciation of what Eve Kosofsky Sedgwick has called "male homosocial desire," or in a liberation from what, with a more carceral but no less erotic shade of meaning, we might also call male bonds. After Sedgwick's (here, actively) inspiring demonstration that men's desire for men is the very motor of patriarchally given social structures, it might seem implausible even to entertain the possibility of such a renunciation or liberation, which would amount to a withdrawal from the social *tout court*. Yet this is apparently what the endings of many nineteenth-century novels paradigmatically stage: the hero's thorough-going disenchantment with the (homo)social, from which he is resigned to isolate himself. By and large, nineteenth-century fiction is no less heavily invested than Sedgwick's analysis of it in luridly portraying the dysphoric effects—particularly on men—of homosocial desire, and this fact must raise the question of the status of such effects within the general rhetorical strategy of the fiction that cultivates them. If, for example, *The Woman in White* obligingly constitutes a "pathology" of male homosocial desire, this is evidently not because the novel shares, say, Sedgwick's ambition to formulate a feminist/gay critique of homophobically patriarchal structure; but neither is it because the novel so naively embraces this structure that it recounts-without-counting the latter's psychological costs. Rather, as we will see, the novel puts its homosocial pathology in the service of promoting a familiar homosocial cure: a cure that has the effect of a renunciation of men's desire for men only because, in this treated form, and by contrast, such desire exists in a "normal" or relatively silent state.

The novel's most obvious specimen of an abnormal male homosocial *Bund*—the one it adduces at the end, as though at last to consolidate the freely floating homoerotics of the text and thus to name and contain them—is that secret Italian political association which (Walter is quite correct in saying) is "sufficiently individualized" for his purposes if he calls it, simply, "The Brotherhood." The novel tolerates this exotic freemasonry on two ideological conditions, which, if they were not so inveterately combined in a policy of quarantine, might otherwise strike us as incompatible. On the one hand, The Brotherhood owes its existence to the political adolescence of Italy, to which, in case the point is lost, Pesca correlates his own immaturity when he became a member. The advanced nation as well as the enlightened parent may rest assured imagining that The Brotherhood is only a phase that in the normal course of political or personal development will be superseded. Yet on the other hand, no possible course of development can retrieve someone once he has been admitted into this society of fellows and bears its "secret mark," which, like his membership, lasts for life. Strange as it may be for Walter to learn that one of his best friends belongs to the secret fraternity, the revelation occasions no alarm (lest, for instance, an attempt be made to initiate *him*), since the pathos of Pesca's case is well cultivated by Pesca himself, who admits to suffering still from those youthful impulses ("I try to forget them—and they will not forget *me!*") which forever condemn him to consort in such dubious company. (In the usual distribution of roles, Walter's mother, but not his sullenly nubile sister, has welcomed Pesca into the household.) A congenial point is borne in the activities of The Brotherhood itself, whose in-house purges are the "outside" world's best protection against it. Walter's sword need never cross with Fosco's—a mercy given the impressive estimates we are invited to make of the "length" of the latter—in the duel that "other vengeance" has rendered unnecessary. The Brotherhood has mortally called the Count to "the day of reckoning"—not for his offences against Walter, but for his all-too-promiscuous fraternizing within and without its organization. The wound struck "exactly over his heart" hints broadly at the "passional" nature of the crime in which—for which—Fosco is murdered. Thus, at the exhibition of his naked and knifed corpse (the former "Napoleon," now, as it were, the dead Marat, and the rueful Parisian morgue, also as it were, the gayer continental baths), we hear the curator's familiarly excited double discourse, in which a flushed moralism never quite manages to pacify the sheer erotic fascination that hence remains available to incite it: "There he lay, unowned, unknown, exposed to the flippant curiosity of a French mob! There was the dreadful end of that long life of degraded ability and heartless crime! Hushed in the sublime repose of death, the broad, firm, massive face and head fronted us so grandly that the chattering Frenchwomen about me lifted their hands in admiration, and cried in shrill chorus, 'Ah, what a handsome man!' "

"And all men kill the thing they love": what is often taken for Wilde's gay depressiveness (though in Reading Gaol, what else is left to intelligence but to read its prison?) provides a not-so-oddly apt formula for the novel's pathology of male bonds, whose godforsaken expression coincides with its providential punishment in death. (Besides the murder of Fosco, we may cite the "suicide" of his boon companion: it is no accident that, having locked himself in the vestry, Sir Percival accidentally sets it on fire.) A couple of reasons obtain for bringing out, as I have pseudo-anachronistically been doing, the continuities between the novel's representation of "brotherhood" and our media's no less sensational staging of male homosexuality. One would be to begin measuring the extent to which nineteenth-century culture has contributed to the formation of the context in which an uncloseted gayness is popularly determined. (Thus, the homophobic virulence that dispreads in rivalrous response to homosexual immunodeficiency is "only" the most recent, extreme, and potentially catastrophic figure of an interpretative framework that precedes AIDS by well over a century.) Another would be to recognize that if our culture can only "think" male homosexual desire within a practice of aversion therapy, this is because—for a long while and with apparently greater efficacy—it has routinely subjected male homosocial desire to the same treatment.

Representationally, this treatment consists of a diptych, in which the baleful images of homosocial apocalypse on one panel confront a comparatively cheering family portrait on the other. The fact that Fosco and Sir Percival are both married is far from making them what *The Woman in White* understands by family men. For as the novel's final tableau makes abundantly clear, what is distinctively cheering about the family portrait is less the connection between husband and wife (Marian, not Laura, holds up his son to Walter's charmed gaze) than the bond between father and son. Thus, the aim of what we have called aversion therapy is not to redirect men's desire for men onto women, but, through women, onto boys: that is, to privatize homosocial desire within the middle-class nuclear family, where it takes the "normal" shape of an Oedipal triangle. Yet the twinned projects whose achievement the novel makes *precede* the establishment of a family curiously correspond to what, at least since Freud's summation of nineteenth-century culture, we may recognize as the family's own defining features: (1) shut up the woman—or, in the rivalry between father and son of which she is the object, keep mother from becoming the subject of a desire of her own; and (2) turn from the man—or, in that same rivalry, develop an aversion therapy for home use. The foundation of the Hartright family, therefore, cannot put an end to the brutalities of its prehistory, nor will these brutalities have dialectically prepared the way for a civilizing familialism, since the violent workings of an Oedipal family organization (Sir Percival is a much older man than Walter, and so forth) have implicitly generated the narrative that this organization is explicitly constituted to conclude. At the end, then, the novel has merely discovered its beginning, in the family matrix where such violence has acquired its specific structure and whence it has made its fearful *entrée dans le monde*. "And there is more where that came from," if only because where that came from is also where that eventually returns. As though refusing to cease shocking us, even where it least surprises us, *The Woman in White* "ends" only by recurring to that family circle which will continue to relay—with no end in sight—a plot that still takes many people's breath away. (Like the woman's, or the homosexual's, or [for she has figured in both roles] Marian's: "Let Marian end our Story," but—these are the text's last words, as well as Walter's—what follows is dead silence.)

V

Note on the author's body: shortly after I began writing this essay, the muscles on my shoulders and back went into spasm. Referring this thoracic pain to other matters (excessive working out, an affair of the heart) than the work on which it continually interrupted my progress, I consulted physical and psychological therapists. Only when the former at last pronounced that a rib was out of place (which may have been what the latter was getting at when he diagnosed, on the insurance form, a personality disorder), was I willing to entertain the possibility that I had become, in relation to my own writing, an improbably pat case of hysteria. Now that a practised hand has put the fugitive rib back into its cage, my spine tingles to have borne out my assumption of that "non-recognition" which evidently also obtains between the somatics of writing and what is written about. I am less pleased (though still thrilled) to understand that, on the same assumption, what dumbfounds me also lays the foundation for my dumbness: too stupid to utter what has already been said in the interaction between body and text, and in the traces of that interaction within body or text; and too mute to do more than designate the crucial task of identifying in this writing the equivocal places where "sensation" has gone, not to say love.

George MacDonald and the Tender Grandmother

Humphrey Carpenter

On July 9, 1862, Charles Dodgson wrote in his diary: "To Tudor Lodge, where I met Mr MacDonald coming out. I walked a mile or so with him, on his way to a publisher, with the MS. of his fairy tale "The Light Princess" in which he showed me some exquisite drawings by Hughes."

It is rather striking coincidence that Dodgson, who only a few days earlier had told the story of *Alice* to the Liddell children, should happen to call on George MacDonald at his London home on the morning when MacDonald was taking to the publisher the short story that began his career as a children's writer. Charles Kingsley, meanwhile, was writing *The Water-Babies*. In other words, these three men began to make their contributions to children's literature within weeks of each other. Moreover, all three were ministers of religion—if of very different types—and all three had intense scientific or mathematical interests. A pattern begins to emerge, particularly when we realise that religious uncertainty, a thread which seems to run through *The Water-Babies* and *Alice*, played a central part in the life of George MacDonald.

He was born at Huntly in Aberdeenshire in 1824, and claimed descent from a MacDonald who escaped the massacre of the clan by the Campbells at Glencoe in 1692. His great-grandfather was a piper in the 1745 rebellion, and fought at Culloden. The piper's son, George's grandfather, founded a spinning factory and bleaching business at Huntly, on the River Bogie—an appropriate setting for the childhood of a boy whose writings were largely to concern water and bogeys. But by the time George was born, the Industrial Revolution had made the family businesses obsolete and unprofitable, and his father had become a tenant farmer. The family was

From *Secret Gardens: A Study of the Golden Age of Children's Literature.* © 1985 by Humphrey Carpenter. Allen & Unwin, 1985.

conscious of its social position: George and his three brothers were not allowed to speak the Aberdeenshire dialect at table or before their elders, although among themselves and with social inferiors they would lapse into the vernacular. MacDonald's novels would, in time, help to establish what has been called the "Kailyard" school of literature, with their homely picture of Scottish village and small-town life. But he can scarcely be called a deeply Scottish writer: he wrote for the English public, and when he included Scottish dialect in his books he did so self-consciously. When writing from the depths of his imagination, in his fantasies, he inhabited a country of the mind which had nothing to do with Scotland—except with regard to the religious and spiritual questions which hung over it. His paternal grand-mother had left the parish church and taken herself to the ferociously Calvinistic "Missionar Kirk," and Calvinism was the *datum* of George's religious experience.

His mother, invalided for many years with tuberculosis, died when he was eight, and at least one critic has used this fact to interpret all Mac-Donald's fiction. Certainly mother-figures haunt his stories, and one cannot doubt that the loss affected him deeply: all his life he treasured a letter written by her, in which she described her regret at having to wean him when he was only a few weeks old. But one should not press this Freudian interpretation of his imagination too hard, at least not to the point of de-ducing that he hated and feared his father. The very opposite seems to have been true: the father, not apparently a stern Calvinist in character, seems to have run a happy home after his wife's death, allowing the four boys (of whom George was the second) to run about the place as they wished; and when he eventually remarried, seven years later, he chose a wife who is reported to have been unfailingly kind and loving to the boys. George said that he "had never asked his father for anything . . . but it was given," and there are strikingly lovable fathers in his stories: Diamond's kindly father, Joseph, in *At the Back of the North Wind*; and, in the Curdie books, Peter the miner (Curdie's own father) and Irene's "King-papa," who is seen more than once stooping down from his great white horse to enfold his child in his arms, a memorable image of strong and loving fatherhood. There is a similarly loving father in MacDonald's near-autobiographical novel *Ranald Bannerman's Boyhood*.

In fact, in the childhood years after the death of his mother, George seems to have been full of high spirits. At about the age of twelve he wrote to his father that

> tho' I would be sorry to displease you in any way, yet I must tell you that the sea is my delight and that I wish to go to it as soon as possible, and I hope that you will not use your parental au-thority to prevent me, as you undoubtedly can.

We know almost nothing about his childhood reading matter, but perhaps the urge to leave home and travel was fostered by *The Pilgrim's Progress*, a favourite book all his life, and one which profoundly influenced his fantasy writing.

He won a bursary to King's College, Aberdeen, where he found himself particularly drawn into the study of natural science, and for a time thought of becoming a chemist or a doctor. He was attracted less by scientific knowledge itself than by its metaphysical implications. One may assume there is autobiography in the passage in his fantasy novel *Lilith* where the narrator says of his obsession with scientific studies:

> It was chiefly the wonder they woke that drew me. I was constantly seeing, and on the outlook to see, strange analogies, not only between the facts of different sciences of the same order, or between physical and metaphysical facts, but between physical hypotheses and suggestions glimmering out of the metaphysical dreams into which I was in the habit of falling. I was at the same time much given to a premature indulgence of the impulse to turn hypothesis into theory.

This sounds like a description of the mind of a writer of science fiction, and indeed many of MacDonald's stories border on that genre or actually cross into it. *Lilith* itself, for example, touches on the notion of several different worlds or time zones co-existing on the same physical plane; when first published (in 1895) it was read with great interest by H. G. Wells, who had simultaneously explored the same notion in *The Time Machine*, published the same year.

MacDonald's absorption in metaphysical speculation perhaps dates from, and was certainly encouraged by, a vacation from his studies at Aberdeen, when he took a job cataloguing a neglected library in some great mansion or castle in the far north of Scotland. This place has never been identified, but it became a permanent feature of his imagination, and was undoubtedly the original of Princess Irene's home in *The Princess and the Goblin*, "a large house, half castle, half farmhouse, on the side of [a] mountain, about halfway between its base and its peak." Such a house becomes a symbol, in this novel and in others of MacDonald's tales, for the universe itself—too large to be explored thoroughly by anyone, containing forgotten stairs and turrets and distant, dusty rooms, not to mention dark unknowable cellars; both frightening and, in its middle regions, homelike and comforting. The image of the library-within-a-castle recurs too; in *Lilith*, the story into which, at the end of his life, MacDonald tried to pack all his metaphysical obsessions, the character of Adam himself, the first man, takes the form of Mr. Raven, a librarian in a castle.

What MacDonald found in that library galvanised his imagination. It was there that he read many of the English poets for the first time, but he also knew German, and the library's owner had stocked the shelves with the German Romantic writers of the late eighteenth and early nineteenth centuries. This led him to discover E. T. A. Hoffmann, author of many ornate fairy stories, such as the tale of Coppelia, the doll who comes alive; La Motte Fouqué, whose tale of Undine the water sprite MacDonald thought "the most beautiful" of all fairy stories; and "Novalis," the poet Friedrich von Hardenberg, whose own life was as tragically romantic as his verse—at the age of twenty-two he fell in love with a twelve-year-old girl, who not long afterwards died of tuberculosis. Of these three writers, Novalis was the one who exercised the most powerful attraction to MacDonald. He set himself to making translations of Novalis's poems, and his own first prose work, *Phantastes*, was a ractical demonstration of Novalis's principle of fantasy writing, itself quoted as an epigraph to MacDonald's book:

> . . . narratives without coherence but rather with association like dreams . . . [which] can at best have an allegorical meaning in general, and an indirect effect like music.

Very probably within the same library MacDonald found the works of Swedenborg, which were certainly to influence his metaphysical-scientific speculations. Possibly it was now too that he first read the writings of the late sixteenth-century German mystic Jacob Boehme, from whom he was to derive many ideas found in his fantasy stories: among them, that of water as "the primordial principle of nature," and the notion of a perpetual state of evolution within the created universe, so that creatures may evolve upwards towards God, or downwards. So, in MacDonald's stories, we have the air-fish in "The Golden Key" which, as a reward for goodness, is cooked and eaten but in the process becomes a higher being, "a lovely little creature in human shape, with large white wings"; and the red worm in *Lilith*, which Mr Raven plucks from the ground and tosses in the air: "It spread great wings, gorgeous in red and black, and soared aloft." And there are also the Uglies in *The Princess and Curdie*, human beings relegated to the shapes of grotesque beasts as a punishment, and, in *The Princess and the Goblin*, the goblins themselves, who were once "very like other people," but in consequence of spiritual corruption have become "ludicrously grotesque both in face and form." MacDonald, in other words, explored the idea that Kingsley had touched on in *The Water-Babies*—that souls make bodies, and outward appearances indicate inward spiritual states. It was an ingenious answer of the imagination to Darwin.

Alongside such discoveries as Novalis and Boehme, the English poets may have seemed a little tame to someone of MacDonald's turn of mind, though one can see from *Phantastes* that he digested Spenser eagerly enough. And Blake made a deep mark on him; in later years there hung in his study an engraving, taken from Blake, of an aged man entering a tomb, and the same man emerging from it young, vigorous, and radiant. He adapted the same picture for his bookplate, and the notion of death not as an end but as a process of cleansing and revitalising runs through his stories. Anodos and Mr Vane, heroes of *Phantastes* and *Lilith*, both die to rise again, and Diamond's death at the end of *At the Back of the North Wind* is obviously a prelude to his return to the North Wind's mysterious country (Purgatory). The cleansing fire of roses in the Curdie books, administered by the old Princess, who is the nearest MacDonald came to a representation of God, is similarly purgatorial. Here, of course, we are in Dante's territory, and MacDonald absorbed the *Divine Comedy* deeply. It provides much of the structure of *Lilith* and *The Golden Key*, and is referred to openly in *At the Back of the North Wind*.

Inevitably, the young George MacDonald, having discovered this rich literary hoard in the castle library, began to write poetry. His son Greville describes his father's first efforts as "so weird and obscure that it is difficult to detect their motive"; we know that the dominant mood of them was that of gothic gloom and a romanticised death-wish—a contemporary at Aberdeen speaks of MacDonald walking up and down the seashore, "addressing the sea and the waves and the storm," and he was in the habit of saying, "I wish we were all dead." There are hints here of the destructiveness that was eventually to dominate his writing. But he also got on efficiently with the business of earning a living.

He went south and took a tutorship with a Congregationalist family in London, and soon afterwards became engaged to a girl whose family were of the same religious persuasion—Louisa Powell, daughter of a leather merchant. He was to make what seems to have been a very happy marriage with her, but one cannot help speculating about his romantic-sexual nature. Love plays a strikingly large part in his fantasy stories—striking because it is by no means an essential element in the genre (for example, Tolkien and C. S. Lewis, in many respects close to MacDonald, managed almost entirely without it in their books). It is usually one of two kinds: the love of a child or childlike person for a maternal figure (Diamond for the North Wind, Irene and Curdie for the old princess, and many similar instances in the shorter fairy stories), or—and this is just as striking—the love of child for child. MacDonald is one of the very few children's authors who make a success of portraying romantic feelings between a boy and a girl. Irene and Curdie are strongly attracted to each other from their first meeting in *The Princess and the Goblin*, and MacDonald's unselfconscious description of this is paralleled by many instances in his other tales: Tangle and Mossy's love for each other in "The Golden Key," Colin's love for a girl stolen by the fairies in "The Carasoyn," Diamond's affection for the crossing-sweeper Nanny in *At the Back of the North Wind*, to cite just a few. Even more striking is the love of the adult hero, Mr Vane, for the motherly child Lona in *Lilith*.

Her hair was much longer, and she was become almost a woman, but not one beauty of childhood had she outgrown. When first we met after our long separation, she laid down her infant, put her arms round my neck, and clung to me silent, her face glowing with gladness; the child whimpered; she sprang to him, and had him in her bosom instantly. To see her with any thoughtless, obstinate, or irritable little one, was to think of a tender grand-mother. I seemed to have known her for ages—for always—from before time began! I hardly remembered my mother, but in my mind's eye she now looked like Lona; and if I imagined sister or child, invariably she had the face of Lona! My every imagination flew to her; she was my heart's wife!

"A tender grandmother": not "a tender mother." The difference may seem slight, almost casual, but it is not. Again and again the women who dominate MacDonald's books are not mother-figures so much as grand-mother-figures. His very first work of prose fiction, *Phantastes,* opens with its hero discovering in a locked drawer of an old desk a tiny fairy-figure who grows in a moment into a beautiful full-sized woman; he is drawn to her beauty "by an attraction as incomprehensible," but she warns him:

> "Foolish boy, if you could touch me, I should hurt you. Besides, I was two hundred and thirty-seven years old, last Midsummer eve; and a man must not fall in love with his grandmother, you know."

This grandmother-fairy is the first of a long line of such beings in Mac-Donald's stories, the two most notable being the old Princess in the Curdie books, and the North Wind. Each is aged, indeed timeless; each can shrink to child-size, and the next moment stand giantlike and terrible. Within the terms of the stories such beings are expressions of the nature of God or Providence, but one cannot help supposing that the grandmother-figure who can also become a child had a private psychological meaning for MacDonald. It seems impossible to guess what that was; one can only note that his wife was two years older than him, and seems to have treated him largely with amused maternal (even grand-maternal) tolerance; that he was especially deeply attached to his daughter Lilia, and—perhaps most strik-ing—that in 1872 he arranged for John Ruskin to meet the adolescent Rose La Touche secretly at the MacDonald house, despite the fact that Rose's parents had forbidden such a meeting, and that most people considered Ruskin to be sexually abnormal. Did he share something of Ruskin's (and Dodgson's, and Novalis's) obsession with the beauty of young girls? Was this one of the poles of his romantic-sexual feelings, and was the other a need for a grandmotherly love?

Soon after arriving in London he decided that he should become a Congregational minister; not, apparently, because he had a firm religious faith but because this seemed a way of finding one. He spoke of himself, in a letter to his father, as "always searching for faith in place of contem-plating the truths of the gospel which produce faith," and in this respect he remained entirely Protestant throughout his life. In other ways, though, he had a more Catholic, sacramental imagination. His stories deal with spiritual transformations achieved through sacramental means (baptismal immersions in water, cleansing fires, and suchlike), and bread and wine feature often in them; Curdie, who in *The Princess and Curdie* has become somewhat Christ-like, cures the weak and poisoned king with a diet of fresh bread and good wine (as opposed to the adulterated wine the corrupt court has been giving him). The one religious state of mind MacDonald never experienced was secure orthodoxy; his books show how he was constantly in search of some new spiritual experience which would test him, and the few references in them to conventional religion are chiefly contemptuous. The preacher in *The Princess and Curdie* is described as a "sermon-pump," devoted to upholding the rottenness of the secular state; and one may find a similar notion in *Lilith*, where there is a description of the Bags, a race of grotesque giants, worshipping "the biggest and fattest of them,"

> so proud that nobody can see him; and the giants go to his house at certain times, and call out to him, and tell him how fat he is, and beg him to make them strong and eat more and grow fat like him.

One can find the same sort of contempt for official or organised religion in MacDonald's realistic adult novels; for example the preacher to the London congregation in *David Elginbrod* is portrayed as chiefly interested in keeping his rich parishioners happy.

MacDonald's chief religious difficulty has usually been represented, by those who have written about him, as an inability to accept the Calvinist doctrine that only the elect will achieve salvation, while the rest of humanity will be damned. MacDonald, it is said, was fretting at the Calvinist chains of his childhood. Certainly this is true as far as it goes, and his failure as a minister was due most obviously to this doctrinal problem. He was appointed to a Congregational chapel at Arundel in Sussex, but was soon in trouble with his hearers for expressing the opinion that the heathen might find salvation, and even that animals might go to heaven. His differences with them eventually led him to resign, and he and his family thereafter lived in various parts of England, sometimes supported by the charity of rich benefactors, while MacDonald made what he could by lecturing on science and literature, and by preaching where he could hire a hall. In the end he gave up being a nonconformist minister altogether, settled in London, and found some sort of sanctuary in the Church of England, among the congregation of Charles Kingsley's mentor F. D. Maurice. But whereas Kingsley had embraced Maurice's teaching because of its liberalism and social concern, MacDonald apparently found it acceptable to him because it approached his own view of the nature of good and evil.

He portrayed Maurice under thin disguise in *David Elginbrod,* where he said of him: "He believes entirely that God loves, yea *is* love, and, therefore, that hell itself must be subservient to that love, and but an embodiment of it." The notion of hell, and indeed of all evil, as an embodiment of God is pervasive in MacDonald's writing. Among the children's books, one may perceive it in *At the Back of the North Wind*, where North Wind performs an apparently evil action—sinking a ship—as part of the larger divine plan. It is the central notion in *The Wise Woman*, a children's novella written by MacDonald in the interval between his two Curdie books, which describes the sufferings imposed upon two selfish little girls by a "wise woman" who clearly represents God. The Curdie stories themselves, on the other hand, seem to deal with embodiments of evil which cannot be workings of the divine plan—the goblins beneath the mountain in *The Princess and the Goblin*, and the wicked courtiers in *The Princess and Curdie*. But both the goblins and courtiers are stagey, ridiculous villains, necessities of a rather crude plot rather than serious characterisations of evil. There must *be* villains, so that Curdie and Irene are in peril; but the point of the story is their reaction to that peril, and the trust and love that they come to put in the Godlike old princess, who is never there when they go and look for her, but always appears when she is least expected and most needed. By the end of MacDonald's life and *Lilith*, this notion that God is everything and everything is God (which he very probably first acquired from Boehme) had become explicit. Lilith herself, the demon creature who according to Jewish folklore was Adam's first wife, is in MacDonald's story both devil and god, temptress and eternal mother. There is no evil; and the reader of *Lilith* may feel that there is no good either.

Yet we should not suppose that MacDonald, turning his back on Calvinist theology and embracing a universe where "good" and "evil" were not true distinctions, had rejected the idea of the wicked receiving punishment. In fact the castigation of evil-doers plays a large part in his fiction. At times, indeed, he bears a resemblance to one of his wife's aunts, of whom it was said that "she could never lie comfortable in bed if she might not believe in hellfire and everlasting pains." Perhaps this element of Calvinism ran too deep in MacDonald to be eradicated by his changes of religious opinion; perhaps he simply had what we would now call a sadistic streak. At any rate he presents us in one story with a little girl who declares: "If I was a man, I would kill all the wicked people in the world," and this clearly has the author's approval. The old princess in the Curdie books, Godlike and all-loving as she is, nevertheless remarks that "There are plenty of bad things that want killing," and the punishments she metes out to the evil courtiers who have tried to poison Irene's king-father are about as unpleasant as anything in children's literature: one has his leg bitten to pieces, another has a finger twisted off, and MacDonald hints that even worse is going on. "The terrors of the imagination were fast yielding to those of sensuous experience," he says; a sentence that seems to relish physical pain. Even the saintly Curdie kills dogs by hitting them through the brain with his mattock, and disables the palace cook with the same instrument. *Lilith* and the short story "The Cruel Painter" contain a great deal of practical detail about vampirism, while the latter describes an artist whose delight is to depict terrible tortures on his canvases. The suspicion grows that this may be a portrait of MacDonald himself. Perhaps nastiest of all, because of the simplicity and apparent innocence of its style, is "The Giant's Heart," a short story about two children (the nauseatingly named Buffy-Bob and Tricksey-Wee) who torture a giant by squeezing drops of "spider-juice" on to his heart:

> The giant had given an awful roar of pain the moment they anointed his heart, and had fallen down in a fit. . . . The first words he uttered were,—
> "Oh, my heart! my heart! . . . "
> Here he fainted again; for Tricksey-Wee, finding the heart beginning to swell a little, had given it the least touch of spider-juice.

MacDonald began to make his name as a writer by publishing *Within and Without* (1855), a blank verse play describing the attempts of one Count Julian, a former monk, to reconcile earthly with heavenly love. Charles Kingsley was among its admirers. Next, in 1857, MacDonald spent a mere two months writing "a kind of fairy tale . . . in the hope that it will pay me better than the more evidently serious work." This was *Phantastes*, which did not prove a money-spinner, but was an act of self-discovery. In it, with astonishing sureness and fluency, he mapped out the imaginative territory which he would explore in closer detail in his later fantasy stories.

Phantastes is nowadays best known as the book which introduced C. S. Lewis to MacDonald's writings, and set him on his own course as a writer of fantasy. Lewis's admirers, coming to it hopefully, are often puzzled by its extraordinary style and content. Lewis spoke of it as "baptising" his imagination, which implies that it is a holy book. It is actually very unholy, but reading it is rather like experiencing some sort of total immersion, so that the baptismal metaphor is not entirely inappropriate.

A modern reader may suppose the book to be largely about sexuality, and in fact *Phantastes*, unlike most of MacDonald's writings, may be interpreted almost entirely in sexual terms. The hero Anodos, whose name is Greek for "pathless," is on his twenty-first birthday initiated by a fairy mother- (or grandmother-) figure into a Fairyland whose features and events seem to stand for sexual experience and a child's or young man's reactions to it. He is menaced by the masculine, perhaps father-like, Ash tree, but is saved by the maternal Beech (" ' Why, you baby!' said she, and kissed me with the sweetest kiss of winds and odours"). The experience of lying in her arms leaves him feeling "as if new-born." But he is tricked into the arms of the Maid of the Alder, who he has been told "will smother you with her web of hair, if you let her near you at night"; and this and subsequent experiences with other female inhabitants of Fairyland give Anodos a sense of guilt and pollution which seem to be symbolic of a young man's guilty reaction to sexuality. Later he comes to a strange palace, where, in a library (the library-in-the-castle), he reads of a land where children are born without conception and there is no physical love between the sexes; he also reads of a young man who can only see the woman he loves by means of a mirror. In the palace he discovers a womblike hall to which he returns again and again; later, he brings a female statue to life by chanting a startlingly erotic ballad to it, commanding each part of her body to come to life, from her feet gradually upwards:

> Rise the limbs, sedately sloping,
>   Strong and gentle, full and free;
> Soft and slow, like certain hoping,
>   Drawing nigh the broad firm knee . . .
> Temple columns, close combining,
>   Lift a holy mystery.

The whole of *Phantastes,* indeed, may be interpreted as being about the "holy mystery" of sex—with the possible exception of the climactic scene, where Anodos dies in the act of exposing a false religion whose god devours its worshippers; this would appear to be autobiography of a different sort, and may refer to MacDonald's resignation from his Arundel ministry.

In fact *Phantastes* is many things, and an exclusively sexual interpretation ignores many other layers of meaning—or at least, layers of implied meaning, for MacDonald was not usually an allegorist. He denied that *Phantastes* was an allegory, called it simply a "fairy tale," and elsewhere asserted that fairy stories such as he wrote did not have one specific meaning. He continued: "Everyone, however, who feels the story, will read its meaning after his own nature and development. . . . A genuine work of art must mean many things; the truer its art, the more things it will mean." MacDonald, in other words, wished to be a myth-maker rather than an allegorist. C. S. Lewis judged him to have succeeded in this more than any other modern writer, and indeed it is hard to think of any other nineteenth- or twentieth-century author who excelled him in sheer fertility of mythic imagination.

Not surprisingly, after *Phantastes,* which appeared in print in 1858, MacDonald found himself uncertain what to do next. He had poured everything into the book; where could he go next, and how could he make a living as a writer? No immediate answer was apparent, and he tried his hand at several projects which failed. Meanwhile *Phantastes* brought him a number of admirers. We do not know what C. L. Dodgson thought of it, but it was in the year after its publication that he first met MacDonald, and the book's reputation probably encouraged him to get to know its author. Though the two men had little in common as writers, there were points of correspondence. Was the original idea of *Through the Looking-Glass* possibly suggested by the lover-in-the-mirror story in *Phantastes?* (The young man in this story looks into the mirror and sees that the room reflected in it is his own room—and yet not his own.) MacDonald apparently had Lewis Carroll in mind when he wrote the short story "Cross Purposes" (1867), a rambling dreamlike tale about two children who wander into a very Wonderland-like fairy world—one of them is even called Alice. And did he take the mirror idea back again from Lewis Carroll in *Lilith*, where Vane the hero passes more than once from one world to another by means of a looking-glass? But such points of connection are slight, and Dodgson had more interest in the MacDonald children, particularly Lilia, than in their father's writings. He showed them the manuscript of *Alice's Adventures Underground* at quite an early stage in its composition—the spring of 1863—and asked if they thought it worth publishing. His son, Greville, declared that he "wished there were 60,000 volumes of it," and the family's enthusiasm played a large part in encouraging "Uncle Dodgson" to put it into print. Later, Dodgson delighted in watching the public performances of *Pilgrim's Progress* for which the family became celebrated, Lilia playing Christiana and MacDonald himself Mr Greatheart, a role for which his bearded, increasingly patriarchal appearance was entirely suited.

MacDonald's next full-length work of fiction after *Phantastes* was *David Elginbrod* (1863), a partly autobiographical novel about a young Scot coming south, which descends at times to gothic hack-writing—there is a mesmerist in it called Funkelstein, who has an evil power over the hero's beloved, Euphrasia Cameron. It was the first of many "realistic" works of fiction by MacDonald, dealing with the theological worries of young Scotsmen, or based on memories of his childhood. The adult novels are now entirely forgotten; several of the realistic novels for children, or about them, have survived on the shelves of public libraries. None of them contains the essential MacDonald.

However, by the time that *David Elginbrod* was published he had begun to discover an outlet for his fantasy imagination in the form of short stories for children. The first of these seems to have been "The Light Princess," the tale that Dodgson accompanied on its travels to the printer. It is MacDonald's most cheerful, and therefore least characteristic, fairy story— a pun on the word "gravity," for the princess has no *gravitas* (she is perpetually laughing) and also no physical gravity; eventually she acquires both after a prince has nearly sacrificed himself for her. Among the next to be written were "The Giant's Heart" (the sadistic piece about the spider-juice) and "The Castle," which seems like an early sketch for *The Princess and the Goblin* with its account of a family of children inhabiting an enormous castle. MacDonald does not seem to have known what to do with these stories at first, for he printed them in *Adela Cathcart* (1864), a loosely knit novel for adults with a good deal of fireside story-telling in it. This, no doubt, was partly because he always liked the story-within-a-story method: there is scarcely a full-length book of his that does not contain at least one secondary story within it, told by one of the characters. But it was also because his short fantasy stories were not exclusively for children; along with "The Light Princess," "The Giant's Heart," and "The Castle," *Adela Cathcart* contained "The Cruel Painter," the grisly story about the artist who delights in painting pictures of torture. Indeed for the rest of his life MacDonald had a habit of producing Poe-like grotesque tales that sit oddly alongside his fairy stories. There was a blackness in his imagination which could not be contained in his writings for children.

His first specifically children's book was *Dealings with the Fairies* (1867), in which "The Light Princess" and "The Giant's Heart" were reprinted alongside "Cross Purposes" (his *Alice* imitation), "The Shadows" (an early sketch for *At the Back of the North Wind*), and "The Golden Key." This last-named story has been called MacDonald's masterpiece, and is certainly his most perfectly crafted piece of work, a miniature *Phantastes* for children. It is at once very simple and very complicated: the tale of a boy and a girl, Mossy and Tangle, and their pilgrimage through life to the grave and beyond, all told in richly symbolic terms, as they go beneath sea and land, and visit the elements of the earth before passing out of this world.

Again, sexual symbolism pervades the narrative, but this is only one level of its meaning. "The Golden Key" is the pure essence of MacDonald; but it is, perhaps, the nucleus of a great story rather than one which itself achieves greatness. Like *Phantastes* it is too dense, too symbolic, and too lacking in ordinary, comprehensible events to communicate much at a first or even a second reading. Few children are likely to be moved by it.

MacDonald might, indeed, have remained merely an interesting foot-note to children's literature had he not, in his search for an adequate income, begun to write for a children's magazine, *Good Words for the Young*, published in London by a fellow Scot, Alexander Strahan. His involvement with this magazine (which he actually edited himself for a few months) made him begin something he had not attempted before, a full-length children's fantasy. *At the Back of the North Wind* appeared in the pages of *Good Words for the Young* in 1868, and Strahan published it as a book three years later, by which time MacDonald had produced another serial for the paper, *The Princess and the Goblin*.

These are the two books by which MacDonald is now chiefly remembered. They are both compromises between the "essential" MacDonald—the author of *Phantastes, Lilith,* and "The Golden Key"—and the writer with eleven children who had to earn a living. They were obviously written in a hurry, without much revision, and both are rambling and repetitive. *At the Back of the North Wind* owes rather a lot—too much for present day taste—to the sentimental evangelical novels for children which had been popular since the 1850s; Diamond, the poor illiterate half-invalid boy who is befriended by North Wind, would not be out of place in the pages of Hesba Stretton's *Jessica's First Prayer* or other mid-Victorian Sunday School diehards; and "Good Words for the Young" might not be a bad subtitle for the whole book. MacDonald the Congregationalist preacher has temporarily taken over from MacDonald the myth-maker, as he was inclined to do when a story was being written to make money. But even this diluted form of the MacDonald imagination has a powerful appeal, and no one who has read the story in early childhood will forget the account of the land "at the back of the North Wind," a place of utter stillness where "nothing went wrong . . . neither was anything quite right . . . but everything was going to be right some day." *At the Back of the North Wind* is no less than a rewriting of the *Purgatorio* for children.

The Princess and the Goblin is as rambling as *At the Back of the North Wind*. Its scene shifts with almost monotonous predictability between the mines, where Curdie the miner's boy is struggling to discover what horrid plot the goblins are hatching, and the turret room in the castle—the room where little Princess Irene meets and is amazed by her great-great-grandmother, who sits for ever spinning, has a great white globe like the moon, and a flock of pigeons that come and go at her command. But now there is nothing out of key, not a whiff of the Sunday School; instead, the story is redolent of Grimm and Perrault. It was in fact the first original British children's book to make an utterly confident, fresh use of such traditional materials as an old fairy spinning in a tower, and a race of wicked dwarfs beneath a mountain—or rather, beneath the castle itself; for MacDonald uses the stuff of folklore to construct a parable about the Christian universe. There are demons down below gnawing at the foundations; a precarious security within the main rooms; and a divine being high above who sometimes holds aloof from events, sometimes intervenes dramatically. Really, *The Princess and the Goblin* is as powerful a piece of religious teaching as ever came the way of a Sunday School child.

MacDonald was doing what Kingsley had tried to do but largely failed, and what Dodgson had refused to do: creating an alternative religious landscape which a child's mind could explore and which could offer spiritual nourishment. It was a positive achievement, not an act of destruction, and MacDonald was almost unique in it. Hans Andersen had done something of the same, but, despite MacDonald's example, almost no British writer for children seemed prepared to face the challenge until C. S. Lewis, an avowed disciple of MacDonald, began his Narnia cycle nearly eighty years later.

In fact, MacDonald himself quickly lost the touch for it, and began to become a destroyer rather than a creator. Something went wrong between the two Curdie books. *The Wise Woman*, which emerged in 1875 (after *The Princess and the Goblin* and before *The Princess and Curdie*) is a very unpleasant book. Where there should be lightness of touch in the story of the Wise Woman's handling of the two selfish girls, there is something closer to horror. She abducts them both without telling their parents what has happened to them, and subjects them to treatment which is not only frightening and unpleasant, but keeps failing to cure them. Finally she blinds two of the parents and puts a third into a coma. If this is a parable about God, as clearly it is, then MacDonald's view of the Creator seems to have become black and despairing.

The Princess and Curdie, written as a serial in 1877, confirms that this is so. A disproportionate amount of the book—about the first third—is taken up once again with Irene's great-great-grandmother, the old princess, as if MacDonald needs to reassure himself that the benevolent God of the first Curdie book is still there. It is evident that she is not, or at least that she is changed. She now tends to appear not as a beautiful maiden, but as "a small withered creature . . . like a long-legged spider holding up its own web." Even when rejuvenating herself and standing up to her full height she is still "plainly very old." Eventually she reappears as young and beautiful, but by this time we have been told that the miners regard her as a witch, "an old hating witch, whose delight was to do mischief." They call her Old Mother Wotherwop, and associate her with calamities in the mine. Curdie rejects these stories, but it seems that the miners are not entirely wrong; she tells him: "It is one thing what you or your father may think about me, and quite another what a foolish or bad man may see in me." She is not so very far, perhaps, from Lilith.

The second Curdie book is largely a parable about appearances and how they may deceive—Curdie is given the power of detecting the beast-natures which lurk in apparently good people—and also a reworking of the story of Christ. Curdie is "one who is come to set things right in the king's house," like Christ coming into the world, and his purging of the evil courtiers in the palace is preceded by a servant-girl telling her fellows, John-the-Baptist-like, "If you do not repent of your bad ways, you are going to be punished—all turned out of the palace together." But Mac-Donald will not allow them to repent; he prefers that they should wallow in their iniquities, and so be punished by physical torture (mauling by the dreadful beasts whom Curdie has brought with him), and even when this is complete he will not let humanity alone. Curdie and Irene duly marry and become king and queen, but they have no children, and the kingdom passes into bad hands after their death; its foundations are undermined by the greedy populace, eager for gold and jewels from the mines, and "one day at noon, when life was at its highest, the whole city fell with a roaring crash. The cries of men and the shrieks of women went up with its dust, and then there was a great silence." The parable is, of course, being followed through to its end; this is the Last Judgement. But it is a very strange Last Judgement: no one is saved. In fact the conclusion of *The Princess and Curdie* is reminiscent not of the book of Revelation but of the fall of Sodom and Gomorrah.

With the destruction of the city at the end of *The Princess and Curdie,* MacDonald's writing for children in effect came to an end. Almost all the books he was to produce for the remainder of his life were for adults. That he should stop regarding himself as a children's author is not in itself surprising; he had never indeed really done so, declaring that "I do not write for children, but for the childlike, whether of five, or fifty, or seventy-five." What is striking is the increasingly pessimistic, even sinister, character of his spiritual vision. That pessimism is all too clear in *A Rough Shaking* (1891), his one remaining book for young readers, which is a nightmarish account of the maltreatment of a boy who has lost his mother in an earthquake. At the very end of his life as a writer, in *Lilith*, which was published in 1895, the old visionary power returned, but with more disturbing results than ever; for this final fantasy, with its vision of evil-as-good and good-as-evil, its wild, uncontrolled symbolism, and its hotchpotch of gnostic religions and sinister folklore, is evidence of a mind in disintegration. One is not surprised to learn that, soon after *Lilith* was published, MacDonald withdrew into total silence, not speaking even to members of his family. He died in 1905, at the age of eighty-one.

Like Lewis Carroll, he had looked over the brink, and had examined the darkness which lay beyond the religious beliefs of his day. Like Kingsley, his writing for children was largely a search for a positive religious experience that could replace conventional Christianity. At first he found that experience in *At the Back of the North Wind* (though really that book scarcely departs from the normal Christian world-view), and in *The Princess and the Goblin*, with its marvellous image of the all-powerful grandmother presiding over the rambling, half-known, mysterious mansion—an image that is at once Arcadian in its suggestion of a paradisal landscape set apart from the real world, and also a clever parable for the whole universe. But MacDonald's visionary power would not let him stop there, and, like Kingsley, he found that destruction of the old certainties was easier than the creation of new ones.

He did, however, leave one positive trail that may have been discovered by a later author for children, a fellow Scot and an exponent of the Kailyard school of novels. In *Lilith*, Mr Vane finds himself in a country inhabited by children who have not grown up. Lona, whom Vane loves and who is eventually killed by Lilith, is one of these. The children are full of pranks and quite unafraid of anything—except the possibility that some of them after all may begin to grow. One of them is called Peter. We do not know whether J. M. Barrie read *Lilith*, but *Peter Pan*, an outstanding piece of quasi-religious myth-making for children, began to form itself in his imagination no more than six years after it was published.

Becoming a Heroine in *The Egoist* and *Diana of the Crossways*

Rachel M. Brownstein

Thackeray can only have been teasing when he called Vanity Fair *"a novel without a hero," as though that were a contradiction in terms. It is the heroine who is indispensable.*

—MARY LASCELLES

George Meredith kept it a secret that his grandfather and his father had been tailors. But the protagonist of his early novel, *Evan Harrington,* has a tailor grandfather conspicuously named Melchizedec and called "The Great Mel," just like Meredith's. The nature of the skeleton in his closet, and the fact that he half-closed the door to it and later pretended he hadn't, are suggestive details about Meredith. He was a snob ashamed of his humble Welsh origins, but he took pride in them, on the side—pride in being a Celt more witty and passionate than Englishmen, being George Meredith, the grandson of Mel. He lied about his grandfather in life, but told the truth in literature; it was like him to do such a thing, like him to use for fiction, at no matter what cost, the preposterous and ironic, therefore irresistible, revealing fact. The tailor as heroic patriarch is, like the best things in Meredith, a little bit too good, but true.

The tailors in the novelist's background are material beautifully cut out for the Comic Spirit, the goddess Meredith invented to worship. Her celebrated silvery laughter insists on them. No connection of hers was ever touched by a hint of vulgar trade! She is to be imagined by the reader as surrounded by irreverent gamboling naked imps, but calm and poised herself, well-dressed, high-nosed, absolutely *comme il faut*. Her domain is the drawing room of high comedy, her laughter a clear celestial-aristocratic tinkle. She stands aloof to mock the multitude, and shows the deserving few the high road from the seething caldron of the world to a level Meredith called civilization. There, men and women spar with bright, honed wits; they are equals and complements, freed from the hot narrowings of getting and spending, blood relatives, need, and desire.

From *Becoming a Heroine.* © 1982 by Rachel M. Brownstein. Penguin, 1982.

The Comic Spirit is an apotheosis of the English lady: she is graceful and accomplished, aloof from the world in the high style of the upper classes, impeccable. She is a made-up, semiclassical deity, a Diana with impish children, a virgin mother nurturing with disdain, female yet sexless. The goddess of fortuitously fastidious grandsons of tailors is the corrective to God the funless father. It is her pleasure and her special pride to distinguish high bright spirits in the mass; she is never fooled by the mere garments of greatness, or, for that matter, the deceptive plain broadcloth of tailors' descendants. Her realm is the lofty, snowy Alps: at the end of Meredith's *The Egoist* she appears there and looks down at the world, compressing her lips as she gracefully and generously abstains from further mockery of men.

The Alps by themselves are not quite the whole picture of the Meredithian heights. Another image softens and complicates, the double-blossomed cherry tree of *The Egoist*. Meredith marries the images when Clara, the heroine, first sees the tree:

> the load of virginal blossom, whiter than summer-cloud on the sky, showered and drooped and clustered so thick as to claim colour and seem, like higher Alpine snows in noon-sunlight, a flush of white. From deep to deeper heavens of white, her eyes perched and soared. Wonder lived in her . . . wonder so divine, so unbounded, was like soaring into homes of angel-crowded space, sweeping through folded and on to folded white fountainbow of wings, in innumerable columns.
>
> (chap. 11)

As the Alps are, the tree is an astonishing, exhilarating, awesome natural wonder: the sight of it helps liberate Clara from her oppressive personal situation. In their softness and abundance the blossoms epitomize sensual beauty, and yet their whiteness, which recalls flushed Alpine snows, is cold and chaste. The tree is the creature of a gardener, not of nature, beautiful but fruitless. "Call this the Vestal of civilization," Clara's classicist father declares. Like the Comic Spirit, the cherry tree is feminine but not female, the image of a lady.

Meredith imagined himself a champion of women. His feminism was romantic, involving a passion for personal distinction more than one for equality. The heads of the fiercely sexual wag sadly over his revealing sort of hankering after a paradise furnished with silver sugar-tongs and fresh table linens; and his personal history of not having been able to live with his first, clever wife, Thomas Love Peacock's daughter Mary, would seem to bear out their suspicions. When Sir Willoughby Patterne, at the end of *The Egoist*, tries to assure himself that the marital booby prize he gets is the best bride after all, the narrator's inflection is ominous: "But he had the lady with brains! He had: and he was to learn the nature of that possession in the woman who is our wife" (chap. 49). Meredith wrote a sequence of poems, *Modern Love*, about the break-up of his marriage. Like *The Angel in the House*, Coventry Patmore's celebration of Victorian family life and the ideal domestic female at its center, this long poem written in the great age of the long novel is about life after the wedding. Meredith's poem is the antithesis of Patmore's: it is analytic and meditative rather than simply narrative. And the marriage it analyzes is bad. The ordinary life of a couple has become a monstrous mockery that masks the truth of mistrust and despair. The writer of lyrical, lapidary prose made this painful story out of plain verse. *Modern Love* clings tenaciously to a variation on the sonnet form as the couple whose story it chronicles hold on to the form of their marriage:

> At dinner, she is hostess, I am host.
> Went the feast ever cheerfuller? She keeps
> The Topic over intellectual deeps
> In buoyancy afloat. They see no ghost.
> With sparkling surface-eyes we ply the ball:
> It is in truth a most contagious game:
> HIDING THE SKELETON, shall be its name.
> Such play as this, the devils might appal!
> But here's the greater wonder; in that we
> Enamoured of an acting nought can tire,
> Each other, like true hypocrites, admire;
> Warm-lighted looks, Love's ephemerioe,
> Shoot gaily o'er the dishes and the wine.
> We waken envy of our happy lot.
> Fast, sweet, and golden, shows the marriage-knot.
> Dear guests, you now have seen Love's corpse-light shine.

Modern Love concludes that "passions spin the plot," and that we are "betrayed by what is false within." Meredith's is a novelist's vision of the fatal implication of appearances in feelings. The self-consciousness that marks his style is his subject.

There is no defending *The Egoist* against the charge of extreme artificiality and linguistic denseness: that high-handed pyrotechnique is there to enjoy or reject, a matter of taste. But against the common charge that the novel is cold and heartless, or the nearly opposite accusation that it lets its victim off too lightly in the end, defending is in order. Sir Willoughby Patterne, the eponymous Egoist, is a man-membrane, whose self-regard is inordinately, inextricably involved with the regard others have or pretend to have for him. He is a poseur; he is his appearance. The membrane is elaborately wrought and very fragile—and it is all there is to poor Willoughby. As a satirical portrait, he is not unfamiliar: for centuries writers have pilloried persons overly dependent on others and on artifice, and celebrated the strong man who remains himself, come what or who may. The heroine, in contrast, has been described sympathetically as by nature implicated in artifice, and involved with others and what they think of her. The heroine-centered novel since *Clarissa* defines extreme susceptibility to the estimate of others, and an inextricable connection with artifice, as the feminine and also the quintessentially human condition. Read as a development of this tradition, *The Egoist* is something more than a satirical portrait of a monster. Willoughby Patterne stands very specifically for the upper-class Englishman of the nineteenth century, and Meredith satirizes in him the fatuousness and smugness, the callousness and heartlessness, of the type. But as a beautiful creature dependent on appearances and destined only for marriage, he is a version—a travesty—of the heroine. *The Egoist* is a sort of transvestite novel, the tailor's grandson's brilliant alteration of a genre to fit a radical critique of its assumptions. Liberating the heroine from the center of the courtship plot for feminist purposes, it puts in her place a "hero" who is her mirror-image. Like Clarissa, Sir Willoughby is the pride of his world and its creature, profoundly committed to what Lovelace might call a "mere notional" self—which is to say, a notion that has little connection with an emotional center of identity. But unlike Clarissa or any heroine, Willoughby also has real power in the world. Therefore he is seriously dangerous. Meredith exposes him, with glee but not without sympathy.

The Egoist turns the heroine's story on its head. It is both a send-up of the heroine-centered novel and a variation on it. It is about the breaking, not the making, of an engagement. This is the story: a beautiful virgin—well-born, intelligent, charming, wealthy, and eighteen, by objective standards the most desirable young woman in England, unaffected, lively, and witty—is being forced to marry a man she finds physically, spiritually, and morally repellent. There has been a formal engagement; preparations for the wedding are proceeding; time is on the man's side, and space, for the girl is virtually imprisoned in a house in the country. She feels, painfully, her littleness and weakness. Meanwhile the man's awareness of her reluctance to marry him whets his sexual appetite; her own feelings are turned, like her beauty, against her. Locked in a situation she has unwittingly produced, she feels guilty, constrained, claustrophobic; she wants freedom, she fights for air. She sees herself in horror as a heroine: "Dreadful to think of! she was one of the creatures who are written about!" (chap. 15). She thinks of herself with a heroine's doubleness of mind, as someone who must stand for her whole sex and at the same time distinguish herself from it: "for her sex's sake, and also to appear an exception to her sex, this reasoning creature desired to be thought consistent" (chap. 19). Along with her reputation and her fate, her identity, or idea of herself, is at risk.

Nobody will understand or indeed hear her objections to a marriage objectively grand, thoroughly approved by custom and convention. All the people around her suppose it will make her happy. Her father, her natural protector, is for his own reasons on her suitor's side. Seeking help, she makes several confidants. Her mind seems to her unreliable; she has doubts about the accuracy of her perceptions of a world grown hostile and flat;

raised to submit, she condemns herself for feeling rebellious, and is nearly ready to give in. She is a lady and therefore she has been brought up to be a coward: the blunt assessment is Meredith's. But her woman's nature asserts itself. By stealth she escapes from the place where she is immured, intending to seek the protection of a female friend. A very charming young man offers to help her escape, but it turns out he wants to have her in the other man's place. It becomes clear to her (and us) that Woman's natural adversary is Man, whose lust is as unnatural as the civilized ploys he uses to entrap her. It becomes clear that civilization is the tool of lust. As she is civilization's creature, she seems destined to be lust's victim. It becomes evident that she must stoop to the world's ways in order to save herself, to make other people understand how she feels, who she is, to articulate that self the whole world conspires to ignore and destroy, and meanwhile not to be compromised in the world's eyes.

I have nearly exhausted the parallels. *The Egoist* is a comedy; Clara's story only recalls Clarissa's. A single sentence suggests how faintly:

> In a dream somehow she had committed herself to a lifelong imprisonment; and, oh terror! not in a quiet dungeon; the barren walls closed round her, *talked*, called for ardour, expected admiration.
>
> (chap. 10)

The italics are mine: "talked" contains Meredith's insight and emphasis.

Meredith is vague about what led Clara Middleton to engage herself to Sir Willoughby Patterne, and to make an extended prenuptial visit to his house with her father. (His name suggests he is the very pattern of a Willoughby—the name *par excellence* of a romantic gentleman, as the author of *Sense and Sensibility* thought early on. Like the heroine's name—Clara is not Clarissa, she is the inhabitant of the middle not the highest realm of being—the "hero's" deliberately reminds us of other novels. It is reminiscent of the popular Willow Pattern of china, and a story connected with that, as well. The heroine is also linked with china, underscoring the feminine connotations of the association and connecting the couple that will eventually break up.) We are expected to take it for granted that an inexperienced girl would be dazzled by an offer from the handsome and wealthy scion of a great English family, a matrimonial prize, apparently charming— charming, that is, in public. Clara discovers the private man after the engagement. This is entirely logical, as the worst thing about Willoughby is the difference between his public and private selves. There is a screaming, greedy baby inside the gentleman's skin. In the privacy of Patterne Hall, he drops his plausible manner and expects his beloved to admire what he conceals from the world. Clara thinks, "How must a man despise women, who can expose himself as he does to me!" When he confides in her and says, "This is not a language I talk to the world," she begs, "But do, do talk to me as you talk to the world, Willoughby; give me some relief!" (chap. 10). The private Willoughby is a primitive, a brute; marrying him, a girl must encounter the odious inner man. In the intimate sexual relation, the Egoist is exposed. Clara experiences the question "Can a woman have an inner life apart from him she is yoked to?" as "a sharp physical thought" (chap. 21). Mind and body, language and love, are confounded; therefore marriage is a situation like no other.

The conceit basic to *The Egoist* is that a man may be considered as women commonly are, as generic. Commenting on one of Willoughby's fatuous pronouncements about the nature of women, the intelligent Laetitia Dale observes tartly, "The generic woman appears to have an extraordinary faculty for swallowing the individual" (chap. 14). Blind and deaf to all but the most superficial and measurable distinctions among women, Willoughby has sought a perfect bride. The dashing Constantia Durham has already jilted him when he meets Clara; Clara soon plans to do so, too, and eventually even Laetitia Dale decides not to marry him before (not because she wants to) she does. For the Egoist, for generic man, that is, "there is no individual woman. He grants her a characteristic only to enroll her in a class. He is our immortal dunce at learning to distinguish her as a personal variety, of a separate growth" (chap. 19). Like a heroine, Willoughby is representative, part person, part pattern. He is an anti-exemplar, an anti-Grandison. Like Sir Charles, he is described as sunlike, most hilariously when his adoring female relatives recall his standing on the chair as a child, crying, "I am the sun of the house!" (chap. 44). He surrounds himself with women: faded, thirty-year-old Laetitia Dale, who has waited years to marry him; the dowagers Mrs. Mountstuart Jenkinson, Lady Culmer, and Lady Busshe, who delight in competing as prophets of his glorious fate; his slavish maiden aunts, Eleanor and Isabel. The Egoist is wedded to the social world as the conscious heroine is: like her he depends on reflection and on reputation to be sure of his value and to keep his grip on his valuable self.

Willoughby Patterne is partly exonerated by Meredith as not himself responsible for what he is. He is "a gentleman nurtured in idolatry," the product of hereditary aristocracy and primogeniture, of generations of Patternes. Centuries of ruthless egoism have produced him; he is owned by his House. All England encourages its idle gentlemen to pursue only their own pleasure on their own extensive lands the way Willoughby does, and it admires them for feeling no responsibility to the rest of the world, for thinking nothing of those who think so much of them. The social system that places Willoughby apart from the world in his artificial Eden at Patterne Hall makes him inhuman; and partly because he thinks *of* little else, he is unable to think *for* himself. He is the centerpiece, the result, of a corrupt social structure. His relationship to women epitomizes his society's; to analyze women's importance to him is to illustrate the importance of feminism for England. The story of Sir Willoughby Patterne's marrying is based on the condition of England as it is described in John Stuart Mill's *On the Subjection of Women* (1869), which Meredith had read with interest.

The novel turns on the illogical premise that an engagement must be unmade the way it is made, through a mutual understanding. Unlike Clarissa, Clara has engaged herself all by herself. The genteel world she lives in is like Jane Austen's world: there are clearly defined courtship customs, and a definable group of eligible men to choose from, and some very bad bets among them, and no one at all to save a girl from falling for one of those. Her fate is in her hands. Only Clara's word binds her to Willoughby. Her widower father, scholarly, polysyllabic, and bibulous, has amiably gone along with her decision to marry this unexceptionable if stupid young man, and he is enjoying the pleasures of a visit to palatial Patterne Hall, where there is a well-stocked library and a magnificent wine cellar, and the company of Willoughby's intellectual cousin and secretary, Vernon Whitford. Dr. Middleton is an accessory to the Egoist, as he is an egoist himself. Meredith's argument that Willoughby is a monstrously enlarged part of all of us is made as he shows a plurality, a conspiracy, of egoists.

Dr. Middleton very casually thinks little of women, tossing off classical references to support his stock ideas. Among the formulas and accepted ideas that bind Clara to Willoughby, therefore, are the misogynistic lines of Roman poets. It is part of the wall of words between them that prevents them from separating. Clara, for instance, is bound by a lady's language:

> She could not, as in a dear melodrama, from the aim of a pointed finger denounce him, on the testimony of her instincts, false of speech, false in deed. She could not even declare that she doubted his truthfulness. The refuge of a sullen fit, the refuge of tears, the pretext of a mood, were denied her now by the rigour of those laws of decency which are a garment to ladies of pure breeding.
>
> (chap. 43)

She is too corseted with customs to tell the truth, so she cannot break her engagement. Meanwhile Sir Willoughby, in secret, recalls the plots of pulp fiction to salve his pride. He imagines "romances" in which Clara is ruined and comes back to him on her knees. In her company, he uses conventional polite formulas to feign incomprehension and fuddle his antagonist—another use of language in the service of misunderstanding. Stock phrases and standard images of women throng to his aid and make him almost clever. For instance, when she is bored with him Clara yawns and then feebly explains,

> "I am sleepier here than anywhere."
> "Ours, my Clara, is the finest air of the kingdom. It has the effect of sea-air."
> "But if I am always asleep here?"
> "We shall have to make a public exhibition of the Beauty."
>
> (chap. 10)

Meredith keeps us mindful of the power of language by using it flamboy-antly. Willoughby is perverse: he has, it is said, a "burning wish to strain her in his arms to a flatness provoking his compassion" (chap. 23). *The Egoist* begins with a slow essay-chapter that ends with an epitaph for the hero, a line that kills him off before his story begins: "Through very love of self himself he slew." Its backfiring movement is the novel's: Sir Wil-loughby gets himself into his pickle of a plot by getting down on his knees once too often, and so, in the end, he is forced back down where he began, forced to marry the woman he jilted after being jilted himself.

Remembering *Modern Love,* and invoking Victorian euphemism, some readers have argued that *The Egoist* only pretends to be about the breaking of an engagement, and is really the veiled story of a divorce. This is not the case. Sir Willoughby himself makes the distinction:

> "You know, to me, Clara, plighted faith, the affiancing of two lovers, is a piece of religion. I rank it as holy as marriage; nay, to me it is holier; I really cannot tell you how; I can only appeal to you in your bosom to understand me. We read of divorces with comparative indifference. They occur between couples who have rubbed off all romance."

> (chap. 15)

The Egoist is about the undoing of a romance; therefore it mirrors the court-ship plot. What has placed Clara in Willoughby's house and hands is only her word—Yes—and she is constrained by logic to extricate herself by another word—No—which she cannot say and he cannot hear. The rela-tionship of the couple is purely verbal; they are bound only by a promise.

Yet Willoughby wants Clara for her body. She is qualified to be the mother of the sons (not daughters) of Patterne because she has health, wealth, and beauty, and is a virgin. When Richardson identified woman's adversary as the rake, a rebel and an outlaw, he spoke on behalf of both women and society; an attack on the Egoist satirizes the establishment, and identifies woman with the outsider and the satirist with her cause. Wil-loughby's fetish for feminine chastity is implicated in the selfishness of his lust: to maintain himself and propagate his kind, he must possess the natural world's finest creature, a "quick nature," and assert his overlordship of the earth. Clara is saved in the end by the health that enables her to fight back with energy, and the beauty that finds her an alternative lover. He is Vernon Whitford, Willoughby's cousin. Vernon is a scholar and an accomplished pedestrian (like Meredith himself and Leslie Stephen, the literary Alpinist who was a model for Vernon, who became the father of Virginia Woolf). Where Sir Willoughby's favorite posture, on horseback, bespeaks the man who aims to be master, his cousin Vernon's prowess as a walker suggests his doggedness and simplicity, his closeness to the earth. Sacrificing realism to romantic fantasy, Meredith idealizes the rational and perfect love between the young scholar and an older scholar's daughter.

Clara and the charming, half-Irish Horace de Craye are delightfully witty together, but the novelist arranges for the quieter man—not the Celt—to get the heroine in the end. Vernon is a humanist and a human being; his devotion to flowering trees and to the Alps prove he is worthy of a heroine who can race a twelve-year-old boy without getting winded, a girl who, like Elizabeth Bennet, is impervious to mud and English weather. De Craye, like Willoughby, has a history of casually exploiting women of the lower classes; Vernon, in contrast, once went so far as to marry one (she is conveniently dead). The fact shadows him, ever so lightly, with the glamour of sexual experience; in contrast, the shadow on Willoughby, who has once been jilted, is impotence. Vernon is poor, and scholarly, and tactful, and modest—the literary man as a perfect Perseus, "Phoebus Apollo as fasting friar," as Mrs. Mountstuart Jenkinson has it.

In Mrs. Mountstuart, the reigning matron of the Egoist's universe, the powers of the word, the world, and woman are imagined as one. She is the icing on the cake of this epigrammatic novel. Her specialty is the devastating one-liner. Of Laetitia Dale she says, for instance, "Here she comes, with a romantic tale on her eyelashes." Her epigrams, like caricatures, depend on the tiniest bit too emphatic a focus on a single feature, often a good one the epigram calls into question by attending to it. Vernon is too thin and ascetic, but basically, we are meant to think, he is perfect, has the soul of a saint and is made like a pagan god. Laetitia, who writes poems and romances to support herself and her father, has long eyelashes—what can that mean? Is she batting off a romantic tale? Trembling on the brink of tears? Of Sir Willoughby himself Mrs. Mountstuart says heart-stoppingly little: *"You see he has a leg."* Not two legs but one. It "will walk straight into the hearts of women." Is it a phallus or the leg made in bowing, made for dancing attendance? Does it suggest his deep subservience to women, and to conventions? Far commoner synecdoches for the whole man are "a head," "a heart." Is "leg" to suggest that Sir Willoughby has neither? He is physically a perfect specimen; nonetheless, "leg" mystifies. The observation is repeated; Mrs. Mountstuart, who relishes her phrases, cracks that one like a whip. There is no way to ask what it might mean. Sir Willoughby, terrorized, interprets her *mot* as a flattery. Much depends on tone: *"You see,"* is how she puts it, *"he has a leg."* ("You *see* it; or, you see, *he* has it. Miss Isabel and Miss Eleanor disputed the incidence of the emphasis, but surely, though a slight difference of meaning may be heard, either will do: many, with a good show of reason, throw the accent upon *leg"* [chap. 2].) We are supposed to see, and we pretend to, or think we do. Or do we?

About Mrs. Mountstuart's epigram for Clara, Willoughby very circumlocutiously attempts to inquire, delicately concealing distress: what *does* dear Mrs. Mountstuart mean by "a dainty rogue in porcelain"? Why rogue? he wants to know, complacently accepting the rest of it, his fiancée hit off as an ornamental figurine. The lady does not say, chary like any sibyl of talking too much, waiting like her rival Lady Busshe for the event to prove her a prophet. Questions proliferate about whether Clara (her heart? her hymen?) or the engagement will break, and then the brittle wedding presents begin to arrive. One is a broken vase; the other, a dinner service, comes legitimately in several pieces. The matter of patterns on porcelain is loaded with significances. Is the point only that Clara will not accept her woman's place? Or is Mrs. Mountstuart merely putting some people on by seeming to send others up?

Mrs. Mountstuart is a worldly widow—she has lived in British India. The savage point is delicately made that, being British, she has handily escaped suttee. Her only amusement is to be amusing. She aims to defeat better-born and better-married rivals by her native wit. As Sir Willoughby is the chief young man in her world, she defines herself as his chief supporter, chronicler, chorus: she depends on him to provide plot and characters on which to base her *bons mots*, to lend his importance to her statements by being their subject. To keep him at her side she must seem to be on his but also she must keep him awed, and afraid that she will lose the respect she pretends to have for him, or that she will stop feigning it. The Egoist's dominance depends on the egoism, or at least on the selfishness, of others. Willoughby has more than Mrs. Mountstuart to lose. She explains him to Clara, explaining herself:

> The secret of him is, that he is one of those excessively civilized creatures who aim at perfection: and I think he ought to be supported in his conceit of having attained it; for the more men of that class, the greater our influence. . . . We must be moderately slavish to keep our place; which is given us in appearance; but appearances make up a remarkably large part of life, and far the most comfortable.
>
> (chap. 35)

It is in the interest of ladies like Mrs. Mountstuart that men be artificial creatures like Willoughby. The high place of women in drawing rooms, Mrs. Mountstuart knows, is only "given us in appearance," and therefore she values appearances, which not only make up a large part of life but also affect the disposition of realities. In reality, Sir Willoughby is a slave to the sex he would enslave; aware of this, Mrs. Mountstuart can manipulate him. The acknowledged mistress of ceremonies, she is, in a ceremonious world, mistress of considerable power. Willoughby's terror of her tongue is critical in the process by which he is outmaneuvered and forced to save face by letting Clara go. For the women band together against him, Mrs. Mountstuart and Laetitia on Clara's side, in a sisterhood to be reckoned with. The glutton who aimed to eat up the world's fairest flower and fruit finds himself "in the jaws of the world, on the world's teeth," brought to sacrifice himself "for the favourable looks and tongues of those women whose looks and tongues he detested" (chap. 46), Mrs. Mountstuart and her friends. The consumer is consumed. Clara is allowed to disengage herself for the reason she would have been married—for his appearance's sake. And Sir Willoughby, jilted a second time, is obliged to marry Laetitia, whom he has jilted twice. The romances Mrs. Mountstuart observed trembling on her eyelashes have fallen like scales from Laetitia's eyes in the course of Sir Willoughby's courtship of Clara; she agrees to marry him because she is poor, so as to be able to stanch the flow from her pen. By marrying him as she does, reluctantly, she reduces the grandiose Sir Willoughby to his goods and chattels; because she includes them in her mind, those will not include her. All the victorious women in the novel defeat the Egoist by the way they think of and look at him.

The first time Clara Middleton feels the impulse to laugh at Willoughby Patterne she has to stifle it. The giggle swells in her when, after her father praises the rod as an instrument of education, Miss Eleanor and Miss Isabel murmur to each other that Willoughby in his youth "would not have suffered it!" Clara sighs and Meredith interprets her silence:

> She sighed and put a tooth on her underlip. The gift of humourous fancy is in women fenced round with forbidding placards; they have to choke it; if they perceive a piece of humour, for instance, the young Willoughby grasped by his master, and his horrified relatives rigid at the sight of preparations for the deed of sacrilege, they have to blindfold the mind's eye. They are society's hard-drilled soldiery, Prussians that must both march and think in step. It is for the advantage of the civilized world, if you like, since men have decreed it, or matrons have so read the decree; but here and there a younger woman, haply an uncorrected insurgent of the sex matured here and there, feels that her lot was cast with her head in a narrower pit than her limbs.
>
> Clara . . . asked for some little, only some little, free play of mind in a house that seemed to wear, as it were, a cap of iron.
>
> (chap. 9)

The repression of the maiden's mind is analogous to the physical punishment administered to boys, which little Willoughby escaped. It is as formative. The Egoist's iron cap is made to match that other uncomfortable garment for girls, the iron maiden: armored uncomfortably in invisible versions of both, well-bred English girls are preserved for their possessors, and impressed as the foot soldiers of their repressive society. At Patterne Clara is made to stifle her physical self—her desire, her impulse to run swiftly, her laughter—by an enclosure of her mind. But as it turns out in the end, "Miss Middleton owed it to Sir Willoughby Patterne that she ceased to think like a girl" (chap. 10). Accurately perceived, the Egoist cures the ills he causes. Tickled by his absurdity, infuriated by his presumptions, terrified by suffocating in his caresses, and seeing that her whole life is at stake, Clara begins to think no longer like a girl but like a woman—but not one of those servile women of whom Meredith writes that "a shadow of the male Egoist is in the chamber of their brains overawing them" (chap. 11). To begin to laugh at the Egoist is to banish his shadow, burst the iron cap. One need not laugh out loud, Meredith cautions timorously; one can retain good manners, decent dress, aristocratic attitudes. Clara breaks free, gracefully, allowing Sir Willoughby what shreds of his dignity remain. The novel's final image is of the cool Comic Spirit. Vernon and Clara, who have married, have gone to the Alps; the Spirit sits beside them there, and looks from her eminence down and across Europe to Patterne, to Willoughby. She says nothing; instead "she compresses her lips," like Elizabeth Bennet when just before her marriage she swallows a sharp remark and reflects that Darcy "had yet to learn to be laught at." Willoughby lacks the capacity to learn; the Spirit is simply through with him. Gracefully, she restrains herself. Her silence is not imposed by an iron cap, but freely chosen.

As the last volleys of silvery laughter echo and die away in the Alps, it is a little hard to say who laughs last. *The Egoist* ends conventionally, with marriages. There is some obvious irony: one is meant to doubt that Laetitia and Willoughby will be happy ever after. But in the face of Clara Middleton's happiness with Vernon Whitford, we seem to be meant to be misty-eyed. Yet Clara, for all of Meredith's assertions that she has begun to think, never quite breaks free enough of the novelist's hovering analytic intelligence to acquire a mind recognizably her own; she is too well supervised and well monitored to be a convincing character. The indispensable Whitford, too, is a shadowy figure, as hard to picture as Mrs. Mountstuart's impossible image, Phoebus Apollo as fasting friar. So far as one can see him he looks gray. Meredith praises the scholar in him, and the Alpinist, and the modest, helpful man. Are we meant to observe the hypocrisy and passivity that enable him to coexist with Willoughby, or to find his remoteness and lack of sparkle unattractive? I suspect not. Vernon and Clara are idealized as a perfect couple for the top of the obligatory wedding cake at the novel's end. Having put Willoughby in a heroine's place, and satirized his pretensions to perfect selfhood, Meredith gives himself room to idealize Clara—to have the heroine both ways, as the novel form is calculated to have her, as a subject and an ideal object, a person and a metaphor, at once. The Comic Spirit finds nothing to laugh at in the happy couple in the Alps. But why does she haunt their honeymoon?

Meredith was both critical of the prevailing sexual myths of his time and embroiled in them. From the story of *Diana of the Crossways* (1897)—the story in the novel and some stories that hang around it—we can gather some illustrations of this, and of related matters I have been discussing.

Meredith was a prolific but not a popular novelist until his beautiful, brilliant Diana captured the imagination of English readers. "There is a large and beautiful conception of womanhood in Diana rather than a single woman," Virginia Woolf wrote astutely of this heroine, in whom the generic and the particular urgently combine and clash, as they do in Sir Willoughby, but not to satiric effect. A delicate "portrait" of Diana was featured in a book of sketches of chaste and lovely heroines of popular fiction, drawn as if they were so many actual society belles, which was published as a coffee-table folio around the turn of the century. *Diana of the Crossways* got attention partly because it revived a scandal about a real woman, the Hon. Caroline Norton, who had been dead some twenty years when the novel appeared, but who was still well enough remembered to be recognized as Meredith's model. (The novelist had once met her.) Rather like Byron, whom she physically resembled, Mrs. Norton had lived a myth, and therefore was susceptible to fictionalization. One of three beautiful granddaughters of the playwright Richard Brinsley Sheridan, she was brilliant as well, dashing. As her 1909 biographer put it, "the lyric touch, too often wanting in her verses, is never lacking in her life; her story, told in her own dramatic words, is her real contribution to the literature of her century." Caroline Norton wrote poems and novels and tracts, and she was a witty and charming conversationalist. The stories told about her by envious enemies contributed to her notoriety: in the elaborately periphrastic introductory chapter of *Diana*, Meredith analyzes, with sympathy, a talking woman's special vulnerability to talk.

A lawsuit brought by Mrs. Norton's estranged husband made her the victim of serious slander as well as mere envious insinuations. Separated from his wife, Norton sued the Prime Minister, Lord Melbourne, for enjoying her favors. In that time women were so little recognized as persons that Caroline figured in the lawsuit as a piece of property. The case was dismissed; Mr. Norton had no evidence. But the suit intensified Caroline Norton's sense of the wrongs that had been done her under sanction of law. When her husband left her he had taken the children. Under England's law, they belonged entirely to him, and for years he prevented her from seeing them. Mrs. Norton wrote tracts and attempted to charm powerful politicians in an effort to alter the laws regulating the property of married women and the custody of children.

Meredith's Diana is, like Caroline Norton, the sort of woman women envy; a society belle, well born and well placed, she is beautiful, witty, and spirited, and furthermore a published writer. Diana is also an unhappy wife, a (chaste) intimate of great politicians, and the subject of gossip, again like Mrs. Norton. But there are inevitable differences between life and novels: while the fictitious Diana's husband dies and she marries again, happily, while she is still young, Caroline Norton was not free to marry until shortly before her death, when she was in her sixties. And Diana is not a mother. Literary convention made Meredith strip Mrs. Norton of her three children as the laws of England had allowed Mr. Norton to do the same thing. Finally, Diana writes romances, not tracts. I suppose a childless Diana could not convincingly be shown as passionately directing her mind's best efforts toward reforming the laws of child custody. Obvious other reasons too made Meredith soften her from a pamphleteer to the most acceptable type of literary lady, a popular novelist.

The plot of *Diana of the Crossways* turns on an episode in which the heroine sells to a newspaper editor a political secret that has been told her by Percy Dacier, the young politician she loves. More than enough motive is provided for Diana's act: in dramatic scenes we see her out of money and blocked at writing a novel that is to release her from debt, and horror-struck by a sudden attempt Percy has made on her chastity. At an earlier crisis in her life she had also reacted like the chaste goddess Diana to a man's sexual assault: then maidenly flight had led to the disaster of her first marriage. If we grant that she has been badly scarred by that earlier overture of her best friend's husband, and grant also that her long relationship with Percy Dacier has been intimate yet "pure," we must believe in her terror. But Meredith wants us to believe in addition that she would go on from terror to utter intellectual confusion—that a sophisticated woman, an accomplished hostess wise in the ways of political life, would not know it was wrong to sell a political secret to the newspapers. Meredith asks us to believe that Diana has no idea she is engaged in a serious act of betrayal. Committed to idealizing his heroine, he is unable to let us think she knowingly performed a base act: so instead he suggests she is unimaginably naïve. A "real" Diana, we suspect, would have known what she was doing; Mrs. Norton, for example, would certainly have known.

But as it turns out, Mrs. Norton was accused of doing precisely what Diana does in the novel. When *Diana of the Crossways* appeared, Meredith was accused of reviving false rumors about her. (All subsequent editions of the novel were prefaced by a note insisting the story was a fiction.) Faithful to gossip, the novel is false to historical truth and psychological plausibility, and so it founders. What is the moral? Is there a moral?

The heroine of *Diana of the Crossways* is adorably a sexual being because she is a literary woman: her wit, her being a novelist, make her attractive. Meredith insists on his brilliant writer-heroine's difference from the docile and dull blond heroines of romance, but he writes, nevertheless, with the worshipful delight of a dreamer adoring a Rose. The point of the novel about her is Diana's deliciousness. If, on rereading, she proves not quite so wonderfully witty as Meredith says she is, we must still believe in her brilliance if we would give ourselves at all to the fiction. Diana is the fantasy of a man who adored witty women. She is a novelist. But when she sells the truth to the newspapers, she uses language as witty women novelists never use it. She uses the language of politics and newspapers, the language of men's world. Diana breaks the rule that separates domestic or private language (bedroom, drawing-room, novel language) from public language. In effect she claims for her own purposes a language women are barred from using. But the feminist point is obscured in *Diana of the Crossways* because selling the secret is by any standards wrong and even contemptible, and because Meredith's argument that Diana knew not what she did is unconvincing. What Meredith pretends to present as evidence of his heroine's bold spirit identifies radical action with treason and moral cowardice, with hysteria, selfishness, and even stupidity. Meanwhile the fabric of the fiction is rent because the novelist blindly and sentimentally protects his heroine.

Tracts like the ones Caroline Norton wrote aim to change the world by language; novels like George Meredith's aim to delight and to civilize. Two different kinds of change, two different languages, are involved. A novelist's playful language is, like Diana's wit, an agent of Eros. Meredith shows us his heroine intoxicating herself, writing alone in her room, as she transmutes facts into fictions. She pleasurably changes herself into her lover when she writes a novel about a Young Minister of State (Percy Dacier). We can imagine George Meredith in a similar frame of mind as by language he transformed a dead Caroline Norton (and a male wit named Meredith) into a vivid, female, fictitious Diana, romantically Celtic like himself. The novel changes reality into fictions, makes lies into effective truths, and perilously calls attention to its own processes, and reverses them. But it avoids the function of language Caroline Norton's tracts reached for: it lacks the ability to effect real social change, the aim that statements and secrets of statesmen have. Affirming the mythical character of a heroine named for a mythical goddess, Meredith reaffirms the conservative message the bourgeois novel has usually transmitted, identifying the traditional conflation of the domestic, the private, the separate, the individual, the unique, and the conventionally feminine, as an ideal. Because he cared more for myth than for history, he changed Caroline Norton's story; he used gossip as the basis of a fiction. Is there a lesson in the fact that, so doing, he flawed his novel? Is there another in the fact that *Diana of the Crossways* deliberately raises the issues that undermine it?

Ironies compound themselves outside the fiction, too. Biographies of Mrs. Norton have since *Diana* included a chapter on Meredith's novel; a heroine of feminism, who did good work for her sex, is best remembered as the prototype of a glamorous character in fiction. On the other hand, the historical Mrs. Norton, Mary Shelley's friend, a novelist and a wit, was in fact glamorous in precisely the old, high way Meredith adored, and celebrated in making Diana. The question of what in fact is fair, not to mention what is fact, is dizzying.

Alice and Wonderland:
A Curious Child

Nina Auerbach

"What—is—this?" he said at last.
"This is a child!" Haigha replied eagerly, coming in front of Alice to
introduce her . . . "We only found it today. It's as large as life, and twice
as natural!" "I always thought they were fabulous monsters!" said the
Unicorn. "Is it alive?"

For many of us Lewis Carroll's two *Alice* books may have provided the first
glimpse into Victorian England. With their curious blend of literal-mind-
edness and dream, formal etiquette and the logic of insanity, they tell the
adult reader a great deal about the Victorian mind. Alice herself, prim and
earnest in pinafore and pumps, confronting a world out of control by
looking for the rules and murmuring her lessons, stands as one image of
the Victorian middle-class child. She sits in Tenniel's first illustration to
Through the Looking-Glass and What Alice Found There in a snug, semi-foetal
position, encircled by a protective armchair and encircling a plump kitten
and a ball of yarn. She seems to be a beautiful child, but the position of
her head makes her look as though she had no face. She muses dreamily
on the snowstorm raging outside, part of a series of circles within circles,
enclosures within enclosures, suggesting the self-containment of innocence
and eternity.

Behind the purity of this design lie two Victorian domestic myths:
Wordsworth's "seer blessed," the child fresh from the Imperial Palace and
still washed by his continuing contact with "that immortal sea," and the
pure woman Alice will become, preserving an oasis for God and order in
a dim and tangled world. Even Victorians who did not share Lewis Carroll's
phobia about the ugliness and uncleanliness of little boys saw little girls as
the purest members of a species of questionable origin, combining as they
did the inherent spirituality of child and woman. Carroll's Alice seems sister
to such famous figures as Dickens's Little Nell and George Eliot's Eppie,
who embody the poise of original innocence in a fallen, sooty world.

From *Victorian Studies* 18, no. 1 (September 1973). © 1972 by the Trustees of Indiana
University.

Long after he transported Alice Liddell to Wonderland, Carroll himself deified his dream-child's innocence in these terms:

> What wert thou, dream-Alice, in thy foster-father's eyes? How shall he picture thee? Loving, first, loving and gentle: loving as a dog (forgive the prosaic simile, but I know of no earthly love so pure and perfect), and gentle as a fawn: . . . and lastly, curious—wildly curious, and with the eager enjoyment of Life that comes only in the happy hours of childhood, when all is new and fair, and when Sin and Sorrow are but names—empty words, signifying nothing!

From this Alice, it is only a step to Walter de la Mare's mystic icon, defined in the following almost Shelleyan image: "She wends serenely on like a quiet moon in a chequered sky. Apart, too, from an occasional Carrollian comment, the sole medium of the stories is *her* pellucid consciousness."

But when Dodgson wrote in 1887 of his gentle dream-child, the real Alice had receded into the distance of memory, where she had drowned in a pool of tears along with Lewis Carroll, her interpreter and creator. The paean quoted above stands at the end of a long series of progressive falsifications of Carroll's first conception, beginning with Alice's pale, attenuated presence in *Through the Looking-Glass*. For Lewis Carroll remembered what Charles Dodgson and many later commentators did not, that while *Looking-Glass* may have been the dream of the Red King, *Wonderland* is Alice's dream. Despite critical attempts to psychoanalyze Charles Dodgson through the writings of Lewis Carroll, the author of *Alice's Adventures in Wonderland* was too precise a logician and too controlled an artist to confuse his own dream with that of his character. The question "who dreamed it?" underlies all Carroll's dream tales, part of a pervasive Victorian quest for the origins of the self that culminates in the controlled regression of Freudian analysis. There is no equivocation in Carroll's first *Alice* book: the dainty child carries the threatening kingdom of Wonderland within her. A closer look at the character of Alice may reveal new complexities in the sentimentalized and attenuated Wordsworthianism many critics have assumed she represents, and may deepen through examination of a single example our vision of that "fabulous monster," the Victorian child.

Lewis Carroll once wrote to a child that while he forgot the story of *Alice*, "I think it was about 'malice.' " Some Freudian critics would have us believe it was about phallus. Alice herself seems aware of the implications of her shifting name when at the beginning of her adventures she asks herself the question that will weave through her story:

> "I wonder if I've been changed in the night? Let me think: *was* I the same when I got up this morning? I almost think I can remember feeling a little different. But if I'm not the same, the next question is, 'Who in the world am I?' Ah, *that's* the great puzzle!"

Other little girls traveling through fantastic countries, such as George Macdonald's Princess Irene and L. Frank Baum's Dorothy Gale, ask repeatedly *"where* am I?" rather than *"who* am I?" Only Alice turns her eyes inward from the beginning, sensing that the mystery of her surroundings is the mystery of her identity.

Even the above-ground Alice speaks in two voices, like many Victorians other than Dodgson-Carroll:

> She generally gave herself very good advice, (though she very seldom followed it), and sometimes she scolded herself so severely as to bring tears into her eyes; and once she remembered trying to box her own ears for having cheated herself in a game of croquet she was playing against herself, for this curious child was very fond of pretending to be two people.

The pun on "curious" defines Alice's fluctuating personality. Her eagerness to know and to be right, her compulsive reciting of her lessons ("I'm sure I can't be Mabel, for I know all sorts of things") turn inside out into the bizarre anarchy of her dream country, as the lessons themselves turn inside out into strange and savage tales of animals eating each other. In both senses of the word, Alice becomes "curiouser and curiouser" as she moves more deeply into Wonderland; she is both the croquet game without rules and its violent arbiter, the Queen of Hearts. The sea that almost drowns her is composed of her own tears, and the dream that nearly obliterates her is composed of fragments of her own personality.

As Alice dissolves into her component parts to become Wonderland, so, if we examine the actual genesis of Carroll's dream child, the bold outlines of Tenniel's famous drawing dissolve into four separate figures. First, there was the real Alice Liddell, a baby belle dame, it seems, who bewitched Ruskin as well as Dodgson. A small photograph of her concludes Carroll's manuscript of *Alice's Adventures under Ground,* the first draft of *Wonderland.* She is strikingly sensuous and otherworldly; her dark hair, bangs, and large inward-turned eyes give her face a haunting and a haunted quality which is missing from Tenniel's famous illustrations. Carroll's own illustrations for *Alice's Adventures under Ground* reproduce her eerieness perfectly. This Alice has a pre-Raphaelite languor and ambiguity about her which is reflected in the shifting colors of her hair. In some illustrations, she is indisputably brunette like Alice Liddell; in others, she is decidedly blonde like Tenniel's model Mary Hilton Badcock; and in still others, light from an unknown source hits her hair so that she seems to be both at once.

Mary Hilton Badcock has little of the dream child about her. She is blonde and pudgy, with squinting eyes, folded arms, and an intimidating frown. In Carroll's photograph of her, the famous starched pinafore and pumps appear for the first time—Alice Liddell seems to have been photographed in some sort of nightdress—and Mary moves easily into the clean, no-nonsense child of the Tenniel drawings. Austin Dobson wrote,

Enchanting Alice! Black-and-white
Has made your charm perenniel;
And nought save "Chaos and old Night"
Can part you now from Tenniel.

But a bit of research can dissolve what has been in some ways a misleading identification of Tenniel's Alice with Carroll's, obscuring some of the darker shadings of the latter. Carroll himself initiated the shift from the subtly disturbing Alice Liddell to the blonde and stolid Mary Badcock as "under ground" became the jollier-sounding "Wonderland," and the undiscovered country in his dream child became a nursery classic.

The demure propriety of Tenniel's Alice may have led readers to see her role in *Alice's Adventures in Wonderland* as more passive than it is. Although her size changes seem arbitrary and terrifying, she in fact directs them; only in the final courtroom scene does she change size without first wishing to, and there, her sudden growth gives her the power to break out of a dream that has become too dangerous. Most of Wonderland's savage songs come from Alice: the Caterpillar, Gryphon and Mock Turtle know that her cruel parodies of contemporary moralistic doggerel are "wrong from beginning to end." She is almost always threatening to the animals of Wonderland. As the Mouse and birds almost drown in her pool of tears, she eyes them with a strange hunger which suggests that of the *Looking-Glass* Walrus who weeps at the Oysters while devouring them behind his handkerchief. Her persistent allusions to her predatory cat Dinah and to a "nice little dog, near our house," who "kills all the rats" finally drive the animals away, leaving Alice to wonder forlornly—and disingenuously—why nobody in Wonderland likes Dinah.

Dinah is a strange figure. She is the only above-ground character whom Alice mentions repeatedly, almost always in terms of her eating some smaller animal. She seems finally to function as a personification of Alice's own subtly cannibalistic hunger, as Fury in the Mouse's tale is personified as a dog. At one point, Alice fantasizes her own identity actually blending into Dinah's:

> "How queer it seems," Alice said to herself, "to be going messages for a rabbit! I suppose Dinah'll be sending me on messages next!" And she began fancying the sort of thing that would happen: " 'Miss Alice! Come here directly, and get ready for your walk!' 'Coming in a minute, nurse! But I've got to watch this mousehole till Dinah comes back, and see that the mouse doesn't get out.' "

While Dinah is always in a predatory attitude, most of the Wonderland animals are lugubrious victims; together, they encompass the two sides of animal nature that are in Alice as well. But as she falls down the rabbit-hole, Alice senses the complicity between eater and eaten, looking-glass versions of each other:

"Dinah, my dear! I wish you were down here with me! There are no mice in the air, I'm afraid, but you might catch a bat, and that's very like a mouse, you know. But do cats eat bats, I wonder?" And here Alice began to get rather sleepy, and went on saying to herself, in a dreamy sort of way, "Do cats eat bats? Do cats eat bats?" and sometimes, "Do bats eat cats?" for, you see, as she couldn't answer either question, it didn't matter which way she put it.

We are already halfway to the final banquet of *Looking-Glass*, in which the food comes alive and begins to eat the guests.

Even when Dinah is not mentioned, Alice's attitude toward the animals she encounters is often one of casual cruelty. It is a measure of Dodgson's ability to flatten out Carroll's material that the prefatory poem could describe Alice "in friendly chat with bird or beast," or that he would later see Alice as "loving as a dog . . . gentle as a fawn." She pities Bill the Lizard and kicks him up the chimney, a state of mind that again looks forward to that of the Pecksniffian Walrus in *Looking-Glass*. When she meets the Mock Turtle, the weeping embodiment of a good Victorian dinner, she restrains herself twice when he mentions lobsters, but then distorts Isaac Watts's *Sluggard* into a song about a *baked* lobster surrounded by hungry sharks. In its second stanza, a Panther shares a pie with an Owl who then becomes dessert, as Dodgson's good table manners pass into typical Carrollian cannibalism. The more sinister and Darwinian aspects of animal nature are introduced into Wonderland by the gentle Alice, in part through projections of her hunger onto Dinah and the "nice little dog" (she meets a "dear little puppy" after she has grown small and is afraid he will eat her up) and in part through the semi-cannibalistic appetite her songs express. With the exception of the powerful Cheshire Cat, whom I shall discuss below, most of the Wonderland animals stand in some danger of being exploited or eaten. The Dormouse is their prototype: he is fussy and cantankerous, with the nastiness of a self-aware victim, and he is stuffed into a teapot as the Mock Turtle, sobbing out his own elegy, will be stuffed into a tureen.

Alice's courteously menacing relationship to these animals is more clearly brought out in *Alice's Adventures under Ground*, in which she encounters only animals until she meets the playing cards, who are lightly sketched-in versions of their later counterparts. When expanding the manuscript for publication, Carroll added the Frog Footman, Cook, Duchess, Pig-Baby, Cheshire Cat, Mad Hatter, March Hare, and Dormouse, as well as making the Queen of Hearts a more fully developed character than she was in the manuscript. In other words, all the human or quasi-human characters were added in revision, and all develop aspects of Alice that exist only under the surface of her dialogue. The Duchess's household also turns inside out the domesticated Wordsworthian ideal: with baby and pepper flung about indiscriminately, pastoral tranquillity is inverted into a whirlwind of savage sexuality. The furious Cook embodies the equation between eating and killing that underlies Alice's apparently innocent remarks about Dinah. The violent Duchess's unctuous search for "the moral" of things echoes Alice's own violence and search for "the rules." At the Mad Tea Party, the Hatter extends Alice's "great interest in questions of eating and drinking" into an insane *modus vivendi*; like Alice, the Hatter and the Duchess sing savage songs about eating that embody the underside of Victorian literary treacle. The Queen's croquet game magnifies Alice's own desire to cheat at croquet and to punish herself violently for doing so. Its use of live animals may be a subtler extension of Alice's own desire to twist the animal kingdom to the absurd rules of civilization, which seem to revolve largely around eating and being eaten. Alice is able to appreciate the Queen's savagery so quickly because her size changes have made her increasingly aware of who she, herself, is from the point of view of a Caterpillar, a Mouse, a Pigeon, and, especially, a Cheshire Cat.

The Cheshire Cat, also a late addition to the book, is the only figure other than Alice who encompasses all the others. William Empson discusses at length the spiritual kinship between Alice and the Cat, the only creature in Wonderland whom she calls her "friend." Florence Becker Lennon refers to the Cheshire Cat as "Dinah's dream-self," and we have noticed the subtle shift of identities between Alice and Dinah throughout the story. The Cat shares Alice's equivocal placidity: "The Cat only grinned when it saw Alice. It looked good-natured, she thought: still it had *very* long claws and a great many teeth, so she felt it ought to be treated with respect." The Cat is the only creature to make explicit the identification between Alice and the madness of Wonderland: " '. . . we're all mad here. I'm mad. You're mad.' 'How do you know I'm mad?' said Alice. 'You must be,' said the Cat, 'or you wouldn't have come here.' Alice didn't think that proved it at all." Although Alice cannot accept it and closes into silence, the Cat's remark may be the answer she has been groping toward in her incessant question, "who am I?" As an alter ego, the Cat is wiser than Alice—and safer—because he is the only character in the book who is aware of his own madness. In his serene acceptance of the fury within and without, his total control over his appearance and disappearance, he almost suggests a post-analytic version of the puzzled Alice.

As Alice dissolves increasingly into Wonderland, so the Cat dissolves into his own head, and finally into his own grinning mouth. The core of Alice's nature, too, seems to lie in her mouth: the eating and drinking that direct her size changes and motivate much of her behavior, the songs and verses that pop out of her inadvertently, are all involved with things entering and leaving her mouth. Alice's first song introduces a sinister image of a grinning mouth. Our memory of the Crocodile's grin hovers over the later description of the Cat's "grin without a Cat," and colors our sense of Alice's infallible good manners:

> How cheerfully he seems to grin,
>   How neatly spreads his claws,
> And welcomes little fishes in,
>   With gently smiling jaws!

Walter de la Mare associates Alice with "a quiet moon" which is by implication a full moon. I think it is more appropriate to associate her with the grinning crescent that seems to follow her throughout her adventures, choosing to become visible only at particular moments, and teaching her the one lesson she must learn in order to arrive at a definition of who she is.

Martin Gardner pooh-poohs the "oral aggressions" psychoanalysts have found in Carroll's incessant focus on eating and drinking by reminding us of the simple fact that "small children are obsessed by eating, and like to read about it in their books." Maybe his commonsense approach is correct, but Lewis Carroll was concerned with nonsense, and throughout his life, he seems to have regarded eating with some horror. An early cartoon in *The Rectory Umbrella* depicts an emaciated family partaking raptly of a "homœopathic meal" consisting of an ounce of bread, half a particle of beer, etc.; young Sophy, who is making a pig of herself, asks for another molecule. Throughout his life, Carroll was abstemious at meals, according to his nephew and first biographer, Stuart Dodgson Collingwood: "the healthy appetites of his young friends filled him with wonder, and even with alarm." When he took one of his child-friends to another's house for a meal, he told the host: "Please *be careful*, because she eats a good deal too much." William Empson defines his attitude succinctly: "Dodgson was well-informed about foods, kept his old menus and was winetaster to the College; but ate very little, suspected the High Table of overeating, and would see no reason to deny that he connected overeating with other forms of sensuality." To the man who in *Sylvie and Bruno* would define EVIL as a looking-glass version of LIVE, "gently smiling jaws" held teeth which were to be regarded with alarm; they seemed to represent to him a private emblem of original sin, for which Alice as well as the Knave of Hearts is finally placed on trial.

When the Duchess's Cook abruptly barks out "Pig!" Alice thinks the word is meant for her, though it is the baby, another fragment of Alice's own nature, who dissolves into a pig. The Mock Turtle's lament for his future soupy self later blends tellingly into the summons for the trial: the lament of the eaten and the call to judgment melt together. When she arrives at the trial, the unregenerate Alice instantly eyes the tarts: "In the very middle of the court was a table, with a large dish of tarts upon it: they looked so good, that it made Alice quite hungry to look at them—'I wish they'd get the trial done,' she thought, 'and hand round the refreshments!' " Her hunger links her to the hungry Knave who is being sentenced: in typically ambiguous portmanteau fashion, Carroll makes the trial both a pre-Orwellian travesty of justice and an objective correlative of a real sense of sin. Like the dog Fury in the Mouse's tale, Alice takes all the parts. But unlike Fury, she is accused as well as accuser, melting into judge, jury, witness, and defendant; the person who boxes on the ears as well as the person who "cheats." Perhaps the final verdict would tell Alice who she is at last, but if it did, Wonderland would threaten to overwhelm her. Before it comes, she "grows"; the parts of her nature rush back together; combining the voices of victim and accuser, she gives "a little scream, half of fright and half of anger," and wakes up.

Presented from the point of view of her older sister's sentimental pietism, the world to which Alice awakens seems far more dream-like and hazy than the sharp contours of Wonderland. Alice's lesson about her own identity has never been stated explicitly, for the stammerer Dodgson was able to talk freely only in his private language of puns and nonsense, but a Wonderland pigeon points us toward it:

> "You're a serpent; and there's no use denying it. I suppose you'll be telling me next that you never tasted an egg!"
>
> "I have tasted eggs, certainly," said Alice, who was a very truthful child; "but little girls eat eggs quite as much as serpents do, you know."
>
> "I don't believe it," said the Pigeon, "but if they do, why, then they're a kind of serpent: that's all I can say."
>
> This was such a new idea to Alice, that she was quite silent for a minute or two.

Like so many of her silences throughout the book, Alice's silence here is charged with significance, reminding us again that an important technique in learning to read Carroll is our ability to interpret his private system of symbols and signals and to appreciate the many meanings of silence. In this scene, the golden child herself becomes the serpent in childhood's Eden. The eggs she eats suggest the woman she will become, the unconscious cannibalism involved in the very fact of eating and desire to eat, and finally, the charmed circle of childhood itself. Only in *Alice's Adventures in Wonderland* was Carroll able to fall all the way through the rabbit hole to the point where top and bottom become one, bats and cats melt into each other, and the vessel of innocence and purity is also the source of inescapable corruption.

Alice's adventures in Wonderland foreshadow Lewis Carroll's subsequent literary career, which was a progressive dissolution into his component parts. Florence Becker Lennon defines well the schism that came with the later books: "Nothing in *Wonderland* parallels the complete severance of the Reds and Whites in *Through the Looking-Glass*. In *Sylvie and Bruno*, author and story have begun to disintegrate. The archness and sweetness of parts, the utter cruelty and loathsomeness of others, predict literal decomposition into his elements." The Alice of *Through the Looking-*

Glass, which was published six years after *Wonderland,* represents still another Alice, Alice Raikes; the character is so thinned out that the vapid, passive Tenniel drawing is an adequate illustration of her. *Wonderland* ends with Alice playing all the parts in an ambiguous trial which concludes without a verdict. *Looking-Glass* begins with an unequivocal verdict: "One thing was certain, that the *white* kitten had nothing to do with it—it was the black kitten's fault entirely." Poor Dinah, relegated to the role of face-washer-in-the-background, has also dissolved into her component parts.

Throughout the books, the schism between Blacks (later Reds) and Whites is developed. Alice's greater innocence and passivity are stressed by her identification with Lily, the white pawn. The dominant metaphor of a chess game whose movements are determined by invisible players spreads her sense of helplessness and predestination over the book. The nursery rhymes of which most of the characters form a part also make their movements seem predestined; the characters in *Wonderland* tend more to create their own nursery rhymes. The question that weaves through the book is no longer "who am I?" but "which dreamed it?" If the story is the dream of the Red King (the sleeping embodiment of passion and masculinity), then Alice, the White Pawn (or pure female child) is exonerated from its violence, although in another sense, as she herself perceives, she is also in greater danger of extinction. Her increasing sweetness and innocence in the second book make her more ghost-like as well, and it is appropriate that more death jokes surround her in the second *Alice* book than in the first.

As Carroll's dream children became sweeter, his attitude toward animals became increasingly tormented and obsessive, as we can see in the hysterical antivivisection crusade of his later years. In one of his pamphlets, "Vivisection as a Sign of the Times," cruelty to animals, which in the first Alice was a casual instinct, becomes a synecdoche for the comprehensive sin of civilization:

> "But the thing cannot be!" cries some amiable reader, fresh from an interview with the most charming of men, a London physician. "What! Is it possible that one so gentle in manner, so full of noble sentiments, can be hardhearted? The very idea is an outrage to common sense!" And thus we are duped every day of our lives. Is it possible that that bank director, with his broad honest face, can be meditating a fraud? That the chairman of that meeting of shareholders, whose every tone has the ring of truth in it, can hold in his hand a "cooked" schedule of accounts? That my wine merchant, so outspoken, so confiding, can be supplying me with an adulterated article? That my schoolmaster, to whom I have entrusted my little boy, can starve or neglect him? How well I remember his words to the dear child when last we parted. "You are leaving your friends," he said, "but you will have a father in

me, dear, and a mother in Mrs. Squeers!'' For all such rose-coloured dreams of the necessary immunity from human vices of educated men the facts in last week's *Spectator* have a terrible significance. ''Trust no man further than you can see him,'' they seem to say. ''Qui vult decipi, decipiatur.''

''Gently smiling jaws'' have spread themselves over England. The sweeping intensity of this jeremiad shares the vision, if not the eloquence, of Ruskin's later despairing works.

As the world becomes more comprehensively cruel, the Carrollian little girl evolves into the impossibly innocent Sylvie in *Sylvie and Bruno* and *Sylvie and Bruno Concluded*, who is more fairy or guardian angel than she is actual child. Here, the dream belongs not to Sylvie but to the strangely maimed narrator. Any hint of wildness in Sylvie is siphoned off onto her mischievous little brother Bruno, whom she is always trying to tame as the first Alice boxed her own ears for cheating at croquet; and any real badness is further placed at one remove in the figure of the villainous Uggug, an obscenely fat child who finally turns into a porcupine. Uggug's metamorphosis recalls that of the Pig-baby in *Wonderland*, but in the earlier book, the Cook let us know that Alice was also encompassed by the epithet—a terrible one in Carroll's private language—''Pig!''

Like Alice's, Sylvie's essential nature is revealed by her attitude toward animals. But while Alice's crocodile tears implicated her in original sin, Sylvie's tears prove her original innocence. In a key scene, the narrator tries to explain to her ''innocent mind'' the meaning of a hare killed in a hunt:

> ''They hunt *foxes*,'' Sylvie said, thoughtfully. ''And I think they *kill* them, too. Foxes are very fierce. I daresay men don't love them. Are hares fierce?''
> ''No,'' I said. ''A hare is a sweet, gentle, timid animal—almost as gentle as a lamb.'' [Apparently no vision of the snappish March Hare returned to haunt Lewis Carroll at this point.]
> ''But, if men *love* hares, why—why—'' her voice quivered, and her sweet eyes were brimming with tears.
> ''I'm afraid they *don't* love them, dear child.''
> ''All *children* love them,'' Sylvie said. ''All *ladies* love them.''
> ''I'm afraid even *ladies* go to hunt them, sometimes.''
> Sylvie shuddered. ''Oh, no, not *ladies*!'' she earnestly pleaded.
> . . . In a hushed, solemn tone, with bowed head and clasped hands, she put her final question, ''Does GOD love hares?''
> ''Yes!'' I said. ''I'm *sure* He does. He loves every living thing. Even sinful *men*. How much more the animals, that cannot sin!'' [Here the whole *Wonderland* gallery should have risen up in chorus against their creator!]

"I don't know what 'sin' means," said Sylvie. And I didn't try
to explain it.

"Come, my child," I said, trying to lead her away. "Wish good-
bye to the poor hare, and come and look for blackberries."

"Good-bye, poor hare!" Sylvie obediently repeated, looking
over her shoulder at it as we turned away. And then, all in a
moment, her self-command gave way. Pulling her hand out of
mine, she ran back to where the dead hare was lying, and flung
herself down at its side in such an agony of grief I could hardly
have believed possible in so young a child.

Sylvie's weeping over a dead hare is an unfortunate conclusion to
Alice's initial underground leap after a live rabbit. Dodgson has been driven
full circle here to embrace the pure little girl of Victorian convention, though
he is ambivalent in this passage about "ladies." But his deterioration should
be used as a yardstick to measure his achievement in the first of the *Alice*
books, which a brief survey of some typical portraits of children in nineteenth-century literature may help us to appreciate.

Victorian concepts of the child tended to swing back and forth between
extremes of original innocence and original sin; Rousseau and Calvin stood
side by side in the nursery. Since actual children were the focus of such
an extreme conflict of attitudes, they tended to be a source of pain and
embarrassment to adults, and were therefore told they should be "seen
and not heard." Literature dealt more freely with children than life did, so
adult conflicts about them were allowed to emerge more openly in books.
As Jan Gordon puts it:

The most amazing feature of, say, Dickens's treatment of children,
is how quickly they are transformed into monsters. Even Oliver
Twist's surname forces the reader to appreciate the twisting condition normally associated with creatures more closely akin to the
devil! One effect of this identification with evil adults . . . is that
the only way of approaching childhood is by way of the opposite
of satanic monstrosities—namely, the golden world of an edenic
wonderland whose pastoral dimension gives it the status of a primal scene.

(*Aspects of Alice*, edited by Robert Phillips)

In its continual quest for origins and sources of being, Victorian literature
repeatedly explores the ambiguous figure of the child, in whom it attempts
to resolve the contradictions it perceives much as *Sylvie and Bruno* does: by
an extreme sexual division.

Little boys in Victorian literature tend to be allied to the animal, the
Satanic, and the insane. For this reason, novels in which a boy is the central
focus are usually novels of development, in which the boy evolves out of

his inherent violence, "working out the brute" in an ascent to a higher spiritual plane. This tradition seems foreshadowed by the boy in Wordsworth's *Prelude,* whose complexity undercuts the many Victorian sentimentalizations about Wordsworth's children. The predatory child in the first two books, traveling through a dark landscape that seems composed largely of his own projected fears and desires, has in fact a great deal in common with Carroll's Alice. Carroll is truer than many of his contemporaries to the ambiguities of Wordsworth's children, but he goes beyond Wordsworth in making a little girl the focus of his vision. Wordsworth's little girls tend to be angelic, corrective figures who exist largely to soothe the turbulence of the male protagonists; his persona in the *Prelude* is finally led to his "spiritual eye" through the ministrations of an idealized, hovering Dorothy.

David Copperfield must also develop out of an uncontrolled animality that is close to madness—early in the novel, we learn of him that "he bites"—and he can do so only through the guidance of the ghostly Agnes, pointing ever upward. Dr. Arnold's Rugby, which reflected and conditioned many of the century's attitudes toward boys, was run on a similar evolutionary premise: the students were to develop out of the inherent wickedness of "boy nature" into the state of "Christian gentleman," a semidivine warrior for the good. In the all-male society of Rugby, Dr. Arnold was forced to assume the traditionally female role of spiritual beacon, as the image of the Carlylean hero supplanted that of the ministering angel. Thomas Hughes's famous tale of Rugby, *Tom Brown's School Days,* solves this problem by making Tom's spiritual development spring from the influence of the feminized, debilitated young Arthur and his radiantly ethereal mother: only after their elaborate ministrations is the young man able to kneel by the Doctor's casket and worship the transfigured image of the-Doctor-as-God. Women and girls are necessary catalysts for the development of the hero out of his dangerously animal state to contact with the God within and without him.

Cast as they were in the role of emotional and spiritual catalysts, it is not surprising that girls who function as protagonists of Victorian literature are rarely allowed to develop: in its refusal to subject females to the evolutionary process, the Victorian novel takes a signficant step backward from one of its principal sources, the novels of Jane Austen. Even when they are interesting and "wicked," Victorian heroines tend to be static figures like Becky Sharp; when they are "good," their lack of development is an important factor in the Victorian reversal of Pope's sweeping denunciation—"most women have no characters at all"—into a cardinal virtue. Little girls in Victorian literature are rarely children, nor are they allowed to grow up. Instead, they exist largely as a diffusion of emotional and religious grace, representing "nothing but love," as Dodgson's Sylvie warbles. Florence Dombey in Dickens's *Dombey and Son* may stand as their paradigm. Representing as she does the saving grace of the daughter in a world dominated by the hard greed and acquisitiveness of men—the world that kills her tender brother Paul—Florence drifts through Mr. Dombey's house in a limbo of love throughout the book, waiting for her father to come to her. She ages, but never changes, existing less as a character than as a "spiritual repository into which Mr. Dombey must dip if he is to be saved." Dickens's Little Nell and Little Dorrit are equally timeless and faceless. Though both are in fact post-pubescent—Little Nell is fourteen, Little Dorrit, twenty-two—they combine the mythic purity and innocence of the little girl with the theoretical marriageability of the woman, diffusing an aura from a sphere separate from that of the other characters, a sphere of non-personal love without change.

Charlotte Brontë's Jane Eyre and George Eliot's Maggie Tulliver are two more sharply-etched little girls who grow into women, but even they represent, in an angrier and more impassioned way, "nothing but love." Neither develops in the course of her book, because neither needs to change: all both need is acceptance of the love they have to offer, which in Jane Eyre's case is fervently erotic and ethical, and in Maggie Tulliver's is passionately filial and engulfing. Both triumph at the end of their novels because they are allowed to redeem through their love the men they have chosen, who, as Victorian convention dictated, have undergone a process of development up to *them*. This reminds us once more that in Victorian literature, little boys were allowed, even encouraged, to partake of original sin; but little girls rarely were.

We return once more to the anomaly of Carroll's Alice, who explodes out of Wonderland hungry and unregenerate. By a subtle dramatization of Alice's attitude toward animals and toward the animal in herself, by his final resting on the symbol of her mouth, Carroll probed in all its complexity the underground world within the little girl's pinafore. The ambiguity of the concluding trial finally, and wisely, waives questions of original guilt or innocence. The ultimate effect of Alice's adventures implicates her, female child though she is, in the troubled human condition; most Victorians refused to grant women and children this respect. The sympathetic delicacy and precision with which Carroll traced the chaos of a little girl's psyche seems equalled and surpassed only later in such explorations as D. H. Lawrence's of the young Ursula Brangwen in *The Rainbow*, the chaos of whose growth encompasses her hunger for violence, sexuality, liberty, and beatitude. In the imaginative literature of its century, *Alice's Adventures in Wonderland* stands alone.

The Educated Ego: Samuel Butler's *Way of All Flesh*

Thomas L. Jeffers

The Erewhonian myth of pre-existence may be read at two different levels. On one, it is an amusing *reductio* of the Church's "legal fiction" of original sin: birth is the result of a criminal blunder on the part of the pure spirit who desires to put on flesh, in expiation for which he is forced to sign, by proxy, a statement admitting the depravity of his wish to come into the world, and enslaving himself to his parents in payment for their trouble in having him—the whole procedure being "confirmed" in a ceremony at age fourteen. On a second level, the myth is a serious, quasi-Platonic version of a truth darkly understood in the Christian doctrine of original sin and analyzed by some psychoanalysts in their discussion of birth trauma: namely, that being born *is* calamitous. Not that it is a literal fall from the realm of pure spirit into the realm of matter: a spirit or an intelligence—the words are synonymous for Butler—doesn't exist until sperm and ovum meet and a new organism gets under way. It is instead a fall from life in the womb, where one knows perfectly what's what and where all necessary provisions are piped in, into the life outside, where one must build one's own establishment in the face of strange contingencies and at the not always tender mercy of grown-ups. A myth about this sort of fall is no mere elaboration of a pointless lament: it is a valuable attempt to tell what goes "wrong" at birth, in order better to comprehend, once the irrevocable has happened, what the duties of child and parents are.

Having made the binding decision to be born, the child's duty clearly is to stay at his post and try to realize the amenities of life in the womb in terms appropriate to the new life outside. That doesn't mean a return to the fetal sleep. It means an active engagement with the different conditions

From *Samuel Butler Revalued.* © 1981 by the Pennsylvania State University. Pennsylvania State University Press, 1981.

417

of pleasure which the extra-uterine world sets. As the counselors in the realm of pure spirit are supposed to say to the departing: If you recall the bliss of your prior state, if, suicidally, you yearn for it as Orpheus yearned for the fading Eurydice, then "fly—fly—if you can remember the advice—to the haven of your present and immediate duty, taking shelter incessantly in the work which you have in hand." The work the child has in hand is that of securing his own happiness, a work which, as we shall see, breaks down into a number of relatively simple "jobs." It is the parents who have the larger and more complex duty, appropriate to their opportunity to do something to repair the calamity that has befallen their children. They are "to remember how they felt when they were young, and actually to behave towards their children as they would have had their own parents behave towards themselves" (*Erewhon*). One usually images the golden rule's "Do unto others" as though the "others" were grown-ups. Butler suggests that they might also be children, which is to stretch the grown-ups' powers of empathy in directions that had been too strange for the Twelve, and have been too strange for the millions since. And no wonder. "For [though] all children love their fathers and mothers, if these last will only let them," and though parents do often have an instinct to "let them" love, there is "no talisman in the word[s] 'parent' [or 'child'] which can generate miracles of affection," nor can affection be compelled by law (*The Fair Haven*; *Erewhon*). Affection must be earned by both parties. That is their final duty, which they have a good, if rarely perceived, incentive to perform: in affectionate families the father of fifty and the son of twenty are friends, and the father of sixty doesn't feel that the son of thirty is impatient for him to die.

I

I want first to consider in some detail the child's "present and immediate duty," asking not only what must be done, but what faculties are needed to do it. "What shall I do?" This particular interrogative is several times on the lips of lawyers and plutocrats who want to know from Jesus how they shall inherit eternal life. Without reference to inheriting anything, it is what the conscience-stricken Jews ask of Peter when he tells them that the man they crucified has been made "both Lord and Christ" (Acts 2:36–37), a passage which Bunyan alludes to at the end of the first paragraph of *The Pilgrim's Progress*, where Christian, burdened by his sins and their wages, "brake out with a lamentable cry, saying, *What shall I do?*" There are, as many readers have noticed, several incidental parallels between *The Pilgrim's Progress* and *The Way of All Flesh*—the motif of a "progress" along a "way," Butler's early thought of calling his hero "Christian," the series of helpers through various trials, etc.—but the essential parallel is here, in the distress of asking how one is to escape death and come to life. And on the surface, Bunyan and Butler give the same answer: one must forsake one's kin, for the gate leading to the celestial city is too strait to admit a family crowd. Only the lean individual can fit through.

In the first half of Bunyan's book Christian has forsaken his wife and children, who see the light in the second half; in Butler's book it is the child who must forsake his parents and siblings, who never see the light. One must give up *all* for Christ, whether they follow one's lead or not. Bunyan has in mind Jesus' saying that "If any man come to me, and hate not his father and mother, and wife, and children, and brethren, and sisters, yea, and his own life also, he cannot be my disciple" (Luke 14:26). Butler has the same saying in mind, but by identifying Christ, as we have seen, with the inward intelligence of "his own life," he radically changes Bunyan's (and Luke's) meaning. The coincidence of theme breaks down when we come to particular theologies; yet Luke, Bunyan, and Butler are tied together by the surprise, not to say the disgust, with which the ordinary reader hears the command to "hate" the near ones whom he is usually told he should love. Luke or Bunyan would be quick to explain that he is telling the believer to subordinate all to one goal, which is incorporation with Christ. With rather extensive transvaluation of terms, Butler ultimately gives the same explanation, but he fills in the immediate details more than either Luke or Bunyan is concerned to do. He says, in effect, that a man is to hate his family because they are devouring his soul between morning business and evening prayers.

Butler's rule of thumb is that one should never trouble to learn anything till one has been made very uncomfortable for a very long time by not knowing it. After such a wide invitation to quietism, his injunction to learn something as desperate as the severing of family ties—the giving up of that which ought to be a present help—indicates a situation which must be very uncomfortable, wherein the family members' duty of earning one another's affection has been altogether shirked. The trouble in the Pontifex family lies precisely in the parents' overinsistence on *being* a present help. They don't let Ernest do anything for himself, because they regard him as a mere duplication of themselves—or if he isn't, he ought to be.

Theobald expects the infant Ernest to be a "full grown clergym[a]n—of moderate views, but inclining rather to Evangelicism." When he finds that the boy is at first nothing of the sort, but only a squirming amalgam of Pontifex and Allaby juices, he drives him into the rectory greenhouse, weeding out all signs of self-will in order to cultivate a little J.S.Mill minus the radicalism: "Before he was three years old he could read, and after a fashion, write. Before he was four he was learning Latin, and could do rule of three sums" (*The Way of All Flesh*). Ernest refuses to be forced. He first quarrels with his father and pitches his own tent when, as a fetus, he attaches himself to the uterine wall. And once the umbilical cord has been cut, he may be said to have begun his quarrel with his mother too. He wants to have a separate self, but it takes him years consciously to realize that he does, and years more to realize that he *ought*—the latter illumination beginning at Roughborough when he puts the torch to Theobald's effigy, and culminating in London when he hears Overton say that his parents are awful. There is no contradiction, Jerome Buckley notwithstanding, between Butler's emphasis on the influence of heredity and his emphasis on the need for differentiation. Ernest is continuous with his parents both biologically (their genes are his) and socially (their naivety and religiosity are his), but he is also separate from them. Biologically, it is *his* stomach that must be fed; socially, it is *his* emotions, *his* purposes that must steer his life as he moves into waters beyond his parents' ken. Theobald assumes that, since "ordination was the road [he] knew and understood, and indeed the only road about which he knew anything at all," then it must be the one for Ernest, too. Such a road will lead Ernest into his grave. He must live his life as a good metaphor lives its life, by functioning within a convention, yet being sufficiently strange to stand out against it. If he repeats the convention and no more, he is dead.

What does Ernest require to stand out against his parents? As I have intimated, he requires luck, in both its circumstantial and its biological aspects. He also requires cunning—the power of intelligence which 1) is one form of biological luck, 2) is activated by circumstantial luck, and 3) is free to improve upon both. Let us look at these requirements more closely.

Ernest's circumstantial luck comes to him in the external stimuli of Towneley's triple *No*'s, of Mr. Shaw's lesson in Form Criticism, of a pleasant six months in jail, of the glorious £70,000, and so on. These stimuli appear to be a series of lottery numbers, Ernest seeming less to have purchased the winning tickets than to have had them thrust into his hands. Lacking the fortitude and energy necessary to create his own advantages, he can only stand and wait: "He should not have had the courage to give up all for Christ's sake, but now Christ had mercifully taken all; and lo! it seemed as though all were found." If this apparent predestinarianism were everything, Ernest's break-through wouldn't be as interesting as it is. But "Christ" is no external deity whose last resource is shock treatment—the golden, amnesiac lightning which obliterates the awful Battersby past and makes possible a blessed, fairly unprescribed future. Rather, "Christ" is Butler's nonce-word for the unconscious intelligence Ernest's biological luck has given him. His "Christian" knowledge consists of his instinct for what gives pleasure, and his impulse to put himself into situations where he is likely to get it. "Christ" deflects his course into opportunities disguised as predicaments, wherein the "all" which hinders his seeking his own truest happiness will be swept away.

Think of the particulars of the Miss Maitland episode which precipitates Ernest's imprisonment. He advances upon her as he supposes Towneley to have advanced upon Miss Snow, trying thus to satisfy a hunger that is at once sexual and spiritual—to spend himself inside a woman, and thereby to achieve something of the lightness and eager virility of Towneley, who has "come before [his] time" with "a hurried step . . . [which] bound[ed] up the stairs as though . . . the force of gravity had little power" over him. "Christ" knows that these satisfactions can be got only by kicking into the corner "the Bible given him at his [false] christening by his affectionate godmother and aunt Elizabeth Allaby," and by marching off straight to do what the Bible forbids. "Christ" doesn't know tactically how to proceed beyond this—to determine, e.g., whether Miss Maitland is really like Miss Snow, as Mrs. Baxter says, or whether, as Mrs. Jupp says, she isn't. Tactical knowledge is important, but it is secondary to the unconscious conviction that the restraints of clerical respectability must be cut. It is not too much therefore to say that Ernest's unconscious self drives him to an extremity wherein he either will commit the fornication he longs for, or will land himself in jail—which institution will effectually defrock him, that he might seek his satisfaction with a lighter tread. Nor do I think it too much to say that his unconscious self is what prompts him to ask Towneley whether he doesn't like poor people—a question which his conscience may suppose to be a righteous challenge, but which in fact is a request for Towneley to set that conscience straight by showing him how nobody is nicer for being poor, etc. Finally, in the conversation with Mr. Shaw it is Ernest's unconscious self which urges him to wield his conscience's greatest weapon, the Bible, to see how strong it actually is. He is like a man driving hard an engine he really wants to break—so that he can go get a new and different one.

One would be going too far in attributing so much cunning to the curate's unconscious self, were it not that the child's has shown so much already. When Ernest is ill and is encouragingly told by mama that he needn't be afraid of dying, because, if he promises never to vex papa anymore, he will go to heaven and be with Grandpapa Pontifex and Grandmama Allaby and sing beautiful hymns to Jesus, he feels no "wish to die, and was glad when he got better, for there were no kittens in heaven, and he did not think there were cowslips to make cowslip tea with." He enjoys the things of this life very well: he is not going to be easily tricked into preferring those of some other. Then there is his reaction to his first meeting with Dr. Skinner, whose office is lined with books two rows deep "from floor to ceiling": "It was horrible." And a while later Ernest provides himself an escape from Dr. Skinner's factious talk by beginning to cry—"doubtless through an intense but inarticulate sense of boredom greater than he could bear." At school he shirks fights of every species, including football, because, as "a mere bag of bones, with upper arms about as thick as the wrists of other boys his age," and with a "pigeon-breasted" "little chest," he always gets beaten up. He despises himself for shirking, assuming that "the timidity natural to childhood" is evidence of his "cowardice." But in truth "the instinct which made him keep out of games for which he was ill adapted was more reasonable than the reason which would have driven him into them." In the same way he avoids the sofa conversations offered by his mother, not because he is a worse coward than his fellows, but because "all sensible people are cowards when they are off their beat, or when they think they are going to be roughly handled." It is precisely this discretion which rescues him from his parents' inquisition, as it has from Dr. Skinner's miasmal pleasantries: Theobald and Christina probe and probe into the misdemeanors of the Roughborough boys, "till they were on the point of reaching subjects more delicate than they had yet touched upon. Here Ernest's unconscious self took the matter up, and made a resistance to which his conscious self was unequal, by tumbling him off his chair in a fit of fainting."

"Sapiens suam si sapientiam nôrit": the young Ernest usually does know his own wisdom, but rarely can he articulate it. Dwelling within him as deep as it does, it ultimately defies full articulation, though the copious essays which interrupt Butler's narrative prove that it can be pointed to— articulated in approximate terms which are quite sufficient. In young Ernest, though, even approximate articulation is shouted down by the voice of his father—his "conscious self . . . begotten of prigs, and trained in priggishness." This "outward and visible old husk" may do all the talking for a while, but it has no vital influence on Ernest's actions. Vital influence belongs to the unconscious self, inward and unseen, which is "the God who made [him]."

Butler's distinction between selves is of course analogous to that which Freud draws between the parties flanking the conscious ego: the conscience above ("super") and the id below. The Freudian terms are useful. What Butler calls Ernest's "conscious self" is what we should call his "conscience," though he is indeed so dominated by the voice of his father that in him the two are identical. But the psychology Butler is anticipating is less Freud's than Lawrence's. The issue is between those who regard the unconscious as rapacious and heedless, an energy which is necessary but always in need of governance, and those who regard it as moderating and trustworthy, an energy which, as long as novel dilemmas don't put it off the scent, can govern itself. Lawrence writes: "The Freudian unconscious is the cellar in which the mind keeps its own bastard spawn. The true unconscious is the well-head, the fountain of real motivity," which in its pristine state one knows not through concepts, but wholly and directly, as one knows the sun, or one's mother, or anything primal, the senses reaching out and "lovingly roving like the fingers of an infant or a blind man over the face of the treasured object." One cannot, however, just live in intimacy with one's unconscious self, like an infant eternally at his mother's breast. When novel dilemmas arise, as they assuredly will, one needs an intelligently conscious ego, not just to hear the demands of the now bewildered unconscious, but to chart a course which will satisfy them. The conscious ego in Ernest's case is the implied addressee of the speech on p. 116 [of Daniel F. Howard's 1964 edition]. Butler is emphatic about the intelligence of the unconscious self, and I have suggested how Ernest's pushes him into situations where, one way or other, the obstacles between him and his richest pleasures will be cleared away. What Butler leaves to implication is the need someone as distressingly placed as Ernest must have for a shrewd ego to act as prophet for the "Christ" or "God" within.

Consider how Ernest's conscious ego performs "God's" work. At Roughborough he wittingly schemes to sell an old Sallust in order to buy copies of the Handel oratorios. He chooses to aid the other boys in burning his father's effigy, thus "confirming" his election as "the huge old bishop" who has visited the school that day never could. At Cambridge he allows "God" to find out what aesthetically he really likes, and then articulates it, thereby completing the movement from taste, the province of the unconscious, to criticism, the province of the ego. Most notably, he decides upon leaving prison that he won't see his "most dangerous enemies," his parents, and when they outwit him by showing up in the receiving room, he firmly commands his father not to speak to him, and scrambles away. This crossing of the Rubicon is "not perhaps very heroically or dramatically" done, but done it is, with an effort which causes Ernest, once he is outside, to lean against the prison wall and weep. It is a crossing that is demanded by "God," and effected by his prophet—an act of *deliberate* rebellion which has moved even the grudging Arnold Kettle to admiration, and which proves that "God" will be unseeing as well as unseen till he has an "I" who can watch and act for him.

Do the decisions of the intelligent ego therefore accumulate toward the formation of a new superego? In some ways it seems so: Theobald and Pryer are replaced by Overton and Towneley, new objects of emulation. But that is only a psychologically convenient first stage. The true conscience is not above the ego, but below it: the conscientious man lives in obedience to the divine commandments of his provident unconscious. And Ernest's unconscious is finally different not only from Towneley's, as we have noted, but from Overton's. As the latter's name suggests, he is "super" to Ernest— a figure who is obviously more congenial to him than Theobald, yet who must also be surpassed. Ernest must, for instance, write the serious theological and moral tracts which his own genius needs to write, and to do so in spite of Overton's call for something more entertaining. His unconscious self *can't* be entertaining till he has slain his enemies. Butler then is portraying a psyche which, in its healthy state, is not the tripartite affair which Freud portrays, wherein the ego strives to achieve a balance of power between its partners. It is a bipartite affair between the ego and the unconscious, the latter having a trustworthy wisdom of its own which renders a superior "governour" unnecessary. In someone like Ernest the role of the ego is substantial: it is uncomfortably circumstanced and must be as conniving as it can. In someone like Towneley, though, the ego has very little to do: it is so well set up that it can cruise on automatic pilot.

It isn't till Ernest is fairly grown that his ego displays any intelligence. When he is very young, it is at the mercy of his father's voice, and he has to rely on his unconscious self to pull him out of scrapes—whether by crying or by fainting. At one moment his inchoate ego may feel righteous in disobeying his father, but at the next it feels overwhelmed by its utter depravity. It won't be secure till, years later, it has succeeded in locating its true conscience. It is to grown-ups, therefore, that Butler is usually speaking when he pronounces the *do*'s and *don't*s of family life. In a still more or less Puritan culture, they alone have lived long enough perhaps to have seen through the false divinity and to have got acquainted with the true, the inscape of the self. They are in a position to avoid the mistakes made on them, and from the beginning to promote with their own children the message of Psalm 82: though "ye shall die like men," yet "Ye are gods; and all of you are children of the most High." What Shaw called a ceremony in "parricide [sic] and matricide long drawn out" is then also a program against infanticide, no less drawn out.

II

What practical things should grown-ups do for the "children of the most High" who are their charge? They should guide them in matters of money and sex, the bivium, so to speak, of the Butlerian university, the branches of which we must discuss first separately, then together.

Parents should give their children lots of money, or if no large legacy can be brought together, give them the sort of training that will put them in the way of making money for themselves. Butler is sure that the individual talent, properly tutored, will rise to its own level in the marketplace. But proper tutoring is precisely what the English public schools and ancient universities don't provide for the youth who must earn his own living. Dead languages, abstract mathematics, far-away history, and Church dogmatics are certainly not taught for their utilitarian value; nor, Butler feels, are they taught especially for their "own sake" (whatever that would mean: what is Latin, that is should have a sake?). Rather, they are just the sorts of complex superfluities which are expensive and difficult to acquire, and which therefore are the perfect signs whereby one can distinguish the quality from the commoner. So much the worse for the quality: such an education is costly to the parents, who naturally resent the drain on their capital, but more costly to the children, whose "retreat" is thereafter cut off. They can no longer turn to a trade or to manual labor, which alone could secure their independence. Because Ernest's training in carpentry is aborted, he has nothing to fall back on when his curacy and his money are gone. He does train as a tailor in prison—luckily he is still young and eager enough to learn—but as Overton's own tailor Mr. Larkin sees, it is too late for him to begin. A public school boy can't be happy mixing with tailors, nor they with him: "A man must have sunk low through drink or natural taste for low company before he could get on with those who have had such a different training from his own." That sentence may sound like quintessential Victorian snobbery, but in fact it points to a psychological reality that keeps most people from being more than theoretical egalitarians.

Butler joins a chorus of Victorians—Macaulay, Carlyle, Kingsley, Froude—who insist that education be materially useful; young people who have no great property coming to them, the majority after all, must get from their masters the know-how to enable them to earn honest livings. Even if a boy stands to inherit an independence, Butler argues, apprenticeship in a trade would still be prudent, for who knows what will happen at the "place they call the stock exchange"? Moreover, a good grounding in economics will help him look *out* for what will happen there, and protect himself against the worst. Overton gives Ernest a belated introduction to the rules of double-entry bookkeeping ("the most necessary branch of any young man's education after reading and writing"), which is indeed but the instrument for the profounder art of speculation. Butler would have a course in speculation taught in every public school, the boys reading the financial papers and playing a sort of Monopoly with pence standing for pounds: "There might be a prize awarded by the headmaster to the most prudent dealer, and boys who lost their money time after time should be dismissed." Such a course might be continued at university, except that it would entail the creation of a professorship in speculation, and nothing that the universities do well—cricket, rowing, cooking—is taught by professors. So the course had better end at the sixth form.

Butler is not jesting, nor, as far as the training of young *rentiers* goes, should he be. He is echoing the sound advice Locke offers on teaching boys the details of estate management—advice worth quoting at length:

> Many Fathers, though they proportion to their Sons liberal Allowances, according to their Age and Condition; yet they keep the Knowledge of their Estates, and Concerns from them, with as much reservedness, as if they were guarding a secret of State from a Spy, or an Enemy. . . . Nothing cements and establishes Friendship and Good-will, so much as *confident Communication* of Concernments and Affairs. Other Kindnesses without this, leave still some Doubts: But when your Son sees you open your Mind to him, when he finds that you interest him in your Affairs, as Things you are willing should in their Turn come into his Hands, he will be concerned for them, as for his own; wait his Season with Patience, and Love you in the time, who keep him not at the distance of a Stranger. This will also make him see, that the Enjoyment you have is not without Care; which the more he is sensible of, the less will he envy you the Possession, and the more think himself Happy under the Management of so favourable a Friend, and so careful a Father.

Neither George nor Theobald Pontifex has read Locke's book: whenever money is at issue between them and their sons, they can only clutch and threaten. George's favorite threats are to say that he will apprentice his boys to greengrocers, which they wish he would, or to shake his will at them, which they wish he wouldn't: "He would in his imagination cut them all out one after another and leave his money to found almshouses, till at last he was obliged to put them back, so that he might have the pleasure of cutting them out again next time he was in a passion." Theobald follows suit, though by shaking his will a little less, he perhaps a little more makes the rudiment of allowances, inheritances, and yearly expenses greater mysteries than they are.

"[M]ake no mysteries where nature has made none." The violation of that commandment with respect to money is discomfiting to Ernest both when he must go without his *"menus plaisirs"* at school and when he is shorn clean by Pryer in London. Its violation with respect to sexuality, however, is ruinous to him. Aunt Alethaea has wrapped a nest egg with Bank of England notes, to be kept warm for Ernest till he is ready to be "born" at age twenty-seven, and Overton has taught him how to husband it. No one, however, can do much for him sexually. As a schoolboy he has his bout of what Robert Graves calls pseudo-homosexuality, yet about heterosexuality he is completely innocent. Indeed, when the servant girl Ellen, who in order to prepare for confirmation ought to have been studying the routes of Paul's missionary journeys, is discovered to have got pregnant and Ernest is momentarily suspected, he turns out to be "not only innocent, but deplorably—I might even say guiltily—innocent." Innocence is what prevents him from distinguishing between the characters of Miss Snow and Miss Maitland, and what, once he has been punished for that error, leads him to suppose that the new-found Ellen is the right woman to help him: "I had learnt as a boy things that I ought not to have learnt, and had never had a chance of that which would have set me straight." It may be that "Gentlefolks is always like that," as Ellen says, but Ernest is so "like that," so "starving for something to love and lean upon," that he can't detect that this particular female "something" is too gin-ridden to hold him up for long. Like his father before him, he has been kept from knowing any females besides his mother and sister. At Roughborough he has been lectured on the sanctity of the spirit's temple, and at Cambridge he has been denied both the opportunity to see "abandoned" women, and the money to buy them:

> At night [the judge at Ernest's trial ironically says] proctors patrolled the street and dogged your steps if you tried to go into any haunt where the presence of vice was suspected. By day the females who were admitted within the college walls were selected mainly on the score of age and ugliness. It is hard to see what more can be done for any young man than this.

Ernest's parents and masters have only been following the advice of the best ecclesiastical authorities. And were they here to turn to the secular pundits whose wisdom, as I have argued, contributed so greatly to Butler in other matters, they would not be much better off.

Locke had nothing to say about the sex education of young Englishmen. Throwing up his hands in disgust at how fast vice ripened among schoolboys and indeed among the whole of Restoration society, and planning for himself removal to America, he recommended that boys be tutored at home, regardless of expense. Cobbett, for all his earthiness, faced the problem no more squarely. Chesterfield, though also insisting that boys not be thrown into the vicious company of other boys, was a little bolder about the vicious company of women: he got so far as to allow Philip to lay out money on Italian courtesans, as long as they were reputable. And that is the advanced position, the latitudinarian remedy for lust between the succubae of puberty and the chaste sheets of marriage. Exploitative and joyless, it is the path for sexual discovery which Butler recommends: while others close their eyes and immure their sons, he proclaims (very quietly, it is true) the satisfactions of well-heeled whoremongering. He ought to be credited with having the candor to acknowledge the need for sexual discovery, but pitied—if that isn't too impudent—for failing to acknowledge the need for sexual maturation, which involves a delicacy and a fidelity to which a carefully folded pound note to Mlle. Dumas, once a week for many years, does not answer.

III

Butler does little, then, to dissipate the mysteries surrounding the growing youth's sexuality. He does a great deal, however, to dissipate those surrounding his need for money, and it is worth returning to the subject, not only because it is ultimately linked with that of sexuality, but because in its own immediate terms it has been so frequently misperceived. Butler's constant calls for money from his swindling and long-lived father, the wish-fulfilling bonanza he contrives for Ernest, his insistence on allowances, legacies, and a pre-money education all go rather shrill in the ears of most readers. Like Mr. Micawber he resolves his personal crises into the question of whether he has enough money: if yes, he is content; if no, he is miserable. Other variables seem not to count.

In *The Way of All Flesh* the fathers and sons go to war over great expectations and greater expenditures; even friends first meet each other as if through a teller's window, as when Overton introduces himself to little Ernest by giving him and Joey twopence halfpenny to buy "sweeties," and waiting for them to figure out how to make change. Everyone with lots of money—Towneley, Alethaea, or Overton—is supposed prima facie to be affable, successful, and virtuous; even Ernest's father and grandfather are thus respected by their neighbors, and with Butler's general concurrence. Small wonder, therefore, that Edmund Wilson should complain that "five years after *Das Kapital*, eighteen years after Dickens's *Hard Times*," Butler's class prejudices deflected his powers of satire away from the evils of capitalism; or that Arnold Kettle should mockingly say that Butler's famous "common sense . . . finds its level at fifteen hundred a year"; or that Miss Savage should indomitably lecture him as follows:

> I call you a most unreasonable man. Let the poor stupid disagreeable people have the money (I think they very often do); they want it poor things. When you get that modest competence you speak of, I shall look upon you as defrauding somebody or other.

Small wonder that these voices should be raised, yet Butler is hardly as myopic as they suggest. He knows that, given nature's limited resources, somebody's good luck in the struggle for existence entails somebody else's bad: it is not his fault, it is the system's—meaning by "system" not any particular economics, but nature itself. Butler is aware of the tenor of the socialist critique of capitalism, which decries "the unearned increment of land [values]," and which ought to extend to the similarly unearned increment of railway stock. But since inequities between the haves and the have-nots are simply a function of the pressure of large populations on small reserves, he takes them for granted and is happy that, for the time being, the socialists are rating landowners instead of stockholders. Yet though he isn't as toadyingly myopic as his critics imply, he isn't as liberally far-sighted as he might be, either. He sees economics with the eyes of a Victorian *rentier*—Wilson is quite right about that. He is exceptional in his criticism of Darwin's metaphysical assumptions, but drearily ordinary in his acceptance of the economic corollaries of those assumptions which men like Charles Graham Sumner and Herbert Spencer were cheerlessly formulating.

Still, Darwin had something extremely valuable to teach Butler about economics, something which Butler elaborated in ways that went on to be valuable for others. Darwin taught him, in a word, that economics is inescapable. Life on this planet is stubbornly material—not totally so, as Darwin thought, but mostly so nonetheless. We have got to live on *something* a year, and Butler's "money" is only a summary word for those material goods which we will produce, distribute, and consume according to whatever system we can devise, but which, if we want to survive, we can't forego. Darwin grounded this truth in natural science; Hume and Dr. Johnson had, a century earlier, grounded it in associational psychology and social ethics. Each formulation finds a place in Butler, and each is necessary because there are rich people who, preferring not to struggle for their money, want the poor to find virtue in submission, and because there are people, rich and poor, who, ashamed at having to live in the flesh, want us to be like them and find beauty in the spirit alone.

Hume speaks of our "natural" respect for the wealthy and aversion to the poor, based upon the pleasant "ideas" accompanying the one, and the unpleasant the other:

When we approach a man who is, as we say, at his ease, we are presented with the pleasing ideas of plenty, satisfaction, cleanliness, warmth; a cheerful house, elegant furniture, ready service, and whatever is desirable in meat, drink, or apparel. On the contrary, when a poor man appears, the disagreeable images of want, penury, hard labor, dirty furniture, coarse or ragged clothes, nauseous meat and distateful liquor immediately strike our fancy. What else do we mean by saying that one is rich, the other poor?

Hume knows perfectly well that wealth is no guarantee of virtue, and that one doesn't measure out esteem in proportion to income. Personally, one judges the characters of men according to their intrinsic qualities, not according to the "capricious favors of fortune." But publicly, one pays "a superior deference to the great lord above the vassal, because riches are the most convenient, being the most fixed and determinate source of distinction." Riches are a "convenient" and "determinate" criterion because they are what *enable* a man to be virtuous—to please and to be useful—as a man without riches almost never can be.

In this, if in little else, Hume and Dr. Johnson agree. The latter is emphatic on money's being prior to personal merit—prior instrumentally, not ontologically. "Go into the street," he says, "and give one man a lecture on morality, and another a shilling, and see which will respect you most." Those who argue for the advantages of poverty, as he himself did when he was young, are found to be very sorry to be poor. A large income, rightly spent, can bring happiness; a small income is likely to keep happiness from coming at all:

> Poverty takes away so many means of doing good, and produces so much inability to resist evil, both natural and moral, that it is by all virtuous means to be avoided. Consider a man whose fortune is very narrow; whatever be his rank by birth, or whatever his reputation by intellectual excellence, what good can he do? or what evil can he prevent? That he cannot help the needy is evident; he has nothing to spare. But, perhaps, his advice or admonition may be useful. His poverty will destroy his influence: many more can find that he is poor, than that he is wise; and few will reverence the understanding that is of so little advantage to its owner.

That is precisely Butler's contention. Money is nothing in itself, it is useful only when we part with it. Like the words of our language, coins are the outward signs of "an inward and spiritual purchasing power" which is realized when they are exchanged. And what we exchange them for are the necessaries of food, clothing, shelter, etc., which ensure our material comfort, that we may go on to learn amiability, to exercise our genius, or to gain whatever reputation we desire. Since we can't cultivate any of these if we are materially pinched, Butler concludes that no loss can be as serious as the loss of money—money, again, being the covenanted sign of our ability to buy the material goods we can't do without.

We can summon more courage against terminal illness or the death of our loved ones than we can against financial ruin. In the first instance, as long as we have money to pay for a warm bed and a nurse, we will die quietly enough, living life to the dregs no matter what the pain. In the second instance, we are like Job, who "probably felt the loss of his flocks and herds more than that of his wife and family—for he could enjoy his flocks and herds without his family, but not his family—not for long—if he had lost all his money." Loss of money can prevent us from maintaining or repairing our health; it can turn friends and family against us in anger, when they discover that we are no sure stay after all, but "have been obtaining esteem under false pretences." After loss of money comes loss of health, then loss of reputation—the latter being, in spite of Cassio, a bad third, since it is usually based on violations of "*parvenues* conventions," not on violations of the established canons of material and carnal well-being. With health and money, we can live happy "without any reputation at all." But suppose, out of a desire to exert our reputation for others' good, we grow a new one, "as a lobster grows a new claw": what chance [to echo Dr. Johnson] does our new reputation have to influence them if we are poor, and they see how little material good it has done us?

It is hard to deny the cogency of this, once we realize that Butler is arguing not for money's ontological value—it has none—but for its instrumental value. Job's "flocks and herds" are instruments for obtaining the tokens with which he can obtain a mule for his wife and a doctor for himself. These things secured, he will be free to study God's mighty works, and to worship. Job's more-than-material ends were, in a different theological key, Butler's also. That is why he made it a point of honor to be wealthy—to be set up in a way which allowed him to pursue his moral and aesthetic campaigns, whether in the reading room of the British Museum or in the nooks along the coast of Sicily. Like Darwin, Hume, and Dr. Johnson, Butler turned the truism "We need material goods" into a truth, and gave it a grounding in which his precursors' interests in natural science, associational psychology, and social ethics overlap.

He was least percipient about the branch of the latter called political economy, but even there he was so refreshingly candid and unapologetic that, as E. M. Forster says, no one who read him could afterwards ignore the importance of money, or pretend it was vulgar. It is from Butler that Shaw, for instance, learned to be unhypocritical about a good life's requiring money. In his "Preface" to *Major Barbara* he honors Froissart's knight for claiming "a good life" as his birthright, and for being honest enough to say that the way to get it was "to rob and pill." The problem with medieval society was that robbing and pilling actually did lead to "a good life," when they should have led to the gallows. If modern society were properly organized, those who quietly robbed and pilled [i.e., lived on what are called independent incomes] *would* go to the gallows—or as Shaw aseptically puts it, "to the lethal chamber."

> But as [he continues], thanks to our political imbecility and per-
> sonal cowardice (fruits of poverty, both), the best imitation of a
> good life now procurable is life on an independent income, all
> sensible people aim at securing such an income, and are, of course,
> careful to legalize and moralize both it and all the actions and
> sentiments which lead to it and support it as an institution. What
> else can they do? They know, of course, that they are rich because
> others are poor. But they cannot help that: it is for the poor to
> repudiate poverty when they have had enough of it.

The passage makes one think of Margaret Schlegel in *Howards End*, self-consciously clipping her coupons and cashing them in on concerts, pictures, tours, books, and tea. She sees her money as an island holding her up over the flood of the "unthinkable" poor; she shocks Mr. Wilcox by specifying the size of her island, and by expecting him to specify the size of his. She is in effect Alethaea Pontifex's progressively modified descendant, the intelligent woman for whom Shaw wrote his guide to socialism and capitalism. She doesn't pretend that she can live without her island, and, wanting others to have islands just as beautifully furnished, she vaguely feels that they will get them as soon as they want them badly enough. And the sooner the better, since the abundance of life on one island finally depends on that throughout the whole archipelago.

Once more we have seen Butler as a mediator between the assumptions of his created precursors and those of his heirs. In economics he advances the wisdom of the former either by expressing it more wittily, or by interpreting it according to Victorian conditions, or by eluding the Mammon-worshipper's trap of supposing that material realities are the only realities. In turn, his heirs advance his ideal of the moneyed life to the point where it applies explicitly to everyone—an egalitarian dream the realization of which he himself would believe more distant than even the Fabian Shaw predicts, but the importance of which he would salute because it *is* a dream, an attempt to subvert the Malthusian equations. What his heirs conceive in economics is in principle not alien to what he himself says about the importance of money: they simply take him at his word and look for ways to get everyone well set up. The distance between Butler and his heirs is therefore not intellectual; it is emotional. Neither Shaw nor Forster ever confuses economic and sexual struggle, but Butler does, and to such a degree as to disable some critics from taking seriously anything he writes on either head. It is here that the branches of the Butlerian bivium sadly collapse into one another.

After Ernest has come into his inheritance, he returns to Battersby to see his dying mother. Theobald has heard nothing about the legacy, and has sent a check for the train fare and for a suit of clothes. Ernest is dandied up—as finely as "Towneley himself." Theobald stands aghast and Ernest "put out his hand and said laughingly, 'Oh it's all paid for—I am afraid you do not know that Mr. Overton has handed over to me Aunt Alethaea's money.' Theobald flushed scarlet . . ." and so on. It is obvious that Butler is using his novel to over-indulge his wish to revenge himself against his father for the years of financial insecurity which a bit of generosity and a more obligingly early death might have relieved. But there is worse behind. Having failed to assert himself sexually against his father, whether by literally usurping his mother's affection or by transferring the struggle to another relationship, Ernest quarrels with him on economic grounds, where "Oh, it's all paid for" shouts defiance. All vital, erotic pugnacity is missing— and no doubt because Theobald is himself such a sexual nonentity that he doesn't in the least call Ernest out. Their quarrel *has* to be economic, since there isn't enough emotional energy to fuel any other kind. Even the ethico-theological quarrel, of which Butler has made a great deal, seems at the moment of Ernest's return to Battersby to have been subsumed under the economic quarrel—as though his new ideas about divinity needed to be reified "in grey Ulster and blue and white necktie." The scene is a facer for anyone who respects Butler: the man could evidently be extraordinarily petty. But was he also self-deluded? Did he think Ernest's appearance, and the sharp words which turn his father an ashen color, amount to a happy coming of age? At one level, yes: the teller of the tale was no doubt smugly conscious of having "won" against the father. But as Lawrence says, we don't want to trust the teller, for he doesn't necessarily know what he has told. Trust the tale instead. At that level, where the teller's unconscious has been busy, a truer sort of knowledge resides, just as Butler insisted from *Erewhon* on. At that level, he may be said to understand his occasional pettiness, affectional exhaustion, and confusion of Eros and Mammon, and to understand with an immediacy which his urbanity only half-hides. His unconscious gives him away, just as Ernest's has given him away in the Miss Maitland episode, by pushing him into a desperate attempt to grasp the object of his desire, wherein he may triumph, but will more likely discover both the inadequacy of the object and the awkwardness with which he is reaching for it.

The Refusal of Involvement
in Hardy's Writing

J. Hillis Miller

Nowhere in Hardy's writings is there a description of an originating act in which the mind separates itself from everything but itself. His self-awareness and that of his characters are always inextricably involved in their awareness of the world. Their minds are turned habitually outward. Almost every sentence Hardy ever wrote, whether in his fiction, in his poetry, or in his more private writings, is objective. It names something outside the mind of which that mind is aware. A man, in his view, should even look at his own interior life as something detached and external, not as something known from the inside with special intimacy. "A naturalist's interest in the hatching of a queer egg or germ is the utmost introspective consideration you should allow yourself," he says in a private notebook entry of 1888.

In spite of this distaste for introspection, there is a passage in Florence Emily Hardy's *Life* which takes the reader close to the intrinsic quality of his mind. This text, like most of the *Life,* was probably composed by Hardy himself:

> One event of this date or a little later [when Hardy was about six] stood out, he used to say, more distinctly than any [other]. He was lying on his back in the sun, thinking how useless he was, and covered his face with his straw hat. The sun's rays streamed through the interstices of the straw, the lining having disappeared. Reflecting on his experiences of the world so far as he had got, he came to the conclusion that he did not wish to grow up. Other boys were always talking of when they would be men; he did not

From *Thomas Hardy: Distance and Desire.* © 1970 by the President and Fellows of Harvard College. Harvard University Press, 1970.

want at all to be a man, or to possess things, but to remain as he was, in the same spot, and to know no more people than he already knew (about half a dozen).

This episode does not constitute a genetic moment. Two events have preceded it and are reflected in it. The first is certain "experiences of the world." The nature of these is suggested by a passage at the opening of *Jude the Obscure* which so closely resembles the text in the *Life* that it may be called an anticipatory comment on it. The young Jude, like the young Hardy, finds that a man is not born free. Each person is ushered into the world in a certain spot in space and time. He has certain ancestors. He finds himself with a certain role to play in his family, in his community, in his social class, in his nation, even on the stage of world history. Like the young Jude, who is shown in the middle of a "vast concave" cornfield which goes "right up towards the sky all round, where it [is] lost by degrees in the mist that shut[s] out the actual verge and accentuate[s] the solitude," each man finds himself at the center of a receding series of contexts which locates him and defines him. This imprisonment is all the more painful for being so intangible. Jude stands alone and in the open, but he is nonetheless bound by the situation he has inherited. Like Pip in Dickens's *Great Expectations,* he is an orphan. Like Pip, he has been told by his foster mother that he is "useless" and would be better dead. Along with so many other heroes of nineteenth-century novels, Hardy's protagonists find themselves "living in a world which [does] not want them." Though Hardy himself was not an orphan and seems to have had a fairly happy childhood, he too, in the passage from the *Life,* broods over how "useless" he is. The conventional motifs of the orphan hero and the indifferent foster parent express his general sense that no man's situation is of his making or satisfies his desire.

Hardy's response to this experience of life is so instinctive that it is never recorded, but always precedes any record, though it is repeated again and again in his own life and in that of his characters. It precedes any record because it makes consciousness and the recording of consciousness possible. This response is a movement of passive withdrawal. Like a snail crawling into its shell, or like a furtive animal creeping into its burrow, he pulls his hat over his face and looks quietly at what he can see through the interstices of the straw. The gesture objectifies an act of detachment which, for him, is involuntary and antedates any gesture which embodies it. The separation which is natural to the mind may be lost by a man's absorption in the world or it may be maintained by a willful standing back, but initially it is given with consciousness itself. To be conscious is to be separated. The mind has a native clarity and distinctness which detaches it from everything it registers.

Though Hardy finds that his consciousness separates him from the world, he does not turn away from what he sees to investigate the realm of interior space. He and his characters are distinguished by the shallowness of their minds. They have no profound inner depths leading down to the "buried self" or to God. They remain even in detachment oriented toward the outside world and reflecting it, mirrorlike. Though Hardy remains turned toward the exterior, looking at it or thinking about it, his movement of retraction separates him from blind engagement and turns everything he sees into a spectacle viewed from the outside.

A passage in *The Mayor of Casterbridge* demonstrates further this superficiality of consciousness. The act of coming to self-awareness does not lead to a recognition of the intrinsic quality of the mind. It is a revelation about the outside world, a recognition of the mute detachment of external objects and of the inexplicable fact that this particular power of knowing, which might be anywhere or beholding any scene, happens to be imprisoned by one environment rather than by another. The mind is held entranced by a vision of objects which seem themselves entranced, constrained. The passage describes Elizabeth-Jane Henchard's experience as she sits late at night by the bedside of her dying mother. She hears one of those odd sounds audible in a silent house in the small hours: one clock ticking against another clock, "ticking harder and harder till it seemed to clang like a gong." This revelation of the fact that a clock's ticking is a mechanical noise, not a natural expression of the passage of time, leads her to recognize the paradoxical nature of her situation. She is both within her immediate environment and outside it. She is in bondage to it in the sense that if she looks at anything she must look at what happens to be there to see. She is free of it in the sense that what she sees has no necessary connection to her watching mind. Seeing this causes her consciousness to spin incoherently with unanswerable questions about why things around her are as they are. Though the passage registers as acute an awareness of self as is expressed anywhere in Hardy's writing, it shows the mind still turned chiefly toward the outside world, still asking why things are as they are rather than why the mind is as it is. The question of the nature of the mind arises only after a confrontation of the helpless objectivity of external things:

> And all this while the subtle-souled girl [was] asking herself why she was born, why sitting in a room, and blinking at the candle; why things around her had taken the shape they wore in preference to every other possible shape. Why they stared at her so helplessly, as if waiting for the touch of some wand that should release them from terrestrial constraint; what that chaos called consciousness, which spun in her at this moment like a top, tended to, and began in.

The spontaneous withdrawal of the mind to a position of detached watchfulness is ratified by an act of will. Rather than choosing to lose himself in one or another of the beguiling forms of engagement offered by the world, Hardy, like many of his characters, chooses to keep his distance. Like Herman Melville's Bartleby, he decides he "would prefer not to"—prefer not to grow up, prefer not to take responsibility, prefer not to move out of his own narrow circle, prefer not to possess things, prefer not to know more people. The young Jude also experiences this desire to remain on the periphery of life. He too pulls his hat over his eyes and lies "vaguely reflecting": "As you got older, and felt yourself to be at the centre of your time, and not a point in its circumference, as you had felt when you were little, you were seized with a sort of shuddering, he perceived. All around you there seemed to be something glaring, garish, rattling, and the noises and glares hit upon the little cell called your life, and shook it, and warped it. If he could only prevent himself growing up! He did not want to be a man." The motif recurs once more when the speaker in a late poem, a poem characteristically craggy in diction, remembers as a child crouching safely in a thicket of ferns and asking himself: "Why should I have to grow to a man's estate,/ And this afar-noised World perambulate?" ("Childhood among the Ferns"). The world is noise and glare, the threat of an engulfing violence which will shake and twist a man's life. Only if he can remain self-contained, sealed off from everything, can he escape this violence. He must therefore refuse any involvement in the world. Hardy's fundamental spiritual movement is the exact opposite of Nietzsche's will to power. It is the will not to will, the will to remain quietly watching on the sidelines.

Having given up the virile goals which motivate most men, Hardy can turn back on the world and watch it from a safe distance, see it clearly with a "full look at the Worst" ("In Tenebris, II"), and judge it. This way of being related to the world is the origin of his art. Such an attitude determines the habitual stance of his narrators, that detachment which sees events from above them or from a time long after they have happened. Or it might be better to say that these spatial and temporal distances objectify a separation which is outside of life, outside of time and space altogether, as the speaker in "Wessex Heights" seems "where I was before my birth, and after death may be." The tone of voice natural to a spectator who sees things from such a position imparts its slightly acerb flavor throughout his work as a compound of irony, cold detachment, musing reminiscent bitterness, an odd kind of sympathy which might be called "pity at a distance," and, mixed with these, a curious joy, a grim satisfaction that things have, as was foreseen, come out for the worst in this worst of all possible worlds.

Such a perspective is also possessed by many of the protagonists of Hardy's novels, those watchers from a distance like Gabriel Oak in *Far from the Madding Crowd*, Christopher Julian in *The Hand of Ethelberta*, Diggory Venn in *The Return of the Native*, or Giles Winterborne in *The Woodlanders*. The detachment of such characters is expressed in the recurrent motif of spying in his fiction. He frequently presents a scene in which one character sees another without being seen, watches from an upper window or a hill, peeks in a window from outside at night, or covertly studies a reflection in a mirror.

In the lyric poetry too a stance of detachment is habitual. The speaker of the poems is "The Dead Man Walking," to borrow the title of one of them. He is withdrawn from the present, "with no listing or longing to join" ("In Tenebris, III"). From this separation he focuses his attention on the ghosts of the past. He sees things from the perspective of death, and as a consequence is so quiet a watcher, so effaced, that birds, animals, and forlorn strangers pay no attention to him, knowing that his vision is as distant as the stars (" 'I Am the One' "). This detachment is most elaborately dramatized in the choruses of spirits in *The Dynasts*. These spirits, says Hardy, are not supernatural beings. They "are not supposed to be more than the best human intelligences of their time in a sort of quint-essential form." From this generalization he excludes the Chorus of Pities. They are "merely Humanity, with all its weaknesses." The careful attention to details of optical placement in *The Dynasts*, which John Wain has associated with cinematic technique, is more than a matter of vivid presentation. It is an extension of the implicit point of view in the novels and in the lyric poems. It has a thematic as well as technical meaning. The choruses in *The Dynasts* are able to see the whole expanse of history at a glance. When they focus on a particular event they see it in the context of this all-encompassing panoramic vision. The spirits in the "General Chorus of Intelligences" at the end of the "Fore Scene" boast that they are everywhere at once and can contract all time and space to a single spot of time:

> We'll close up Time, as a bird its van,
> We'll traverse Space, as spirits can,
> Link pulses severed by leagues and years,
> Bring cradles into touch with biers;
> So that the far-off Consequence appears
> Prompt at the heel of foregone Cause.

The narrative voice and perspective in the fiction, the attitude natural to many characters in the novels, the location of the speaker habitual in the poems, the epic machinery of *The Dynasts*—all these express the detachment of consciousness which is fundamental to Hardy's way of looking at the world. Such separation allows him and his spokesmen to see reality as it is. From a detached point of view the environment no longer seems so close that one can only be aware of its dangerous energy, its glare and garish rattling. The man who is pursuing some immediate goal is too close to life to see it whole. Only from a distance are its patterns visible. In *Desperate Remedies*, for example, Aeneas Manston is paradoxically granted by the intensity of his involvement the insight born of a momentary detachment. From the point of view of the man involved in a concrete situation, such a perspective is trivial, a momentary wandering of the mind.

The narrator and the reader, however, can see that the character has by a fortuitous inattention been briefly granted a glimpse of the true pattern of existence. Here the view of the protagonist approaches, in a moment of vision which recurs in Hardy's fiction, the wide view of the narrator:

> There exists, as it were, an outer chamber to the mind, in which, when a man is occupied centrally with the most momentous question of his life, casual and trifling thoughts are just allowed to wander softly for an interval, before being banished altogether. Thus, amid his concentration did Manston receive perceptions of the individuals about him in the lively thoroughfare of the Strand; tall men looking insignificant; little men looking great and profound; lost women of miserable repute looking as happy as the days are long; wives, happy by assumption, looking careworn and miserable. Each and all were alike in this one respect, that they followed a solitary trail like the inwoven threads which form a banner, and all were equally unconscious of the significant whole they collectively showed forth.

The same image appears in *The Woodlanders*. Though Giles Winterborne and Marty South walking in the early morning are completely "isolated" and "self-contained," their lives form part of the total fabric of human actions being performed all over the globe: "their lonely courses formed no detached design at all, but were part of the pattern in the great web of human doings then weaving in both hemispheres from the White Sea to Cape Horn."

What Manston has for an instant, Hardy and his narrators have as a permanent possession. They see each individual life in the context of the whole cloth of which it is part. This superimposition of the engaged view and the detached, wide view pervades Hardy's writing and is the source of its characteristic ironies. If much of his work is made up of careful notation of immediate particulars—the weather, the landscape, a house or a room, the colors of things, apparently irrelevant details, what the characters say, think, or do as they seek satisfaction of their desires—the narrative perspective on these particulars, present in the steady and cool tone of the language, is a vision so wide that it reduces any particular to utter insignificance. Such a view reveals the fact that "winning, equally with losing," in any of the games of life, is "below the zero of the true philosopher's concern."

The nature of the universe seen from this perspective is expressed figuratively in the key images of *The Dynasts*. The motif of the single thread in a cloth reappears there when the Spirit of the Years says that the story of the Napoleonic Wars is "but one flimsy riband" of the "web Enorm" woven by the Immanent Will through "ceaseless artistries in Circumstance/ Of curious stuff and braid." Along with this image goes another, that of a monstrous mass in senseless motion. The writhing of the whole includes in its random movement all men and women driven by their desires and intentions. *Desperate Remedies* anticipates this motif too. In one scene Aeneas Manston looks into a rain-water-butt and watches as "hundreds of thousands of minute living creatures sported and tumbled in its depth with every contortion that gaiety could suggest; perfectly happy, though consisting only of a head, or a tail, or at most a head and a tail, and all doomed to die within the twenty-four hours." Perfect image of man's life as Hardy sees it! In *The Dynasts*, published over thirty years after *Desperate Remedies*, the image reappears in Hardy's picture of the people of the earth, "distressed by events which they did not cause," "writhing, crawling, heaving, and vibrating in their various cities and nationalities," or "busying themselves like cheesemites," or advancing with a "motion . . . peristaltic and vermicular" like a monstrous caterpillar, or "like slowworms through grass." The actions of man are controlled by the unconscious motion of the universe, "a brain-like network of currents and ejections, twitching, interpenetrating, entangling, and thrusting hither and thither the human forms." Dreaming brain, network, web, mass of writhing, intertwined creatures—these images describe a universe in which each part is a helpless victim of the weaving energy which unconsciously knits together the whole.

Hardy's conception of human life presupposes a paradoxical form of dualism. There is only one realm, that of matter in motion, but out of this "unweeting" movement human consciousness, that "mistake of God's" (" 'I Travel as a Phantom Now' "), has arisen accidentally, from the play of physical causes. Though the detached clarity of vision which is possible to the human mind has come from physical nature, it is radically different from its source. It sees nature for the first time as it is, has for the first time pity for animal and human suffering, and brings into the universe a desire that events should be logical or reasonable, a desire that people should get what they deserve. But of course the world does not correspond to this desire. This is seen as soon as the desire appears. Knowledge of the injustice woven into the texture of things does not require extensive experience. The young Jude musing under his hat perceives already the clash of man's logic and nature's: "Events did not rhyme quite as he had thought. Nature's logic was too horrid for him to care for. That mercy towards one set of creatures was cruelty towards another sickened his sense of harmony." Like little Father Time in *Jude the Obscure*, Hardy is already as old as the hills when he is born, foresees the vanity of every wish, and knows that death is the end of life. To see the world clearly is already to see the folly of any involvement in it.

In Hardy's world there is no supernatural hierarchy of ideals or commandments, nor is there any law inherent in the physical world which says it is right to do one thing, wrong to do another, or which establishes any relative worth among things or people. Events happen as they do happen. They have neither value in themselves nor value in relation to any end beyond them. Worse yet, suffering is certain for man. In place of God there is the Immanent Will, and this unthinking force is sure to inflict pain on a man until he is lucky enough to die. Birth itself is "an ordeal of degrading personal compulsion, whose gratuitousness nothing in the result seemed to justify." Best of all would be not to be born at all, as Hardy affirms poignantly in "To an Unborn Pauper Child."

Both halves of the term "Immanent Will" are important. The supreme power is immanent rather than transcendent. It does not come from outside the world, but is a force within nature, part of its substance. It is a version of the inherent energy of the physical world as seen by nineteenth-century science: an unconscious power working by regular laws of matter in motion. Though what happens is ordained by no divine lawgiver, the state of the universe at any one moment leads inevitably to its state at the next moment. Existence is made up of an enormous number of simultaneous energies each doing its bit to make the whole mechanism move. If a man had enough knowledge he could predict exactly what will be the state of the universe ten years from now or ten thousand. All things have been fated from all time.

The term "Will" is equally important. Hardy's use of this word supports Martin Heidegger's claim that a dualistic metaphysics leads to the establishment of volition as the supreme category of being. Hardy recognizes that his nomenclature may seem odd, since what he has in mind is not conscious willing. Nevertheless he defends "will" in a letter of 1904 to Edward Clodd as the most exact word for his meaning: "What you say about the 'Will' is true enough, if you take the word in its ordinary sense. But in the lack of another word to express precisely what is meant, a secondary sense has gradually arisen, that of effort exercised in a reflex or unconscious manner. Another word would have been better if one could have had it, though 'Power' would not do, as power can be suspended or withheld, and the forces of Nature cannot." Though the Immanent Will is not conscious, it is still will, a blind force sweeping through the universe, urging things to happen as they do happen, weaving the web of circumstances, shaping things in patterns determined by its irresistible energy.

The only hope for a change from this situation would be a gradual coming to consciousness of the Immanent Will. This odd version of "evolutionary meliorism," which Hardy considered himself to have invented, is expressed in a number of his poems, most powerfully in *The Dynasts*, where the Spirit of the Years, after the reader has been shown all the senseless carnage of the Napoleonic Wars, foresees a time when all will be changed—"Consciousness the Will informing, till It fashion all things fair!" Hardy takes great pleasure in a number of his poems, for example, in "The Blow," or in "Fragment," in describing the anguish of the Immanent Will if it should become conscious and understand what exquisite tortures of suffering it has unwittingly imposed on man and on the animals over the centuries:

Should that morn come, and show thy opened eyes
All that Life's palpitating tissues feel,
How wilt thou bear thyself in thy surprise?—

Wilt thou destroy, in one wild shock of shame,
Thy whole high heaving firmamental frame,
Or patiently adjust, amend, and heal?
                              ("The Sleep-Worker")

"If Law itself had consciousness, how the aspect of its creatures would terrify it, fill it with remorse!" At this point in world history, however, the long expected event has not yet occurred. Mankind is "waiting, waiting, for God *to know it*" ("Fragment"). This earnest expectation may or may not be fulfilled. Meanwhile man must endure things as they are. This endurance is made more painful by knowledge that if the Immanent Will does not come to consciousness the best man can hope for is that he will be lucky enough to "darkle to extinction swift and sure." The development of man is a mistake on the part of the vital energy of earth. Man is no more fit for survival than the dinosaur or the saber-toothed tiger.

This vision of the universe is presupposed throughout Hardy's writing. The philosophical passages in *The Dynasts* only make explicit what is implicit in his novels and early poems. His vision of things is one version of a world view widely present in the late nineteenth century. Its sources in his reading of Tyndall, Huxley, Darwin, Spencer, Schopenhauer, Comte, and others have been often discussed. It is impossible to demonstrate, however, that any one of these sources is uniquely important in determining Hardy's view of things. He read many of the writers who formulated the late Victorian outlook, and his notions were undoubtedly also acquired in part from newspapers, periodicals, and other such reading. What matters most is to identify the idiosyncratic emphases in his version of a current view, the personal elements in his response to this view, and the way all the aspects of his world view are involved with one another.

They are involved not in the sense that all flow from some single presupposition, but in the sense that the various elements might be spoken of as implying one another. Beginning with any one of them leads to the others as natural if not inevitable accompaniments. They form a system or structure. If consciousness is a lucid, depthless, anonymous awareness of what is outside it, a "point of view," a reflecting mirror, then the mind sees the world from a distance as something different from it in nature. The wider, the more detached, the more impersonal, the more disinterested, the more clear and objective a man's view is the closer he will come to seeing the truth of things as they are. This is the scientific or historical point of view, a natural associate of the bifurcation of the world into subject and object. Mind is seen as detached lucidity watching a world of matter in motion.

This motion in things appears to be caused by an intrinsic power within them, a power to which Hardy, like Schopenhauer or Nietzsche, gives the name will. If a man is separated from the universe by the detached clarity of his mind, he participates in the motion of nature through his body, through the emotions that body feels, and through the energy of desire which engages him in the world. This energy seems to be within his control, but is actually only the working through his body of the universal will in its unconscious activities of self-fulfillment. For Hardy, man has a double nature, a power of thinking and understanding, and a power of doing, feeling, and willing. If through the latter he takes part in the endless physical changes of the world, through the former he recognizes that these transformations, even those "willed" by man, leave nature still indifferent to human needs, unstructured by any inherent system of value. If the world view of nineteenth-century science accompanies naturally the separation of mind from world, along with the scientific view goes that draining of value from the essence of matter of fact which Alfred North Whitehead has described in *Science and the Modern World*. Objects are merely objects. They behave as they do behave, according to universal and impersonal laws. Any human value they may appear to have is a subjective illusion cast over them by man's instinctive desire that the world should provide him with an environment corresponding to his needs.

The emptying of human significance from things is often associated with loss of religious faith. Only a world of hierarchical levels in participation easily allows for a God who is both within His world and outside it. In the dispersal which is likely to accompany the separation of existence into two realms, subject and object, mind and world, God may at first be seen as separating himself from his creation. He withdraws to a distant place and watches the universe from afar. The scientist in his all-embracing objectivity apes this conception of God. If the division of realms of existence appears complete, if there seems no inherence of God in my consciousness, in nature, or in other people, if there remain open no more avenues of mediation by which a distant God may be reached, however indirectly, as in the forlorn echo from an infinite distance in Matthew Arnold's "The Buried Life," then I may experience not the "disappearance of God" but the death of God, that death which Hardy announces in "God's Funeral."

The experience of the death of God seems a natural concomitant of a definition of man as pure consciousness and of everything else as the object of that consciousness. To the "deicide eyes of seers" ("A Plaint to Man") God seems no more than a "man-projected Figure" ("God's Funeral"). God is killed by the attainment of that all-embracing vision which makes man a seer. The span of perfected human consciousness, separate, pure, clear-seeing, is as wide as the infinite universe it beholds, a universe now revealed to be made of blazing suns in a black void. Such a universe is shown to Lady Constantine by the young astronomer, Swithin St. Cleeve, in *Two on a Tower*. "Until a person has thought out the stars and their interspaces," says Swithin, "he has hardly learnt that there are things much more terrible than monsters of shape, namely, monsters of magnitude without known shape. Such monsters are the voids and waste places of the sky." In such a view the detachment of the watching mind corresponds to the infinite breadth of the universe it beholds. Both are equally null, nullity reflecting nullity, man and all his concerns reduced by the terrible impersonality of space to infinitesimal specks in a measureless hollow. "There is a size," says Swithin,

> at which dignity begins . . . ; further on there is a size at which grandeur begins; further on there is a size at which solemnity begins; further on, a size at which awfulness begins; further on, a size at which ghastliness begins. That size faintly approaches the size of the stellar universe. . . . [If] you are restless and anxious about the future, study astronomy at once. Your troubles will be reduced amazingly. But your study will reduce them in a singular way, by reducing the importance of everything. . . . It is quite impossible to think at all adequately of the sky—of what the sky substantially is, without feeling it as a juxtaposed nightmare.

Such a sense of man's place in the universe is not too different from that of his contemporary, Friedrich Nietzsche, but Hardy's response to this vision is radically different. It is in this response that his special quality must be sought. As a number of critics have seen, his attitude is in some ways strikingly similar to that of Nietzsche's predecessor, Arthur Schopenhauer, the philosopher whose dissertation *On the Four-fold Root of the Principle of Sufficient Reason* Hardy read in 1889 or 1890 in Mrs. Karl Hillebrand's translation. Nietzsche defines man as the will to power. In a world of amoral determinism man should take matters into his own hands, become a center of force organizing the world into patterns of value. The man of relentless will can turn his life from fated repetition into willed repetition and so escape into a paradoxical freedom. Hardy, like Schopenhauer's saint or artist who has lifted the veil of Maya, is more passive and detached. Like so many of his countrymen, like Dickens for example, he fears the guilt involved in becoming the value-giving center of his world. Willing means yielding to those emotions which orient a man toward other people. The longing for power and ownership involves a man in the swarming activity of the Immanent Will, and so alienates him from himself, as Napoleon in *The Dynasts,* surely a man of will, is nevertheless only an instrument of impersonal forces working through him.

Each man, in Hardy's view, has a paradoxical freedom. His own power of willing is, as in Schopenhauer's system, only his embodiment of a tiny part of the vast energy of the Immanent Will. Even so, a man's will is apparently under the control of his mind, or at least it expresses the intentions of that mind. This means that if the other powers around him are in a momentary equilibrium he can act freely rather than being pushed by external energies. Hardy returns frequently to this notion and always expresses it in the language of physical forces in interaction, as when he speaks of "the modicum of free will conjecturally possessed by organic life when the mighty necessitating forces—unconscious or other—that have 'the balancings of the clouds,' happen to be in equilibrium," or as in a stanza from a poem of 1893, "He Wonders about Himself":

> Part is mine of the general Will,
> Cannot my share in the sum of sources
> Bend a digit the poise of forces,
> And a fair desire fulfil?

The language here reveals how little free Hardy's concept of free will is. As part of the general will his individual will expresses that of which it is a part. It is moved with the whole, even though in unusual circumstances of balance it may be the part of the general will which gives the push to things. His freedom is in fact servitude, as the note of interrogation in this poem suggests. Another text on the theme makes this even clearer. It uses an odd metaphor which suggests that the free will of the individual is no more than his power to move independently, but automatically, according to patterns that have been implanted previously by the "Great Will": "whenever it happens that all the rest of the Great Will is in equilibrium the minute portion called one person's will is free, just as a performer's fingers are free to go on playing the pianoforte of themselves when he talks or thinks of something else and the head does not rule them." Once more the image of the digit occurs. Man is at best no more than a forefinger of the universal sleep-walking giant. Another such text describes the Will as "like a knitter drowsed,/ Whose fingers play in skilled unmindfulness." Even when the individual will acts with the paradoxical freedom of a self-acting finger it is still no more than a portion of the universal Will. As a result, the more powerfully a man wills or desires, the more surely he becomes the puppet of an all-shaping energy, and the quicker he encompasses his own destruction. As soon as he engages himself in life he joins a vast streaming movement urging him on toward death and the failure of his desires.

Safety therefore lies in passivity, in secrecy, in self-effacement, in reticence, in the refusal of emotions and of their temptations to involvement. These temptations, however, are almost irresistibly strong, even for a man naturally so clear-headed as Hardy. Though the mind is different in essence from the physical motion of things as they are driven by the Immanent Will, it does not constitute a realm altogether apart. The mind of even the most detached and far-seeing man is still oriented toward the world, watching it, dwelling within it, open to its solicitations, subject to its glare and garish rattling. Like Joseph Conrad in *Victory* and elsewhere, Hardy frequently turns to a theme which is for both writers not without its grimly comic aspects: the story of a man who by luck or by deliberate effort of will has kept himself apart from other men and women, but is in spite of his aloofness lured into involvement and suffering. Boldwood in *Far from the Madding Crowd* is a good example of such a character. Nor was Hardy himself exempt from such experiences, in spite of his reticence and self-control.

In his fiction and in his life this loss of self-possession takes two principle forms: falling in love and yielding to the magical power of music. His love affair with his cousin Tryphena Sparks, if this indeed took place, and his love for his first wife seem to have been, in their ambiguous complexity, the central events of his personal life. These events are reflected with varying degrees of obliquity in his writing, most directly in the poem "Thoughts of Phena, at News of Her Death," and in the poems he wrote after the death of his wife, the "Poems of 1912–13." Certainly these infatuations were the most important cases in which Hardy broke his instinctive reserve. The suffering which seems to have followed in both cases can be glimpsed here and there in the sparse evidence about his private life. This suffering gives his life a pattern much like the recurrent form of his fiction. It was not only Tryphena Sparks or Emma Gifford to whom he responded, however. A number of examples are given in the *Life* of his penchant, as a boy and as a young man, for falling passionately in love with girls he had glimpsed from a distance. The poem "To Lizbie Browne" commemorates one of these episodes:

> But, Lizbie Browne,
> I let you slip;
> Shaped not a sign;
> Touched never your lip
> With lip of mine,
> Lost Lizbie Browne!

As for Hardy's response to music, a curious passage in the *Life*, a passage almost adjacent to the text describing the young boy's retreat under his hat, shows how he shared with the characters in his fiction a strong susceptibility to it:

> He was of ecstatic temperament, extraordinarily sensitive to music, and among the endless jigs, hornpipes, reels, waltzes, and country-dances that his father played of an evening in his early married years, and to which the boy danced a *pas seul* in the middle of the room, there were three or four that always moved the child to tears, though he strenuously tried to hide them. . . . This peculiarity in himself troubled the mind of "Tommy" as he was called, and set him wondering at a phenomenon to which he ventured not to confess. He used to say in later life that, like Calantha in Ford's *Broken Heart*, he danced on at these times to conceal his weeping. He was not over four years of age at this date.

An admirably suggestive and revealing passage! He was of "ecstatic temperament"—the phrase is a strong one. In spite of his self-enclosure, his cultivation of a watchful detachment, Hardy was so subject to the lure of the outside world that music could draw him out of himself, destroy his self-control, and reduce him to helpless tears. His response to music, however, is more than a reaction to the objective beauty of a moving melody. It is also a mediated reaction to other people, those who have invented the tune or who play it. The boy weeping as he listens to music is as much subject to his father as to the melody. It is this double enslavement which so troubles him. The power of music is like the power of a beautiful woman. In both cases an overwhelming emotional reaction draws his soul involuntarily out of his body and makes him the puppet of someone outside himself, as the children were entranced by the Pied Piper of Hamelin.

This association between music and love is dramatized in that admirable short story, "The Fiddler of the Reels" (1893). The Fiddler, "Mop" Ollamoor, plays so magically that he could "well-nigh have drawn an ache from the heart of a gate-post. He could make any child in the parish, who was at all sensitive to music, burst into tears in a few minutes by simply fiddling one of the old dance-tunes he almost entirely affected—country jigs, reels, and 'Favourite Quick Steps' of the last century." Mop's power is also sexual, and his sexual magnetism works by way of his music. Like a young girl Hardy once heard whose singing had the power of "drawing out the soul of listeners in a gradual thread of excruciating attention like silk from a cocoon," Mop can "play the fiddle so as to draw your soul out of your body like a spider's thread." The story tells how he enthralls a young country girl, Car'line, steals her away from her betrothed, seduces her, and some years later once more hypnotizes her with his playing so that he can abduct the child born of their union. Music and love—both are an irresistible fascination.

Rather than yielding in complete abnegation of will to the lure of music and love, as does Car'line, Hardy fights for his independence. This is not easy to do. It is one thing to withdraw under his hat in a moment of solitude and decide not to involve himself in the world. It is quite another to remain in possession of himself while his father is playing the fiddle or when he sees a pretty girl. In fact it is impossible. The tears flow involuntarily; his soul goes out of his body. The best he can do is to hide his tears, keep his love secret, as he did from the various girls he loved when he was an adolescent.

This hiding takes a curious form. In the passage cited above Hardy dances on to conceal his weeping. The dancing is a response to the emotive power of the music, but it is an indirect, covert response, a transposition of the helpless and self-betraying tears into a more or less impersonal and socially accepted form of behavior. In dancing the uncontrolled tears and the lax flowing out of the soul into the world are turned into the controlled expression of art. This art is a way of being involved in the world and of responding to it without being swallowed up by it. It holds things at a distance and imitates in another pattern the objective patterns in the outside world which have held his attention through their power to generate an emotional fascination. Such an art is at once a reaction to the external world, and a protection against it. It is a transformation of the reaction into a shape which imitates it at a distance.

Exactly this pattern can be seen in another passage from the early pages of the *Life*. Once more there is a strong emotional response to the qualitative aspects of an experience. The experience is accepted and yet held at arm's length through its change into the objective form of a work of art. The text comes between the one about the young Hardy's response to music and the one about his desire not to grow up:

> In those days the staircase at Bockhampton (later removed) had its walls coloured Venetian red by his father, and was so situated that the evening sun shone into it, adding to its colour a great intensity for a quarter of an hour or more. Tommy used to wait for this chromatic effect, and, sitting alone there, would recite to himself "And now another day is gone" from Dr. Watts's Hymns, with great fervency, though perhaps not for any religious reason, but from a sense that the scene suited the lines.

The same elements are here: the bright red wall which draws him to watch for its special intensity at sunset; the holding back from the danger of his response not by destroying the response or by turning away from it, but by transmuting it into another form which matches it at a distance, the fervency of the singing corresponding to the intensity of the red wall at sunset. The fundamental structure of Hardy's relation to the world may be identified through the juxtaposition of these homologous texts. In all of them the mind confronts in detachment a world which is seen as possessing dangerous energies, energies which are yet ambiguously attractive. There is a refusal of direct involvement, but there is also discovery of a means of indirect response. Hardy's preference for such responses may help to explain why he became a writer and what relation to the world his writing expresses.

Tess of the D'Urbervilles:
A Novel of Assertion

Jean R. Brooks

> "What's the use of learning that I am one of a long row only—finding
> out that there is set down in some old book somebody just like me, and to
> know that I shall only act her part; making me sad, that's all. The best is
> not to remember that your nature and your past doings have been just like
> thousands' and thousands', and that your coming life and doings 'll be like
> thousands' and thousands'."
>
> —Tess of the D'Urbervilles

Tess of the D'Urbervilles is not about a pure woman betrayed by man, morality, and the President of the Immortals; her fight for re-acceptance and
happiness; "the incessant penalty paid by the innocent for the guilty"
(*Academy* review) or the decay of the peasantry. All these aspects are there,
but all are contributory to the major conflict suggested by the two parts of
the title. " 'Call me Tess,' she would say askance" when Angel Clare "called
her Artemis, Demeter, and other fanciful names half teasingly," and it is
as the dairymaid Tess, an individual human being, that she "had set herself
to stand or fall by her qualities." But she is also Tess "of the D'Urbervilles,"
and the novel is shaped by the tension between the personal and impersonal
parts of her being. The right to be human is not easy to assert against the
laws of nature, heredity, society and economy which abstract from people
"the differences which distinguished them as individuals."

The surface story of Tess narrates the events that defeat her struggle
for personal happiness. But the poetic underpattern reveals "underneath
the resolute purpose of the planning animal, the victim of circumstance
and the doomed or sanctified being"—a more archetypal direction to her
life, hostile to personal claims.

The plot is simple and unoriginal. Its familiarity springs from two
sources. The eternal triangle, the wronged woman who cannot escape her
past, "the woman pays," the double standard of morality for men and
women, were themes known to Victorian literature. Balladry can produce
Patient Griselda, the highborn lady in disguise, the seduced milkmaid, the
murder of a betrayer, and retribution on the gallows. Hardy's poetic power
lies first of all in crossing and challenging the Victorian moral tale with the
ethic of folk tradition. The Victorian assumption that the fallen woman did

From *Thomas Hardy: The Poetic Structure.* © 1971 by Jean R. Brooks. Grafton Books, 1981.

not rise again is questioned by the timeless values of the ballad world, closer to natural law.

> Though a knave hath by me leyne,
> Yet am I noder dede nor slowe;
> I trust to recouer my harte agayne,
> And Crystes curse goo wyth yow!
> ("Crow and Pie")

The ballad mode, non-naturalistic and poetic, also lends belief to those unlikely incidents which disturb a naturalistic view of the novel but fall into place as manifestations of "the indomitable unconscious will" that directs the underpattern. Angel's sleepwalking, Alec's conversion and his blood soaking through the ceiling, the gift of an empty mansion in the New Forest; the impish operations of time, chance, coincidence and cross-purpose, mock the resolute purpose of the planning animal with intimations of her archetypal destiny. Such are the collision of the mailcart with the Durbeyfield waggon, the coincidence of Chaseborough Fair with the market, the drunken revel and Tess's fatigue; the mistiming that dooms Tess "to be seen and coveted that day by the wrong man," and Angel to dance with the wrong girl and return from Brazil too late; the events which frustrate her attempts to confess and seek aid from Angel's parents; the tenant-farmer of the "starve-acre" farm turning out to be the Trantridge man who owed her a grudge; Angel's chance glimpse of the D'Urberville portraits as he hesitates outside Tess's bedroom; the build-up of her family's misfortunes just after she has refused Alec's help; and the omens—all add up to an impressive vision of the workings of a Fate familiar to folklore, irrational and unknowable, ordering the affairs of men to a nonhuman rhythm.

The plot is organized round the seven "phases" of Tess's personal story to give pointers to the direction in which her impersonal life is moving. Her first phase as "The Maiden" ends when Alec seduces her.

> An immeasurable social chasm was to divide our heroine's personality thereafter from that previous self of hers who stepped from her mother's door to try her fortune at Trantridge poultry farm.

The second phase follows Tess's return home with the consciousness of original sin on her—"she looked upon herself as a figure of Guilt intruding into the haunts of Innocence"—to the birth and death of her baby, and her reintegration into country ritual. "The past was past; whatever it had been was no more at hand."

> On one point she was resolved: there should be no more D'Urberville air-castles in the dreams and deeds of her new life. She would be the dairymaid Tess, and nothing more.

In Phase the Third, "The Rally," the experience and personality of the dairymaid Tess are enlarged at Talbothays by Angel Clare. The unpremeditated kiss that ends this phase means that "something had occurred which changed the pivot of the universe for their two natures." That "something," in the next phase, is that Tess hands over part of her self to the impersonal force of love. This phase follows the maturing natural relationship of two lovers "converging, under an irresistible law, as surely as two streams in one vale," until Tess's fatal confession on her wedding night. In Phase the Fifth, "The Woman Pays," the personal Tess is gradually depersonalized, first of all by the abstract ideal of purity which Angel prefers to her real human self, and secondly, when he has abandoned her, by the increasingly automatic mode of her life.

> There was something of the habitude of the wild animal in the unreflecting instinct with which she rambled on—disconnecting herself by littles from her eventful past at every step, obliterating her identity.

Now seeking not happiness, but mere survival, she has a second recovery through endurance of winter weather and rough work at Flintcombe Ash. This time it is halted on her return from Emminster, when a meeting with Alec gives her "an almost physical sense of an implacable past which still engirdled her."

The closing in of her implacable past to submerge her personal identity occupies the sixth phase. She makes her last helpless gesture as an independent woman in the D'Urberville vaults, where her homeless family have camped for the night. "Why am I on the wrong side of this door!" In the last phase, the "coarse pattern" that had been traced "upon this beautiful feminine tissue, sensitive as gossamer," is fulfilled at Stonehenge, a place of religious sacrifice, and Wintoncester, ancient social capital of Wessex. Alec's murder and Tess's execution identify the personal Tess with the D'Urberville family type, the scapegoat victim of fertility rites, and those innate and external pressures which level down the human being into something less than human—"her breathing now was quick and small, like that of a lesser creature than a woman."

The pivotal points in Tess's fight to be herself show fundamental parallels that compel comparisons and contrasts. These draw the lines of the "coarse pattern" for us. Tess has three "deaths" and three rebirths: the first at Talbothays into the fullness of human and natural existence; the second at Flintcombe Ash into a lower plane of animal survival; the third in a metaphysical sense, when she hands over the meaning of her life to 'Liza-Lu and Angel standing, significantly, in the position of Giotto's *Two Apostles*. Her two violations, physical and spiritual, invite comparison as well as contrast between Alec D'Urberville and Angel Clare. Both deny Tess the right to be human, Alec in obedience to the subhuman impulse of sex, Angel to the superhuman power of the image that substitutes essence for existence. Both are incompletely characterized when compared with the rounded humanness of Tess, but this is surely stratagem rather than error. Alec's resemblance to the Victorian stage villain and the morality Vice, and Angel's to one of his own unreal (angelic) conceptions of human nature, indicate their role as complementary agents of dehumanization. Both betray Tess in a world of paradisal lushness, though the resemblance should not blind one to the essential differences between Trantridge and Talbothays. Both feed her with fruit (chap. 5, chap. 30). Both are associated in action and commentary with fire; Alec in its red, murky aspect and Angel with its radiance—the fire of hell and heaven.

There are other parallels stressed by radiation outwards from the central crisis of Tess's confession. The fertility of her experience at Talbothays in Phase the Third, rising to its climax of hope in her engagement to Clare, is balanced in Phase Five by the sterility at Flintcombe Ash, which touches the bottom of despair at Alec's return. Her reintegration into natural rhythms in Phase Two is offset by her increasing subjection to mechanical rhythms in Phase Six, and pointed up by the repetition of the word "past" at the end of each phase. The final swallowing up of the particular aim in the general doom in Phase the Seventh is an ironical development of John Durbeyfield's claim to definition by family in Phase the First.

Such parallels suggest a rich layer of archetypal myth directing the course of Tess's life. Hardy's rich poetic and narrative resources combine to bring out the deeper meaning of the novel by imaginative description of the way characters move and speak and relate to their environment. The central events are described in Darwinian terms of struggle and adaptation, extinction and renewal of the species. But the discovery of Tess's ancestry initiates all the myths about the meaning of being human; myths that are explored in the rest of the novel through an intricate network of poetic cross-references. It may be dismissed as top dressing, but a responsiveness to poetic overtones in the first chapters reveals why Hardy placed the D'Urberville theme in a key position.

"Sir John D'Urberville—that's who I am," declares shiftless peasant Jack Durbeyfield. His prostrate position "upon the bank among the daisies" suggests the effigies in the D'Urberville vault. The attempt of insecure man, no longer able to give himself meaning by reference to a creator with a holy plan, to define himself through the name and fame of his human pedigree, becomes an ironical definition through death. "I've—got—a—gr't—family—vault—at—Kingsbere—and—knighted-forefathers-in-lead-coffins-there!" Ancestry becomes a metaphor for all the impersonal forces which swallow up individual effort and lethargy alike in the final and inclusive impersonality of death.

Hardy's poetic and dramatic presentation of the various layers of Tess's past prepares us to view her in the double aspect indicated by the title. The lyrical meditation that begins chapter 2, on the "fertile and sheltered tract of country" where Tess was born gives way to a shot, nearer in space and time but still distanced, of the transformed fertility rite that connected primitive man to the cycle of nature. Jack Durbeyfield's mock-heroic progress, with its absurd hero chanting his meaningless identification with things that are dead, provides an ironical backdrop to this "local Cerealia"—an inheritance older than the D'Urbervilles that once gave religious and social definition, if a violent one, to man in the mass—and draws attention to Tess taking part. The colour combination which picks her out—"She wore a red ribbon in her hair, and was the only one of the white company who could boast of such a pronounced adornment"—persistently links her with a complex of passion, guilt, sacrifice, and purity. Here it associates her with the noble white hart killed violently in the forest, the first of the hunting images that run through the book as types of Tess's fate. As we move to close-up in the present moment, Tess comes before us not only as herself, but also as a product of the same nonhuman forces that produced landscape, ritual and heredity. On the outskirts of the scene stands Angel Clare, urban invader of the unconscious harmony with his disease of modern thought and "creeds which futilely attempt to check what wisdom would be content to regulate," watching a primitive try at regulation. The dramatic composition is masterly.

The need for wisdom to regulate is made clear in chapter 3, where the picture of Tess's inheritance is completed. Joan Durbeyfield, fixed forever at the cradle and the washtub, opposes "the muck and muddle of rearing children" to the memory Tess brings with her of an ordered ritual that once gave religious significance to fertility. Tess, as a budding woman, is cast for the role of childbearer too. But the dramatic juxtaposition questions the value of the primitive, unaware fertility of shiftless Marlott for modern conditions of self-conscious responsibility.

The dramatic and poetic vision that links Tess to her inheritance as animal, woman, and human being has already suggested the three fundamental and interconnecting myths that she will be lived by. They are the fertility scapegoat, Paradise Lost, and that twentieth century response to the "ache of modernism," the exile. Marlott and Trantridge, sheltered and languorous, smaller in scale than the Valley of the Great Dairies where Tess reaches maturity, present the first of these, the world of fertility myth, or primal harmony before the birth of consciousness. (Richard Beckman, in "A Character Typology for Hardy's Novels,"*ELH*, 30 [1963], suggests that the pattern of moods built up in the novels parallels the pattern of evolution in "Before Life and After"—Nescience—Consciousness—Nescience.)

> They followed the road with a sensation that they were soaring along in a supporting medium, possessed of original and profound thoughts, themselves and surrounding nature forming an organ-

ism of which all the parts harmoniously and joyously interpenetrated each other. They were as sublime as the moon and stars
above them, and the moon and stars were as ardent as they.

The figures in this world take on the Dionysian attributes of vegetation
gods:

> Of the rushing couples there could barely be discerned more
> than the high lights—the indistinctness shaping them to satyrs
> clasping nymphs—a multiplicity of Pans whirling a multiplicity of
> Syrinxes; Lotis attempting to elude Priapus, and always failing . . .

and it is on this night of traditional licence that Tess is seduced. But Hardy's
poetic presentation casts doubt on the meaning of fertility myth for modern
man. The elements of the "supporting medium" which contribute to the
harmony of all the parts—moonlight, candlelight, pollen dust (the first of
the many pollen images that link Tess with fertility throughout the book),
fog, and "the spirit of wine" lend it a nightmare quality, and distance it
as an illusion of the irresponsible. Tess becomes aware of the need for a
more advanced harmony, which will not affront the dignity of a self-conscious human being by ignoring the dissonance of personal pain, when
the inharmonious accident to Prince proves the universe's "serene dissociation from these two wisps of human life." The birds, who "shook themselves in the hedges, arose, and twittered" as usual, and the incongruous
beauty of spilt blood in the sunrise suggest a duplicity in the cosmos too
complex for communal fertility ritual to cope with.

Nevertheless, the sexual guilt of causing life subconsciously demands
a scapegoat whose purity will carry off the sins of the world. Tess's role
as victim is stressed in those scenes where the symbolic overtones of red
and white set up rich dissonances of pain and purity, guilt and innocence,
life and death, the paradox of living. The red is often the red of real blood.
Prince's blood glares against the paleness of dawn, the lane, and Tess's
white features as she tries to stop the hole with her hand. The violent
colour contrast, the crimson stain Tess receives as the result of her effort,
the suggestion of sexual guilt in the blood ("Princely" but worn-out like
the D'Urbervilles) that pours from a hole pierced by the phallic spike on a
dark night, foreshadow her seduction and doom of murder and sacrifice.
Such foreshortenings of reality, as Morrell points out in *Thomas Hardy: The
Will and the Way*, are not necessarily images of what *must* happen, but of
what *may* happen if steps are not taken to avert disaster. Tess's association
with blood is often neutral, or at least ambivalent. Another dawn scene,
when she humanely kills the bleeding pheasants, reveals to her not only
her own predicament in the cosmos as a creature "brought into being by
artificial means" in order to be killed, but also her superior freedom as a
human being not to hurry to her destiny. The nest she had made for herself
under the boughs recalls the nest of leaves Alec made for her in The Chase

but the plight of the pheasants restores her to human nature from the animal nature Alec's act implied: "I be not mangled, and I be not bleeding, and I have two hands to feed and clothe me." As she stands hesitant at the door of Emminster Vicarage,

> a piece of bloodstained paper, caught up from some meat-buyer's dustheap, beat up and down the road without the gate; too flimsy to rest, too heavy to fly away; and a few straws kept it company.

The blood-stained paper and straw, here literally a floating omen, is transmuted by her crucial loss of courage at Emminster into a fixed image of the fate she has helped to release. When she strikes Alec on the rick with a gauntlet, "the blood began dropping from his mouth upon the straw," and Tess, "with the hopeless defiance of the sparrow's gaze before its captor twists its neck," accepts the domination of her impersonal role. "Once victim, always victim—that's the law!"

Even Hardy's figurative description of Alec, when Tess first meets him, as "one who stood fair to be the blood-red ray in the spectrum of her young life" modulates before long through the forced strawberries and early roses he has given her to another blood omen in the thorn that pricks her chin. The suspicion that he has been decking a sacrificial victim, in this region "wherein Druidical mistletoe was still found on aged oaks" (a phrase recalled when Tess confesses to an impulse of suicide under Angel's ironical gift of mistletoe over the wedding bed) is strengthened when Joan washes her daughter's hair (a fertility symbol) for the second visit to Trantridge, and

> put upon her the white frock that Tess had worn at the club-walking, the airy fulness of which, supplementing her enlarged *coiffure,* imparted to her developing figure an amplitude which belied her age, and might cause her to be estimated as a woman when she was not much more than a child.

She is wearing the same white dress when she is seduced.

Descriptions of natural phenomena, used so variously in Hardy's work, combine with colour symbolism to define Tess's role as ritual victim. The sun-god, who demanded blood to perpetuate his life-giving powers, is much in evidence. Hardy's accuracy in conveying the effect of sunlight at different times of the day and year make these effects a poetic correlative to Tess's acceptance of her role. At Wellbridge Manor, just before she confesses, the low afternoon winter sunlight "stretched across to her skirt, where it made a spot like a paint-mark set upon her." The stain sets up reverberations not only of Prince's blood, which splashed her "from face to skirt," but also of the text-painter who embodied her conventional sense of guilt in red letters, "THY, DAMNATION, SLUMBERETH, NOT." At Flintcombe Ash, where the red threshing machine drives Tess with the impersonality of immutable law, "a wrathful shine" from the March sunset dyes the tired faces of the enslaved threshers with "a coppery light," giving to the human features the look of ritual masks that marked the men who surrounded Tess on the Stone of Sacrifice at sunrise, "their faces and hands as if they were silvered, the remainder of their figures dark." Even the benevolent morning sun of the Marlott harvest, "a golden-haired, beaming, mild-eyed, God-like creature," throws "stripes like red-hot pokers" on cottage furniture and intensifies the ruddy hue of the "revolving Maltese cross" on the reaping machine, reminding us that sun worship had its sacrificial aspect. At all times Tess is linked intimately to the natural world from which her consciousness isolates her. Hardy's double vision presents her both as an extension of nature moved by forces beyond her control— most obviously in the Talbothays idyll, where her sexuality blossoms with the maturing season—and as a subjective being whose moral awareness pushes her beyond the world of fertility myth to the world of knowledge gained and Paradise lost.

One world can be seen modulating into the other in chapter 14. The Marlott harvest shows the highest achievement possible to a way of life still closely linked to fertility ritual. It is a good life. All the details contribute to a picture of natural harmony: the youthful sun-god, taking a personal interest in the ritual, the reaping machine which starts with a non-mechanical ticking "like the love-making of the grasshopper," and the horses who pull it, made as much a part of the sun-directed pattern by their glistening brasses as the men by their twinkling trouser buttons. The women too are "part and parcel of outdoor nature," timing their dance-like movements to the unhurried pace of machine and horses. Once again, as in chapter 2, Tess is seen first as an integral part of landscape and ritual; as one of the field-women, who has "somehow lost her own margin, imbibed the essence of her surrounding, and assimilated herself with it." As Hardy describes the "clock-like monotony" of Tess's work in great detail, the tense changes to the eternal present (a common feature of Hardy's style when describing the unchanging rhythms of country labour) and the rhythm of binding controls the rise and fall of the sentences. The quiet rhythms, soft consonants and subtle vowel progressions are halted abruptly by the hardness of the last word as Hardy draws attention to the girl's bare arm: "and as the day wears on its feminine smoothness becomes scarified by the stubble, and bleeds." The abrupt halt serves to remind us of Tess's connection, by now well-established through colour imagery, with the motif of sacrifice. The undertones are strengthened by the red "Maltese cross" to which Hardy draws attention and the ritual encirclement of small animals, which tallies closely with Frazer's description in *The Golden Bough* of the killing of the corn spirit/vegetation god/scapegoat at harvest. But even this does not destroy the harmony. It is distanced by time, "the doom that awaited them later in the day," and by the ritual pattern of their death, that abstracts individuality from participants in the dance. The choreography is continued by the children carrying the baby, who "rose above the stubbly convexity of the hill" to repeat the earlier movement pattern of the reaper and horses. Feeding the baby adds another feminine rhythm to the eternal ritual. The baby, the friendliness of the rustics, the unhurried rhythm of work and repose where nature, animal, man and machine work together in unforced harmony, build up a vision of a world where primal rightness has not yet taken the tinct of wrong.

The good life, doing what it must, with no hope, no despair, no human awareness or choice of action, has its own dignity. But certain elements in the scene—the moonlight progress, the sense of oneness with nature— throw the mind back to the drunken revel at Chaseborough, and the two scenes held in balance with Hardy's comment on Tess's subjective sensations demonstrate the falseness of a philosophy of harmony for the modern thinking and feeling human being, who has emerged from innocence to awareness of alienation. "The familiar surroundings had not darkened because of her grief, nor sickened because of her pain."

There is something in Tess at war with nature which she needs the qualities denoted by Angel's name to bring out. Communal fertility ritual cannot cope with a personal "misery which transcended that of the child's simple loss." Her concern for the baby's individual soul belongs to the kind of Christianity practised, if not preached, by Angel's parents. Her passage thus from "simple girl to complex woman" is embodied in a striking visual image in the second half of the chapter, the baptism of her baby, which carries overtones still sounding from the harvest ritual. The modulation begins in the paragraph that joins the two parts. The picture of Tess taking part in the traditional ride home on the harvest wagon, at one with her ballad-singing companions and the rhythms of life and death denoted by harvest and balladry, is lit by

> a broad tarnished moon that had risen from the ground to the eastwards, its face resembling the outworn gold-leaf halo of some worm-eaten Tuscan saint.

The worm-eaten saint superimposed on the symbol of fertility/purity prepares both for Tess's growth towards a more advanced kind of religion and for the deadness of its outer forms. The eye moves from the moonlit and sunlit communal ritual to the solitary candlelit figure of Tess performing a sacred rite of the Christian church. "The ecstasy of faith almost apotheosized her." The priest-like white nightgown, the basin and jug and other properties of this "act of approximation" are made divine and meaningful not by any virtue in the rite of baptism itself, but by the value of the individual human being that stands at the centre of Christ's religion.

> The children gazed up at her with more and more reverence, and no longer had a will for questioning. She did not look like Sissy to them now, but as a being large, towering, and awful—a divine personage with whom they had nothing in common.

The sign of the cross that marks the baby baptizes Tess as a suffering human being. Conception in sorrow, toil for daily bread, frailty, freedom of will and awareness of human alienation are to define the new-created woman in place of nobility human and divine and innocence lost. Her "desires are limited to man and his humble yet formidable love" (*The Plague*)—the basic human rights to live, love, work and be happy. She also takes with her to Talbothays an inheritance of vital animal instincts with which human values must come to terms. These are constantly present in Hardy's minutely detailed evocations of the maturing summer in the fertile Valley of the Great Dairies, where growth is felt as an active sexual force that affects vegetation, animals, maids and men alike. The details that denote the observant naturalist are selected by the poet to evoke simultaneously the mystery of the "great passionate pulse of existence" that orders the movement of the natural world, and a solid sense of everyday reality.

> Rays from the sunrise drew forth the buds and stretched them into long stalks, lifted up sap in noiseless streams, opened petals, and sucked out scents in invisible jets and breathings.

> During the day the animals obsequiously followed the shadow of the smallest tree as it moved round the stem with the diurnal roll; and when the milkers came they could hardly stand still for the flies.

> On the gray moisture of the grass were marks where the cows had lain through the night—dark-green islands of dry herbage the size of their carcases, in the general sea of dew. From each island proceeded a serpentine trail, by which the cow had rambled away to feed after getting up, at the end of which trail they found her; the snoring puff from her nostrils, when she recognized them, making an intenser little fog of her own amid the prevailing one.

The sense of reality is vital to the novel. It is the reality of the physical world in which a human being without God finds meaning and definition. Tess's response to it takes the obvious form of response through a lover. Angel and Tess are constantly seen as an image of the highest fulfilment in the human pair not divorced from the natural setting that is their present meaning and past history.

> The sun was so near the ground, and the sward so flat, that the shadows of Clare and Tess would stretch a quarter of a mile ahead of them, like two long fingers pointing afar to where the green alluvial reaches abutted against the sloping sides of the vale.

Talbothays stands fair to become Paradise regained. It is a fully human paradise, that does not exclude moral awareness and unmerited personal suffering. It provides constant reminders of the doom of death and the shortness of life: butterflies trapped in the milkmaids' gauze skirts, "another year's instalment of flowers, leaves, nightingales, thrushes, finches, and such ephemeral creatures,"

> wooden posts rubbed to a glossy smoothness by the flanks of infinite cows and calves of bygone years, now passed to an oblivion almost inconceivable in its profundity.

Work is transformed from God's curse to a harmony with country rhythms and one of the factors in the growth of love, for every emotional crisis happens during the course of the dairy chores. The three milkmaids, suffering as individuals from a gratuitous passion which reduces each to "portion of one organism called sex" accept their pain with dignity and generosity. Sex itself is not evil at Talbothays: only thinking makes it so. Tess's spiritual quality of purity is rooted in her vital sexual nature. Talbothays gives hope of reconciliation between the natural harmony of a preconscious state and a respect for the conscious human self.

Angel Clare is seen as the "god-like" Adam to Tess's Eve. With his modern consciousness, advanced views and vaunted respect for the variegated Hodge, he has qualities of spiritual delicacy that could benefit an untutored Paradise. But the poetic undercurrents flowing through his encounters with Tess suggest that his angelic qualities have some kinship with the snake that deceived her in the earlier unconscious Eden. The snake is still there, in the form of her sex. "She was yawning, and he saw the red interior of her mouth as if it had been a snake's." It was a moment "when the most spiritual beauty bespeaks itself flesh." The unweeded garden where Tess "undulated upon the thin notes of the second-hand harp" looks back to the sinister lushness of Marlott. Her inability to leave the spot, "like a fascinated bird" looks forward to her bird-like submission to her sexual master Alec on the rick. The distortion of reality produced by Angel's music on her subjective consciousness—

> The floating pollen seemed to be his notes made visible, and the dampness of the garden the weeping of the garden's sensibility. Though near nightfall, the rank-smelling weed-flowers glowed as if they would not close for intentness, and the waves of colour mixed with the waves of sound

—the confusion of senses and distances, the pollen, the sense of exaltation—"Tess was conscious of neither time nor space"—even the rhythm of the sentences, echo the self-deception of the Trantridge revellers. Yearning for absolute harmony is the other side of the coin of sexual attraction.

Hardy's double stress on the objective reality of the garden, full of attractive but foul-smelling weeds and sticky blights that stain Tess as she is drawn towards the angelic music (played, as Hardy is careful to point out, on a *second-hand* harp and with poor execution) and its subjective beauty when filtered through Tess's unweeded emotions, point the dangers as well as the advantages of the angelic power to transform the physical world into the spiritual. Tess's comment, after confessing her fears of life, "But *you*, sir, can raise up dreams with your music, and drive all such horrid fancies away!" marks the kind of deceiver Angel will be in this new conscious garden of Eden. The sham D'Urberville raised hopes of definition by human pedigree; the sham angel appeals to the human yearning for the absolute, which leads likewise to death. But ideal dreams persist. Angel is introduced into the story by a typically idealistic remark on William Dewey's deception of the bull with the Nativity hymn, which caricatures Angel's attempts to impose his superhuman vision on the living physical world. In a godless world human beings depend on each other for definition. But Angel betrays the humanness of Tess by his distorted perception. To him she "was no longer the milkmaid, but a visionary essence of woman"— Artemis, Demeter, Eve, a goddess. His preference of essence to existence adds a modern Existentialist slant to Hardy's version of the Paradise myth.

Angel's replacement of the living Tess by a lifeless image is realized in a closely-woven poetic texture. It links together the various manifestations of automatic impulsion which drive Tess to her death when she leaves Talbothays. This can be seen clearly in chapter 20, where the identification with Adam and Eve is explicit. The chapter is built on tension between physical reality and distorted perception of it which is central to the novel.

> Whilst all the landscape was in neutral shade his companion's face, which was the focus of his eyes, rising above the mist stratum, seemed to have a sort of phosphorescence upon it. She looked ghostly, as if she were merely a soul at large. In reality her face, without appearing to do so, had caught the cold gleam of day from the north-east; his own face, though he did not think of it, wore the same aspect to her.

The strange poetic effects of light and mist are just as natural, and just as neutral, as the physical solidity of the cows. It is the self-deceiving mind of Angel that takes appearance for reality. Hardy stresses the "preternatural" "non-human" quality of those early morning hours, yet "it was then . . . that [Tess] impressed him most deeply," not as a human being who craved warmth but as "a visionary essence of woman." The "dignified largeness both of disposition and physique" which "Tess seemed to Clare to exhibit" compels comparison not only with the physical "luxuriance of aspect" that rivets Alec's eyes, but also with the baptism of the baby, where the divinity of this being, "large, towering, and awful" is created by what Angel forgets—the imperfect human being at the centre of the ritual. The "minute diamonds of moisture" that temporarily give Tess a "strange and ethereal beauty" look back to "the miniature candle-flame inverted in her eye-pupils," in the baptism scene, which "shone like a diamond," and forward to the brilliants which help Angel to create another Tess. The unreal essence of fine lady he has created, dramatically embodied in the debased

D'Urberville portraits "builded into the wall" like his fixed definition of purity, moves him to turn from the living woman.

> Sinister design lurked in the woman's features, a concentrated purpose of revenge on the other sex—so it seemed to him then. The Caroline bodice of the portrait was low—precisely as Tess's had been when he tucked it in to show the necklace; and again he experienced the distressing sensation of a resemblance between them.

The fog in chapter 20, and the remoteness imposed on human figures by effects of light and distorted subjective perception, carry echoes of the confused, unreflective life of Marlott and Trantridge, which add overtones of the subhuman to this scene of superhuman harmony with nature.

> At these non-human hours they could get quite close to the waterfowl. Herons came, with a great bold noise as of opening doors and shutters, out of the boughs of a plantation which they frequented at the side of the mead; or, if already on the spot, hardly maintained their standing in the water as the pair walked by, watching them by moving their heads round in a slow, horizontal, passionless wheel, like the turn of puppets by clockwork.

Like the heron that Mrs Yeobright watches as she lies near death on Egdon Heath, these herons, with their "noise as of opening doors and shutters," suggest the freedom of the absolute. The mechanical similes that describe their movements fuse the unreflecting animal life with that other mode of automatic impulsion, machinery, to imply the mechanical nature of the universe that crushes the vital qualities of Tess's nature after Angel's rejection of her personal self for a "passionless" "non-human" image of purity.

Careful attention to the details of such scenes where Angel is a chief actor reveals his archetypal role as human agent of the impersonal powers which, once released, will destroy Tess's life. In chapter 20 the poetic force comes from the accumulation of lyrical details: in the sleepwalking scene, from dramatic details which form a poetic image. This scene, like the Stonehenge episode, has been criticized for its theatricality. But they are theatrical for a purpose. The staginess reinforces Hardy's Aeschylean image of Tess as "sport" for the President of the Immortals. Tess at Stonehenge and Angel in the sleepwalking episode are playing roles assigned to them by their buried selves. Psychology bears witness to the theatrical nature of the subconscious. Movement, gesture, speech, positioning, and props of the scene grow rings of evocation. The rigid stone coffin of an abbot in which Tess's living body is placed suggests the logical end of absolute aspirations, and the destructive force of the ascetic image which will hound Tess to the Stone of Sacrifice. To Angel, the human Tess is "Dead! Dead! Dead!" and his unconscious actions are eloquent of the repressed sexual guilt and fear of the powers of life that demand a sacrifice to purity. The precariousness of their position on the plank, Tess's trust and impassivity, and her failure to follow up her chance to take control, are all dramatic correlatives of the poetic underpattern which drives Tess from Paradise a second time.

Tess's expulsion from the human Paradise thrusts her into the modern myth of the lonely, rootless exile from meaning. Talbothays has given her human awareness, meaning through love, and roots in the natural rhythms of life and work in a simple traditional community. Hardy's poetic treatment of Tess's new relationship to her surroundings after Angel's betrayal—the betrayal of god-in-man—shows what Camus calls "this divorce between man and his life, the actor and his setting" which constitutes the feeling of absurdity. The divorce begins immediately after Tess's confession. "All material objects around announced their irresponsibility with terrible iteration." Angel's absolute mode of perceiving is revealed as inadequate. The physical world that took its meaning from human emotion now exists only as a lumpish, alien factor in the elemental struggle to survive and endure.

Flintcombe Ash brings sharply to the senses the bleak sterility of life without illusions, without love, without God, without a future goal or anything that gives a reason for living to the human being, irrelevant and abandoned on the surface of the earth in a wintry death-marked universe that does not add up. A patient accumulation of the manifestations of rain, wind and snow and their physical effects on Tess and Marian builds up a feeling of the obliteration of human identity by the "achromatic chaos of things." Tess's mutilation of her distinctive beauty is reflected in the huge, high swede field, over which the two girls crawl like flies: "it was a complexion without features, as if a face, from chin to brow, should be only an expanse of skin." Once again she is part of the landscape. But the arrival of apocalyptic Northern birds, "gaunt spectral creatures with tragical eyes" but no memory of the cataclysmic horrors they had witnessed, gives the lie to the impression that she is "a thing scarcely percipient, almost inorganic." The human consciousness that has brought Tess pain and exile has also brought her knowledge and memories of the Talbothays paradise which define her as a human being against the levelling flintiness of trivial existence.

Flintcombe Ash also provides the modern false gods which step into the void created by lack of roots in heaven and earth. The threshing should be compared in every detail with the Marlott reaping as processes that are respectively meaningless and meaningful. The dawn of the cold March morning is "inexpressive" in contrast to the August sunrise which gave definition to men, horses and furnishings. The personal sun-god has been replaced by the impersonal "engine which was to act as the *primum mobile* of this little world": the horses and local driver who understood every stage of the reaping ritual, by an itinerant Northern engineer, described less as a person than as a mechanical function, who "had nothing to do with preparatory labour" and remained isolated from the agricultural scene. His engagement on another farm the following day forces the breakneck pace of the work; a sad reminder of the unhurried rhythm of the Marlott harvest. The friendly rick which gave Tess shelter as she ate her lunch and fed her baby in harmonious companionship has been transformed into a threatening abstract "trapezoidal" shape which exposes her to Alec's attentions. The thresher is a soulless "red tyrant" that gears all the workers to its insatiable demands and drives Tess by its incessant throbbing to a state of puppet-like action independent of will. The dominance of the mechanical image over the vital qualities of life suggests that the patterned ritual dance which gave harmonious meaning to life and death has been replaced by the order of immutable law which, like the engineer, does not require process to have purpose.

> His fire was waiting incandescent, his steam was at high pressure, in a few seconds he could make the long strap move at an invisible velocity. Beyond its extent the environment might be corn, straw, or chaos; it was all the same to him.

The details that evoke a mechanistic universe include all the impersonal forces that abstract meaning from a human being unprotected by providential design, ritual pattern, or love. One of them is time. The accelerated motion of the machine that dominates Tess, reinforced by Alec's renewed attentions, warns that time will not stand still. Nothing but her submission to conventional judgements stands in the way of another visit to Emminster; yet still Tess fails to stamp a meaningful pattern on the flow of time by decisive action. The pathos of Tess practising Angel's favourite ballads against his return should not hide Hardy's comment: "Tess was so wrapt up in this *fanciful dream* [my italics] that she seemed not to know how the season was advancing." Time in the shape of heredity controls her actions in the prophetic blow she deals to Alec with a gauntlet. Time combines with another false god of the void, economic interest, to rob the human being of significance. Hardy's metaphysical meaning, as usual, comes out of a physical situation. The dominance of machinery in late nineteenth-century Wessex was one of the factors which exiled man from work rooted in nature, and defined him by the profit motive and the production schedule. The homelessness of Tess's family ties the metaphysical sense of exile from meaning to concrete economic pressures which drive man unresting over the earth with no place to go.

The logical end of all depersonalizing forces is the D'Urberville vaults where Tess, in terms of the hunt metaphor, is run to earth. The reproachful gleam of the unloaded furniture, and the spoliation of the D'Urberville tombs, build up a powerful picture of a world dead to human values. It is completed when the sham D'Urberville rises from the "mere stone reproduction" on the oldest altar tomb, to challenge the "hollow echo from below" with the false values that too often define the modern exile in a universe shaped by death—money and sex uncontrolled by meaningful ritual. The scene looks back to the stone coffin in which Angel places a Tess who is dead to him in her human aspect, and forward to the Stone of Sacrifice.

Alec's role as devil of negation in an absurd universe (his loud clothes, diabolical disguises, and sudden manifestations call to mind the negating devils of Dostoevsky and Thomas Mann) is defined by his poetic connection with the threshing. He turns up at the rat-hunt which is done not by harvesters engaged in the ritual dance of life and death as at Marlott, but by "men unconnected with the threshing" as a casual sport, "amid the barking of dogs, masculine shouts, feminine screams, oaths, stampings, and confusion as of Pandemonium." The Plutonic engineer foreshadows Alec's satanic association with fire and smoke on the Marlott allotment, where they isolate him in a *pas de deux* with Tess. The "red tyrant" recalls the colour through which he is linked to Tess's fate: his red house, just as alien to the landscape, "built for enjoyment pure and simple," where strawberries, roses, fowls and Tess are forced out of the order of nature for pleasure. His element is chaos. Tess kills him, and takes responsibility (like Camus's Meursault), to assert human purpose against the temptations of purposeless process. The murder, while it aligns Tess with inherited automatic tendencies which direct the cosmic process towards death (a *Daily Chronicle* review of Galton's *Hereditary Genius* in 1892 called heredity "the scientific equation of the theological dogma of original sin"), paradoxically restores to her life an order she has chosen; to live and love with an intensity sharpened by knowledge of the imminent death sentence she had pronounced on herself.

After Alec's murder, Tess and Angel re-live with the poetic intensity of a drowning man a telescoped and accelerated version of Tess's life, which points her archetypal role by blending motifs from all three myths. Tess's lonely journeys over the surface of Wessex have defined her archetypal exile from harmony. Since leaving Talbothays all her journeying, with the significant exception of the abortive trip to Emminster, has pointed in the direction of Stonehenge. In a universe shaped by death, it is the only journey to end in fulfilment. The realization that "to stay, or make a move— it came to much the same" (Camus, *The Outsider*) when all effort ends in death adds a dissonant undermelody to the paradisal interlude in the New Forest with an Angel fallen to human virtues—"Tenderness was absolutely dominant in Clare at last." The lush woodland which recalls the richness of Talbothays and the barren Salisbury plain which recalls the Flintcombe Ash period flank the belated fulfilment of the wedding night in a mansion whose furnishings recall Wellbridge Manor. The fulfilment is as childlike, as "temporary and unforefending" as their plans of escape. Ironical echoes of the earlier innocence at Marlott—seclusion, the dream-like atmosphere, the sense of suspended time—hint at the impossibility of Paradise for two responsible living human beings. "Within was affection, union, error forgiven: outside was the inexorable." Tess and Angel can only achieve absolute harmony by "ignoring that there was a corpse."

Tess's fate acknowledges the power of death, which allows no-one to remain unsoiled.

> We can't stir a finger in this world without the risk of bringing death to somebody . . . each of us has the plague within him; no one, no one on earth, is free from it. . . . What's natural is the microbe. All the rest—health, integrity, purity (if you like)—is a product of the human will, of a vigilance that must never falter.
>
> (Camus, *The Plague*)

Tess, in spite of her vigilance, collaborates at times with the power of death—with her desire for oblivion, her submission to impersonal forces and concepts through her love for Angel, her relapses to waiting on Providence when her responsible consciousness tells her that there is no Providence to wait on. Stonehenge and Wintoncester, with their symbols of an order based on death defined blackly against the empty sky, provide a fitting end to this modern myth about the maintenance of human identity against the void. Hardy gives full weight to the impersonal agents of that order. Yet while his cosmos robs the human individual of meaning, his poetry puts it back again.

The poetic vision gives supreme importance to Tess's inner, unique experience of the world through her sensations and emotions; unusually detailed for Hardy. She is also defined by the poetry of her work. Even the harsh work at Flintcombe Ash borrows poetic beauty from the transformations of frost and snow and the tragic evocations of the Northern birds who share and universalize Tess's will to live. The differing kinds of work take their special rhythm from the rhythms of her life, sensitively realized in narrative and speech structure. The rhythms of Talbothays, slow and contemplative or simple and passionate, reflecting her sweep to maturity with its hesitations, crises, reprieves and rallies, build up a very different emotional response from the monotonous, consonantal rhythm of mechanical work at Flintcombe Ash, or the deadness of shocked existence, detail after dragging detail in flat bald sentences, at Wellbridge Manor. Hardy's dialogue is not always inspired: perhaps even Angel would hardly have met the greatest crisis of his life with "My God—how can forgiveness meet such a grotesque—prestidigitation as that!"—but Tess's stupefied simplicity in the quarrel, her bare statements of truth—"It is in your own mind what you are angry at, Angel; it is not in me"—catch the intimate cadences of a noble and passionate woman. Her qualities even infect the rougher speech of her companions. Izz Huett's "She would have laid down her life for 'ee. I could do no more," and "Her mind can no more be heaved from that one place where it do bide than a stooded wagon from the hole he's in" have the noble ballad simplicity of Tess's personal rhythms. This personal rhythm is set frequently against the dance-like rhythm of scenes where human beings become part of an automatic process—the harvest, the garlic picking, the threshing. Yet the personal rhythm prevails in an overwhelming sense of Tess's beauty of character.

Tess dies, but the meaning of her life, and of the whole book, lies in her vibrant humanity, her woman's power of suffering, renewal, and compassion, which has restored Angel to his rightful nature as Man, conscious of guilt and imperfection. One could not wish to be angel or animal while Tess exists in her human love, passion, beauty, trust, forgiveness, pity, sensitivity, responsibility, endurance, dignity, integrity, and spiritual light. To accept her mortality and the terrible beauty of the earth, to discover the absurdity of immutable law that makes of her fineness a death-trap, and yet to oppose her will against the universe as she found it and make moral choice that it is better to do this than that, is to answer the question of "The Blinded Bird," "Who is divine?"

Chronology

1803   Edward Bulwer-Lytton born, son of General Bulwer and Elizabeth Lytton, heiress of the estate of Knebworth, Herts. He is educated at Fulham, Rottingdean, Ealing, and Cambridge, and supports himself by writing until he comes into his inheritance, whereupon he adds his mother's name to his own.

1804   Benjamin Disraeli born to literary historian Isaac D'Israeli. He is educated by his father and at schools at Islington and at Walthamstow. Is articled at Lincoln's Inn, where he writes romances to support himself. Later elected to Parliament, where he becomes the head of a radical Tory group. Twice made Prime Minister and three times Chancellor of the Exchequer; eventually Queen Victoria makes him Earl of Beaconsfield.

1810   Elizabeth (Stevenson) Gaskell born to William Stevenson, a Unitarian Minister and Keeper of Treasury Records. She is reared by her aunt and educated at Stratford-upon-Avon. Upon her marriage to William Gaskell, a Unitarian minister, she moves to Manchester, where she works with the poor and writes.

1811   William Makepeace Thackeray born in Calcutta to a civil servant working with the East India Company. At the age of three he returns, upon his father's death, to England, where he is educated at Charterhouse and at Trinity College, Cambridge, which he leaves without a degree. Enters the Middle Temple, but never practices law and after various professional failures takes up a lifetime career of journalism.

1812   Charles Dickens born in Portsea to John Dickens, a clerk in the Navy Pay Office. Indifferently educated because of his father's continual insolvency, he works as a child at a blacking factory and later as a solicitor's clerk and as a freelance reporter before launching a career as a novelist, a journalist, and a lecturer.

1815   Anthony Trollope born, son of a struggling barrister and Frances Trollope, who supports the family with her prolific writing. He is educated

467

at Harrow and Winchester. He works as an official for the Post Office, which involves considerable travel, for much of his adult life.

1816   Charlotte Brontë born to the Reverend Patrick Brontë in Yorkshire; she is educated with her sisters, Emily (born 1818) and Anne (born 1820), at the Clergy Daughters' School at Cowan Bridge, where their two elder sisters die of tuberculosis. The sisters spend much of their adult lives alternately teaching, either in schools or as governesses, and caring for their father and brother. Charlotte eventually marries her father's curate, the Reverend A. B. Nicholls.

1819   Mary Anne Evans (George Eliot) born to Robert Evans, a Warwickshire estate manager; educated at Miss Franklin's school in Coventry, and at other boarding schools. Supports herself as a journalist and translator until the inception of her career as a novelist, which her common-law husband, author and critic George Henry Lewes, encourages her to take up.
　　　　Charles Kingsley born, son of the Reverend Charles Kingsley. He is educated at Helston Grammar school in Cornwall, at King's College in London, and at Magdalene College, Cambridge. Becomes curate and later rector of Eversley, Hampshire. In later life becomes Professor of Modern History at Cambridge and canon of Chester and Westminster.

1824   William Wilkie Collins born, son of landscape painter William Collins. Educated for a time in private schools in London, his real education comes from a two-year tour of Italy with family. He is apprenticed to a firm of tea merchants, studies law and is called to the Bar, but never practices. Later writes numerous short stories and articles for periodicals, as well as novels.
　　　　George MacDonald born to a Scottish miller, and educated at Huntley School, Aberdeenshire, and at King's College, Aberdeen. Works variously as a teacher and a minister before appointment as Professor of English Literature at Bedford College, London.

1827   Disraeli publishes *Vivian Grey*.
　　　　Bulwer-Lytton publishes *Falkland*.

1828   George Meredith born, son of a Portsmouth tailor. Receives little formal education, most of it at a school in Moravia. After apprenticeship to a lawyer in London, he takes up a literary career, serving as a reader for Chapman and Hall publishers after he becomes a successful novelist and poet.
　　　　Bulwer-Lytton publishes *Pelham, or The Adventures of a Gentleman*.

1829   Bulwer-Lytton publishes *The Disowned* and *Devereux*.

1830   Bulwer-Lytton publishes *Paul Clifford*.

1831   Disraeli publishes *The Young Duke*.

1832   Charles Dodgson (Lewis Carroll) born, son of a clergyman; educated at Richmond, Yorkshire, at Rugby School, and at Christ Church College, Oxford. He is ordained deacon at Oxford, and teaches mathematics until becoming Curator of the Senior Common Room at Christ Church. Publishes throughout his life on mathematics and logic.

Disraeli publishes *Contarini Fleming.*
Bulwer-Lytton publishes *Eugene Aram.*

1833   Disraeli publishes *The Wondrous Tale of Alroy.*
Bulwer-Lytton publishes *Godolphin.*

1834   Bulwer-Lytton publishes *The Last Days of Pompeii.*

1835   Samuel Butler born, son of the rector of Langar, Nottinghamshire, and grandson of Bishop Samuel Butler. He is educated at Shrewsbury School and at St. John's College, Cambridge. Breeds sheep in New Zealand and begins career as a writer. Later attends art school, exhibiting his work at the Royal Academy. Throughout his life writes extensively on subjects of scientific controversy. Also writes on religious and classical subjects.
Bulwer-Lytton publishes *Rienzi, the Last of the Tribunes.*

1836   Dickens publishes *Sketches by Boz.*

1837   Queen Victoria ascends the throne.
Dickens publishes *Pickwick Papers.*
Disraeli is elected to Parliament; publishes *Venetia* and *Henrietta Temple.*
Bulwer-Lytton publishes *Ernest Maltravers.*
Thackeray joins the staff of *Fraser's Magazine.*

1838   Bulwer-Lytton publishes *Alice.*
Dickens publishes *Oliver Twist.*

1839   Dickens publishes *Nicholas Nickleby.*
Thackeray serializes *Catherine* in *Fraser's.*

1840   Thomas Hardy born, son of a mason, in Dorset. Educated at the local school, then in Dorchester. Articled to a local architect and church restorer, he later works as an assistant architect in London, where he begins his writing career.

1841   Dickens publishes *Barnaby Rudge* and *The Old Curiosity Shop.*

1842   Dickens publishes *American Notes.*

1843   Dickens publishes *A Christmas Carol.*

1844   Dickens publishes *Martin Chuzzlewit.*
Disraeli publishes *Coningsby, or The New Generation.*
Thackeray becomes officially connected with *Punch* magazine; serializes *The Luck of Barry Lyndon* in *Fraser's.*

1845   Disraeli publishes *Sybil, or The Two Nations.*

1846   Eliot translates Strauss's *Life of Jesus Critically Examined.*
The Brontë sisters publish *Poems* under the pseudonyms of Currer, Ellis, and Acton Bell.

1847   Charlotte Brontë publishes *Jane Eyre*, Emily Brontë publishes *Wuthering Heights*, and Anne Brontë publishes *Agnes Grey.*
Disraeli publishes *Tancred, or The New Crusade.*
Trollope publishes *The Macdermots of Ballycloran.*

1848   Thackeray publishes *Vanity Fair*.
       Trollope publishes *The Kellys and the O'Kellys*.
       Kingsley publishes *Yeast* in *Fraser's*.
       Gaskell publishes *Mary Barton*.
       Dickens publishes *Dombey and Son*.
       Anne and Charlotte Brontë travel to London to make their identity
       known; Anne publishes *The Tenant of Wildfell Hall*. Emily Brontë dies at
       Haworth of tuberculosis.

1849   Eliot becomes assistant editor for the *Westminster Review*; begins trans-
       lation of Spinoza's *Tractatus Theologico-Politicus*.
       Bulwer-Lytton publishes *The Caxtons*.
       Charlotte Brontë publishes *Shirley*. Anne Brontë dies of tuberculosis at
       Scarborough.

1850   Kingsley publishes *Alton Locke* and a pamphlet, *Cheap Clothes and Nasty*.
       Dickens founds *Household Words* and publishes *David Copperfield*.
       Collins publishes *Antonina*.
       Charlotte Brontë meets Gaskell (her future biographer) and Thackeray.
       Thackeray publishes *The History of Pendennis* and *Rebecca and Rowena*.

1851   Wilkie Collins and Dickens become friends.
       Thackeray leaves *Punch*.

1852   Thackeray publishes *Henry Esmond*.
       Collins publishes *Basil*.

1853   Charlotte Brontë publishes *Villette*.
       Dickens publishes *Bleak House*.
       Gaskell publishes *Cranford* and *Ruth*.
       Bulwer-Lytton publishes *My Novel, or Varieties in English Life*.

1854   Eliot takes up residence with Lewes; translates Ludwig Feuerbach's *Es-
       sence of Christianity*, Spinoza's *Ethics*.
       Dickens publishes *Hard Times*.

1855   Gaskell publishes *North and South*.
       Kingsley publishes *Westward Ho!* and *Glaucus, or The Wonders of the Shore*.
       Thackeray publishes *The Newcomes*.
       Trollope publishes *The Warden*.
       Charlotte Brontë dies of toxemia of pregnancy in Yorkshire.

1856   Meredith publishes *The Shaving of Shagpat*.

1857   Trollope publishes *Barchester Towers*.
       Dickens publishes *Little Dorrit*.
       Kingsley publishes *Two Years Ago*.
       Charlotte Brontë's *The Professor* published posthumously.
       Gaskell publishes *The Life of Charlotte Brontë*.

1858   *Scenes of Clerical Life*, the first work published under the name "George
       Eliot"; the author's identity established publicly later in the year.
       Bulwer-Lytton installed as Colonial Secretary in Derby's Tory govern-
       ment; publishes *What Will He Do with It?*
       MacDonald publishes *Phantastes*.

Trollope publishes *Doctor Thorne*.
Thackeray quarrels with Dickens.

1859   Butler decides against ordination.
Dickens founds the magazine *All the Year Round*.
Eliot publishes *Adam Bede*.
Meredith publishes *The Ordeal of Richard Feverel*.
Thackeray publishes *The Virginians*.
MacDonald made Professor of Literature at Bedford College, London.

1860   Thackeray becomes editor of *Cornhill Magazine*.
Meredith publishes *Evan Harrington*.
Eliot publishes *The Mill on the Floss*.
Collins publishes *The Woman in White*.
Kingsley accepts the Regius Chair of Modern History at Cambridge.

1861   Dickens publishes *Great Expectations*.
Eliot publishes *Silas Marner*.
Trollope publishes *Framley Parsonage*.

1862   Bulwer-Lytton publishes *A Strange Story*.
Thackeray publishes *The Adventures of Philip*.
Collins publishes *No Name*.

1863   Butler publishes *A First Year in Canterbury Settlement*.
Eliot publishes *Romola*.
Kingsley publishes *The Water Babies: A Fairy Tale for a Land-Baby*.
Gaskell publishes *Sylvia's Lovers*.
Trollope publishes *Rachel Ray*.
MacDonald publishes *David Elginbrod*.
William Makepeace Thackeray dies suddenly at his home in London of "disordered digestion" and "cerebral effusion."

1864   Trollope publishes *The Small House at Allington*.
MacDonald publishes *Adela Cathcart*, a novel which contains interpolated fairy tales—"The Light Princess," "The Giant's Heart," "The Castle," etc.

1865   Carroll publishes *Alice's Adventures in Wonderland*.
Meredith publishes *Rhoda Fleming*.
Dickens publishes *Our Mutual Friend*.
Trollope publishes *Can You Forgive Her?* and *Miss Mackenzie*.
Elizabeth Gaskell dies of heart failure at her home in Hampshire, leaving *Wives and Daughters: An Every-day Story* unfinished.

1866   Eliot publishes *Felix Holt, the Radical*.
Collins publishes *Armadale*.
Kingsley publishes *Hereward the Wake*.
Bulwer-Lytton made Baron Lytton of Knebworth.

1867   Trollope publishes *The Last Chronicle of Barset* and resigns as head Post Officer of the Eastern district.
MacDonald publishes *Dealings with the Fairies*, a collection of fairy tales which contains "The Golden Key."

1868   Disraeli made Prime Minister for the first time.
Collins publishes *The Moonstone*.

Eliot publishes *The Spanish Gypsy.*
Hardy finishes his first novel (now lost), titled "The Poor Man and the Lady."

1869   Trollope publishes *Phineas Finn* and *He Knew He Was Right.*

1870   Disraeli publishes *Lothair.*
Charles Dickens dies of a stroke, after several years of ill health, at his home in Gad's Hill, leaving *The Mystery of Edwin Drood* unfinished.

1871   Hardy publishes *Desperate Remedies.*
MacDonald publishes *At the Back of the North Wind* and *Ranald Bannerman's Boyhood.*
Carroll publishes *Through the Looking-Glass, and What Alice Found There.*
Bulwer-Lytton publishes *The Coming Race.*
Meredith publishes *The Adventures of Harry Richmond.*

1872   Eliot publishes *Middlemarch.*
Butler publishes *Erewhon.*
Hardy publishes *Under the Greenwood Tree.*
MacDonald publishes *The Princess and the Goblin.*

1873   Kingsley appointed Chaplain to the Queen.
Hardy publishes *A Pair of Blue Eyes.*
Trollope publishes *The Eustace Diamonds.*
Edward Bulwer-Lytton publishes *Kenelm Chillingly;* dies at Knebworth of an epileptic fit brought on by an ear infection, leaving *Pausanias the Spartan* unfinished.

1874   Hardy publishes *Far from the Madding Crowd.*
Trollope publishes *Phineas Redux.*

1875   Trollope publishes *The Way We Live Now.*
MacDonald publishes *The Wise Woman.*
Charles Kingsley dies at his home in Eversley of severe hemorrhage following pneumonia.

1876   Carroll publishes *The Hunting of the Snark.*
Eliot publishes *Daniel Deronda.*
Trollope publishes *The Prime Minister.*
Meredith publishes *Beauchamp's Career.*
Hardy publishes *The Hand of Ethelberta.*
Disraeli made Earl of Beaconsfield.

1877   Meredith presents lecture *On the Idea of Comedy.*

1878   Hardy publishes *The Return of the Native.*

1879   Meredith publishes *The Egoist.*
Eliot publishes *Impressions of Theophrastus Such.*

1880   Hardy publishes *The Trumpet-Major.*
Disraeli publishes *Endymion.*
Trollope publishes *The Duke's Children.*
George Eliot dies after a very brief illness at her new home in Chelsea.

1881   Hardy publishes *A Laodicean.*
Trollope publishes *Ayala's Angel.*

Benjamin Disraeli dies of asthma-related illness at his London home, leaving the incomplete "Falconet."

1882   Hardy publishes *Two on a Tower*.
Anthony Trollope dies of a stroke at his home in London.

1883   Trollope's *Autobiography* published posthumously.
MacDonald publishes *The Princess and Curdie*.

1885   Meredith publishes *Diana of the Crossways*.

1886   Hardy publishes *The Mayor of Casterbridge*.

1887   Hardy publishes *The Woodlanders*.

1888   Hardy publishes *Wessex Tales*.

1889   Carroll publishes *Sylvie and Bruno*.
William Wilkie Collins dies of a paralytic stroke, following a long affliction with gout compounded by opium addiction, at his home in London.

1891   Hardy publishes *Tess of the D'Urbervilles*.

1892   Hardy serially publishes the first version of *The Well-Beloved*.

1893   Carroll publishes *Sylvie and Bruno Concluded*.

1895   Hardy publishes *Jude the Obscure*; its failure leads him to give up novel writing for poetry.
MacDonald publishes *Lilith*.
Meredith publishes *The Amazing Marriage*.

1897   The second version of Hardy's *The Well-Beloved* published.

1898   Lewis Carroll dies of a bronchial infection at his sisters' home, "The Chestnuts," in Guildford.

1901   Queen Victoria dies.
Butler publishes *Erewhon Revisited*.

1902   Samuel Butler collapses in Rome; dies in a London nursing home of intestinal catarrh and pernicious anaemia.

1903   Butler's *The Way of All Flesh* published posthumously.

1905   Meredith accepts the Order of Merit.
George MacDonald dies of tuberculosis, compounded by chronic eczema.

1909   George Meredith dies at home at Box Hill of a heart condition following years of ill health.

1910   Hardy accepts the Order of Merit, having refused a knighthood.

1928   Thomas Hardy dies of cardiac syncope at his home, "Max Gate." Florence Hardy publishes the first part of Hardy's autobiography, *The Early Life of Thomas Hardy, 1840–1891*.

1930   Florence Hardy publishes *The Later Years of Thomas Hardy, 1892–1928*, the last four chapters of which were her composition.

Contributors

Harold Bloom, Sterling Professor of the Humanities at Yale University, is the author of *The Anxiety of Influence, Poetry and Repression,* and many other volumes of literary criticism. His forthcoming study, *Freud: Transference and Authority,* attempts a full-scale reading of all of Freud's major writings. A MacArthur Prize Fellow, he is general editor of five series of literary criticism published by Chelsea House. During 1987–88, he served as Charles Eliot Norton Professor of Poetry at Harvard University.

Elliot Engel is Professor of English at North Carolina State University. Together with Margaret F. King, he is the author of *The Victorian Novel before Victoria.*

Margaret F. King is Associate Professor of English at the University of North Carolina, Chapel Hill.

Donald D. Stone is Professor of English at the City University of New York in Queens. He is author of *The Romantic Impulse in Victorian Fiction* and *Novelists in a Changing World.*

Catherine Gallagher is Associate Professor of English at the University of California, Berkeley, and is author of *The Industrial Reformation of English Fiction: Social Discourse and Narrative Form 1832–1867.*

Jack P. Rawlins is Professor of English at California State University and author of *Thackeray's Novels: A Fiction That Is True.*

George Levine is Professor of English at Rutgers University. He is the author of *The Boundaries of Fiction* and *The Realistic Imagination: English Fiction from* Frankenstein *to* Lady Chatterley.

475

Garrett Stewart, Professor of English at the University of California at Santa Barbara, is the author of *Dickens and the Trials of Imagination* and *Death Sentences: Styles of Dying in British Fiction*.

John Carey is Merton Professor of English Literature at Oxford University. He is author of several books, including *Thackeray: Prodigal Genius* and *John Donne: Life, Mind and Art*.

John Kucich is Associate Professor of English at the University of Michigan. He is the author of *Excess and Restraint in the Novels of Charles Dickens*.

Michael Riffaterre is University Professor at Columbia University. His books which have appeared in English are *Semiotics of Poetry* and *Text Production*.

Tony Tanner is a Fellow of King's College, Cambridge. His books include *The Reign of Wonder: Naivety and Reality in American Literature, City of Words: American Fiction 1950–1970*, and *Adultery in the Novel: Contrast and Transgression*.

Jan B. Gordon is Professor of English at Tokyo University of Foreign Studies. He has most recently published articles on Anne Brontë, Mark Twain, and on English poetry in polylingual Singapore.

Barry V. Qualls is Professor of English at Rutgers University and author of *The Secular Pilgrims of Victorian Fiction*.

Daniel Cottom is Assistant Professor of English at Wayne State University. He has published on Defoe, George Eliot, Hawthorne, and Melville.

T. B. Tomlinson is Reader in English Language and Literature at the University of Melbourne and author of *The English Middle-Class Novel* and *A Study of Elizabethan and Jacobean Tragedy*.

Valentine Cunningham is Lecturer in English at Corpus Christi College, Oxford. He is the author of *Everywhere Spoken Against: Dissent in the Victorian Novel*.

D. A. Miller is Professor of English and Comparative Literature at the University of California, Berkeley. He is the author of *Narrative and Its Discontents: Problems of Closure in the Traditional Novel*.

Humphrey Carpenter is the author of *The Inklings* and *Secret Gardens: A Study of the Golden Age of Children's Literature*.

Rachel M. Brownstein is Assistant Professor of English at Brooklyn College and author of *Becoming a Heroine: Reading about Women in Novels*.

Nina Auerbach is Associate Professor of English at the University of Pennsylvania. She is the author of *Communities of Women: An Idea in Fiction* and *Woman and the Demon: The Life of a Victorian Myth*.

Thomas L. Jeffers is Professor of English at Marquette University and author of *Samuel Butler Revalued*.

J. Hillis Miller is Professor of English at the University of California, Irvine. His influential studies of Victorian and modern literature include *The Disappearance of God, Poets of Reality, The Linguistic Moment,* and *Fiction and Repetition.*

Jean R. Brooks is the author of *Thomas Hardy: The Poetic Structure.*

Bibliography

GENERAL

Abel, Elizabeth, et al., eds. *The Voyage In: Fictions of Female Development*. Hanover, N.H.: University Press of New England, 1983.

Allen, Walter. *The English Novel*. New York: Dutton, 1955.

Auerbach, Nina. *Communities of Women: An Idea in Fiction*. Cambridge, Mass.: Harvard University Press, 1978.

———. *Romantic Imprisonment: Women and Other Glorified Outcasts*. New York: Columbia University Press, 1985.

———. *Woman and the Demon: The Life of a Victorian Myth*. Cambridge, Mass.: Harvard University Press, 1982.

Avery, Gillian. *Nineteenth Century Children: Heroes and Heroines in English Children's Stories 1780–1900*. London: Hodder & Stoughton, 1965.

Barker, Francis, et al., eds. *1848: The Sociology of Literature*. Colchester, England: University of Essex Press, 1977.

Bedient, Calvin. *Architects of the Self*. Berkeley: University of California Press, 1972.

Beer, Gillian. *Darwin's Plot: Evolutionary Narrative in Darwin, George Eliot, and Nineteenth-Century Fiction*. London: Routledge & Kegan Paul, 1983.

Beer, Patricia. *Reader, I Married Him: A Study of the Women Characters of Jane Austen, Charlotte Brontë, Elizabeth Gaskell and George Eliot*. London: Routledge & Kegan Paul, 1974.

Briggs, Asa. *Victorian People: A Reassessment of Persons and Things 1851–67*. Harmondsworth: Penguin, 1965.

Brownley, Martine Watson, ed. *Mothering the Mind: Twelve Studies of Writers and Their Silent Partners*. New York: Holmes & Meier, 1984.

Brownstein, Rachel M. *Becoming a Heroine: Reading about Women in Novels*. New York: Viking Press, 1982.

Buckley, Jerome H. *Season of Youth: The Bildungsroman from Dickens to Golding*. Cambridge, Mass.: Harvard University Press, 1974.

———, ed. *The Worlds of Victorian Fiction*. Cambridge, Mass.: Harvard University Press, 1975.

Carpenter, Humphrey. *Secret Gardens: A Study of the Golden Age of Children's Literature*. London: Allen & Unwin, 1985.

Cazamian, Louis. *The Social Novel in England: 1830–1850: Dickens, Disraeli, Mrs. Gaskell, Kingsley*. Translated by Martin Fido. London: Routledge & Kegan Paul, 1973.

Cecil, David. *Early Victorian Novelists*. Harmondsworth: Pelican, 1948.

Chandler, Alice, et al., eds. *From Smollett to James: Studies in the Novel and Other Essays Presented to Edgar Johnson*. Charlottesville: University Press of Virginia, 1981.

Chesterton, G. K. *The Victorian Age in Literature*. London: Williams & Norgate, 1913.

Cockshut, A. O. J. *Man and Woman: A Study of Love and the Novel*. New York: Oxford University Press, 1978.

Cohan, Steven. *Violation and Repair in the English Novel*. Detroit: Wayne State University Press, 1986.

Coveney, Peter. *The Image of Childhood: The Individual and Society: A Study of the Theme in English Literature*. Rev. ed. Baltimore: Penguin, 1967.

Cunningham, Valentine. *Everywhere Spoken Against: Dissent in the Victorian Novel*. Oxford: Oxford University Press, 1975.

Dawson, Carl. *Victorian Noon: English Literature in 1850*. Baltimore: Johns Hopkins University Press, 1979.

Edwards, Lee R. *Psyche as Hero: Female Heroism and Fictional Form*. Middletown, Conn.: Wesleyan University Press, 1984.

Eigner, Edwin. *The Metaphysical Novel in England and America: Dickens, Bulwer, Hawthorne, Melville*. Berkeley: University of California Press, 1978.

Engel, Elliot, and Margaret F. King. *The Victorian Novel before Victoria: British Fiction during the Reign of William IV, 1830–37*. London: Macmillan, 1984.

Ermath, Elizabeth Deeds. *Realism and Consensus in the English Novel*. Princeton: Princeton University Press, 1983.

Fleishman, Avrom. *Fiction and Ways of Knowing*. Austin: University of Texas Press, 1978.

————. *Figures of Autobiography: The Language of Self-Writing in Victorian and Modern England*. Berkeley: University of California Press, 1983.

Freadman, Richard. *Eliot, James, and the Fictional Self*. London: Macmillan, 1986.

Gallagher, Catherine. *The Industrial Reformation of English Fiction: Social Discourse and Narrative Form 1832–1867*. Chicago: University of Chicago Press, 1985.

Garrett, Peter K. *The Victorian Multiplot Novel: Studies in Dialogical Form*. New Haven: Yale University Press, 1980.

Gilbert, Sandra, and Susan Gubar. *The Madwoman in the Attic: The Woman Writer in the Nineteenth-Century Imagination*. New Haven: Yale University Press, 1979.

Gregor, Ian, ed. *Reading the Victorian Novel: Detail into Form*. New York: Barnes & Noble, 1980.

Hardy, Barbara. *The Appropriate Form: An Essay on the Novel*. London: Athlone Press, 1964.

————. *Forms of Feeling in Victorian Fiction*. London: Peter Owen, 1985.

————. *Tellers and Listeners: The Narrative Imagination*. London: Athlone Press, 1975.

Hawthorn, Jeremy, ed. *The Nineteenth-Century British Novel*. London: Edward Arnold, 1986.

Helsinger, Elizabeth K., Robin Lauterbach Sheets, and William Veeder. *The Woman Question: Society and Literature in Britain and America, 1837–1883*. 3 vols. New York: Garland, 1983.

Henkle, Roger B. *Comedy and Culture: England 1820–1900*. Princeton: Princeton University Press, 1980.

Homans, Margaret. *Bearing the Word: Language and Female Experience in Nineteenth-Century Women's Writing*. Chicago: University of Chicago Press, 1986.

————. *Woman Writers and Poetic Identity*. Princeton: Princeton University Press, 1980.

Hughes, Winifred. *The Maniac in the Cellar: Sensation Novels of the 1860s*. Princeton: Princeton University Press, 1980.

Jay, Elisabeth. *The Religion of the Heart*. Oxford: Clarendon Press, 1979.

King, Jeannette. *Tragedy in the Victorian Novel: Theory and Practice in the Novels of George Eliot, Thomas Hardy, and Henry James*. Cambridge: Cambridge University Press, 1980.

Knoepflmacher, U. C. *Laughter and Despair: Readings in Ten Novels of the Victorian Era*. Berkeley: University of California Press, 1971.

————. *Religious Humanism and the Victorian Novel: George Eliot, Walter Pater, and Samuel Butler*. Princeton: Princeton University Press, 1965.

Landow, George P. *Victorian Types, Victorian Shadows: Biblical Typology in Victorian Literature, Art, and Thought*. London: Routledge & Kegan Paul, 1981.

Leavis, F. R. *The Great Tradition*. London: Chatto & Windus, 1948.

Levine, George. *The Realistic Imagination: English Fiction from* Frankenstein *to* Lady Chatterley. Chicago: University of Chicago Press, 1981.

Massey, Irving. *The Gaping Pig: Literature and Metamorphosis*. Berkeley: University of California Press, 1976.

Mellor, Anne K. *English Romantic Irony*. Cambridge, Mass.: Harvard University Press, 1980.

Miller, D. A. *Narrative and Its Discontents: Problems of Closure in the Traditional Novel*. Princeton: Princeton University Press, 1981.

Miller, J. Hillis. *The Disappearance of God*. Cambridge, Mass.: Harvard University Press, 1963.

————. *Fiction and Repetition: Seven English Novels*. Cambridge, Mass.: Harvard University Press, 1982.

————. *The Form of Victorian Fiction: Thackeray, Dickens, Trollope, George Eliot, Meredith, and Hardy*. Notre Dame, Ind.: University of Notre Dame Press, 1968.

Polhemus, Robert M. *Comic Faith: The Great Tradition from Austen to Joyce*. Chicago: University of Chicago Press, 1980.

Postlethwaite, Diana. *Making It Whole: A Victorian Circle and the Shape of Their World*. Columbus: Ohio State University Press, 1984.

Praz, Mario. *The Hero in Eclipse in Victorian Fiction*. London: Oxford University Press, 1956.

Qualls, Barry V. *The Secular Pilgrims of Victorian Fiction: The Novel as Book of Life*. Cambridge: Cambridge University Press, 1982.

Ragussis, Michael. *Acts of Naming: The Family Plot in Fiction*. New York: Oxford University Press, 1986.

Rathburn, Robert C., and Martin Steinmann, Jr., eds. *From Jane Austen to Joseph Conrad*. Minneapolis: University of Minnesota Press, 1958.

Sadoff, Diane. *Monsters of Affection: Dickens, Eliot, and Brontë on Fatherhood*. Baltimore: Johns Hopkins University Press, 1982.

Sale, Roger B. *Fairy Tales and After: From Snow White to E. B. White*. Cambridge, Mass.: Harvard University Press, 1978.

Sanders, Andrew. *The Victorian Historical Novel, 1840–1880*. London: Macmillan, 1978.

Sedgwick, Eve Kosofsky. *Between Men: English Literature and Male Homosocial Desire*. New York: Columbia University Press, 1985.

Showalter, Elaine. *A Literature of Their Own: British Women Novelists from Brontë to Lessing*. Princeton: Princeton University Press, 1977.

Siegle, Robert. *The Politics of Reflexivity*. Baltimore: Johns Hopkins University Press, 1986.

Stevenson, Lionel. *The English Novel: A Panorama.* Boston: Houghton Mifflin, 1960.

Stewart, Garrett. *Death Sentences: Styles of Dying in British Fiction.* Cambridge, Mass.: Harvard University Press, 1984.

Stone, Donald D. *The Romantic Impulse in Victorian Fiction.* Cambridge, Mass.: Harvard University Press, 1980.

Tillotson, Geoffrey. *A View of Victorian Literature.* Oxford: Clarendon Press, 1978.

Tillotson, Kathleen. *Novels of the Eighteen-Forties.* Oxford: Clarendon Press, 1954.

Vargish, Thomas. *The Providential Aesthetic in Victorian Fiction.* Charlottesville: University Press of Virginia, 1985.

Wagenknecht, Edward. *Cavalcade of the English Novel: From Elizabeth to George VI.* New York: Holt, 1943.

Weinstein, Philip M. *The Semantics of Desire: Changing Models of Identity from Dickens to Joyce.* Princeton: Princeton University Press, 1984.

Williams, Raymond. *The Country and the City.* New York: Oxford University Press, 1973.

———. *Culture and Society 1780–1950.* New York: Columbia University Press, 1983.

———. *The English Novel from Dickens to Lawrence.* London: Chatto & Windus, 1970.

Wilt, Judith. *Ghosts of the Gothic: Austen, Eliot, and Lawrence.* Princeton: Princeton University Press, 1980.

Yeazell, Ruth Bernard, ed. *Sex, Politics, and Science in the Nineteenth-Century Novel.* Baltimore: Johns Hopkins University Press, 1985.

EDWARD BULWER-LYTTON

Bell, E. G. *Introduction to the Prose Romances, Plays and Comedies of Edward Bulwer, Lord Lytton.* Chicago: W. M. Hill, 1914.

Blake, Robert. "Bulwer-Lytton." *Cornhill Magazine* 1077 (1973): 67–76.

Christensen, Allan Conrad. *Edward Bulwer-Lytton: The Fiction of New Regions.* Athens: University of Georgia Press, 1976.

Dahl, Curtis. "Bulwer-Lytton and the School of Catastrophe." *Philological Quarterly* 32 (1953): 428–42.

Escott, T. H. S. *Edward Bulwer, First Baron Lytton of Knebworth: A Social, Personal, and Political Monograph.* London: George Routledge & Sons, 1910.

Fleishman, Avrom. *The English Historical Novel: Walter Scott to Virginia Woolf.* Baltimore: Johns Hopkins University Press, 1971.

Fradin, Joseph I. " 'The Absorbing Tyranny of Every-day Life': Bulwer-Lytton's *A Strange Story.*" *Nineteenth-Century Fiction* 16 (1961): 1–16.

Greenberg, Martin H., et al., eds. *No Place Else: Explorations in Utopian and Dystopian Fiction.* Carbondale: Southern Illinois University Press, 1983.

Hollingsworth, Keith. *The Newgate Novel, 1830–1847: Bulwer, Ainsworth, Dickens, and Thackeray.* Detroit: Wayne State University Press, 1963.

Lytton, Victor Alexander, second earl of. *Bulwer-Lytton.* Denver: Alan Swallow, 1948.

———. *The Life of Edward Bulwer, First Lord Lytton, by His Grandson.* 2 vols. London: Macmillan, 1913.

Moers, Ellen. *The Dandy: Brummell to Beerbohm.* New York: Viking, 1960.

Rosa, Matthew Whiting. *The Silver-Fork School: Novels of Fashion Preceding Vanity Fair.* New York: Columbia University Press, 1936.

Sadleir, Michael. *Bulwer, a Panorama: Edward and Rosina, 1803–1836.* Boston: Little, Brown, 1931.

Simmons, James C. "The Novelist as Historian: An Unexplored Tract of Victorian Historiography." *Victorian Studies* 14 (1971): 293–305.

Wagner, Geoffrey. "A Forgotten Satire: Bulwer-Lytton's *The Coming Race*." *Nineteenth-Century Fiction* 19 (1965): 379–85.

Wolff, Robert Lee. *Strange Stories and Other Explorations in Victorian Fiction*. Boston: Gambit Press, 1971.

Zipser, Richard A. *Edward Bulwer-Lytton and Germany*. Berne: Peter Lang, 1974.

BENJAMIN DISRAELI

Bewley, Marius. "Towards Reading Disraeli." *Prose* 4 (1972): 5–23.

Blake, Robert. *Disraeli*. London: Eyre & Spottiswoode, 1966.

Bradford, Susan. *Disraeli*. New York: Stein & Day, 1983.

Braun, Thom. *Disraeli: The Novelist*. London: Allen & Unwin, 1981.

Cecil, David. *Early Victorian Novels*. London: Constable, 1934.

Fido, Martin. " 'From His Own Observation': Sources of Working Class Passages in Disraeli's *Sybil*." *Modern Language Review* 72 (1977): 268–84.

Holloway, John. *The Victorian Sage*. London: Macmillan, 1953.

Jerman, B. R. *The Young Disraeli*. Princeton: Princeton University Press, 1960.

Levine, Richard A. *Benjamin Disraeli*. New York: Twayne, 1968.

Maurois, André. *Disraeli*. London: Bodley Head, 1927.

Merrit, James D. "The Novelist St. Barbe in Disraeli's *Endymion*: Revenge on Whom?" *Nineteenth-Century Fiction* 23 (1968): 85–88.

Monypenny, W. F., and G. E. Buckle. *Life of Benjamin Disraeli*. 2 vols. Rev. ed. New York: Macmillan, 1929.

Nickerson, Charles. "Disraeli's *The Young Duke*." *The Disraeli Newsletter* 3, no. 2 (Fall 1978): 18–38.

O'Kell, Robert. "Disraeli's *Coningsby*: Political Manifesto or Psychological Romance?" *Victorian Studies* 23 (1979): 57–78.

Roth, Cecil. *Benjamin Disraeli*. New York: Philosophical Library, 1952.

Schwarz, Daniel R. *Disraeli's Fiction*. London: Macmillan, 1979.

Stewart, R. W. *Disraeli's Novels Reviewed 1836–1968*. Metuchen, N.J.: Scarecrow Press, 1975.

ELIZABETH GASKELL

Aina, Rubenius. *The Woman Question in Mrs. Gaskell's Life and Works*. Cambridge, Mass.: Harvard University Press, 1950.

Bald, Marjory A. *Women Writers of the Nineteenth Century*. Cambridge, Mass.: Harvard University Press, 1923.

Barry, James D. "Elizabeth Cleghorn Gaskell." In *Victorian Fiction*. New York: Modern Language Association of America, 1974.

Basch, Françoise. *Relative Creatures: Victorian Women in Society and the Novel*. Cambridge: Cambridge University Press, 1974.

Bodenheimer, Rosemarie. "*North and South*: A Permanent State of Change." *Nineteenth-Century Fiction* 34 (1979): 281–301.

———. "Private Griefs and Public Acts in *Mary Barton*." *Dickens Studies Annual* 9 (1981): 195–216.

Briggs, Asa. *Chartist Studies*. London: Macmillan, 1959.

Calder, Jenni. *Women and Marriage in Victorian Fiction*. London: Thames & Hudson, 1976.

Chapple, J. A. V., and Arthur Pollard, eds. *The Letters of Mrs. Gaskell*. Manchester: Manchester University Press, 1966.

Craik, W. A. *Elizabeth Gaskell and the English Provincial Novel*. London: Methuen, 1975.

Duthie, Enid L. *The Themes of Elizabeth Gaskell*. London: Macmillan, 1980.

Easson, Angus. *Elizabeth Gaskell*. London: Routledge & Kegan Paul, 1979.

Fryckstedt, Monica Correa. *Elizabeth Gaskell's* Mary Barton *and* Ruth: *A Challenge to Christian England*. Stockholm: Almqvist & Wiksell, 1982.

Ganz, Margaret. *Elizabeth Gaskell: The Artist in Conflict*. New York: Twayne, 1969.

Gill, Stephen. "Price's Patent Candles: New Light on *North and South.*" *Review of English Studies* 27 (1976): 313–21.

Hopkins, A. B. *Elizabeth Gaskell: Her Life and Work*. London: John Lehmann, 1952.

———. "Mrs. Gaskell in France 1849–1890." *PMLA* 53 (1938): 545–74.

Lansbury, Coral. *Elizabeth Gaskell*. Boston: Twayne, 1984.

———. *Elizabeth Gaskell: The Novel of Social Crisis*. London: Paul Elek, 1975.

Lucas, W. J. *The Literature of Change: Studies in the Nineteenth Century Provincial Novel*. New York: Harper & Row, 1977.

McVeagh, John. *Elizabeth Gaskell*. London: Routledge & Kegan Paul, 1970.

Martin, Carol. "Gaskell, Darwin, and *North and South.*" *Studies in the Novel* 15 (1983): 97–107.

Pollard, Arthur. *Mrs. Gaskell: Novelist and Biographer*. Manchester: Manchester University Press, 1965.

Sanders, Andrew. *The Victorian Historical Novel, 1840–1880*. London: Macmillan, 1978.

Sharps, John Geoffrey. *Mrs. Gaskell's Observation and Invention*. Fontwell, Sussex: Linden Press, 1970.

Shelston, A. J. "*Ruth*: Mrs. Gaskell's Neglected Novel." *Bulletin of the John Rylands Library* 58 (1975): 173–92.

Weiss, Barbara. "Elizabeth Gaskell: The Telling of Feminine Tales." *Studies in the Novel* 16 (1984): 274–87.

Wheeler, Michael D. "The Writer as Reader in *Mary Barton.*" *Durham University Journal* 67 (1974): 92–106.

Wolfe, Patricia. "Structure and Movement in *Cranford.*" *Nineteenth-Century Fiction* 23 (1968): 161–76.

Wright, Edgar. *Mrs. Gaskell: The Basis for Reassessment*. London: Oxford University Press, 1965.

WILLIAM MAKEPEACE THACKERAY

Bloom, Harold, ed. *Modern Critical Interpretations: William Makepeace Thackeray's* Vanity Fair. New Haven: Chelsea House, 1987.

———, ed. *Modern Critical Views: William Makepeace Thackeray*. New Haven: Chelsea House, 1987.

Burch, Mark H. " 'The World Is a Looking-Glass': *Vanity Fair* as Satire." *Genre* 15 (1982): 265–79.

Carey, John. *Thackeray: Prodigal Genius*. London: Faber & Faber, 1977.

Colby, Robert A. *Thackeray's Canvass of Humanity: An Author and His Public*. Columbus: Ohio State University Press, 1979.

———. "Thackeray Studies 1979–1982." *Dickens Studies Annual* 12 (1983): 341–56.

Collins, Philip, ed. *Thackeray: Interviews and Recollections*. New York: St. Martin's Press, 1983.

Costerus, n.s. 2 (1974). Special Thackeray issue.

Craig, G. Armour. "On the Style of *Vanity Fair.*" In *Style in Prose Fiction: English Institute Essays*, edited by Harold C. Martin. New York: Columbia University Press, 1958.

Dodds, J. W. *Thackeray: Critical Portrait*. London: Oxford University Press, 1941.

Ennis, Lambert. *Thackeray: The Sentimental Cynic*. Evanston: Northwestern University Press, 1950.

Ferris, Ina. *William Makepeace Thackeray*. Boston: Twayne, 1983.

Fisher, Judith Law. "Siren and Artist: Contradiction in Thackeray's Aesthetic Ideal." *Nineteenth-Century Fiction* 39 (1985): 392–419.

Garret-Goodyear, Joan. "Stylized Emotions, Unrealized Selves: Expressive Characterization in Thackeray." *Victorian Studies* 22 (1979): 173–92.

Greig, J. Y. T. *Thackeray: A Reconsideration*. London: Oxford University Press, 1950.

Hagan, John. "*Vanity Fair*: Becky Brought to Book Again." *Studies in the Novel* 7 (1975): 479–505.

Harden, Edgar F. *Thackeray's English Humourists and Four Georges*. Newark: University of Delaware Press, 1985.

———. *The Emergence of Thackeray's Serial Fiction*. Athens: University of Georgia Press, 1979.

Hardy, Barbara. *The Exposure of Luxury: Radical Themes in Thackeray*. Pittsburgh: University of Pittsburgh Press, 1972.

Loofbourow, John. *Thackeray and the Form of Fiction*. Princeton: Princeton University Press, 1964.

Manning, Sylvia. "Incest and the Structure of *Henry Esmond*." *Nineteenth-Century Fiction* 34 (1979): 194–213.

McMaster, Juliet. *Thackeray: The Major Novels*. Toronto: University of Toronto Press, 1971.

McMaster, R. D. "The Pygmalion Motif in *The Newcomes*." *Nineteenth-Century Fiction* 29 (1974): 22–39.

Monod, Sylvère. "Brother Weavers of Motley." *Essays and Studies* 26 (1973): 66–82.

Monsarrat, Ann. *An Uneasy Vision: Thackeray the Man, 1811–1863*. New York: Dodd, Mead, 1980.

Peters, Catherine. *Thackeray's Universe*. New York: Oxford University Press, 1987.

Phillips, K. C. *The Language of Thackeray*. London: André Deutsch, 1978.

Rawlins, Jack P. *Thackeray's Novels: A Fiction That Is True*. Berkeley: University of California Press, 1974.

Ray, Gordon N. *The Buried Life: A Study of the Relation between Thackeray's Fiction and His Personal History*. Cambridge, Mass.: Harvard University Press, 1952.

———. *Thackeray: The Age of Wisdom 1847–1863*. New York: McGraw-Hill, 1958.

———. *Thackeray: The Uses of Adversity 1811–1846*. New York: McGraw-Hill, 1955.

———, ed. *The Letters and Private Papers of William Makepeace Thackeray*. Cambridge, Mass.: Harvard University Press, 1946.

Studies in the Novel 13, nos. 1–2 (1981). Special Thackeray issue.

Sudrann, Jean. "The Philosopher's Property: Thackeray and the Use of Time." *Victorian Studies* 10 (1967): 359–88.

Sundell, M. G., ed. *Twentieth-Century Interpretations of* Vanity Fair: *A Collection of Critical Essays*. Englewood Cliffs, N.J.: Prentice-Hall, 1969.

Sutherland, J. A. *Thackeray at Work*. London: Athlone Press, 1974.

Tillotson, Geoffrey. *Thackeray the Novelist*. Cambridge: Cambridge University Press, 1954.

Tillotson, Geoffrey, and Donald Hawes, eds. *Thackeray: The Critical Heritage*. London: Routledge & Kegan Paul, 1968.

Welsh, Alexander, ed. *Thackeray: A Collection of Critical Essays*. Englewood Cliffs, N.J.: Prentice-Hall, 1968.

Wheatley, James H. *Patterns in Thackeray's Fiction*. Cambridge, Mass.: M.I.T. Press, 1969.

Wilkinson, Ann Y. "The Thomeavesian Way of Knowing the World: Technique and Meaning in *Vanity Fair*." *ELH* 32 (1965): 370–87.

CHARLES DICKENS

Amalric, Jean-Claude, ed. *Studies in the Later Dickens*. Montpellier: Université Paul Valéry, 1973.

Arac, Jonathan. *Commissioned Spirits: The Shaping of Social Motion in Dickens, Carlyle, Melville, and Hawthorne*. New Brunswick, N.J.: Rutgers University Press, 1979.

Axton, William F. *Circle of Fire: Dickens's Vision and Style and the Popular Victorian Theatre*. Lexington: University of Kentucky Press, 1966.

Barnard, Robert. *Imagery and Theme in the Novels of Dickens*. Oslo: Universitetsforlaget, 1974.

Bloom, Harold, ed. *Modern Critical Interpretations: Charles Dickens's* A Tale of Two Cities. New Haven: Chelsea House, 1987.

———, ed. *Modern Critical Interpretations: Charles Dickens's* Bleak House. New Haven: Chelsea House, 1987.

———, ed. *Modern Critical Interpretations: Charles Dickens's* David Copperfield. New Haven: Chelsea House, 1987.

———, ed. *Modern Critical Interpretations: Charles Dickens's* Hard Times. New Haven: Chelsea House, 1987.

———, ed. *Modern Critical Views: Charles Dickens*. New Haven: Chelsea House, 1987.

Brook, G. L. *The Language of Dickens*. London: André Deutsch, 1970.

Butt, John, and Kathleen Tillotson. *Dickens at Work*. Fairlawn, N.J.: Essential Books, 1958.

Carey, John. *The Violent Effigy: A Study of Dickens's Imagination*. London: Faber & Faber, 1973.

Chesterton, G. K. *Appreciation and Criticisms of the Works of Charles Dickens*. London: Dent, 1933.

Churchill, R. C., comp. and ed. *Bibliography of Dickensian Criticism 1836–1975*. New York: Garland, 1975.

Cockshut, A. O. J. *The Imagination of Charles Dickens*. London: Collins, 1961.

Collins, Philip, ed. *Dickens: The Critical Heritage*. London: Routledge & Kegan Paul, 1971.

Connor, Steven. *Charles Dickens*. London: Basil Blackwell, 1985.

Daldry, Graham. *Charles Dickens and the Form of the Novel*. London: Croom Helm, 1987.

Daleski, H. M. *Dickens and the Art of Analogy*. London: Faber & Faber, 1970.

Dickens Studies Annual: Essays in Victorian Fiction. Vols. 1–7 (1970–78), Carbondale: Southern Illinois University Press; vols. 8–13 (1980–85) New York: AMS Press.

Dickens Studies Newsletter (1970–83). Changed to *Dickens Quarterly*, 1984–.

Dickensian, The, 1905–.

Dyson, A. E. *The Inimitable Dickens: A Reading of the Novels*. London: Macmillan, 1970.

Ford, George H. *Dickens and His Readers: Aspects of Novel Criticism since 1836*. Princeton: Princeton University Press, 1955.

Ford, George H., and Lauriat Lane, Jr., eds. *The Dickens Critics*. Ithaca: Cornell University Press, 1961.

Forster, John. *The Life of Charles Dickens*. Edited by A. J. Hoppé. 2 vols. London: Dent, 1966.

Frank, Lawrence. *Charles Dickens and the Romantic Self*. Lincoln: University of Nebraska Press, 1984.

Garis, Robert E. *The Dickens Theatre: A Reassessment of the Novels*. Oxford: Oxford University Press, 1965.

Gill, Stephen C. "*Pickwick Papers* and the 'Chroniclers by the Line': A Note on Style." *Modern Language Review* 63 (1968): 33–36.

Gray, Paul Edward, ed. *Twentieth Century Interpretations of* Hard Times: *A Collection of Critical Essays.* Englewood Cliffs, N.J.: Prentice-Hall, 1969.

Gross, John, and Gabriel Pearson, eds. *Dickens and the Twentieth Century.* London: Routledge & Kegan Paul, 1962.

Hardy, Barbara. *Charles Dickens: The Writer and His Work.* Windsor, Berkshire: Profile Books, 1983.

————. *Dickens: The Later Novels.* London: Longman, 1968.

————. *The Moral Art of Dickens.* London: Athlone Press, 1979.

Hollington, Michael. *Dickens and the Grotesque.* Totowa, N.J.: Barnes & Noble, 1984.

Horton, Susan R. *The Reader in the Dickens World.* London: Macmillan, 1981.

House, Humphrey. *The Dickens World.* 2d ed. London: Oxford University Press, 1961.

Johnson, Edgar H. *Charles Dickens: His Tragedy and Triumph.* Rev. ed. London: Allen Lane, 1977.

Johnson, Wendell Stacy, ed. *Charles Dickens (New Perspectives).* Englewood Cliffs, N.J.: Prentice-Hall, 1982.

Kincaid, James R. *Dickens and the Rhetoric of Laughter.* Oxford: Clarendon Press, 1971.

Kucich, John. *Excess and Restraint in the Novels of Charles Dickens.* Athens: University of Georgia Press, 1981.

Langer, Suzanne. *Feeling and Form.* London: Routledge & Kegan Paul, 1953.

Lansbury, Coral. ''Dickens's Romanticism Domesticated.'' *Dickens Studies Newsletter* 3 (1972): 36–46.

Leavis, F. R. and Q. D. *Dickens the Novelist.* London: Chatto & Windus, 1970.

Magnet, Myron. *Dickens and the Social Order.* Philadelphia: University of Pennsylvania Press, 1985.

Manning, Sylvia Bank. *Dickens as Satirist.* New Haven: Yale University Press, 1971.

Marcus, Steven. *Dickens: From Pickwick to Dombey.* London: Chatto & Windus, 1965.

————. ''Language into Structure: Pickwick Revisited.'' *Daedalus* 101 (1972): 183–202.

Miller, J. Hillis. *Charles Dickens: The World of His Novels.* Cambridge, Mass.: Harvard University Press, 1958.

Moers, Ellen. ''*Bleak House*: The Agitating Women.'' *The Dickensian* 69 (January 1972): 13–24.

Monod, Sylvère. *Dickens the Novelist.* Norman: University of Oklahoma Press, 1968.

Newman, S. J. *Dickens at Play.* London: Macmillan, 1981.

Newsom, Robert. *Dickens on the Romantic Side of Familiar Things:* Bleak House *and the Novel Tradition.* New York: Columbia University Press, 1977.

Nineteenth-Century Fiction 24, no. 4 (1970). Charles Dickens centennial issue.

Nisbet, Ada, and Blake Nevius. *Dickens Centennial Essays.* Berkeley: University of California Press, 1971.

Orwell, George. *Dickens, Dali and Others: Studies in Popular Culture.* New York: Harcourt, Brace & World, 1963.

Palmer, D. J. *Comedy: Developments in Criticism.* London: Macmillan, 1984.

Partlow, R. B., Jr., ed. *Dickens the Craftsman: Strategies of Presentation.* Carbondale: Southern Illinois University Press, 1970.

Patten, R. L. *Charles Dickens and His Publishers.* Oxford: Clarendon Press, 1978.

Price, Martin, ed. *Dickens: A Collection of Critical Essays.* Englewood Cliffs, N.J.: Prentice-Hall, 1967.

Raphael, Samuel. *East End Underworld.* London: Routledge & Kegan Paul, 1981.

Sanders, Andrew. *Charles Dickens Resurrectionist.* London: Macmillan, 1982.

Schwarzbach, F. S. *Dickens and the City.* London: Athlone Press, 1979.

Scott, P. J. M. *Reality and Comic Confidence in Dickens.* London: Macmillan, 1979.

Slater, Michael. *Dickens and Women.* London: J. M. Dent, 1983.

———, ed. *Dickens 1970: Centenary Essays*. London: Chapman & Hall, 1970.

Stewart, Garrett. *Dickens and the Trials of Imagination*. Cambridge, Mass.: Harvard University Press, 1974.

Stoehr, Taylor. *Dickens: The Dreamer's Stance*. Ithaca: Cornell University Press, 1965.

Sucksmith, Harvey Peter. *The Narrative Art of Dickens: The Rhetoric of Sympathy and Irony in His Novels*. Oxford: Clarendon Press, 1970.

Thomas, Deborah A. *Dickens and the Short Story*. London: Batsford, 1982.

Welsh, Alexander. *The City of Dickens*. Oxford: Clarendon Press, 1971.

Westburg, Barry. *The Confessional Fictions of Charles Dickens*. DeKalb: Northern Illinois University Press, 1977.

Wilson, Angus. *The World of Charles Dickens*. New York: Viking Press, 1970.

Wilt, Judith. "Confusion and Consciousness in Dickens's Esther." *Nineteenth-Century Fiction* 32 (1977): 285–309.

Zwerdling, Alex. "Esther Summerson Rehabilitated." *PMLA* 88 (1973): 429–38.

ANTHONY TROLLOPE

Adams, Robert Martin. "*Orley Farm* and Real Fiction." *Nineteenth-Century Fiction* 8 (1953): 27–41.

apRoberts, Ruth. *The Moral Trollope*. Athens: Ohio University Press, 1971.

Booth, Bradford A. *Anthony Trollope: Aspects of His Life and Art*. Bloomington: University of Indiana Press, 1958.

Bowen, Elizabeth. *Anthony Trollope: A New Judgement*. New York: Oxford University Press, 1946.

Butte, George. "Ambivalence and Affirmation in *The Duke's Children*." *Studies in English Literature 1500–1700* 17 (1977): 709–27.

Cockshut, A. O. J. *Anthony Trollope: A Critical Study*. London: Collins, 1955.

Davies, Hugh Sykes. *Trollope*. London: Longmans, 1960.

Edwards, P. D. *Anthony Trollope: His Art and Scope*. Brighton: Harvester Press, 1978.

Fredman, Alice Green. *Anthony Trollope*. New York: Columbia University Press, 1971.

Gilmour, Robin. *The Idea of the Gentleman in the Victorian Novel*. London: Allen & Unwin, 1981.

Hagan, John. "The Divided Mind of Anthony Trollope." *Nineteenth-Century Fiction* 14 (1959): 1–26.

Halperin, John. *Trollope and Politics: A Study of the Pallisers and Others*. London: Macmillan, 1977.

Harvey, Geoffrey. *The Art of Anthony Trollope*. London: Weidenfeld & Nicolson, 1980.

Hennedy, Hugh L. *Unity in Barsetshire*. The Hague: Mouton, 1971.

Hughes, Judith M. "Self-Suppression and Attachment: Mid-Victorian Emotional Life." *Massachusetts Review* 19 (1978): 541–55.

Kincaid, James R. *The Novels of Anthony Trollope*. Oxford: Clarendon Press, 1977.

McMaster, Juliet. *Trollope's Palliser Novels: Theme and Pattern*. London: Macmillan, 1979.

Nineteenth-Century Fiction 37 (1982). Special Anthony Trollope issue.

Overton, W. J. *The Unofficial Trollope*. Brighton: Harvester, 1982.

Polhemus, Robert M. *The Changing World of Anthony Trollope*. Berkeley: University of California Press, 1968.

Pollard, Arthur. *Anthony Trollope*. London: Routledge & Kegan Paul, 1978.

Pope-Hennessy, James. *Anthony Trollope*. London: Jonathan Cape, 1971.

Ray, Gordon N. "Trollope at Full Length." *Huntington Library Quarterly* 31 (1968): 313–40.

Skilton, David. *Anthony Trollope and His Contemporaries*. London: Longman, 1972.

Smalley, Donald, ed. *Anthony Trollope: The Critical Heritage*. London: Routledge & Kegan Paul, 1969.

Snow, C. P. *Trollope: His Life and Art*. London: Macmillan, 1975.

Stebbins, Lucy P. and Richard P. *The Trollopes: The Chronicle of a Writing Family*. New York: Columbia University Press, 1945.

Terry, R. C. *Anthony Trollope: The Artist in Hiding*. London: Macmillan, 1977.

Tracy, Robert. *Trollope's Later Novels*. Berkeley: University of California Press, 1978.

Wall, Stephen. "Trollope, Balzac, and the Reappearing Character." *Essays in Criticism* 25 (1975): 123–43.

Walpole, Hugh. *Anthony Trollope*. London: Macmillan, 1928.

Wright, Andrew. *Anthony Trollope: Dream and Art*. Chicago: University of Chicago Press, 1983.

THE BRONTËS

Allott, Miriam, ed. *The Brontës: The Critical Heritage*. London: Routledge & Kegan Paul, 1974.

———, ed. Wuthering Heights: *A Casebook*. London: Macmillan, 1970.

Auerbach, Nina. "Charlotte Brontë: The Two Countries." *University of Toronto Quarterly* 42 (1972–73): 328–42.

Benvenuto, Richard. *Emily Brontë*. Boston: Twayne, 1982.

Bloom, Harold, ed. *Modern Critical Interpretations: Charlotte Brontë's* Jane Eyre. New Haven: Chelsea House, 1987.

———, ed. *Modern Critical Interpretations: Emily Brontë's* Wuthering Heights. New Haven: Chelsea House, 1987.

———, ed. *Modern Critical Views: The Brontës*. New Haven: Chelsea House, 1987.

Burkhart, Charles. *Charlotte Brontë: A Psychosexual Study of Her Novels*. London: Victor Gollancz, 1973.

Chase, Richard. "The Brontës: A Centennial Observance." *Kenyon Review* 9 (1947): 487–506.

———. "The Brontës, or Myth Domesticated." In *Forms of Modern Fiction: Essays Collected in Honor of Joseph Warren Beach*, edited by William Van O'Connor. Bloomington: Indiana University Press, 1962.

Chitham, Edward, and Tom Winnifrith. *Brontë Facts and Brontë Problems*. London: Macmillan, 1983.

Craik, W. A. *The Brontë Novels*. London: Methuen, 1968.

De Grazia, Emilio. "The Ethical Dimension of *Wuthering Heights*." *Midwest Quarterly* 19 (1978): 176–95.

Dessner, Lawrence J. *The Homely Web of Truth*. The Hague: Mouton, 1975.

Dingle, Herbert. *The Mind of Emily Brontë*. London: Martin Brian & O'Keefe, 1974.

Donoghue, Denis. "Emily Brontë: On the Latitude of Interpretation." In *The Interpretation of Narrative: Theory and Practice*, edited by Morton W. Bloomfield, 105–33. Cambridge, Mass.: Harvard University Press, 1970.

Duthie, Enid L. *The Brontës and Nature*. London: Macmillan, 1986.

Eagleton, Terry. *Myths of Power: A Marxist Study of the Brontës*. London: Macmillan, 1975.

Ewbank, Inga-Stina. *Their Proper Sphere: A Study of the Brontë Sisters as Early-Victorian Female Novelists*. London: Edward Arnold, 1966.

Gaskell, Elizabeth. *The Life of Charlotte Brontë*. London: J. M. Dent, 1960.

Gerin, Winifred. *Charlotte Brontë: The Evolution of Genius*. Oxford: Oxford University Press, 1968.

Gregor, Ian, ed. *The Brontës: A Collection of Critical Essays.* Englewood Cliffs, N.J.: Prentice-Hall, 1970.

Hewish, John. *Emily Brontë: A Critical and Biographical Study.* London: Macmillan, 1969.

Jackson, Arlene M. "The Question of Credibility in Anne Brontë's *The Tenant of Wildfell Hall.*" *English Studies* 63 (1982): 198–206.

Jacobus, Mary. "The Buried Letter: Feminism and Romanticism in *Villette.*" In *Women Writing and Writing about Women,* edited by Mary Jacobus, 42–60. London: Croom Helm, 1984.

Keefe, Robert. *Charlotte Brontë's World of Death.* Austin: University of Texas Press, 1979.

Knies, Earl A. *The Art of Charlotte Brontë.* Athens: Ohio University Press, 1969.

Langbridge, Rosamond. *Charlotte Brontë: A Psychological Study.* London: Heinemann, 1929.

Lerner, Lawrence. *Love and Marriage: Literature and Its Social Context.* New York: St. Martin's Press, 1979.

Linder, Cynthia. *Romantic Imagery in the Novels of Charlotte Brontë.* London: Macmillan, 1978.

McMaster, Juliet. " 'Imbecile Laughter' and 'Desperate Earnest' in *The Tenant of Wildfell Hall.*" *Modern Language Quarterly* 43 (1982): 352–68.

Martin, Bernard. *The Accents of Persuasion: Charlotte Brontë's Novels.* New York: Norton, 1966.

Maynard, John. *Charlotte Brontë and Sexuality.* Cambridge: Cambridge University Press, 1984.

Moglen, Helene. *Charlotte Brontë: The Self Conceived.* New York: Norton, 1976.

Ohmann, Carol. *Charlotte Brontë: The Limits of Her Feminism.* Old Westbury, N.Y.: Feminist Press, 1972.

Peters, Margot. *Charlotte Brontë: Style in the Novel.* Madison: University of Wisconsin Press, 1973.

Pinion, F. B. *A Brontë Companion: Literary Assessment, Background, and Reference.* London: Macmillan, 1975.

Ratchford, Fannie E. *The Brontës' Web of Childhood.* New York: Columbia University Press, 1941.

Rigney, Barbara Hill. *Madness and Sexual Politics in the Feminist Novel: Studies in Brontë, Woolf, Lessing, and Atwood.* Madison: University of Wisconsin Press, 1978.

Schreiber, Annette. "The Myth in Charlotte Brontë." *Literature and Psychology* 18 (1968): 48–67.

Scott, P. J. M. *Anne Brontë: A New Critical Assessment.* London: Vision Press, 1983.

Smith, Anne, ed. *The Art of Emily Brontë.* New York: Barnes & Noble, 1976.

Sonstroem, David. "*Wuthering Heights* and the Limits of Vision." *PMLA* 86 (1971): 51–62.

Spark, Muriel, and Derek Stanford. *Emily Brontë: Her Life and Work.* New York: Coward-McCann, 1966.

Visick, Mary. *The Genesis of* Wuthering Heights. Hong Kong: Hong Kong University Press, 1958.

Wilson, F. A. C. "The Primrose Wreath: The Heroes of the Brontë Novels." *Nineteeth-Century Fiction* 29 (1974): 40–57.

Winnifrith, Tom. *The Brontës and Their Background: Romance and Reality.* London: Macmillan, 1973.

GEORGE ELIOT

Adam, Ian, ed. *This Particular Web: Essays on* Middlemarch. Toronto: University of Toronto Press, 1975.

Allen, Walter. *George Eliot*. New York: Macmillan, 1964.

Ashton, Rosemary. *George Eliot*. Oxford: Oxford University Press, 1983.

Auster, Henry. *Local Habitations: Regionalism in the Early Novels of George Eliot*. Cambridge, Mass.: Harvard University Press, 1970.

Baker, William. "George Eliot and Judaism." In *Romantic Reassessment*, no. 45, edited by James Hogg. Salzburg: Institut für Englische Sprache und Literatur, Universität Salzburg, 1975.

Beaty, Jerome. Middlemarch *from Notebook to Novel: A Study of George Eliot's Creative Method*. Urbana: University of Illinois Press, 1960.

Beer, Gillian. *George Eliot*. Bloomington: Indiana University Press, 1986.

Bennett, Joan. *George Eliot, Her Mind and Art*. Cambridge: Cambridge University Press, 1948.

Bloom, Harold, ed. *Modern Critical Interpretations: George Eliot's* Middlemarch. New Haven: Chelsea House, 1987.

———, ed. *Modern Critical Interpretations: George Eliot's* The Mill on the Floss. New Haven: Chelsea House, 1988.

———, ed. *Modern Critical Views: George Eliot*. New York: Chelsea House, 1986.

Bonaparte, Felicia. *The Triptych and the Cross: The Central Myths of George Eliot's Poetic Imagination*. New York: New York University Press, 1979.

———. *Will and Destiny: Morality and Tragedy in George Eliot's Novels*. New York: New York University Press, 1975.

Bullet, Gerald. *George Eliot: Her Life and Books*. London: Collins, 1947.

Carroll, David R. "*Middlemarch* and the Externality of Fact." In *This Particular Web*, edited by Ian Adam. Toronto: University of Toronto Press, 1975.

———. "*Silas Marner*: Reversing the Oracles of Religion." *Literary Monographs* 1, edited by Eric Rothstein and Thomas K. Dunseath. Madison: University of Wisconsin Press, 1967.

———, ed. *George Eliot: The Critical Heritage*. London: Routledge & Kegan Paul, 1971.

Chase, Cynthia. "The Decomposition of the Elephants: Double-Reading *Daniel Deronda*." *PMLA* 93 (1978): 215–27.

Clayton, Jay. "Visionary Power and Narrative Form: Wordsworth and *Adam Bede*." *ELH* 46 (1978): 646–72.

Creeger, George, ed. *George Eliot: A Collection of Critical Essays*. Englewood Cliffs, N.J.: Prentice-Hall, 1970.

Daiches, David. *George Eliot*: Middlemarch. Great Neck, N.Y.: Barron's Educational Series, 1963.

Dentith, Simon. *George Eliot*. Brighton: Harvester Press, 1986.

Doyle, Mary Ellen. *The Sympathetic Response: George Eliot's Fictional Rhetoric*. Rutherford, N.J.: Fairleigh Dickinson University Press, 1981.

Edwards, Michael. "George Eliot and Negative Form." *Critical Quarterly* 17 (1975): 171–79.

Emery, Laura Comer. *George Eliot's Creative Conflict: The Other Side of Silence*. Berkeley: University of California Press, 1976.

Ermath, Elizabeth Deeds. *George Eliot*. Boston: Twayne, 1985.

Graver, Suzanne. *George Eliot and Community: A Study in Social Theory and Fictional Form*. Berkeley: University of California Press, 1984.

Haight, Gordon. *George Eliot: A Biography*. Oxford: Oxford University Press, 1968.

Haight, Gordon, and Rosemary T. VanArsdel, eds. *George Eliot: A Centenary Tribute*. London: Macmillan, 1982.

Hardy, Barbara. *The Novels of George Eliot: A Study in Form*. New York: Oxford University Press, 1959.

———. *Ritual and Feeling in the Novels of George Eliot*. Swansea, Wales: University College of Swansea, 1973.

————, ed. *Critical Essays on George Eliot.* New York: Barnes & Noble, 1970.

————, ed. Middlemarch: *Critical Approaches to the Novel.* London: Routledge & Kegan Paul, 1967.

Harvey, William J. *The Art of George Eliot.* Westport, Conn.: Greenwood Press, 1978.

Herbert, Christopher. "Preachers and the Schemes of Nature in *Adam Bede.*" *Nineteenth-Century Fiction* 29 (1975): 412–27.

Hertz, Neil. "Recognizing Causabon." *Glyph* 6 (1979): 24–41.

Jones, R. T. *George Eliot.* Cambridge: Cambridge University Press, 1970.

Kakar, H. S. *The Persistent Self: An Approach to* Middlemarch. Delhi: Doaba House, 1977.

Knoepflmacher, U. C. *George Eliot's Early Novels: The Limits of Realism.* Berkeley: University of California Press, 1968.

————. "Middlemarch: An Avuncular View." *Nineteenth-Century Fiction* 30 (1975): 53–81.

Kucich, John. "George Eliot and Objects: Meaning as Matter in *The Mill on the Floss.*" *Dickens Studies Annual* 12 (1983): 319–37.

————. "Repression and Dialectical Inwardness in *Middlemarch.*" *Mosaic* 18, no. 1 (1985): 45–63.

Mann, Karen B. *The Language That Makes George Eliot's Fiction.* Baltimore: Johns Hopkins University Press, 1983.

Marcus, Steven. "Literature and Social Theory: Starting In with George Eliot." In *Representations: Essays on Literature and Society.* New York: Random House, 1975.

Miller, J. Hillis. "Narrative and History." *ELH* 41 (1974): 455–73.

Milner, Ian. *The Structure of Values in George Eliot.* Prague: Universita Karlova, 1968.

Mintz, Alan. *George Eliot and the Novel of Vocation.* Cambridge, Mass.: Harvard University Press, 1978.

Myers, William. *The Teaching of George Eliot.* Totowa, N.J.: Barnes & Noble, 1984.

Newton, K. M. *George Eliot: Romantic Humanist: A Study of the Philosophical Structure of Her Novels.* Totowa, N.J.: Barnes & Noble, 1981.

Nineteenth-Century Fiction 35 (1980). Special George Eliot issue.

Pearce, T. S. *George Eliot.* Totowa, N.J.: Rowman & Littlefield, 1973.

Pinion, F. B. *A George Eliot Companion: Literary Achievement and Modern Significance.* Totowa, N.J.: Barnes & Noble, 1981.

Redinger, Ruby V. *George Eliot: The Emergent Self.* New York: Knopf, 1975.

Roberts, Neil. *George Eliot: Her Beliefs and Her Art.* Pittsburgh: University of Pittsburgh Press, 1975.

Shuttleworth, Sally. *George Eliot and Nineteenth-Century Science.* Cambridge: Cambridge University Press, 1984.

Smith, Anne, ed. *George Eliot: Centenary Essays and an Unpublished Fragment.* Totowa, N.J.: Barnes & Noble, 1980.

Stump, Reva. *Movement and Vision in George Eliot's Novels.* Seattle: University of Washington Press, 1959.

Sudrann, Jean. "*Daniel Deronda* and the Landscape of Exile." *ELH* 37 (1970): 433–55.

Thale, Jerome. *The Novels of George Eliot.* New York: Columbia University Press, 1959.

Welsh, Alexander. *George Eliot and Blackmail.* Cambridge, Mass.: Harvard University Press, 1985.

Weisenfarth, Joseph. *George Eliot's Mythmaking.* Heidelberg: Carl Winter, Universitätsverlag, 1977.

Witemeyer, Hugh. *George Eliot and the Visual Arts.* New Haven: Yale University Press, 1979.

CHARLES KINGSLEY

Baker, Joseph. *The Novel and the Oxford Movement.* Princeton: Princeton University Press, 1932.

Baldwin, Stanley. *Charles Kingsley.* Ithaca: Cornell University Press, 1934.

Beer, Gillian. "Charles Kingsley and the Literary Image of the Countryside." *Victorian Studies* 8 (1965): 243–54.

Brinton, Clarence Crane. *English Political Thought in the Nineteenth Century.* London: Ernest Benn, 1933.

Buckley, Jerome H. *The Victorian Temper: A Study in Literary Culture.* Cambridge, Mass.: Harvard University Press, 1951.

Downes, David Anthony. *The Temper of Victorian Belief: Religious Novels of Pater, Kingsley, and Newman.* New York: Twayne, 1972.

Harrington, Henry R. "Charles Kingsley's Fallen Athlete." *Victorian Studies* 21 (1977): 73–86.

Hartley, John Allen. *The Novels of Charles Kingsley: A Christian Social Interpretation.* Folkestone: Hour-Glass, 1977.

Johnston, Arthur. "*The Water-Babies:* Kingsley's Debt to Darwin." *English* 12 (1959): 215–19.

Karl, Frederick R. *An Age of Fiction: The Nineteenth Century British Novel.* New York: Farrar, Straus & Giroux, 1964.

Miyoshi, Masao. *The Divided Self: A Perspective on the Literature of the Victorians.* New York: New York University Press, 1969.

Rogers, Katherine M. *The Troublesome Helpmate: A History of Misogyny in Literature.* Seattle: University of Washington Press, 1966.

Stevenson, Lionel. "Darwin and the Novel." *Nineteenth-Century Fiction* 15 (1960): 29–38.

Sussman, Herbert. *Victorians and the Machine: The Literary Response to Technology.* Cambridge, Mass.: Harvard University Press, 1968.

Sutherland, J. A. *Victorian Novelists and Publishers.* London: Athlone Press, 1976.

Wolff, Robert Lee. *Gains and Losses: Novels of Faith and Doubt in Victorian England.* London: John Murray, 1977.

Young, Michael. "History as Myth: Charles Kingsley's *Hereward the Wake.*" *Studies in the Novel* 17 (1985): 174–88.

WILKIE COLLINS

Ashley, Robert. "Wilkie Collins Reconsidered." *Nineteenth-Century Fiction* 4 (1949–50): 265–73.

Bargainnier, Earl F., ed. *Twelve Englishmen of Mystery.* Bowling Green, Ohio: Popular Press, 1984.

Brantlinger, Patrick. "What Is 'Sensational' about the Sensation Novel?" *Nineteenth-Century Fiction* 37 (1982): 1–28.

Brooks, Peter. *Reading for the Plot.* New York: Knopf, 1984.

Eliot, T. S. "Wilkie Collins and Dickens." In *Selected Essays 1917–1932.* New York: Harcourt, Brace, 1932.

Ellis, S. M. *Wilkie Collins, Le Fanu, and Others.* London: Constable, 1951.

Frick, Patricia Miller. "Wilkie Collins's 'Little Jewel': The Meaning of *The Moonstone.*" *Philological Quarterly* 63 (1984): 313–21.

Gates, Barbara T. "Wilkie Collins's Suicides: 'Truth as It Is in Nature.' " *Dickens Studies Annual* 12 (1983): 303–18.

Hennelly, Mark M. "Detecting Collins's Diamond: From Serpentstone to Moonstone." *Nineteenth-Century Fiction* 39 (1984): 25–47.

Kendrick, Walter M. "The Sensationalism of *The Woman in White.*" *Nineteenth-Century Fiction* 32 (1977–78): 18–35.

Lawson, Lewis A. "Wilkie Collins and *The Moonstone.*" *American Imago* 20 (1963): 61–79.

Leavy, Barbara Fass. "Wilkie Collins's Cinderella: The History of Psychology and *The Woman in White.*" *Dickens Studies Annual* 10 (1982): 91–142.

Lonoff, Sue. *Wilkie Collins and His Victorian Readers: A Study in the Rhetoric of Authorship.* New York: AMS Press, 1982.

Maceachen, Dougald B. "Wilkie Collins and British Law." *Nineteenth-Century Fiction* 5 (1950–51): 121–39.

Marshall, William. *Wilkie Collins.* New York: Twayne, 1970.

Miller, D. A. "From 'roman policier' to 'roman-police': Wilkie Collins's *The Moonstone.*" *Novel* 13 (1980): 153–70.

Murfin, Ross C. " 'The Art of Representation': Collins's *The Moonstone* and Dickens's Example." *ELH* 49 (1982): 653–72.

Nadel, Ira Bruce. "Science and *The Moonstone.*" *Dickens Studies Annual* 11 (1983): 239–60.

Page, Norman, ed. *Wilkie Collins: The Critical Heritage.* London: Routledge & Kegan Paul, 1974.

Richardson, Maurice. Introduction to *The Woman in White,* by Wilkie Collins. New York: Dutton, 1972.

Sucksmith, Harvey Peter. Introduction to *The Woman in White,* by Wilkie Collins. New York: Oxford University Press, 1975.

Symons, Julian. Introduction to *The Woman in White,* by Wilkie Collins. Harmondsworth: Penguin, 1974.

GEORGE MacDONALD

Auden, W. H. Introduction to *Visionary Novels of George MacDonald,* edited by Anne Fremantle. New York: Noonday Press, 1954.

Hein, Rolland. *The Harmony Within: The Spiritual Vision of George MacDonald.* Grand Rapids, Mich.: Christian University Press, 1982.

Holbrook, David. "George MacDonald and Dreams of the Other World." *Seven* 4 (1983): 27–37.

Johnson, Joseph. *George MacDonald: A Biographical and Critical Appreciation.* London: Pitman, 1906.

Lewis, C. S. Introduction to *George MacDonald: An Anthology.* New York: Macmillan, 1947.

Lochhead, Marian. "George MacDonald and the World of Faery." *Seven* 3 (1982): 63–71.

MacDonald, Greville. *George MacDonald and His Wife.* London: Allen & Unwin, 1924.

Manlove, Colin. "George MacDonald's Early Scottish Novels." In *Nineteenth-Century Scottish Fiction: Critical Essays,* edited by Ian Campbell. Manchester: Carcanet New Press, 1979.

——. *The Impulse of Fantasy Literature.* Kent, Ohio: Kent State University Press, 1983.

Mendelson, Michael. "George MacDonald's *Lilith* and the Conventions of Ascent." *Studies in Scottish Literature* 20 (1985): 197–218.

Prickett, Stephen. "The Two Worlds of George MacDonald." *North Wind* 2 (1983): 14–23.

——. *Victorian Fantasy.* Brighton: Harvester Press, 1979.

Rabkin, Eric. *The Fantastic in Literature*. Princeton: Princeton University Press, 1976.

Reis, Richard. *George MacDonald*. New York: Twayne, 1972.

Walker, Jeanne Murray. "The Demoness and the Grail: Deciphering MacDonald's *Lilith*." In *The Scope of the Fantastic: Culture, Biography, Themes, Children's Literature*, edited by Robert Collins and Howard Pearce. Westport, Conn.: Greenwood Press, 1985.

Wolff, Robert Lee. *The Golden Key: A Study of the Fiction of George MacDonald*. New Haven: Yale University Press, 1961.

GEORGE MEREDITH

Baker, Robert S. "Faun and Satyr: Meredith's Theory of Comedy and *The Egoist*." *Mosaic* 9, no. 4 (1976): 173–93.

Beer, Gillian. *Meredith: A Change of Masks: A Study of the Novels*. London: Athlone Press, 1970.

Beer, Gillian, and Margaret Harris, eds. *The Notebooks of George Meredith*. Salzburg: Institut für Anglistik und Amerikanistik, University of Salzburg, 1983.

Calder, Jenni. "Cash and the Sex Nexus." *Tennessee Studies in Literature* 27 (1984): 20–53.

Fletcher, Ian, ed. *Meredith Now: Some Critical Essays*. New York: Barnes & Noble, 1971.

Kelvin, Norman. *A Troubled Eden: Nature and Society in the Works of George Meredith*. Stanford: Stanford University Press, 1961.

Lindsay, Jack. *George Meredith: His Life and Work*. London: Bodley Head, 1956.

Miller, J. Hillis. " 'Herself against Herself': The Clarification of Clara Middleton." In *The Representation of Women in Fiction*, edited by Carolyn G. Heilbrun and Margaret Higonnet, 98–123. Baltimore: Johns Hopkins University Press, 1983.

Moses, Joseph. *The Novelist as Comedian: George Meredith and the Ironic Sensibility*. New York: Schocken Books, 1983.

Pritchett, V. S. *George Meredith and English Comedy*. New York: Random House, 1969.

Stevenson, Lionel. *The Ordeal of George Meredith: A Biography*. New York: Scribner's, 1953.

Stone, Donald D. *Novelists in a Changing World: Meredith, James, and the Transformation of English Fiction in the 1880s*. Cambridge, Mass.: Harvard University Press, 1972.

Swanson, Donald R. *Three Conquerors: Character and Method in the Mature Works of George Meredith*. The Hague: Mouton, 1969.

Wilt, Judith. *The Readable People of George Meredith*. Princeton: Princeton University Press, 1975.

Wright, Walter F. *Art and Substance in George Meredith: A Study in Narrative*. Lincoln: University of Nebraska Press, 1953.

LEWIS CARROLL

Auden, W. H. *The Enchafèd Flood: Or The Romantic Iconography of the Sea*. London: Faber & Faber, 1951.

———. "Lewis Carroll." In *Forewords and Afterwords*, selected by Edward Mendelson, 283–93. New York: Random House, 1973.

Blake, Kathleen. *Play, Games, and Sport: The Literary Works of Lewis Carroll*. Ithaca: Cornell University Press, 1974.

Bloom, Harold, ed. *Modern Critical Views: Lewis Carroll*. New Haven: Chelsea House, 1987.

Bowman, Isa. *The Story of Lewis Carroll*. London: J. M. Dent, 1899.

Clark, Ann. *Lewis Carroll: A Biography*. New York: Schocken Books, 1979.

Cohen, Morton N., and Roger Lancelyn Green, eds. *The Selected Letters of Lewis Carroll*. New York: Pantheon, 1982.

Collingwood, Stuart Dodgson. *The Life and Letters of Lewis Carroll*. London: T. Fisher Unwin, 1898.

Cook, Albert. *The Dark Voyage and the Golden Mean: A Philosophy of Comedy*. Cambridge, Mass.: Harvard University Press, 1949.

Crofte-Cooke, Rupert. *Feasting with Panthers: A New Consideration of Some Late Victorian Writers*. New York: Holt, Rinehart & Winston, 1968.

Dolitsky, Marlene. *Under the Tumtum Tree: From Nonsense to Sense: A Study in Nonautomatic Comprehension*. Amsterdam: Benjamins, 1984.

Empson, William. "*Alice in Wonderland:* The Child as Swain." In *Some Versions of Pastoral*. London: Chatto & Windus, 1935.

English Language Notes 20, no. 2 (December 1982). Special Lewis Carroll issue.

Ettleson, Abraham. *Lewis Carroll's* Through the Looking-Glass *Decoded*. New York: Philosophical Library, 1966.

Gardner, Martin, ed. *The Annotated Alice*. 1960. Rev. ed. Harmondsworth: Penguin, 1970.

———, ed. *The Annotated Snark*. New York: Simon & Schuster, 1962.

Gray, Donald J., ed. *Lewis Carroll:* Alice in Wonderland. A Norton Critical Edition. New York: Norton, 1971.

Green, Roger Lancelyn. *Lewis Carroll*. London: Bodley Head, 1960.

———, ed. *The Diaries of Lewis Carroll*. 2 vols. New York: Oxford University Press, 1953.

———, ed. *The Lewis Carroll Handbook*. London: Oxford University Press, 1962.

Greenacre, Phyllis. *Swift and Carroll: A Psychoanalytic Study of Two Lives*. New York: International Universities Press, 1955.

Guiliano, Edward. "Lewis Carroll: A Sesquicentennial Guide to Research." *Dickens Studies Annual* 10 (1982): 263–310.

———, ed. *Lewis Carroll: A Celebration: Essays on the Occasion of the 150th Anniversary of the Birth of Charles Lutwidge Dodgson*. New York: Clarkson N. Potter, 1982.

———, ed. *Lewis Carroll Observed: A Collection of Unpublished Photographs, Drawings, Poetry, and New Essays*. New York: Clarkson N. Potter, 1976.

Hancher, Michael. *On the Writing, Illustration and Publication of Lewis Carroll's* Alice *Books*. London: Macmillan Children's Books, 1984.

Hudson, Derek. *Lewis Carroll*. London: Constable, 1954.

Huxley, Francis. *The Raven and the Writing Desk*. New York: Harper & Row, 1977.

Jabberwocky: The Journal of the Lewis Carroll Society, 1969–.

Jackson, Rosemary. *Fantasy: The Literature of Subversion*. London: Methuen, 1981.

Kelly, Richard. *Lewis Carroll*. Boston: Twayne, 1977.

Kenner, Hugh. "Alice in Chapelizod." In *Dublin's Joyce*, 276–300. London: Chatto & Windus, 1955.

Kincaid, James R. "Alice's Invasion of Wonderland." *PMLA* 88 (1973): 92–99.

Kirk, Daniel F. *Charles Dodgson: Semeiotician*. Gainesville: University of Florida Press, 1962.

Koelb, Clayton. *The Incredulous Reader: Literature and the Function of Disbelief*. Ithaca: Cornell University Press, 1984.

Lehmann, John F. *Lewis Carroll and the Spirit of Nonsense*. Nottingham: University of Nottingham Press, 1974.

Lennon, Florence Becker. *The Life of Lewis Carroll*. New York: Collier, 1962.

————. *Victoria through the Looking-Glass*. New York: Simon & Schuster, 1945.

Morton, Lionel. "Memory in the *Alice* Books." *Nineteenth-Century Fiction* 33 (1978): 285–308.

Partridge, Eric. "The Nonsense Words of Edward Lear and Lewis Carroll." In *Here, There, and Everywhere*, 162–88. London: Hamish Hamilton, 1950.

Phillips, Robert, ed. *Aspects of Alice: Lewis Carroll's Dreamchild as Seen through the Critics' Looking-Glasses 1865–1971*. New York: Vanguard, 1971.

Pudney, John. *Lewis Carroll and His World*. New York: Scribner's, 1976.

Rackin, Donald. "Corrective Laughter: Carroll's *Alice* and Popular Children's Literature of the Nineteenth Century." *Journal of Popular Culture* 1 (1967): 243–55.

————, ed. Alice's *Adventures in Wonderland: A Critical Handbook*. Belmont, Calif.: Wadsworth, 1961.

Richardson, Joanna. *The Young Lewis Carroll*. London: Parrish, 1964.

Sewell, Elizabeth. *The Field of Nonsense*. London: Chatto & Windus, 1952.

Sutherland, Robert D. *Language and Lewis Carroll*. The Hague: Mouton, 1970.

Taylor, Alexander L. *The White Knight: A Study of C. L. Dodgson (Lewis Carroll)*. Edinburgh: Oliver & Boyd, 1952.

Wood, James. *The Snark Was a Boojum: A Life of Lewis Carroll*. New York: Pantheon, 1966.

SAMUEL BUTLER

Cole, G. D. H. *Samuel Butler and* The Way of All Flesh. London: Home & Van Thal, 1947.

Forster, E. M. "The Legacy of Samuel Butler." *The Listener* (June 12, 1952): 955–56.

Furbank, P. N. *Samuel Butler*. Cambridge: Cambridge University Press, 1948.

Ganz, Margaret. "Samuel Butler: Ironic Abdication and the Way to the Unconscious." *English Literature in Transition* 28 (1985): 366–94.

Grylls, David. *Guardians and Angels: Parents and Children in Nineteenth-Century Literature*. London: Faber & Faber, 1978.

Holt, Lee Elbert. *Samuel Butler*. New York: Twayne, 1964.

Houghton, Walter E. *The Victorian Frame of Mind, 1830–1870*. New Haven: Yale University Press, 1957.

Jones, Joseph. *The Cradle of Erewhon: Samuel Butler in New Zealand*. Austin: University of Texas Press, 1959.

Kettle, Arnold. *An Introduction to the English Novel, Vol. 2*. London: Hutchinson, 1953.

Knoepflmacher, U. C. " 'Ishmael' or Anti-Hero? The Division of Self: *The Way of All Flesh*." *English Literature in Transition* 4 (1961): 28–35.

Levin, Gerald. "Shaw, Butler, and Kant." *Philological Quarterly* 52 (1973): 142–56.

Muggeridge, Malcolm. *The Earnest Atheist: A Study of Samuel Butler*. London: Eyre & Spottiswoode, 1936.

Norrman, Ralf. *Samuel Butler and the Meaning of Chiasmus*. London: Macmillan, 1986.

Pritchett, V. S. "A Victorian Son." In *The Living Novel and Later Appreciations*. New York: Random House, 1964.

Rattray, R. F. *Samuel Butler: A Chronicle and an Introduction*. London: Duckworth, 1935.

Stillman, Clara G. *Samuel Butler: A Mid-Victorian Modern*. New York: Viking Press, 1932.

Willey, Basil. *Darwin and Butler: Two Versions of Evolution*. New York: Harcourt, Brace, 1960.

Wilson, Edmund. *The Triple Thinkers: Ten Essays on Literature*. London: Oxford University Press, 1938.

Wisenthal, J. L. "Samuel Butler's Epistle to the Victorians: *The Way of All Flesh* and Unlovely Paul." *Mosaic* 13, no. 1 (1979): 17–29.

Woolf, Virginia. "A Man with a View." In *The Essays of Virginia Woolf*, ed. Andrew McNellie. San Diego: Harcourt Brace Jovanovich, 1987, Volume 2, pp. 34–39.

Zabel, Morton Dauwen. "Samuel Butler: The Victorian Insolvency." In *The Victorian Novel: Modern Essays in Criticism*, edited by Ian Watt, 446–61. London: Oxford University Press, 1971.

THOMAS HARDY

Abercrombie, Lascelles. *Thomas Hardy: A Critical Study*. London: Martin Secker, 1924.

Alvarez, A. Afterword to *Jude the Obscure*. New York: New American Library, 1961.

Bailey, J. O. *Thomas Hardy and the Cosmic Mind*. Chapel Hill: University of North Carolina Press, 1956.

Bayley, John. *An Essay on Hardy*. Cambridge: Cambridge University Press, 1978.

Bloom, Harold, ed. *Modern Critical Interpretations: Thomas Hardy's* Jude the Obscure. New Haven: Chelsea House, 1987.

———, ed. *Modern Critical Interpretations: Thomas Hardy's* The Mayor of Casterbridge. New Haven: Chelsea House, 1988.

———, ed. *Modern Critical Interpretations: Thomas Hardy's* The Return of the Native. New Haven: Chelsea House, 1987.

———, ed. *Modern Critical Interpretations: Thomas Hardy's* Tess of the D'Urbervilles. New Haven: Chelsea House, 1987.

———, ed. *Modern Critical Views: Thomas Hardy*. New Haven: Chelsea House, 1987.

Brady, Kristin. *The Short Stories of Thomas Hardy*. New York: St. Martin's Press, 1982.

Brooks, Jean R. *Thomas Hardy: The Poetic Structure*. Ithaca: Cornell University Press, 1971.

Blunden, Edmund. *Thomas Hardy*. London: Macmillan, 1951.

Butler, Lance St. John. *Thomas Hardy*. Cambridge: Cambridge University Press, 1978.

Carpenter, Richard. *Thomas Hardy*. New York: Twayne, 1964.

Casagrande, Peter J. *Unity in Hardy's Novels: "Repetitive Symmetries."* Lawrence: Regents Press of Kansas, 1982.

Cox, R. G., ed. *Thomas Hardy: The Critical Heritage*. London: Routledge & Kegan Paul, 1970.

Drabble, Margaret, ed. *The Genius of Thomas Hardy*. London: Weidenfeld & Nicolson, 1976.

Elliot, Ralph W. *Thomas Hardy's English*. Oxford: Basil Blackwell, 1984.

Gerber, Helmut E., and W. Eugene Davis, eds. *Thomas Hardy: An Annotated Bibliography of Writings about Him*. DeKalb: Northern Illinois University Press, 1973.

Giordano, Frank R. *"I'd Have My Life Unbe": Thomas Hardy's Self-Destructive Characters*. University: University of Alabama Press, 1984.

Gittings, Robert. *The Older Hardy*. London: Heinemann, 1978.

Gregor, Ian. *The Great Web: The Form of Hardy's Major Fiction*. Totowa, N.J.: Rowman & Littlefield, 1974.

Guerard, Albert J. *Thomas Hardy: The Novels and Stories*. Cambridge, Mass.: Harvard University Press, 1949.

————, ed. *Hardy: A Collection of Critical Essays*. Englewood Cliffs, N.J.: Prentice-Hall, 1963.

Hardy, Evelyn. *Thomas Hardy: A Critical Biography*. London: Hogarth Press, 1954.

Hardy, Florence Emily. *The Life of Thomas Hardy, 1840–1928*. London: Macmillan, 1962.

Hornback, Bert G. *The Metaphor of Chance: Vision and Technique in the Works of Thomas Hardy*. Athens: Ohio University Press, 1971.

Howe, Irving. *Thomas Hardy*. New York: Macmillan, 1967.

Johnson, Bruce. *True Correspondence: A Phenomenology of Thomas Hardy's Novels*. Tallahassee: University Presses of Florida, 1983.

Kramer, Dale. *Thomas Hardy: The Forms of Tragedy*. Detroit: Wayne State University Press, 1975.

————, ed. *Critical Approaches to the Fiction of Thomas Hardy*. London: Macmillan, 1979.

LaValley, Albert J. *Twentieth Century Interpretations of* Tess of the D'Urbervilles: *A Collection of Critical Essays*. Englewood Cliffs, N.J.: Prentice-Hall, 1969.

Lawrence, D. H. *Phoenix: The Posthumous Papers of D. H. Lawrence*. New York: Viking Press, 1972.

Meisel, Perry. *Thomas Hardy: The Return of the Repressed*. New Haven: Yale University Press, 1972.

Miller, J. Hillis. *Thomas Hardy: Distance and Desire*. Cambridge, Mass.: Harvard University Press, 1970.

Millgate, Michael. *Thomas Hardy: A Biography*. Oxford: Oxford University Press, 1982.

————. *Thomas Hardy: His Career as a Novelist*. New York: Random House, 1971.

Millgate, Michael, and Richard Little Purdy, eds. *The Collected Letters of Thomas Hardy*. Oxford: Oxford University Press, 1978–.

Morrell, Roy. *Thomas Hardy: The Will and the Way*. Kuala Lumpur: University of Malaya Press, 1965.

Page, Norman, ed. *Thomas Hardy: The Writer and His Background*. London: Bell & Hyman, 1980.

Paterson, John. *The Making of* The Return of the Native. Berkeley: University of California Press, 1960.

Peckham, Morse. *Victorian Revolutionaries: Speculations on Some Heroes of a Culture Crisis*. New York: George Braziller, 1970.

Pinion, F. B. *Thomas Hardy: Art and Thought*. London: Macmillan, 1977.

————, ed. *Thomas Hardy and the Modern World: Papers Presented at the 1973 Summer School*. Dorchester, England: Thomas Hardy Society, 1974.

Rutland, William. *Thomas Hardy: A Study of His Writings and Their Background*. Oxford: Basil Blackwell, 1938.

Sherman, G. W. *The Pessimism of Thomas Hardy*. Rutherford, N.J.: Fairleigh Dickinson University Press, 1976.

Smith, Anne, ed. *The Novels of Thomas Hardy*. London: Vision Press, 1979.

Springer, Marlene. *Hardy's Use of Allusion*. Lawrence: University Press of Kansas, 1983.

Stewart, J. I. M. *Thomas Hardy: A Critical Biography*. New York: Dodd, Mead, 1971.

Stone, Donald D. "House and Home in Thomas Hardy." *Nineteenth-Century Fiction* 39 (1984): 231–48.

Thomas Hardy Annual, 1983–.

The Thomas Hardy Society Review, 1975–.

The Thomas Hardy Yearbook, 1970–.

Thurley, Geoffrey. *The Psychology of Hardy's Novels*. Queensland: University of Queensland Press, 1975.

Vigar, Penelope. *The Novels of Thomas Hardy: Illusion and Reality.* London: Athlone Press, 1974.

Zabel, Morton Dauwen. "Hardy in Defense of His Art: The Aesthetic of Incongruity." *Southern Review* 6 (1940–41): 124–41.

Acknowledgments

"The Victorian Novel before Victoria: Edward Bulwer-Lytton" (originally entitled "Edward Bulwer-Lytton") by Elliot Engel and Margaret F. King from *The Victorian Novel before Victoria: British Fiction during the Reign of William IV, 1830–37* by Elliot Engel and Margaret F. King, © 1984 by Elliot Engel and Margaret F. King. Reprinted by permission of Macmillian Press, London and Basingstoke, and St. Martin's Press, Inc.

"Benjamin Disraeli and the Romance of the Will" by Donald D. Stone from *The Romantic Impulse in Victorian Fiction* by Donald D. Stone, © 1980 by the President and Fellows of Harvard College. Reprinted by permission of Harvard University Press, Cambridge, Massachusetts.

"Causality versus Conscience: The Problem of Form in *Mary Barton*" by Catherine Gallagher from *The Industrial Reformation of English Fiction: Social Discourse and Narrative Form 1832–1867* by Catherine Gallagher, © 1985 by the University of Chicago. Reprinted by permission of the University of Chicago Press.

"The Narrative Voice in Thackeray's Novels" (originally entitled "The Narrative Voice") by Jack P. Rawlins from *Thackeray's Novels: A Fiction That Is True* by Jack P. Rawlins, © 1974 by the Regents of the University of California. Reprinted by permission of the University of California Press.

"Thackeray: 'The Legitimate High Priest of Truth' and the Problematics of the Real" by George Levine from *The Realistic Imagination: English Fiction from* Frankenstein *to* Lady Chatterley by George Levine, © 1981 by the University of Chicago. Reprinted by permission of the University of Chicago Press.

"The Pickwick Case: Diagnosis" by Garrett Stewart from *Dickens and the Trials of Imagination* by Garrett Stewart, © 1974 by the President and Fellows of Harvard College. Reprinted by permission of Harvard University Press, Cambridge, Massachusetts.

"The Violent Effigy: A Study of Dickens's Imagination" (originally entitled "Introduction" and "Dickens and Violence" and "Endpiece") by John Carey from *The Violent Effigy: A Study of Dickens's Imagination* by John Carey, © 1973 by John Carey. Reprinted by permission of Faber & Faber Ltd.

"The Fairy-Tale Ending of Dickens's Novels" (originally entitled "The Fairy Tale") by John Kucich from *Excess and Restraint in the Novels of Charles Dickens* by John Kucich, © 1981 by the University of Georgia Press. Reprinted by permission of the University of Georgia Press.

"Trollope's Metonymies" by Michael Riffaterre from *Nineteenth-Century Fiction* 37, no. 3 (December 1982), © 1982 by the Regents of the University of California. Reprinted by permission of the Regents of the University of California.

"Can You Forgive Him?: Trollope's *Can You Forgive Her?* and the Myth of Realism" by George Levine from *Victorian Studies* 18, no. 1 (September 1974), © 1974 by Indiana University. Reprinted by permission of the Trustees of Indiana University.

"Passion, Narrative and Identity in *Wuthering Heights* and *Jane Eyre*" by Tony Tanner from *Teaching the Text*, edited by Susanne Kappeler and Norman Bryson, © 1983 by Tony Tanner. Reprinted by permission of Routledge & Kegan Paul.

"Gossip, Diary, Letter, Text: Anne Brontë's Narrative *Tenant* and the Problematic of the Gothic Sequel" by Jan B. Gordon from *ELH* 51, no. 4 (Winter 1984), © 1984 by the Johns Hopkins University Press, Baltimore/London. Reprinted by permission of the Johns Hopkins University Press.

"Speaking through Parable: George Eliot's Search for a Narrative Medium" (originally entitled "Speaking through Parable: George Eliot") by Barry V. Qualls from *The Secular Pilgrims of Victorian Fiction: The Novel as Book of Life* by Barry V. Qualls, © 1982 by Cambridge University Press. Reprinted by permission of Cambridge University Press.

"The Romance of George Eliot's Realism" by Daniel Cottom from *Genre* 15, no. 4 (Winter 1982), © 1982 by the University of Oklahoma. Reprinted by permission. All rights reserved.

" 'Fits of Spiritual Dread': George Eliot and Later Novelists" by T. B. Tomlinson from *The English Middle-Class Novel* by T. B. Tomlinson, © 1976 by T. B. Tomlinson. Reprinted by permission of Macmillan Press, London and Basingstoke, and Barnes & Noble Books, Totowa, New Jersey.

"Soiled Fairy: *The Water-Babies* in Its Time" by Valentine Cunningham from *Essays in Criticism* 35, no. 2 (April 1985), © 1985 by Stephen Wall. Reprinted by permission of the Editors of *Essays in Criticism*.

"*Cage aux Folles*: Sensation and Gender in Wilkie Collins's *The Woman in White*" by D. A. Miller from *The Nineteenth-Century British Novel* (Stratford-upon-Avon Studies), edited by Jeremy Hawthorn, © 1986 by Edward Arnold (Publishers) Ltd. Reprinted by permission of Edward Arnold (Publishers) Ltd.

"George MacDonald and the Tender Grandmother" by Humphrey Carpenter from *Secret Gardens: A Study of the Golden Age of Children's Literature* by Humphrey Carpenter, © 1985 by Humphrey Carpenter. Reprinted by permission of Allen & Unwin.

"Becoming a Heroine in *The Egoist* and *Diana of the Crossways*" (originally entitled "*The Egoist*") by Rachel M. Brownstein from *Becoming a Heroine* by Rachel M. Brownstein, © 1982 by Rachel M. Brownstein. Reprinted by permission of Penguin Books Ltd. and Richard Scott Simon Ltd.

"Alice and Wonderland: A Curious Child" by Nina Auerbach from *Victorian Studies* 18, no. 1 (September 1973), © 1972 by the Trustees of Indiana University. Reprinted by permission of the Trustees of Indiana University.

"The Educated Ego: Samuel Butler's *Way of All Flesh*" (originally entitled "The Educated Ego") by Thomas L. Jeffers from *Samuel Butler Revalued* by Thomas L. Jeffers, © 1981 by the Pennsylvania State University. Reprinted by permission of the Pennsylvania State University Press.

"The Refusal of Involvement in Hardy's Writing" (originally entitled "The Refusal of Involvement") by J. Hillis Miller from *Thomas Hardy: Distance and Desire* by J. Hillis Miller, © 1970 by the President and Fellows of Harvard College. Reprinted by permission of Harvard University Press, Cambridge, Massachusetts.

"*Tess of the D'Urbervilles*: A Novel of Assertion" by Jean R. Brooks from *Thomas Hardy: The Poetic Structure* by Jean R. Brooks, © 1971 by Jean R. Brooks. Reprinted by permission of Grafton Books, a division of The Collins Publishing Group.

Index